FASHION DRAWING

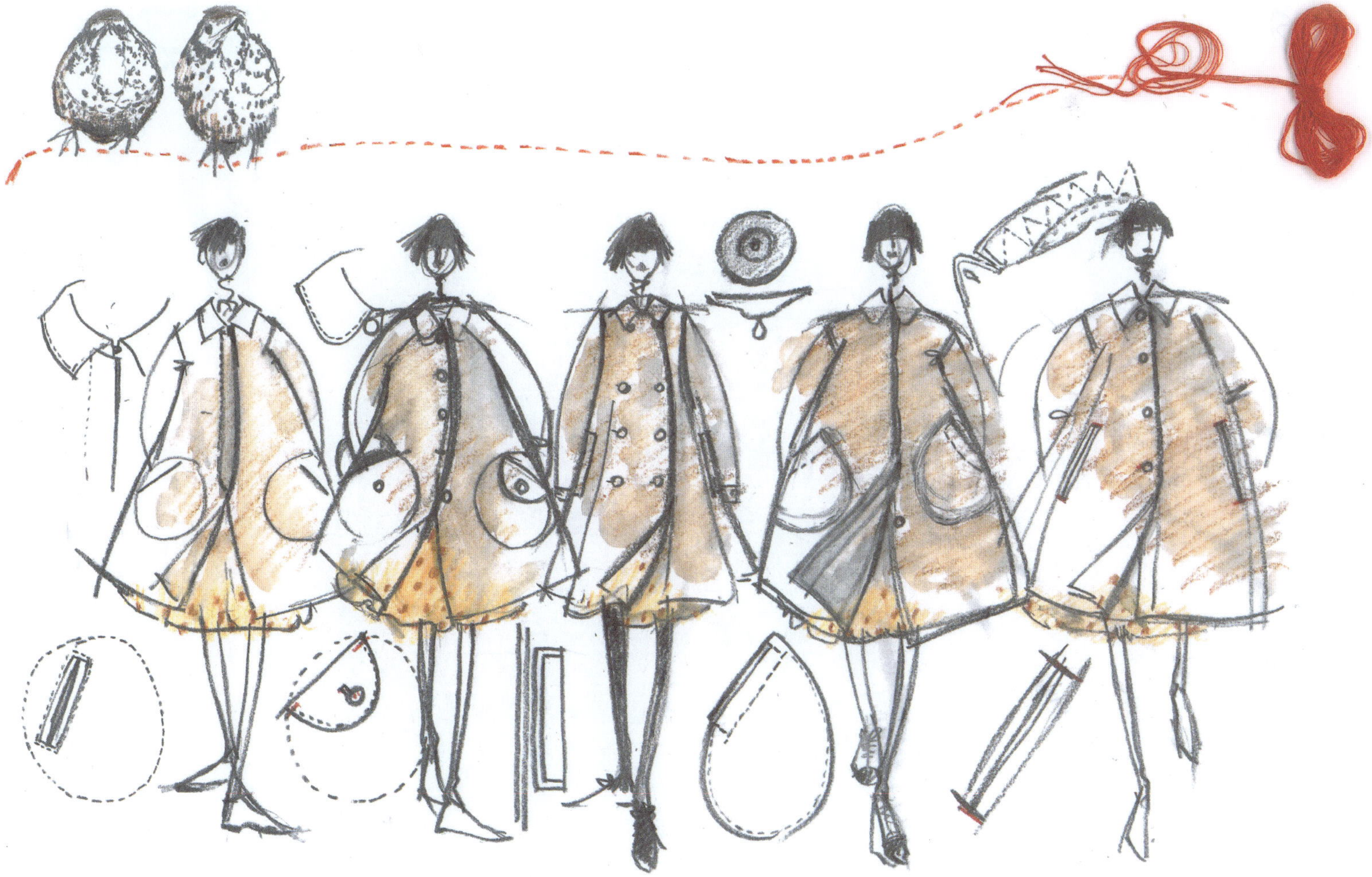

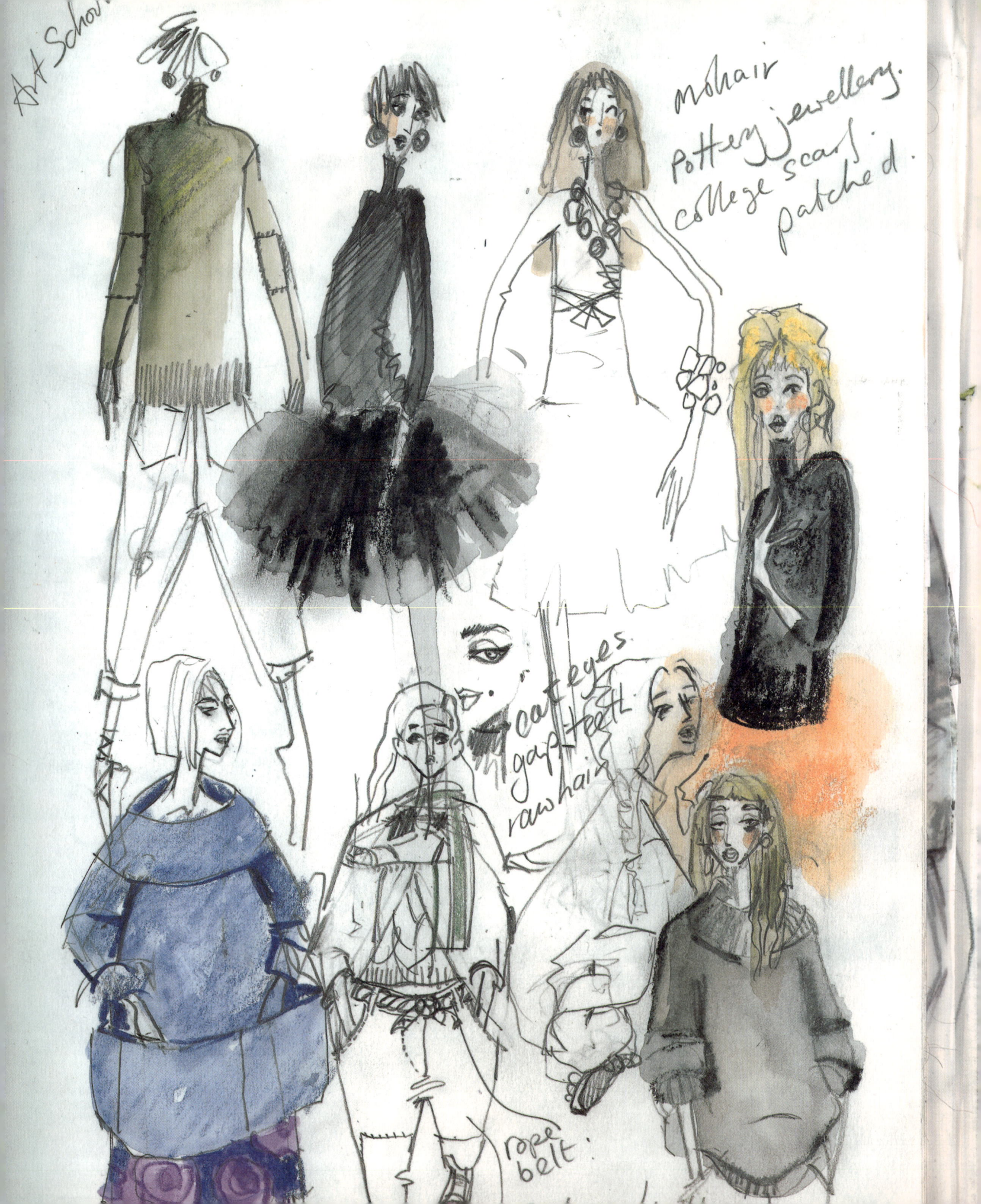

Art School

mohair
pottery jewellery.
college scarf.
patched.

cat eyes.
gap teeth
raw hair

rope
belt.

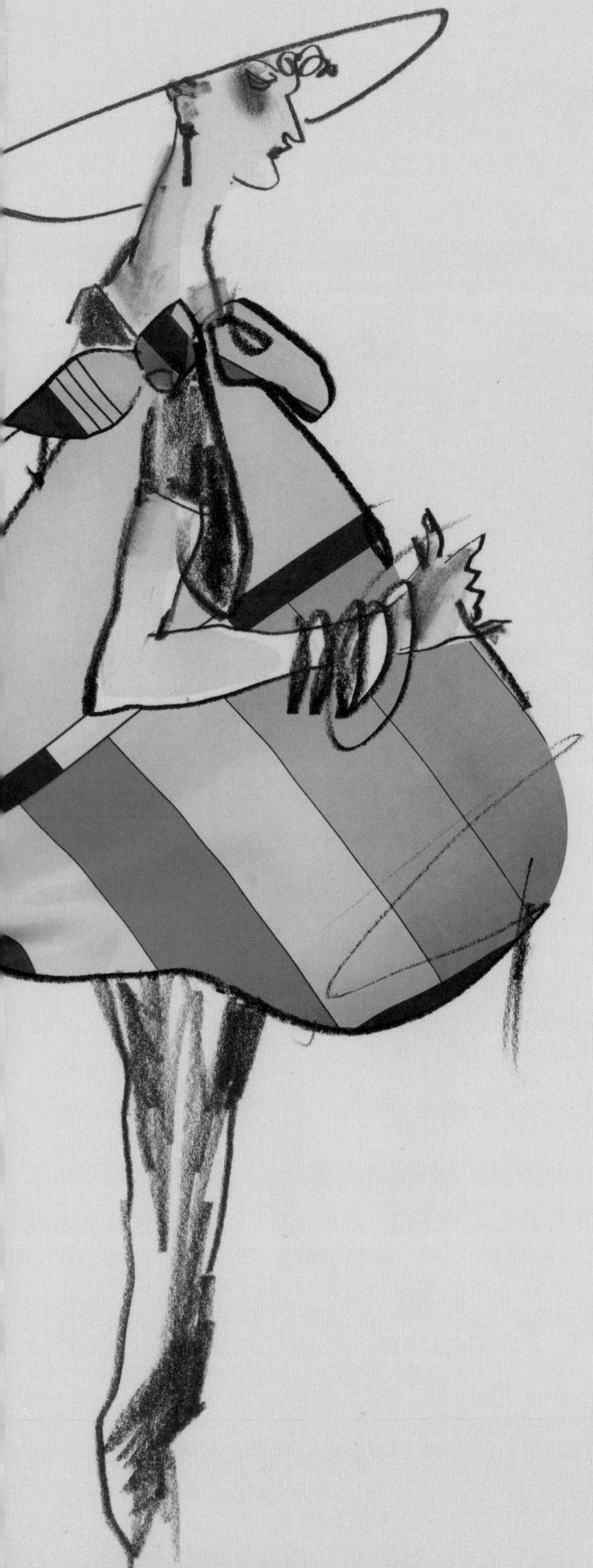

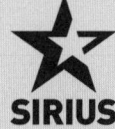

FASHION DRAWING

DISCOVER HOW TO ILLUSTRATE LIKE THE EXPERTS

Noel Chapman & Judith Cheek

SIRIUS

NOEL CHAPMAN trained in fashion and textiles at Liverpool John Moores University. He is a consultant designer specializing in knitwear, market and creative intelligence, who works with a wide range of clients throughout Europe, the USA and the Far East. Noel lectures in fashion, textiles and knitwear design and is a collector/dealer of vintage indigo textiles under the name Bleu Anglais. He is currently researching a book on Chinese folk textiles.

JUDITH CHEEK trained in fashion design at St Martins School of Art before specializing in illustration. She works with a wide range of clients across all levels of the industry and her illustration work covers fashion, beauty, health and exercise, cookery and food.

We would like to thank everyone who has so generously given their time and their work to this book, and would like to say a very special thanks to Yvonne Deacon for her huge contribution, for freely sharing her thoughts and ideas, for her artwork and her tutorials. We would also like to thank Ashley Gray at Gray Modern & Contemporary Art for allowing us to use some of their wonderful collection of vintage fashion illustrations. Without everyone's generosity, this book would never have happened. Sadly, Elizabeth Suter died before the book was finalized. Her drawings are a most valued and stylish contribution – thank you, Elizabeth.

SIRIUS

This edition published in 2026 by Sirius Publishing, a division of Arcturus Publishing Limited,
26/27 Bickels Yard, 151–153 Bermondsey Street,
London SE1 3HA

ISBN: 978-1-3988-5795-7
AD004922UK

Printed in China

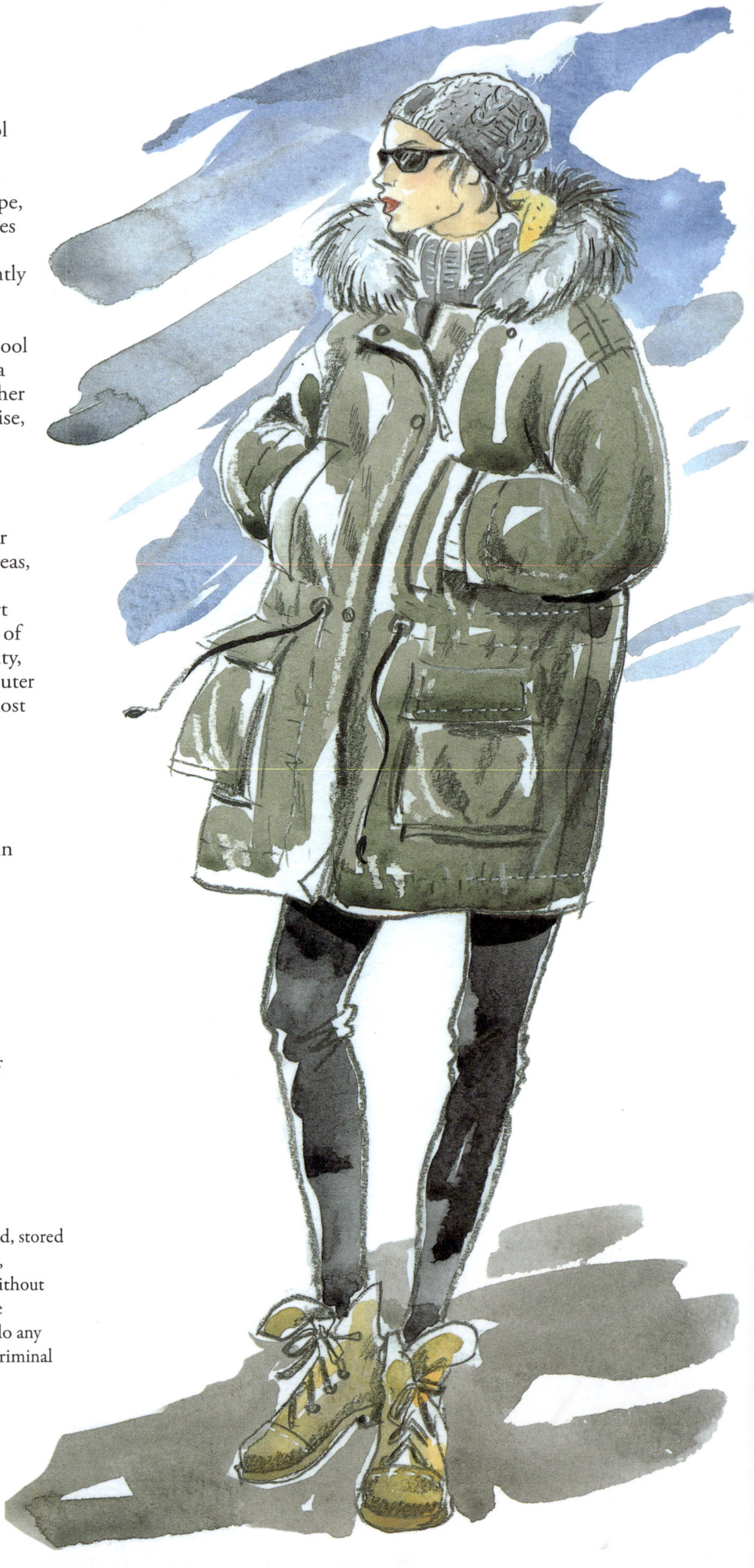

CONTENTS

INTRODUCTION

This book is aimed at designers who want to brush up their fashion drawing and illustration skills, and at would-be designers who want to learn how to draw and illustrate fashion from scratch. It is about learning to draw fashion ideas better, and will show how to record and develop your ideas, whether for your own enjoyment and purposes or to help you on your way towards a career in the industry, where being able to draw and record fashion is a real advantage.

What does the design process involve? What do we mean by inspiration and research, and which comes first? And how do drawing and illustration fit into this puzzle? These are some of the questions this book aims to answer as it charts the processes and activities of fashion drawing and designing.

Whatever the particular discipline of the designer and, arguably, of the artist too, the need to draw reasonably well is paramount, despite popular opinion to the contrary. However, what qualifies as a drawing, and particularly a fashion drawing, depends very much on the individual and whether or not the drawing is 'fit for purpose'. It is at this point that we may meet with some confusion: what is the difference between fashion drawing and fashion illustration? To put it simply, fashion drawing is what designers do to record and develop their design ideas and convey those ideas to others, for example to the machinists and factory workers who will be making the garments. A fashion illustration is often commissioned by a fashion designer, a magazine, or perhaps by a PR team to convey the ideas of the designer. It may be intended to articulate something bigger than simply the clothes – the concept of the collection or, more generally, the idea or desired image of the designer's brand. This idea or image may encompass all kinds of intangibles: it could, for example, be the task of the artist to express an attitude, so while the illustration may break many of the rules of fashion drawing per se, it provides a medium through which a designer may express their ideas. Regardless of the reasoning behind the fashion drawing or fashion illustration, the result needs to fulfil its aim: to be 'fit for purpose'.

Let's start by considering fashion drawing, the art of rendering the human figure, clothes and accessories in an attractive and comprehensible manner. To understand the processes and reasoning behind drawing fashion, it is important to appreciate the stages a designer may go through in the course of the creative journey. The designer may have an idea, and will need to record that idea, to draw it effectively and commit it to paper before it gets away. The idea will then need to be developed and refined, which usually involves a process of redrawing, of questioning and evaluation. Does the image depict what I was trying to express? Are the proportions good? Is the silhouette right? Are the details correct? Does the colour balance work? The cutting and construction of the garment are also part of the design ethos and require due consideration and attention. These are just a few of the many judgements that need to be made, all of which contribute to the successful realization of the design. Both the idea and the final outcome may evolve dramatically from the first sketches, and the processes of drawing and design are inextricably entwined.

This book will guide you through a series of tutorials and aims to help you create better, more professional drawings. It will also endeavour to encourage your own personality to shine through by showing you different possibilities across a range of media, techniques and styles.

Neil Greer

This digitally produced artwork was hand-drawn using a pen and tablet and the computer programme Painter.

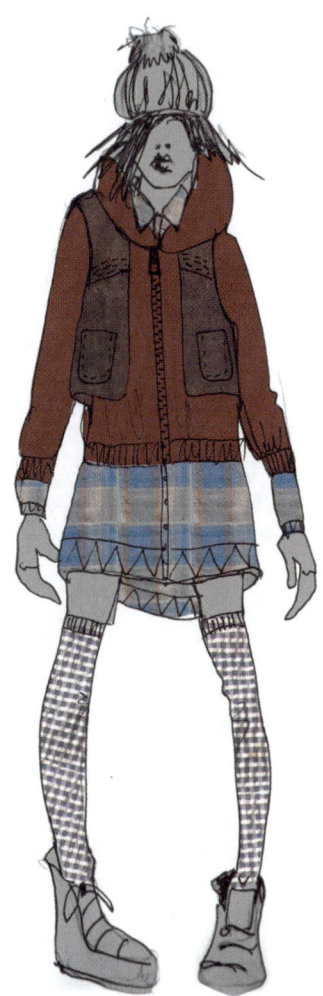

Rosalyn Kennedy

Client: *Bruce Oldfield*
Brush pen and pastel on coloured Ingres paper

Katharina Gulde

Client: *ONLY Bestseller*
Hand and digital drawing combined

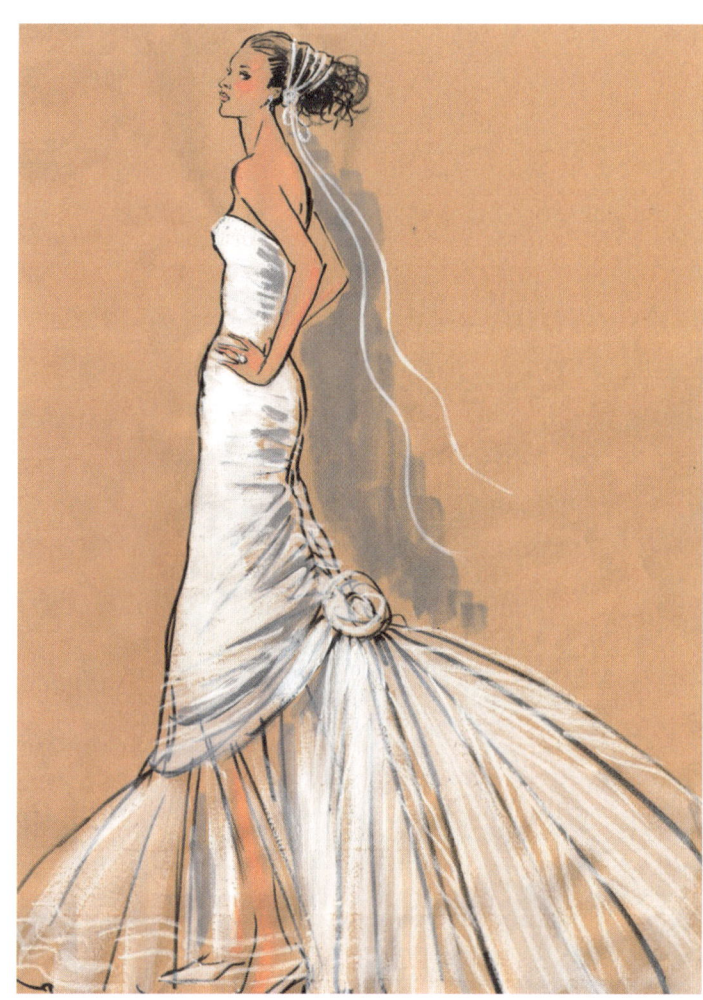

We'll talk about equipment and materials, from the most elementary to a range of more specialist and experimental media, including a little about computer drawings and their use – but first you need to be able to draw by hand. In order to do this we reveal how to draw a model: the human figure – static, posed and in movement – that will later be dressed. This is always the starting point and we shall examine in detail how to accurately depict proportions and details such as hands, feet, heads, hair and faces. It is important to point out at this stage that choosing the styling and look of a drawn figure is just like selecting a live model for real garments; the look and attitude have got to be right for overall success – the wrong model with the wrong hair and look won't wear the designs well.

We'll look at how to draw different fabrics, focusing on their surfaces and qualities, such as whether they are tweedy and chunky or fluid and floaty, and so forth. This is important for plotting the designs of clothes on the figure, getting the silhouette, fit and proportions correct before moving on to the finer points such as styling and construction lines.

Once the design has been refined, the drawing as an artwork needs to be completed with the addition of colour, texture and pattern. We also reveal how to draw 'flats' – the technical or specification drawings necessary for manufacturing – that show clearly and precisely the garment's proportions and construction, the positioning of details and so on. These are drawn off the body, as if the real garments were lying flat on a tabletop. We also describe how to draw accessories, with ideas and techniques to help you depict your ideas clearly.

Later on in the book, we include a fascinating study of colour, discussing its importance in fashion and unveiling some of its mysteries. We also take a look at the language of fashion, using a fun 'dictionary' format to describe many of its elements, together with their origins and uses. And we examine a range of 'finished drawings', showing a wide variety of illustrations by international designers and artists. These are intended both to inspire you and to demonstrate the fabulous range of possible styles, all of which are in their own way 'fit for purpose'.

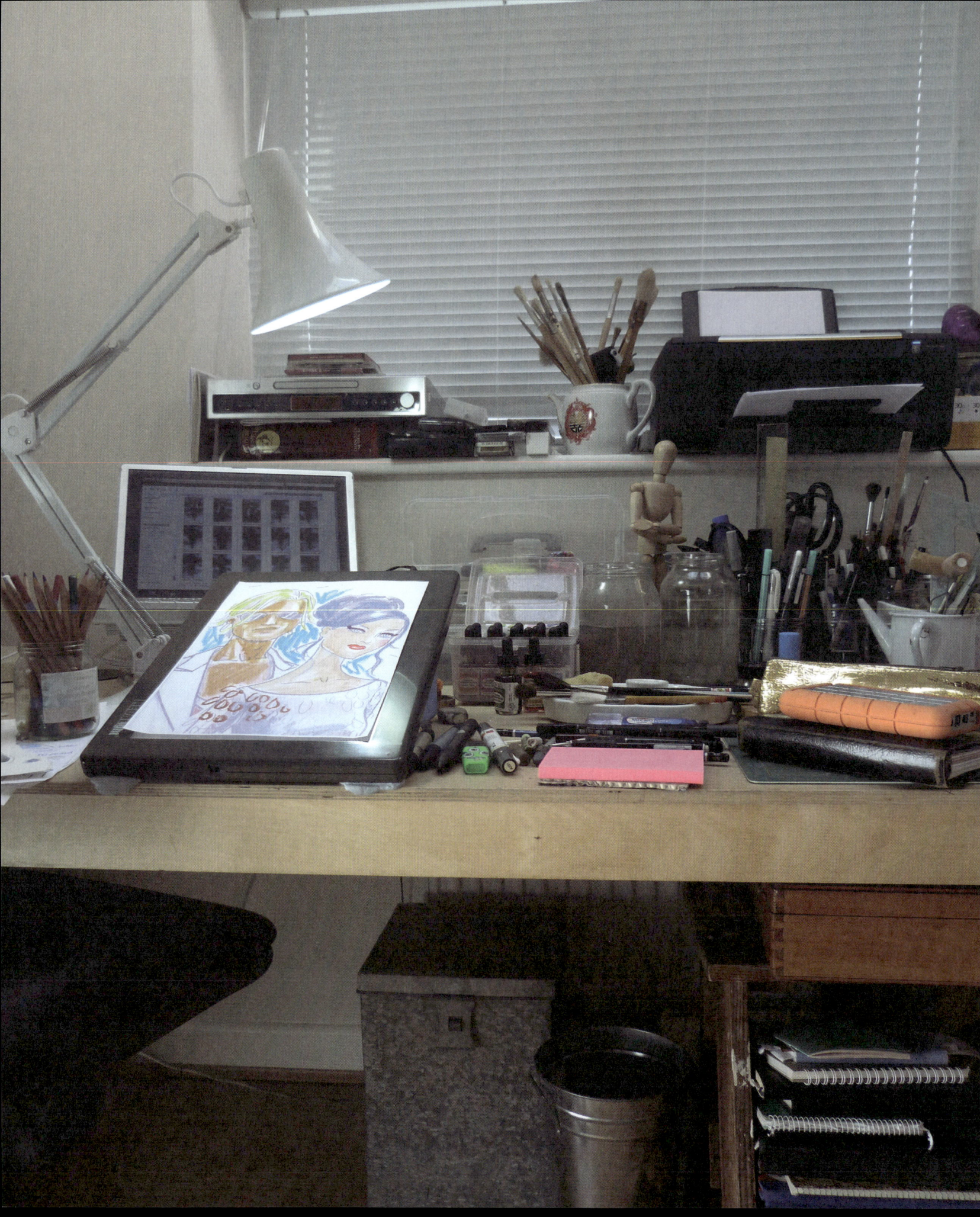

CHAPTER 1

EQUIPMENT AND MATERIALS

Ask any designer what materials and equipment they need to draw and design and you will get a range of different answers. However, many will suggest that you start with a few simple pencils and some ordinary paper. This is fine initially but, as any designer will soon confirm, you will soon begin to favour certain types and brands, both for the way they perform and the marks they make and also how they feel in your hand. The size and shape of your hand, the speed and size at which you draw, and how hard you press all have an influence on your choice of implement, and this is before we even begin to consider the effect you wish to achieve in the actual drawing. Similarly, designers often prefer particular sketchbooks, whether they are large or small, landscape or portrait, spiral-bound or sewn, or zigzag or concertina types. This section aims to reveal the choices on offer and the attributes and benefits of the different types.

YOUR WORKSPACE

While a sketchbook is something you probably use anywhere, including out and about, it is also a good idea to have a dedicated work area – somewhere organized to suit your needs and promote efficiency. It should also have a good natural light source, if possible by a window, and ideally have a movable work lamp fitted with a daylight bulb (full spectrum light) for more accurate colour work. This space should offer you a place in which you can concentrate, where you have everything you need to hand, and where you can safely leave projects out without them being disturbed.

A desk or table that is steady and a comfortable chair with good back support are very important. Many designers like to draw on an angled surface. This does not need to be a sophisticated system – it could simply be a drawing board propped up at the back on a block or a small pile of books or magazines. A wooden A2 drawing board is generally best as it is manageable but has a sufficiently large surface area. The minimum size is A3.

Photograph by Anne-Marie Ward

PAPER

'Drawings are only notes on paper . . . the secret is the paper.'
John Berger, *Drawing on Paper*, 2005

Paper is something we all take for granted, knowing little about its history and failing fully to grasp the range of its uses and possibilities: from the legal documents that control and facilitate our lives, to the products we use and purchase every day and even to the money with which we make those purchases. As creative people, where would we be without it? But even though we may consume great quantities of the stuff, we often under-explore its range and potentials.

The name paper derives from the Ancient Greek *Cyperus papyrus*, a plant from which the Ancient Egyptians created, by lamination, a paper-like material. In the 2nd century BCE, the Chinese invented paper more or less as we know it today, through a process of macerating plant fibres. Hemp and mulberry (a by-product of sericulture) were the chief fibre sources for these early papers. Paper spread slowly westwards from China along the Silk Road, through Samarkand, and by the 10th century had reached Morocco and the Iberian peninsular. Production continued to expand through Europe, where the invention of the printing press in Germany in the 15th century created something of a revolution and paper was its key protagonist. During the Industrial Revolution, mechanization facilitated paper's transition

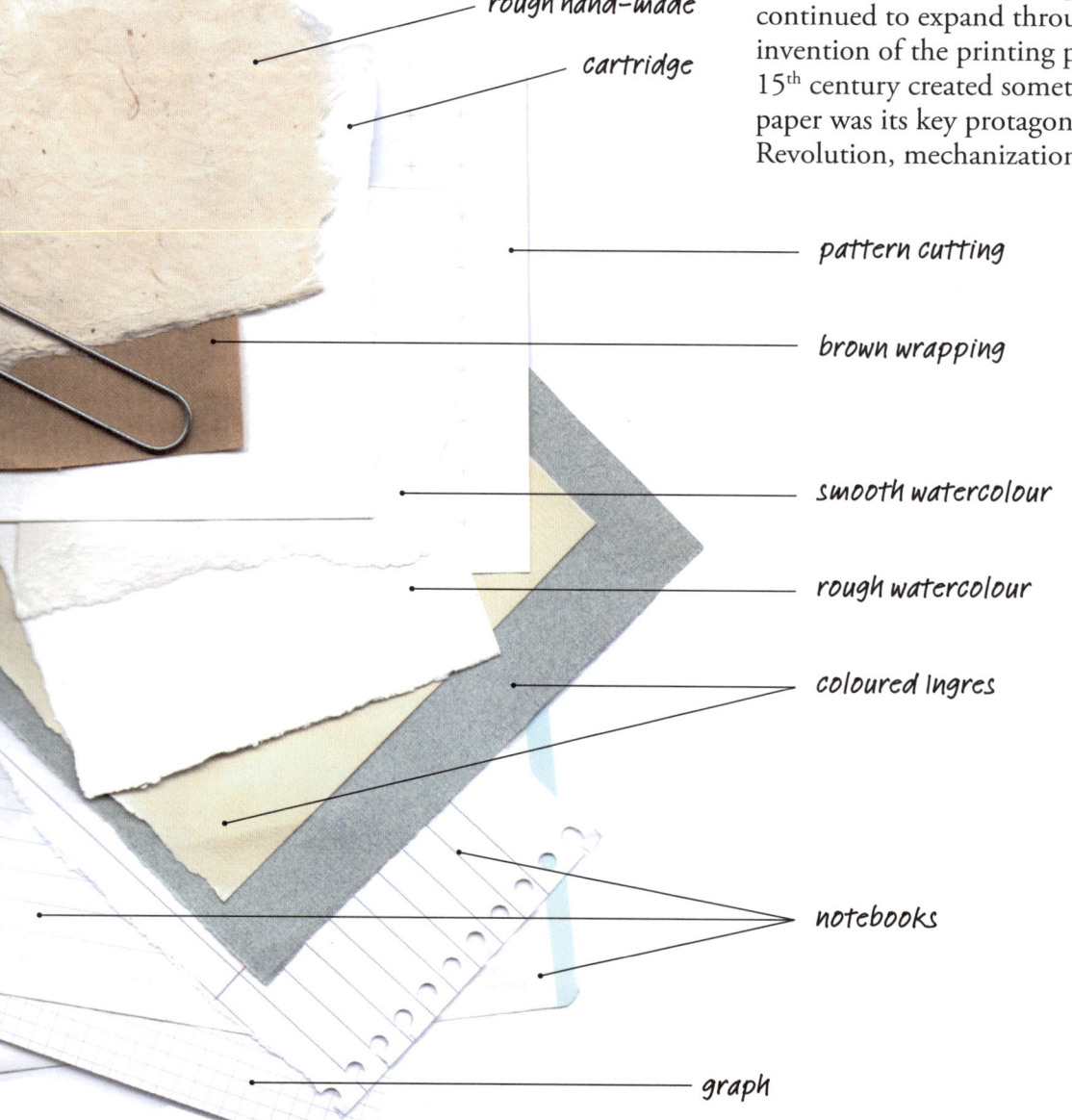

rough hand-made

cartridge

pattern cutting

brown wrapping

smooth watercolour

rough watercolour

coloured Ingres

notebooks

graph

from luxury handmade craft material to ubiquitous, even commonplace, item. To the artist, designer and illustrator it remains an invaluable essential, despite the challenges of our digital age.

The following list offers information about paper's forms, availability and uses. For specialist jobs it's worth doing in-depth research. Some prized types of paper include *lokta* from Nepal and *kozo*, a mulberry-fibre paper from Japan. When travelling you may find local speciality paper sellers or, in little local shops and supermarkets, notebooks and pads of unusual grades and tones.

- Sketch books (various sizes and weights of paper): a small pocket notebook (A5 or such) is good for ideas on the go.
- Basic bulk paper for working out ideas: A4 and A3 size printer paper, weight around 80gsm (grams per square metre). Best bought in ream packs (500 sheets) from office suppliers, etc.
- Layout paper: this is finer than the bulk type (about 45gsm–55gsm) and semi-transparent. You can work through a series of roughs – amending, changing and

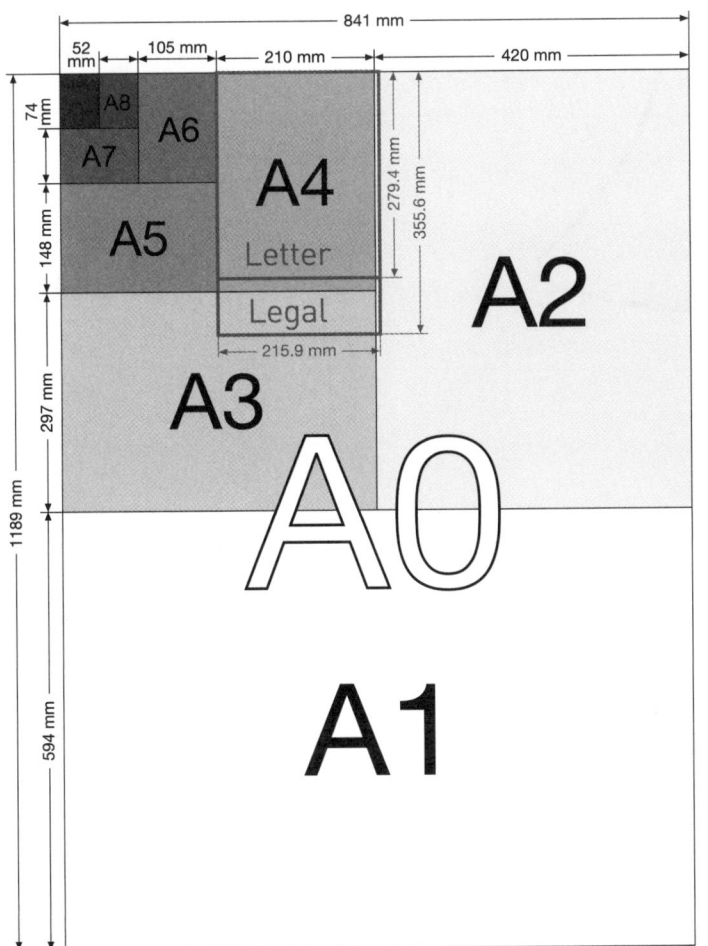

redrawing – just by putting another sheet on top, until you get your 'finished rough'. A good way of doing this is to buy the paper as a pad and begin at the back, working forwards. It's worth remembering that spirit pens and fibre tips will bleed through to the underneath sheet.

- Cartridge paper: a good heavyweight paper that can take various media; an economical choice if you want to experiment with various ways of putting down colour.
- Bleedproof paper: around 70gsm, for use with spirit-based pens (marker pens). It allows you to put down flat colour with a clean edge. In the US there is a heavier weight type called 'Paris' bleedproof paper; in the UK an alternative is Bristol Board (see rag paper below), about 250gsm, a smooth paper, double faced, which can be used either side. Bleedproof paper is excellent for 'air brush' techniques. It is good to use heavier weight paper if the finished drawing is for your portfolio, as thinner paper starts to look shabby quite quickly but is all right for artwork going to print.
- Watercolour paper: for watercolour paints and coloured inks. It comes in two forms: 'cold press' (called NOT), has a rough, textured surface and is good for transparent washes and inks; 'hot press' (HP) gives a smoother finish, which is good for opaque paints such as gouache. All watercolour paper comes in various textures and weights, from fairly lightweight 90gsm to around 300gsm.
- Ingres/coloured papers for pastel work, gouache or collage: this is a beautiful laid paper taking its name from the neoclassical French painter who favoured it. Characterized by its subtle but distinctive lines, produced during milling and available in a wide range of attractively soft colours.
- Rag paper: perhaps one of the oldest examples of recycling, originally made from old clothes – hence its name. More specific versions are linen and cotton paper which are used to make banknotes more durable. Bristol and Somerset are both rag papers whose fibre composition remains the same as when they were first manufactured in the late 19th century. Somerset® is a world leading traditional printmaking paper, mould-made from 100% cotton to high archival standards.
- 'Found' paper: in addition to paper you can buy, you can use scraps torn from magazines, packaging paper and other interesting coloured and textured papers as good stock for drawing and collage work. These make an ideal media mix for fashion illustrations and can be used directly or scanned and used digitally.

ESSENTIAL AND BASIC KIT

The definition of essential equipment depends on whether you are more illustrator than designer, or a little of both. One of the first considerations is what size you should work at. US paper sizes differ from European ones, where standard sizes are formatted from A1 down. This affects whether your work will fit a standard portfolio case and whether you need to scan or copy it for your own records, and also how it will print out in the country you may be sending it to electronically. Most professional European portfolios are A3 maximum, but designers often also have a second smaller A4 version as well as digital files. While a smart digital presentation from an iPad is hugely convenient and can be impressive, for many people technology is no substitute for the touchy-feely experience and accurate colour of a physical portfolio.

The following lists offer guidance to essential and basic kit requirements; you may already own or have easy access to many of these items. Some of what is considered essential depends on individual choice and the type of work you do and includes considerations such as the use of roller and ballpoint pens to facilitate quick mark making and convenience. While the 'Must Have' list contains essentials, the 'Favourites' list is more personal and dependent on the type of work you do. Our 'On the Go' list consists of those few essentials you probably want to have with you always, and the 'Wish' list suggests some of the bigger stuff to save up for – one day. . . . Of course, you can add to or edit these lists to meet your own particular needs and preferences.

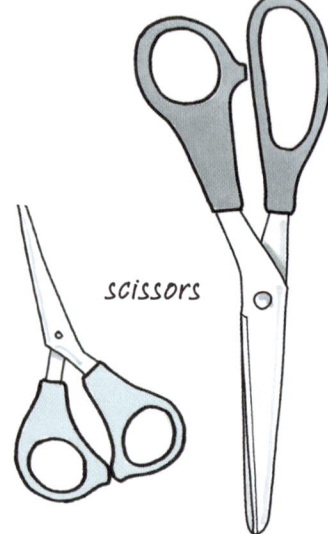

scissors

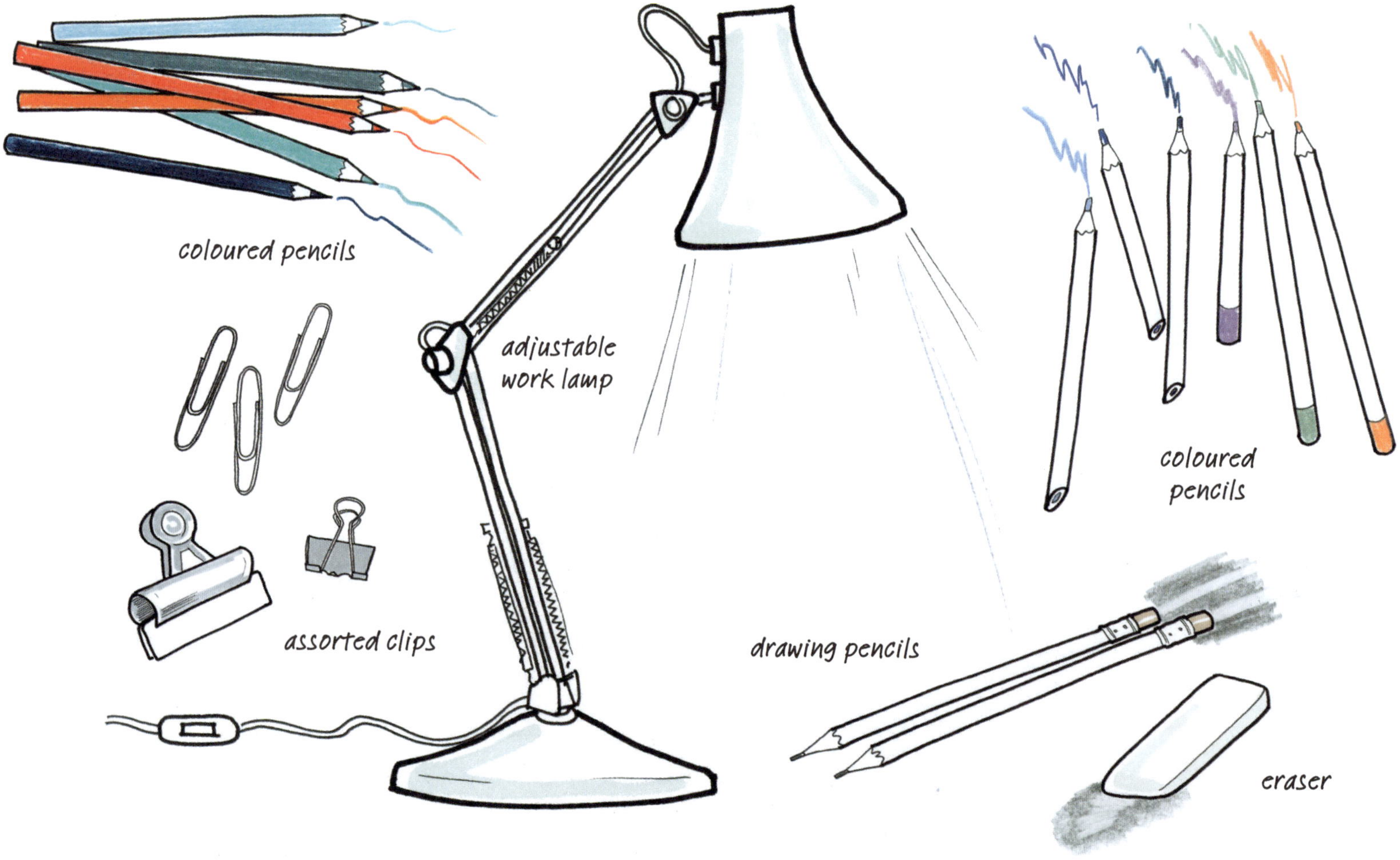

coloured pencils

adjustable work lamp

coloured pencils

assorted clips

drawing pencils

eraser

MUST HAVE LIST

- Adjustable work lamp with a daylight bulb for colour accuracy
- Comfy chair
- Selection of drawing pencils – graded hard to soft
- Pencil sharpener
- Eraser and eraser 'pencil' for finer work
- Coloured pencils
- Ballpoint and rollerball pens
- Scissors
- Assorted clips
- Dip pen and ink
- Fine fibre-tipped pens 0.05 to 0.8
- Brush pen
- Marker pens – perhaps the designer's most useful medium for adding colour speedily and cleanly
- Cutting mat – also good as a drawing surface and to help define a working area on a crowded desk
- Craft knife and blades
- Steel rule – for cutting and measuring
- Perspex rule – for measuring and drawing against
- Corrector pen
- Drawing curve
- Set square
- Masking tape
- Clear sticky tape – for 'ordinary' jobs
- Clear 'magic' removable sticky tape – for specific tasks
- Glue stick
- Sticky notes for notes to self and as positioning guides

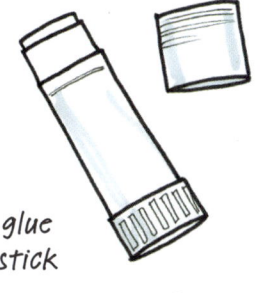

glue stick

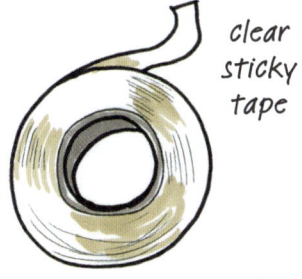

clear sticky tape

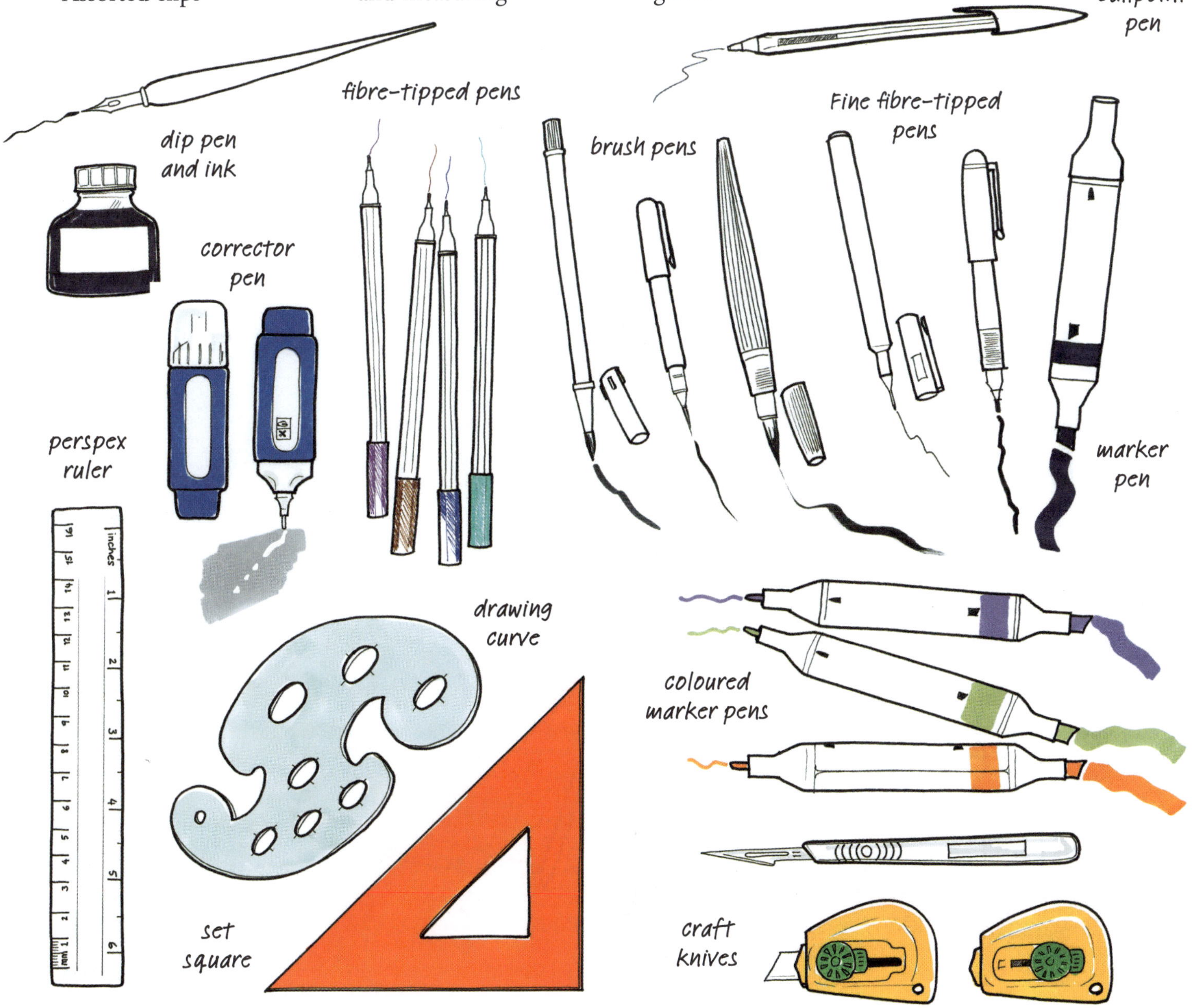

ballpoint pen

dip pen and ink

fibre-tipped pens

brush pens

Fine fibre-tipped pens

marker pen

corrector pen

perspex ruler

drawing curve

coloured marker pens

set square

craft knives

MUST HAVE LIST, CONTINUED

- Layout pad – 50gsm A4 or A3, according to preference
- Laptop or desktop personal computer
- A4 printer/scanner
- Inexpensive printer paper – 60/80gsm for roughs, etc.
- Desk-ready sketchbook
- Higher quality printer paper – 80/90/100gsm, for colour and finished work
- Selection of lined and graph papers – as drawing guides for checks, plaids and stripes, etc. Can be downloaded for free
- Small stapler
- Long-arm stapler
- Pin board – or somewhere you can post important information and reminders to yourself along with inspirational images that will help personalize your workspace

ON THE GO LIST

- Pencil case with your favourite drawing materials – we love automatic pencils because they are sharp, clean and quick!
- Handy size sketchbook – A5 is great for your pocket or bag and can be used as a notebook
- Mobile telephone, for handy camera reference, record-making and notes

FAVOURITES LIST

- Graphite pencil
- Chinagraph pencil
- Conté pencils
- Charcoal pencil
- Chalk pastels
- Oil pastels
- Watercolours
- Acrylics
- Paint brushes for watercolours, acrylics and gouache
- Coloured inks
- Designers' gouache paints
- Soft sponge and roller
- Fixative spray
- Adhesive spray

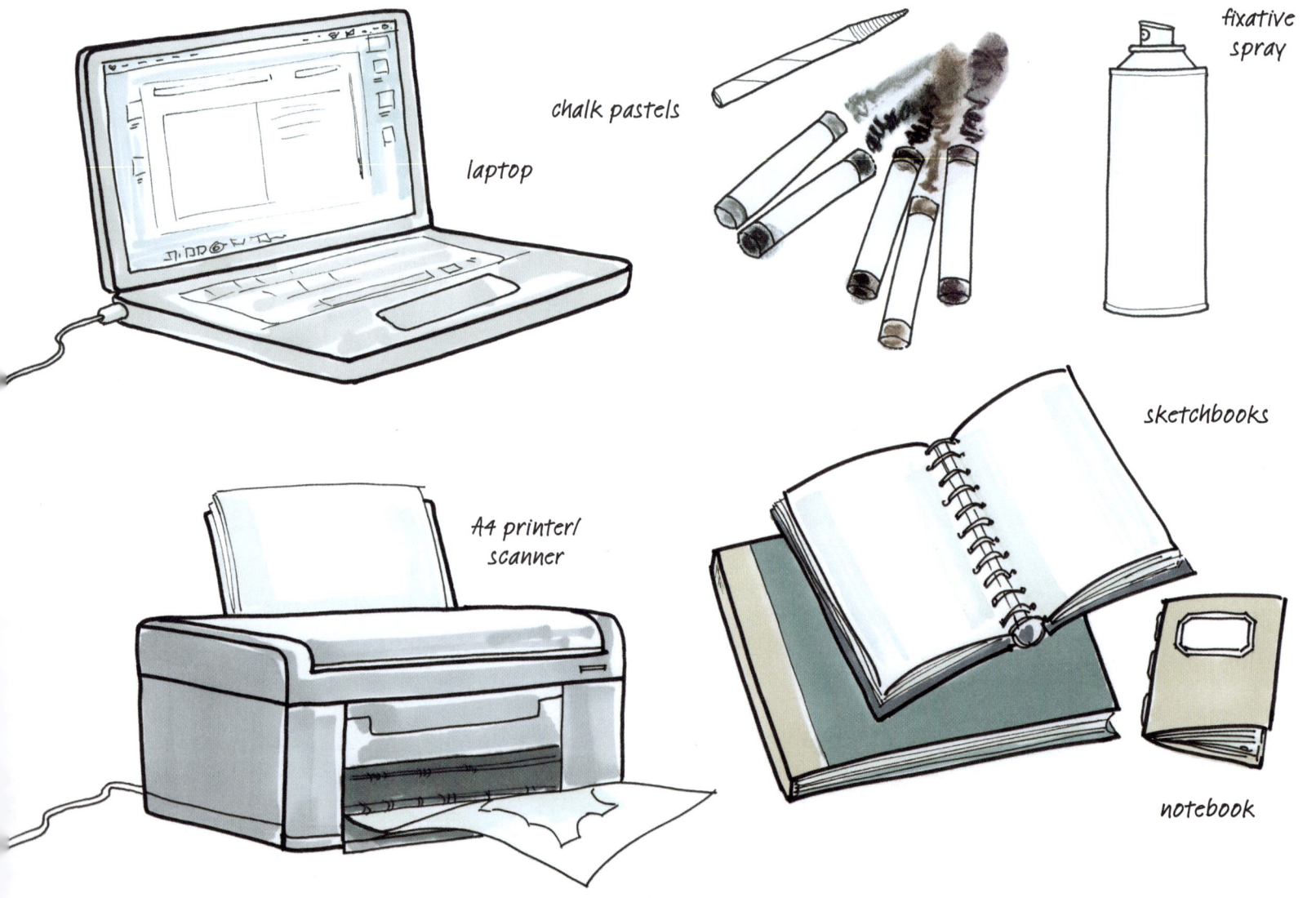

laptop

chalk pastels

fixative spray

A4 printer/ scanner

sketchbooks

notebook

WISH LIST

- A3 printer/scanner
- Light box – for tracing and copying drawings
- Desktop pencil sharpener
- Photoshop program
- Adobe Illustrator (industry preferred) or similar program
- Tablet for drawing and photography
- Professional camera

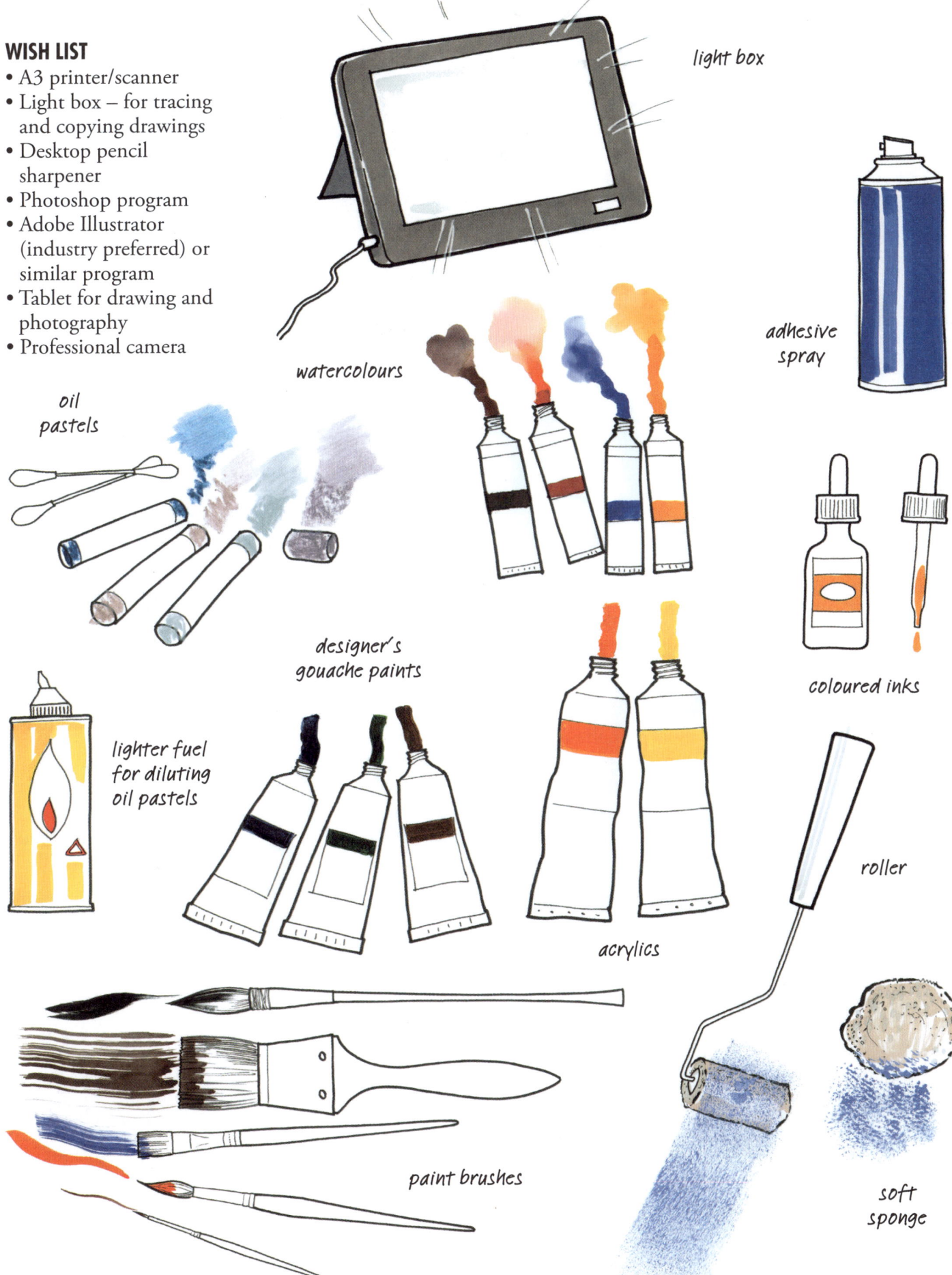

light box

adhesive spray

watercolours

oil pastels

coloured inks

designer's gouache paints

lighter fuel for diluting oil pastels

acrylics

roller

paint brushes

soft sponge

BUILDING UP YOUR KIT: EXPERIMENTAL AND SPECIALIST

Once you have got the hang of some basic skills and are more confident, you can build your range of techniques by experimenting with a broader spectrum of specialist implements. These are termed 'dry' or 'wet'. In addition, there are numerous types of paper which can be explored, producing a range of different finishes.

DRY MATERIALS

- Graphite pencils come in a huge range, from hard leads that give a very fine, faint line, to dark, soft leads that can be smudged with a finger and produce a rougher, more fluid line.
- Chinagraph pencils are waxy and make a bold mark on any surface.
- Conté pencils are very hard pastel crayons with which a variety of effects can be achieved, from very soft to dark and smudgy marks.
- Charcoal pencils are essentially charcoal in a pencil form, which means that they are not as messy to use as lump charcoal. Various grades of charcoal can be bought in this form. It is very fluid, and an extreme variety of lines and marks can be achieved – from the very soft and subtle to dark and bold scribbles – all of which can be easily smudged.
- Chalk pastels are either soft or hard. Pigment is bound together with clay and gum arabic and, as with paints, their price reflects the amount of pure pigment they contain. The first three saturations, containing the most pigment, are the most expensive, and as more white is added to make them paler, so the price reduces. Since they are expensive it is worth trying out just one or two to see if it is a medium you want to use. Soft and subtle effects can be achieved by overlaying, smudging and blending colours.

- Oil pastels comprise pigment bound together with beeswax or mineral wax and non-drying petroleum jelly. They are very waxy and produce a bold, textured line that is excellent for quick life studies. Another feature of these pastels is they can be used to block in large areas of colour and then blended to a flatter colour using lighter fuel, white spirit or turpentine.

WET MATERIALS

- Marker pens are spirit-based and are available in a fantastic range of colours. Each pen usually has two different-sized nibs, making them a versatile, clean and quick way of putting down flat colour.
- Watercolours are blocks of pigment bound together with gum arabic, glycerine, resin and sugar. Water is applied with a brush and the paint can then be transferred to paper to give bold washes of colour, or to build up layers of colour in a tonal way. Once dry, subsequent layers of colour can be added on top.
- Coloured and black inks are essentially concentrated watercolours, and are used in much the same way. They produce very intense colours, which is especially useful if illustrations are going to be reproduced. They can be applied with a brush to create washes of colour or with a pen to produce a lively, scratchy line or to add finer details.
- Gouache, generally called designers' gouache, is an opaque water-based paint that is used for laying down flat colour.
- Fixative spray is used for fixing pencil, crayon, charcoal and pastel once an illustration is complete.
- Adhesive spray is essential for mounting work flat. Make sure you use it in a well-ventilated room to avoid a build-up of fumes.

DRY MATERIALS

Graphite

Chinagraph pencil

Conté pencil

Charcoal pencil

Chalk pastel blended
with finger

Oil-based pastel blended
with white spirit

WET MATERIALS

Nib pen and ink

Marker pen
using a broad nib

Marker pen
using a fine nib

Watercolour over
masking fluid

Concentrated pigment
drawing ink over wax
crayon (wax resist)

Gouache

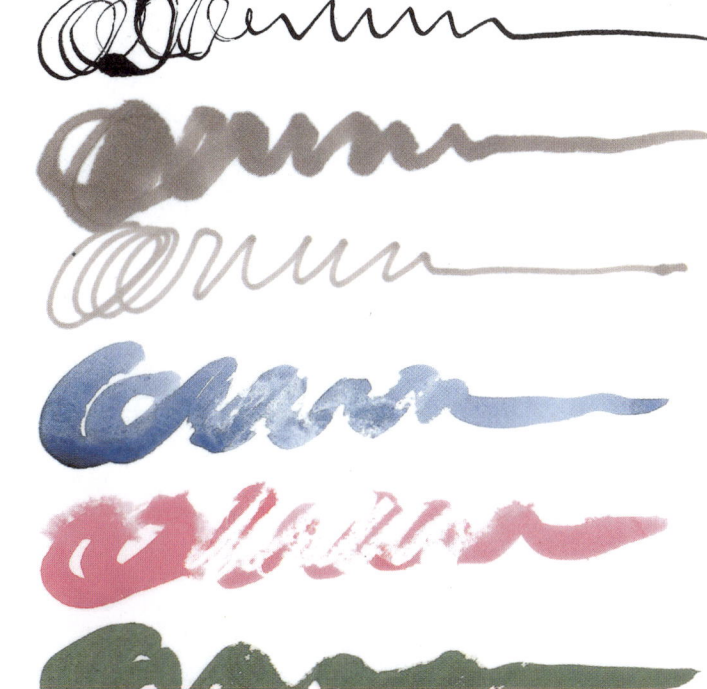

BASIC SKILLS

Fashion drawing requires the ability to draw accurately and symmetrically. Drawing involves the strict coordination of hand and eye. The page or drawing surface must be full-square to the drawer, as having the page at an odd angle or writing diagonally results in distorted hand positions and will spoil your work. It is worth remembering that professional designers may be required to draw all day, for days on end. The tensions that build up in the hand and arm can prove detrimental to long-term health and wellbeing; but they can largely be avoided by correct posture and hand positioning. This is equally as important as a good chair and proper sitting position are for the care of your back.

DRAWING CURVES AND CIRCLES

Following the movements shown here will make drawing easier, simpler and ultimately more successful. They can be broken down into steps – using fingers, hand and arm – and are particularly useful when drawing curves and circles, which can be tricky. There are four key movements, depending on the scale of drawing and size of curve:

- Fingers – for small curves, drawings and details, using the simple manipulation of the fingers
- Wrist and hand – for larger curves, using the basic 'hinge' movement of the wrist back and forth
- Elbow and forearm – for large curves and arcs; the elbow needs to lift off the drawing surface to facilitate freer movement
- Whole arm – for very large drawings, using the swing of the arm and even full body movements.

HOW TO HOLD A PENCIL CORRECTLY

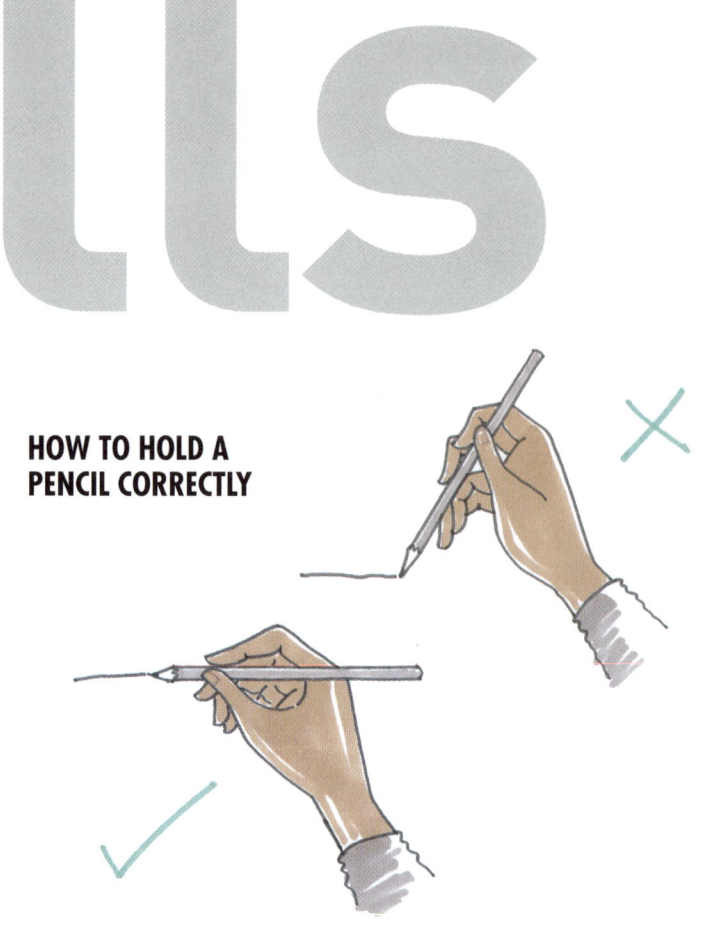

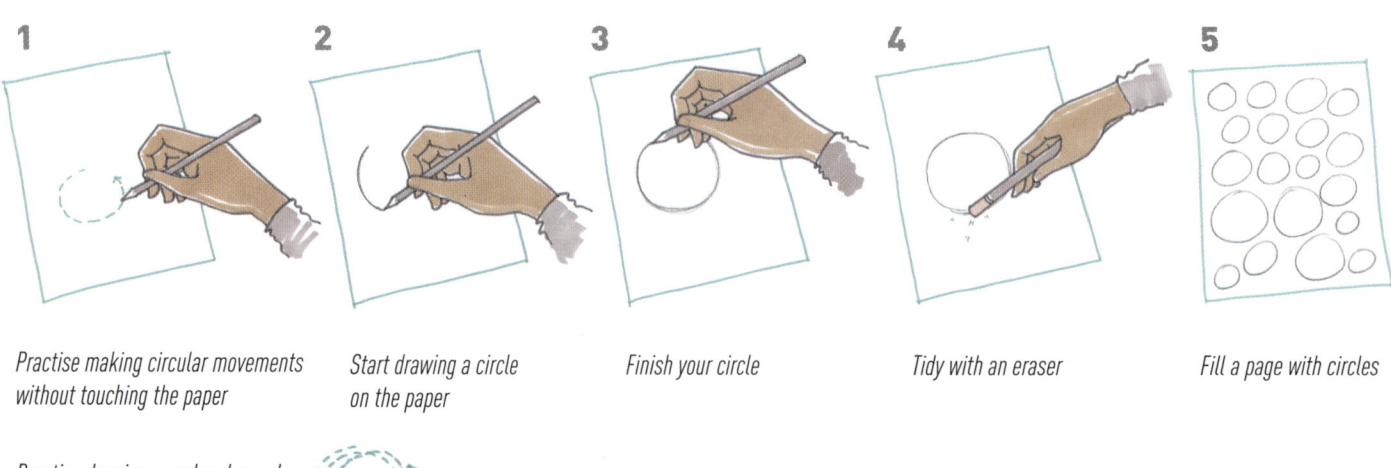

1	2	3	4	5
Practise making circular movements without touching the paper	*Start drawing a circle on the paper*	*Finish your circle*	*Tidy with an eraser*	*Fill a page with circles*

Practise drawing round and round

You can use found objects to draw round – the inside of your roll of sticky tape, a lid or tin can, and not forgetting traditional compasses like the ones you used at school. There are also clever bendable guides you can buy specially for the purpose.

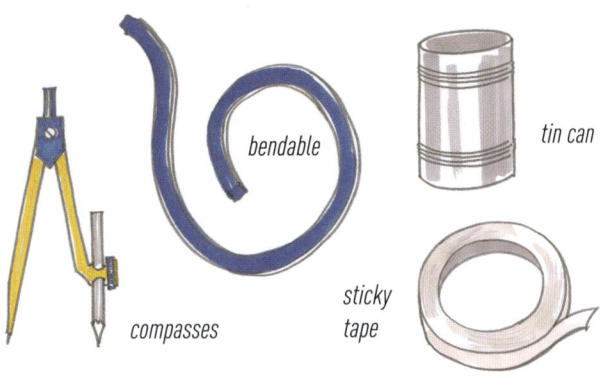

bendable

tin can

sticky tape

compasses

DRAWING CIRCLES USING LITTLE FINGER AS COMPASS

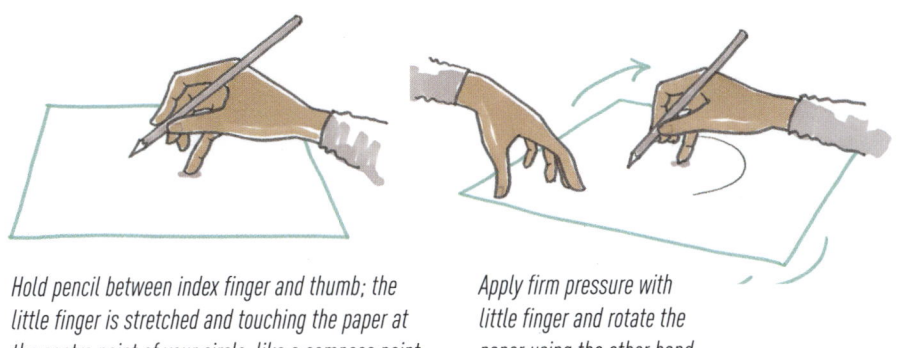

Hold pencil between index finger and thumb; the little finger is stretched and touching the paper at the centre point of your circle, like a compass point

Apply firm pressure with little finger and rotate the paper using the other hand

DRAWING CIRCLES USING WRIST

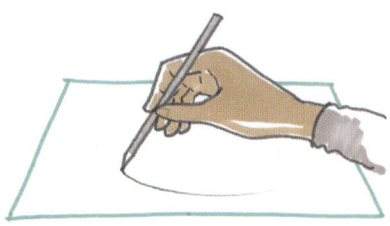

Hold pencil normally, keep fingers still and move your wrist to make the pencil move in an arc

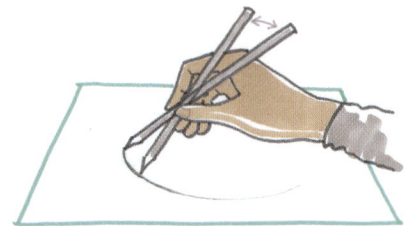

Use lots of little movements to make a large circle and fewer to make a small one, turning the page as necessary

DRAWING CIRCLES USING FOREARM

DRAWING CIRCLES USING WHOLE ARM

To create large circles, move from the elbow to make wide sweeps in either direction

To help understand the range and limitations of these movements it's best to practise a few of them with a small range of equipment and media; pencil, pen, brush, ink and paint, etc. The best, most successful curves are generally drawn in one stroke, from inside the curve – following the body's natural movement – and with a certain amount of speed to keep the stroke fluid. This may be an instance where turning the page can produce a better result. When drawing small curves – a neckline on a garment, for example – there is a point at which, in the action of drawing, the pen changes from being dragged to being pushed. It is at this point that a bump or wobble occurs, so it is important to recognize and if necessary to compensate by moving or turning your drawing page. Of course it may not always be possible to turn your drawing round, you may have to move your body instead. If you are doing a large drawing and want to draw a nice, continuous sweeping curve not only do you need the physical space to work in, you also need suitable media. You've already chosen your paper or board and considered whether it takes wet or dry materials well but if, for example, you are using paint or ink, your brush needs to be large enough to hold enough paint or ink to travel the length of the line.

Of course it's not essential to achieve perfection; sometimes the inaccuracies in a drawing become part of its appeal and character. With practice and growing self-awareness you will be able to judge what adds to and what detracts from the success of a drawing in the context of its end use.

DESIGN LINE-UP

The start of a new drawing or illustration assignment is influenced by personal choice and the nature of the specific job. We used standard cartridge paper for this line-up of drawings – a good all-rounder suitable for the wide choice of media to be deployed. We used a fine fibre-tip pen for the outlines and main details of the drawings and gave considerable thought to the nature and qualities of the fabrics of the various garments, and the suitability of different media for successful rendering.

1 *Magic marker pens were used for areas of flat colour, together with soft chalk pastels blended with a twisted paper pastel blender. Watercolour paints and a fine brush were used to add further texture and highlights.*

2 *Magic marker pens were again used for the flat base colour; dip pen and white ink were used for the pinstripes; and pencil crayons were used for shading and highlights.*

3 *Designers' gouache paints were used for the flat opaque ground with details picked out in fibre tip pen; shadows and highlights were created using pencil crayons.*

4 *Famous for its qualities of good coverage, acrylic paint was applied with a small sponge roller. When the paint was completely dry, shadows and highlights were added with pencil crayons.*

5 *A swatch of 'mock-croc' was used for rubbing over with conté crayon and pencil crayons to create the appropriate textured effect. Finally the drawing was stabilized with spray fixative.*

HEALTH AND SAFETY NOTE

Spray glues and fixatives should ideally be used in an approved fan-assisted spray booth or at least in a well-ventilated room. Remember to wear a protective face mask – available from good art shops or DIY stores.

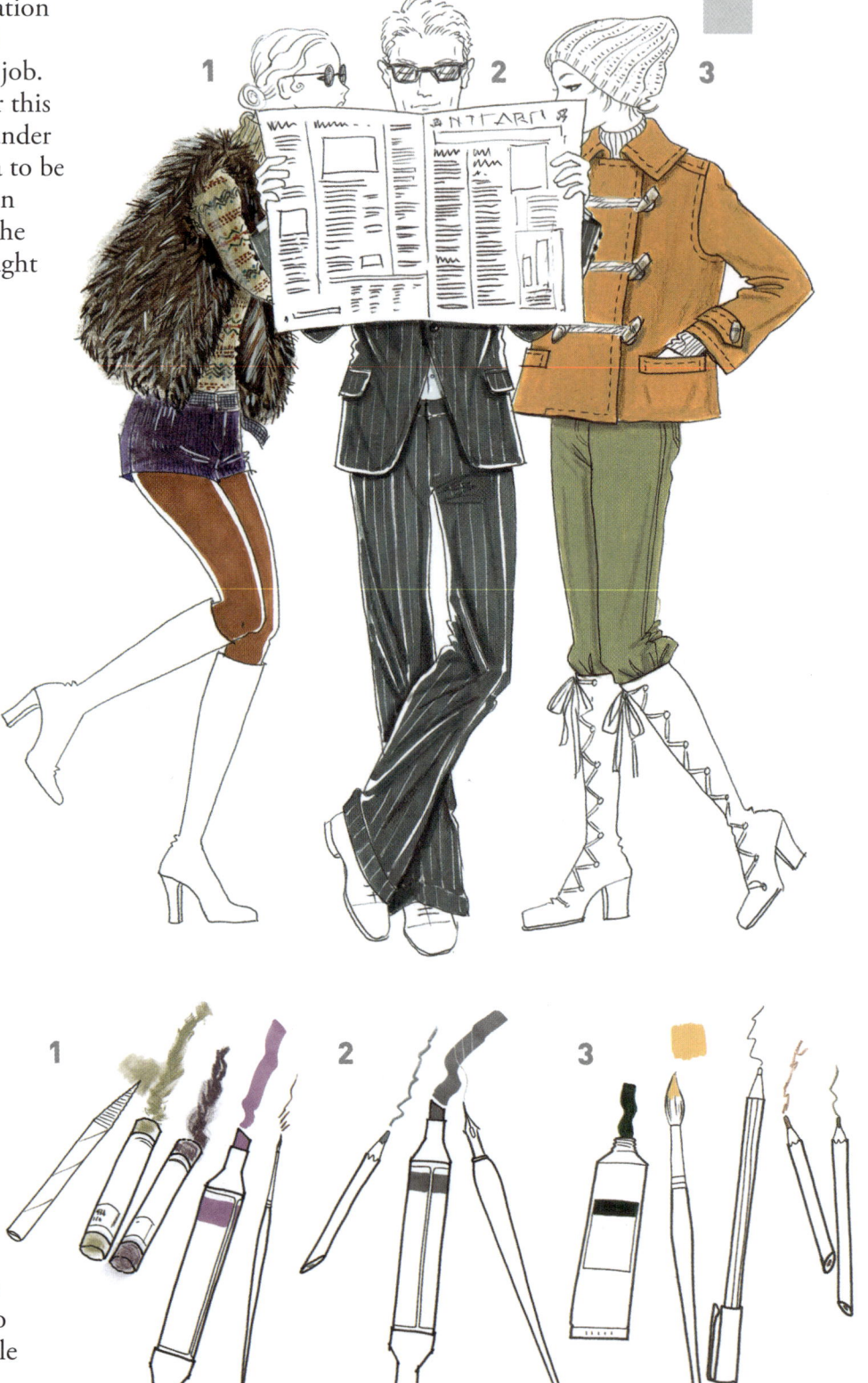

6 *Details of the sweater were coloured with oil pastels blended using cotton buds and a petroleum-based solvent such as lighter fuel, turpentine or white spirit (in a well-ventilated room). For the skirt, scanned fabrics were cut out and collaged using pencil crayons for highlights, definitions and shadows. Finally oil pastels were applied to make the tweed flecks.*

7 *Bold watercolour stroked washes were applied as a base then stippled through a paper doily to create the effect of lace. Pencil crayons were used to add definition; highlights were produced using white ink and dip pen.*

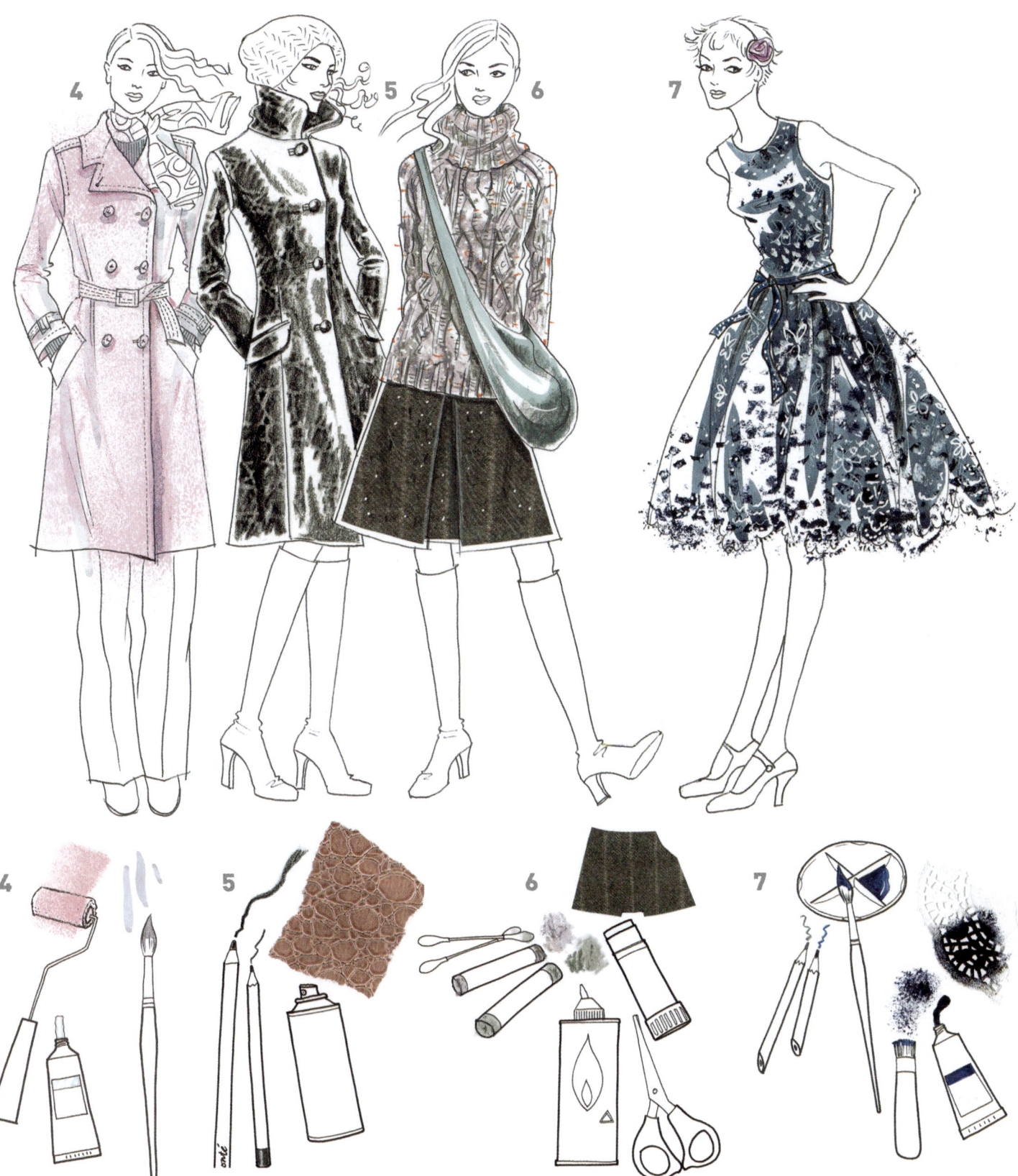

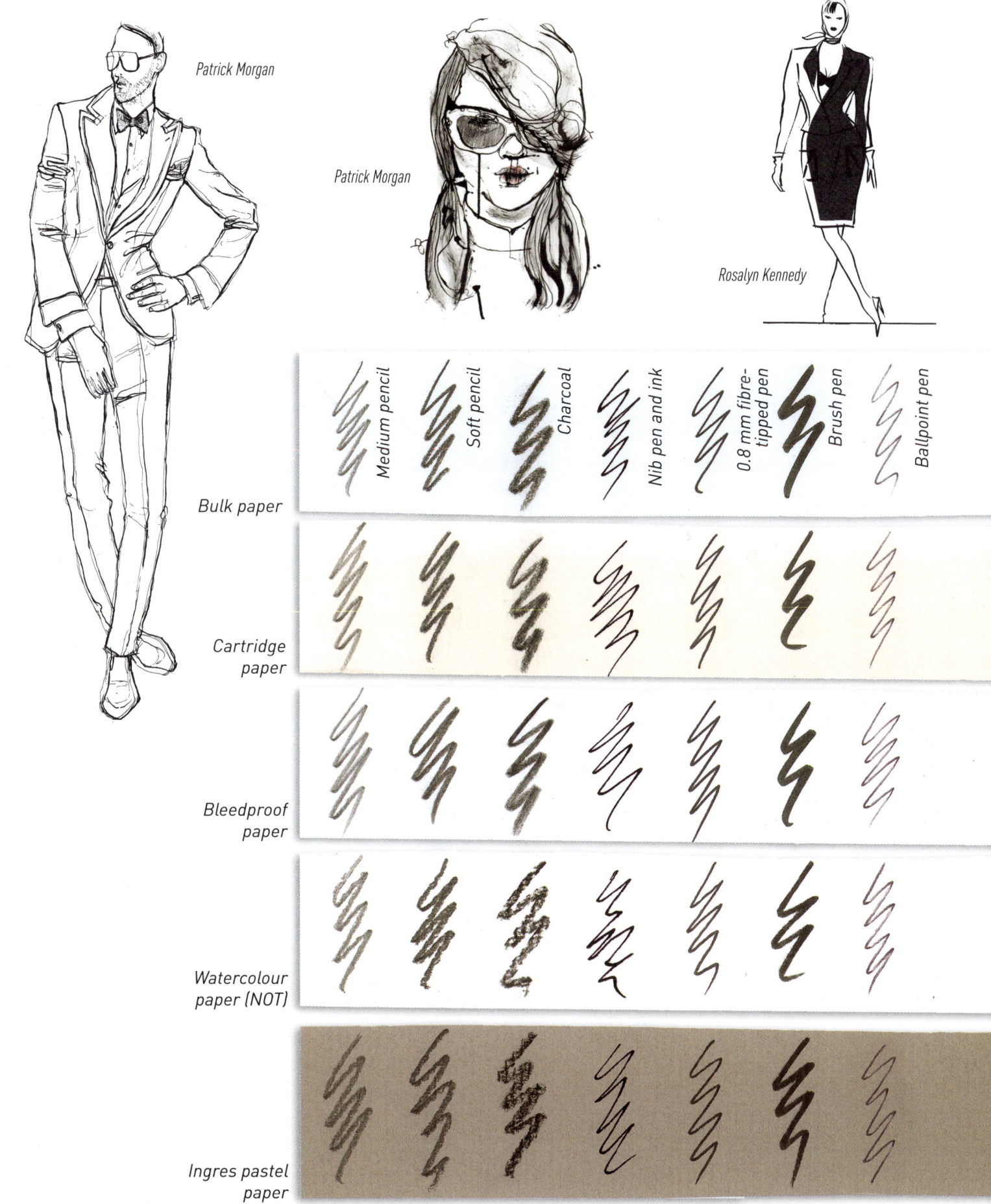

Patrick Morgan

Patrick Morgan

Rosalyn Kennedy

	Medium pencil	Soft pencil	Charcoal	Nib pen and ink	0.8 mm fibre-tipped pen	Brush pen	Ballpoint pen
Bulk paper							
Cartridge paper							
Bleedproof paper							
Watercolour paper (NOT)							
Ingres pastel paper							

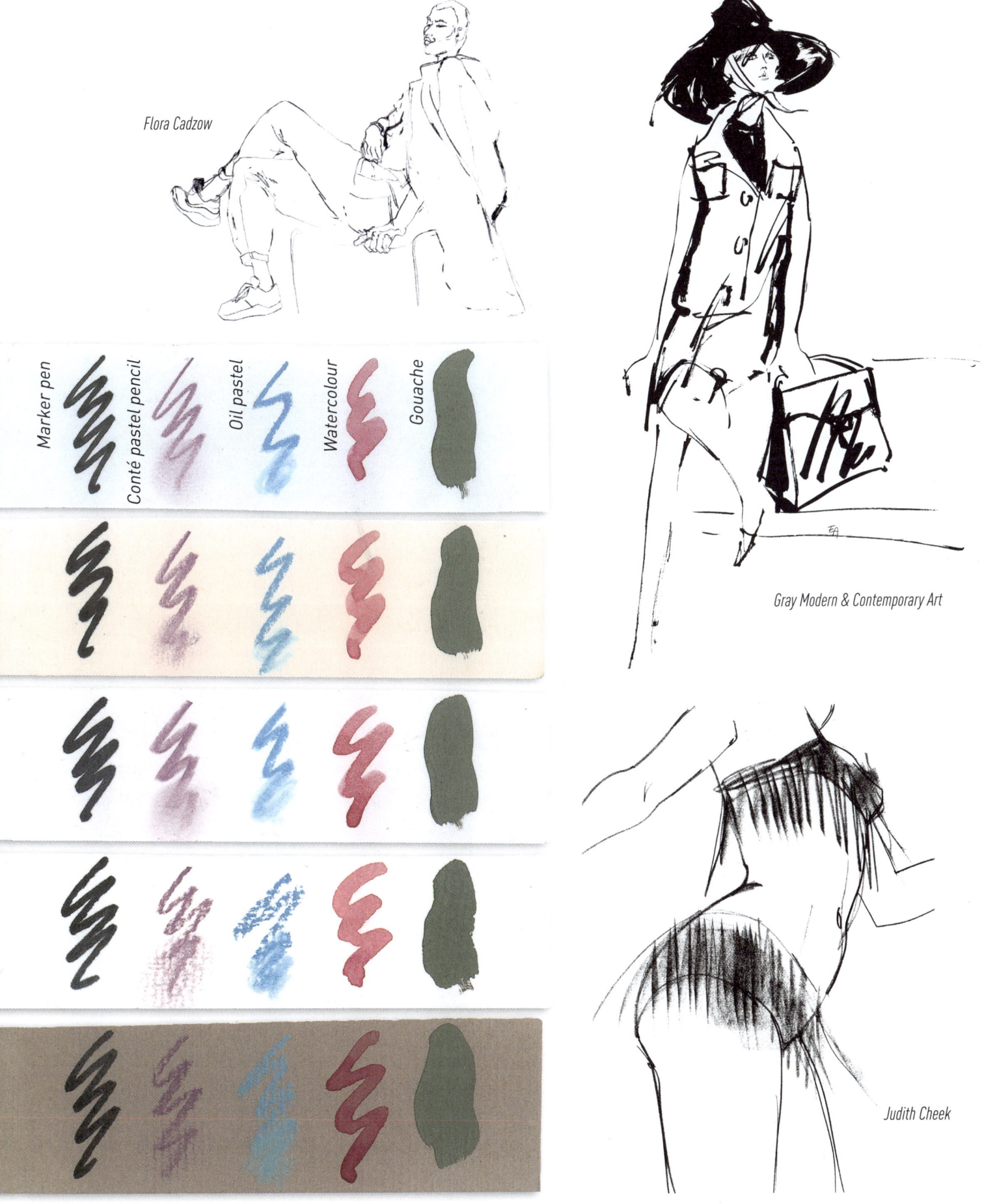

Flora Cadzow

Marker pen

Conté pastel pencil

Oil pastel

Watercolour

Gouache

Gray Modern & Contemporary Art

Judith Cheek

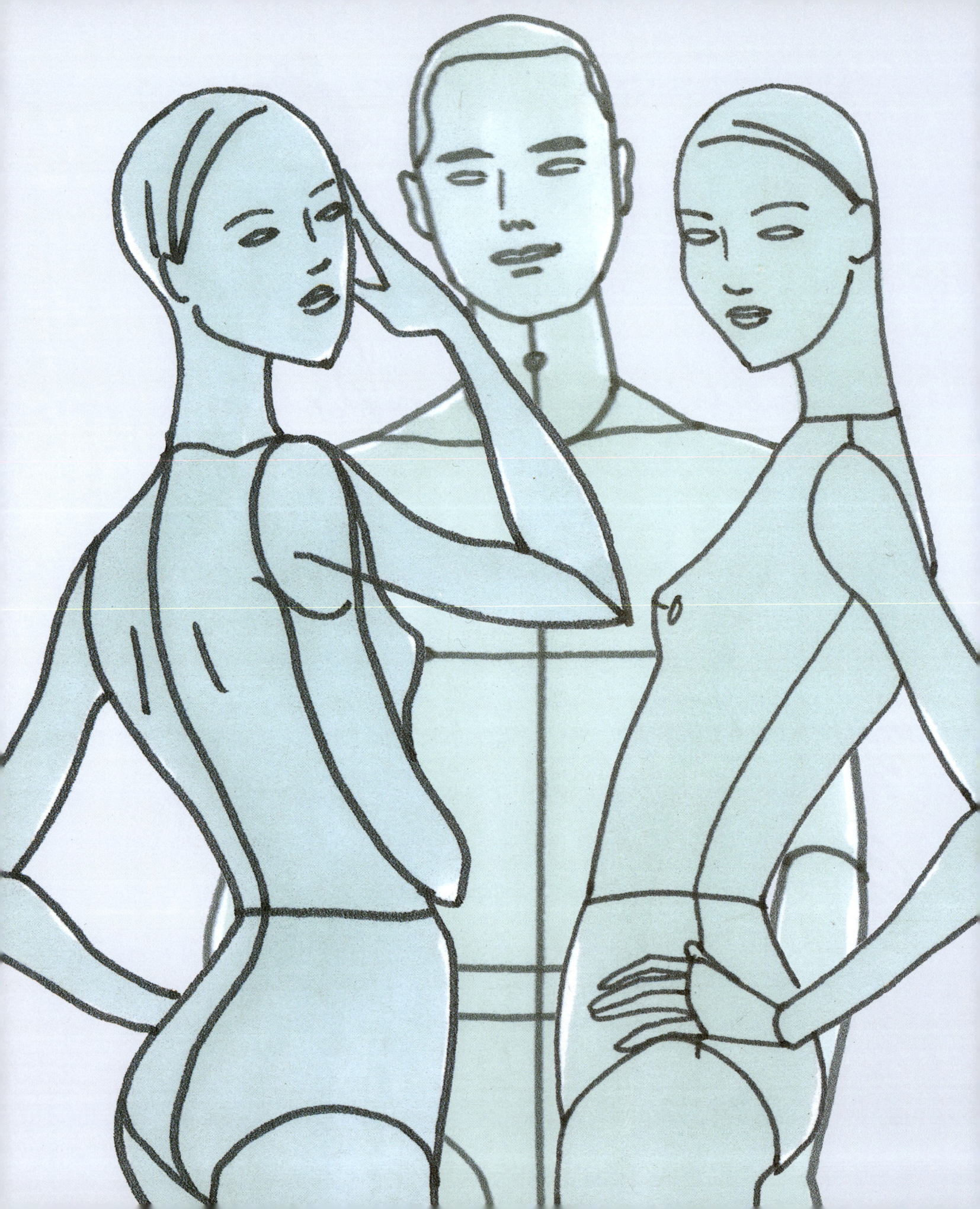

CHAPTER 2

ANATOMY AND POSES

The first step when drawing fashion is to develop a figure – a model that will wear your designs. You may end up with a range of characters that is constantly evolving, but when starting out it is best to perfect one quite basic form that you can adapt to suit different purposes. In this section we shall examine in detail how to get the proportions right for males and females of all ages; how to draw different poses, both static and dynamic; and how to accurately depict details such as hands, feet, heads, hair and faces.

Once you have perfected these skills and achieved a physiologically accurate figure, it is important to allow your individual style to develop, and this chapter contains a wide range of different examples across a mix of mediums and styles that should provide inspiration. It is easy to personalize the figure by varying the skin tone, hair, make-up and so on, and you should try out lots of options. Choosing the styling and look of your drawn figure is just like choosing a live model for real garments; the look and attitude has got to be right for the overall success of the illustration.

Once perfected, this template can be placed underneath a drawing sheet and you can loosely trace the shape of the figure. You can also reduce or enlarge the size of the figure on a photocopier or computer so it can be used for drawings of almost any scale, as well as for replicating numerous forms which can be used to depict a fashion collection.

PROPORTIONS OF THE FASHION FIGURE

All fashion artists apply a certain amount of creative licence to the proportions of a drawn figure – some more so than others. This is because elongating a figure enhances the appeal of the design. The extent of the exaggeration can depend of the final outcome and purpose of the piece, but a fairly standard female fashion figure is seven and a half to eight and a half heads tall, and a male form is around nine heads tall.

It helps when drawing a figure to think of it as a human body, envisaging the skeleton that supports it, the organs it encases and protects, how and where it bends and twists, the joints and muscles that enable those movements, and the distribution of weight and how that shifts as the body moves. It is equally beneficial to consider the physical space that the body occupies, and how perspective affects our view of that space. Taking life-drawing classes can be hugely advantageous as it will expand your knowledge and experience of drawing the human form and probably enable you to try out a range of media too. As with anything, practice makes perfect.

These sketches show a simple static pose and demonstrate how a stylish figure can be drafted using heads as a measurement guide.

Note the characteristic differences that define a male and female form: the female figure has narrower, sloping shoulders, a smaller waist and larger hips (approximately the same as the shoulder width) than the male. Her bust is rounder and placed about midway above the waistline, while the neck and limbs are slimmer and less muscular. The male figure, on the other hand, has shoulders that are wider than his hips, a thicker and perhaps shorter neck, and his body is proportionately a little longer, which results in a lower waistline and a more square-shaped chest that sits a little higher than midway above the waist. The

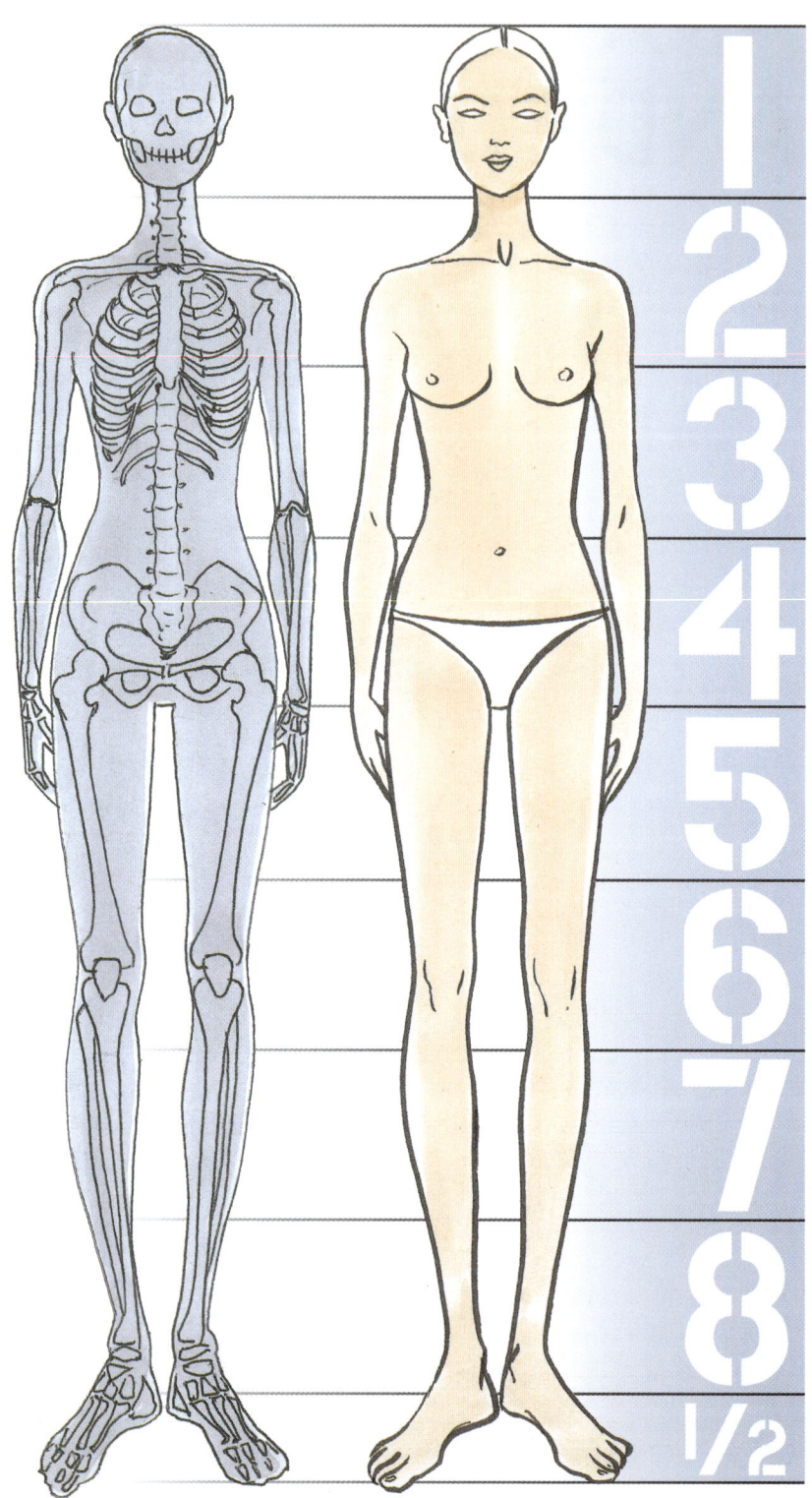

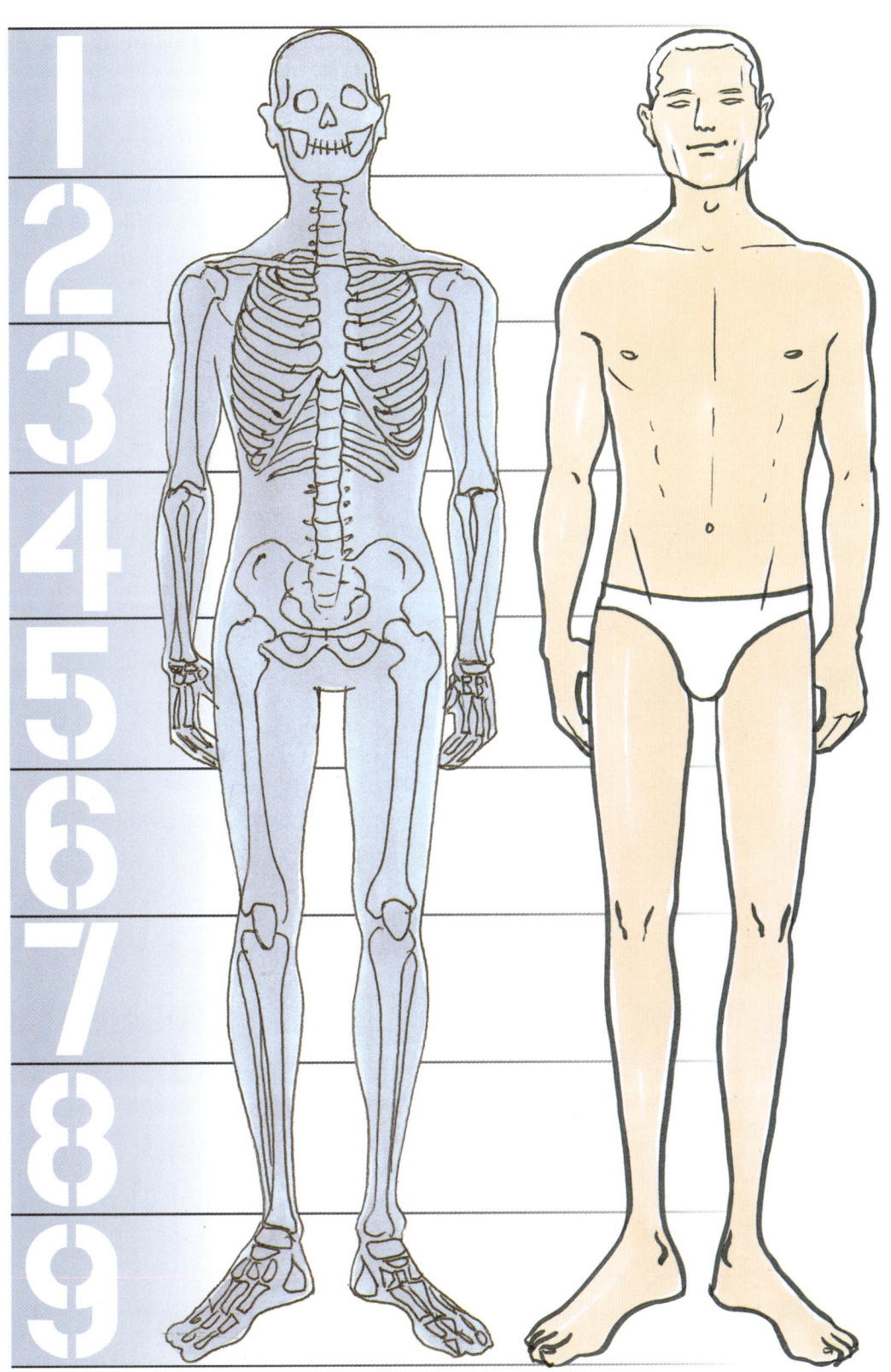

limbs are heavier and generally a little more muscular and larger feet plant him more firmly on the ground. Many designers and illustrators often initially struggle to draw male figures that look convincing yet stylish, but with practice this can be mastered. This straight-on pose is the simplest to draw, and allows numerous easy options for arm positions. It is clear and simple to 'dress' in garments.

DIFFERENT AGES

Here we depict a whole family of figures, each with their own characteristics which must be taken into consideration when drawing in order to depict proportions accurately.

The fact that children have very different growth rates makes it difficult to create a definitive proportion template for each age group. As any parent knows, the size of garments for a specific age range can vary tremendously from brand to brand. If you ever have to design or draw for a childrenswear company they should supply their own size charts. There are, however, some general guidelines:

• A baby's head makes up about one-quarter of the total body length. By the age of one, the head is about two-thirds the size it will be when fully grown, so most of the growth thereafter will be seen in the body and limbs. Babies have short, almost invisible (from an artist's perspective) necks and large round torsos. Their small, chubby limbs are bent rather than straight.

• Toddlers usually have a body that is about four and a half heads high. The shoulders are about the same width as the head height, and they have quite cylindrical bodies, sometimes with quite round tummies. Poses should be fairly static for a toddler, as they are just learning to stand and walk, so the feet are firmly planted on the ground.

• Small children are about five heads tall. Since these lively little people rarely keep still they can be depicted in more active poses.

• Bigger children range in height from six to six and a half heads, although by this age boys and girls can have very different heights. They still have cylindrical torsos and a very straight up-and-down silhouette, although older girls, from about the age of nine or ten, may start to have a slight indentation at the waistline, which is higher than a boy's. Older boys have longer torsos, slimmer hips and slightly wider shoulders than girls.

• By the teenage years (sometimes called Junior in stores), children's height can be seven or eight heads. As hormonal changes take place, male and female forms become more pronounced, and the proportions of the teenage body are quite

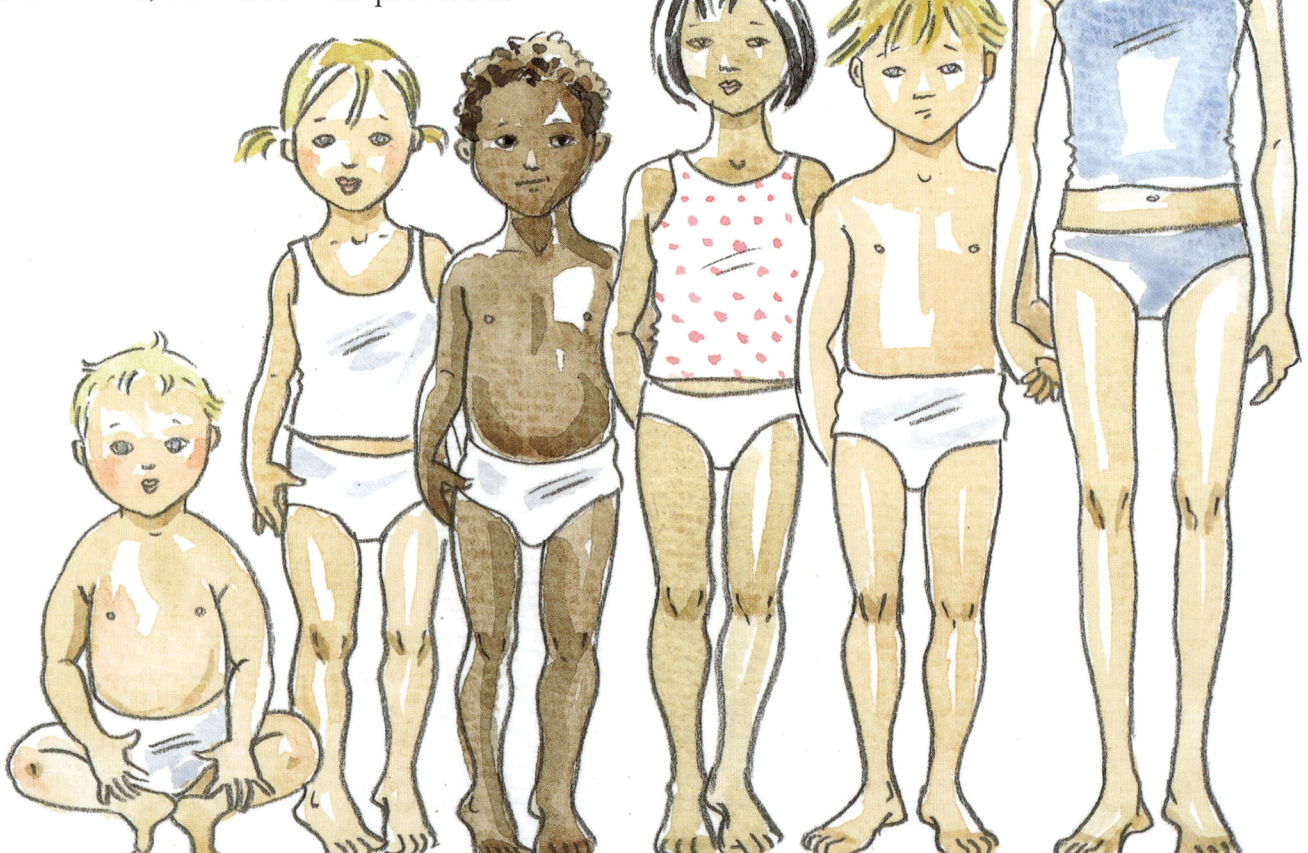

different from a younger child's. Boys have lower, slimmer hips and much longer torsos, which makes the arms and legs appear shorter. The differences are also apparent in head sizes, with girls having smaller heads and more petite facial features, which in boys tend to become more angular. As the body mass increases with age, the difference in muscularity between the genders becomes more apparent.

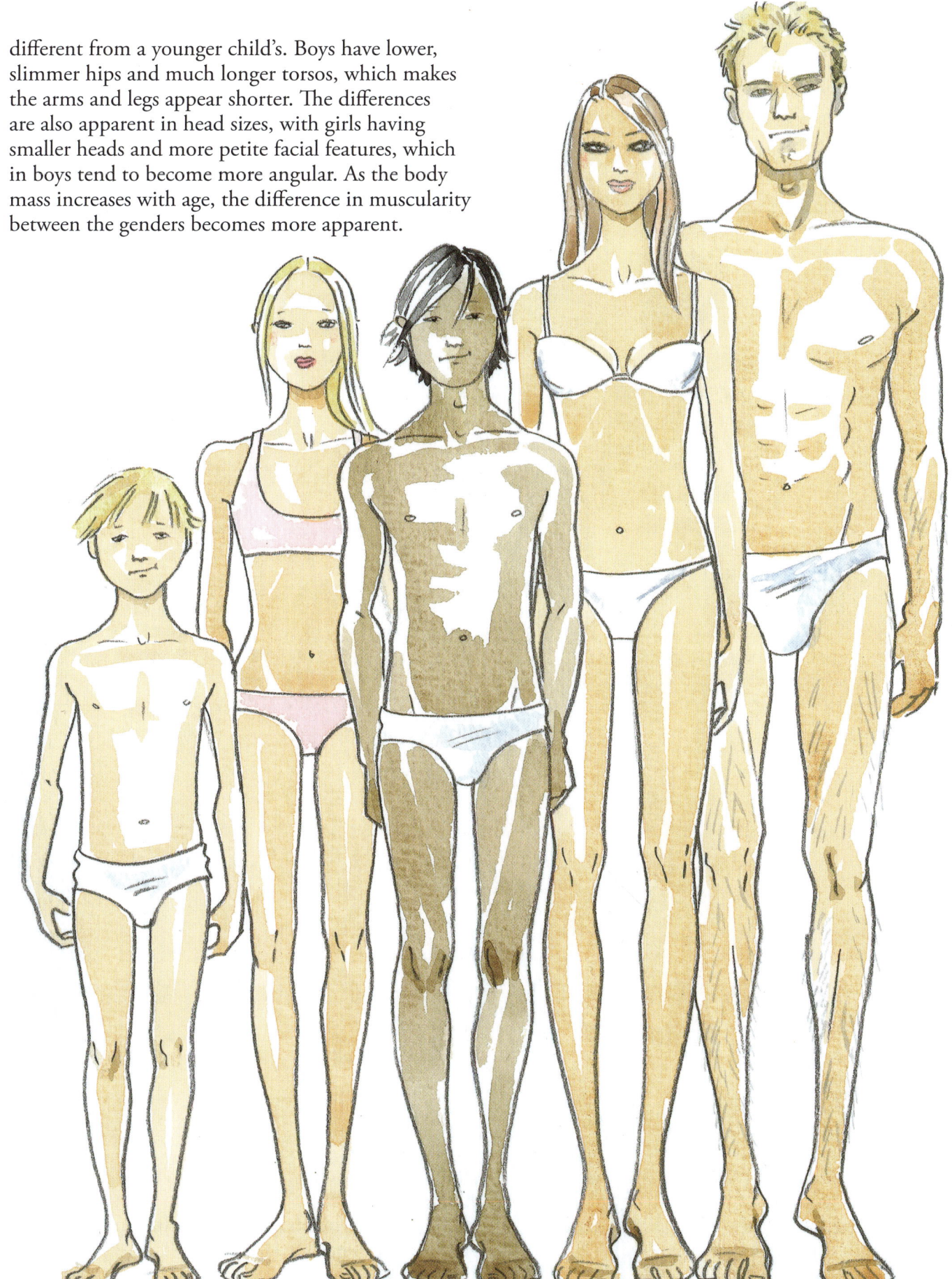

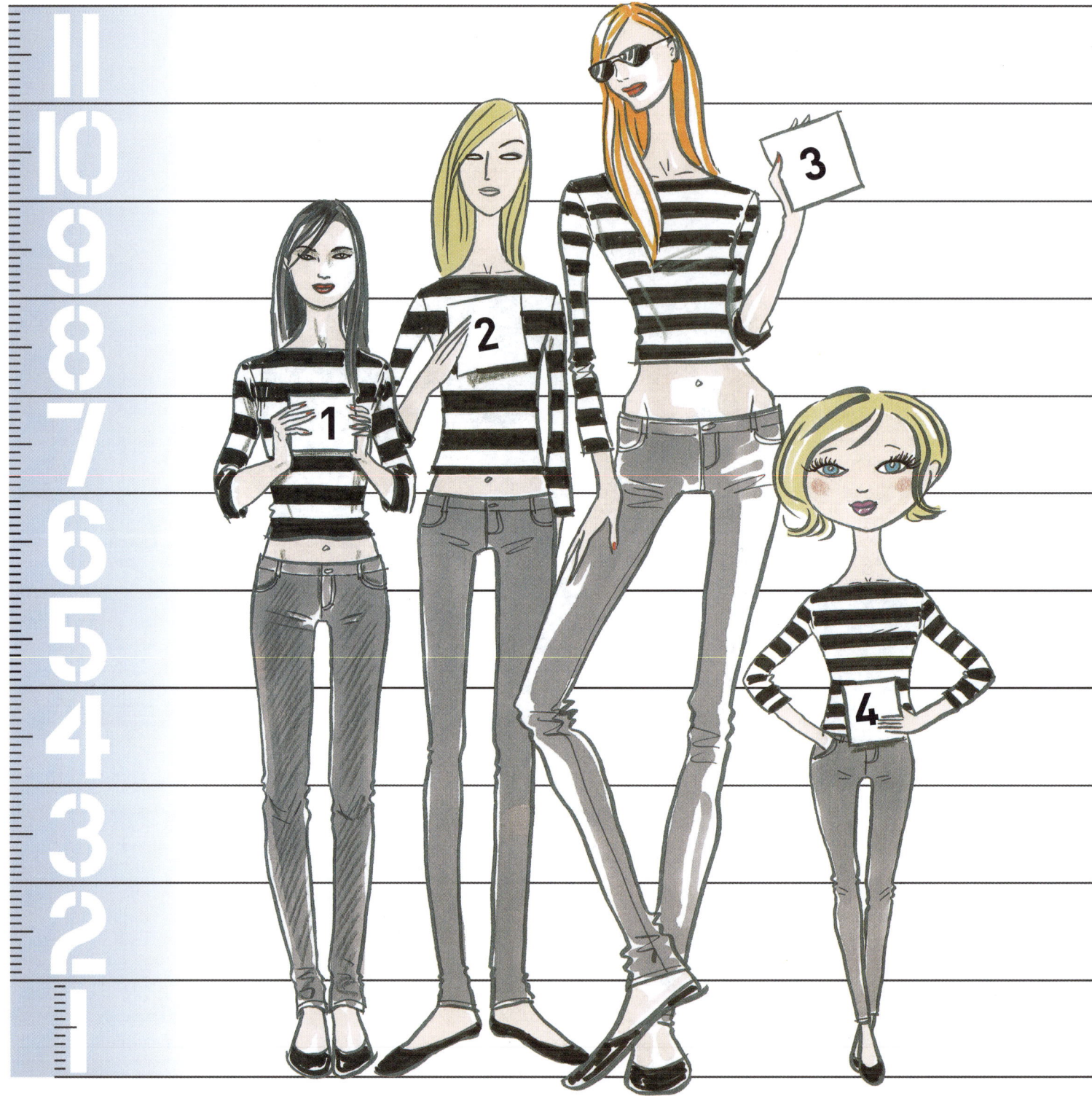

PROPORTION AND CHARACTER

As we have seen, a body height of around seven-and-a-half to eight-and-a-half heads is used for a stylish but not over-stylized female figure, and is pretty much an industry standard. However, having adhered to this basic guide, you can now add individuality and personality with facial features, make-up and hair styling. In addition, when the project allows more scope, you can have some fun with proportions. Large heads can lend a character a funky alien quality or be naïve and endearing. Similarly, heads that are too small can be comic and engaging, or perhaps slightly insect-like or even sinister! Over-elongated and attenuated figures are very striking – think of the sculptures of Alberto Giacometti, which are on the one hand tall and shadowy yet on the other amazingly stylish and elegant.

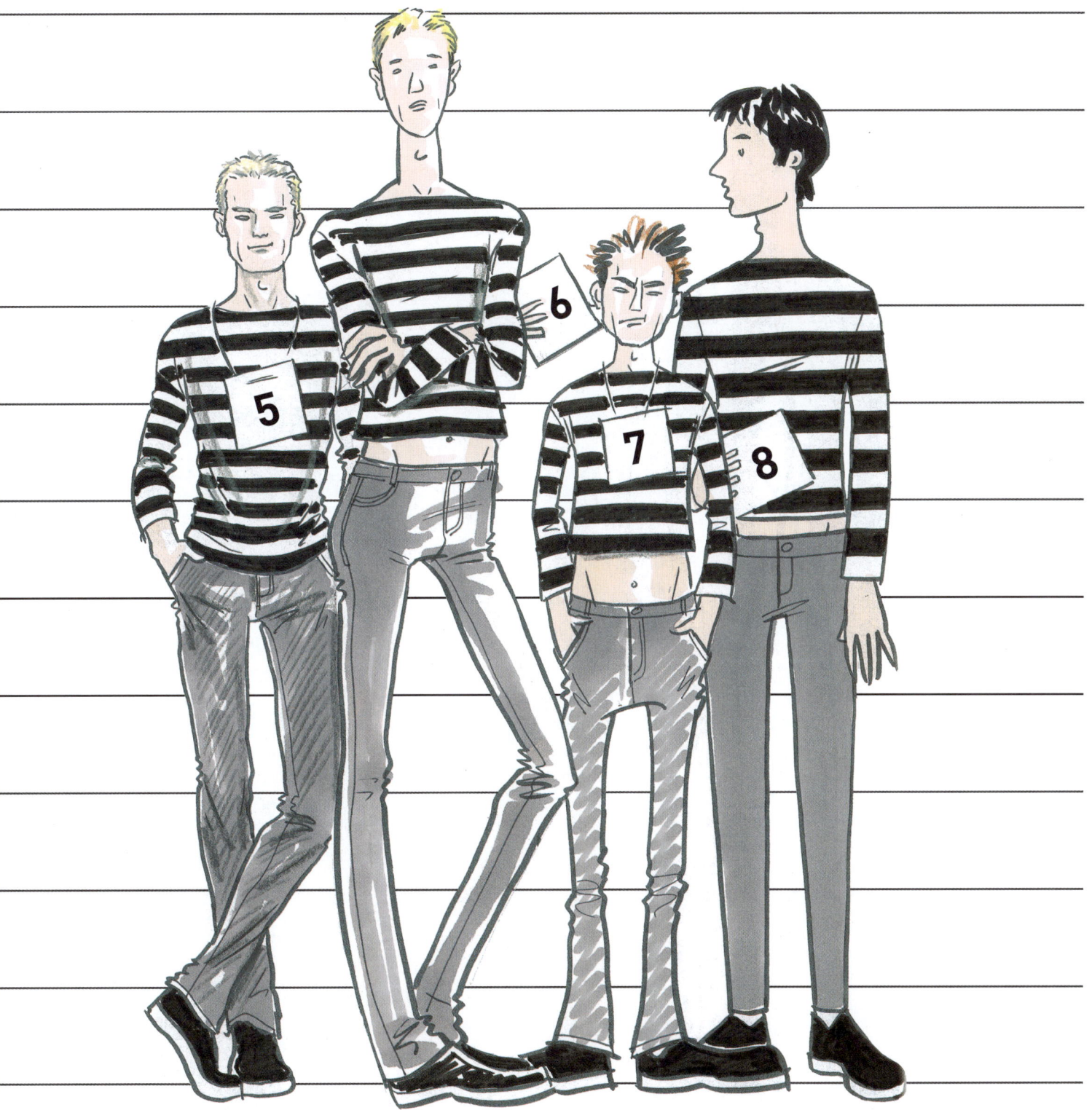

Exaggerated large feet that plant a figure firmly on the ground can make the character appear quite tough or, conversely, surprisingly childlike.

By all means experiment, but keep in mind that if the body is overexaggerated it may be difficult, if not impossible, to fit in important details when you create an outfit. If your template adheres to classic proportions, the design process is usually easier and you will avoid problems. Experimentation and critical evaluation of the drawing style and the content will help you achieve the right balance between wit and individualism and produce artworks that showcase a design in a believable and attractive manner. If you choose to follow a more offbeat path, support the illustration with a set of clear flats (see pages 114–9), to avoid potential difficulties when creating the garments.

CREATING A TEMPLATE

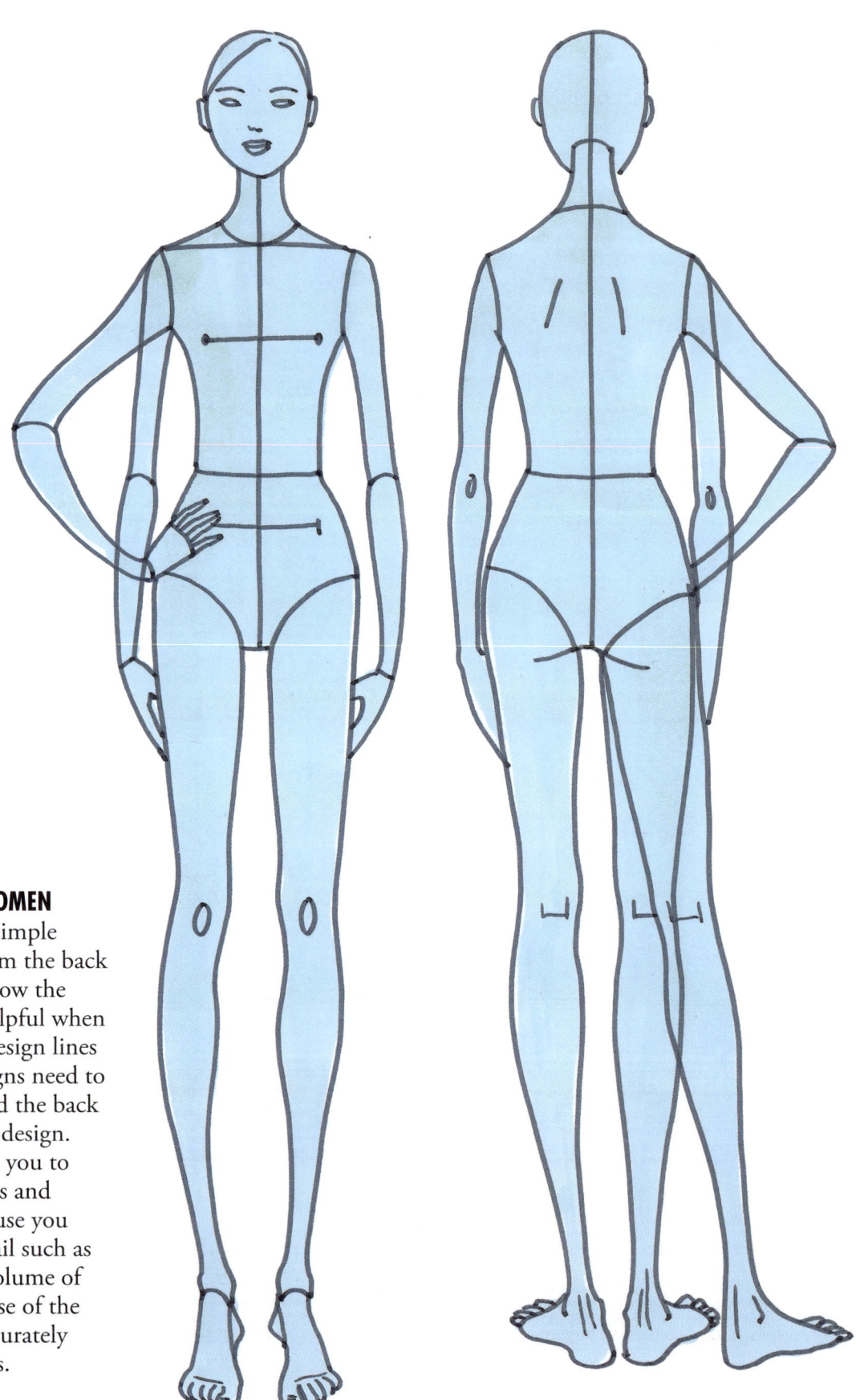

STANDARD STRAIGHT-ON
FRONT AND BACK VIEWS: WOMEN

Here we see how to draft a simple straight-on pose, viewed from the back and the front. You can see how the construction lines can be helpful when establishing the garment's design lines and proportions. Most designs need to be shown from the front and the back in order to fully explain the design.

The template also enables you to vary the position of the arms and legs. This is important because you may need to illustrate a detail such as the drape of a skirt or the volume of a sleeve, and altering the pose of the figure will enable you to accurately portray these design features.

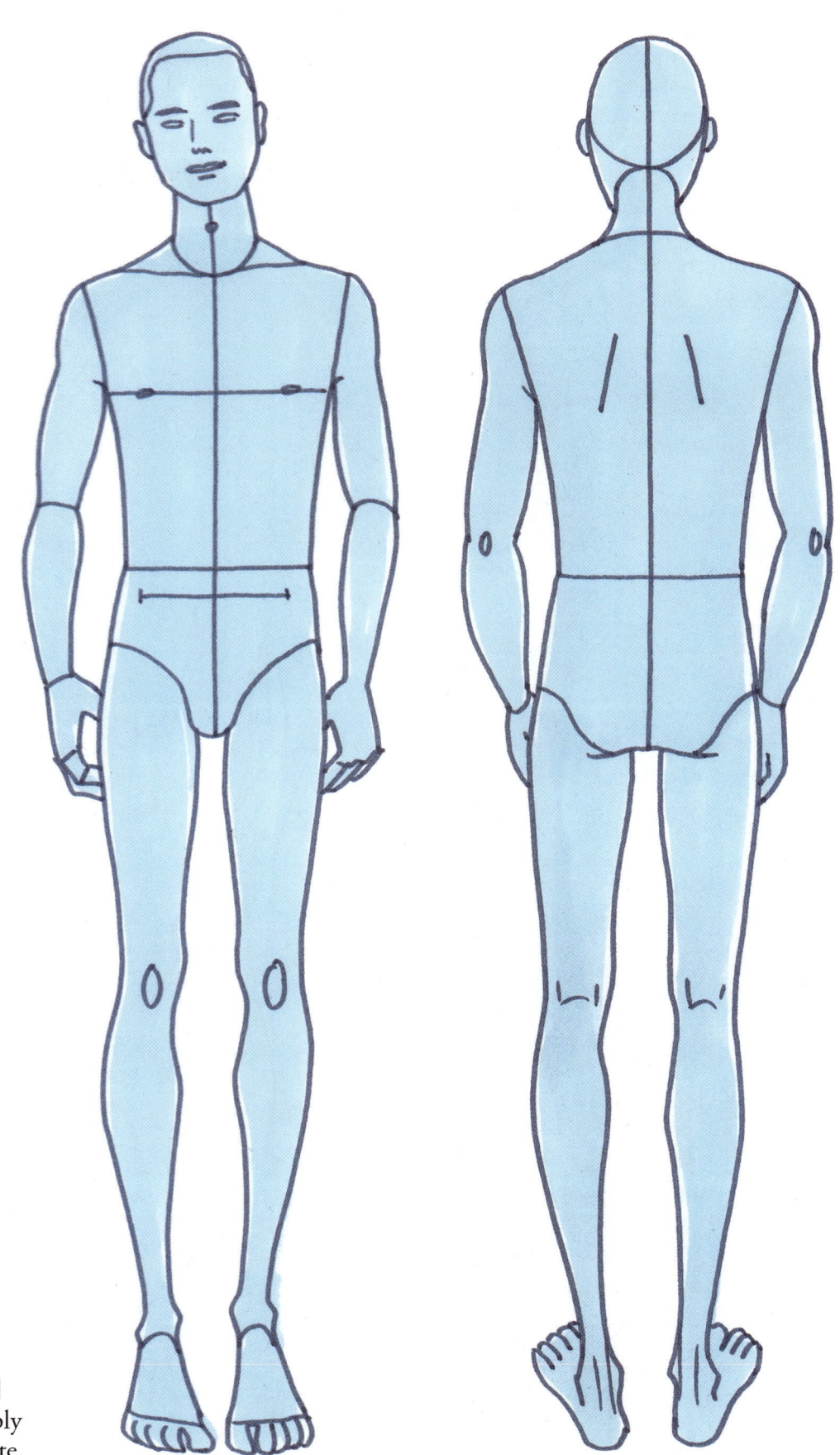

**STANDARD STRAIGHT-ON
FRONT AND BACK VIEWS: MEN**
The same basic guidelines apply
when drafting a man's template.

USING PHOTOGRAPHIC POSES TO CREATE A TEMPLATE

The first step when choosing a photo of a model upon which to base a figure is to look through magazines or a collection of tearsheets and choose a pose you like – one that suits the mood of your project. The next stage is to replicate the pose by tracing the figure. You will probably notice that the proportions of this real model seem too short and inelegant when compared to the templates described on pages 32–3, so you need to impose a little creative licence and adapt the drawing so it is more in keeping with other fashion figures.

Using tracing paper, or layout paper if you have a lightbox, carefully draw slightly inside the outline of the photographed figure to slim it down into a fashion figure. You should also slightly lengthen the neck and make the head a little smaller too. Add proportion and balance lines down the centre of the figure and across the shoulders, waist and hips, as these will help you add clothes to the finished template.

Now look again at your newly outlined figure, without the photograph underneath it. You may need to slightly refine its proportions and appearance.

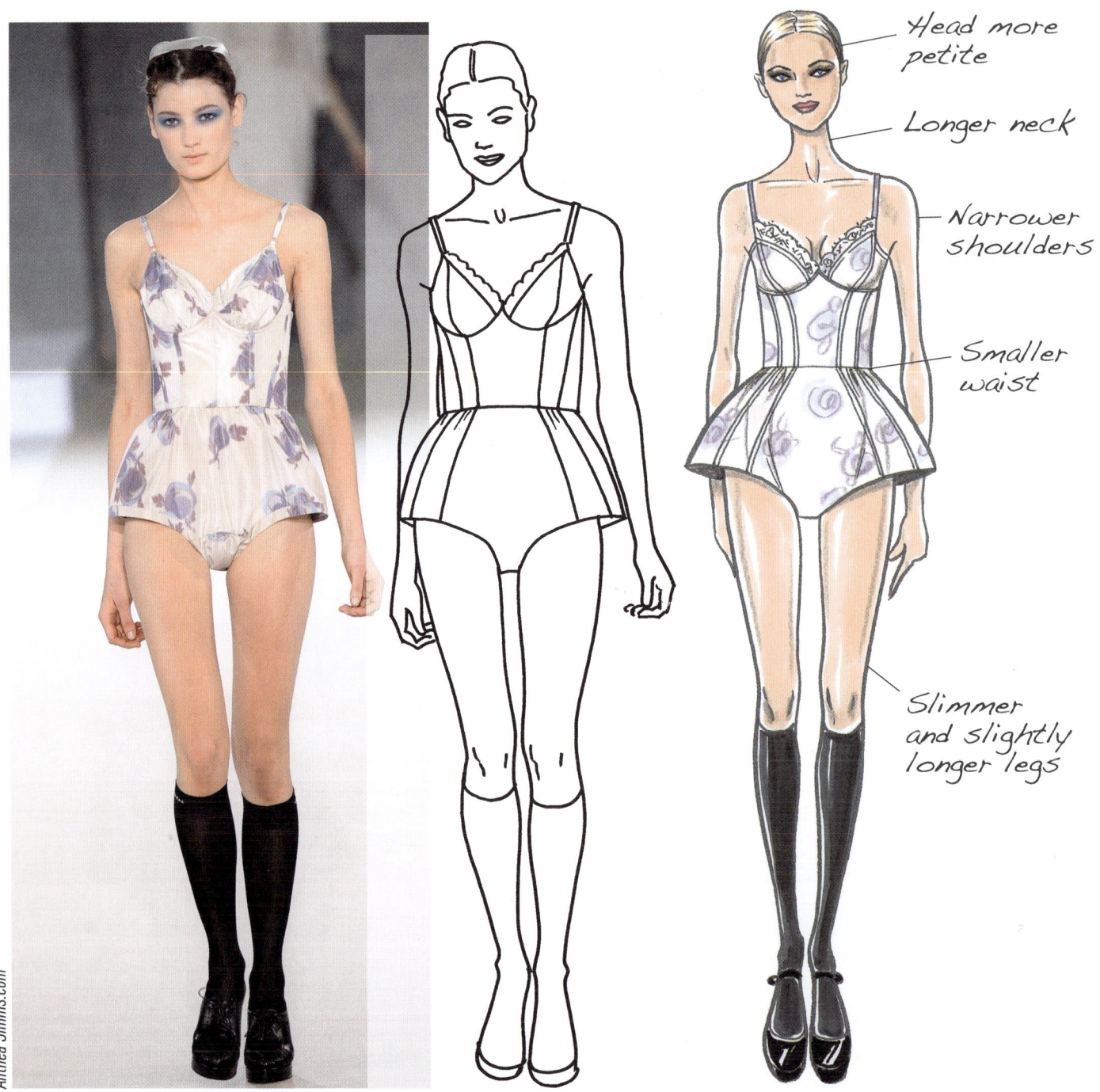

Anthea Simms.com

Head more petite

Longer neck

Narrower shoulders

Smaller waist

Slimmer and slightly longer legs

Once you are happy with the outline, either ink it in with a fine-lined fibre-tipped or rollerball pen and erase the pencil marks, or simply photocopy the pencil drawing – the lines should come out black enough to use the copy as your template.

An alternative method is to use scissors or a craft knife to carefully cut out the model. You can then slice the figure widthways into six pieces, slicing across midway each time between the ankles and knees, the knees and the top of the legs, the wrists and the elbows, the elbows and the armpits and finally across the neck. On a clean piece of paper reposition the photograph, leaving even gaps between the pieces to lengthen the figure to the desired proportions, making sure everything lines up. Once you are happy with the general look, use clear tape to secure the pieces in position and place a sheet of tracing paper on top. You can now trace the outline of the elongated figure. If the final outline is too long, use a photocopier to reduce the template to the correct size.

Both of these techniques can be used for creating templates for men, women and children.

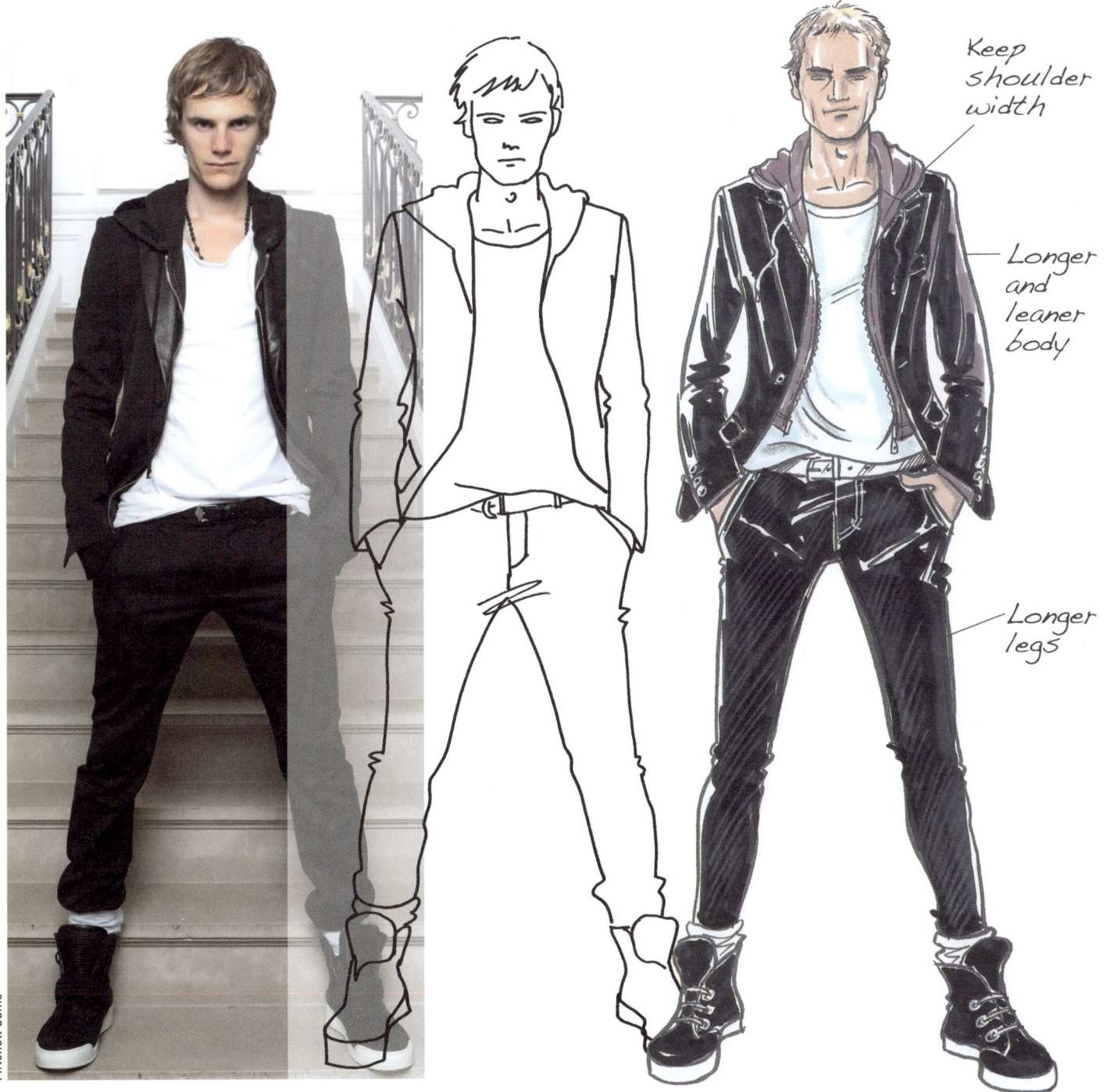

Mitchell Sams

Keep shoulder width

Longer and leaner body

Longer legs

DRAWING HEADS

Having refined the pose of your figure you can now transform it into a model, with an image and identity. Facial expressions are key to creating an attitude or mood, and hair and make-up are strong indicators of period. Collect pages from magazines for ideas and inspiration.

Most heads are roughly egg shaped, and the length of the face is generally the same as that of the hand, which is a useful guide when establishing proportions. Practise drawing a simple, expressionless face to start with, then as your confidence and style develop you can begin to experiment with facial features and expressions to lend the model character.

DRAWING A FEMALE HEAD

1. Draw an egg shape and two lines to mark out a neck. Draw a vertical centre line through the oval. This midline will be used to mark out the position of the features. Remember that if the head tilts to one side, the line will too.

2. Draw a horizontal line halfway down the head.

3. Draw in almond-shaped eyes on the horizontal midline, placing them about an eye's-width apart.

4. Mark the positions of the nose and mouth by dividing the lower half of the face into thirds.

5. To mark out the width of the nose and mouth, draw downward vertical lines from the inner edge of the eye to give the width of the nose, and the inner edge of the iris to show the width of the mouth. You can also roughly check the width of the neck by drawing lines vertically down from the outer edge of the eyes. The top of the ears should roughly align with the eyebrows, and the bottom with the base of the nose.

6. Try adding some hairstyles. Remember, drawing hair does not involve showing every hair on the head – that's not what you see when you look at someone. It's the overall shape, colour and maybe a sense of movement that make an impression, and this overall look is what you should try to produce. The hairstyle you want to draw

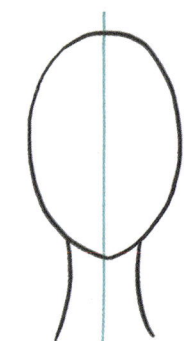

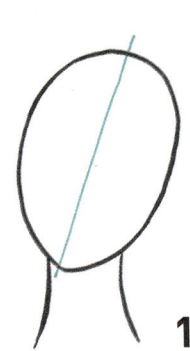

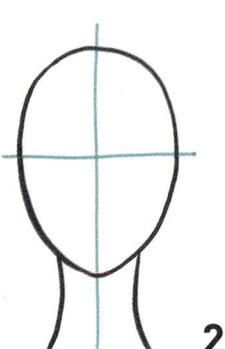

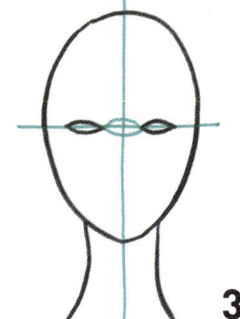

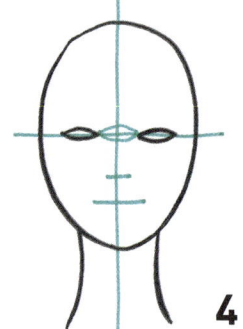

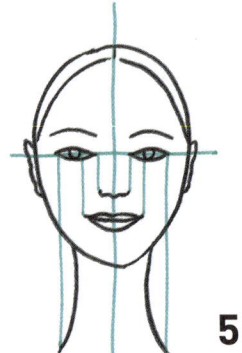

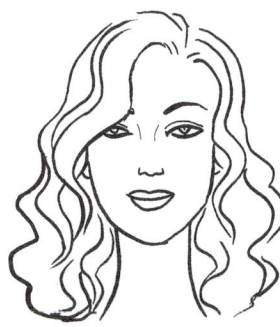

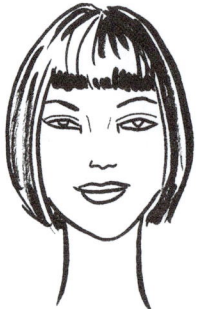

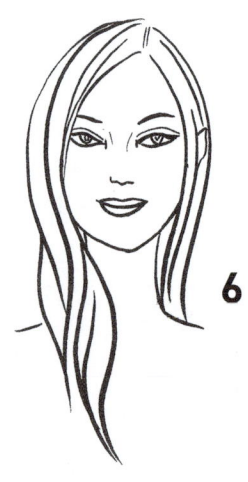

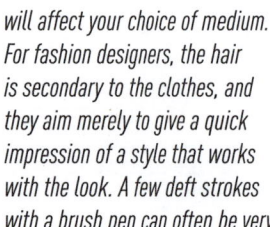

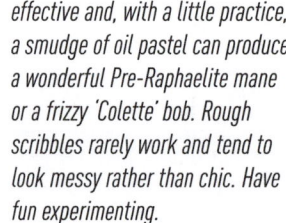

will affect your choice of medium. For fashion designers, the hair is secondary to the clothes, and they aim merely to give a quick impression of a style that works with the look. A few deft strokes with a brush pen can often be very effective and, with a little practice, a smudge of oil pastel can produce a wonderful Pre-Raphaelite mane or a frizzy 'Colette' bob. Rough scribbles rarely work and tend to look messy rather than chic. Have fun experimenting.

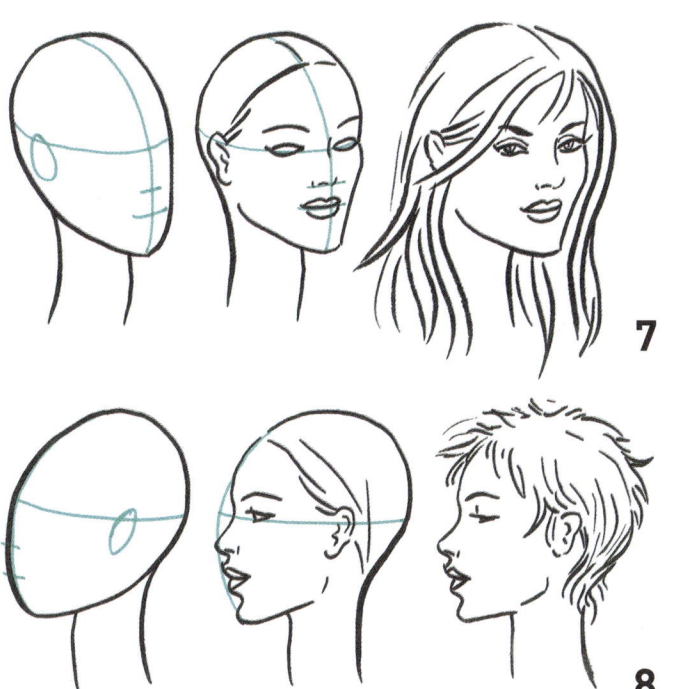

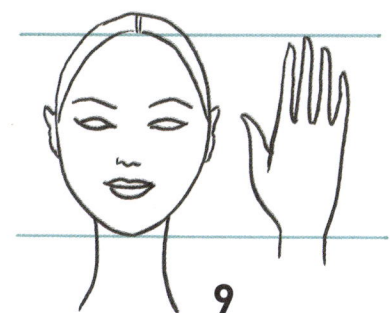

7. The same principles for drawing a head front-on apply when showing a three-quarter view.

8. The same applies to a profile view.

9. Here we can see that the hand is roughly the same length as the face, from the hairline to the chin.

DRAWING A MALE HEAD

Men's heads are frequently proportionally a little larger than women's. Begin with a very basic shape. Here the egg shape is somewhat squared off and the squarer chin and jaw line gives the face a masculine look. The neck will also be a little thicker than a woman's.

Again, when adding hair you're drawing an impression of shape and colour, not every strand. A broad stroke with a marker pen or a few waves drawn with a brush pen should suffice. Practise drawing people you know and using tearsheets from magazines as additional references for styles.

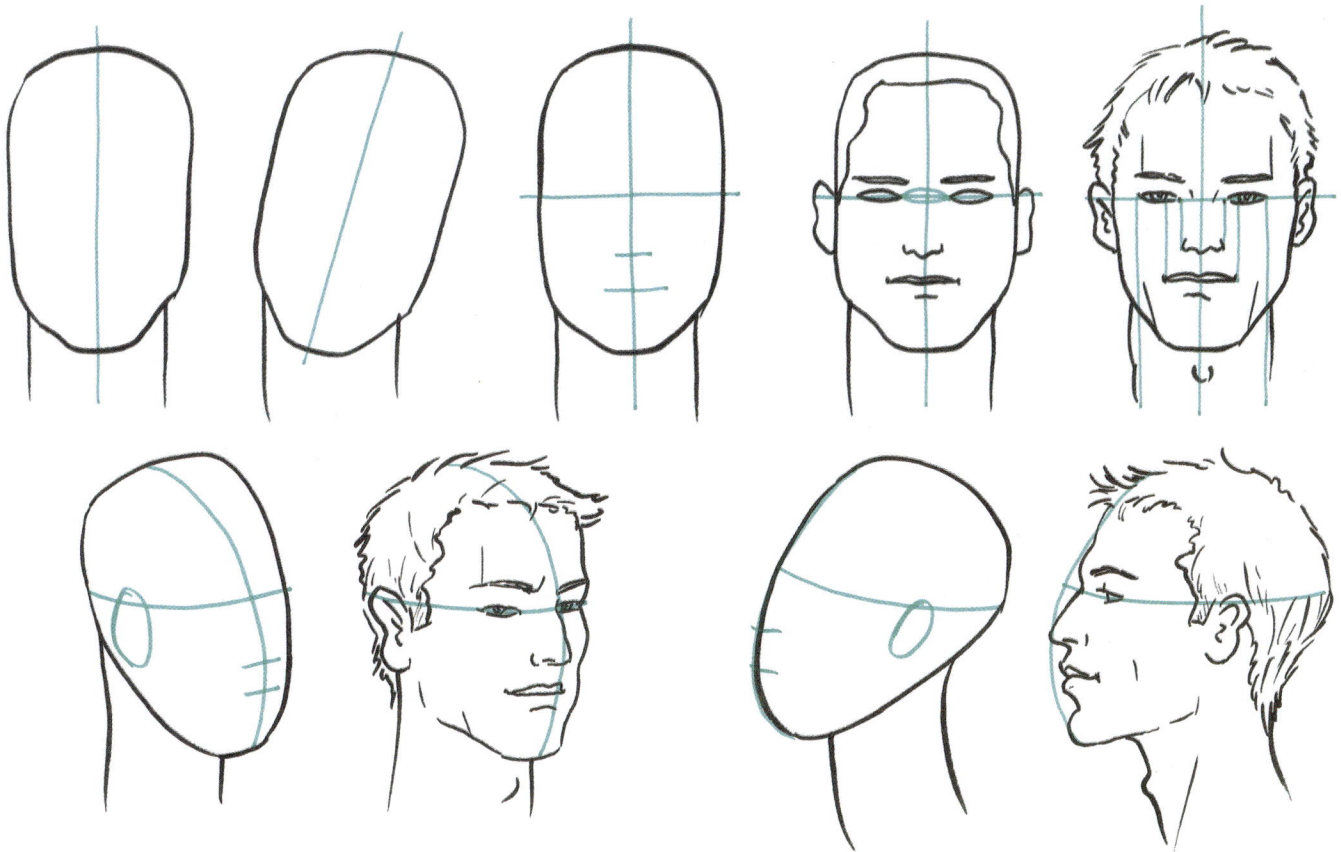

DRAWING HANDS AND FEET

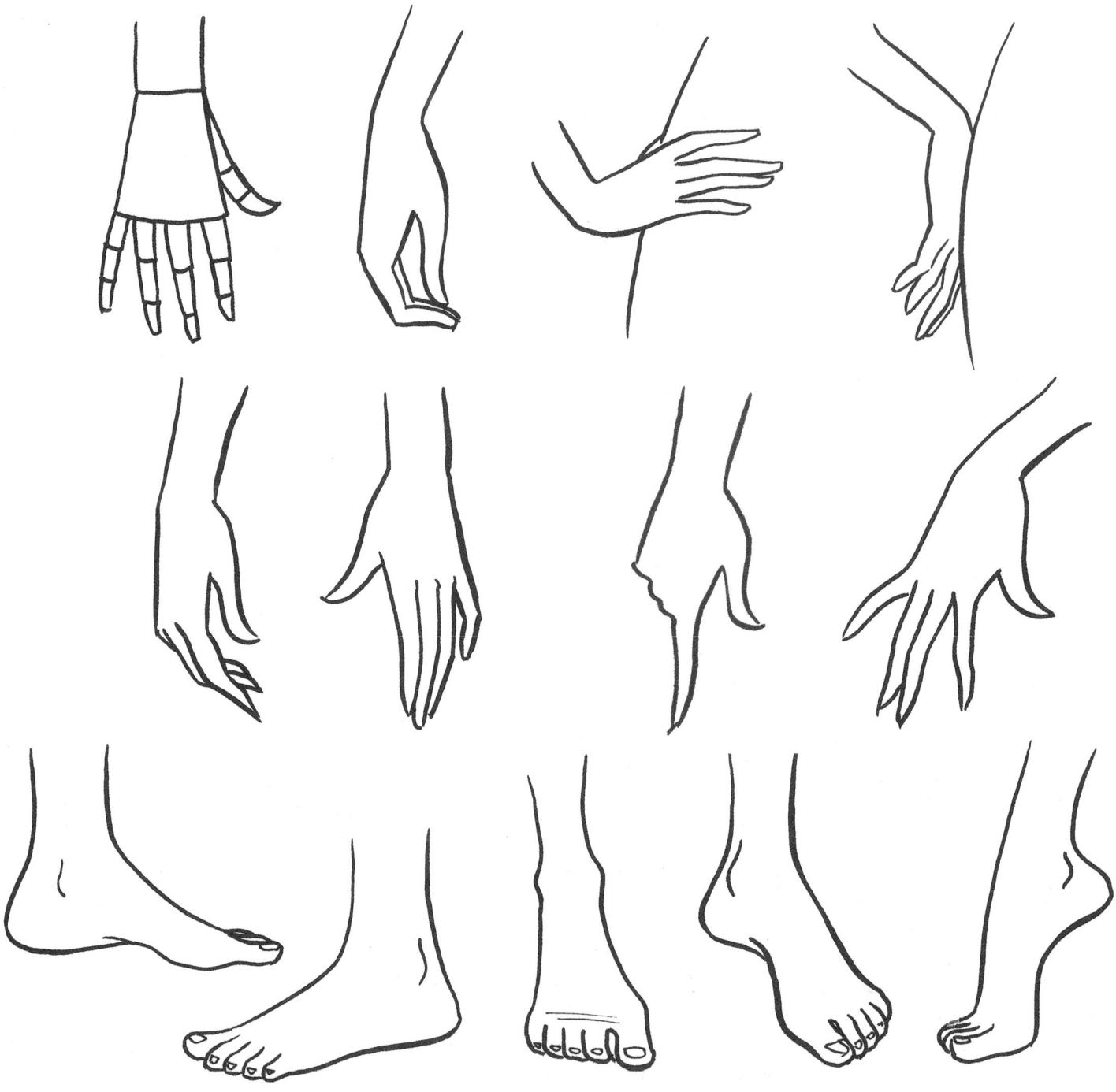

The hands and feet are often the body parts many people struggle to draw, and innumerable half-decent illustrations have been spoiled by the presence of claws or mittens for hands, blobs for feet, or tapering-out legs and no feet whatsoever.

Remembering the guideline that the length of the hand should match the length of the face will help you to get the right scale and proportion. Another useful rule is that the distance from the wrist to the beginning of the fingers is approximately the same as the length of the fingers themselves. The trick is generally to keep it simple, with minimal details, and to break down the construction into basic shapes.

The illustrations above show a female hand and foot in various positions. Have a go at copying the drawings, then try drawing your own hands and feet.

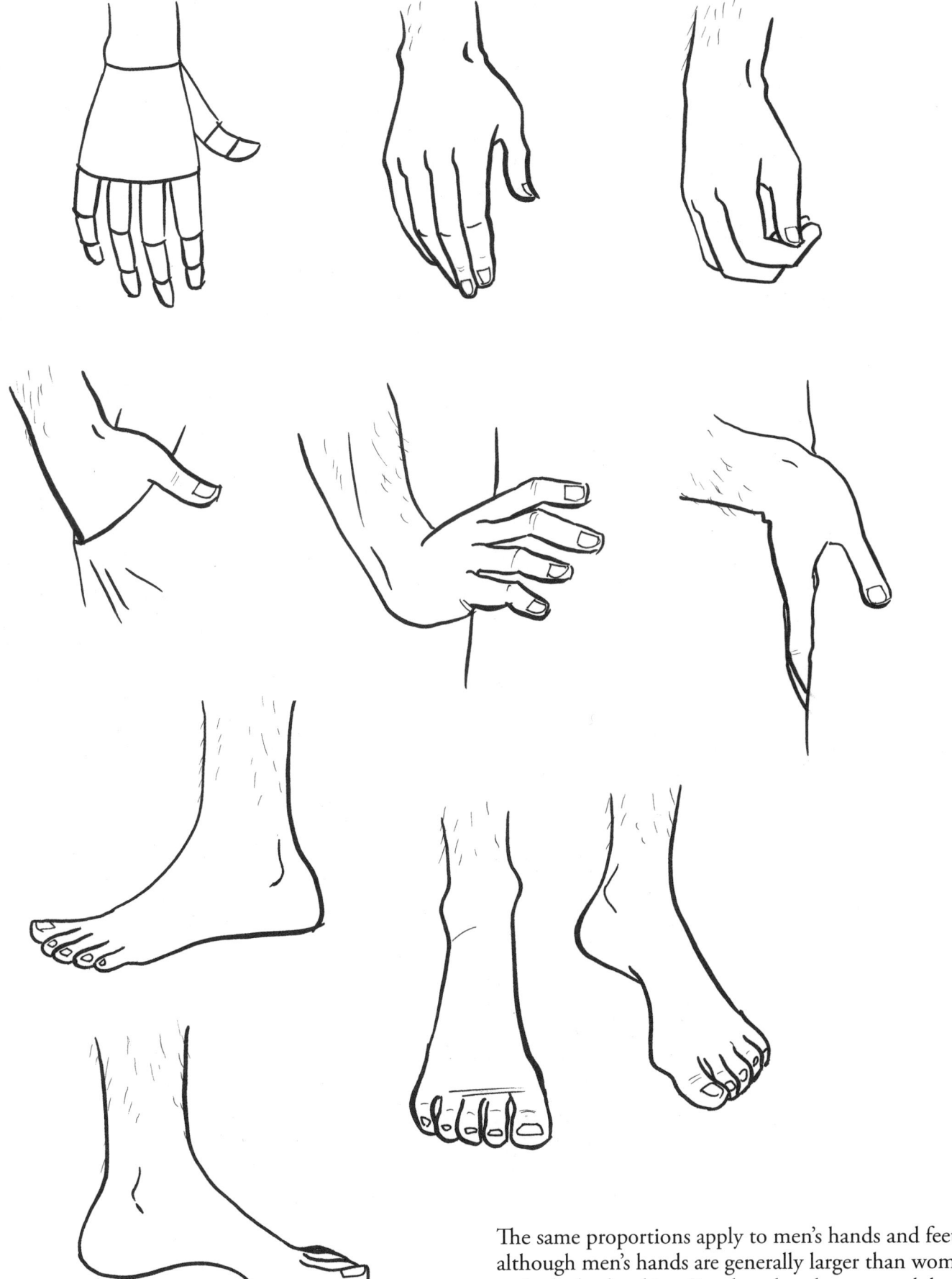

The same proportions apply to men's hands and feet, although men's hands are generally larger than women's and a little chunkier. Simple, relaxed poses work best.

EXTRA POSES AND MOVEMENT: WOMEN

THREE-QUARTER AND SIDE VIEWS

When choosing a pose that best showcases a design, it is often useful to be able to draw three-quarter and side-on views in order to reveal certain design features. The same basic rules used for straight-on or back views apply, but drawing a figure from a three-quarter or side-on angle is a bit trickier as you need to consider perspective more.

When drawing any pose it can be helpful to adopt the position yourself and look in the mirror. Notice whether your body is twisting, the position of your shoulders in relation to your hips, the position of your feet and how the weight is distributed. Ask yourself questions. How are you balanced? Is one leg taking more weight than the other? Which parts of the body are nearest or farthest? As you draw, go over these points in your mind – you'll be surprised how it informs and improves your drawing.

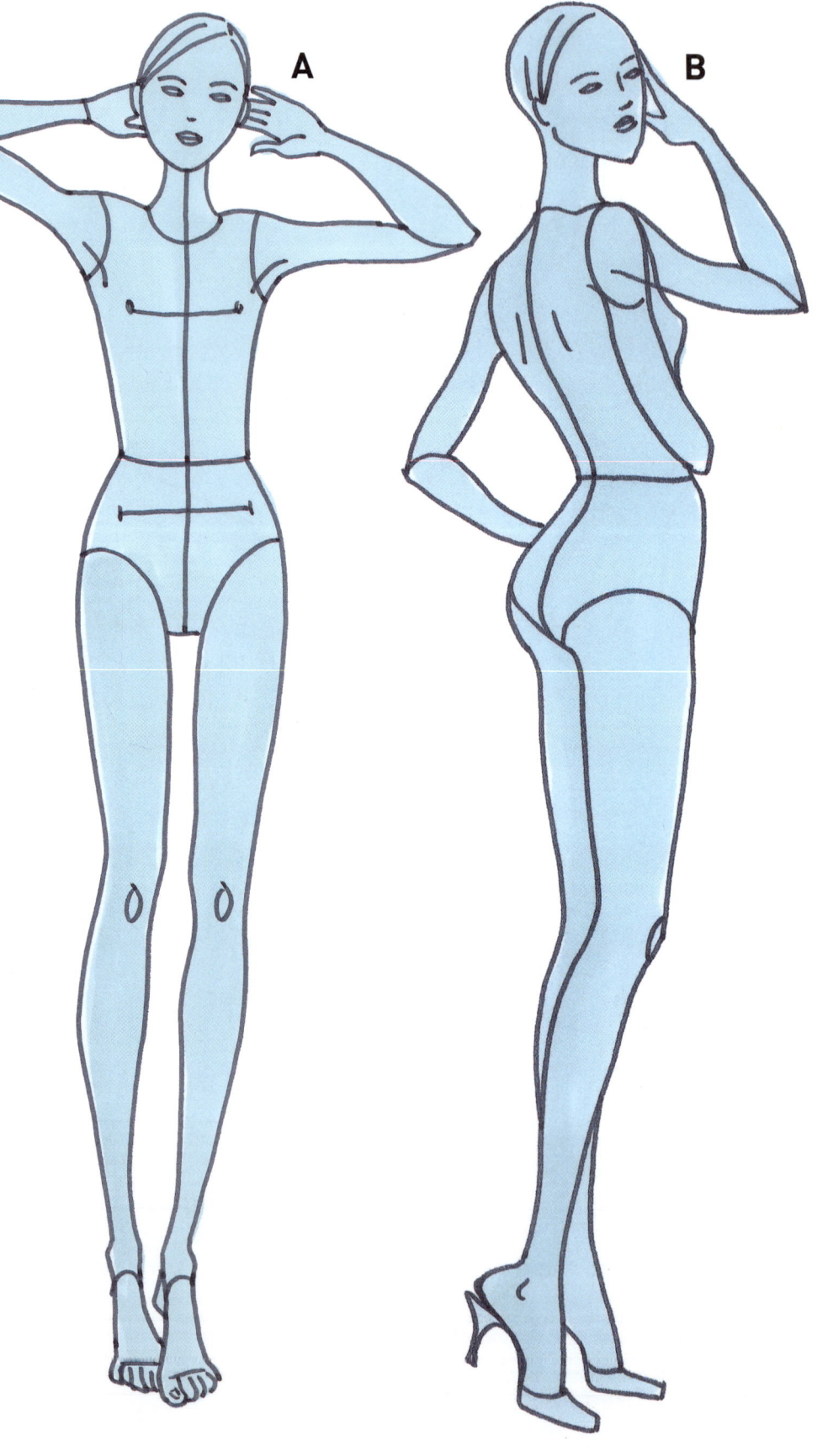

A *Straight-on pose showing raised arms.*

B *As well as looking quite relaxed and natural, three-quarter turned and side-on poses are perfect for showing side details such as pockets and seaming features on jeans and trousers.*

C & D *These may be seen as static poses or, in conjunction with illustration E, as being depictions of how the body looks mid-step. As the body travels through a stride, the spine becomes more tilted and the hips and pelvis move forwards. The weight is carried by one leg as the other steps.*

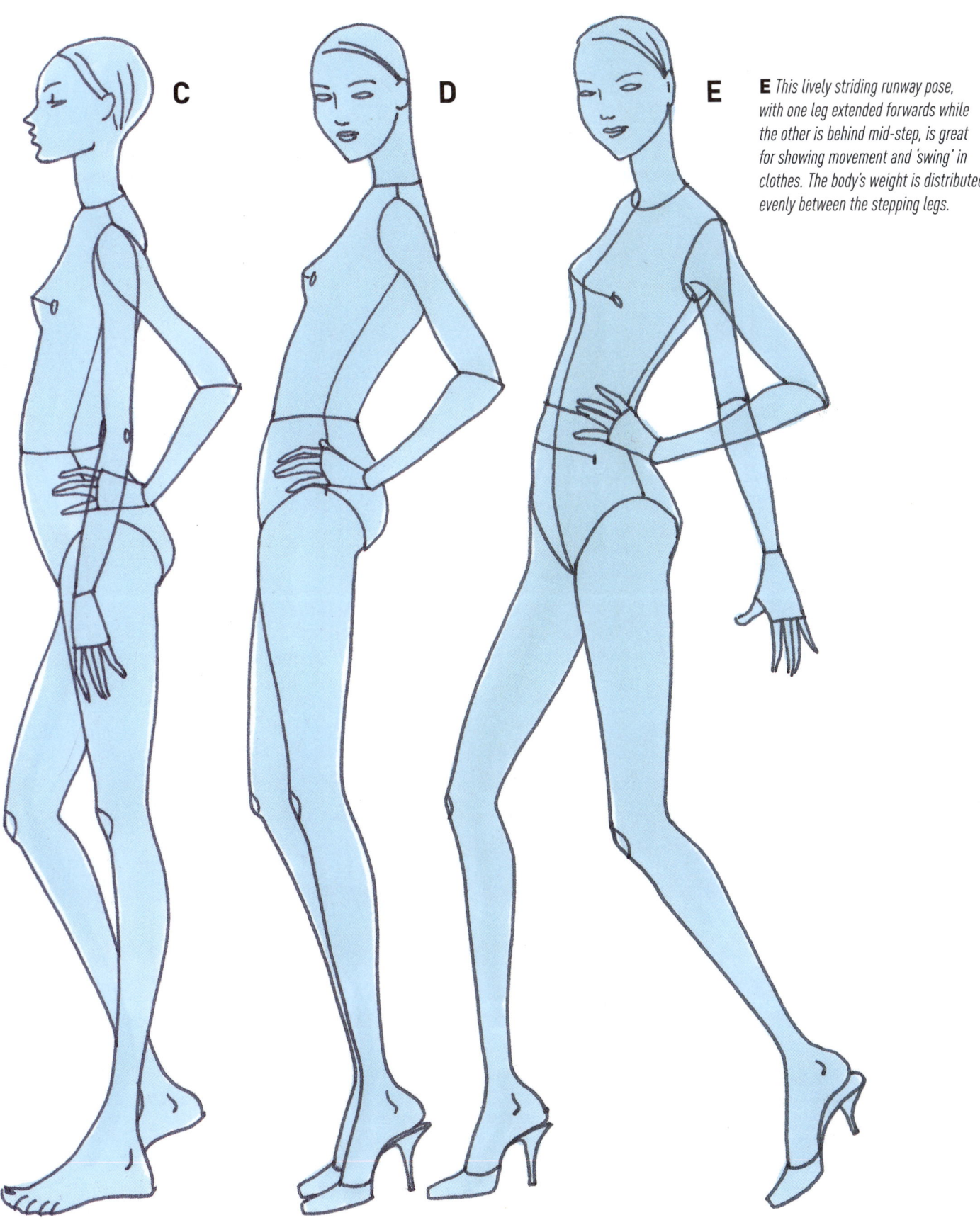

C

D

E

E *This lively striding runway pose, with one leg extended forwards while the other is behind mid-step, is great for showing movement and 'swing' in clothes. The body's weight is distributed evenly between the stepping legs.*

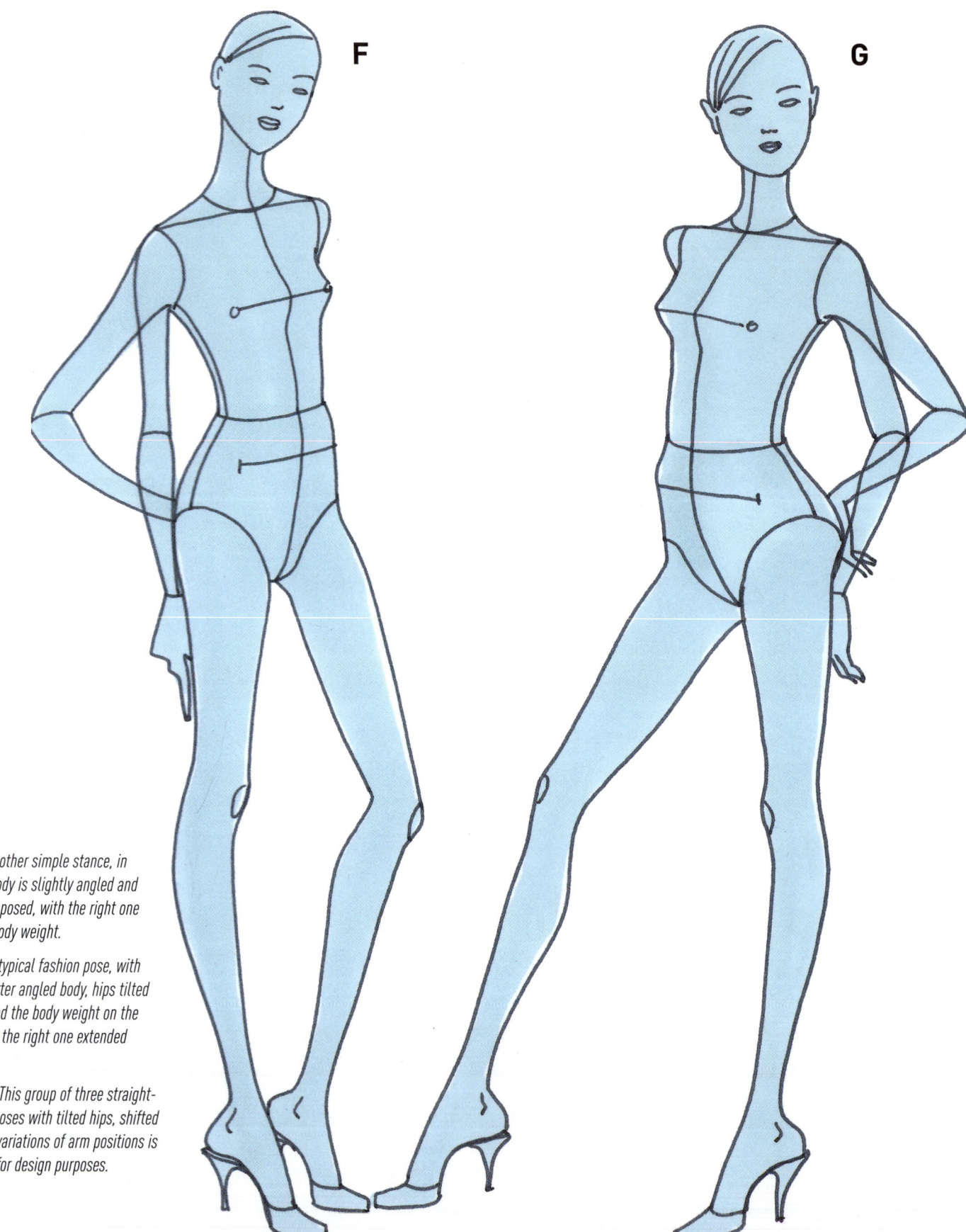

F *This is another simple stance, in which the body is slightly angled and the legs are posed, with the right one taking the body weight.*

G *This is a typical fashion pose, with a three-quarter angled body, hips tilted forwards, and the body weight on the left leg with the right one extended for balance.*

H, I & J *This group of three straight-on fashion poses with tilted hips, shifted weight and variations of arm positions is very useful for design purposes.*

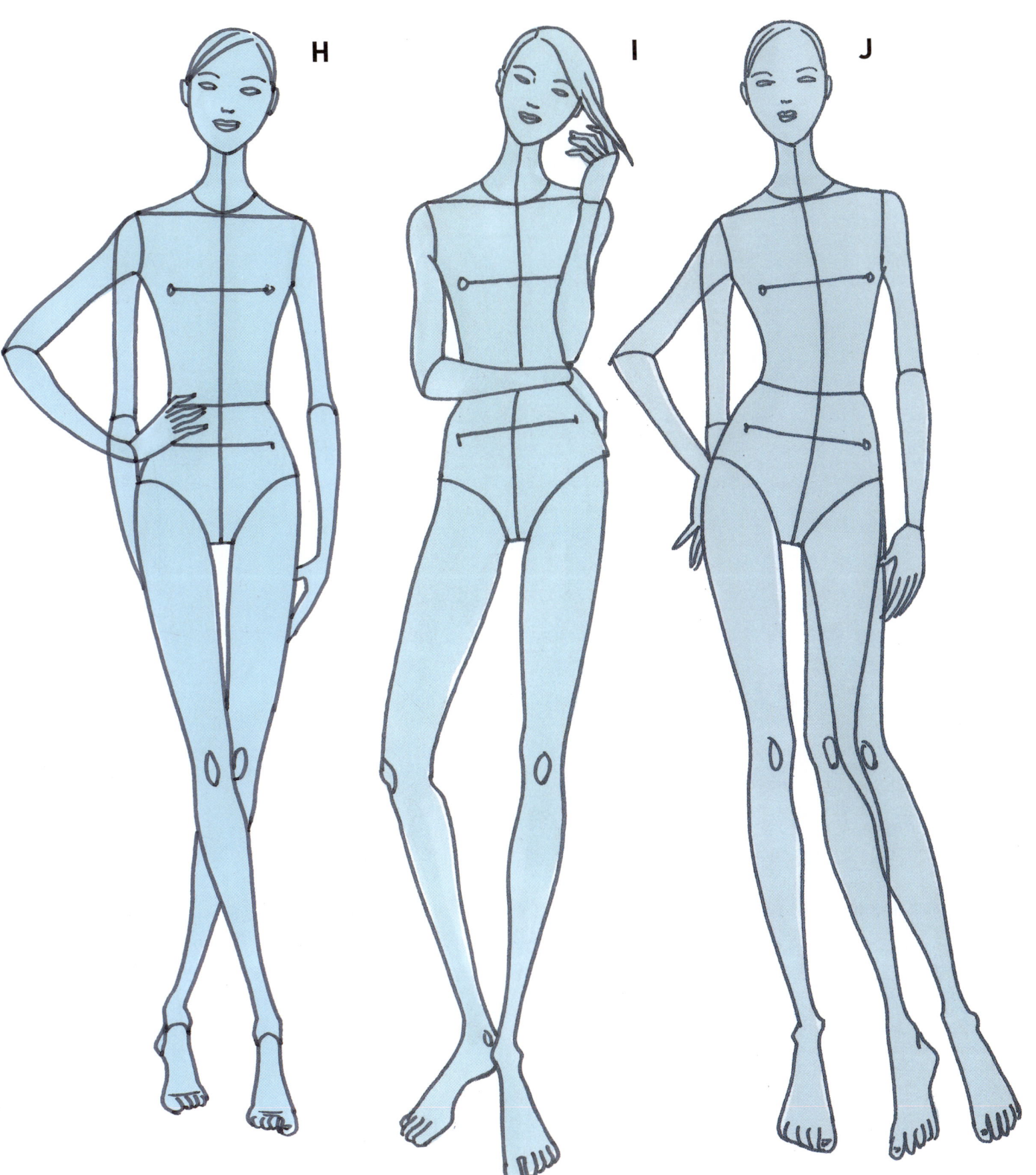

H

I

J

EXTRA POSES AND MOVEMENT: MEN

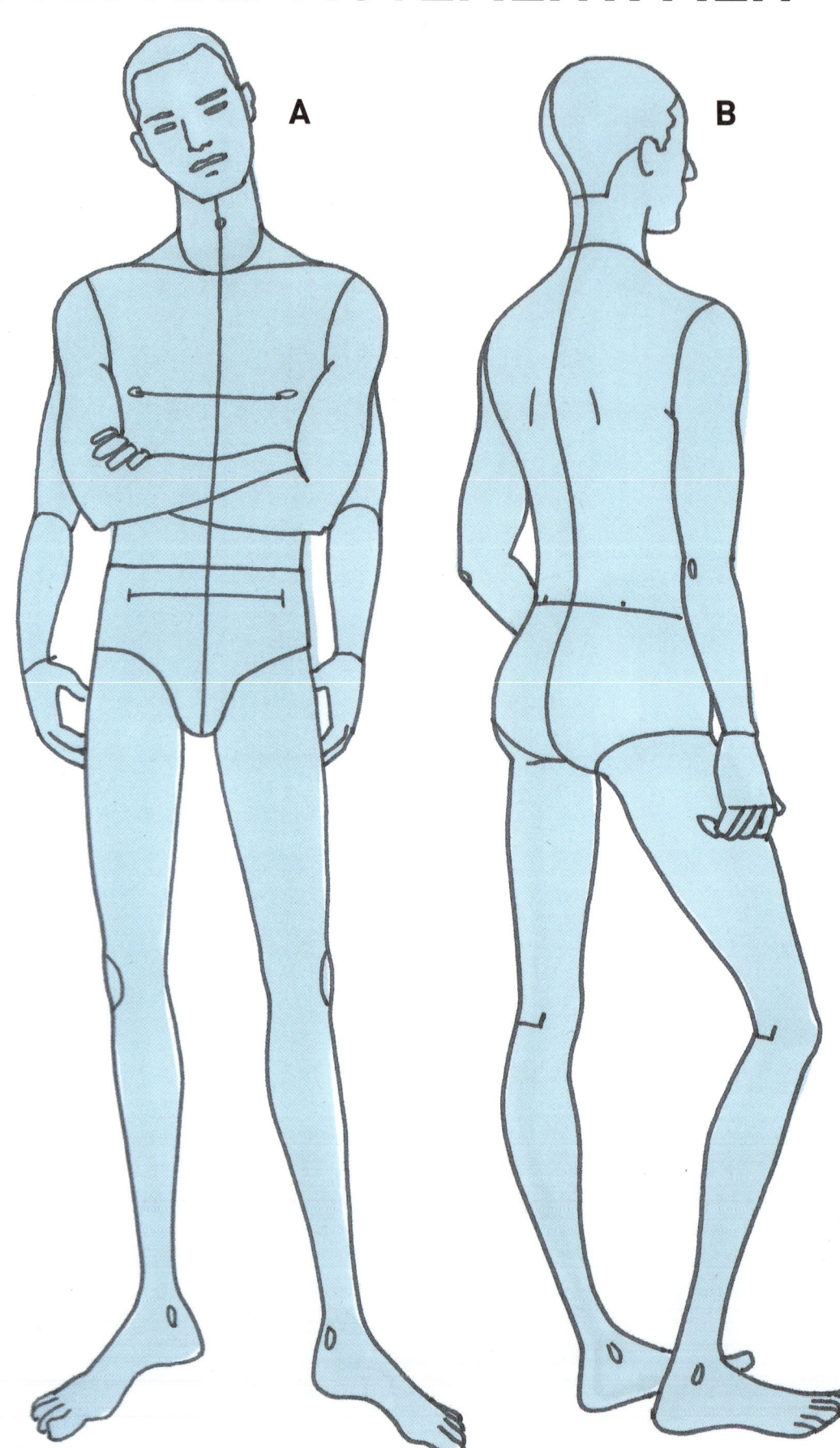

A This is a simple, slightly relaxed straight-on pose that is emphasized by the tilting of the head to one side. Body weight is evenly distributed.

B This slightly three-quarter back view would enable you to show seams and pockets on trousers. The left leg bears most of the body weight.

C Viewed more or less straight-on, this pose is casual and relaxed, with the crossed leg balancing while the right leg takes the body weight. The hand could be positioned behind the back or in a trouser pocket.

D This is quite a relaxed straight-on pose in which the shoulders are slightly tipped and the head is tilted. The right foot is carrying the body weight, while the hands could be buttoning a jacket or fastening a zipper.

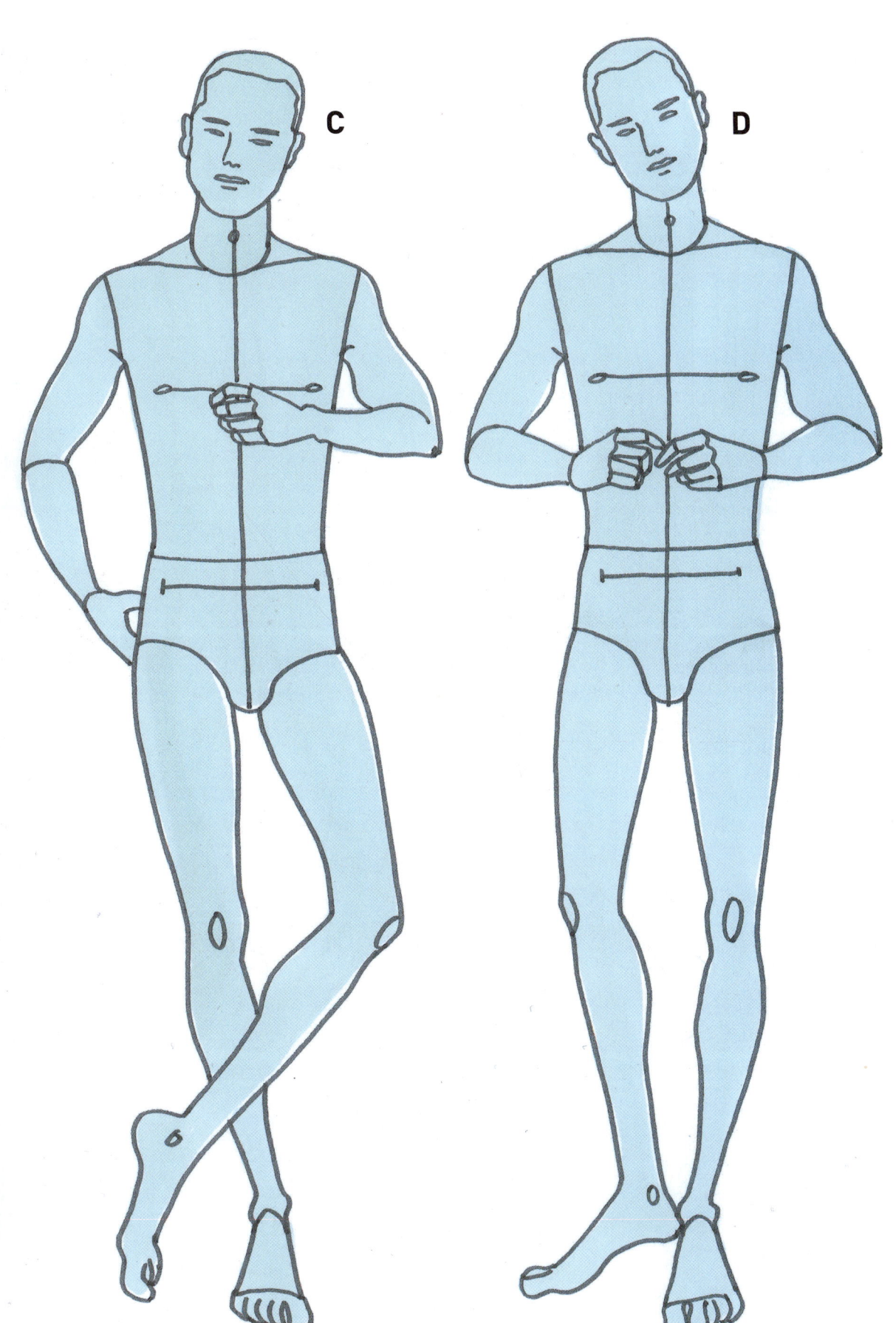

C

D

E *In this three-quarter front pose the head is facing forwards and the crossed leg is casual rather than contrived. The straight right leg carries the body weight while the tipped foot balances.*

F *This three-quarter front pose shows movement as the model is mid-step, with the right leg carrying the majority of the body weight as the left foot lifts slightly. The shoulders are pulled back and the head is also shown from a three-quarter view.*

G *This is a simple side view of a figure mid-step with the left leg taking the body weight. The head is also seen in profile. Seen with illustrations H and I, this pose could be part of a walking or runway sequence.*

H *This mid-step three-quarter pose shows a three-quarter view of the face, the left foot taking the body weight and the right shoulder swinging forwards with the stepping right foot. The shoulders are down as the hands rest on the hips.*

I *This pose depicts the continuation of the movement shown in illustration H. The right foot has landed and the body weight is more evenly distributed, but the left leg still carries more of the weight. The shoulders are pulled back a little and the chest is lifted.*

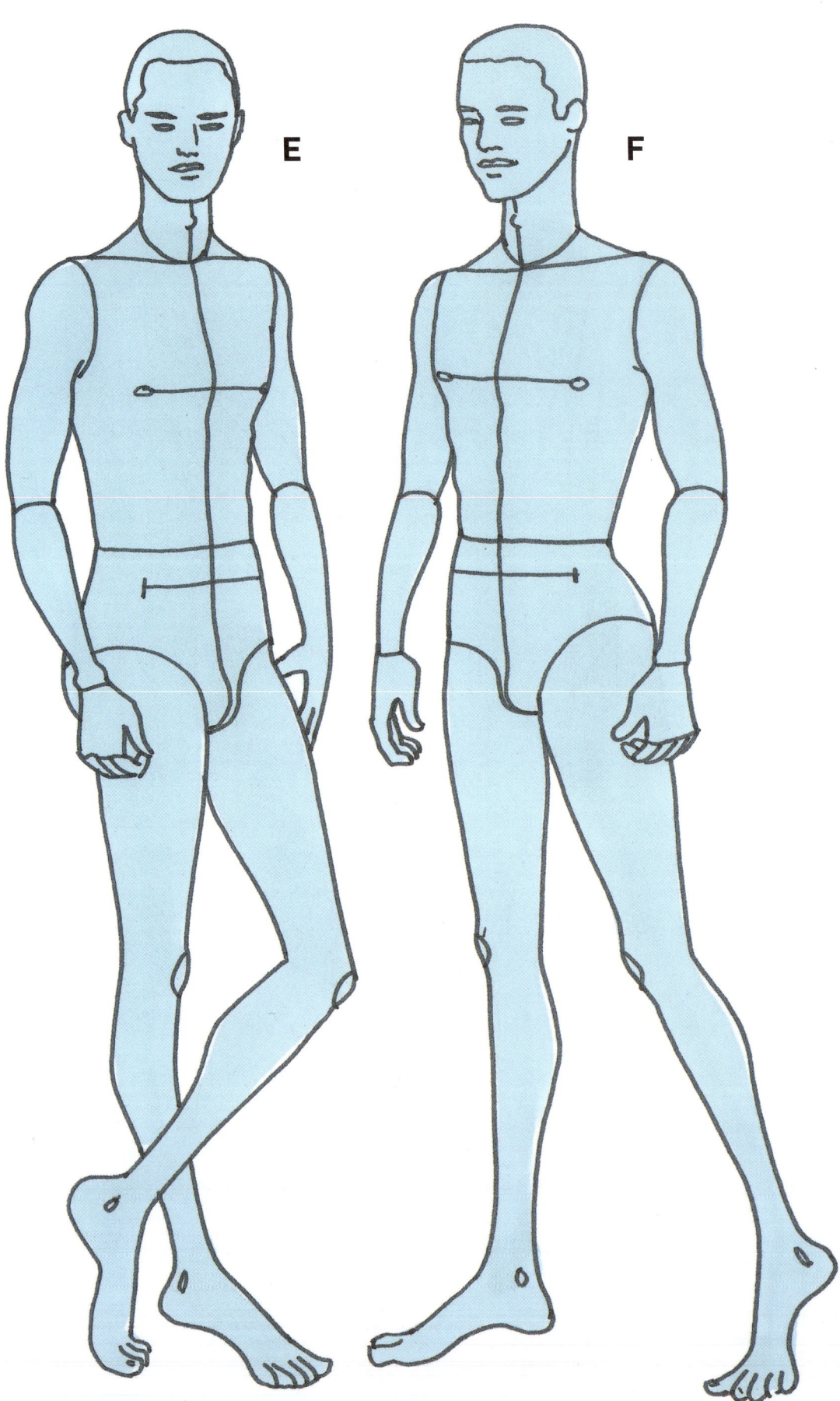

E

F

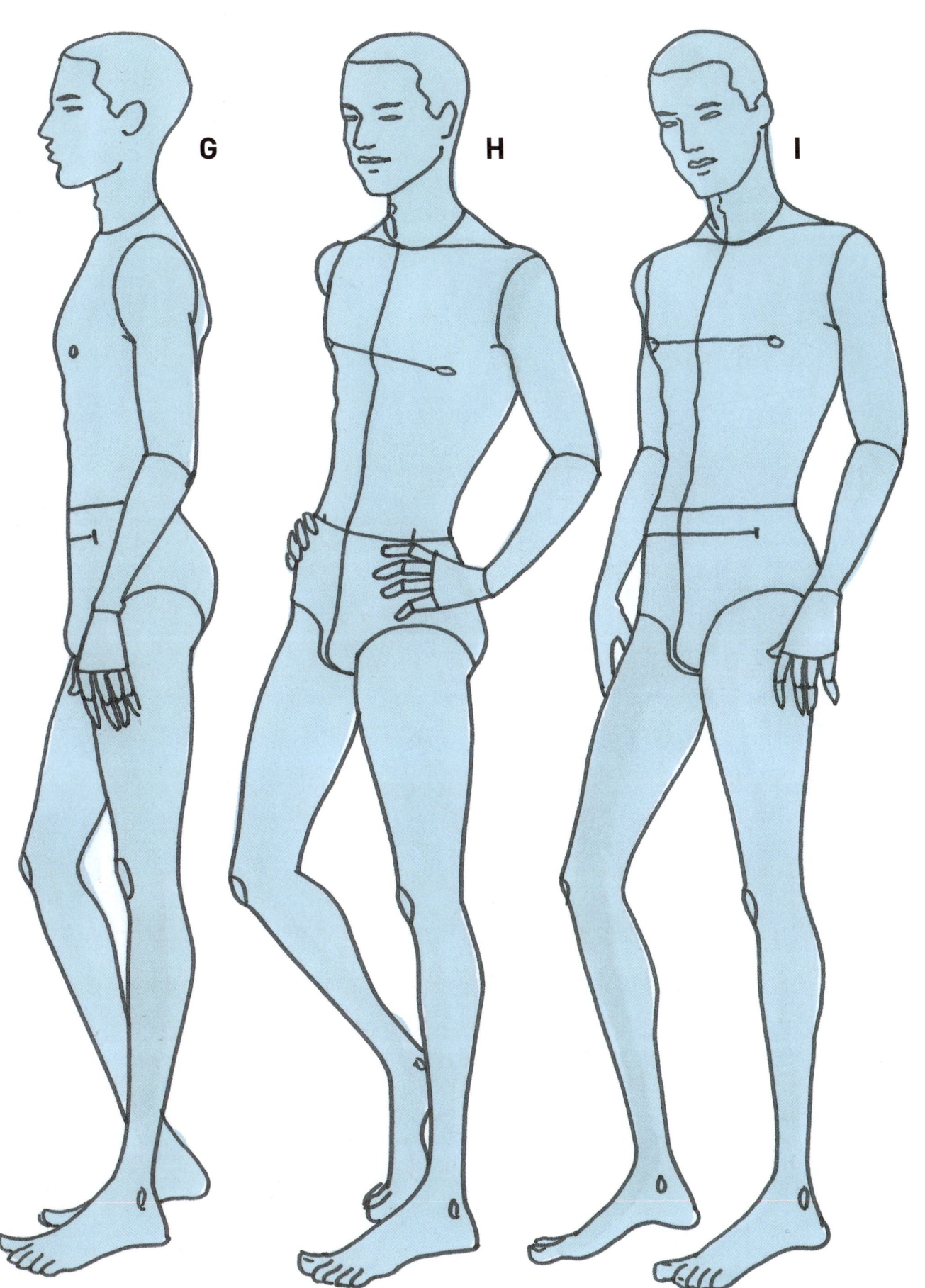

G

H

I

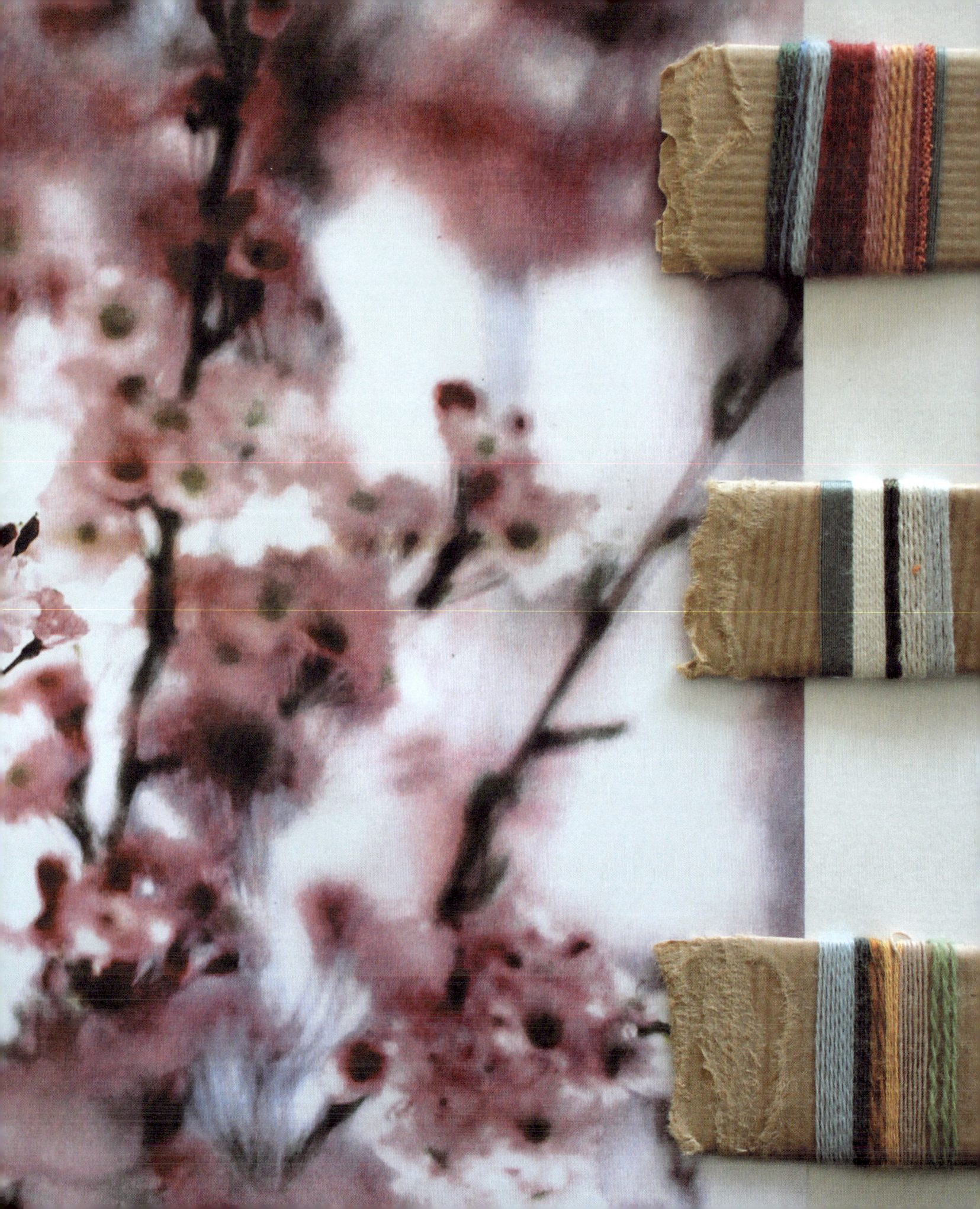

CHAPTER 3

KEEPING AND USING A SKETCHBOOK

We have already covered the different types of sketchbooks available in stores in Chapter 1, but there is nothing to stop you making a sketchbook yourself from an interesting collection of papers, or indeed from finding a vintage book and using that as a starting point. If the book contains images and text that are somehow related to your project then retain them, otherwise you can stick new paper over pages or white out existing material with household emulsion paint. If you choose to buy a new sketchbook, then you should make it your own, especially if it has a company logo on the front. Cover it with interesting paper that works for your project or photocopy one of your own drawings and paste that on to the jacket.

It may be appropriate to have a separate sketchbook for a particular project or assignment, which will allow you a focused space for the development of your designs. But it is also a good idea to have what we might call a 'general sketchbook' or 'ideas book', in which you regularly jot notes and make quick sketches recording a thought, idea or observation. Be a magpie – gather all manner of information in the form of samples of colour, postcards, images, bits of packaging, smudges of paint, snips of fabric, corners torn from magazines, press cuttings and magazine tears, addresses and information about exhibitions and fashion blogs – anything that reminds, records and inspires your creativity. However, whatever else goes in your sketchbook remember that the clue is in the name – you should sketch in it!

When using a sketchbook you should not necessarily consider a possible future reader – it should be the place where you record, create, formulate and document the development of ideas as well as solve problems, either in written or drawn form. However, if you know that a tutor, boss or client is likely to want to see the sketchbook then it is worth ensuring that everything is clear and appealingly presented. Bearing an audience in mind may also help you during the development stages, enabling you to clarify thoughts and consolidate a concept by anticipating reactions and questions.

Finally, a real sketchbook should never be put together at the end of an assignment or project; it should be a progression of ideas that leads to a conclusion in the final designs and ideas, like the logbook of a creative journey or voyage of discovery.

Artwork by Sarah Cunningham

SKETCHBOOK INSPIRATION

Here we can see examples of how, during the early stages of a project, ephemera and 'found images' such as postcards of paintings, magazine tears or photographs can be used to inspire and create the beginnings of ideas in a sketchbook. All the examples shown here are by students from the University of Brighton, UK.

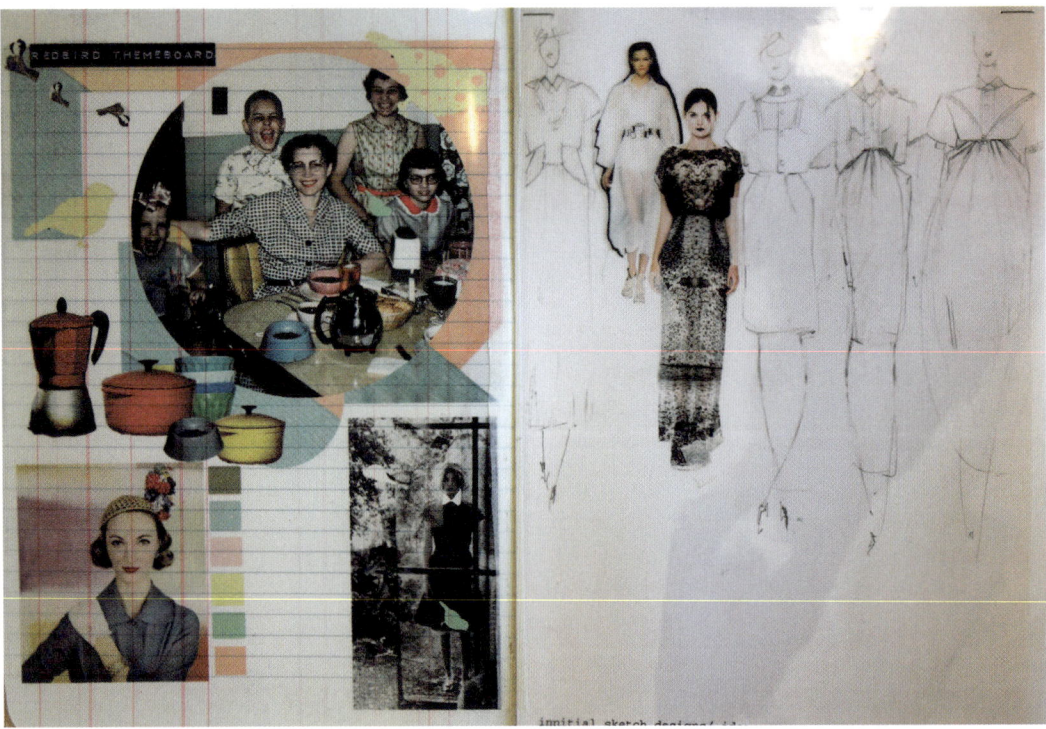

LEFT & BELOW: *This piece by Bryony Cooke builds a charming theme around the story of* I Capture The Castle *by Dodie Smith, and explores a nostalgic, domestic, 1950s 'make-do' look with fresh colours, simple gingham-type fabrics and a quirky little bird motif.*

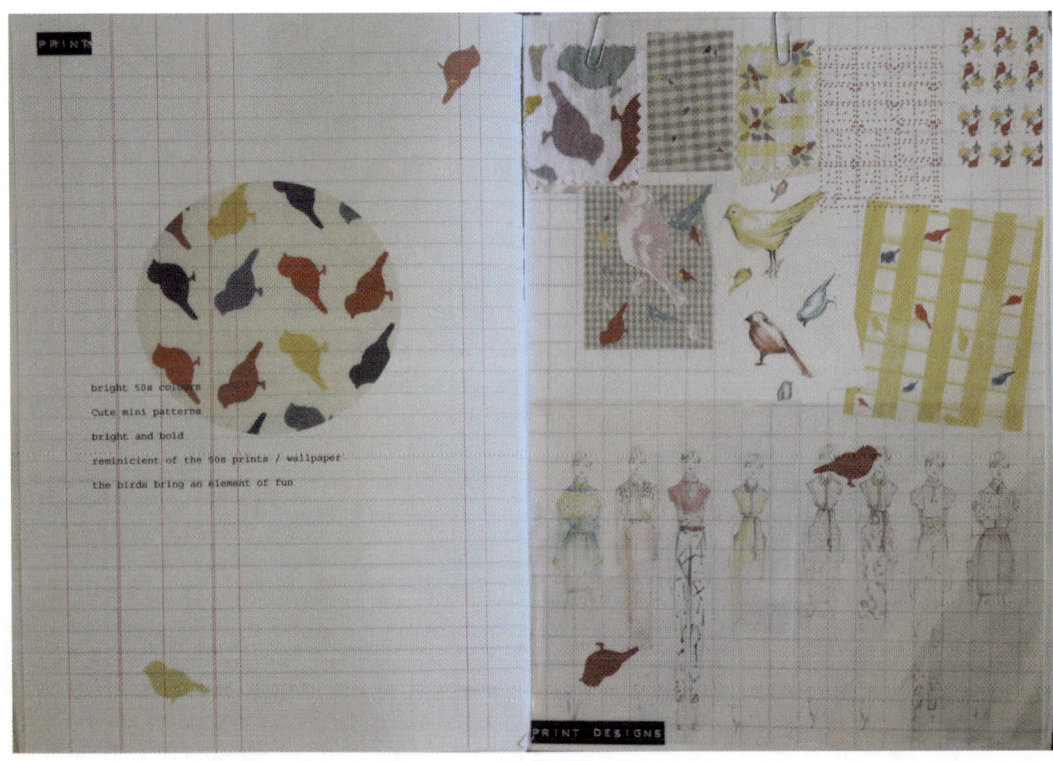

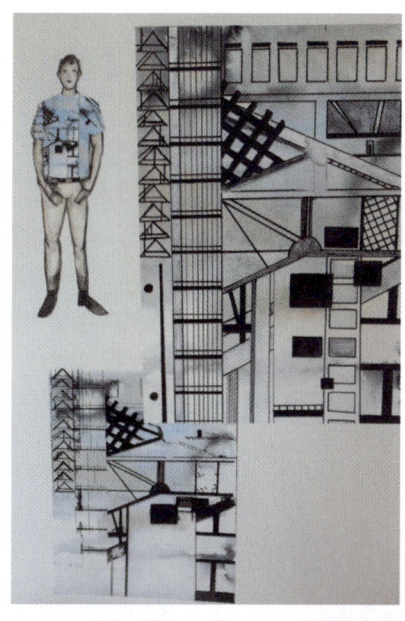

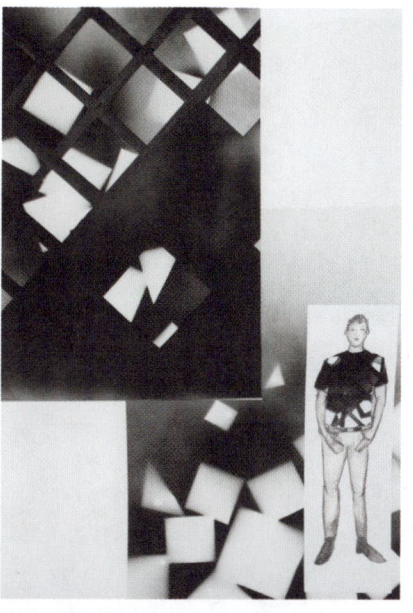

LEFT: *The designer Robert Atkins' photographs of architecture and architectural details reveal an interest in patterns and grid structures, and lead to a series of ideas for prints and patterned menswear in a university CAD (Computer Aided Design) project.*

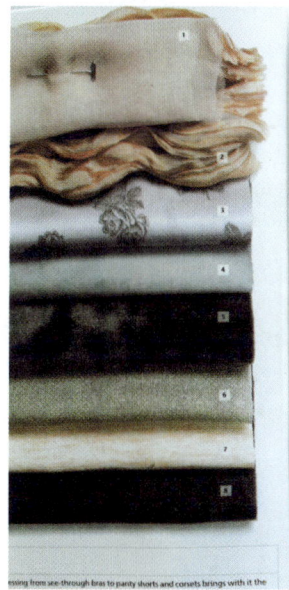

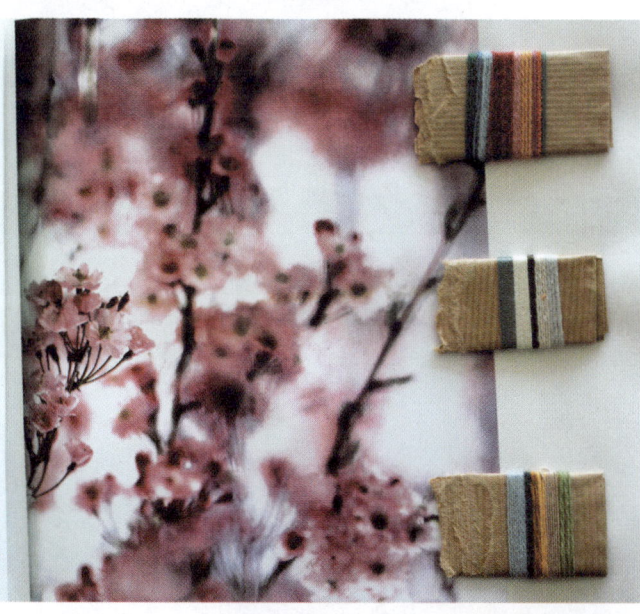

LEFT: *In this sketchbook, Sarah Cunningham uses a found image of blossoms to inspire a colour palette that has been expressed using coloured yarns and embroidery threads. The roughly but thoughtfully torn packing paper is suggestive of soft petal edges and makes a good neutral background for the colour combinations. Embroidery threads are widely available in a range of tones and make a good choice of medium for accurately depicting colours.*

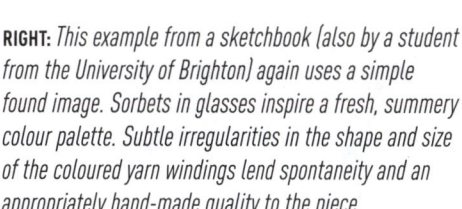

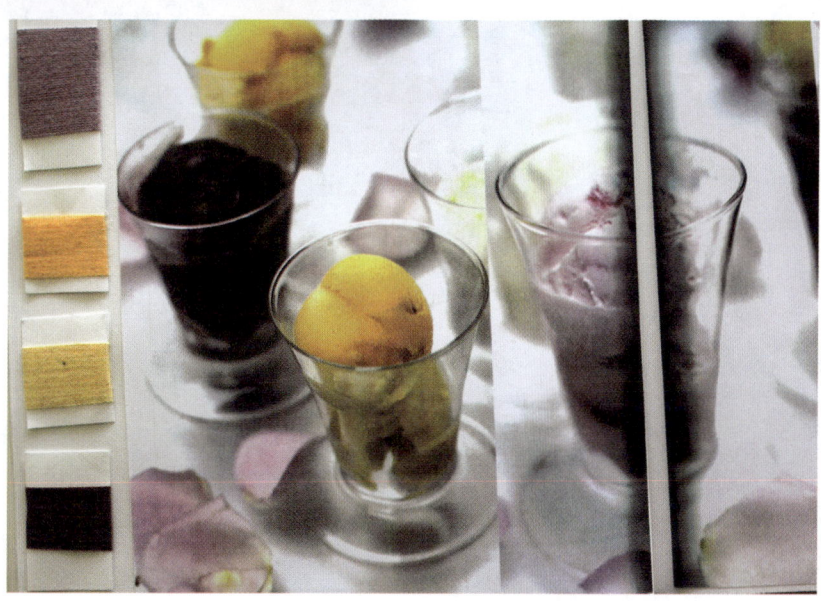

RIGHT: *This example from a sketchbook (also by a student from the University of Brighton) again uses a simple found image. Sorbets in glasses inspire a fresh, summery colour palette. Subtle irregularities in the shape and size of the coloured yarn windings lend spontaneity and an appropriately hand-made quality to the piece.*

CORAL PROJECT by Karen Fehr

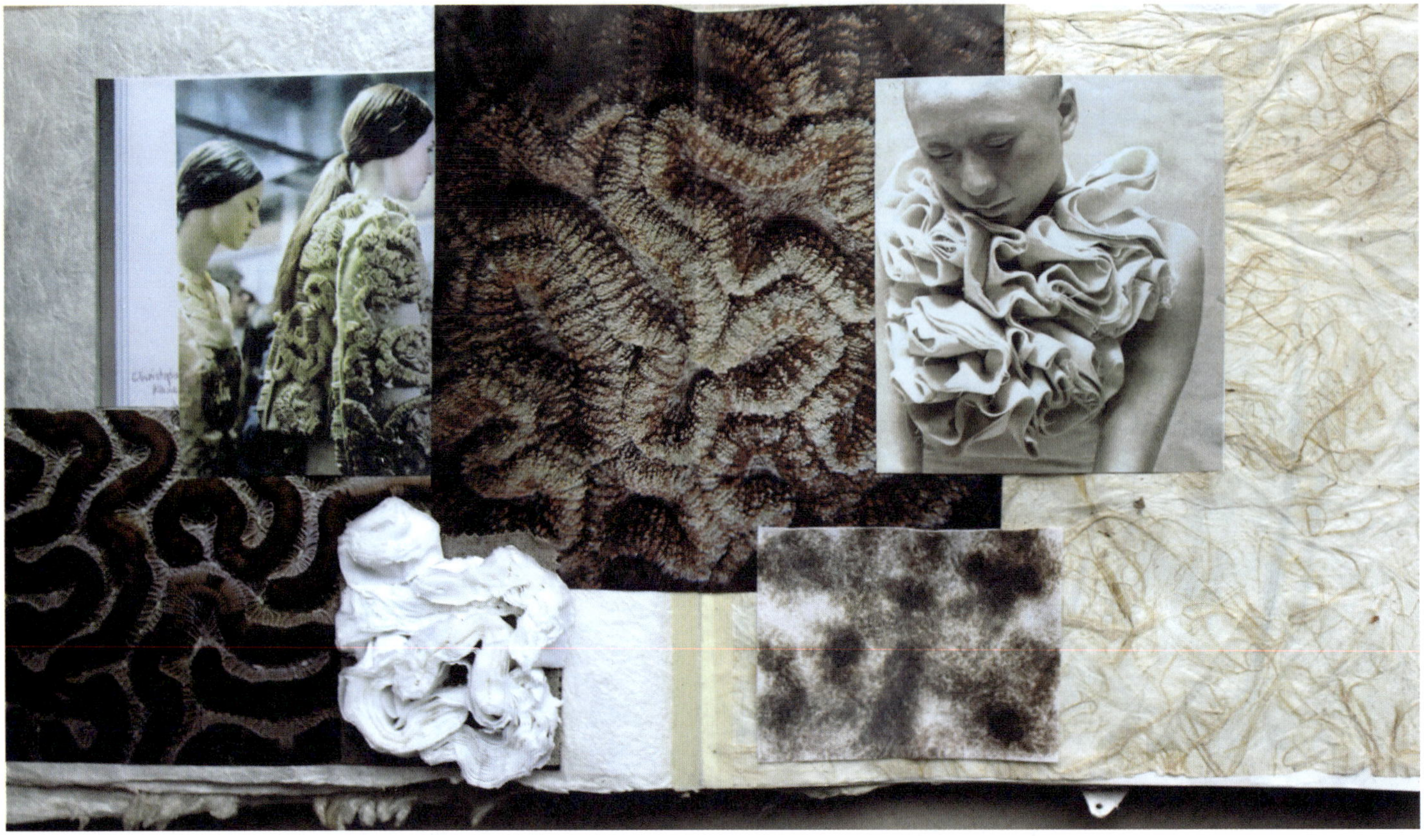

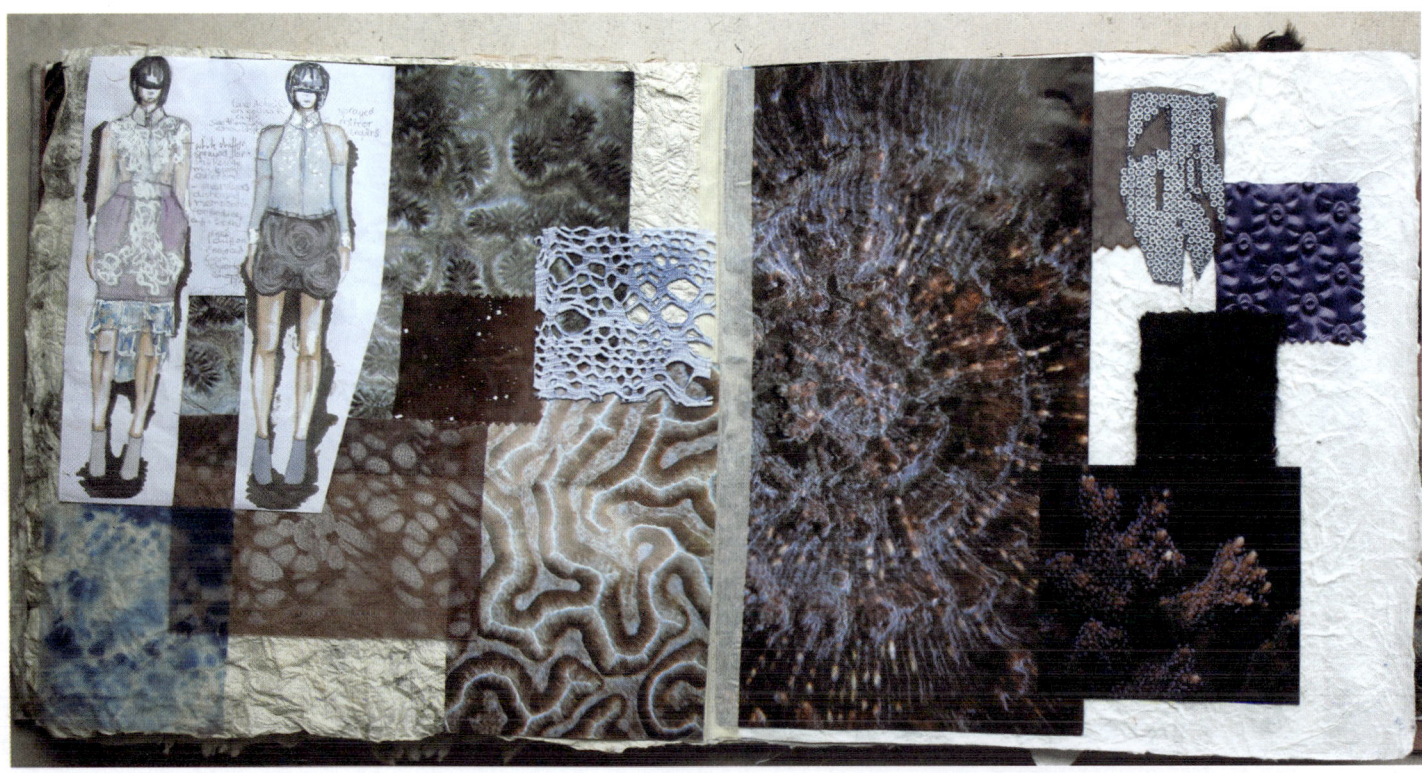

ABOVE: *In this project Karen Fehr (a student at the American Intercontinental University) has chosen coral and the ocean floor as the theme, looking at patterns and textures as the inspiration for fabrics and fabric manipulation techniques. Other found images that are visually related have been added to enrich the imagery.*

BELOW: *Here experiments with fabric painting and simple printing techniques echo and interpret collected photographic images. Found fabrics that evoke the textures and colours have also been added. Garment ideas begin to explore ways of using these fabrics and techniques.*

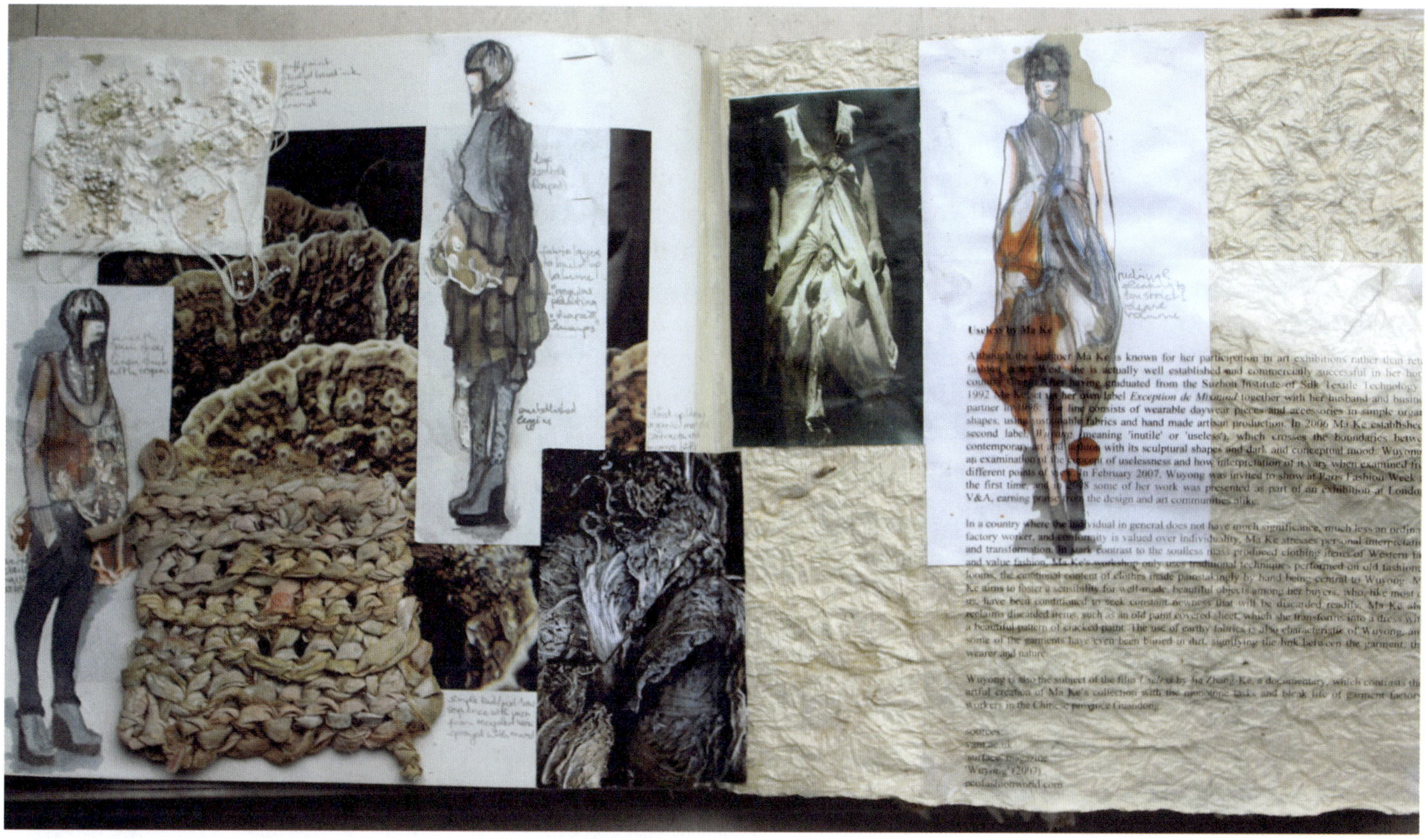

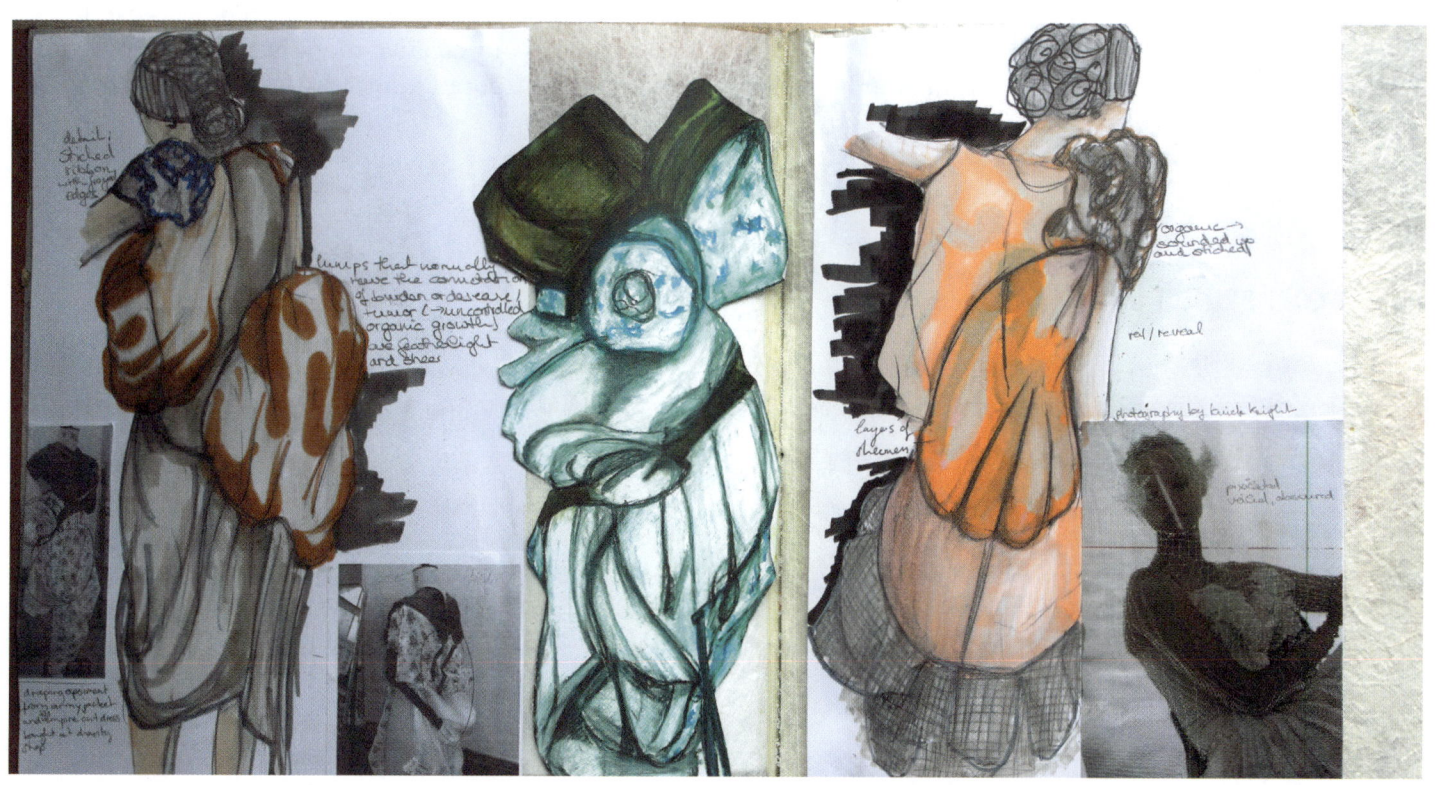

ABOVE: *Additional pages of rough hand-made Indian paper that evoke the rich textures of the theme have been inserted. The forms and structures bring to mind silhouette and volume. Images that suggest fabric textures and inspire knitting using shredded fabric as yarn have been included. Embroidery and embellishment ideas are created using beads, plaster of Paris and paint, for a modern, unconventional interpretation.*

BELOW: *These drawings are inspired by studies of coral, and show initial garment ideas and experiments on the dress stand.*

RESEARCH AND DESIGN

Sketchbooks are inseparable from research and design. If your sketchbook is a logbook of your journey, then research is what you observe, discover and find inspiring on that journey, and design is how you filter, generate and connect ideas and thoughts and focus them into some kind of conclusion; an end concept or product. Research is what stimulates ideas. There is also practical research, which might be enquiry into techniques, processes, fabrics and materials, and this informs and makes those ideas happen. Design development is essentially the aesthetic and practical process of cycling through many permutations of one idea – which will often lead you to more ideas – and by evaluating, refining and critically assessing those themes eventually arriving at a finished design.

Although found material, as already discussed, is very important for stimulating ideas, the work that appears in a sketchbook should be mostly primary research, that is to say things you have drawn and researched first-hand: photographs you have taken, experiments and discoveries made by going, doing, seeing and experiencing things for yourself. The more personal your research, the more individual your creative outcomes will be. Allow yourself to be inspired by almost anything, from a holiday or museum trip to something more obscure and esoteric, and build upon that first spark of an idea, developing a thread that leads from initially random inclusions in your

sketchbook to a definitive conclusion. If your starting point is, for instance, Ancient Egypt, you should eschew obvious mainstream sources of information, such as the innumerable books on the subject, and instead find out whether a collection is being exhibited in a museum or country house and if so go there yourself to draw and photograph (where possible) inspiring artefacts. You might watch some old movies too, and find out about other fashion trends that have been influenced by the same theme over the years, such as the passion for Egyptian styles in France and Regency Britain following Napoleon's campaigns in Egypt and Syria in the late 1700s. Thus it is easy to see how making connections and imaginative leaps and layering influences can help you develop an idea and lend it a personal slant; it's a bit like following a basic recipe and adding some alternative ingredients to give it a twist. Research is exciting: expect the unexpected.

Inclusions in your sketchbook research may be drawings, images or notes or other information about colour, shapes and pattern, form, texture, fabrics and materials, construction, detail, atmosphere, scale, history or background. You should cross-reference or juxtapose images or details within images. The relevance of images and the connections between one image or idea and another should become apparent; as you progress, your creative thought process should be evident and purposeful, not least to you.

DUSTER COAT PROJECT by Yvonne Deacon

1. *This project takes inspiration from a favourite vintage find – a linen duster coat or warehouseman's coat from the 1930s. Other found images were combined to set a mood, including an old grocer's bill and a black and white photograph of a grocer's shop from the early 20th century, with the grocer himself proudly standing in front of his wares. A painting by Cézanne showing a card player wearing a similar coat was also included, together with nostalgic old photographs of a small boy in interesting clothes and a girl on a bike in a print dress. A few swatches of coarse linen and a winding of red thread were later translated into the red stitching feature that appears on the final design.*

2. *A flat or semi-diagrammatical sketch was made of the coat, revealing its lovely details and proportions. The utility aspect was deemed important and this was enhanced by the inclusion of scraps of coarse, hardwearing linen that demonstrated its surface finish, texture and colour after many washes. A charming pencil and crayon sketch of a thrush with its chest puffed-up and wings akimbo provoked ideas about air and volume, and its subtle plumage, along with vintage-look floral fabrics inspired by the bicycling girl, led to the development of the colour story. Loose sketches record and develop initial ideas and silhouettes and combine to build the mood.*

1

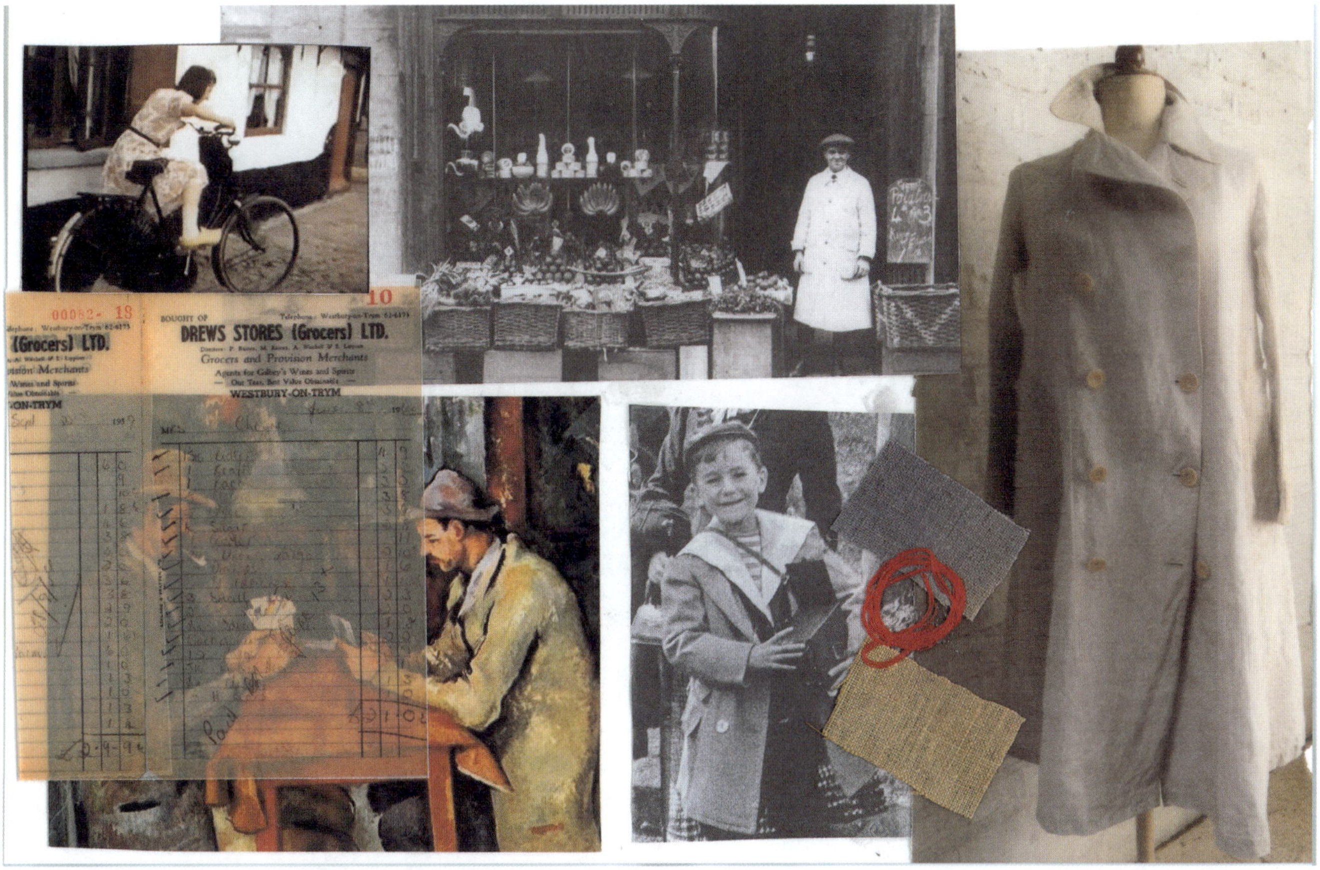

2

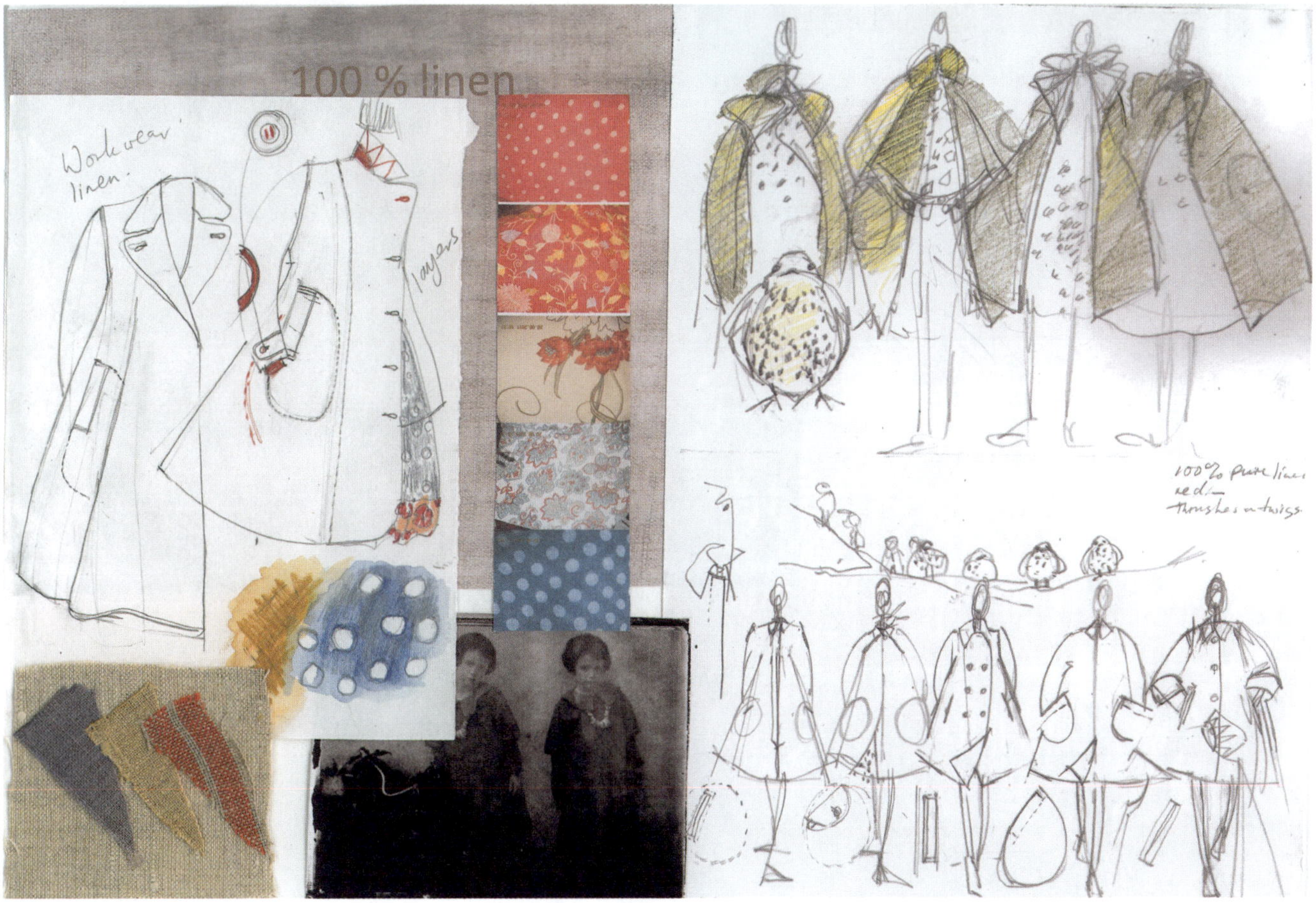

3

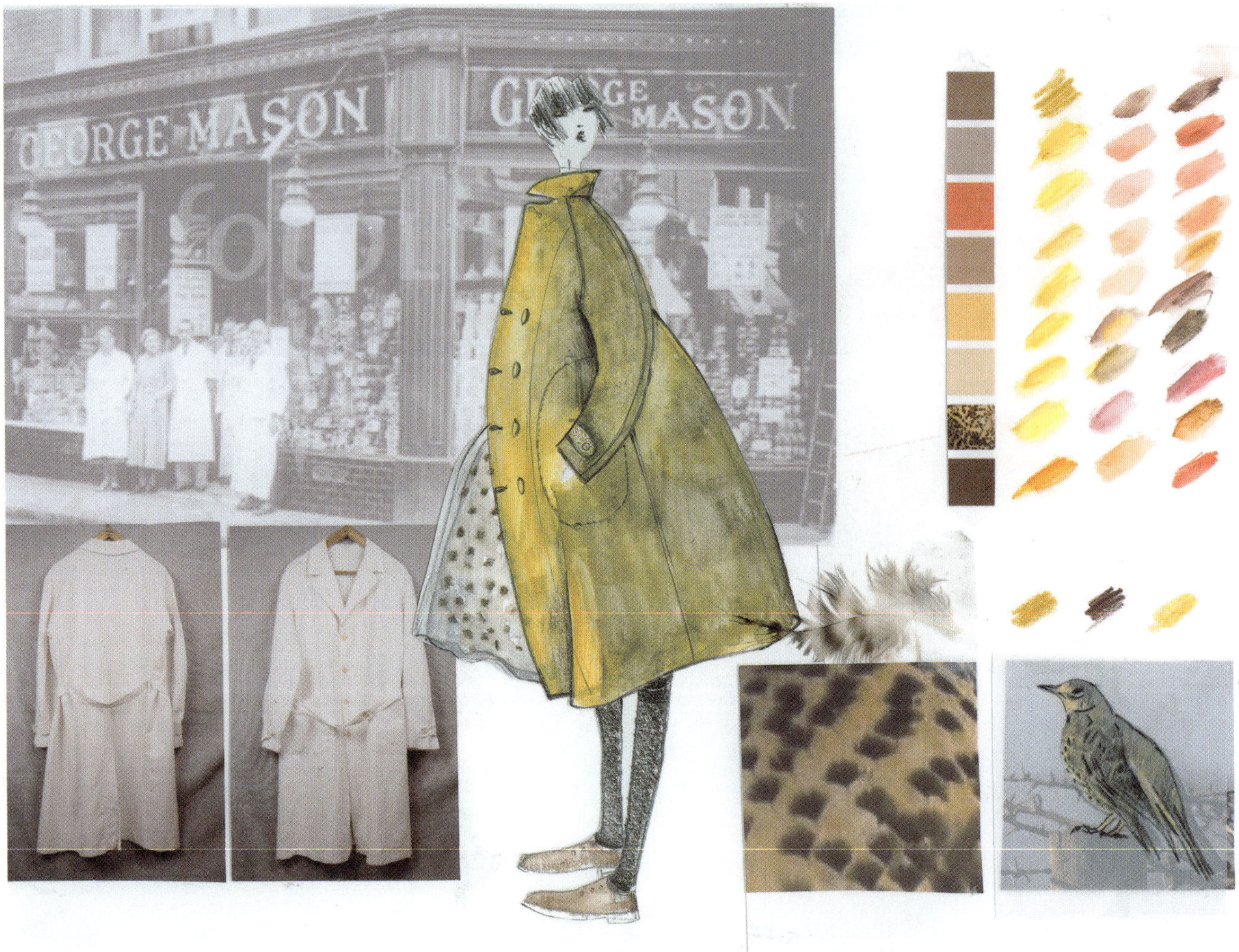

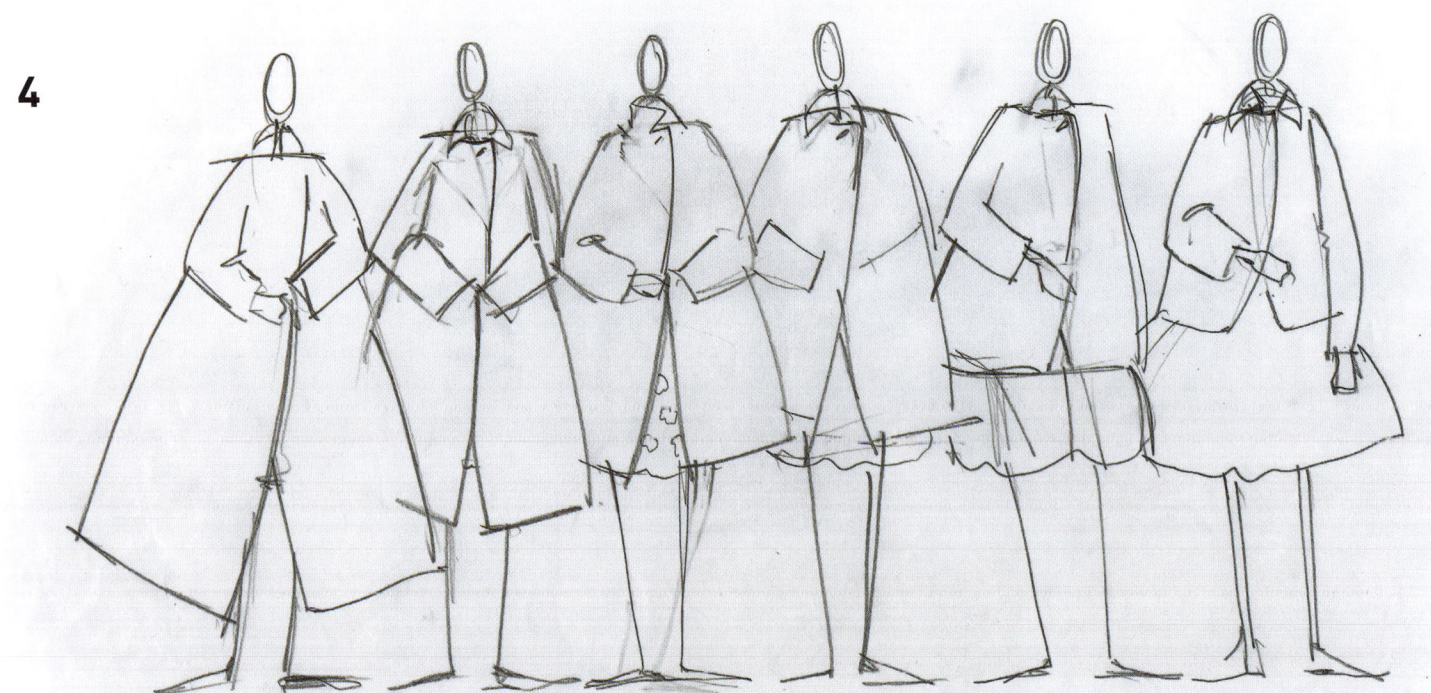

4

3. The theme and atmosphere are clarified in a 'mood board' showing other researched, drawn and found images. Photographs of the actual coat show the thought progression and are supported by a painted and collaged colour palette.

4. 'Design development sheets' show the development of the design ideas. The silhouette is drawn and redrawn, with proportions and details being exaggerated and explored repeatedly.

5. Further series of design developments refine the possibilities for the coat, which is to be the key item in this capsule collection. The functional appeal of its pockets and details are enhanced with bold stitching.

6. The notion of layering – which goes back to the source of the idea in terms of overalls, aprons, protection and volume – is explored in this series of developments.

5

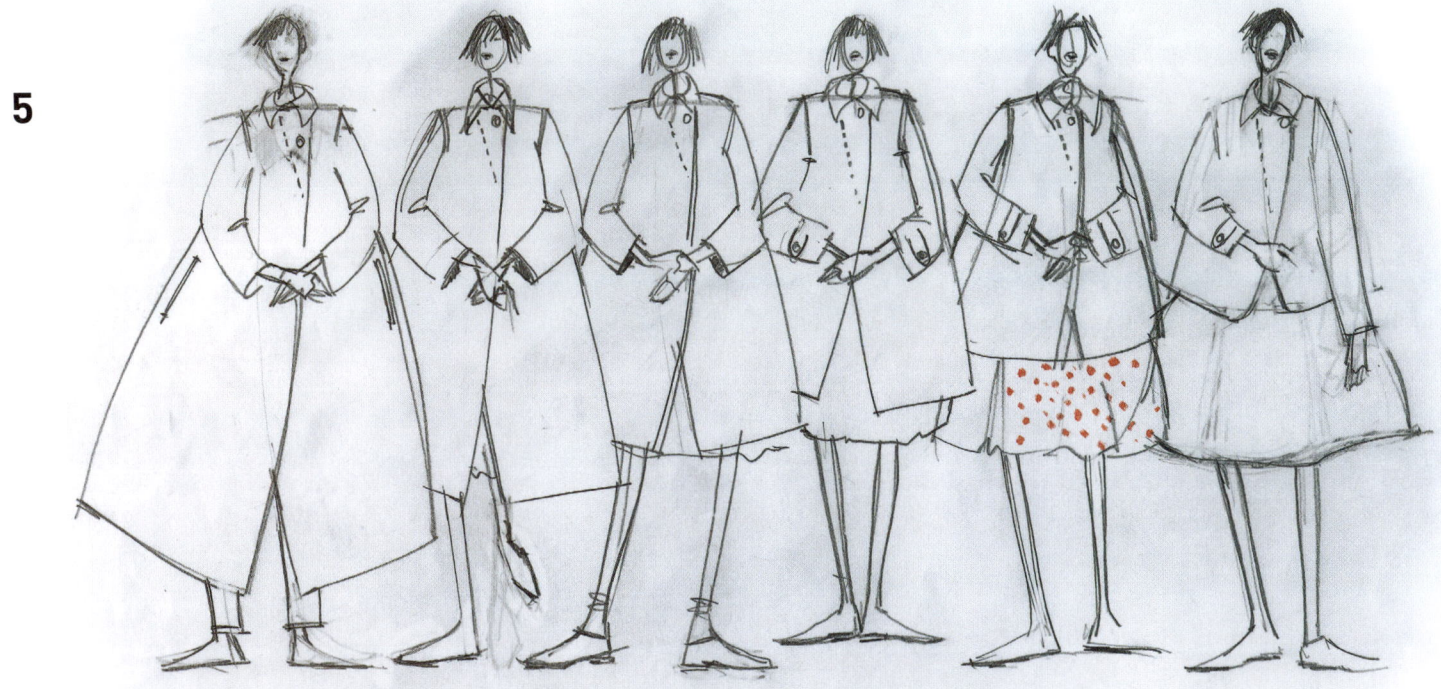

6

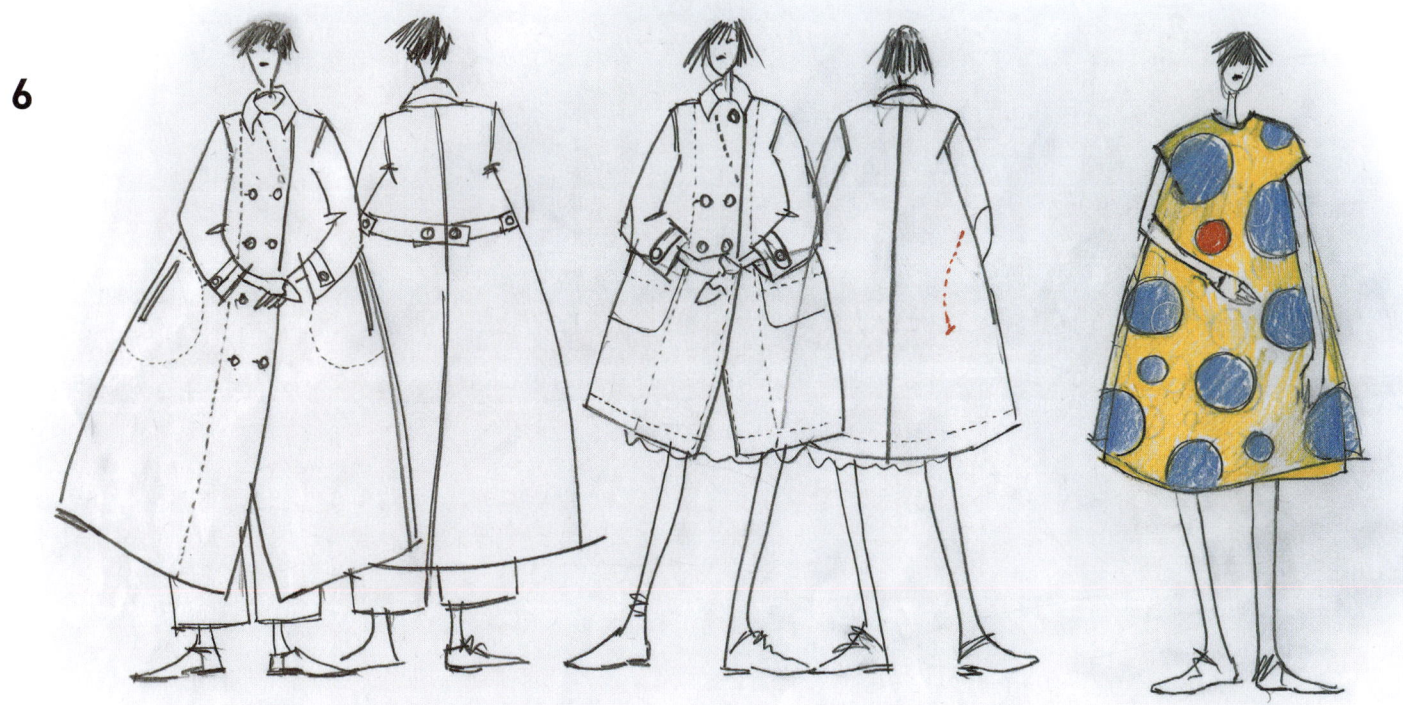

7

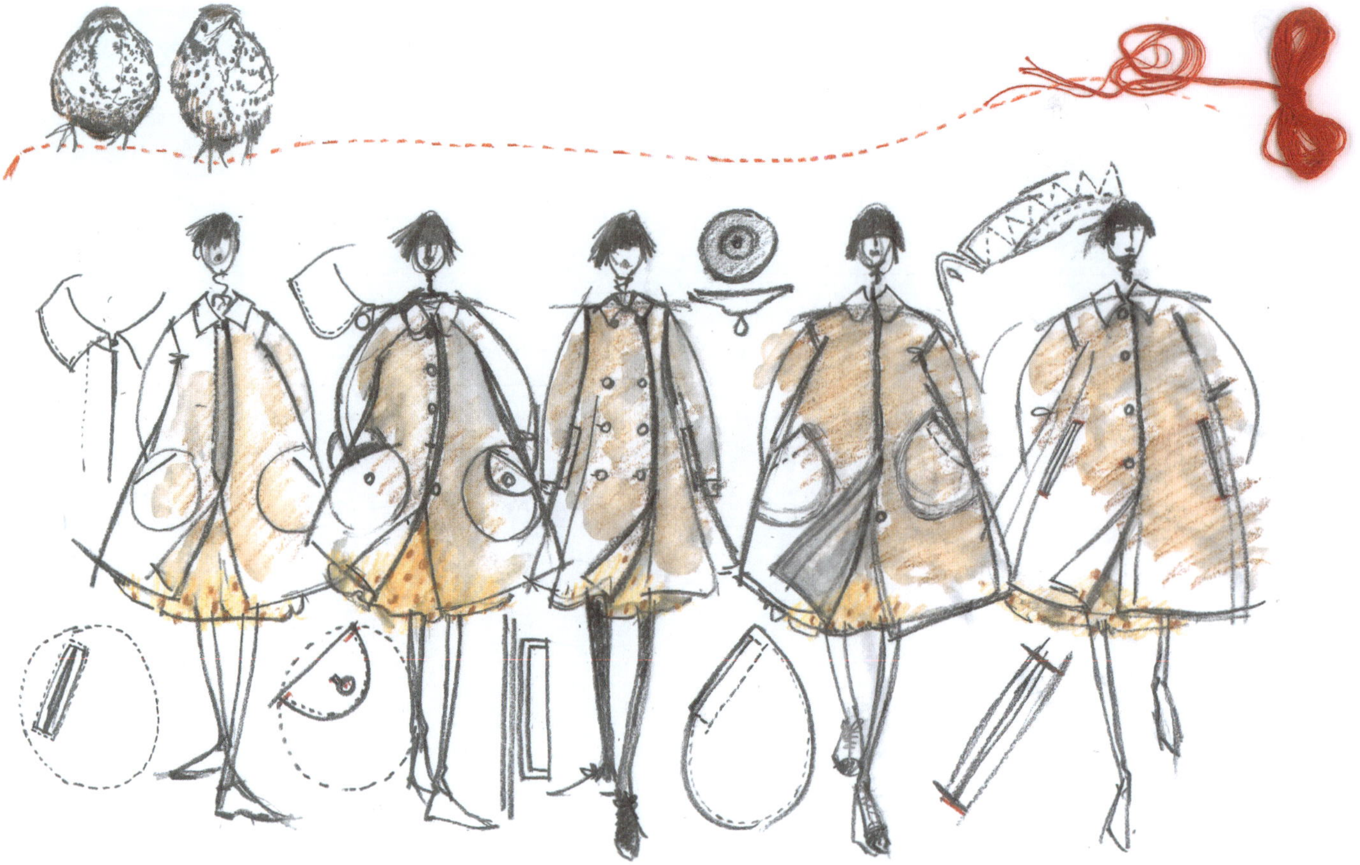

8a

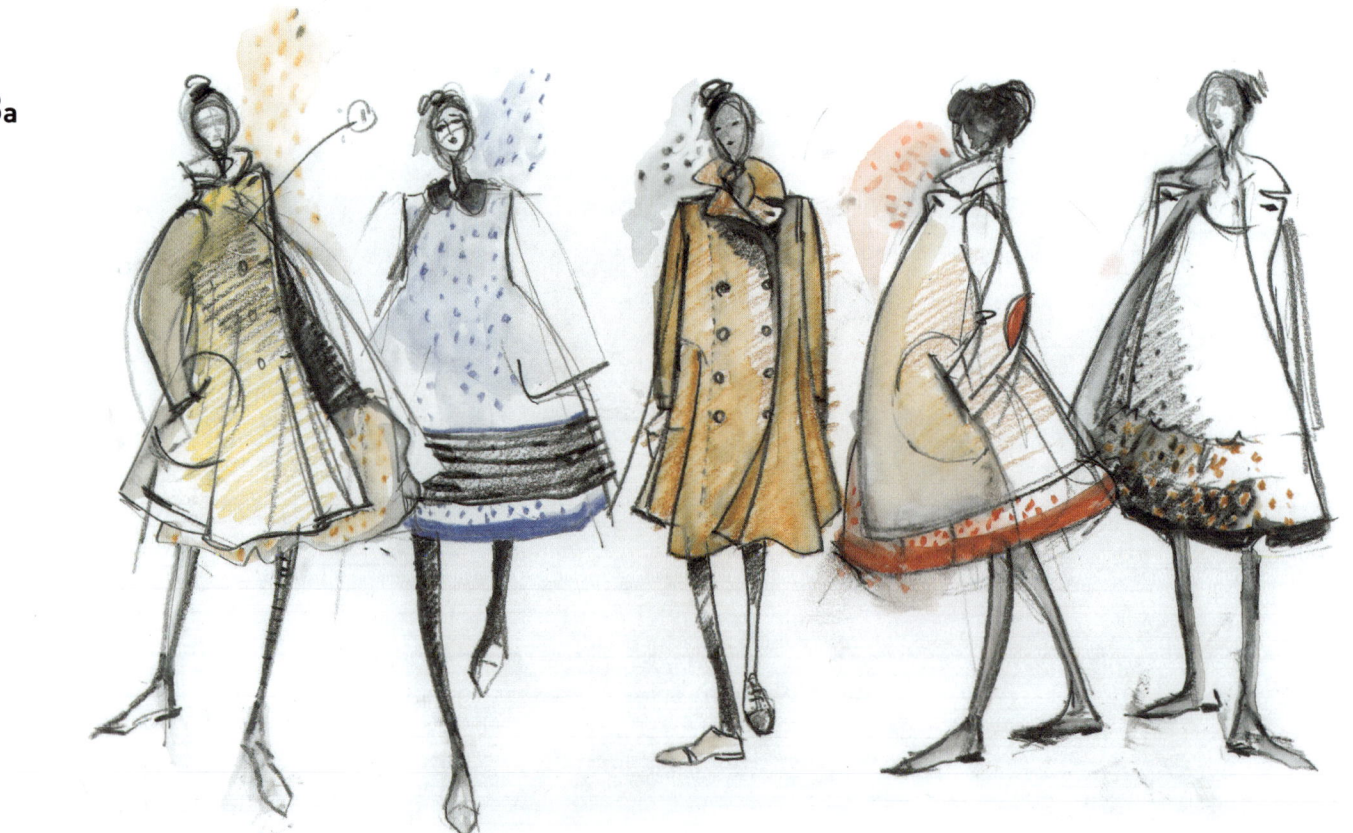

8b

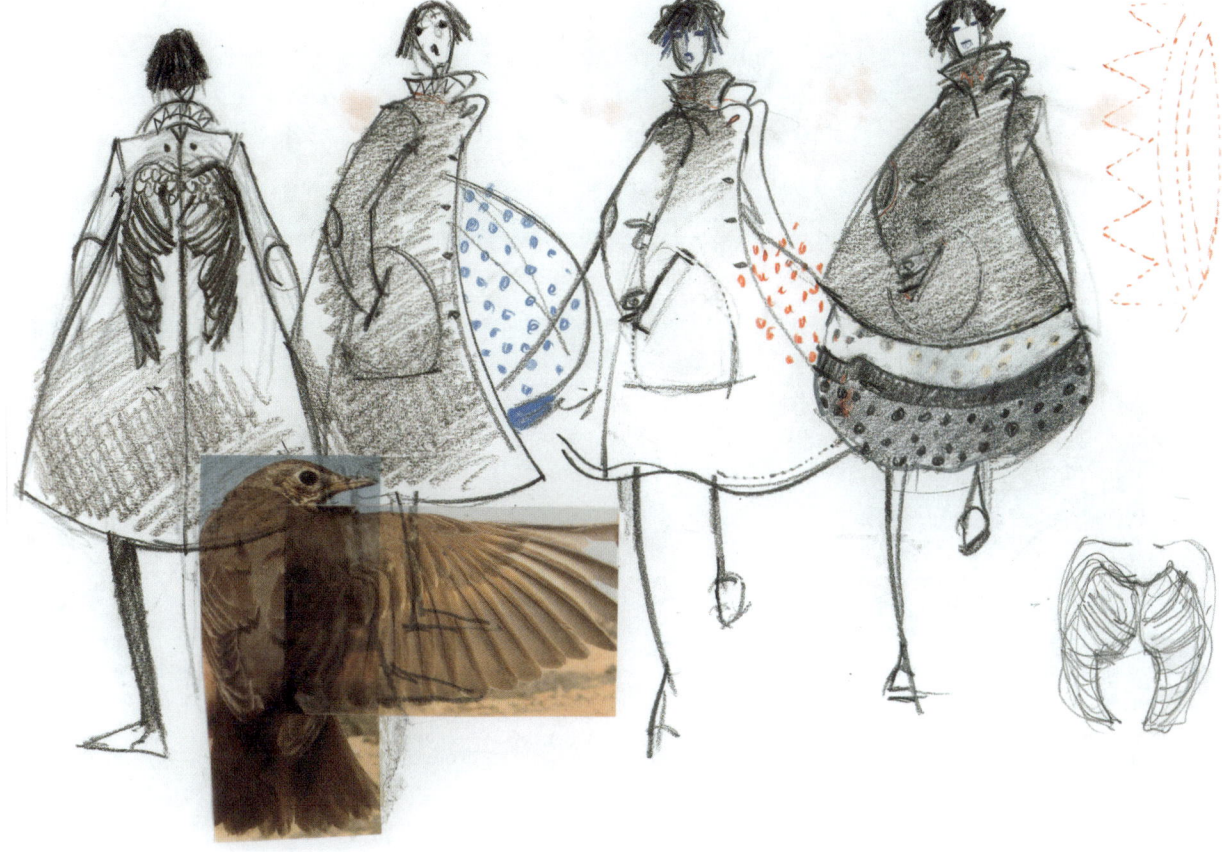

7. The ideas are further developed to include a more literal interpretation of the thrush, with ideas for embroidered wings and speckled and spotted fabrics.

8. The project finishes with a series of more precise design drawings showing the refined ideas and details, and these are clear enough to be used for starting to make up the designs. The last illustration (8c) consists of a precise drawing on tracing paper layered over standard paper on which fabric colour and pattern have been rendered in a loose, interpretive way. This technique complements the layered aspect of the garment's design.

8c

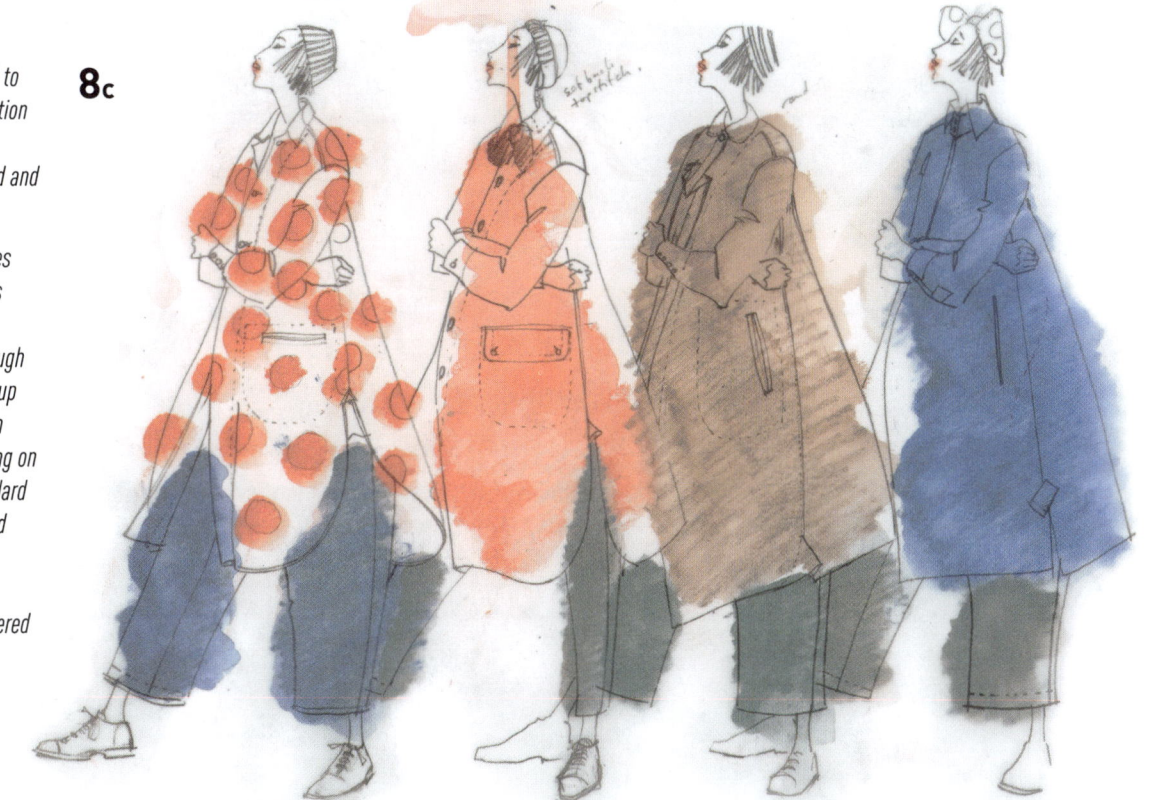

HAMPSTEAD BEATNIKS PROJECT by Yvonne Deacon

1

2

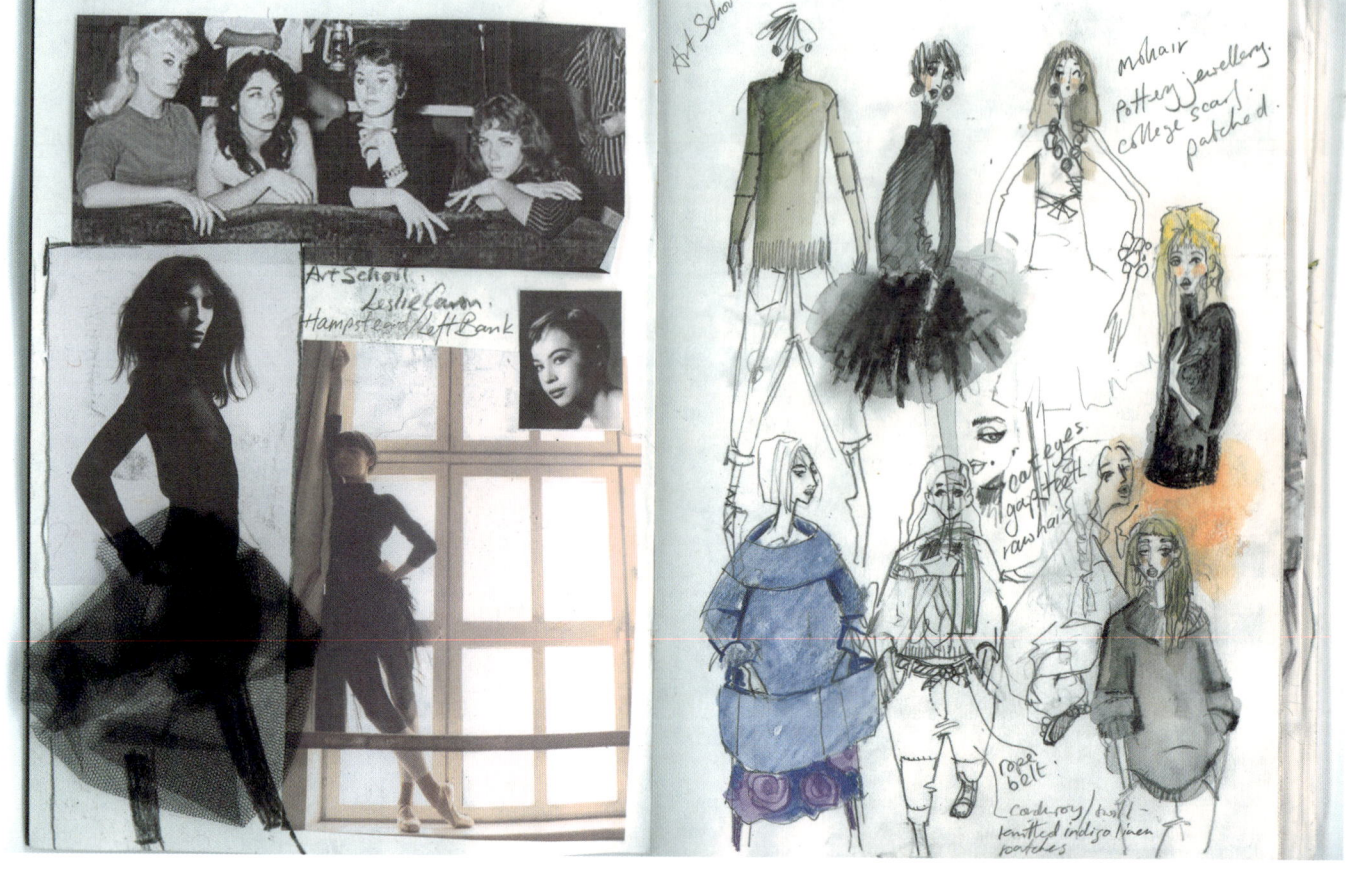

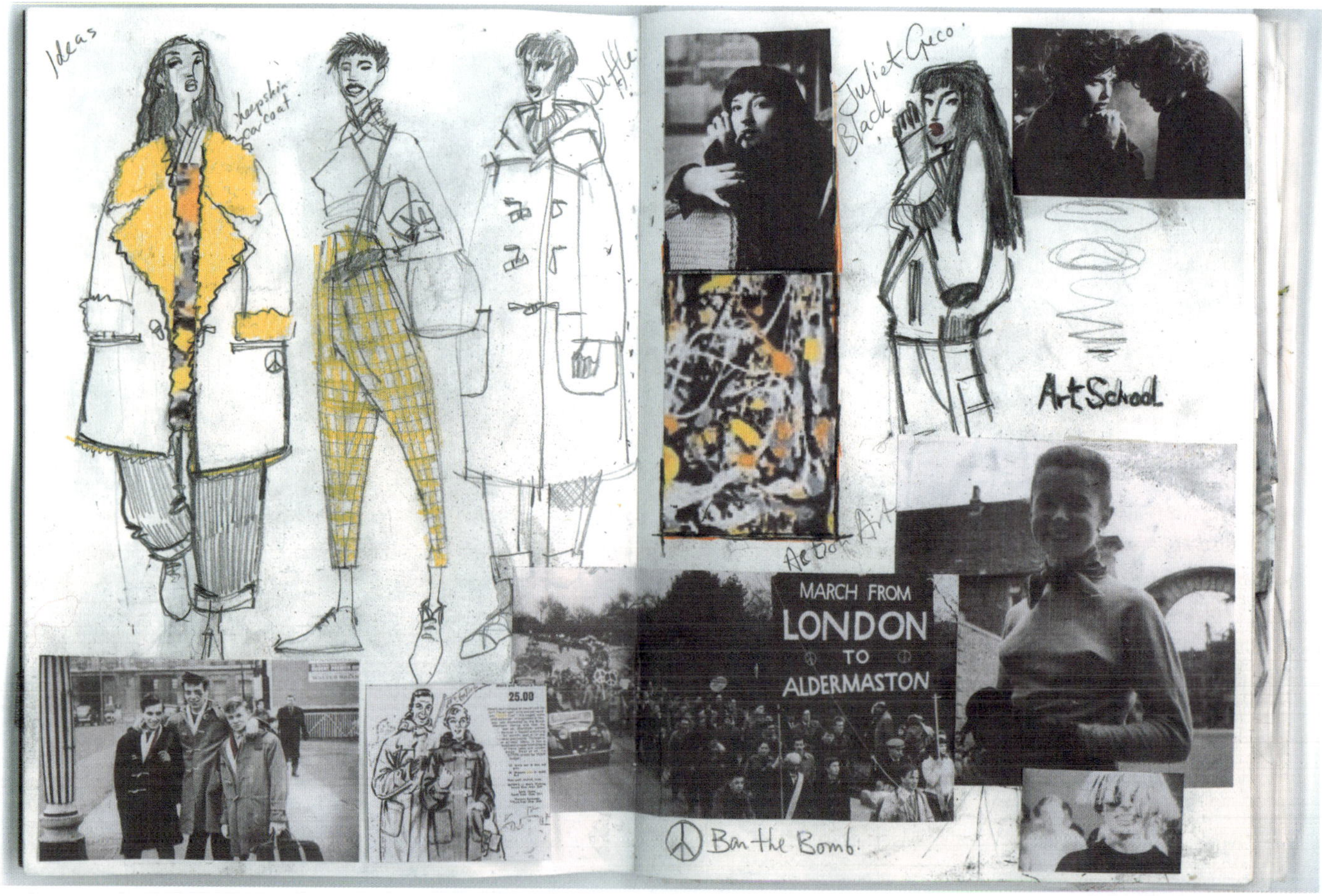

1. This project is based on a theme inspired by the designer's favourite period films and family memories of the artist-bohemians of Hampstead in north London, UK, in the late 1950s. As Hampstead was Britain's answer to the Left Bank in Paris in the same era, images of French film stars and ballet dancers are collaged and combined. Images, sketches and notes for looks, styling and fabrics record initial brainstorming.

2. Nostalgic old photographs of peace marches and vintage advertisements for the beatniks' preferred utility garment, the duffel coat, are collected as the theme develops and broadens.

3. Images of artists and their abstract art, riverside stalls selling paintings, and the bohemian style of the movement's followers inspire more ideas and designs.

4. Artist's painting smocks and the original 'boyfriend' looks of the era begin to combine and suggest silhouettes and styles. An image of a rather wild but stylish young woman recurs and is chosen as a muse/model for design sketches. A small watercolour sketch of a paintbox thematically expresses a colour mood.

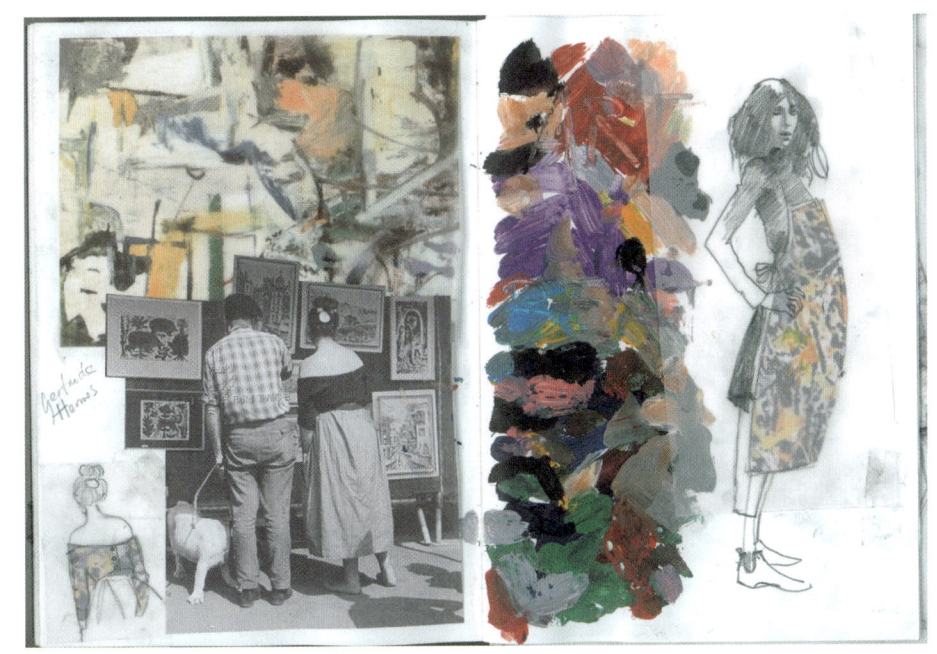

3

4

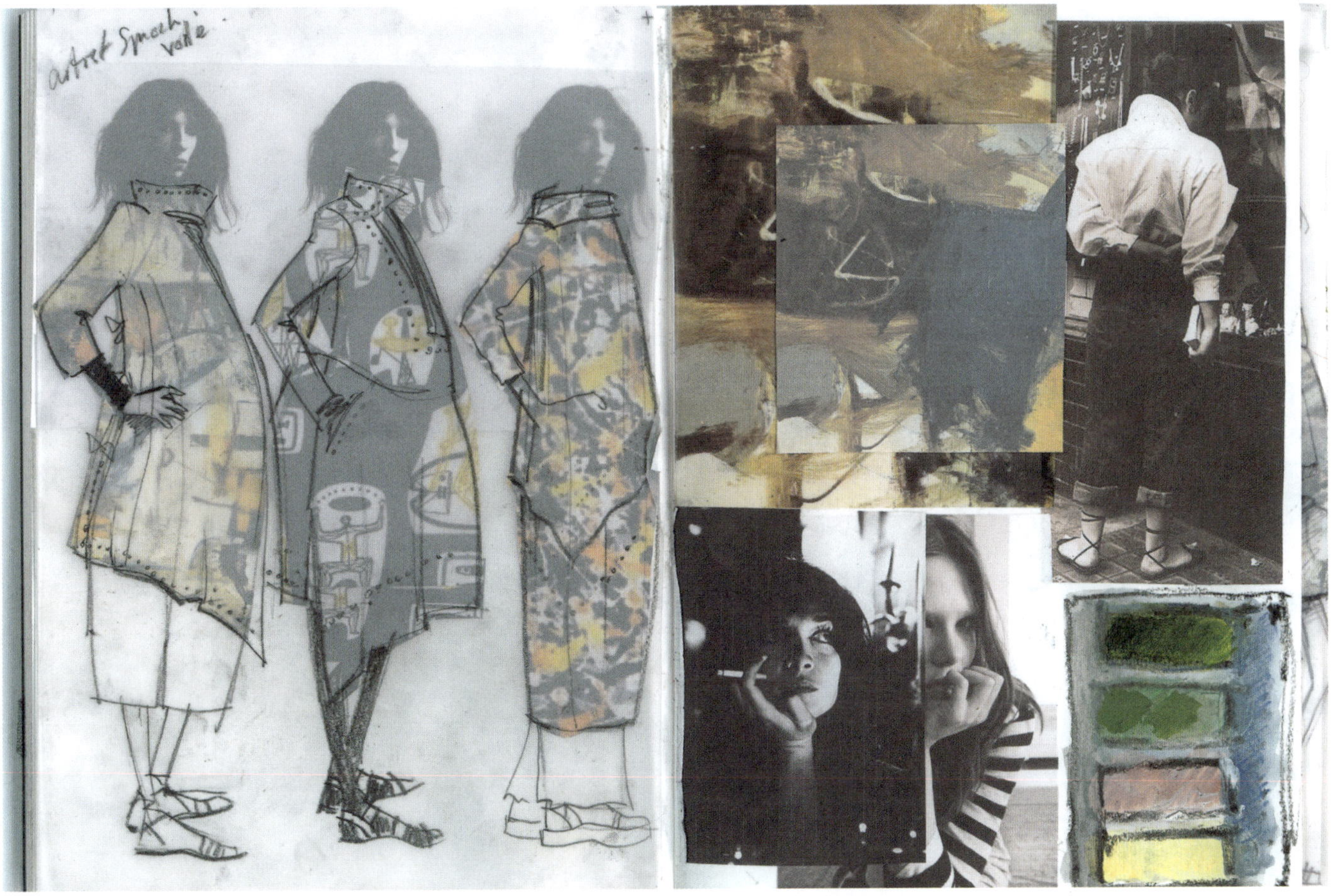

5

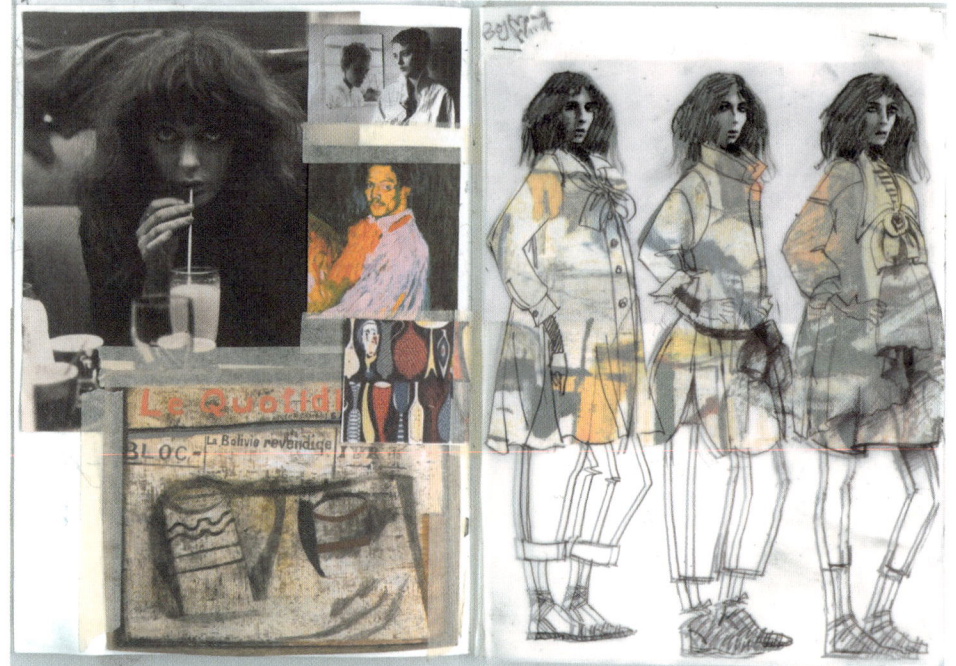

5. *The look is reinforced with images of a 'boyfriend' shirt, vintage printed fabrics and 'coffee bar' style. Design ideas for artist's smocks are developed and refined.*

6. *Other bohemian additions include vintage lace, aprons, oversized proportions and abstract prints, which are collaged together and create another wave of design ideas.*

7. *Ideas of 1950s café society in London and Paris and of the glamorous notion of vintage Parisian fashion combine to upgrade the ideas for a more runway look.*

8. *Finally, a more sophisticated amalgam of all the ideas emerges, embracing all the elements, including the jazz sounds and imagery of the era.*

6

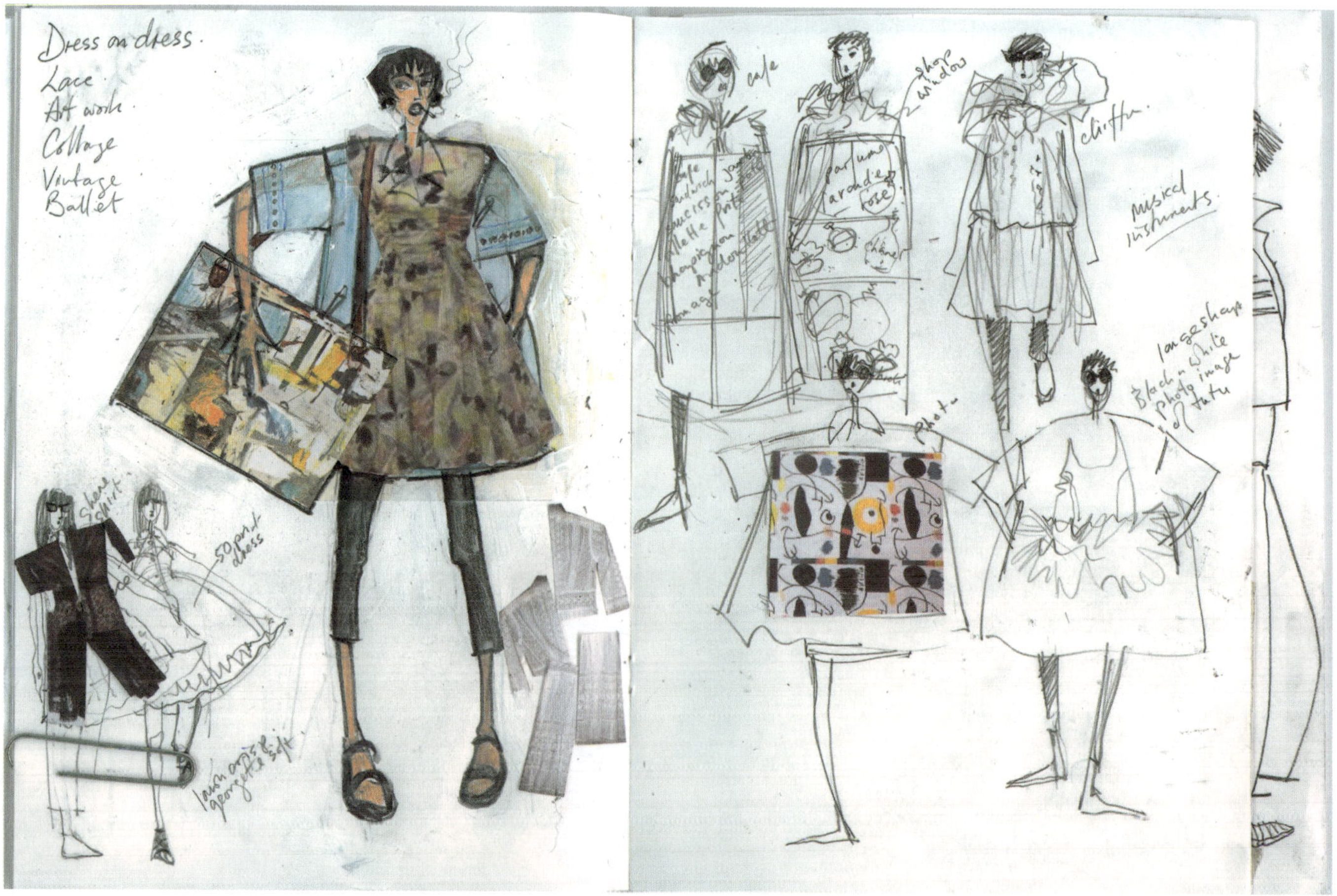

Dress on dress.
Lace
Art work.
Collage
Vintage
Ballet

7

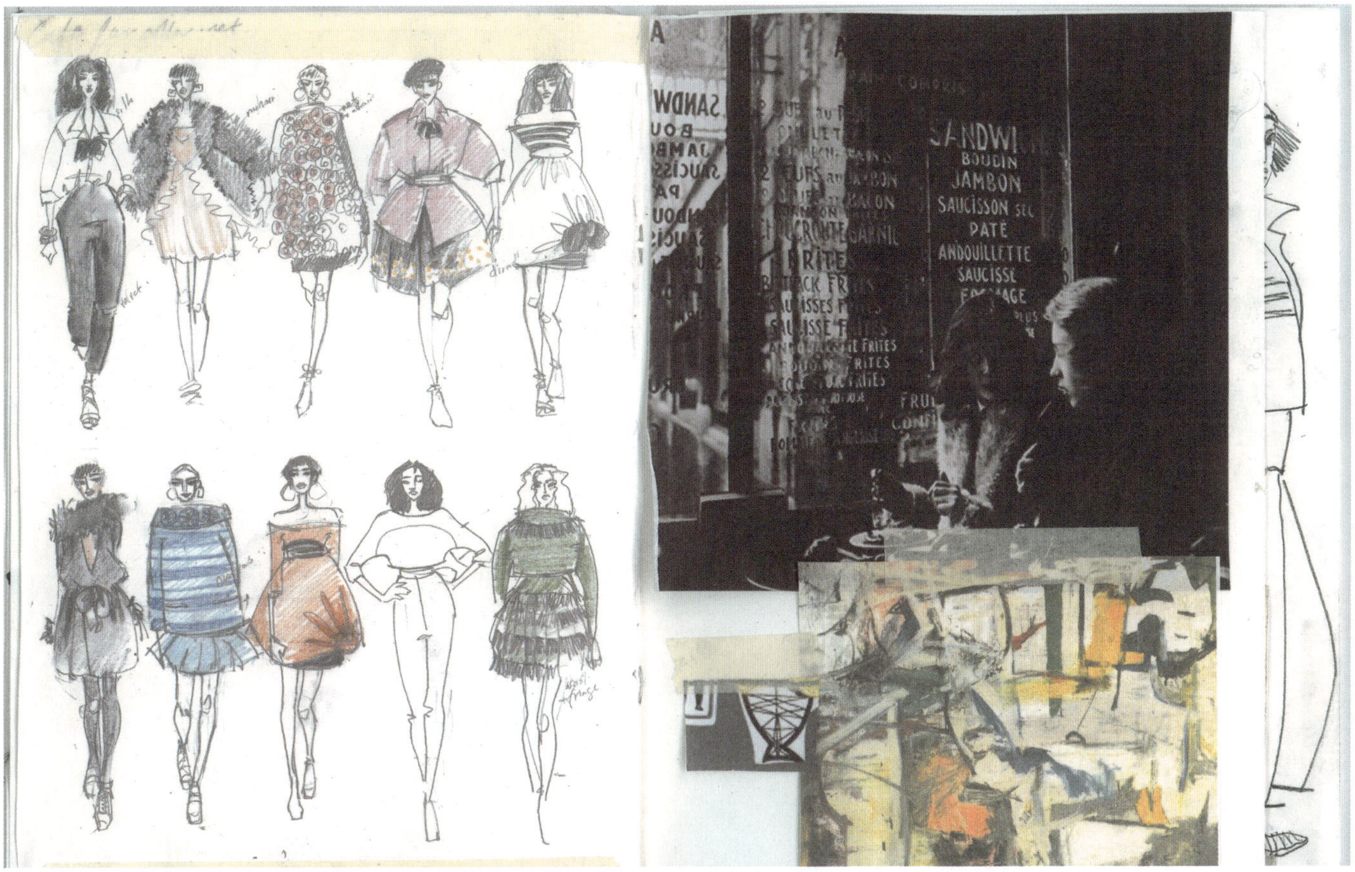

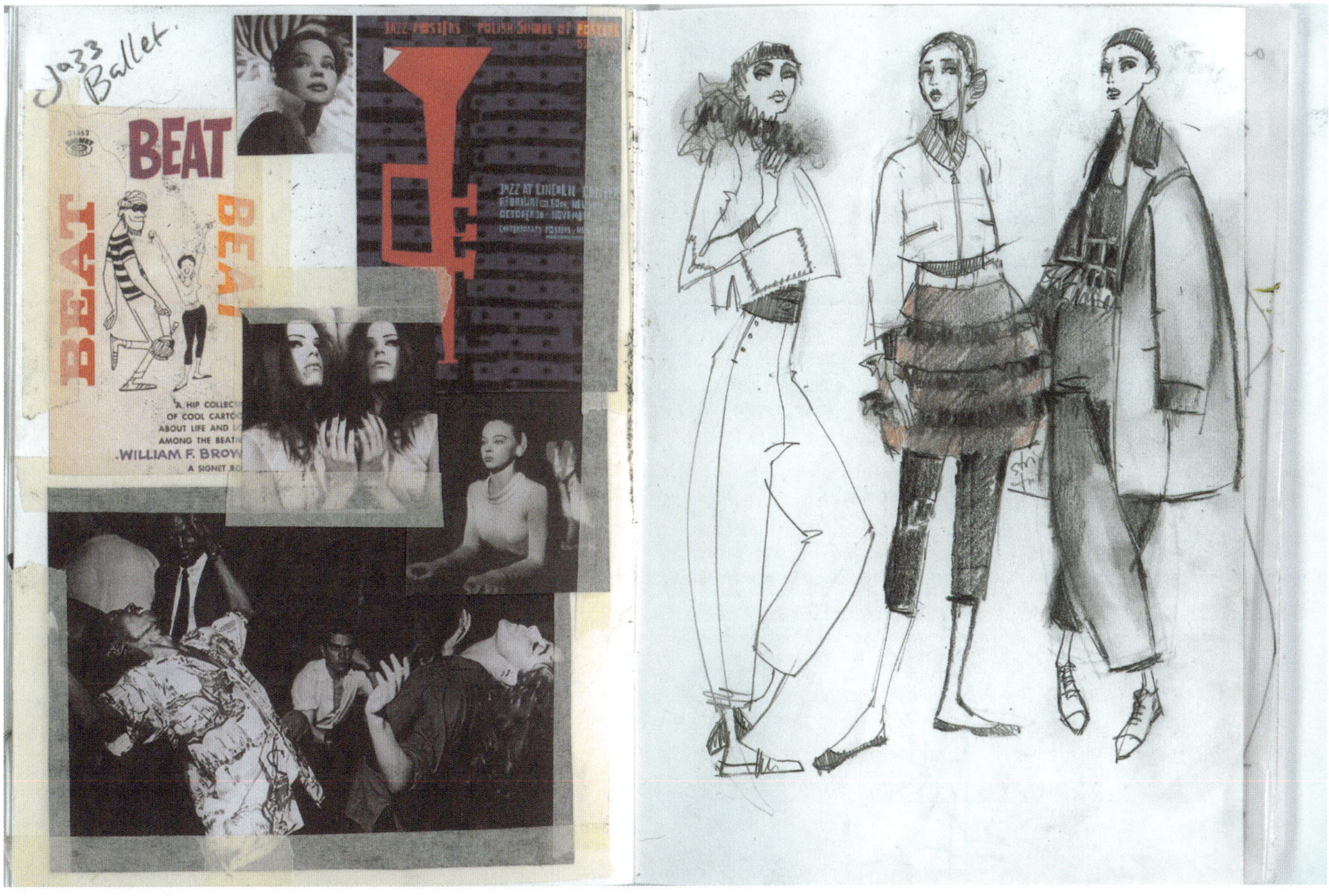

8

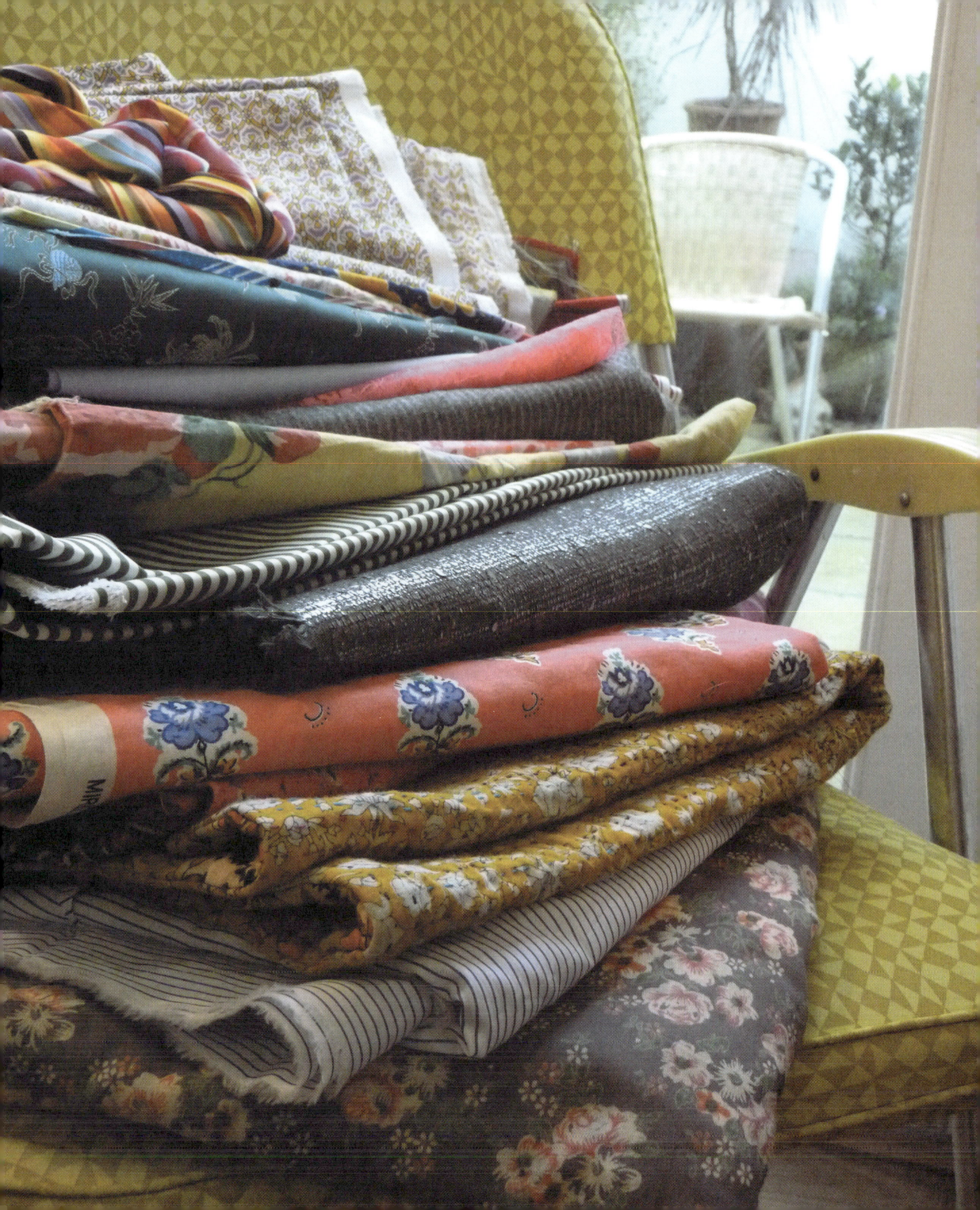

CHAPTER 4

COLOUR

We live in a world of colour. It is a stimulus for our creativity, a trigger for our memory and emotions, a major influence on us all. Almost everyone has some opinion on the subject: a favourite colour, for example, or one they dislike – hate, even. Such are the passions which colour can evoke.

From antiquity, tradition and beliefs have influenced our colour understanding and perceptions. The Ancient Greeks understood the antithesis between black and white and developed a theory of black, white and red as the primary colours. Colour confused even Aristotle, who proposed the opposition of light and dark to be the origin of the intermediate colours. Hippocrates later arrived at the four-colour theory: black, white, red and yellow. It is perhaps surprising, if not extraordinary for a country so deeply associated in our minds with idyllic azure seas and skies, that the Ancient Greeks had no word for the colour blue.

Since these early times there have been many developments in our knowledge and understanding of colour. For anyone wanting to study the science of colour in depth there are libraries devoted to this fascinating subject. However, it is important at this stage to have a basic grasp of what colour is and the way in which we see it.

There are two factors in our perception of colour – light and the human eye – for light is what creates colour in our eyes. The magnetic rays we know as light sit at a frequency somewhere between radio waves at one end of the spectrum and gamma rays at the other, and they include microwaves, infrared, ultraviolet and x-rays. The average human eye can detect only a tiny portion of this vast range, known as 'visible light', and humans can distinguish about ten million variations within it.

In this chapter we look at the fun and fascinating world of colour, and unveil some of its mysteries.

UNDERSTANDING COLOUR

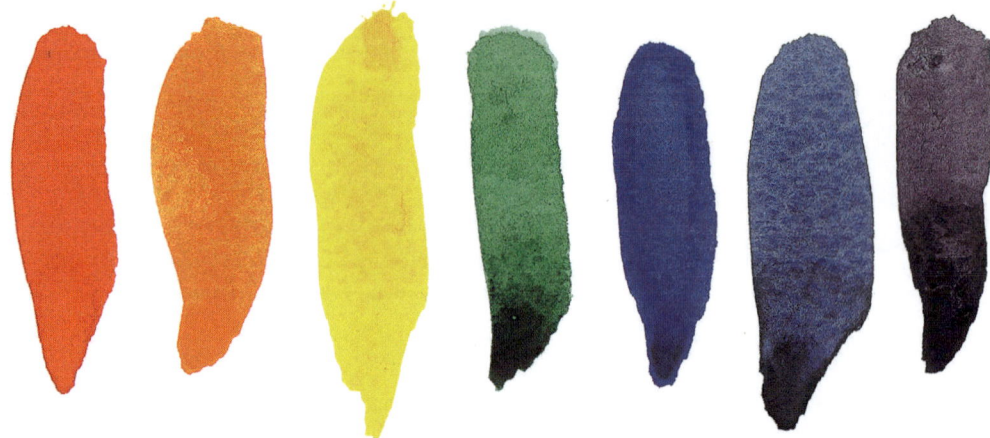

In 1666, English physicist and mathematician Isaac Newton discovered that by using prisms of glass he could refract light and split it into colours. He also found that there was a strict sequence to the colours, which pertained to the angle at which the light was split. The sequence was always the same. You can see this with a rainbow, where light filtered through water droplets produces a pattern of colours identical to those seen using the glass prism.

RODS AND CONES

When our eyes see the whole range of visible light together, they read it as 'white'. When some of the wavelengths are missing, they see it as coloured. The ability to see is what we call vision, and it is achieved by rods and cones in the delicate and complex mechanism of our eyes. Rods recognize black and white and facilitate the most basic part of our vision – black/grey/white. Cones recognize and capture colour and they develop in two stages during early infancy. At first, the baby develops the ability to recognize blue and yellow; next, he or she grows to recognize red and green. What we call colour blindness occurs when the cones fail to develop properly, usually at the second stage of cone development. Cones work best in strong light, which means that our colour vision at night hardly exists. In daylight, as visible (full spectrum) light falls on an object, the physical and chemical properties of its surface allow it to absorb much of the light. The

light that is not absorbed is reflected and bounced back as the colour we see. It is sometimes said that an object is 'doing colour' rather than 'being colour'.

Our eyes see about 80 per cent of the colour range. A small percentage of what we see goes on in our head – it is neurological – and this hints at some of the more emotive aspects of colour.

With a pair of red shoes, for example, the colour atoms of the object behave in such a way that, when light falls on them, they absorb most of the blue and yellow and reflect the red. Paradoxically red shoes contain every wavelength of light – except red.

In 1810, the German writer, dramatist, poet, philosopher and scientist Johann Wolfgang von Goethe published his *Theory of Colours*. Much of this proved later to be scientifically inaccurate, but it was perhaps the poet in him that led him to study systematically the physiological effects of colour. Michael Eugene Chevreal, a chemist who was director of the dye works at the Manufacture des Gobelins in Paris, observed how colours looked differently depending upon the colours they were used next to; this discovery led to his theory of 'simultaneous contrast', which states that context influences the colours we see.

'The learned compute that seven hundred and seven millions of vibrations have to penetrate the eye before the eye can distinguish the tints of a violet.'

EDWARD G. BULWER-LYTTON

'Any white and opaque surface will be partially coloured by reflections from surrounding objects.'

LEONARDO DA VINCI, *THE NOTEBOOKS*, VOL. 1

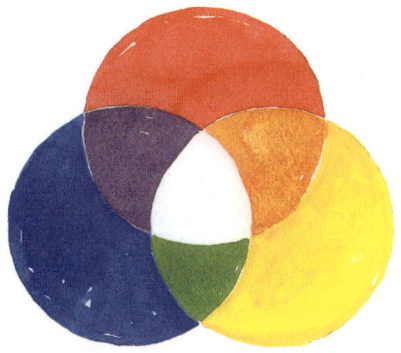

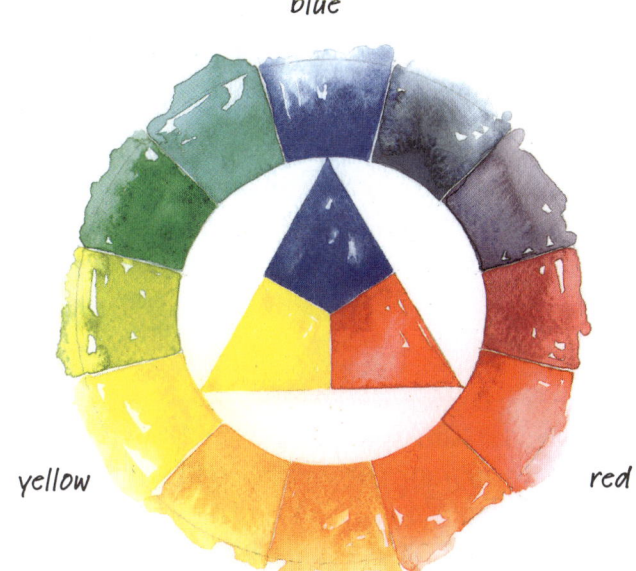

In the early 20th century our understanding of the way colour works was developed by theorists such as Wilhelm Ostwald, a Baltic Latvian chemist who developed the colour wheel as we recognize it today. Albert Munsell, an American painter and art teacher, further developed these ideas and was the first to separate hue (colour), value (lightness) and chroma (purity or shade, sometimes called saturation) into a system that could be illustrated and calibrated. In the language of colour theorists, a tint is the mix of a colour with white, which increases its lightness. Adding black to a colour reduces its lightness and produces a shade. A tone is produced when a colour is mixed with black and white or (in simpler terms) with grey. When a colour is mixed with black, white or grey this reduces its colourfulness, or chroma, though the hue remains the same. However, we tend to use the word shade to mean any variant of a colour, whether it be hue, tint or tone.

COLOUR HARMONY

Colour harmony is when colours are combined in a way that pleases the eye. The simplest colour harmony is analogous, when neighbouring colours are used from the colour wheel, such as yellow-green, yellow and yellow-orange. When directly oppositional colours are combined, such as red and green, blue and orange or yellow and purple, they are known as complementary colours. A third type, known as triadic colour harmony, combines colours evenly spaced around the colour wheel.

'I love colour. I feel it inside me. It gives me a buzz.'

DAMIEN HIRST

METAMERISM

Metamerism is science's way of describing why colours change, appear differently or fail to match in different lights – the cool light of morning or from the north, the warm light of evening and the south, daylight, artificial light, filament, tungsten, fluorescent, and so on. Basically, different materials and surfaces, when combined with different dyes and colourants, will absorb and reflect light differently and appear differently in different lights. We hope you are not confused!

'"Yes!" I answered you last night;
"No!" this morning, Sir, I say!
Colours, seen by candle-light,
Will not look the same by day.'

ELIZABETH BARRETT BROWNING

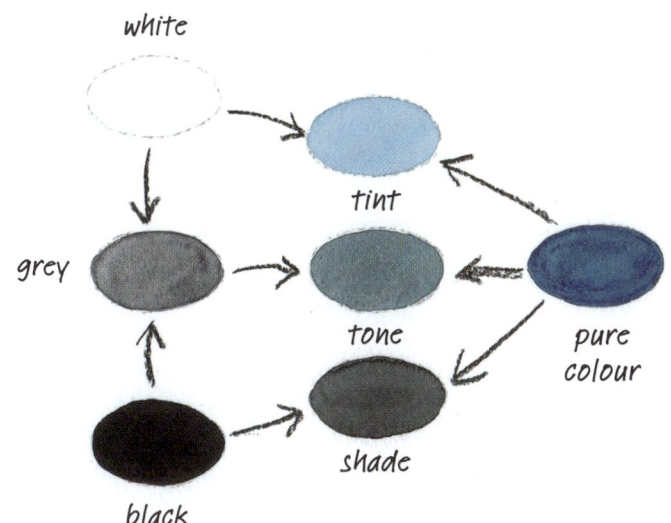

COLOUR & FASHION

In the world of fashion particularly – though this phenomenon is becoming widespread throughout all areas of commerce – colour has always been a major part of the newness offered by designers each season. We frequently hear how fashion has in-built obsolescence; in one season, out the next. Without going into too much depth at this juncture, this can partly be excused by the fact that some colours are perhaps more naturally suited to a particular season – though this appropriateness is more and more often challenged these days as season crossover and *fashion* tends now to influence everything. Colour is, though, the cheapest and easiest way to update anything and, in the interests of commerce, designers do exploit this, as we are well aware. The new colours are usually the main point of curiosity and interest each season.

Looking back in history we can see very definite trends in colours, many of them driven by economic, political and scientific developments and scenarios which as a subject would make for fascinating and enlightening research beyond the scope of this book. More recently we can easily associate colours such as purple with the late 1960s – orange, too. In the 1970s the darker purple and aubergine shades of Biba gave way to brown as part of a huge retro trend. In the 1980s Japanese designers, in particular Yohji Yamamoto, Issey Miyake and Rei Kawakubo with her label Comme des Garçons, converted almost the whole fashion world to black – an influence that still reverberates today.

SIGNATURE COLOURS

Most designers have their 'colour moment', when a colour they show or are associated with is particularly pertinent. Despite changing seasons and over-riding trends, some designers, however, are very much permanently associated with particular colours and in some instances they become ongoing – their signature colour(s) – if not because they regularly show part of their collection or accessories using those colours, then because of the significant colour of their branding and packaging.

In the evolution of fashion brands (as we now know them), designer Jeanne Lanvin was one of the first to be associated with a particular colour. Working in Paris in the early 20th century, Lanvin travelled to Florence where she saw a Fra Angelico fresco and reputedly fell in love with the 'quattrocento blue'. She decorated her home with it and went on to use it extensively in her work. The shade became known as 'Lanvin blue' and, when the label was revived in 2001 with Alber Elbaz as artistic director, the colour became key to the identity through its packaging, branding and perennial inclusion in the ranges.

In 1926 a short, simple black dress by Coco Chanel was featured in American *Vogue* and heralded as the answer to many contemporary dressing dilemmas. As modern as the Model T Ford (which came only in black), elegant and chic, it was soon considered in its essence to be timeless. Chanel herself often broke the severity of black with simple white collar or cuff details, so black and white became the signature house colours until her demise. As she famously stated: 'Women think of all colours except the absence of colour. I have said that black has it all. White too. Their beauty is absolute. It is the perfect harmony.' The label was revived in 1983 under the creative directorship of Karl Lagerfeld. Since then, much has been made of the black and white theme and its contemporary marketing.

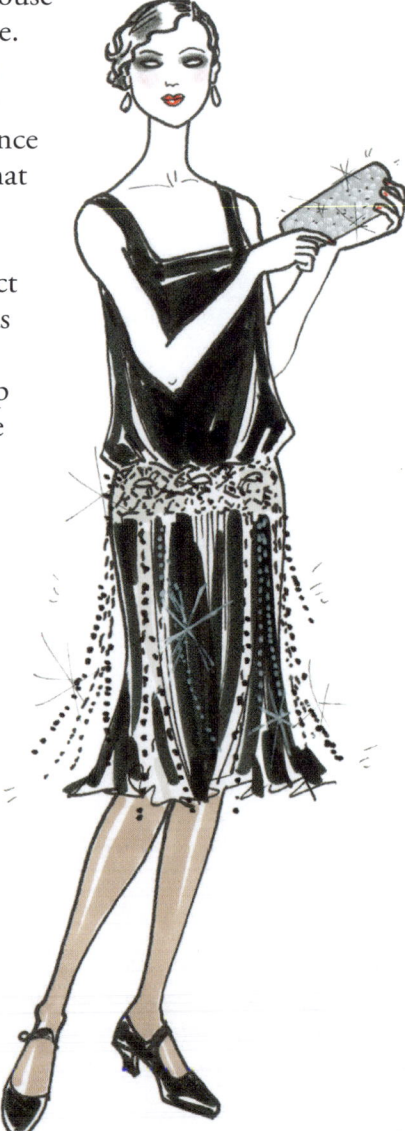

RIGHT: *Chanel's short, elegant little black dress was identified as the 'shape of the future' in 1926.*

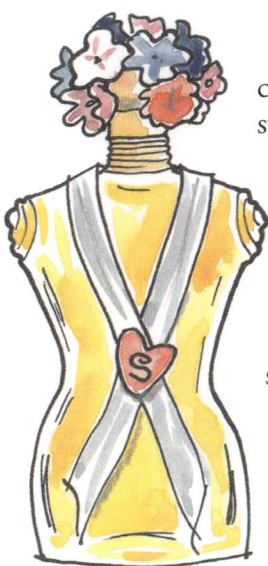

In the 1930s, another Parisian couturier, Elsa Schiaparelli, became synonymous with a particularly fierce shade of bright pink.

When in 1937 she launched her perfume Shocking de Schiaparelli packaged in this shade, the colour became widely known as 'shocking pink' and is still known by this name today.

The French fashion house Hermès was originally a high-end equestrian outfitter and tack-maker, which gradually made the transition to fashion brand. It has maintained and capitalized on its bright orange packaging (reputed to be Pantone 17-1463 Tangerine Tango).

Another early 20th century luggage brand which made the transition to full fashion range is Milan-based Prada. Perhaps still more famous for its bags and accessories than its clothes, Prada has a reputation and association with red, using definitive shades that are never brash or flashy.

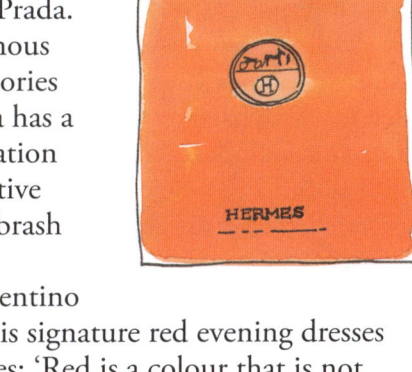

Italian designer Valentino has been known for his signature red evening dresses for at least two decades: 'Red is a colour that is not shy . . . ' he says. 'When I was young, I went to see the opera *Carmen* in Barcelona and the whole set was red – the flowers, the costumes – and I said to myself, "I want to keep this colour in my life." So I mixed a shade with the people who make fabrics – it contains a certain amount of orange – and Valentino Red became an official Pantone colour.'

Red also provides the signature colour for the soles of Christian Louboutin shoes, whatever the style, colour or fabric of the rest of the shoe.

With typical restraint, when Christian Dior opened his couture house on the Avenue Montaigne in Paris in 1946 it was decorated in soft grey Louis XVI style. The colour became the signature colour. When the nose François Demachy recently created a new fragrance in honour of the house and the heritage of the brand, he called it Gris Montaigne.

Yves Saint Laurent, perhaps the greatest of the late 20th century couturiers, was undoubtedly a great colourist. Frequently influenced by fine artists and by traditional costume and dress from exotic corners of the world, which frequently inspired flamboyant colour palettes, he was equally known for his restraint and could just as successfully make a statement in signature navy blue.

The great British designer Jean Muir, who sadly died in 2007, was known for her great confidence with colour on the runway, but was similarly a huge promoter of navy blue, for which she was widely known and adored. She personally wore only navy blue all her life and was widely feted for her clever little navy dresses.

The Italian brand Gucci began its revival and revamp in 1994, with the appointment of Tom Ford as creative director. The signature red and green stripe was revived and Ford changed all the packaging and branding to a chic dark brown, reviving this colour from its dreary 1970s associations and challenging the then ubiquitous black branding of almost all the other big name labels.

Parisian Jean Paul Gaultier has since his 1980s heyday been forever associated with navy and white matelot stripes.

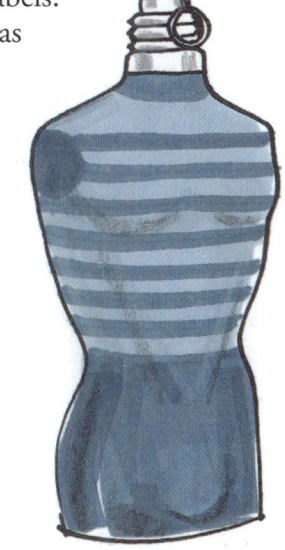

'Colour is the language of poets. It is astonishingly lovely. To speak it is a privilege.' KEITH CROWN

TALKING COLOUR

As we have mentioned, everyone sees colour slightly differently. Lighting and other factors affect how we see colour, so systems have evolved to recognize and standardize colours for industry. The most widely known and popularly used system is Pantone, first developed by Lawrence Herbert in the early 1960s to help an American printing company simplify their stock control.

The Pantone Matching System (PMS) allows designers, industry and manufacturers to colour match, regardless of location and without the need for direct contact with one another. The system is used across an increasingly wide range of industries including print, paint, plastics, yarn, fabric and, consequently, fashion. Pantone colours are identified by a unique serial number and letter suffix which denotes the medium; textile colours have the suffix TPX. New colours are added regularly, responding to fashion trends and innovations. Recent additions include metallics and fluorescents.

TREND FORECASTING

Fashion and colour crossovers aside, colour is a big and important business. Attempts at finding the right colour are the *raison d'être* of the numerous studios and bureaux specializing in trend forecasting, many of which target specific product areas and market levels. One of the biggest of these is the Colour Association, established in 1915. Its founding members were milliners, glove makers and hosiery suppliers who simply recognized that customers needed coordinated, fashionable accessories.

Today it is more complex, as the various influences on consumer tastes and values include economic, environmental and global factors – and fashion is bound up in all of this. When, perhaps rather foolishly, a *New York Times* journalist contacted the Paris office of Alber Elbaz, creative director at Lanvin to ask about fashion forecasts, the newspaper could only report: 'we think we can read "How to Become a Millionaire" or "Find a Gorgeous Husband in Three Weeks", but a book is a book is a book. We have to go with our intuition . . .' Bureaux, studios and style agencies tend to take their lead from the runway shows of influential designers such as Elbaz, not the other way round. Fashion forecasts are for the mass market; for retailers and manufacturers to ensure that they have enough blue sweaters in stock next winter!

Pantone is linked into this circuit, not only supplying the means of accurately disseminating colour information, but also contributing to it. Each year, since 1999, Pantone has declared a 'Colour of the Year', chosen approximately one year in advance. The first of these – Cerulean Blue 15-4020 (chosen for its calming, zen-like qualities) – was for 2000. The choice is discussed and debated by industry, media consultants and creatives and, according to Pantone, 'responds to and reflects the zeitgeist'. For example, the press release declaring Honeysuckle the colour of 2011 said: 'In times of stress, we need something to lift our spirits. Honeysuckle is a captivating, stimulating colour that gets the adrenaline going – perfect to ward off the blues.'

Chosen in the Spring of 2012, the colour for 2013 was Emerald 17-5641, described as: 'Lively. Radiant. Lush . . . A colour of elegance and beauty that enhances our sense of wellbeing, balance and harmony.' For 2014 the choice was Radiant Orchid 18-3224: 'an expressive, creative and embracing purple – one that draws you in with its beguiling charm. A captivating harmony of fuchsia, purple and pink undertones, Radiant Orchid emanates great joy, love and health.' The secrecy around the Colour of the Year is such that the Instagram promotional film for the 2014 colour was made in black and white! More detailed accounts of the colour meetings are published in *Pantone View*, a trade publication used by fashion designers, retailers, florists and other consumer-oriented companies to help inform their design choices and future product planning and coordination.

'Mere colour, unspoiled by meaning, and unallied with definite form, can speak to the soul in a thousand different ways.' OSCAR WILDE

COLOUR PALETTES

'I never met a colour I didn't like.' DALE CHIHULY

Colour is an inspiration – it can create and evoke moods by planting ideas and atmospheres, otherwise intangible, firmly in our minds. A successful colour palette is essential for communicating and referencing colours. Although reference numbers are usually enough for technical purposes, that's not how most people remember colours; we tend to find a name far more evocative and easier to recall. An appropriately named colour can evoke the exact shade in the mind, even though the person may not have necessarily seen it. Once seen together, the connection between name and colour can stay with us forever. So it is worth considering carefully the names you give to your colours; they should be appropriate to your mood or theme and, in the interests of simplicity, be single words only. It is unnecessary, for example, to call a colour 'Rose Pink'; 'Rose' should be enough, and if it isn't you need to pick the appropriate pink flower or object to reference. In industry, many mistakes have been made when one or other of the colour names has been omitted or someone has understood there to be two colours rather than one.

Colours were originally called after their natural pigment names: Ochre, Raw Umber, etc. But colours also readily conjure up images of alchemy and science or historical, geographical and cultural routes; Cadmium Yellow, Prussian Blue, Vermillion, Cardinal, etc. To ponder Ultramarine is to evoke the bluest of oceans – there is magic in the words.

Names and places stimulate the senses, evoke atmospheres and similarly inspire colours themselves. A good colour name can be employed as a powerful communication tool. For example, name a colour Samarkand (you may even conjure up a specific colour as you read this) and it can evoke notions of ancient silk routes – of a mysterious land, part fairytale perhaps, somewhere between Europe, Asia and the Orient. The imagination conjures ikat weaving, exotic silks and even jewels. Find some good reference images and the rest of a wonderful palette falls into place with other colours named from your imaginary adventure. Colours have a volume and intensity that can be generated though themed palettes by balancing, contrasting and orchestrating shades to your own ends and uses.

BELOW: *This old postcard inspired a relaxed casual palette of soft midtones in warm and cool shades (Sunset, Dusk, Sky and Grass). Bank, a soft olive shade, and Sand, a yellow ochre, act as useful neutrals. Mallard and Terroir add richness, with Storm providing definition and sobriety. By giving colours appropriate and evocative names, the palette's identity is reinforced.*

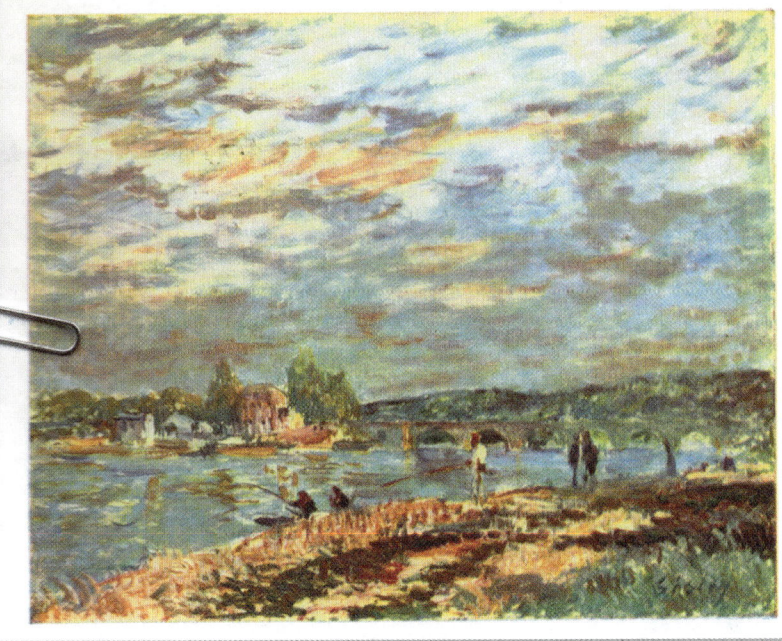

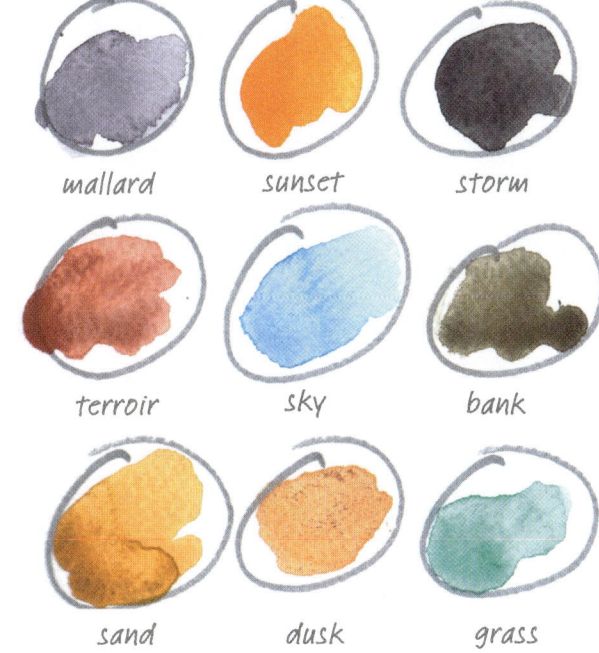

mallard   sunset   storm

terroir   sky   bank

sand   dusk   grass

'Colours, like features, follow the changes of the emotions.' PABLO PICASSO

When designing a colour palette, it is important to think about how it is going to be used. If intended for garments – what season, what type, what market, what materials, even? As some colours will translate differently into different cloths, they may become dull/flat or, conversely, a bit flashy. If the colours are to be used for fabric prints or patterns, how might they be combined? Do you need some highlight or upbeat colours or do you want neutral/quiet colours to set others off to advantage? Maybe you need some darker or richer tones for depth and definition?

Use the following quick, simple exercise to create a colour palette. Begin with an image you feel has a fashion relevance – a postcard of an artwork or a magazine tear that has a colour mood you like – and simply pick out the colours using windings of yarn, small snippets of fabric or coloured tape, etc. You can add small objects – a button, pebble, seashell or seed-head, a small plastic toy – anything that thematically relates and helps build towards the correct feeling and balance of colour.

Here is a fun, novelty colour palette in the form of a jigsaw, running A–Z, from Italian spinning company Millefili Spa. It presents a large colour palette for their range of high-fashion quality knitting yarns. As a designer, rarely would you use more than ten colours in a professional fashion colour palette for a range, but you can cheat a little sometimes and have lighter and darker shades of the same colour – if really necessary! Generally, though, the tighter the palette, the more concise and positive your colour message. A clear, confident message in your work will in turn instil your client's confidence in you.

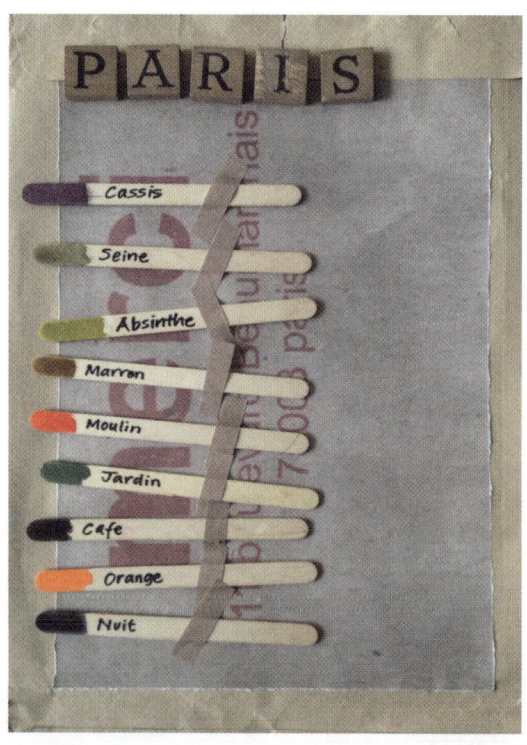

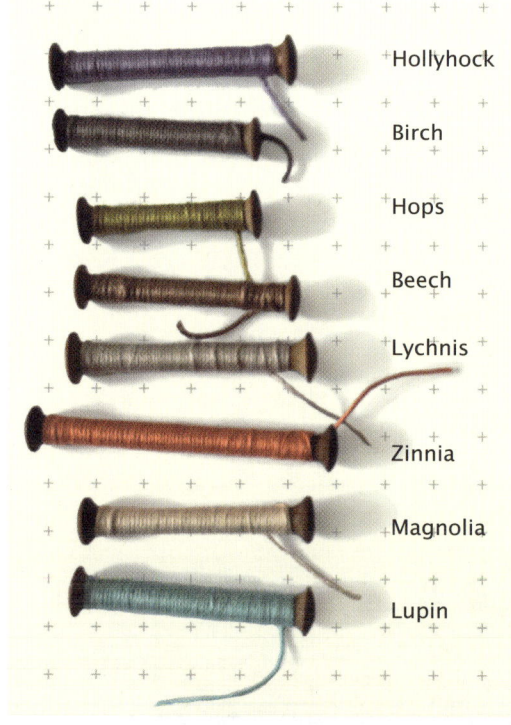

LEFT: *Using old wooden bobbins to wind embroidery threads as colour reference, this palette evokes a vintage needlework theme. It would need to be cross-referenced with Pantone shade numbers for accurate communication internationally.*

'The virtue of a small palette – the limitation stretches you to invent places where they can go.' BRIDGET RILEY

'Often an ugly colour is introduced such as a faded black or drab,
to give counterpoint to colours that are sweet and clean.' JOHN FOWLER

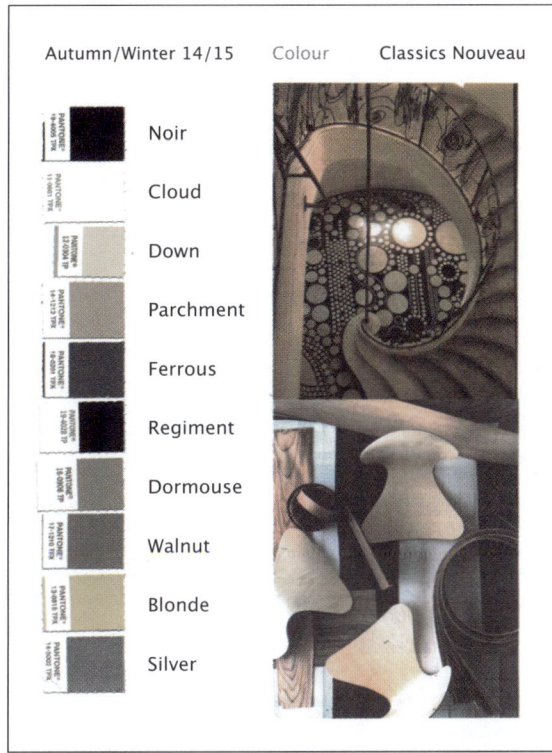

Autumn/Winter 14/15   Colour   **Classics Nouveau**

- Noir
- Cloud
- Down
- Parchment
- Ferrous
- Regiment
- Dormouse
- Walnut
- Blonde
- Silver

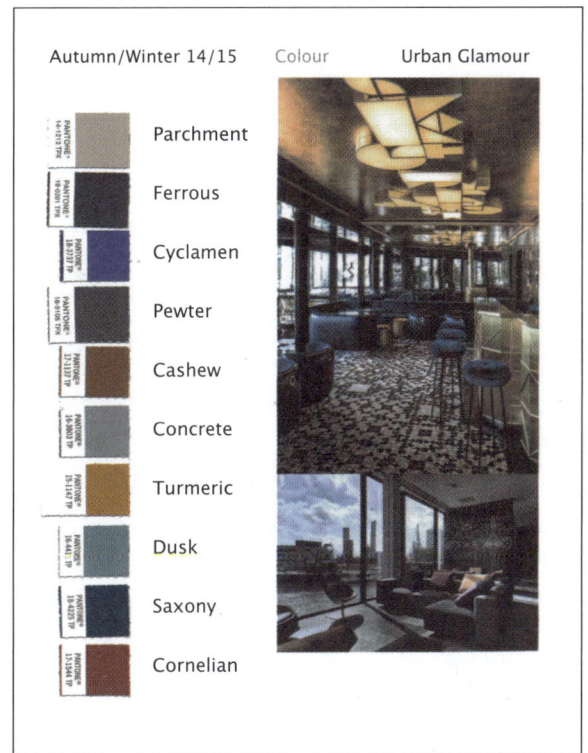

Autumn/Winter 14/15   Colour   **Urban Glamour**

- Parchment
- Ferrous
- Cyclamen
- Pewter
- Cashew
- Concrete
- Turmeric
- Dusk
- Saxony
- Cornelian

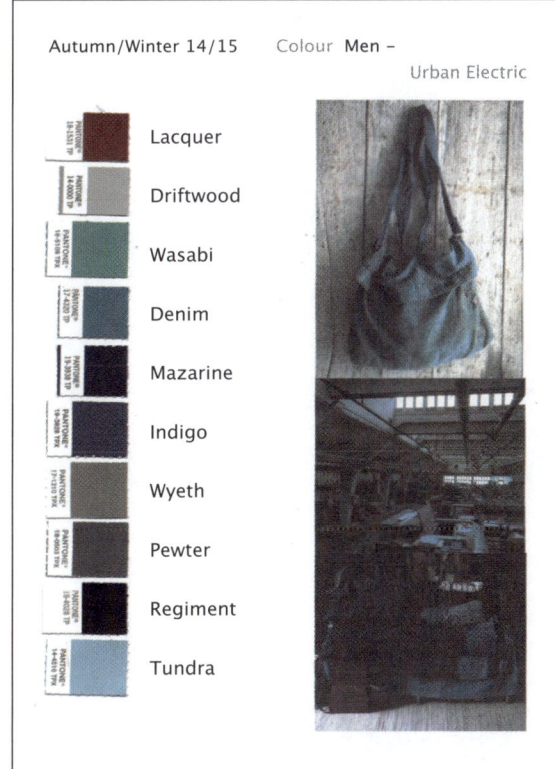

Autumn/Winter 14/15   Colour   **Men –**
Urban Electric

- Lacquer
- Driftwood
- Wasabi
- Denim
- Mazarine
- Indigo
- Wyeth
- Pewter
- Regiment
- Tundra

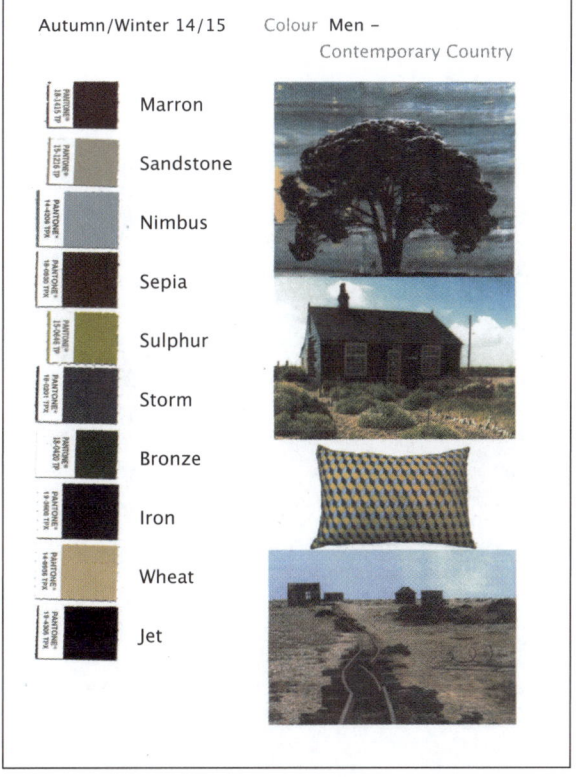

Autumn/Winter 14/15   Colour   **Men –**
Contemporary Country

- Marron
- Sandstone
- Nimbus
- Sepia
- Sulphur
- Storm
- Bronze
- Iron
- Wheat
- Jet

ABOVE: *These colour palettes produced for international clients for Autumn/Winter 14/15 efficiently convey the season's colour moods for their market sector and use industry-standard Pantone colour chips to communicate the specific reference codes accurately and effectively.*

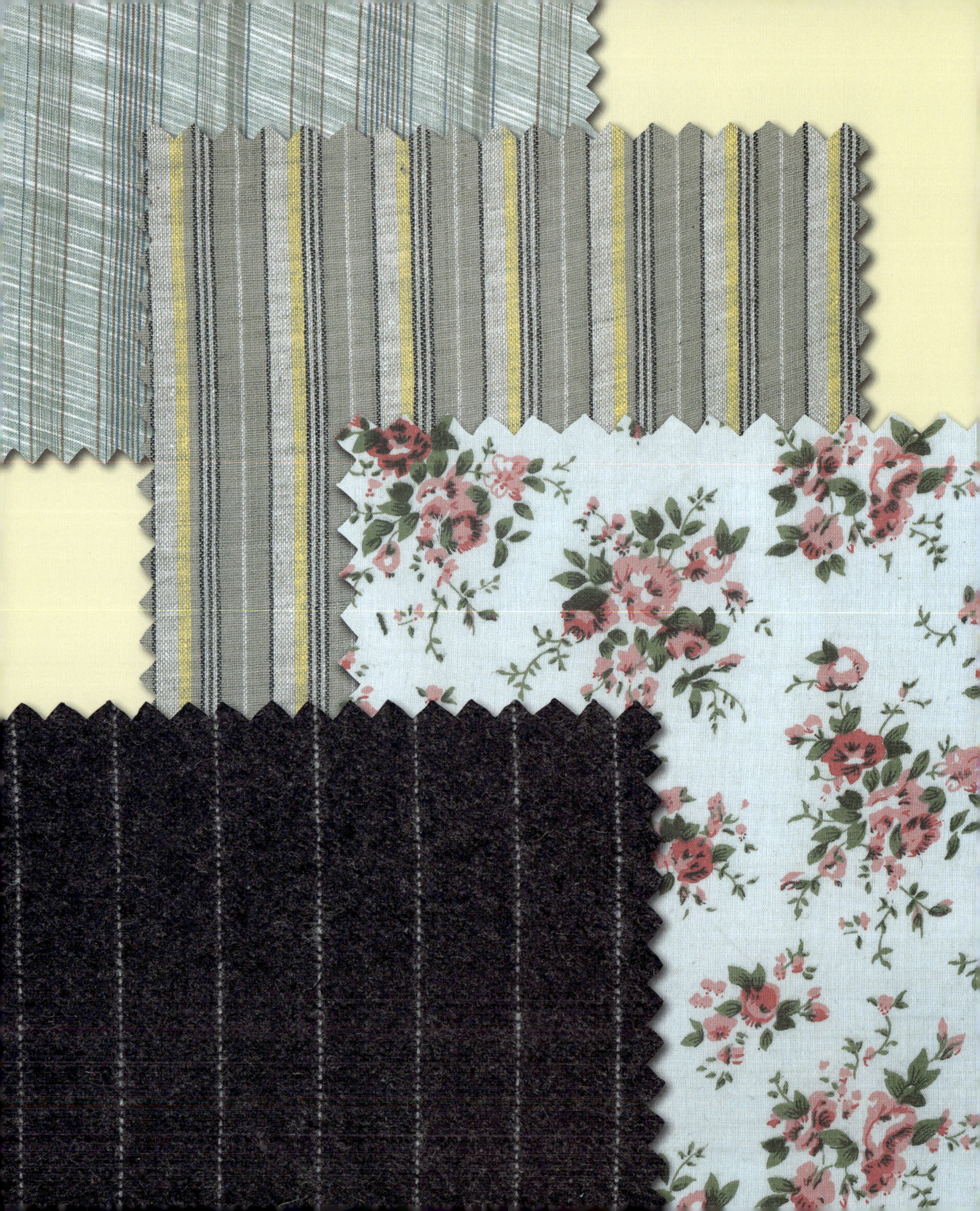

CHAPTER 5

DRAWING FABRIC

Once you have mastered the basics of figure drawing and creating effective poses, the next stage is learning how to draw the clothes. This is rather like making them, so this section reveals how to draw fabric as part of that process. It is a good idea to develop an understanding of the range of fabrics available, as this will enable you to realize how integral cloth is to the character and identity of garments. How this knowledge informs your designs is part of the next step; it is not about replicating a piece of fabric on paper (although that is good practice), it's more about developing your own visual shorthand.

Wherever possible, try to have samples of the fabrics in front of you, or at the very least some magazine tears of similar fabrics so that you know what you are trying to represent. Then try out a range of different mediums until you achieve something you are happy with. Always allow yourself enough time to experiment and to create the actual artwork, taking into account the fact that mediums such as paint and glue will take a while to dry. As with most creative work, a little planning in advance will help you to achieve the best results.

BASIC TECHNIQUES FOR RENDERING FABRIC

Choosing a suitable type of paper is the first stage. Very smooth paper is perfect for depicting satin or shiny fabrics, while watercolour paper may be better for showing rustic tweed or a soft mélange knit. These papers can then be collaged into your drawings. Similarly, you can scan or photocopy the actual fabrics, reduce the scale right down and stick them on to the page as required.

Having drawn an outline of the design, you can lay down a base colour using a marker pen, paint or oil pastel, and then work more detail in with crayon, fibre-tipped pens, ink, gel pens, oil or all of the above! You could also start by using a 'resist' for part of the detail, which involves blocking out an area with wax crayon or a candle or with professional watercolour masking fluid. You then apply a base colour over the top and the detail will remain uncoloured. If you are using masking fluid, remove it once the base paint is dry. You can then add more detail using another medium. This method can work particularly well for damask and lace-type fabrics with shadow or sheen effects, or for those materials with a bolder positive/negative aspect.

Fabrics from The Cloth Shop

WHITE FABRIC

Drawing white fabrics might seem like an easy option, but varying their characteristics brings its own set of challenges that need to be surmounted creatively. In these examples, surface lustre and texture are cleverly suggested using bold strokes and a sensitive choice of mediums that reflect the type of material being depicted.

Voile is a type of fine, sheer fabric. Traditionally, it was always expensive as it was technically more challenging to create fine fabrics, and so was used for special-occasion garments, such as party or wedding dresses, fine shirts and so on. Other sheer fabrics include chiffon, georgette and tulle. These days, thanks to mechanization and man-made fibres, such sheer fabrics have become more affordable and available and are no longer associated exclusively with occasion wear.

Traditionally, lurex and lamé fabrics have metallic threads woven into them, but modern versions of these materials often also incorporate synthetic fibres, and metallic effects are created using foiling and printing techniques.

In the illustration below, good-quality brown wrapping paper was used as drawing paper and after drafting out the design the outline was inked in. Chalk pencil was lightly applied to the dress and further shading was added using marker pen and pencil crayon.

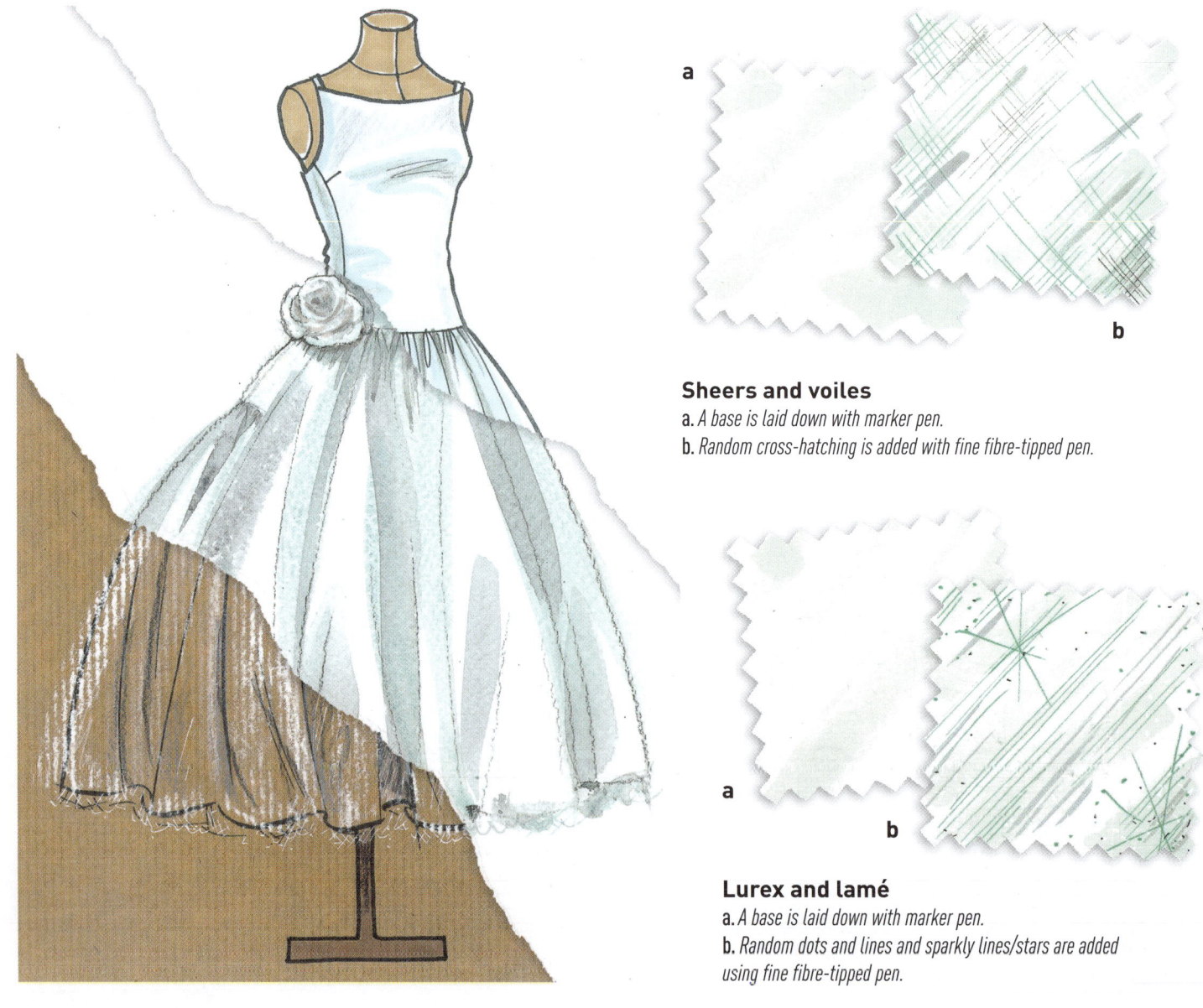

Sheers and voiles
a. A base is laid down with marker pen.
b. Random cross-hatching is added with fine fibre-tipped pen.

Lurex and lamé
a. A base is laid down with marker pen.
b. Random dots and lines and sparkly lines/stars are added using fine fibre-tipped pen.

Broderie anglaise, sometimes known as 'Swiss embroidery', is traditionally a fine white cotton fabric with a pattern of eyelets hand-embroidered onto it, usually in white thread, although European variants often used coloured embroidery threads. Today, there are many variations on this type of fabric, and it is almost always machine-made.

Crochet is a handmade fabric that, unlike knitting, cannot be created by machine even to produce the most simple stitches and designs. Crochet is used to create pretty openwork patterns for decorative trims and finishes, and sometimes to produce clever bas-relief and 3D effects.

Lace, with some variants known as 'thread-lace', covers a broad family of openwork fabrics, including net. The fabric often has strong cultural roots, and particular regions and countries are famous for the different techniques used and the complexity and design of the finished products. While lace was traditionally handmade, machine-made lace began to appear at the height of the Industrial Revolution and mechanized lace production is still developing today.

Guipure lace, despite its name, is a type of embroidery rather than lace, and so is sometimes known by its proper name 'guipure lace embroidery'. It is created by applying a pattern of thread embroidery to a ground fabric, which is then removed by chemical or other means to leave an openwork lace.

In this example of a 1960s-inspired cocktail shift dress, guipure lace is suggested by employing a little stamp to print pattern on the illustration, using irregular pressure to avoid a flat finish.

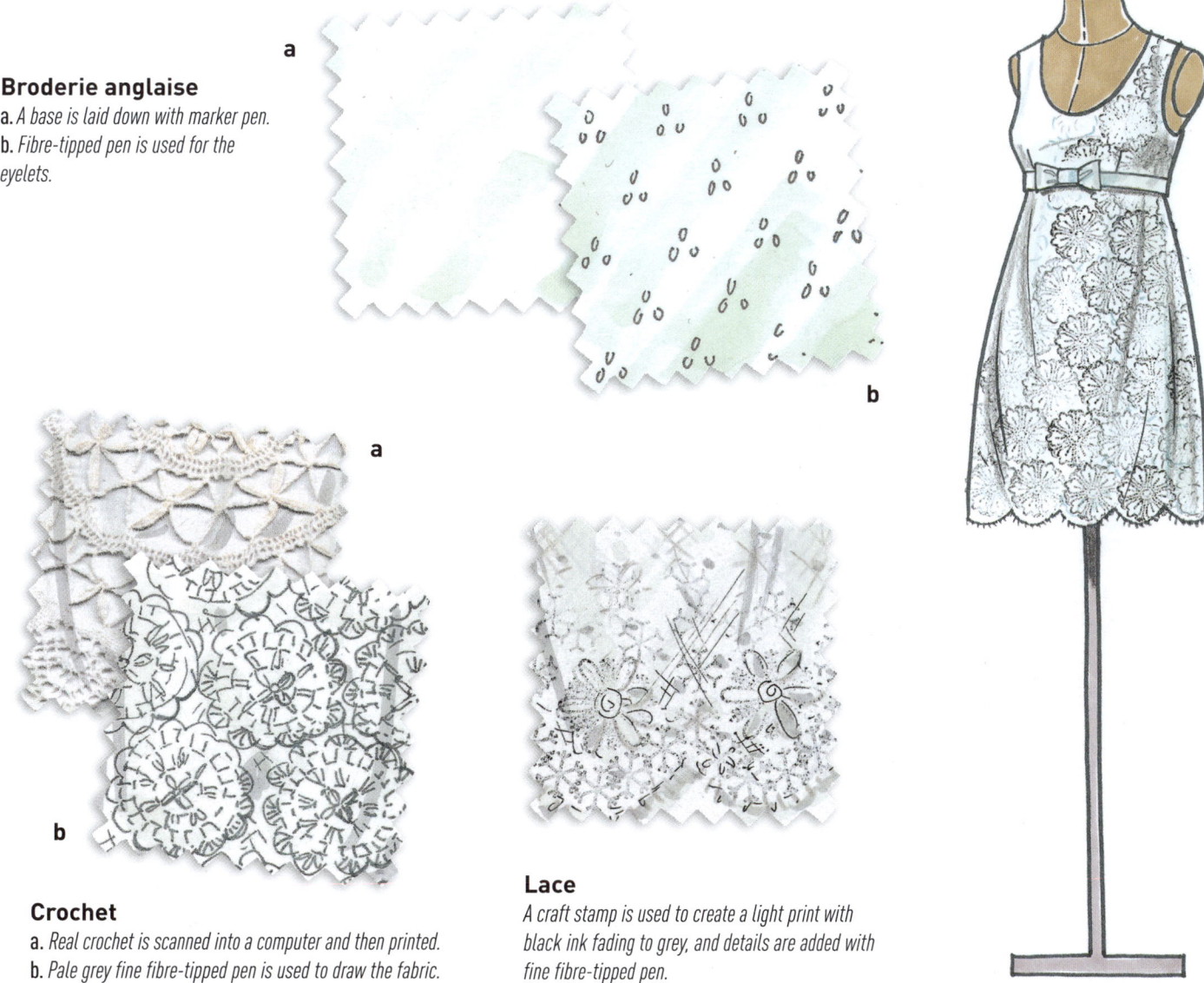

Broderie anglaise
a. *A base is laid down with marker pen.*
b. *Fibre-tipped pen is used for the eyelets.*

Crochet
a. *Real crochet is scanned into a computer and then printed.*
b. *Pale grey fine fibre-tipped pen is used to draw the fabric.*

Lace
A craft stamp is used to create a light print with black ink fading to grey, and details are added with fine fibre-tipped pen.

LUXURY FABRICS

This satin evening dress was drawn on watercolour paper in pencil outline before loose, bold strokes of watercolour were added.

Satin is a smooth, generally lustrous fabric with a close, warp-faced woven surface that catches and reflects the light. Traditionally made from silk, many versions made from synthetic fabrics are also available today. Sateen is similar to satin, but is a weft-faced fabric.

Velvet is fabric woven with a pile surface. This is created during the manufacturing process by lifting the warp over wires to make loops, and then cutting them as the wires are withdrawn. Similar fabrics are plush and velour. Terry, sometimes known as 'terry towelling', is created in a similar way, but the loops are not cut. There are knitted versions of all of these types of pile fabrics, which have the advantage of the degree of stretch associated with most knitted fabrics.

Sequins are sometimes known by their French name, *paillettes*. Traditionally, they are small reflective metallic discs sewn onto fabrics, although modern versions come in all sorts of finishes, including matt, transparent, printed and hologram, and in a wide range of sizes and shapes.

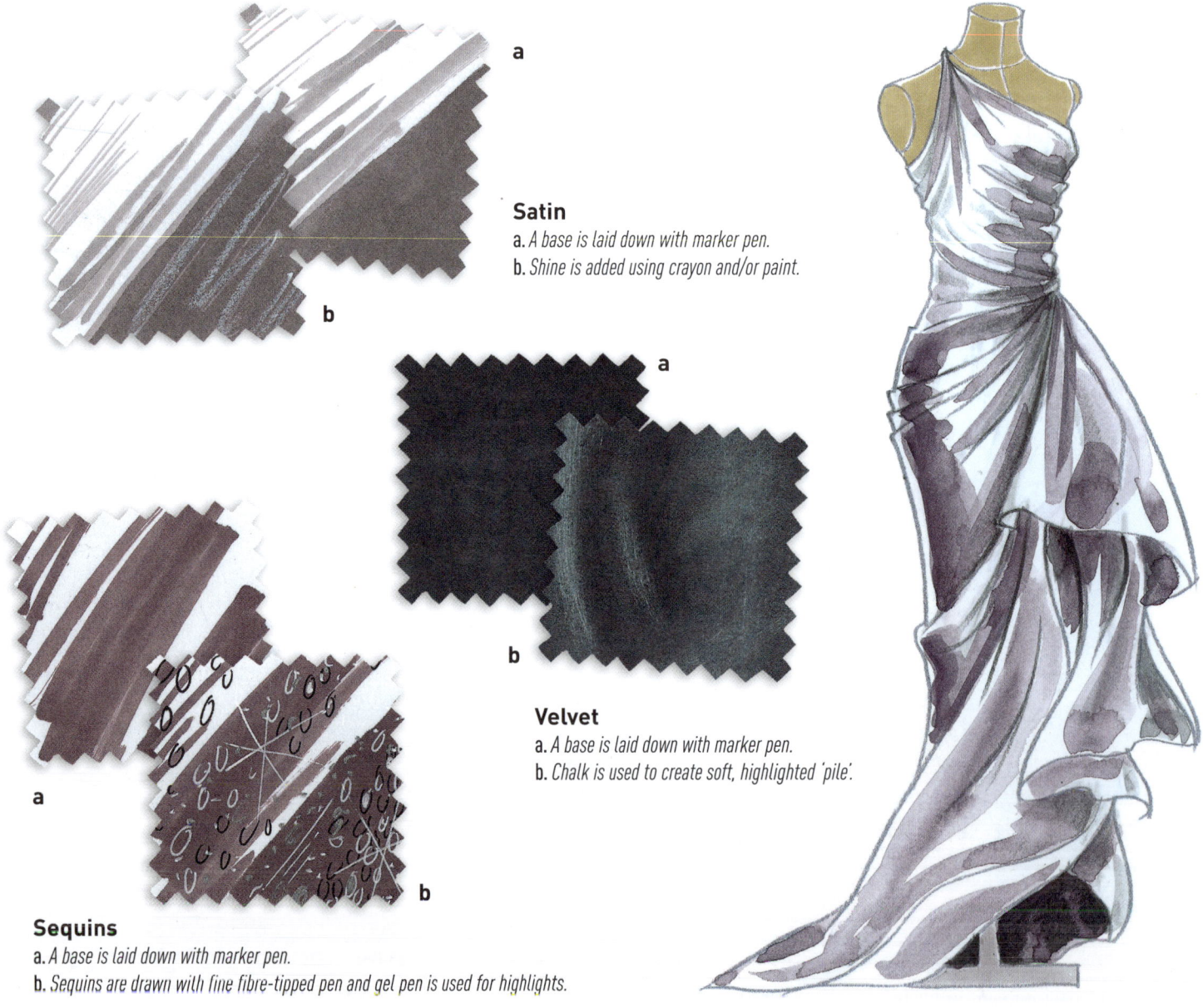

Satin
a. *A base is laid down with marker pen.*
b. *Shine is added using crayon and/or paint.*

Velvet
a. *A base is laid down with marker pen.*
b. *Chalk is used to create soft, highlighted 'pile'.*

Sequins
a. *A base is laid down with marker pen.*
b. *Sequins are drawn with fine fibre-tipped pen and gel pen is used for highlights.*

ANIMAL PATTERNS, FUR AND BROCADE

The loose category of 'animal patterns' covers a range of designs, inspired originally by the markings and textures found on real animal coats. Leopard-skin, cheetah-skin and snakeskin are perennial favourites in the fashion world. New digital printing techniques have resulted in ever-increasing possibilities with regard to the scale of the pattern and repeat. Such has been the popularity of animal prints in recent years that designers are now creating fantasy hybrid patterns that incorporate elements from birds' plumage, patterns found on moths and butterflies, and other variants from the natural world.

Fur, traditionally the skins and coats of dead animals, is used to create very warm garments. The rarity and/or attractiveness of certain animals once elevated these fabrics to luxury status, but the wearing of real fur is now highly contentious, particularly since modern manufacturing can reproduce convincing synthetic versions.

Brocade is a woven fabric related to satin in terms of the technique used to make it. Patterns are usually created by contrasting areas of raised or floated warp threads against a more simply structured ground. Some variants contrast warp threads against weft threads in a similar way.

This eye-catching coat was drawn with a pencil outline on watercolour paper. Masking fluid was used to create a pattern and watercolour paint was applied.

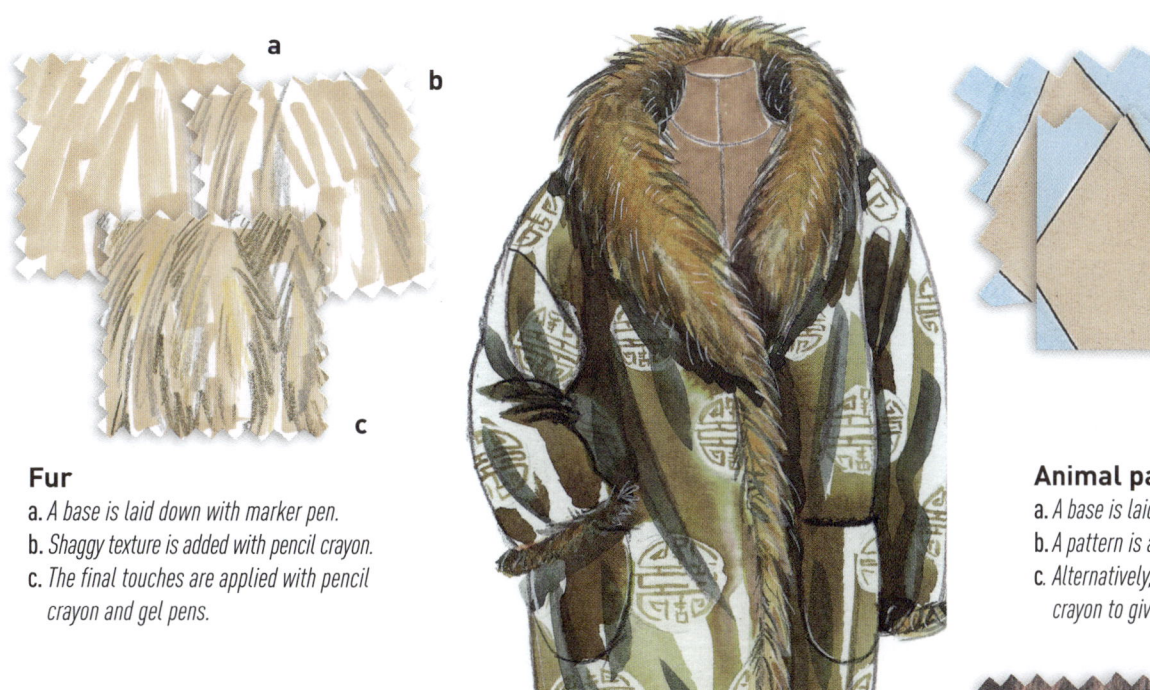

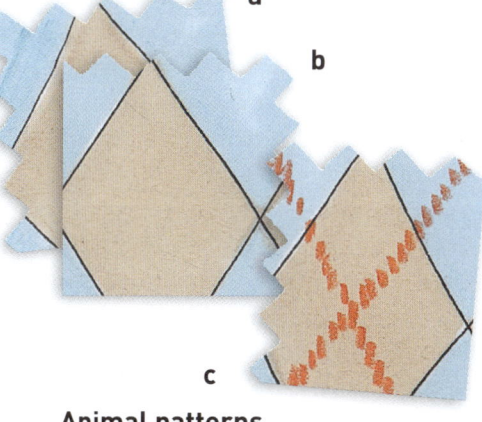

Fur
a. *A base is laid down with marker pen.*
b. *Shaggy texture is added with pencil crayon.*
c. *The final touches are applied with pencil crayon and gel pens.*

Animal patterns
a. *A base is laid down with marker pen.*
b. *A pattern is applied with fibre-tipped pen.*
c. *Alternatively, pattern can be added with pencil crayon to give a softer-looking option.*

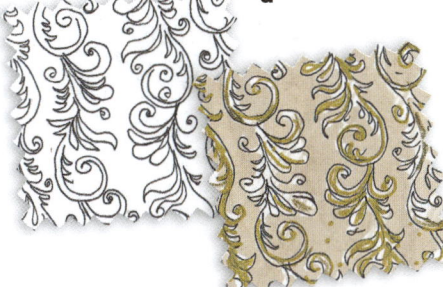

Brocade
a. *An outline is drawn with fine fibre-tipped pen.*
b. *The background is filled in with marker pen and gold gel pen is used to add highlights.*

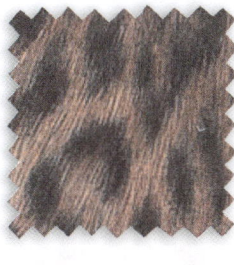

Digital animal prints
Animal-print fabric is scanned into a computer and then printed.

Brocade
A design is drawn in wax resist (see page 75) first, then lightly brushed over with watercolour.

KNIT

Knitting is an ancient method of hand-making fabric and garments that has many cultural roots worldwide, from northern Scotland to Peru and many other countries besides. Most of the knitted patterns such as Fair Isle, Aran or cable which we are familiar with today have origins going back several centuries. Trade and cultural migration has led to many stylistic similarities, resulting in patterns being grouped under a single name, such as 'Nordic', which includes the traditional patterns of Scandinavia, Northern Europe and the Baltic. Since the invention of the earliest knitting machines in the late 16th century for the stocking trade, manufacturers have developed and refined the processes and today machines are able to produce incredibly sophisticated and intricate knitted fabrics and garments. Despite this, perhaps surprisingly, many modern garments are still hand-knitted.

In this men's outfit the soft, warm texture of the Nordic-look sweater is suggested by the subtle colouring, which is applied using marker pens and a little soft pencil crayon for the shadows and the chunky rib trims. The skinny jeans are first rendered with a base of deep blue marker pen, then shadows and highlights are applied with darker and lighter crayons. Fine diagonal pencil crayon marks help to suggest the twill weave of denim.

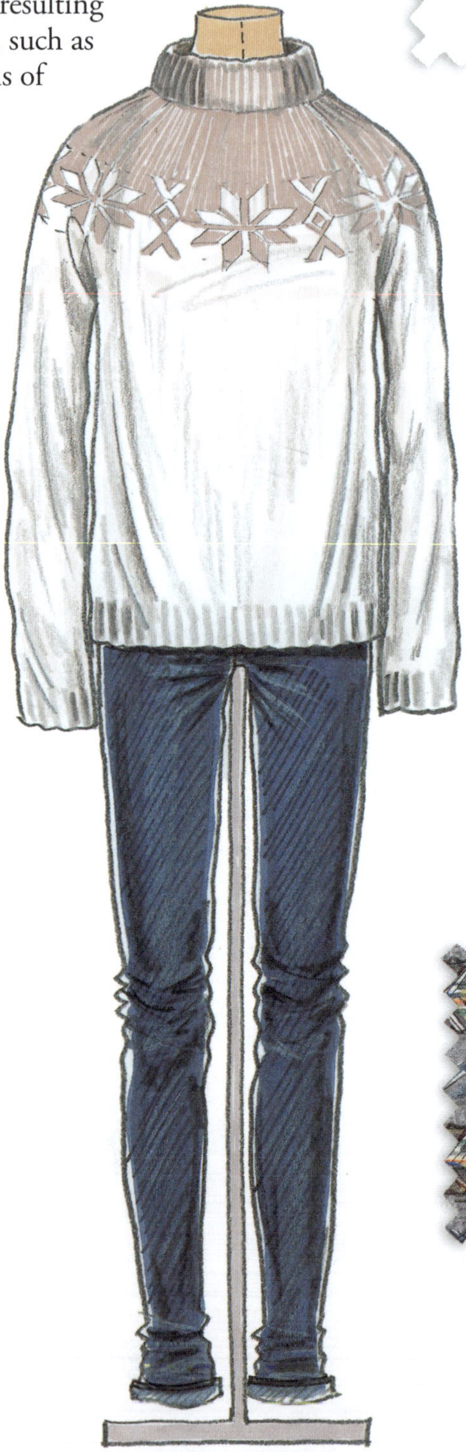

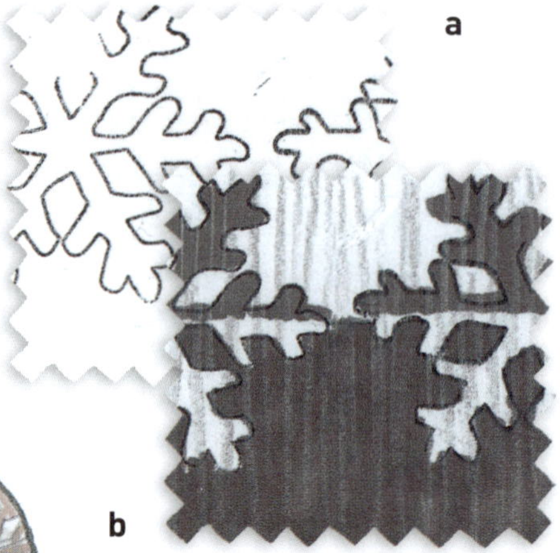

Nordic
a. *A craft stamp is used to apply pattern.*
b. *Marker pen is used to apply colour, then texture is added with a pencil crayon.*

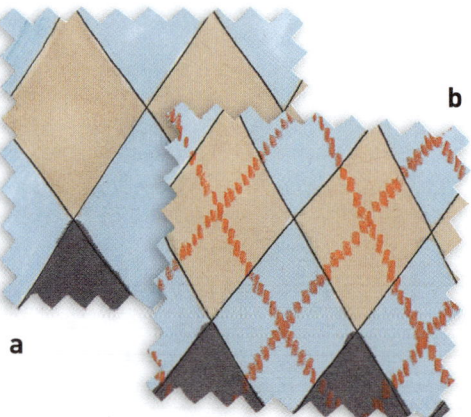

Argyle check
a. *After drafting out a basic pattern in pencil, the diamond shapes are coloured with marker pen.*
b. *Pencil crayon is used to draw in the coloured rakes.*

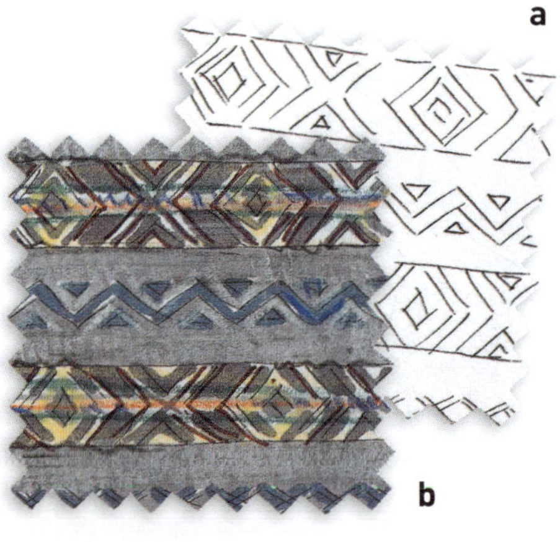

Fair Isle
a. *A pattern is drafted first in pencil, then defined with fine fibre-tipped pen.*
b. *Marker pens and pencil crayons are used to add texture and depth of colour.*

The young woman's outfit combines a soft, semi-sheer fluted skirt – suggested by using delicate brush pen strokes and light crayoning – and a chunky cable-patterned sweater and a simple knitted scarf, both of which are rendered using controlled and restrained pencil crayon marks.

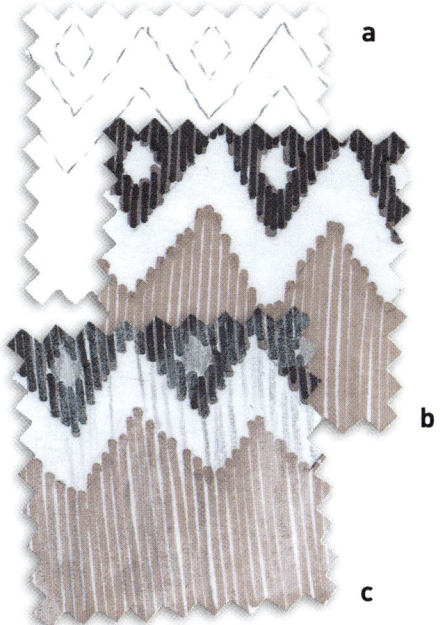

Nordic
a. *A pattern is first drafted out in pencil.*
b. *Marker pen adds delicate colour and the pencil marks are erased.*
c. *Texture and depth of colour are rendered using pencil crayon.*

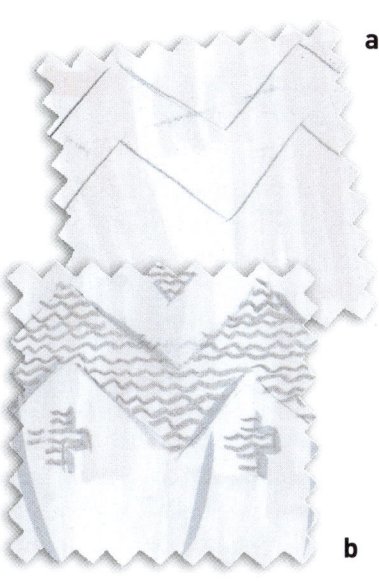

Textured stitches
a. *A pattern is mapped out in pencil, if possible using a real stitch reference for accuracy and clarity.*
b. *The pattern is defined with marker pen, then the pencil is erased. Texture and depth of colour are applied with pencil crayon.*

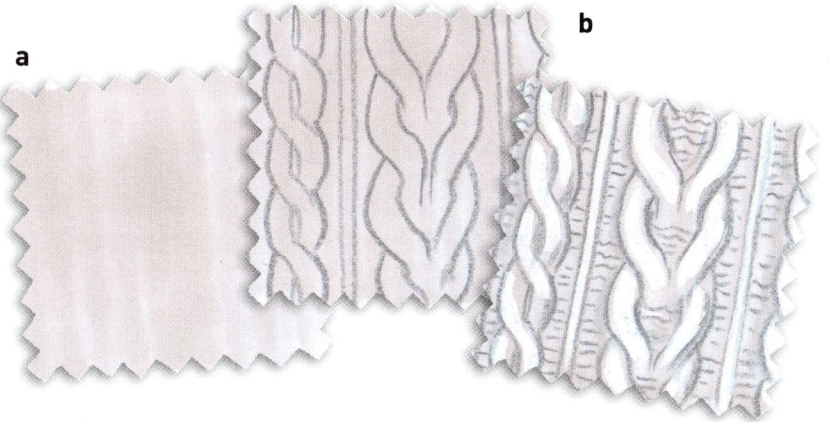

Cable and Aran stitches
a. *A base colour is applied with marker pen.*
b. *A pattern is carefully mapped out in pencil crayon.*
c. *Shading and definition are applied with toning pencil crayons.*

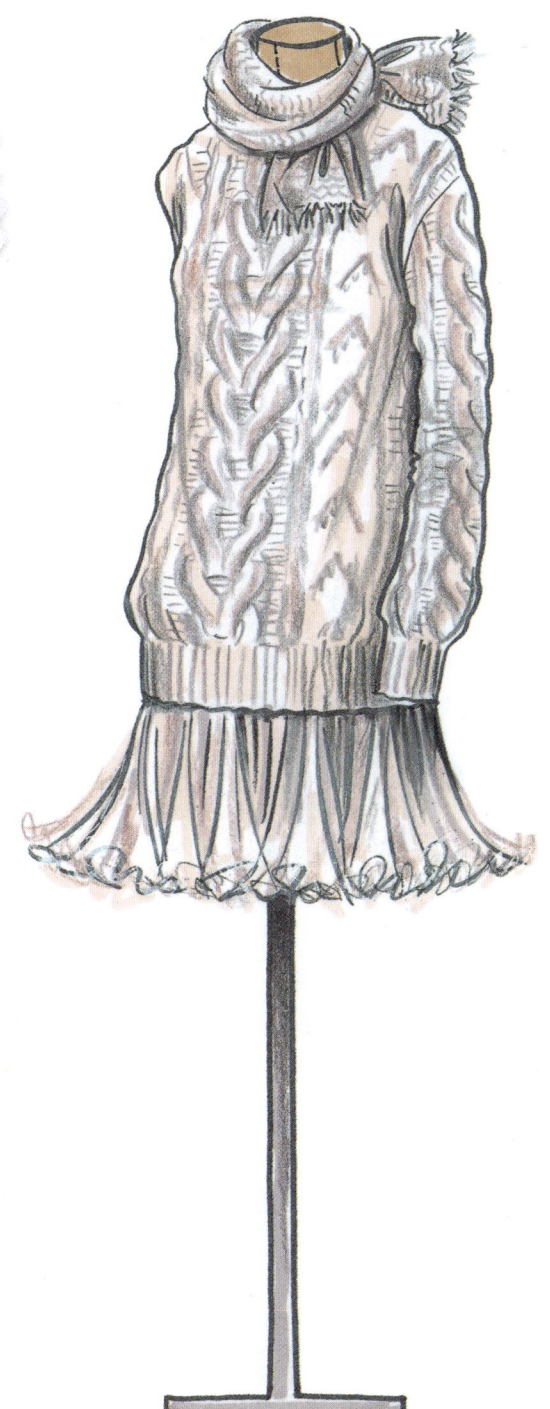

HARD-WEARING FABRIC

Leather
Marker pen is used to create variations of tone.

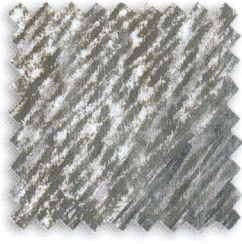

Distressed leather
An oil pastel rubbing on a rough surface creates a distressed effect.

Leather has two principal qualities that fashion perpetually exploits and celebrates: the first is luxury – the depth of colour, supple feel of the fabric and the craftsmanship associated with handling this relatively difficult material; and the second is (perhaps conversely) its tough rebel image, which has its origins in the youth movements of the late 1950s, 60s and 70s, and which is somehow enhanced by signs of wear and tear.

Canvas and denim are tough, relatively coarse-grain fabrics, which have their origins in utility wear. One of the most-loved qualities of denim is the way in which it fades and wears, a quality we associate with individuality and a certain rebel spirit, although much of the denim we buy today is already faded.

Twill is a type of textile weave that repeats on three or more ends or 'picks', which produces the diagonal grain that is characteristic of twill fabric.

For this cool biker girl look, the jeans are again rendered with a base of deep blue marker pen with shadows and highlights applied with darker and lighter crayons. Fine diagonal pencil crayon marks suggest the twill weave of denim, and there are pronounced faded effects as well as delicately drawn and shaded rips and holes. By only partially colouring the jacket, the effect of shine and highlights on softly worn leather is created. Marker pen and a little correction fluid are used to finish a sparkly singlet.

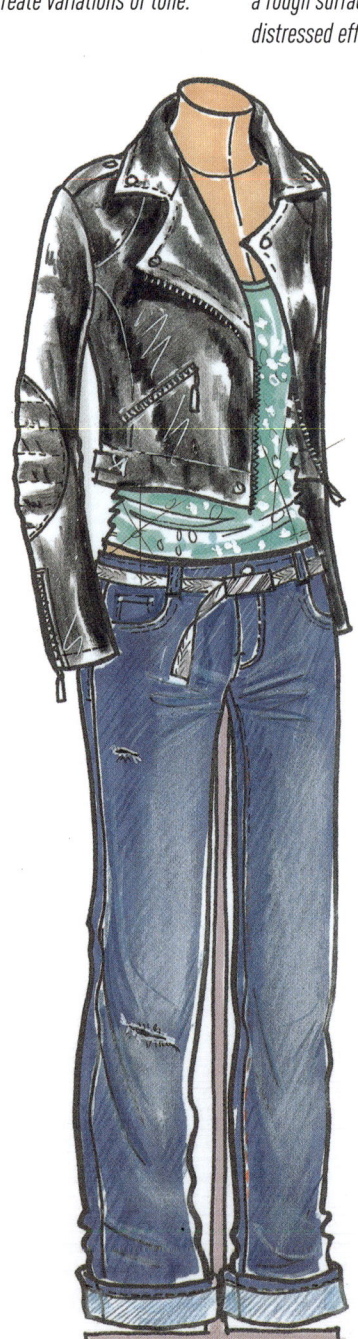

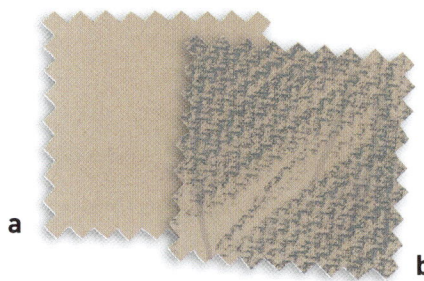

Canvas
a. *A base is applied with marker pen.*
b. *An oil pastel rubbing creates texture.*

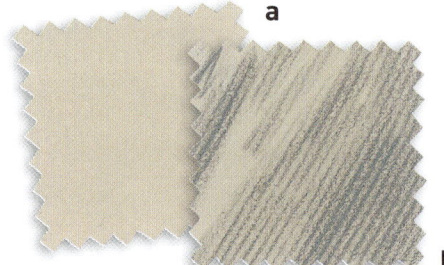

Twill
a. *A base is applied with marker pen.*
b. *A rubbing using marker pen produces a textured finish.*

Denim
a. *A base is applied with marker pen.*
b. *Diagonal twill lines are added with pencil crayon.*
c. *Stitching is rendered with black fibre-tipped pen and worn areas with pastel crayon.*
d. *Pastel crayon and white gel pen are used to add rips.*

The idea of camouflage was first understood by hunters, who took their inspiration from the animals they pursued and their habitats. Although the notion was taken up by the military in the 18th century, it did not really develop into the wide range of specialist fabric patterns we know and recognize today until the First and Second World Wars.

Felt is a dense, textured fabric, the surface of which is compacted and flattened during the manufacturing process to make it very hardwearing.

Corduroy is a woven fabric not dissimilar to velvet in its construction, with a cut weft pile. The vertical lines of the pile, running parallel to the warp, are known as 'wales', as indeed are the vertical lines of rib structures in knitting.

This figure's dark reefer or pea coat could have been flat and lifeless, but deliberately leaving exposed white ground and further highlighting the seams and structure in white pen gave it clarity and definition. The twisted and loosely wrapped striped scarf has been well observed and translated. A base has been applied with marker pen and bold chinagraph pencil lines are used to create the look of soft chunky cord trousers.

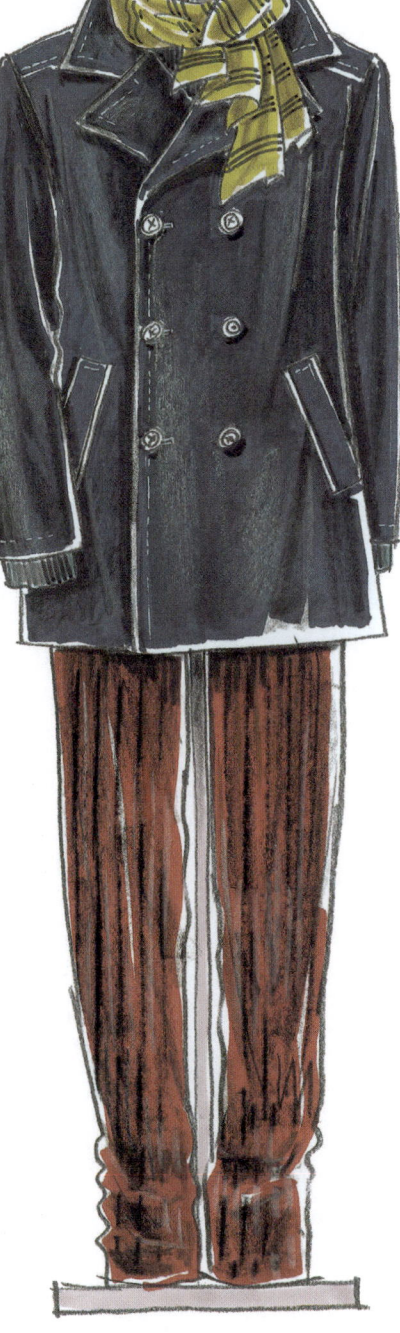

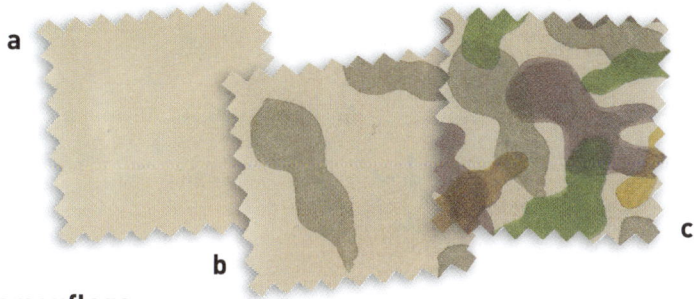

Camouflage

a. *A base is applied with marker pen.*
b. *A pattern is added with another shade of marker pen.*
c. *More overlapping marker pen shapes are layered to create the desired effect.*

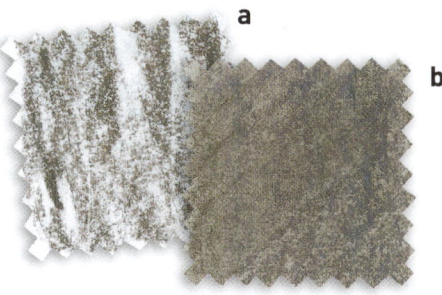

Felted wool

a. *A base is applied with oil pastel.*
b. *A second tone in oil pastel is blended with white spirit, then another rough layer of oil pastel is added on top.*

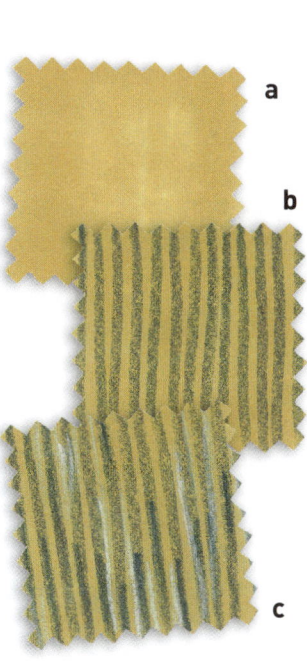

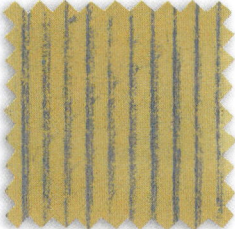

Needle cord and jumbo cord

a. *A base colour is applied with marker pen.*
b. *Vertical strokes in oil pastel indicate the texture.*
c. *White pencil crayon is used to add highlights.*

Cord – alternative method

A base colour is applied with marker pen, then a rubbing on a ribbed surface is made using oil pastel.

MENSWEAR FABRIC

Tweed, originally a heavyweight woollen fabric used for outerwear, was traditionally woven in southern Scotland. The name is taken from the River Tweed, as water from this source was used to wash and finish the fabric. Today the term tweed applies to a wide range of wool, wool blends and wool lookalike fabrics. One of its principal attractions, aside from practicality, is the mix of pleasing colours that are made possible by the dying and weaving techniques used in the production of tweed. Donegal in Ireland lends its name to a speckled, napped, tweed-type fabric that was unique to the area.

The quality of the drawing below and the successful rendering of the fabrics have been greatly helped by the choice of lovely grainy Ingres paper. The pinstripe fabric of the trousers is rendered with a rough background of marker pen to which vertical lines have been applied using white pen.

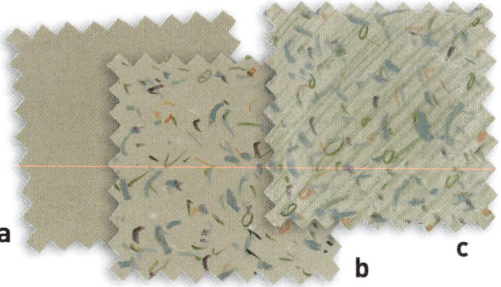

Donegal tweed
a. *A base is applied with marker pen.*
b. *Random dots are added with pencil crayon and pastel.*
c. *The impression of neps (small balls of fibre on the surface of a fabric) and texture is created with pencil crayon.*

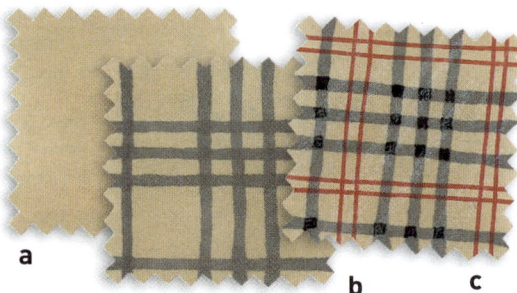

Heritage check
a. *A base is applied with marker pen.*
b. *Check lines are added with marker pen.*
c. *Pencil crayon is used for overlaid check lines.*

Shepherd's check
(and gingham-type structured fabrics)
a. *With a pencilled grid as a guide, diagonal lines are used to create two vertical columns in fibre-tipped pen.*
b. *Horizontal columns of diagonal lines are added to create a check.*
c. *The crossover points of the columns are emphasized by colouring in these areas more solidly.*
d. *The check size can be varied by changing the width of the columns and their distance apart.*

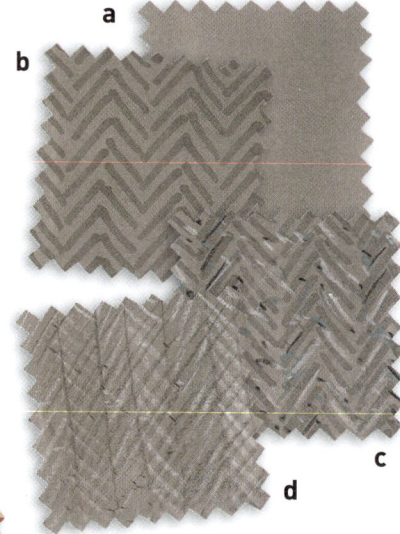

Herringbone tweed
a. *A base is applied with marker pen.*
b. *The basic herringbone structure is added with marker pen.*
c. *Pencil crayon is used to add highlights and tweed effects.*
d. *An alternative technique is to use pencil crayon to mark the pattern on to the marker pen base (see Soft Muted Herringbone on facing page).*

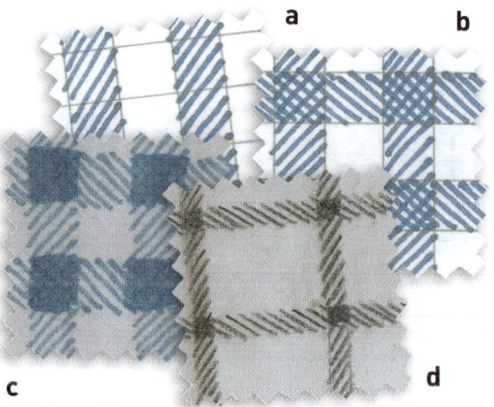

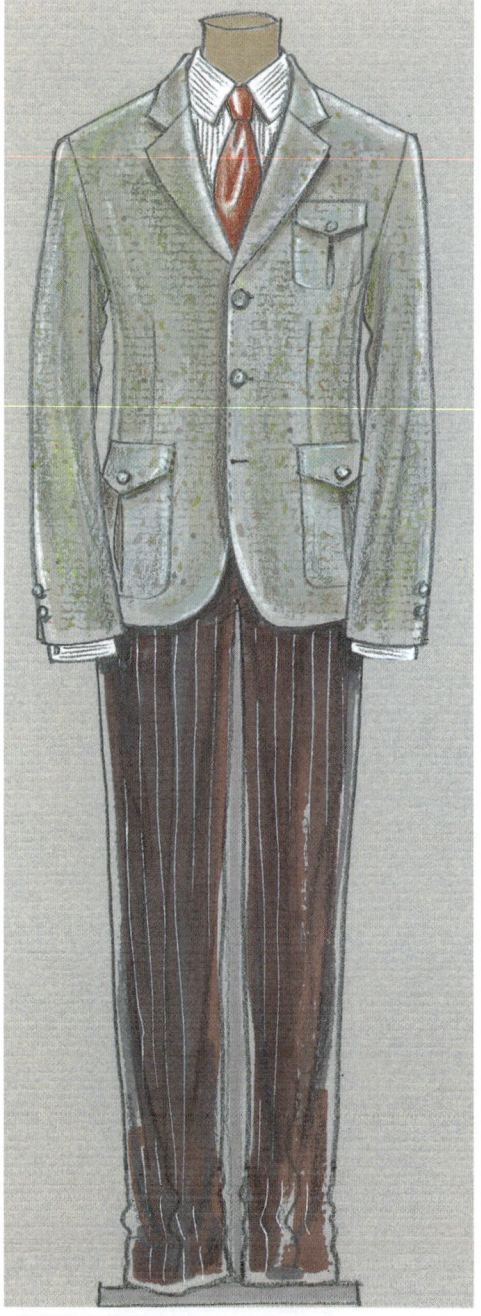

The term herringbone describes a traditional woven pattern, created using a twill (diagonal) weave that is reversed after several courses to produce stripes resembling herringbones.

Shepherd's check is created in contrasting colours by grouping four, six or eight threads of two colours and using a twill weave. The name probably originated from the plaids worn by shepherds in the hills of the Scottish Borders. Houndstooth or dogstooth are variations of this weave. Many of the hunting estates of the British aristocracy developed their own characteristic check colours and patterns that have become known collectively as estate tweeds, or sometimes as estate or heritage checks.

Gingham is a plain weave cotton fabric in which a square construction of dyed yarns is contrasted against white or undyed yarns to form small checks.

On this page, deft lines of marker pen create the ribbed roll-neck sweater. For the overcoat, marker pen was used for the base, with the herringbone pattern completed in fine fibre-tipped pen. White gel pen was used for highlights and lowlights. The trousers were drawn with a base of marker pen, with crayon used for the shadows and highlights.

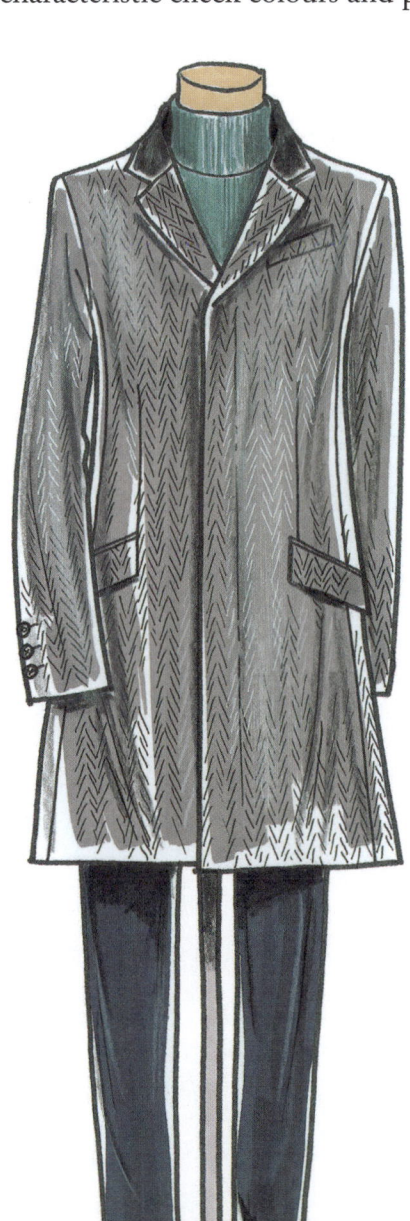

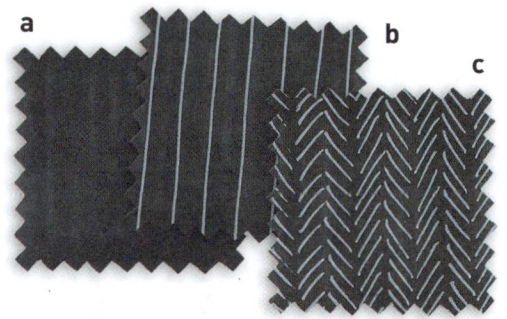

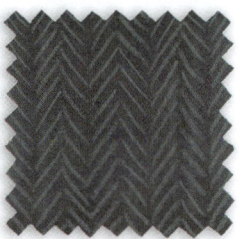

Pinstripe and fine herringbone

a. *A dark base is applied with marker pen.*
b. *The pin stripe is drawn with white gel pen.*
c. *The herringbone pattern is drawn with gel pen for a fine, crisp effect.*

Soft muted herringbone

This tweed version of the herringbone pattern is drawn using soft pencil crayon over a dark marker pen base.

Prince of Wales check

a. *A base is applied with marker pen.*
b. *Bands of vertical lines are added with fine fibre-tipped pen.*
c. *Bands of horizontal lines are similarly added using fine fibre-tipped pen, and pencil crayon over the top adds texture and depth.*

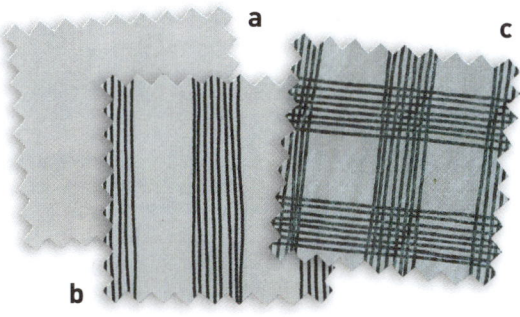

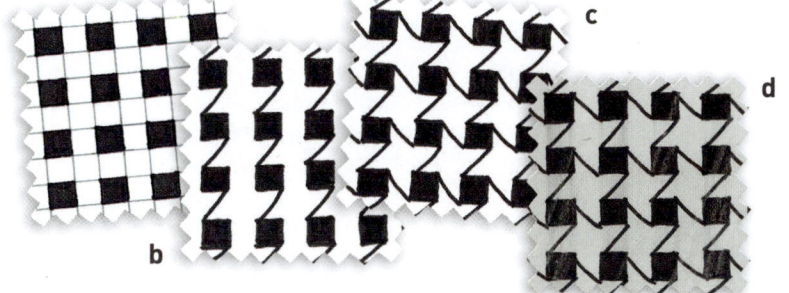

Houndstooth check *(a smaller-scale version of the check is sometimes called puppytooth)*

a. *Using a grid drawn on in pencil, squares are marked out as shown with marker pen.*
b. *The grid is erased and diagonal lines are added to link the boxes vertically using fine fibre-tipped pen.*
c. *Lateral diagonal lines link the boxes horizontally.*

PRINTS

Printing is a way of creating pattern on fabric after it has been woven. Fabric has been printed by various cultures throughout the world for thousands of years. The invention of roller printing at the end of the 18th century revolutionized the process and made patterned fabrics affordable for almost everyone. Modern digital printing processes are again changing the industry, solving problems that have until now restricted the number of colours it is possible to print and the scale of the patterns' repeats.

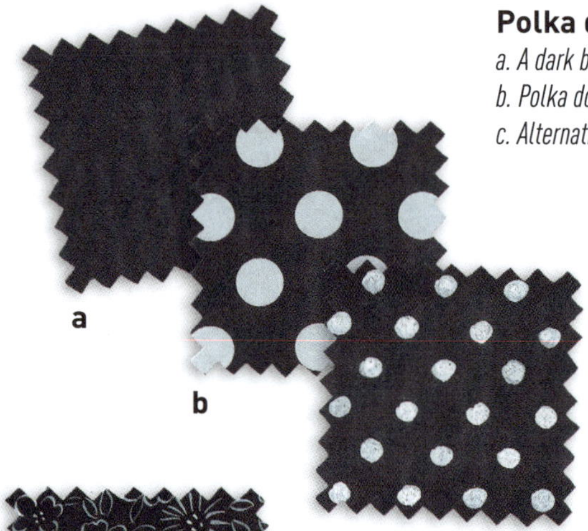

Polka dots
a. A dark base is applied with marker pen.
b. Polka dots can be added using self-adhesive white dots.
c. Alternatively, polka dots can be drawn with designers' gouache.

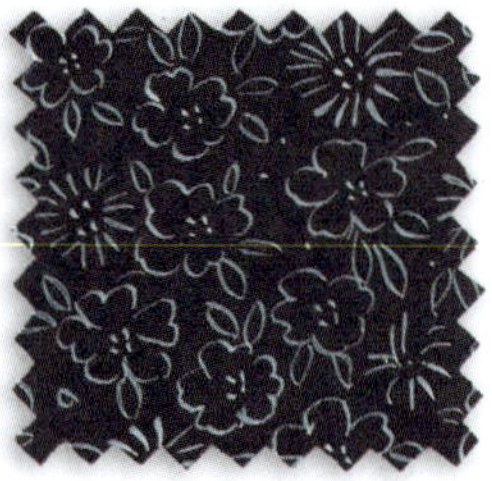

Dolly florals
A floral pattern is drawn on to a dark base using nib pen and ink.

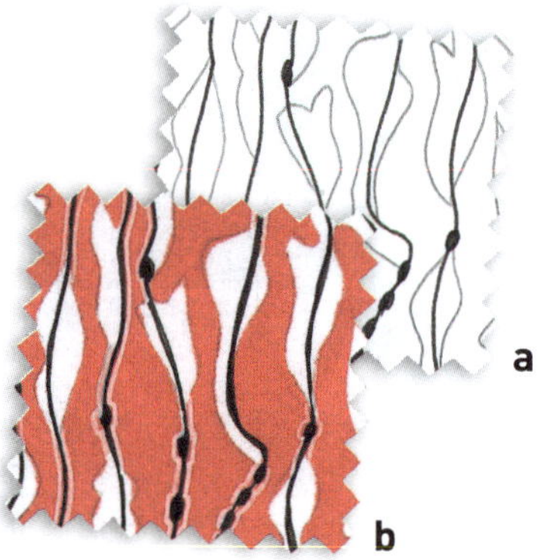

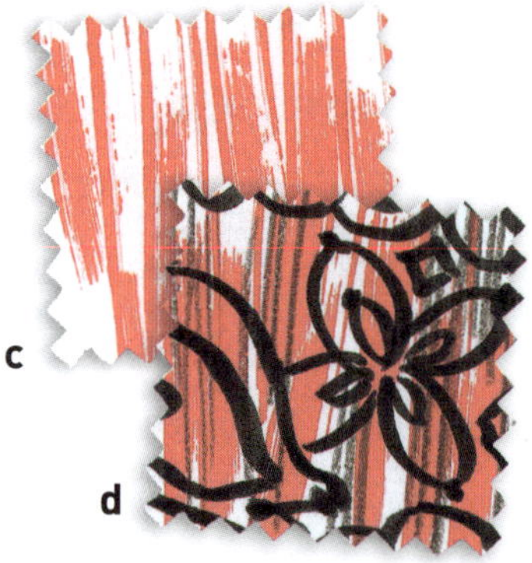

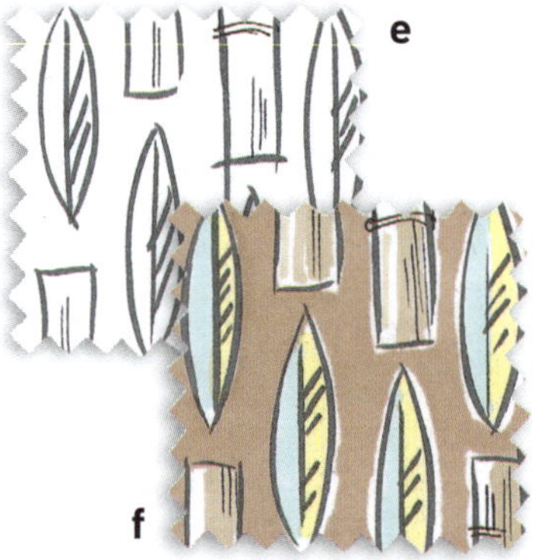

Retro prints
a. A pattern is drawn with pencil, then black lines are added with ink.
b. Marker pen is used to fill in background colour, and the pencil lines are erased.
c. A base is applied with marker pen.
d. Black brush pen is used to apply the pattern.
e. Pattern is drawn in with grey brush pen.
f. Marker pens are used to fill in colour.

Collage
Any existing pattern, such as different fabrics, wrapping paper, craft paper or origami paper, can be scanned and applied.

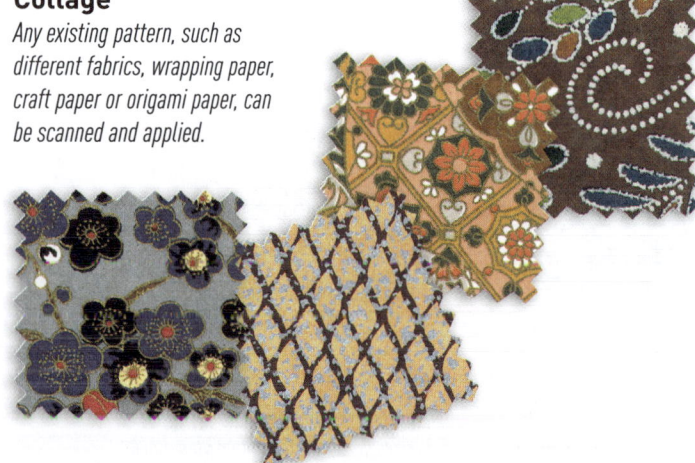

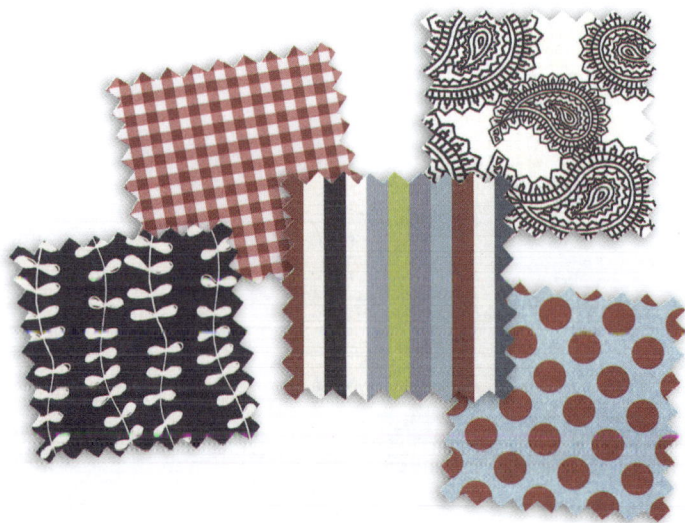

Cotton fabric is woven from cotton fibre, which forms in a boll (protective capsule) around the seeds of a species of plants of the genus *Gossypium* and is unravelled and treated to form the long strands that are used for making fabric. It is grown in many regions of the world, and the cotton fibres vary from country to country, with each having their own particular qualities and advantages. Egyptian cotton plants, for example, produce very long fibres that are woven to create one of the finest cotton fabrics, which is used for making high-quality shirts and fine bed linen. Patterned cotton falls into two distinct categories; woven and printed. Woven patterns include variations of stripes and checks that are created by using contrasting colours of thread in the warp and weft. Printed patterns cover almost every other type of pattern possible.

This floral dress was drawn using a soft pencil outline on watercolour paper. Pattern and some light shadows were added in watercolour. Pencil crayon was used for shading and definition.

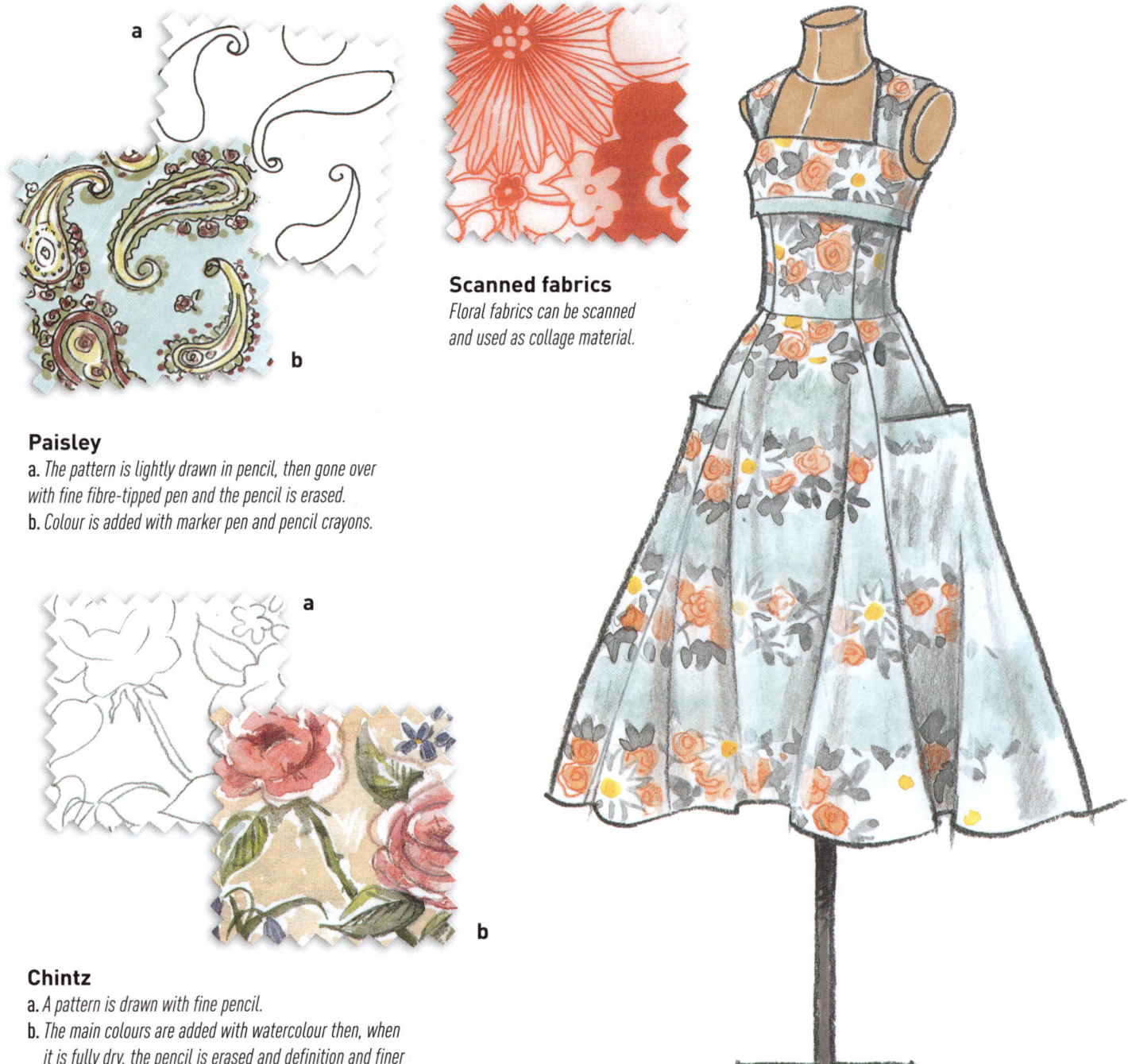

Scanned fabrics
Floral fabrics can be scanned and used as collage material.

Paisley
a. *The pattern is lightly drawn in pencil, then gone over with fine fibre-tipped pen and the pencil is erased.*
b. *Colour is added with marker pen and pencil crayons.*

Chintz
a. *A pattern is drawn with fine pencil.*
b. *The main colours are added with watercolour then, when it is fully dry, the pencil is erased and definition and finer detail are applied on top with pencil crayon.*

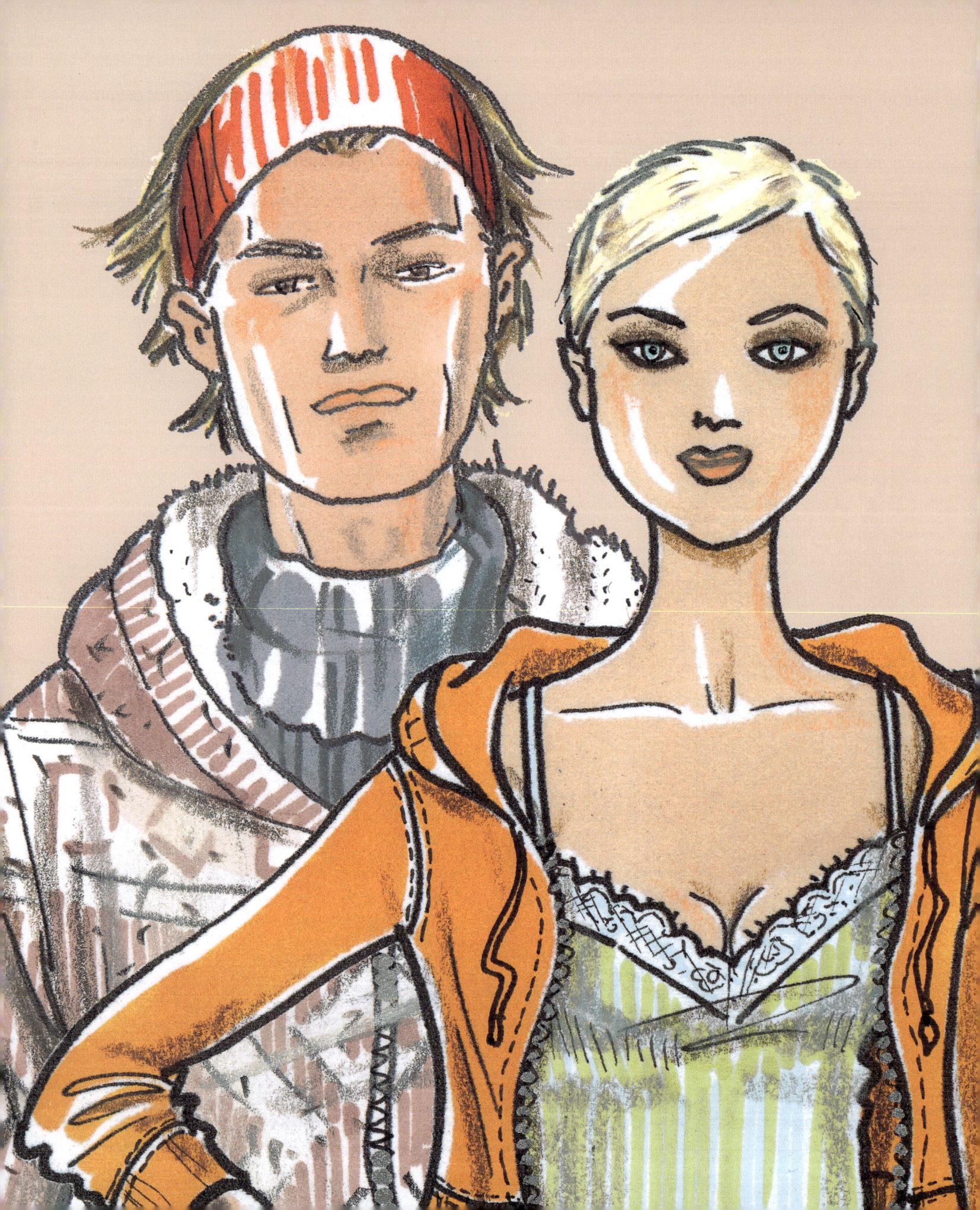

CHAPTER 6

DRAWING GARMENTS AND OUTFITS

With a broader knowledge of fabrics – their qualities, characteristics and behaviour – and a better understanding and appreciation of garment details and construction you can approach the challenge of fashion drawing with confidence. So it follows that the next essential step is to learn something about the construction of clothes, including details such as how a shirt collar works and sits around a neckline, how a jacket rever or lapel folds and rolls, and how shirt cuffs and plackets, pockets, epaulettes, gathers, pleats and so on function. Similarly, you will draw a silhouette better if you understand how the outline is achieved – where the volume comes from and how it is suppressed, reduced or controlled.

You can obtain much of this information simply by paying attention to clothes and studying them with a critical eye, either at home or in stores. Ask questions such as: what is happening here, how is that shape created, how does that neckline or fastening work? There is nothing to stop you trying something on in a store, or asking a friend of the opposite gender to try it on for you, so you can better understand the subtleties and complexities of the construction. Take a closer look and turn the garment inside out, if necessary in the privacy of the changing room. Good drawing comes from good seeing. When it comes to designing, part of the function of drawing is about communicating how the garment is constructed and resolving any issues in order that it can be realized successfully.

Remember, although you may be trying to draw an idea, something new out of your head, there is always something to hand to help you to understand how to draw that notion, be it a real garment with a similar feature or the reference material you have gathered in your scrapbook – your collection of found images, magazine tears, museum and costume drawings and so on. Even draping some fabric in similar fashion across a dress stand or yourself in front of a mirror can assist your imagination and help you to explain and communicate your ideas in your sketches. Keep trying out different variations until you hit upon an illustration that works – ideas evolve as they are drawn and different possibilities present themselves with each adaptation. Above all, have fun!

URBAN GIRL

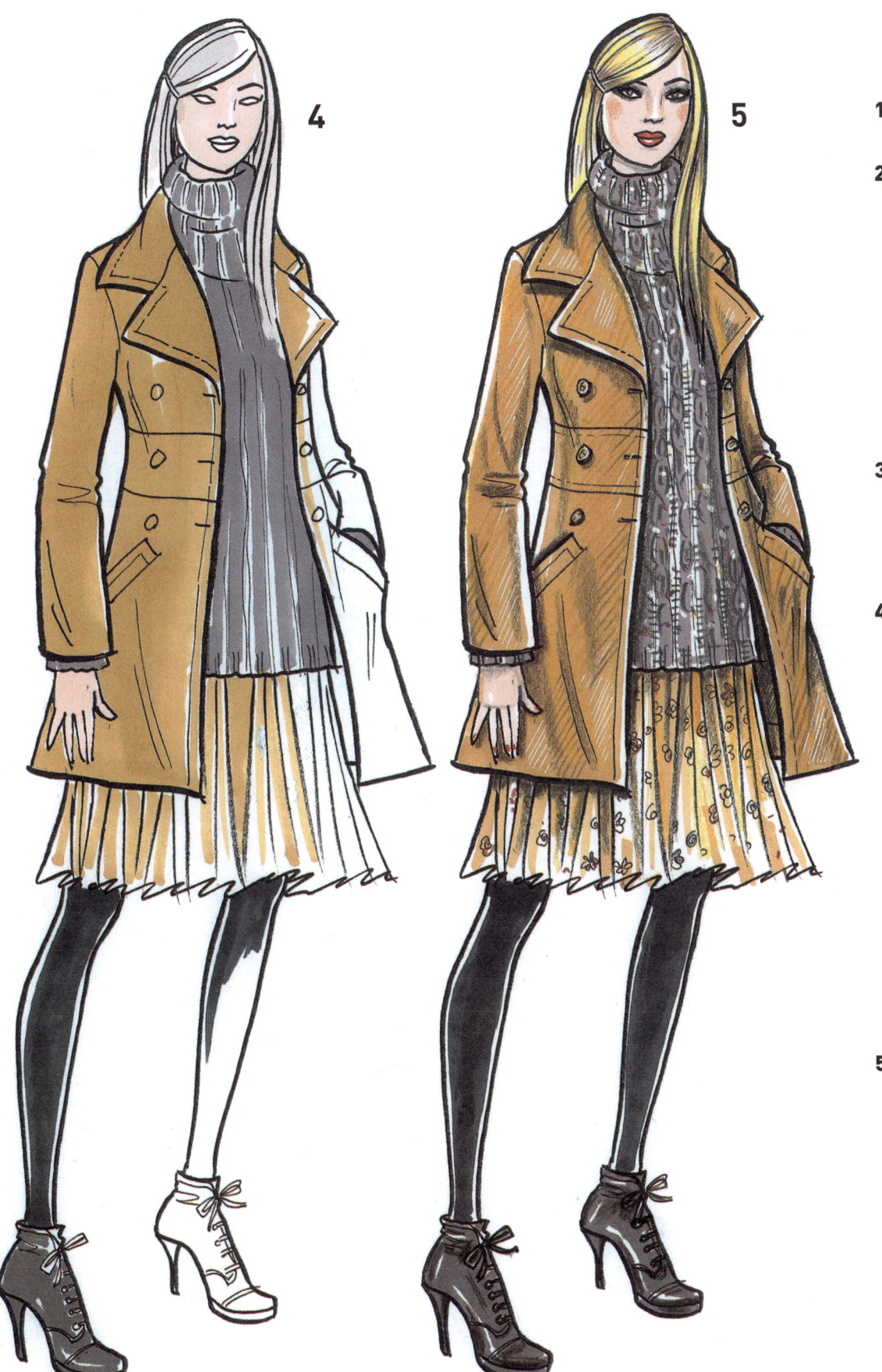

1. *Trace a model from your template, amending limb positions as required.*

2. *Plot out the silhouette of the outfit and the positioning of main details, such as the depth and angle of the neckline and collar. Use a light pencil mark that can be easily erased and altered. Still using pencil, lightly add the hairstyle, facial features and accessories. Remember the clothes should be drawn slightly larger than the figure itself so they look realistic and not skin-tight.*

3. *Once you are happy that everything looks right, ink in the outlines and strongest details with a medium-thickness fibre-tipped pen or a brush pen. Erase the pencil marks.*

4. *Having completed the outline you can add colour using marker pens, watercolour – which produces a more fluid appearance and enables you to mix your own shades – or oil pastel crayons, which give a softer blurred look. Marker pens are ideal for adding skin tones at this stage. Best results are often achieved by not taking the colour right to the edges of the outlines; completely coloured-in drawings can seem very flat and lifeless. Using a marker pen in quick, light directional strokes also helps to enhance the appearance of the pleats in the skirt and gives the effect of movement.*

5. *Add fine fabric details such as texture and print with pencil crayons and wax crayons. Add a little shadowing to help enhance the layering effects and give a more 3D look to collars, pockets and so on. You might want to emphasize topstitching or add shine at the edge of a button. Using white pencil crayon on medium to dark fabrics can help to add definition. Make-up has been added to the face and highlights to the hair.*

VACATION GIRL

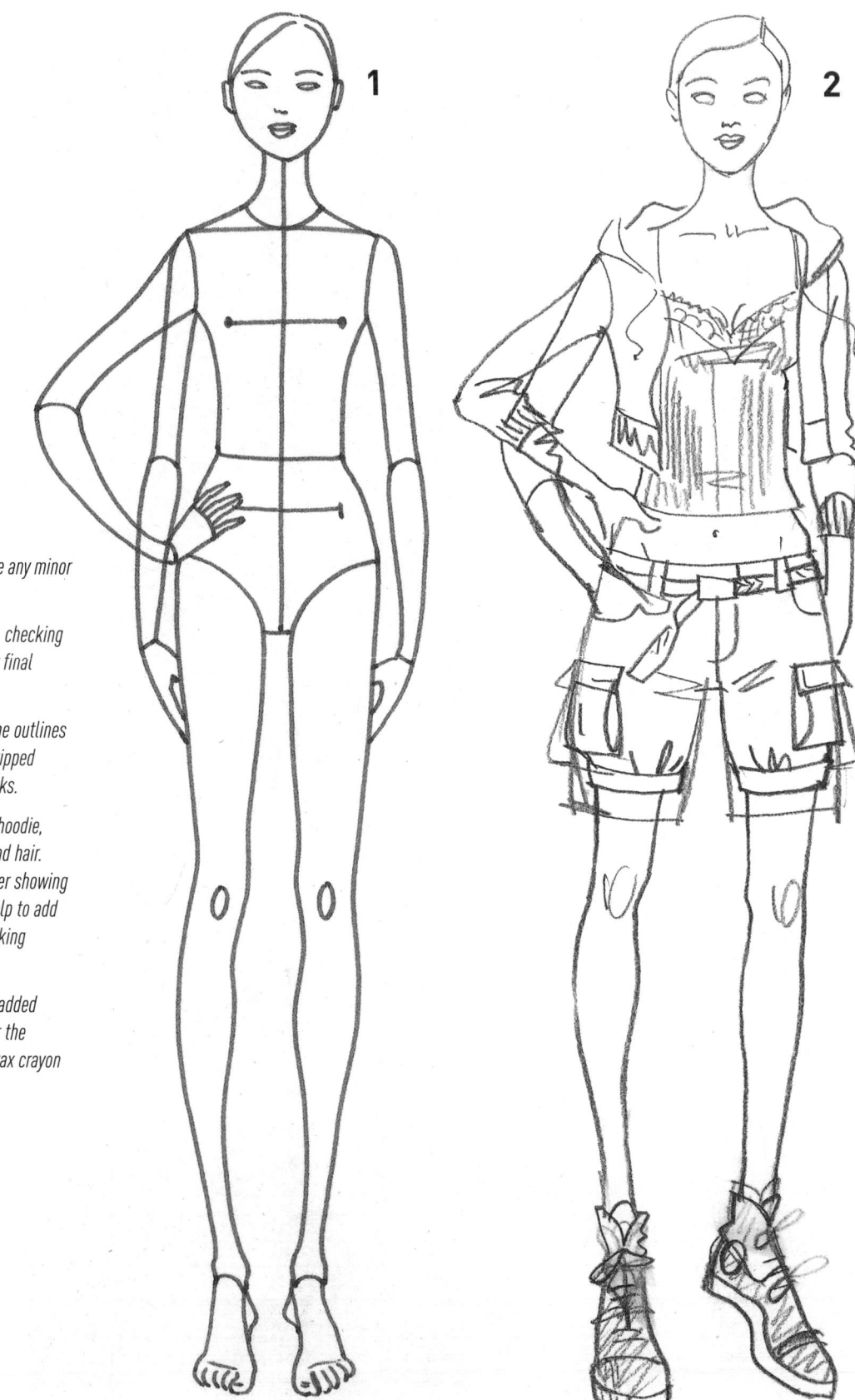

1. *Choose your template and make any minor adjustments to the pose.*

2. *Draw the whole outfit in pencil, checking the proportions and making any final decisions about finer details.*

3. *Once you are satisfied, ink in the outlines using brush pen and fine fibre-tipped pens, then erase the pencil marks.*

4. *Use marker pens to colour the hoodie, camouflage print, skin tones and hair. Leave small areas of white paper showing to suggest highlights, which help to add depth and stop the drawing looking too flat.*

5. *Delicate lines of colour can be added to suggest a rib jersey fabric for the camisole. Use soft pencil and wax crayon for finer details and shading.*

3

4

5

PARTY GIRL

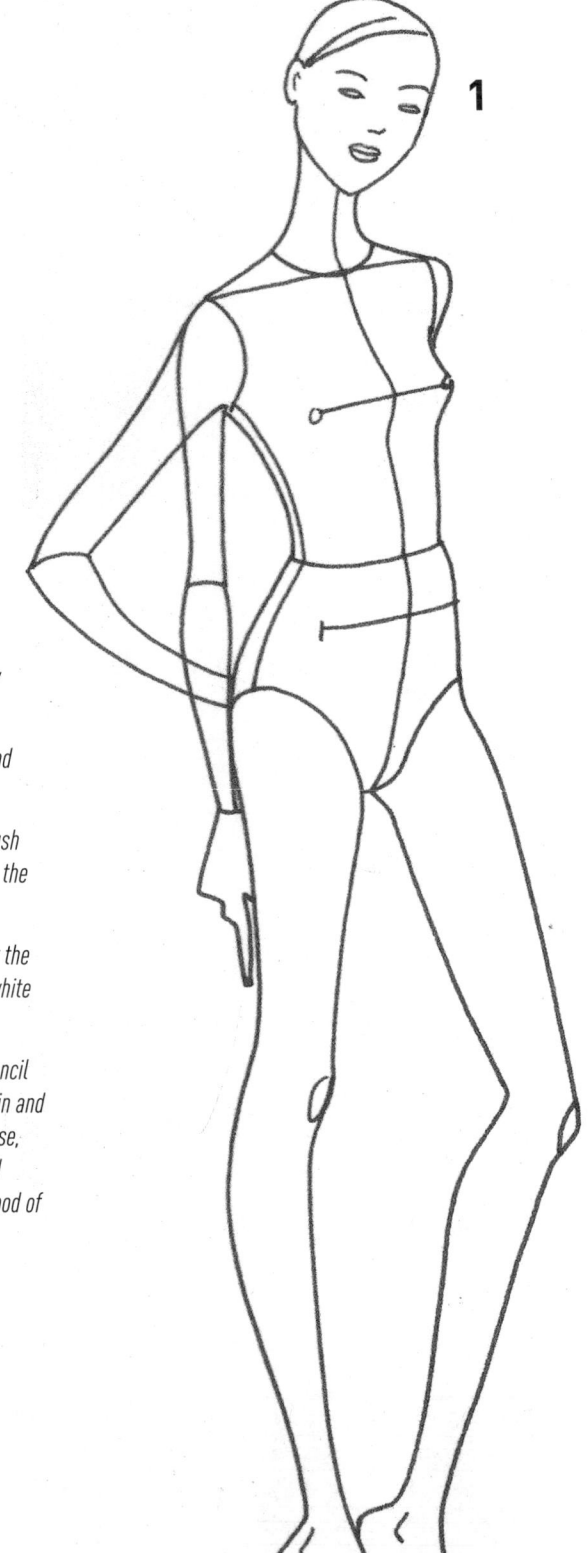

1

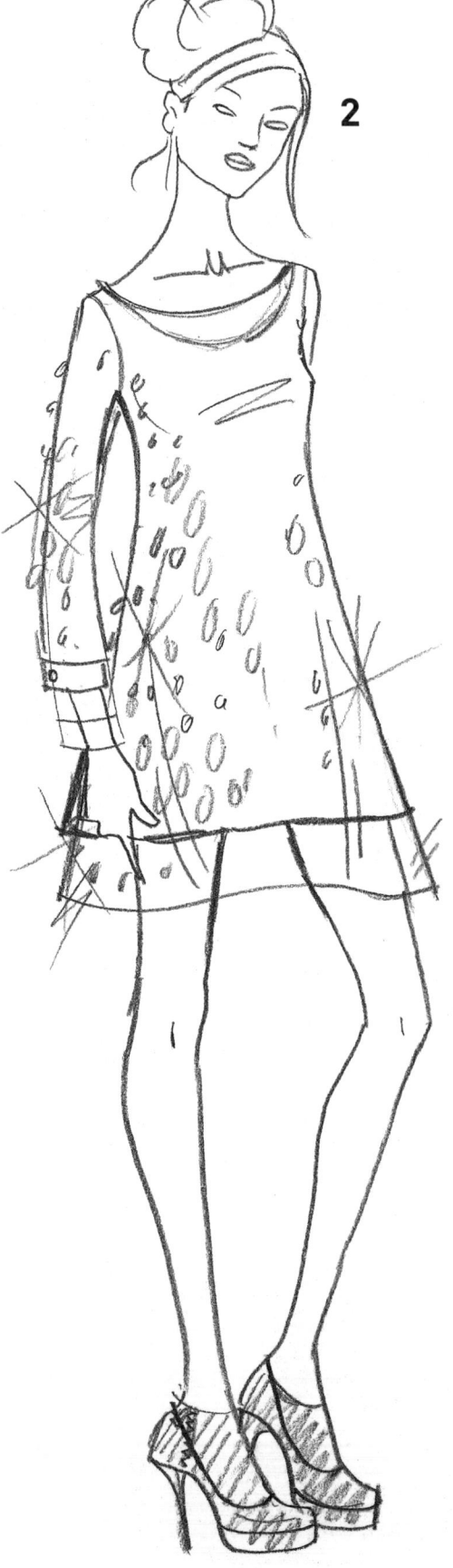

2

1. *Choose your template and make any minor adjustments to the pose.*

2. *Map out and refine the silhouette and proportions in pencil.*

3. *Ink in the dress and figure using brush pen and fine fibre-tipped pen. Erase the pencil marks.*

4. *Use marker pens sparingly to colour the dress, skin tones and hair, leaving white paper showing for highlights.*

5. *Use soft pencil crayon and grainy pencil to add shading, then apply the sequin and sparkle details on the dress in a loose, free style. Use pencil crayons to add make-up and complete the party mood of the outfit.*

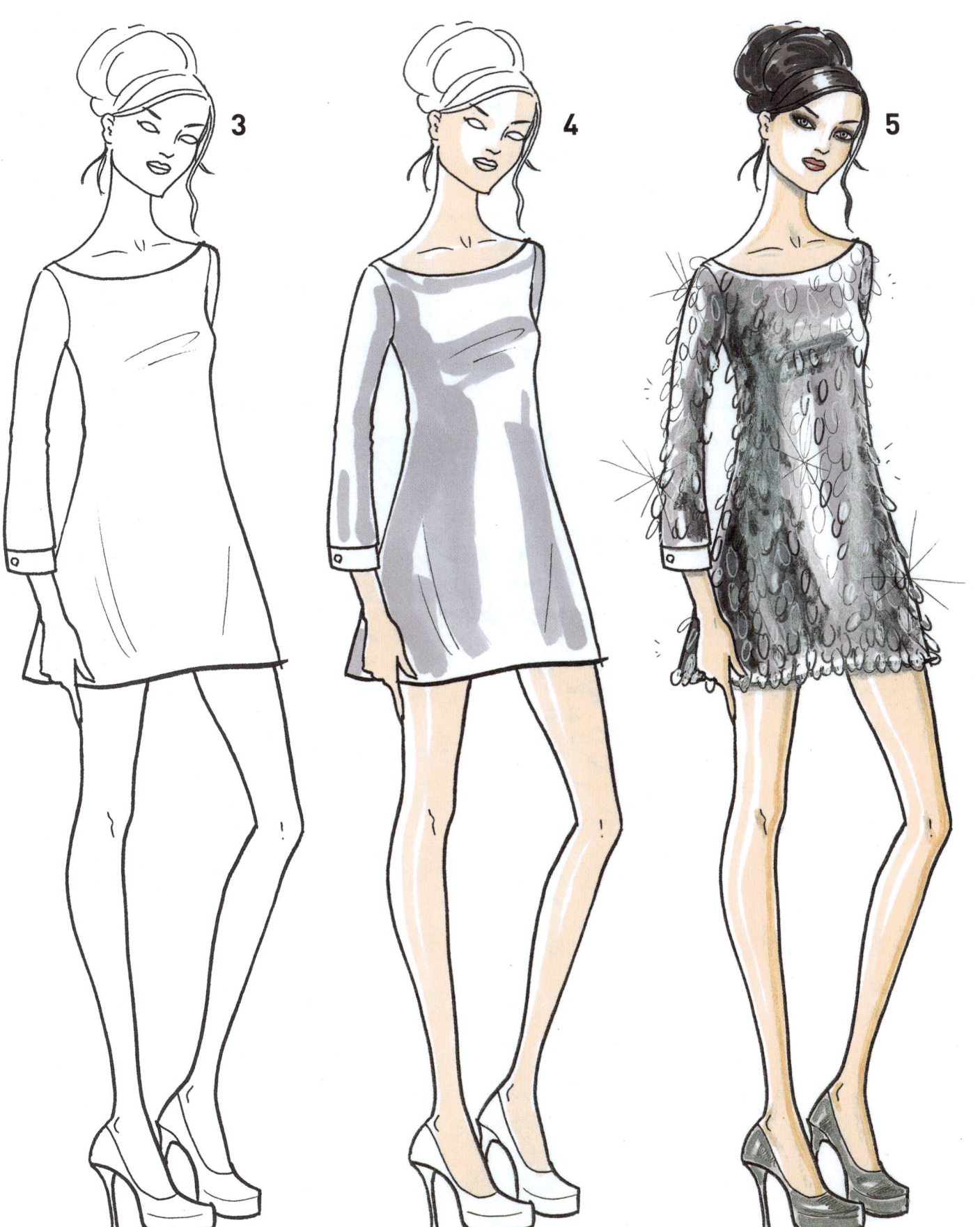

URBAN GUY

1. *Choose your template and make any minor adjustments to the pose.*

2. *Draw the whole outfit in pencil, checking the proportions and making final decisions about details.*

3. *Once you are satisfied, use a brush pen and fine fibre-tipped pens to finalize the outlines, structure and details. Note how small broken lines are used here to suggest the fleece/pile fabric of the hood lining.*

4. *Use light coloured pencil strokes to indicate the relatively complex patterning of the jacquard Nordic-look sweater. Marker pens are best for blocking in base colours for the jeans and roll-neck sweater.*

5. *Continue adding delicate marks with fine fibre-tipped pen to build up the sweater's pattern, keeping the pattern loose and not too defined to indicate a soft, wool-like feel rather than a flat printed look. Use a pencil crayon to add soft shading and highlights to the sweater and jeans. Apply additional diagonal strokes of pencil crayon to the jeans to depict a grainy denim look.*

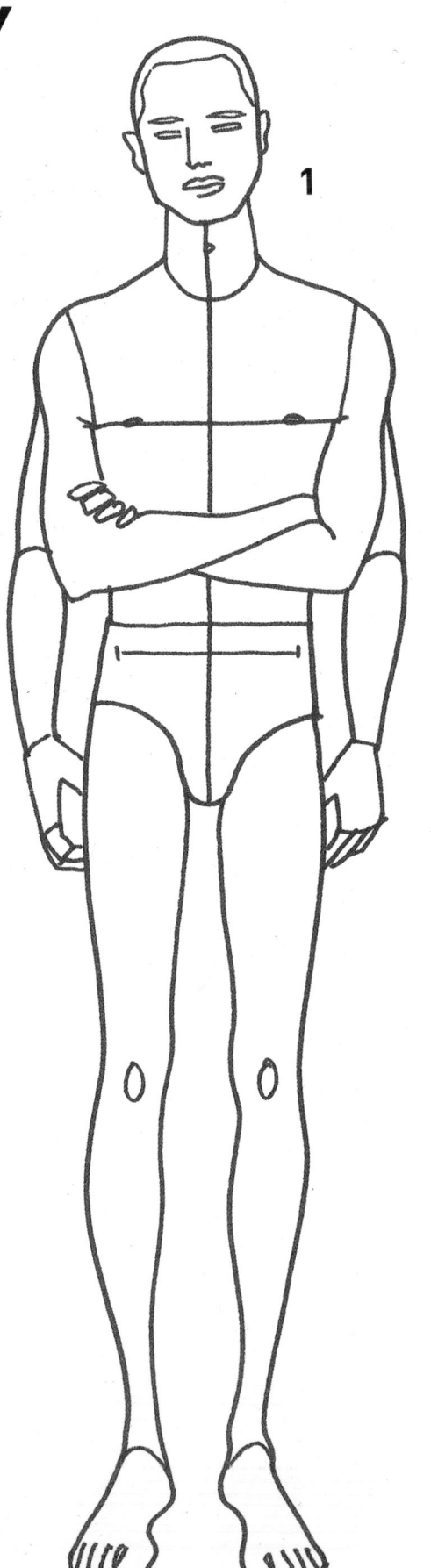

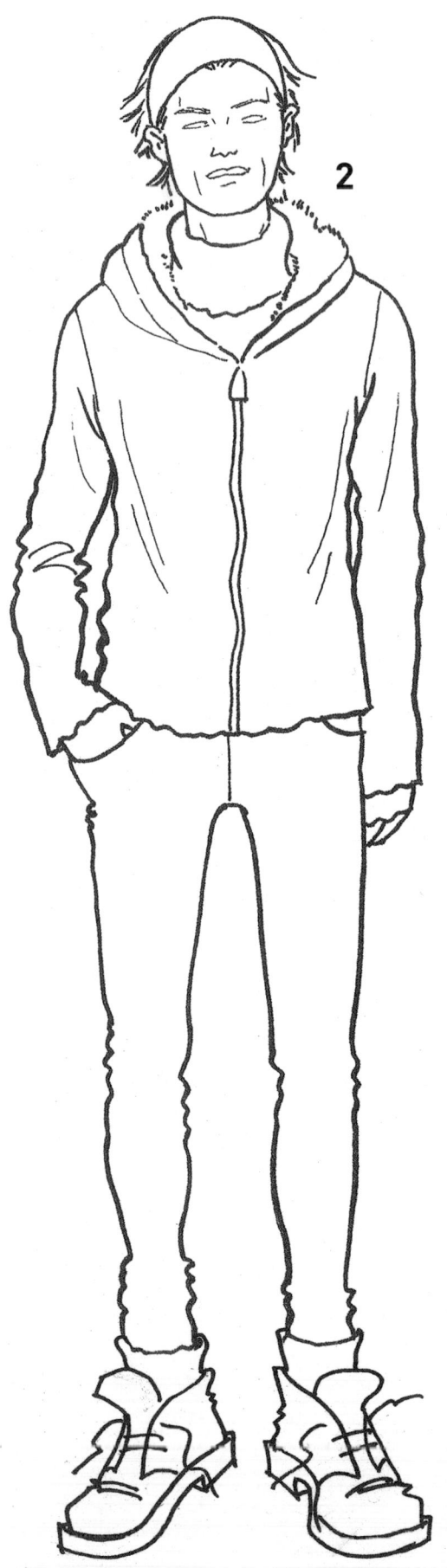

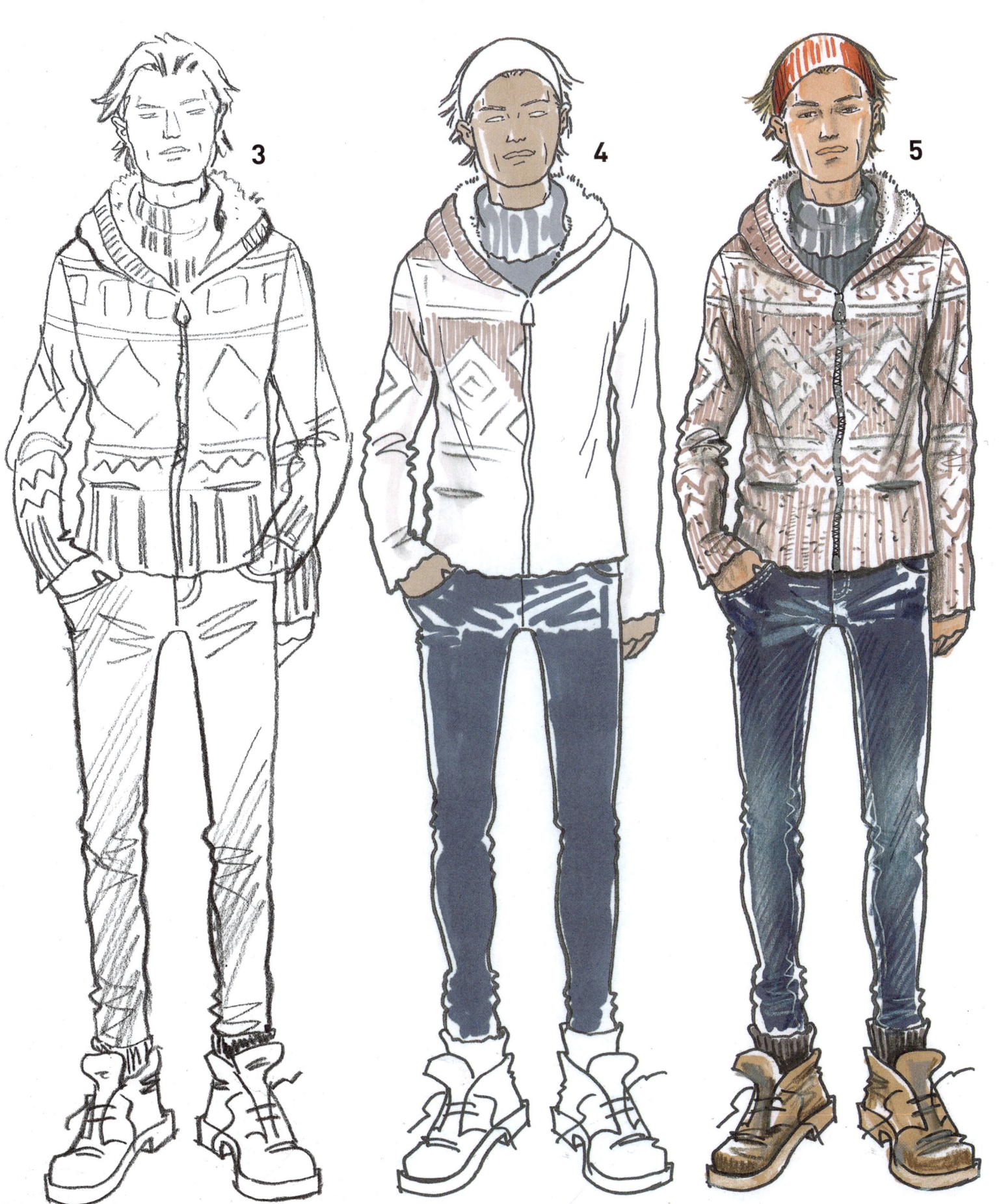

3

4

5

VACATION GUY

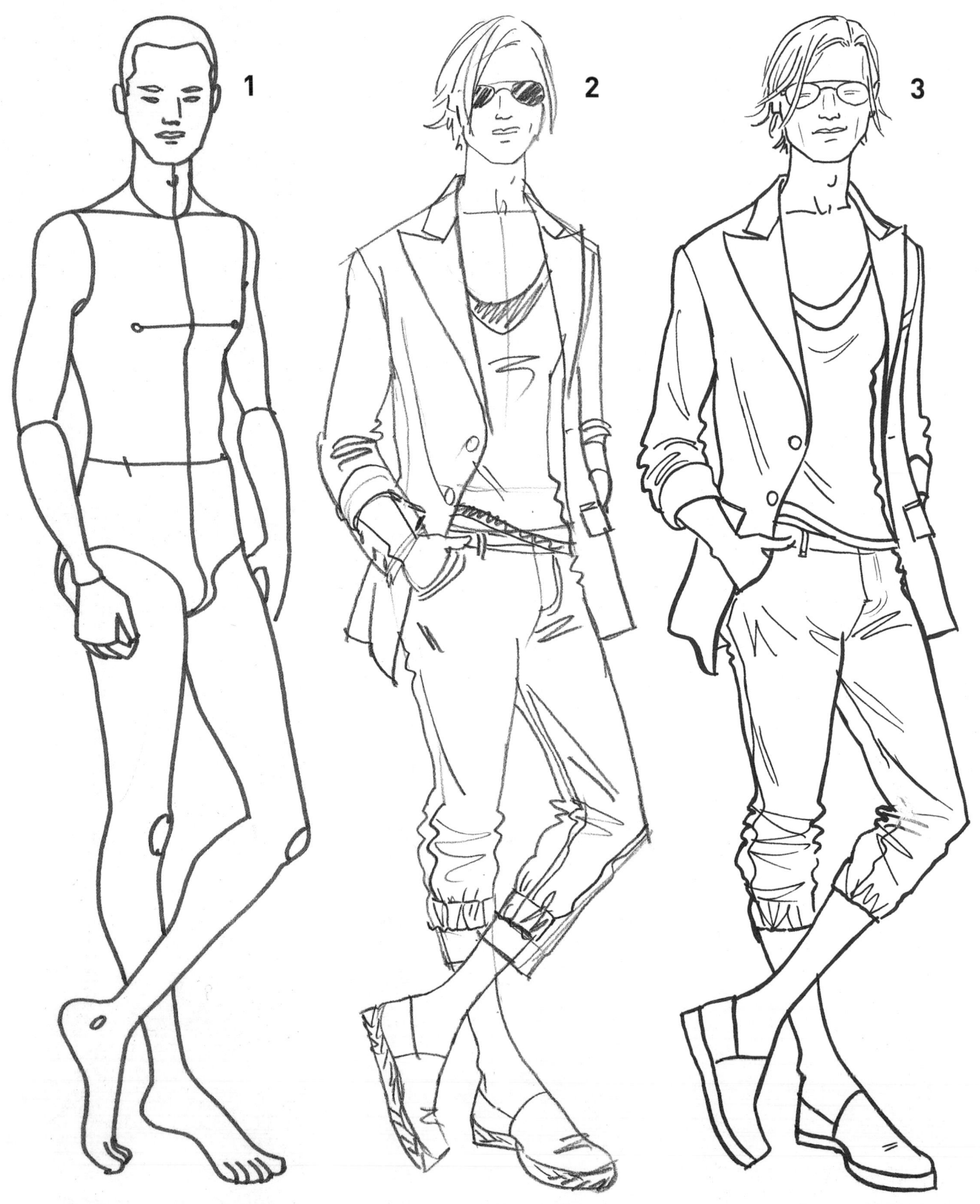

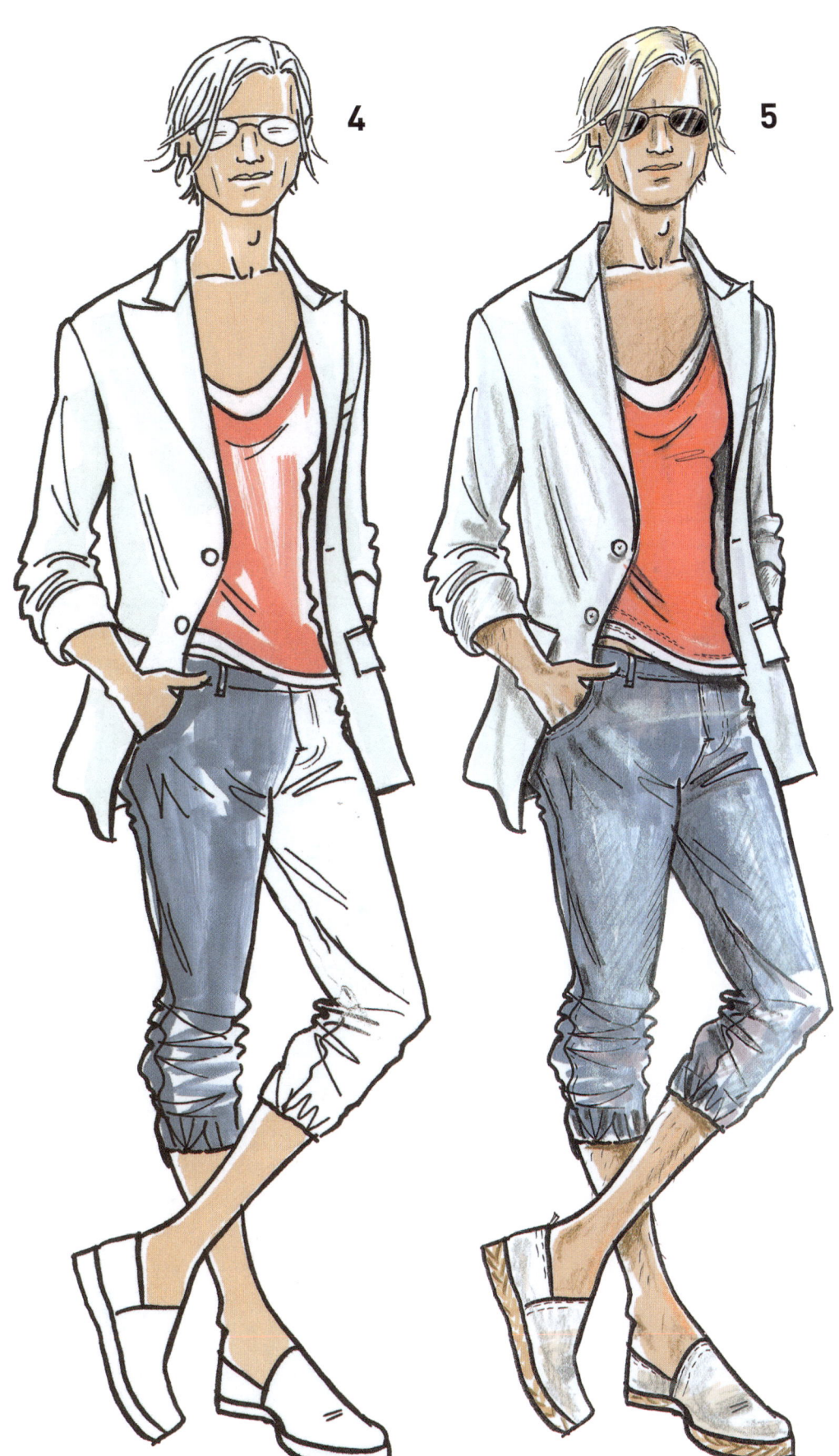

1. *Choose your template and make any minor adjustments to the pose.*

2. *Using pencil, sketch out the silhouette, proportions and finer details.*

3. *Ink in the outline, garments and features with a brush pen and fine fibre-tipped pens. Erase the pencil marks.*

4. *Add ground colour using marker pens, leaving areas of white paper showing to add depth and for highlights. Add finer details with fine fibre-tipped pens.*

5. *Using pencil crayons, add shadows and highlights as required, and use diagonal strokes to create a grain effect on the denim.*

PARTY GUY

1. *Choose your template and make any minor adjustments to the pose.*

2. *Using pencil, sketch out the basic fit, proportions and details of the garments and accessories.*

3. *Use brush pen and fine fibre-tipped pen to ink in the outlines and details, then erase the pencil marks.*

4. *Use marker pens to add colour. Black fabric is always hard to draw, and although marker pens give a good density of colour you must be sure to leave a little more white paper showing than you might at first think necessary, or the garment could look lifeless and flat. Add ground colour only for the trousers at this stage.*

5. *Add the check detail to the trousers using light, controlled pencil crayon strokes; you are aiming to merely give a hint of the pattern. Use marker pens for accessories, hair and skin tones, and correction pen to lend a crisp clarity to the polka-dotted bow tie.*

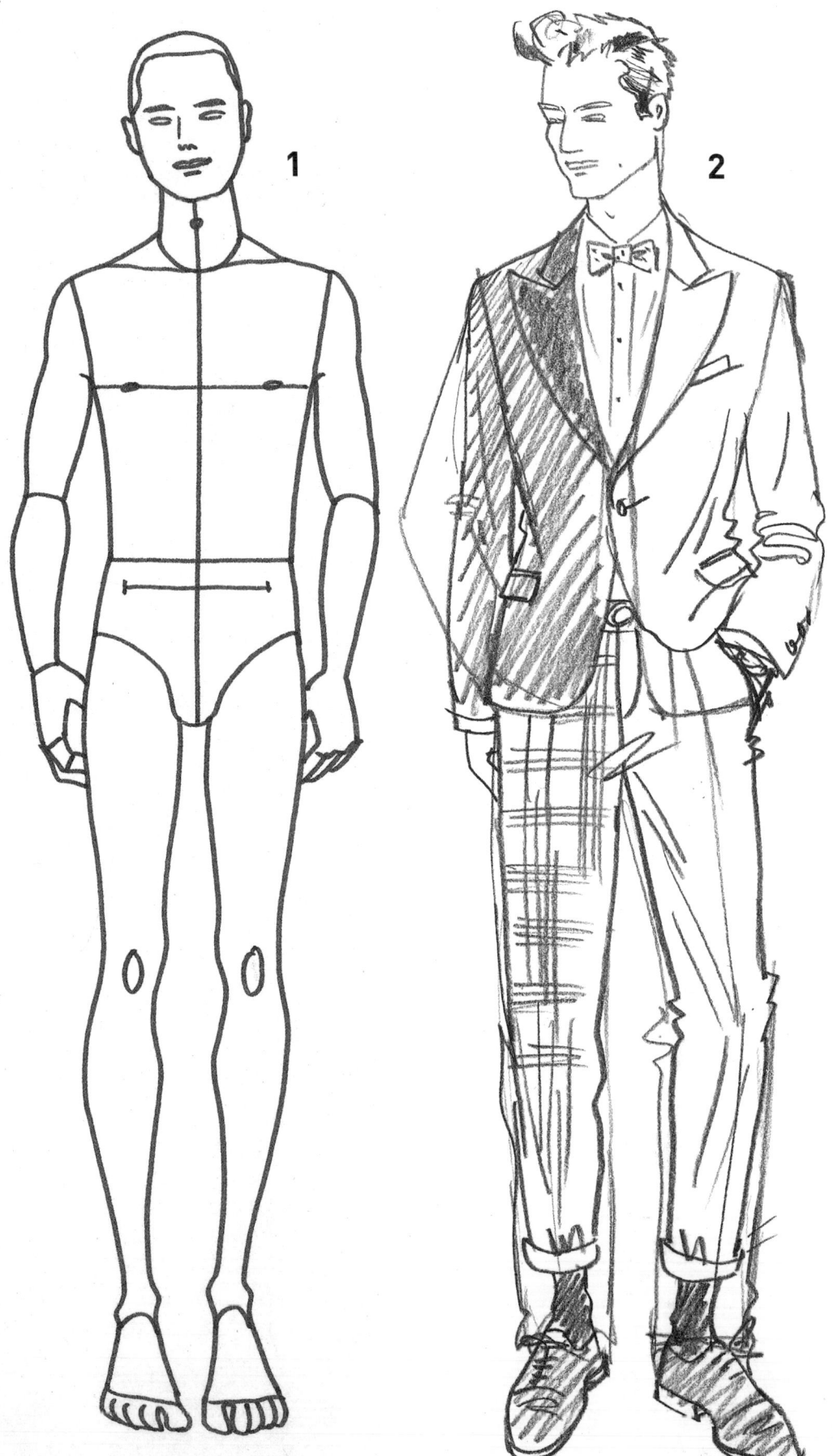

1

2

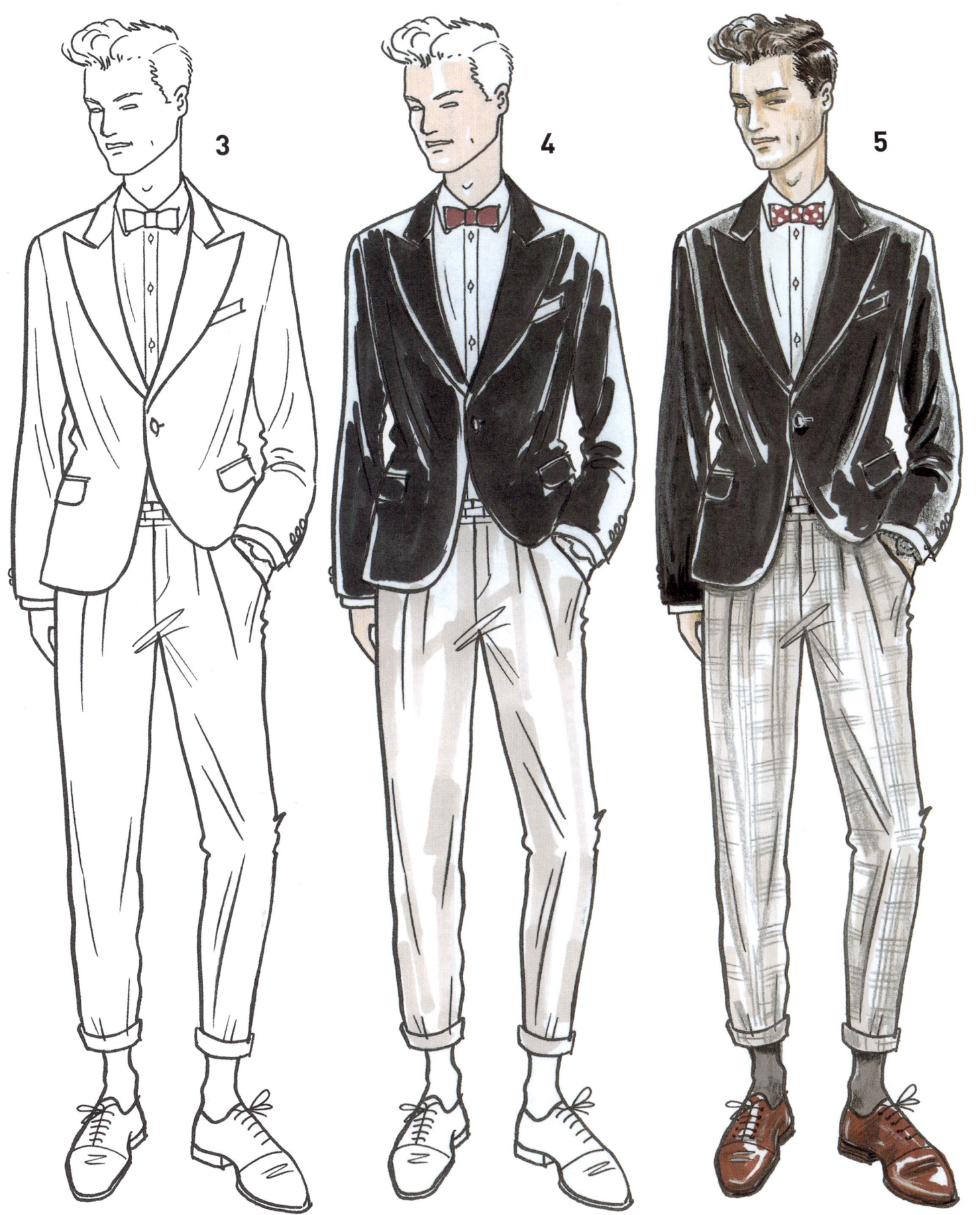

DRAWING EXERCISE: FROM A GARMENT

The subtleties of design are what actually matter most, the elements which update and reinvent something otherwise quite familiar or elevate a retro or costume piece to fashion status. Some of our favourite, most interesting garments are not, nor ever were, what we might call fashionable. Utility and workwear clothing comes into this category – functional garments that are almost timeless, their chief and enduring appeal originating from an authentic, inbuilt utility 'fit-for-purpose' logic which underpins much modern design thinking.

The terms 'timeless' and 'classic' are often used in fashion circles, but they may be nothing more than a convenient handle or journalistic hyperbole. To use 'classic' and 'fashion' in the same breath is, in essence, paradoxical, as fashion demands constant change and updating. Italian writer Italo Calvino's definition – 'A classic is a book that has never finished saying what it has to say' – can comfortably be applied to elements of fashion. A true classic is never static, it evolves and adapts to suit each new era in a fresh and relevant way. It may evolve quite drastically in fit and proportion or with subtlety and nuance through fabrication, detail, context or simply colour. 'Appropriation' is a term we frequently hear in connection with contemporary fashion, and many of today's most successful designers are more master-appropriators than truly creative innovators.

Whatever your approach to design, having a good eye for proportion and detail is key and a successful drawing needs to communicate these subtleties accurately and effectively. The following exercise is an excellent way to refine your eye and hone your drawing skills. You can take a garment from your own wardrobe, borrow one, use an exhibit in a fashion museum or even a series of photographs. You may draw from a hanger or find you need to lay the garment on the floor to see the shape truly.

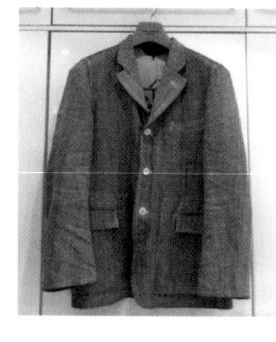 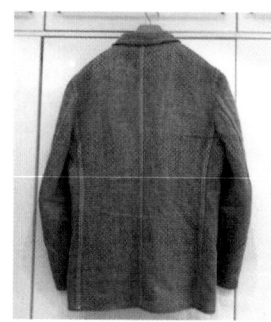

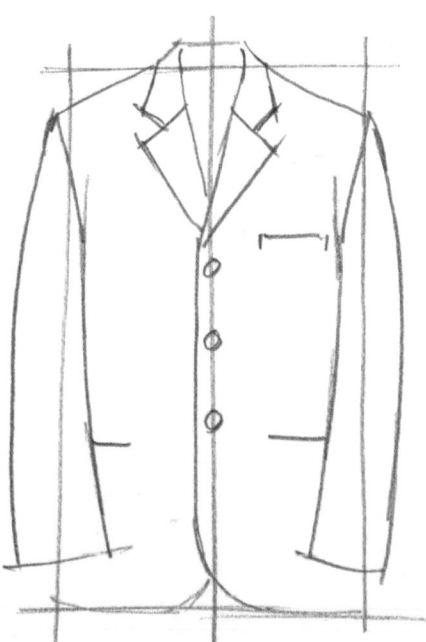

Begin by roughing out the basic shape, paying strict attention to the proportion. In this instance, the break point of the collar and lapels is key, as are the levels of pockets.

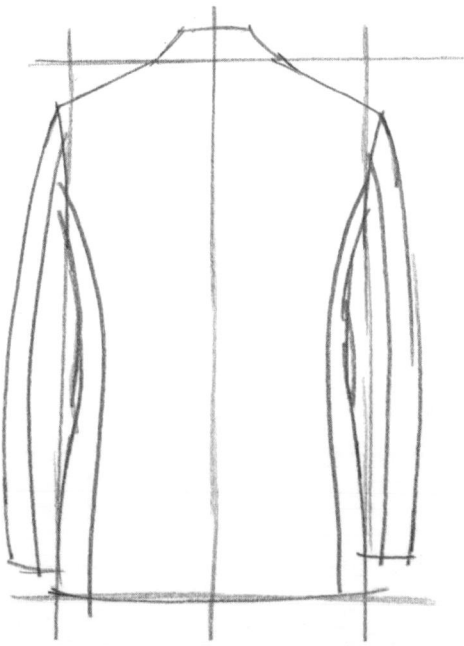

Similarly, the back must echo the front and corroborate all proportions.

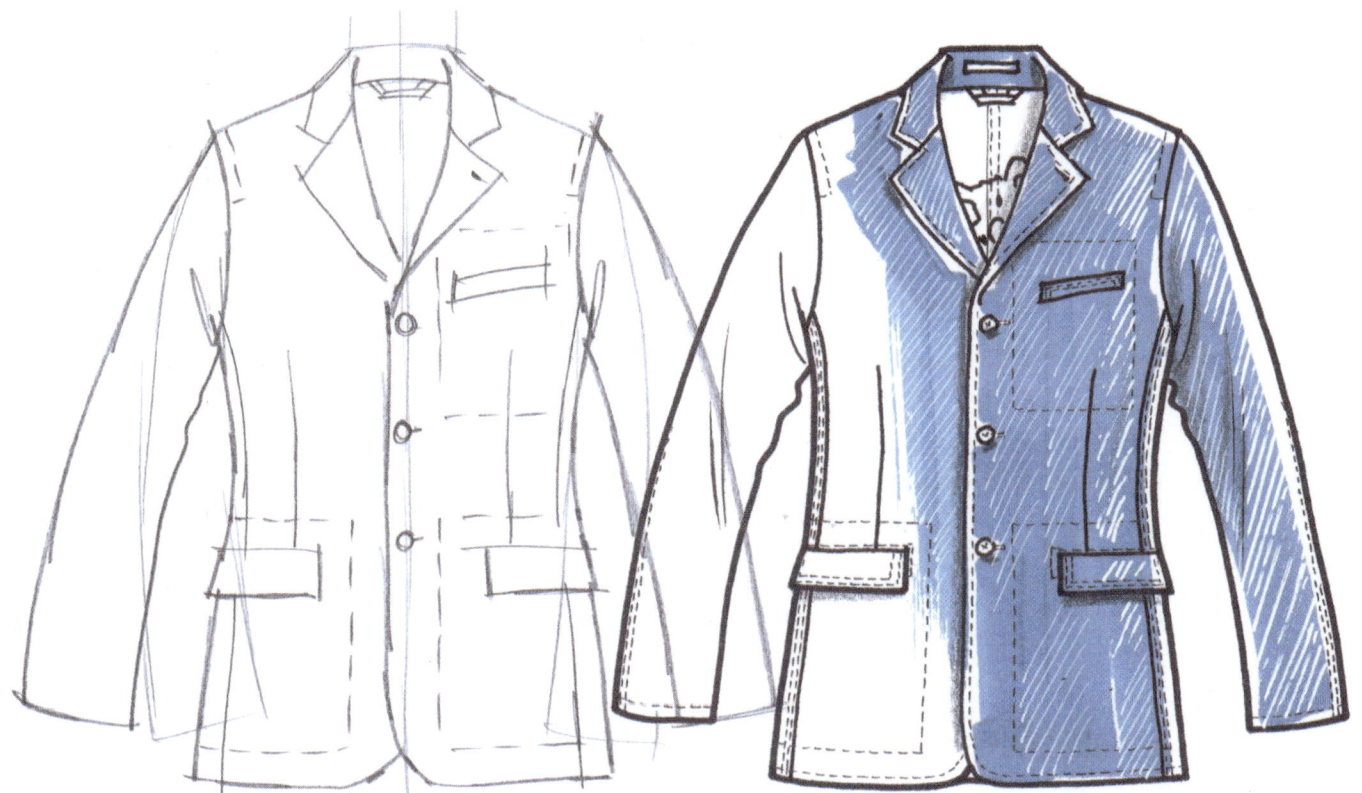

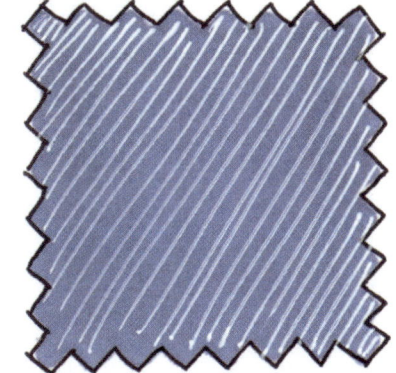

Some adjustment of the garment may be necessary in order to show the clear silhouette and important details. Sleeves can be raised or folded to show quarter seams, cuff details and plackets. The drawing can be folded in half to make sure it is truly symmetrical.

ABOVE: *Once you are happy with the roughed-out drawing, you can experiment with choosing appropriate media.*
RIGHT: *You might draw a swatch of the fabric as further record and reference.*
BELOW RIGHT: *Important details or areas of special interest can be enlarged and highlighted in close-up.*

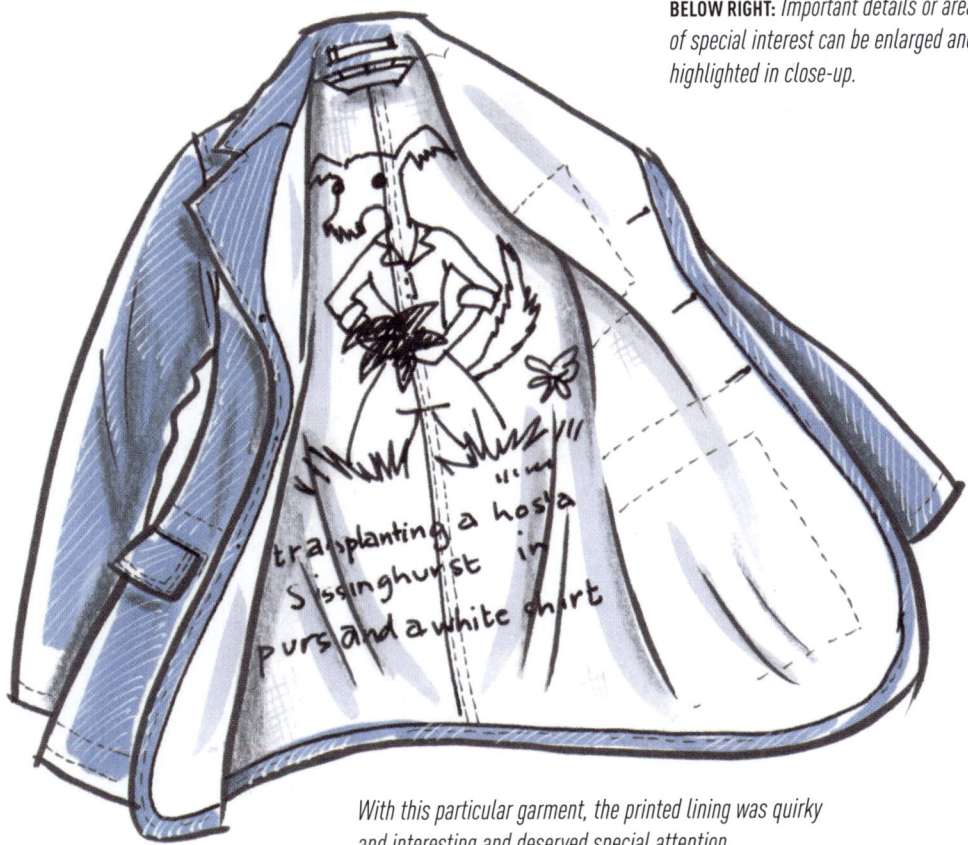

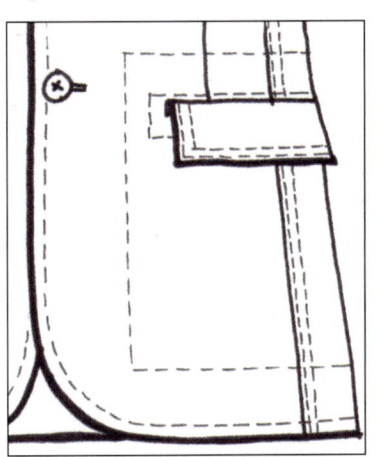

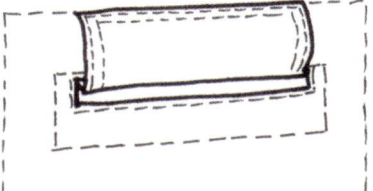

With this particular garment, the printed lining was quirky and interesting and deserved special attention.

DRAWING FROM LIFE

Drawing from life is an enriching experience derived from using a range of materials and understanding angles, movement, form, poses, light and shade. It is good practice, always — a kind of keep-fit exercise that builds an ongoing appreciation of garments, styling, fabric and flow, behaviour, bulk and volume, proportion and detail, as well as of intangible elements such as atmosphere and mood, attitude and energy.

ALL DRAWINGS: *Rosalyn Kennedy*

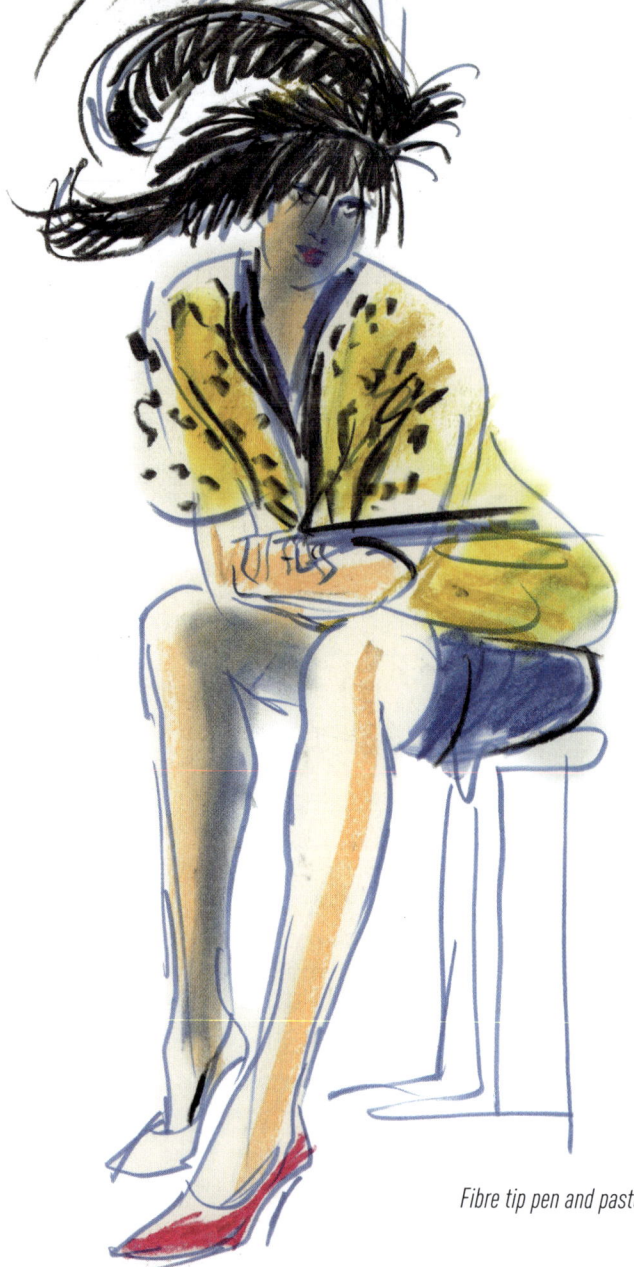

Fibre tip pen and paste

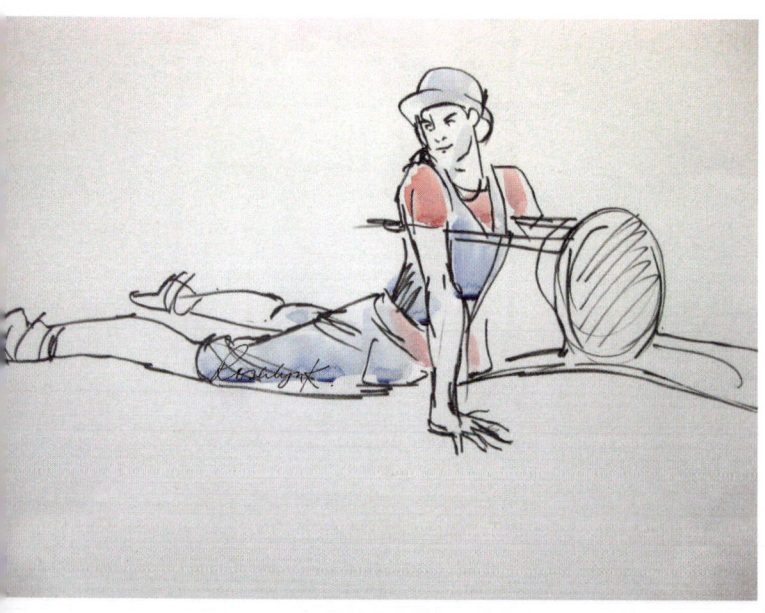

Fibre tip pen and watercolour wash

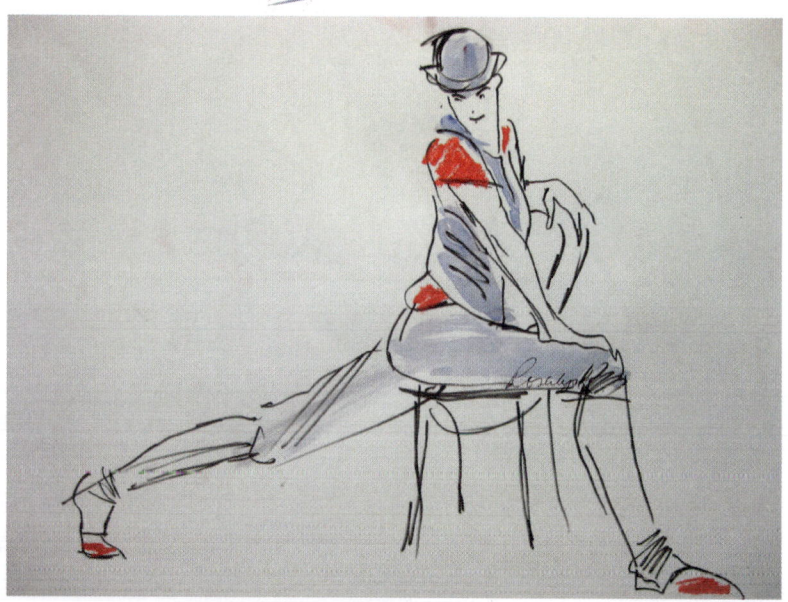

Fibre tip pen, watercolour wash and pastel

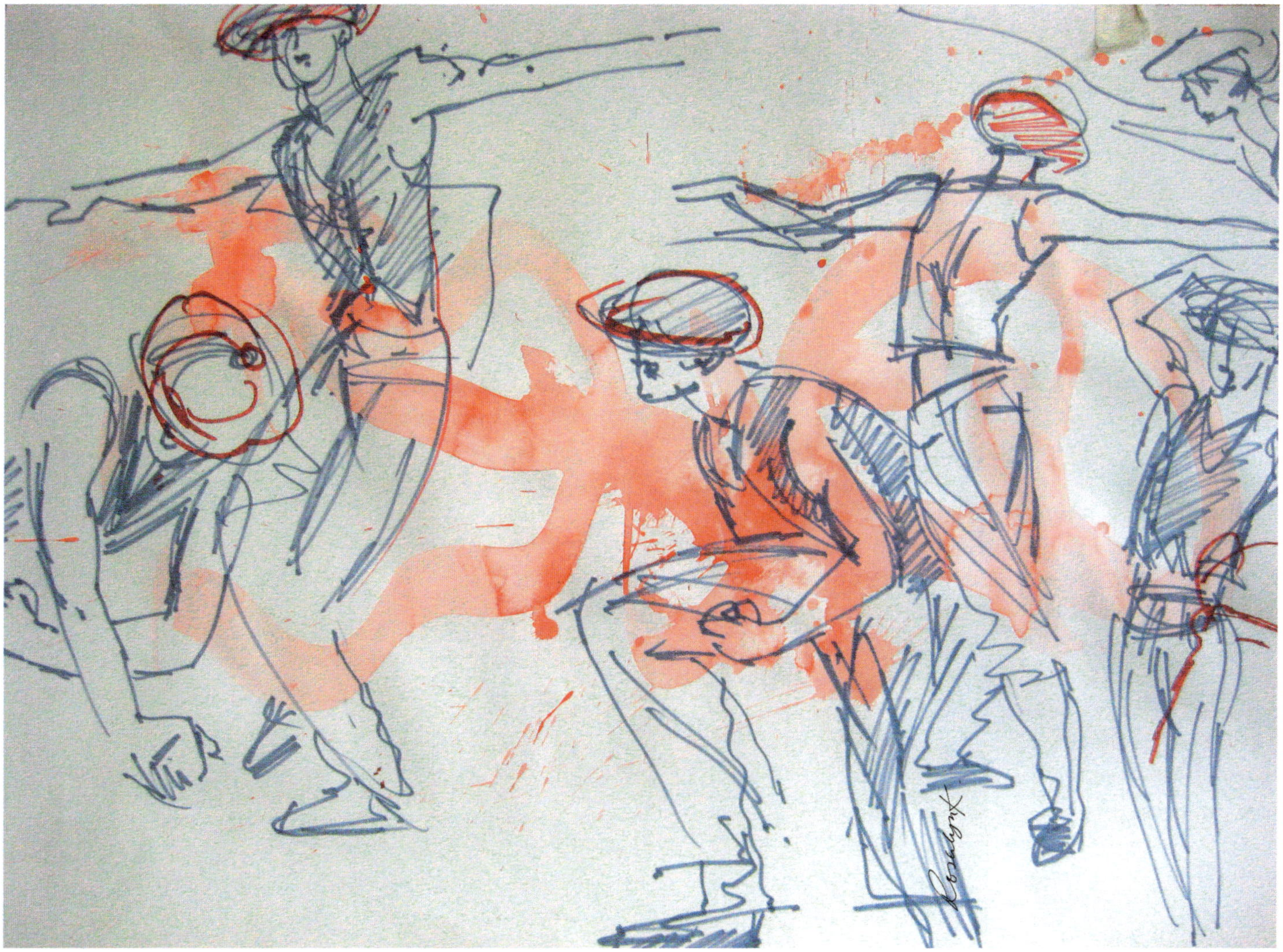

Fibre tip pen and watercolour wash

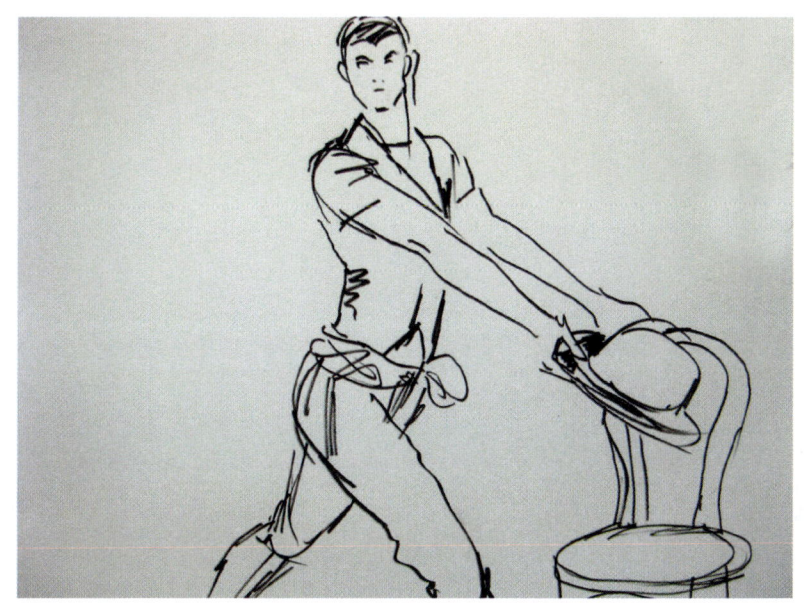

Fibre tip pen

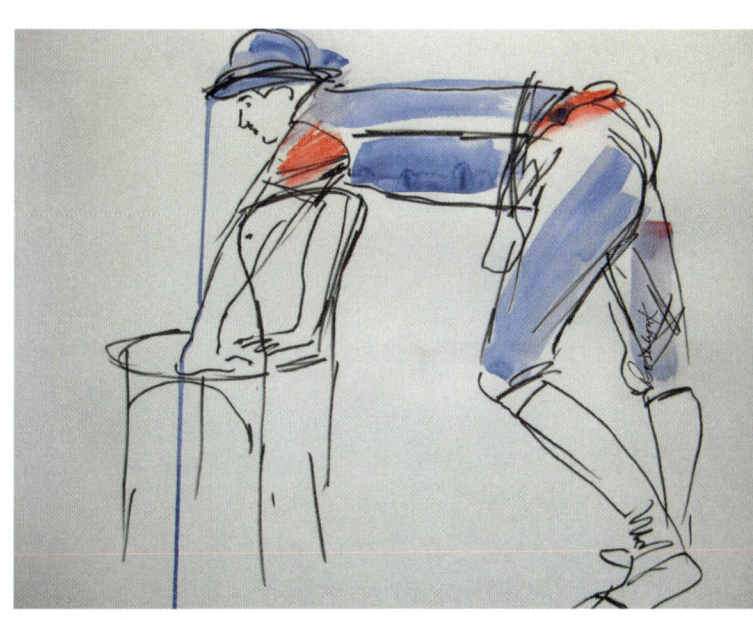

Fibre tip pen, watercolour wash and pastel

RESEARCH & INSPIRATION

'Inspiration is the act of drawing up a chair to the (writing) desk.' ANONYMOUS

Inspiration can be easy when we learn to know ourselves and understand what presses our buttons and stimulates our grey matter. This may be second nature, something that comes naturally and instinctively: a love of art and exhibitions, for example, or period films, visits to museums, learning about history or a personal topic. Travel, theatre and music can be rewarding and effective ways of stimulating the imagination almost automatically. Perhaps most importantly, the research should be actual not simply internet sourced or second-hand from books, but experiential and primary. It should be stuff that is particular to you as an individual (not just the big 'C' cultural experiences): the individual things you are interested in, the quirky objects you collect or the experiences you seek out, the observations you make in the everyday and the humdrum which are particular and personal. These individual characteristics are what are most frequently evident, clearly or otherwise, in the designers and artists we most admire and revere.

Designers have always looked to other creatives for inspiration. Yves Saint Laurent, for instance, created highly original and relevant collections influenced by Matisse, Picasso and others. As we have seen, Jeanne Lanvin was so inspired by the blue of Fra Angelico's frescoes that she made it her signature colour. But taking inspiration from a contemporary fashion designer is different matter; it can be restrictive and may set you on a narrow path

to plagiarism and derivative mediocrity that is best avoided. Many designers have gone down that route, of course, and many have acknowledged it by calling their collection an 'homage'; others, who should have known better, have been less honest about the source of their ideas.

While copying from other designers cannot be described as inspiration, it can be useful to look at fashion eras to keep up with trends, directions and the changing market. But a far more rewarding approach

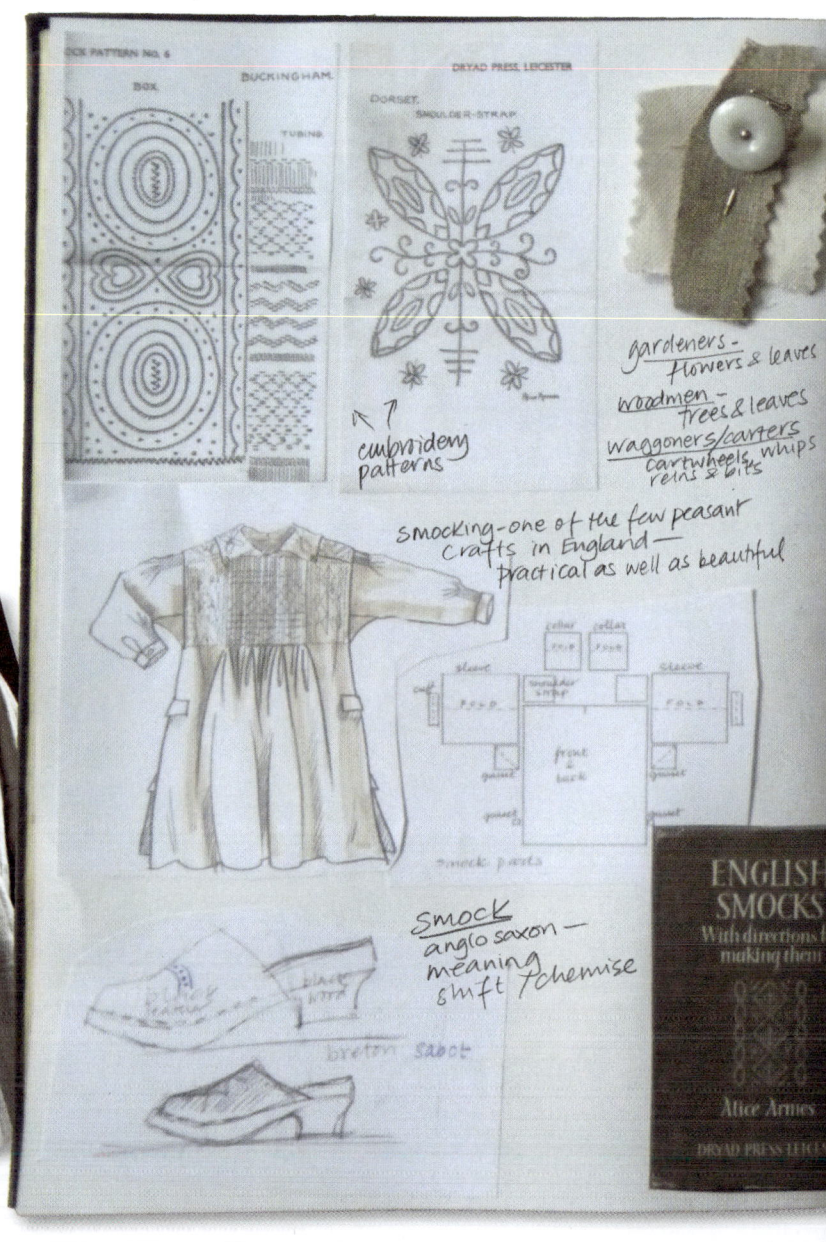

'I always find beauty in things that are odd and imperfect – they are much more interesting.'

MARC JACOBS

is to look at what has inspired other designers; for instance, from looking at many 1940s fashions it is clear that the designers of this decade were, in turn, looking back to the Edwardian and Victorian eras, to what seemed to be (superficially, at least) idyllic, more appealing times before two successive and devastating world wars. Today a designer can avoid parody by cannoning these eras and influences, fusing elements and ideas for a truly contemporary take.

Similarly, if a designer looks at, say, skateboard culture, he or she could examine sources, rather than just the outcomes, adding primary research for a personal, more original result.

Contemporary relevance, though, should be a constant consideration. It is wise to remember that even a collection as revered as Christian Dior's New Look (presented in 1947), which took its inspiration from Victorian dress, drew worldwide criticism at the time for its excessive use of fabric (most of Europe was still under rationing restrictions). It was also criticized for encouraging women back into restrictive, inhibitive clothes. While avoiding the slippery slope of parody, unless your brief is, say, for film or theatre costume where historical authenticity is part of the deal, inspiration can be gained by looking at designers from history and learning about the craft and skills they employed. In this way, in the 1990s John Galliano reinvented the bias cutting techniques pioneered by Madeleine Vionnet in the 1920s, together with a host of other clever cutting tricks from the masters.

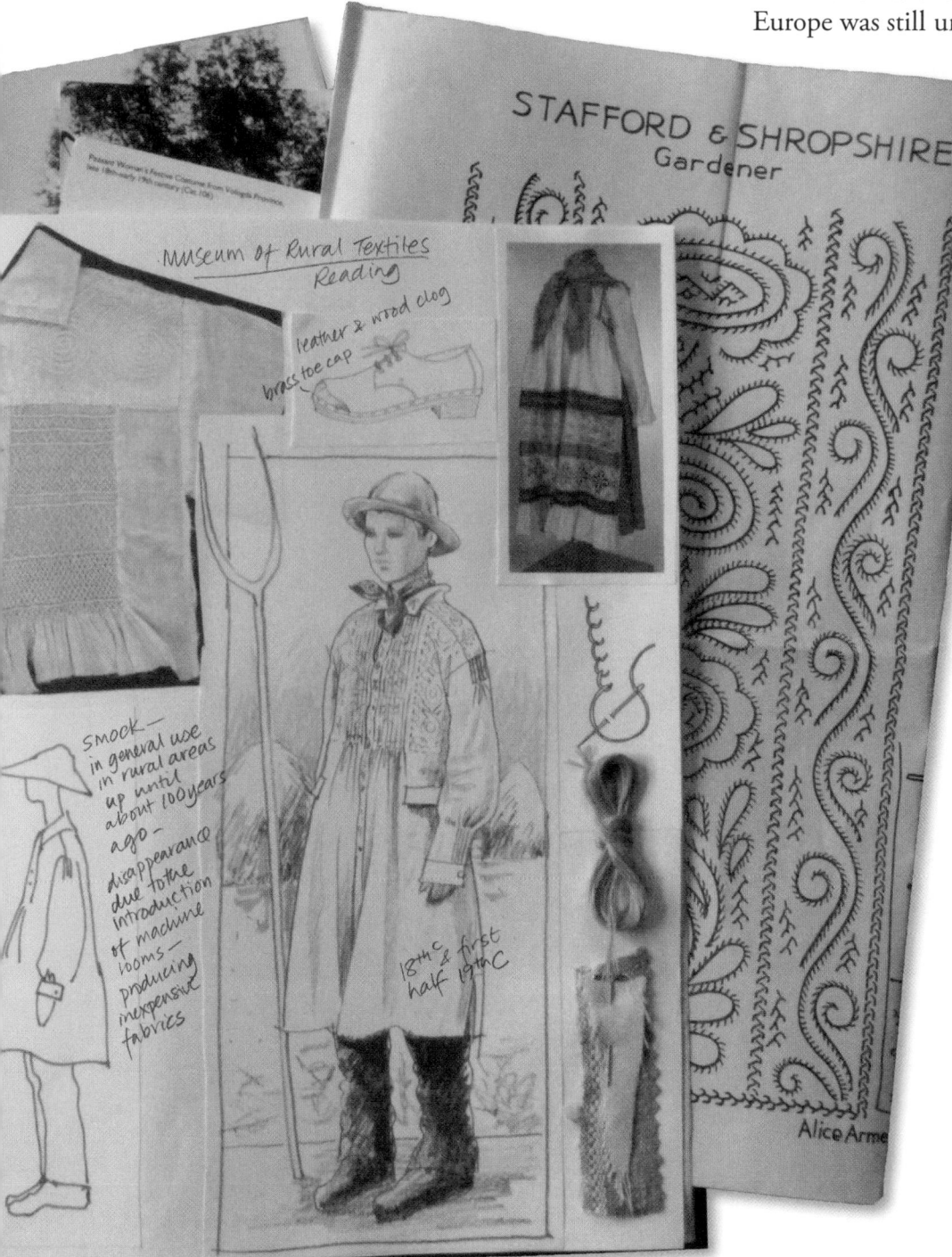

LEFT: *This sketchbook spread shows detailed primary research in the form of museum study drawings of a vintage farmer's smock, with close-ups of features and details, collected vintage reference and photographed back-up. Small but appropriate fabric swatches and comprehensive notes complete the supporting information.*

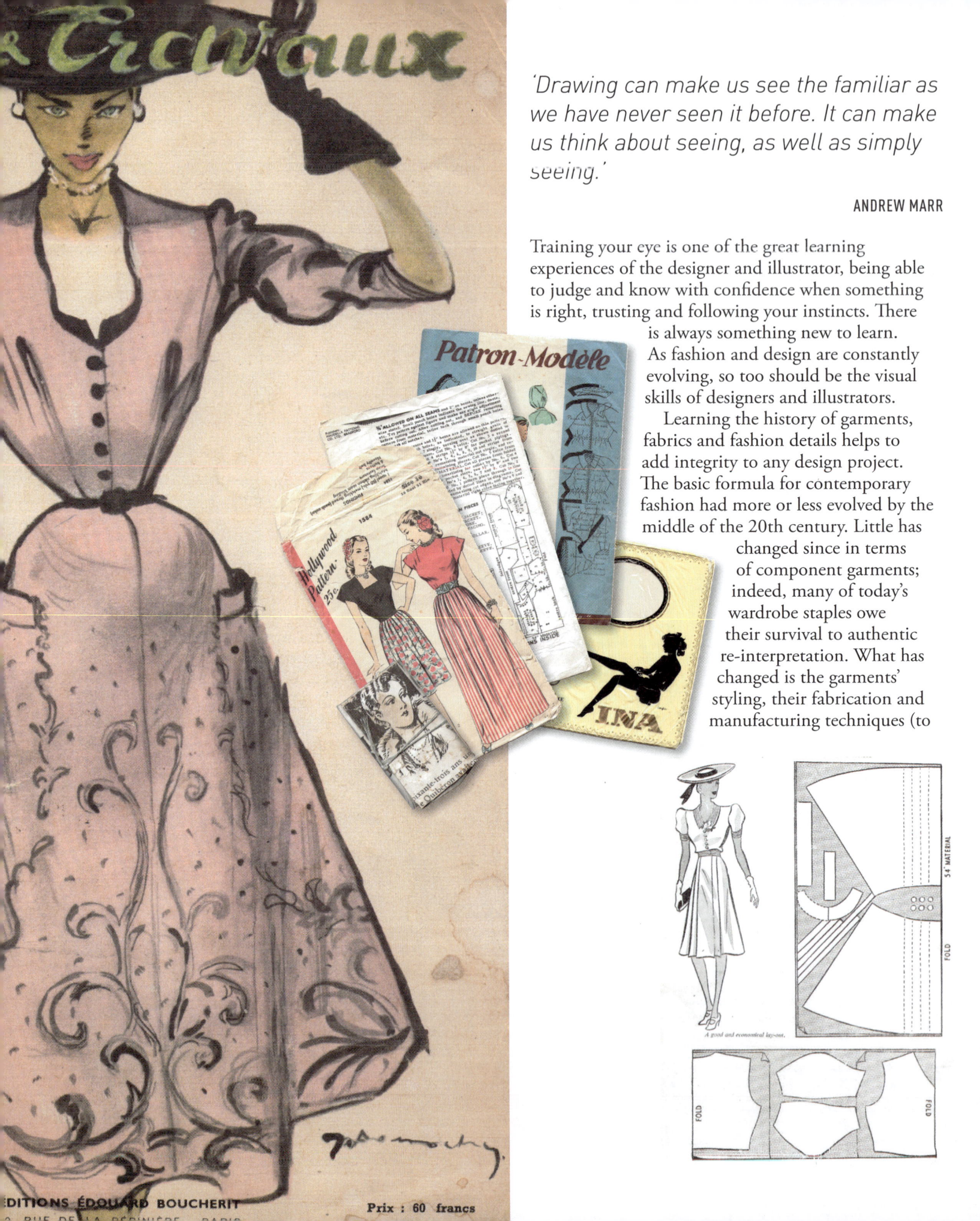

'Drawing can make us see the familiar as we have never seen it before. It can make us think about seeing, as well as simply seeing.'

ANDREW MARR

Training your eye is one of the great learning experiences of the designer and illustrator, being able to judge and know with confidence when something is right, trusting and following your instincts. There is always something new to learn. As fashion and design are constantly evolving, so too should be the visual skills of designers and illustrators.

Learning the history of garments, fabrics and fashion details helps to add integrity to any design project. The basic formula for contemporary fashion had more or less evolved by the middle of the 20th century. Little has changed since in terms of component garments; indeed, many of today's wardrobe staples owe their survival to authentic re-interpretation. What has changed is the garments' styling, their fabrication and manufacturing techniques (to

A good and economical lay-out.

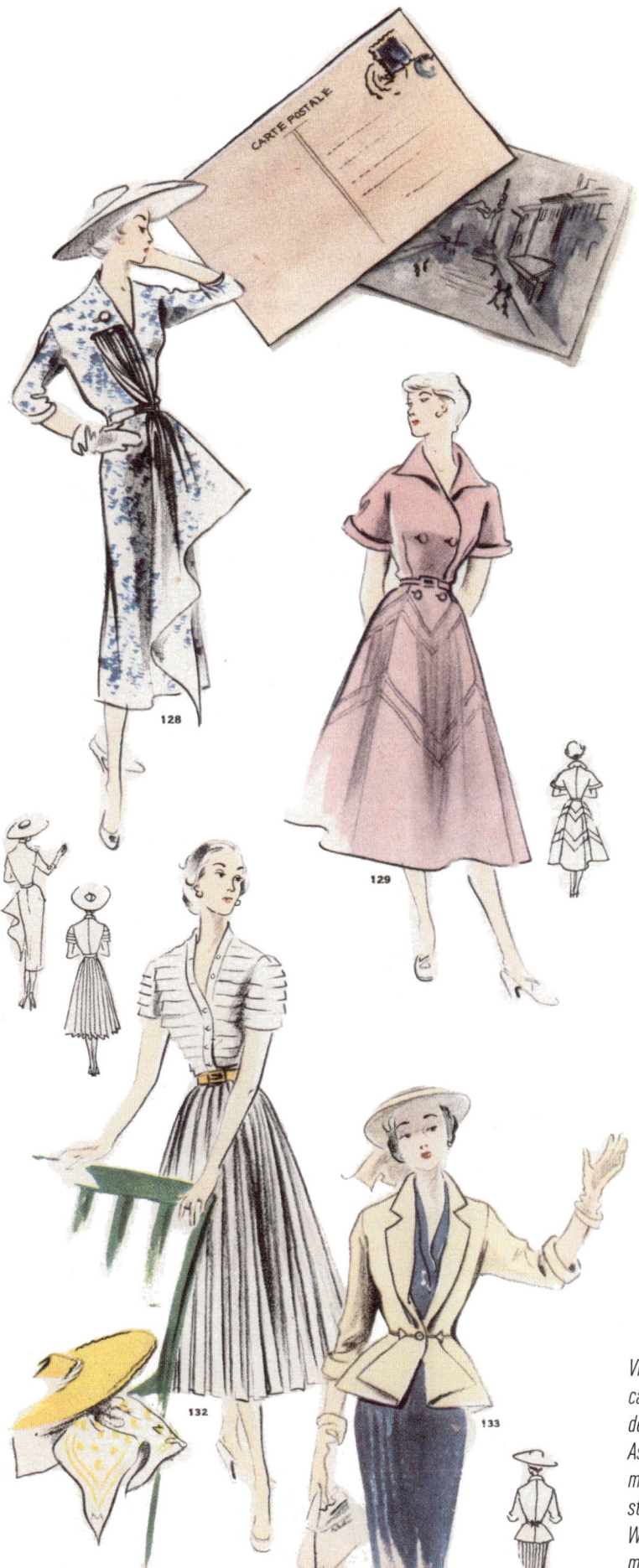

some extent) and, most of all, the democratization and globalization of fashion. It is a truism that, despite all the hype, fashion is more about evolution than revolution.

Learning to spot those subtle but significant details of evolution and appropriation, and to be more analytical, is key. When looking at garments or magazine photographs or at a person in the street, try to think beyond the obvious, the superficial, the non-specific meaningless evaluation – 'she/he looks cool'. A mental checklist can help with your analysis:

• Colour
• Proportions
• Fabrication or fabric mixes
• Embellishments or noticeable techniques
• Silhouette
• Details (lapels or shoulders, for example)

Is it a combination of these elements or a less tangible quality that elevates the look to something a little special – an atmosphere, something evocative of an era, culture or nationality? How about the styling, the accessories? Have the garments been put together in a particular or novel way?

As with the exercise on pages 102–3, drawing helps when researching vintage garments. The ability to draw and record well involves analyzing scale and proportion, and questioning: How wide is right for the lapel? How should a collar actually fall? How full should that sleeve/skirt be? How big should the pockets be and where exactly should they be positioned? Similarly, accuracy is crucial to the task of drawing for illustration purposes.

The subtleties of proportion and scale may be the determining factor that updates a look and makes it current and new or tired and old fashioned – the minute amount by which a shirt collar grows or shrinks, for example. Try standing in front of a mirror, holding a piece of paper up in front of you and drawing or folding the paper to just the right size and angle.

Vintage reference is a rich and easily available source of excellent secondary research that can supply detailed information about silhouette, cut, fabrication, construction, garment details and embellishment, styling and accessories for design and illustration inspiration. Aside from the excellent range of fashion history books available, vintage shops and flea markets can be great sources of old fashion magazines, paper patterns and packaging – still at bargain prices – not to mention garments and fabrics for first-hand study. With special thanks to Niki Zachiadis for the use of her collection of vintage fashion magazines for images.

DRAWING TRICKS

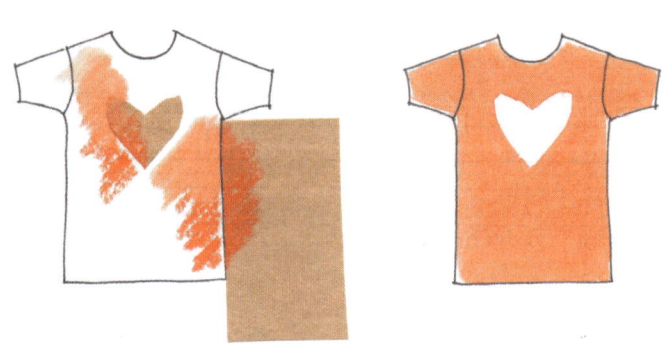
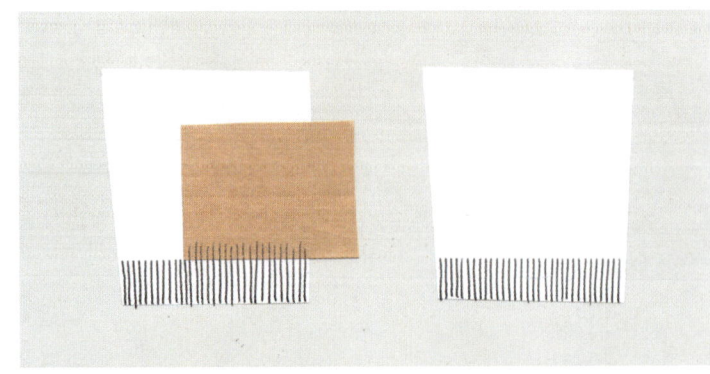

ABOVE: *Use paper masks for adding colour or texture in broad rapid strokes or for bold graphic pattern effects.*

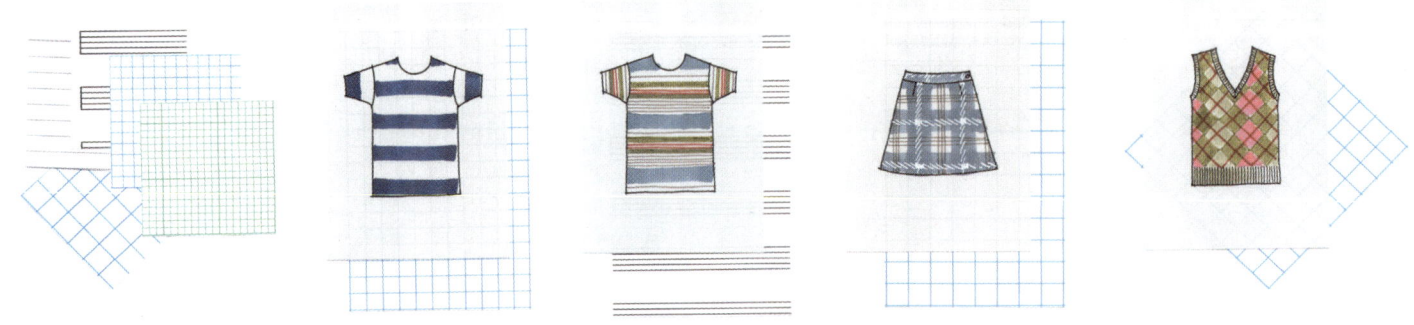

ABOVE: *Use printed papers as guides under layout paper, or on a lightbox, to draw stripes, checks, plaids or argyles. Prints are easy to download in infinite varieties and scale from the internet or can be bought as separate sheets, pads or notebooks. This trick is particularly useful for flats and technical drawings.*

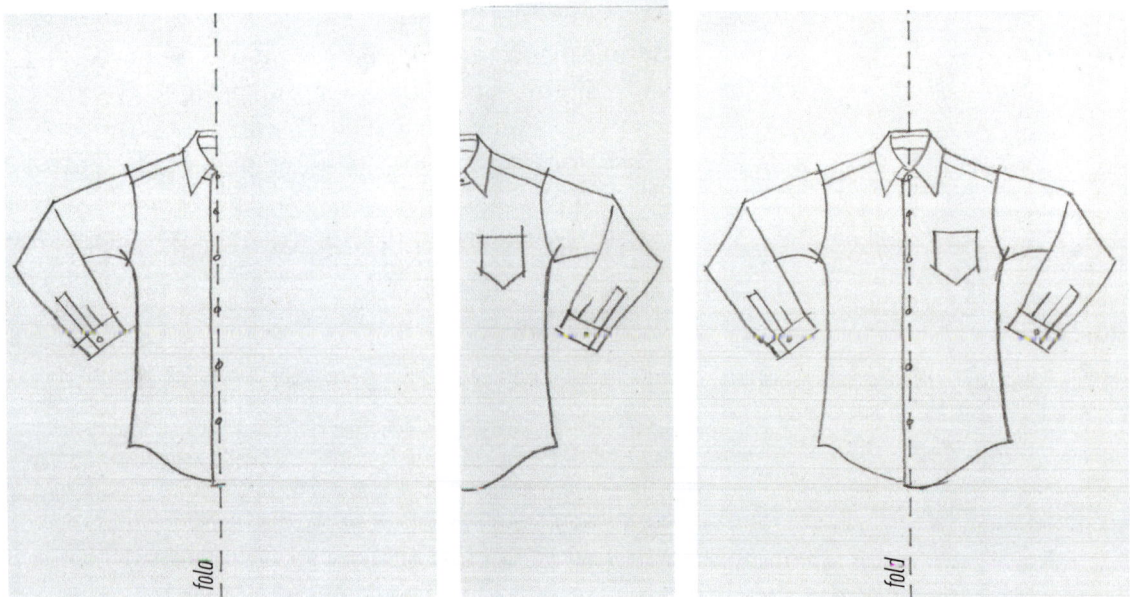

LEFT: *To ensure all hand-drawn flats and technical drawings are completely symmetrical, fold the drawing down the centre line and use a lightbox, layout or transfer paper to trace off the second half.*

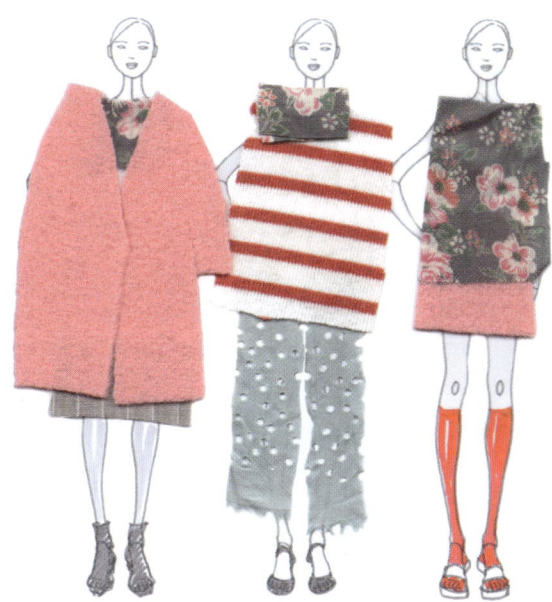

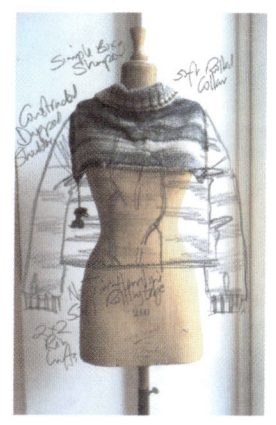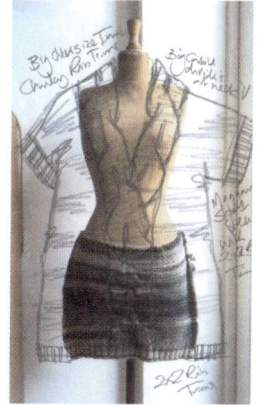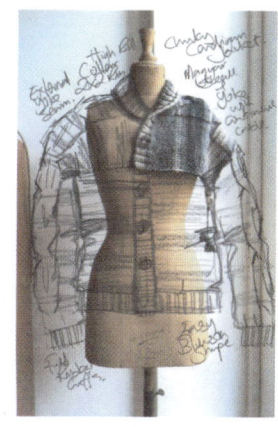

ABOVE: Pin swatches on to a dress stand, how and as you might use them; photograph them using your phone or digital camera; print out and draw the rest of the garment idea on top of the photograph as a quick and easy design tool to extend ideas and possibilities.

ABOVE: Use snips of fabric collaged on to pre-drawn figures or templates to get a quick overall impression of colour balance and proportion.

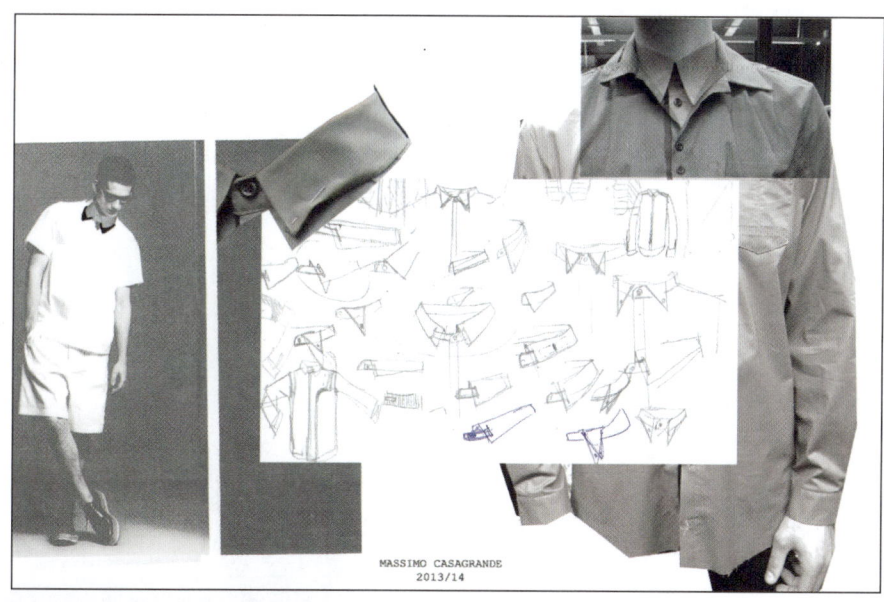

MASSIMO CASAGRANDE
2013/14

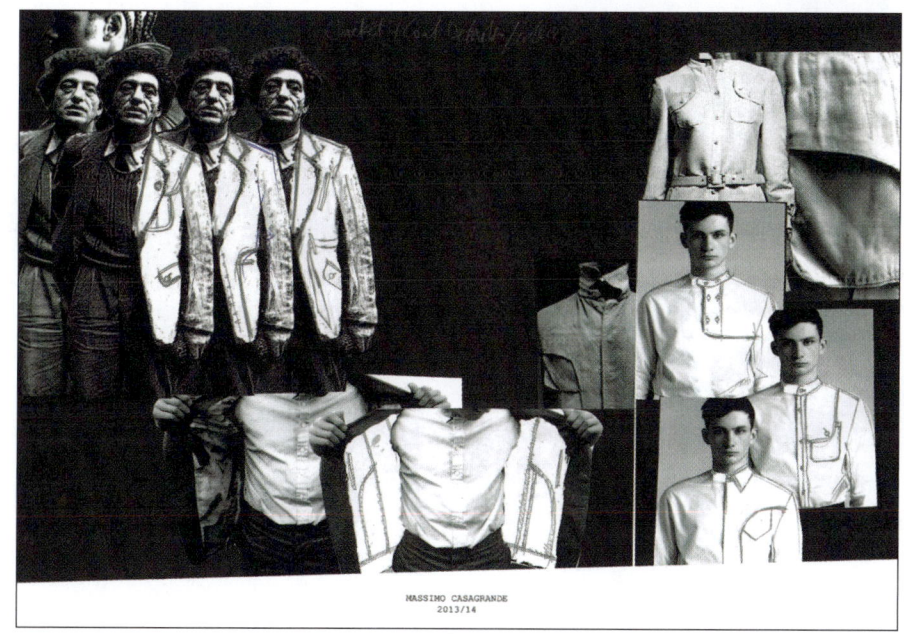

MASSIMO CASAGRANDE
2013/14

ABOVE: Using a similar technique to the above, Massimo Casagrande sometimes manipulates garments on the dress stand, photographs the process and continues to draw ideas and variations on the photographs in his sketchbook.
LEFT: Another technique that is stylish, practical and time efficient – Massimo Casagrande paints white opaque correction fluid on to photocopies or scans of inspirational images in his sketchbook and then draws on top to add his design ideas.

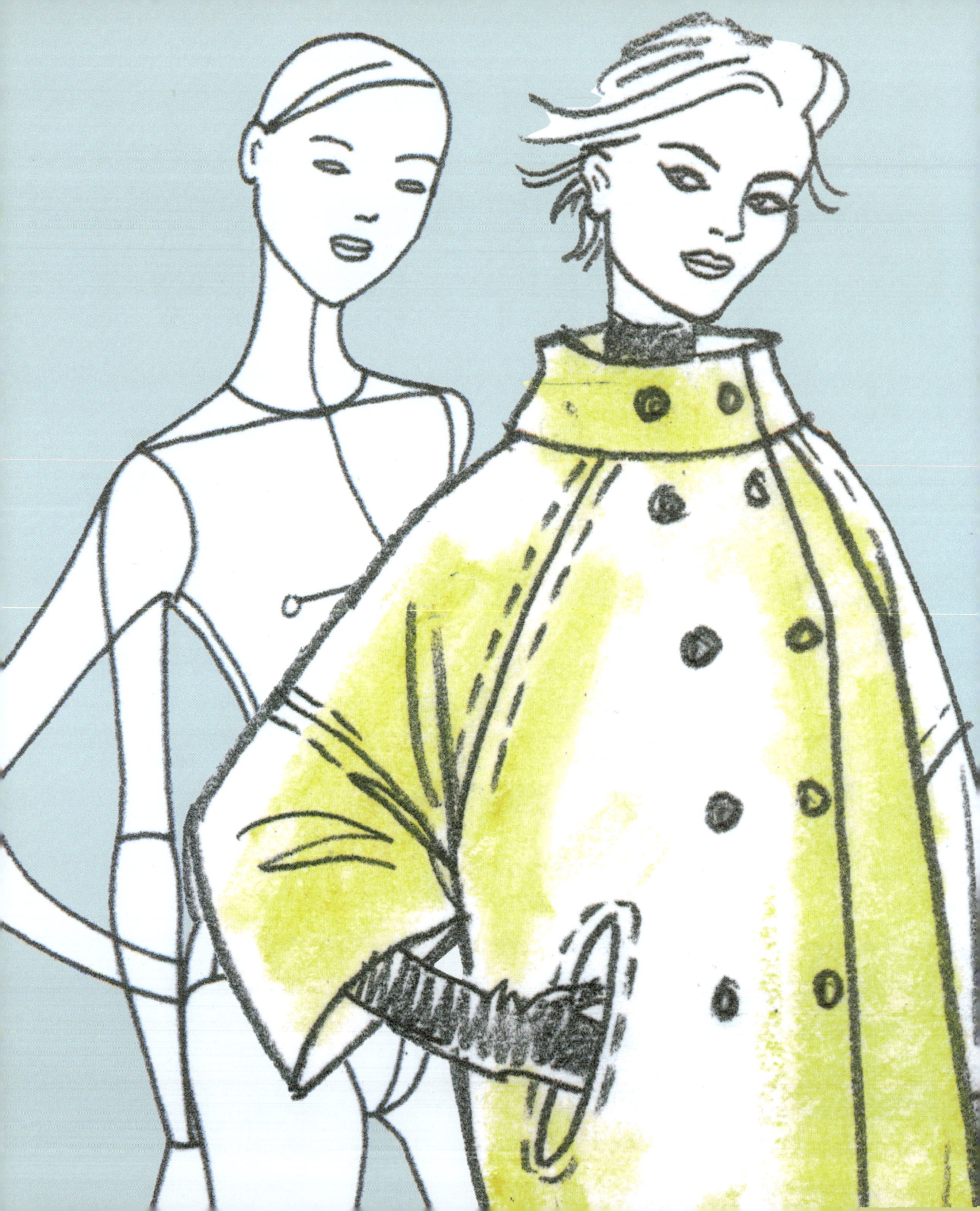

DRAWING AND DESIGNING USING A TEMPLATE

Using a template when illustrating clothes is a great help. Similarly, a template can be a valuable work-in-progress tool for designing clothes, helping to make the creative process more speedy and efficient. By adapting a template that reflects the demographic of your customer in terms of size and proportion you will be able to best portray your designs in an appropriate way.

In addition to figure templates, designers also use templates for drawing 'flats', which are the outlines of garments, rather than figures, that are given to manufacturers when making clothes. Used in a similar way to a figure template, a flat template can be placed under a sheet of paper and quickly traced in order to ensure that the scale and proportion of a range of drawings of the same item are uniform. This makes assessing and comparing the designs much easier.

More detailed flats are commonly termed 'technical drawings', and focus on particular features such as lapels, necklines, drapery and stitching, providing in-depth and accurate guidelines that will ensure the garment is made correctly. Information about the fabric to be used must also be conveyed, whether by being drawn, collaged or scanned, and it is essential that the flow and overall feel of the material are depicted in the illustration. In addition to using traditional methods for creating flats, many modern designers use CAD (Computer Aided Design), which produces very accurate renderings of the garments.

FLATS AND FLOATS

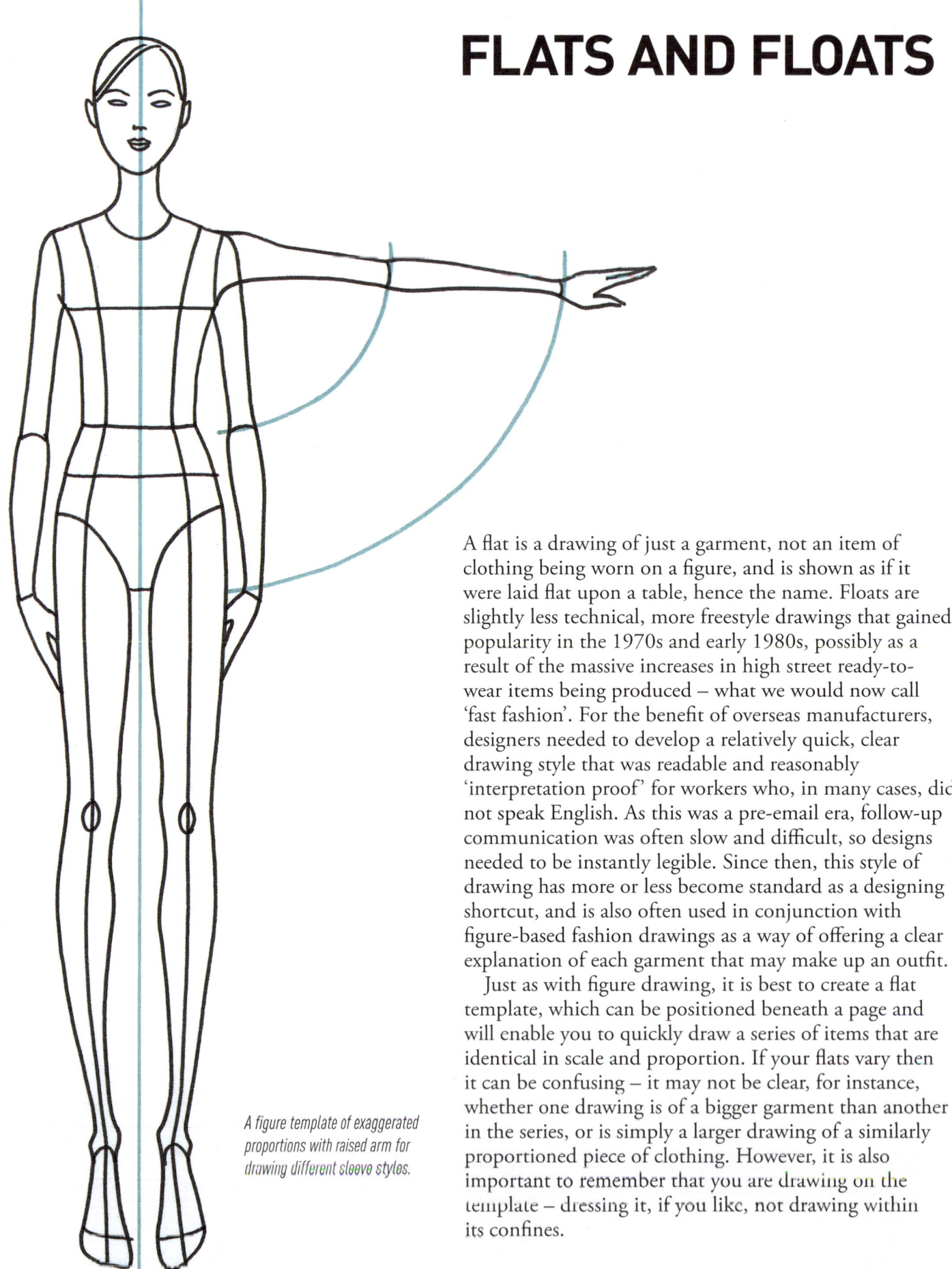

A figure template of exaggerated proportions with raised arm for drawing different sleeve styles.

A flat is a drawing of just a garment, not an item of clothing being worn on a figure, and is shown as if it were laid flat upon a table, hence the name. Floats are slightly less technical, more freestyle drawings that gained popularity in the 1970s and early 1980s, possibly as a result of the massive increases in high street ready-to-wear items being produced – what we would now call 'fast fashion'. For the benefit of overseas manufacturers, designers needed to develop a relatively quick, clear drawing style that was readable and reasonably 'interpretation proof' for workers who, in many cases, did not speak English. As this was a pre-email era, follow-up communication was often slow and difficult, so designs needed to be instantly legible. Since then, this style of drawing has more or less become standard as a designing shortcut, and is also often used in conjunction with figure-based fashion drawings as a way of offering a clear explanation of each garment that may make up an outfit.

Just as with figure drawing, it is best to create a flat template, which can be positioned beneath a page and will enable you to quickly draw a series of items that are identical in scale and proportion. If your flats vary then it can be confusing – it may not be clear, for instance, whether one drawing is of a bigger garment than another in the series, or is simply a larger drawing of a similarly proportioned piece of clothing. However, it is also important to remember that you are drawing on the template – dressing it, if you like, not drawing within its confines.

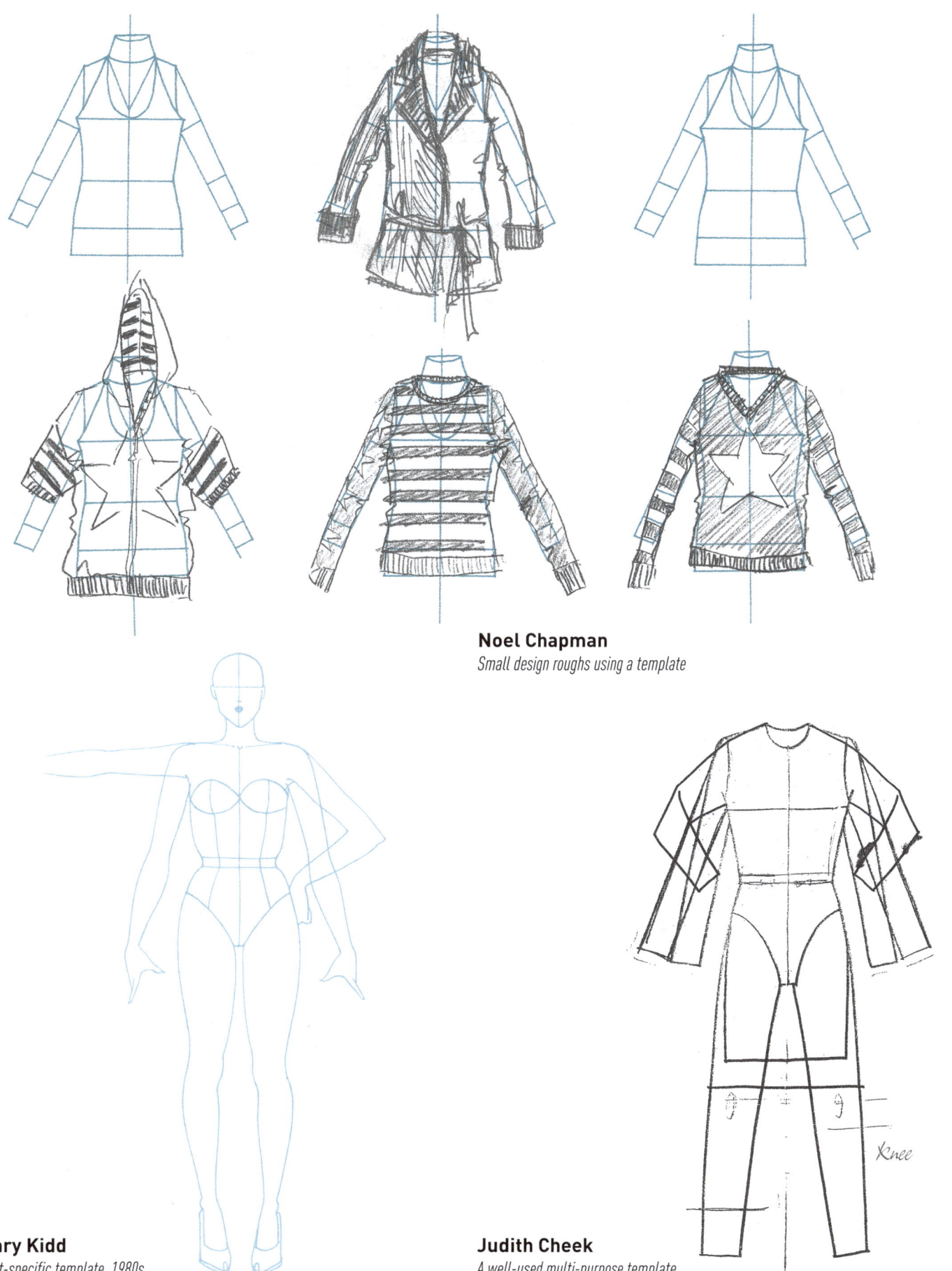

Noel Chapman
Small design roughs using a template

Hilary Kidd
Client-specific template, 1980s

Judith Cheek
A well-used multi-purpose template

Knee

CREATING A TEMPLATE FOR FLATS

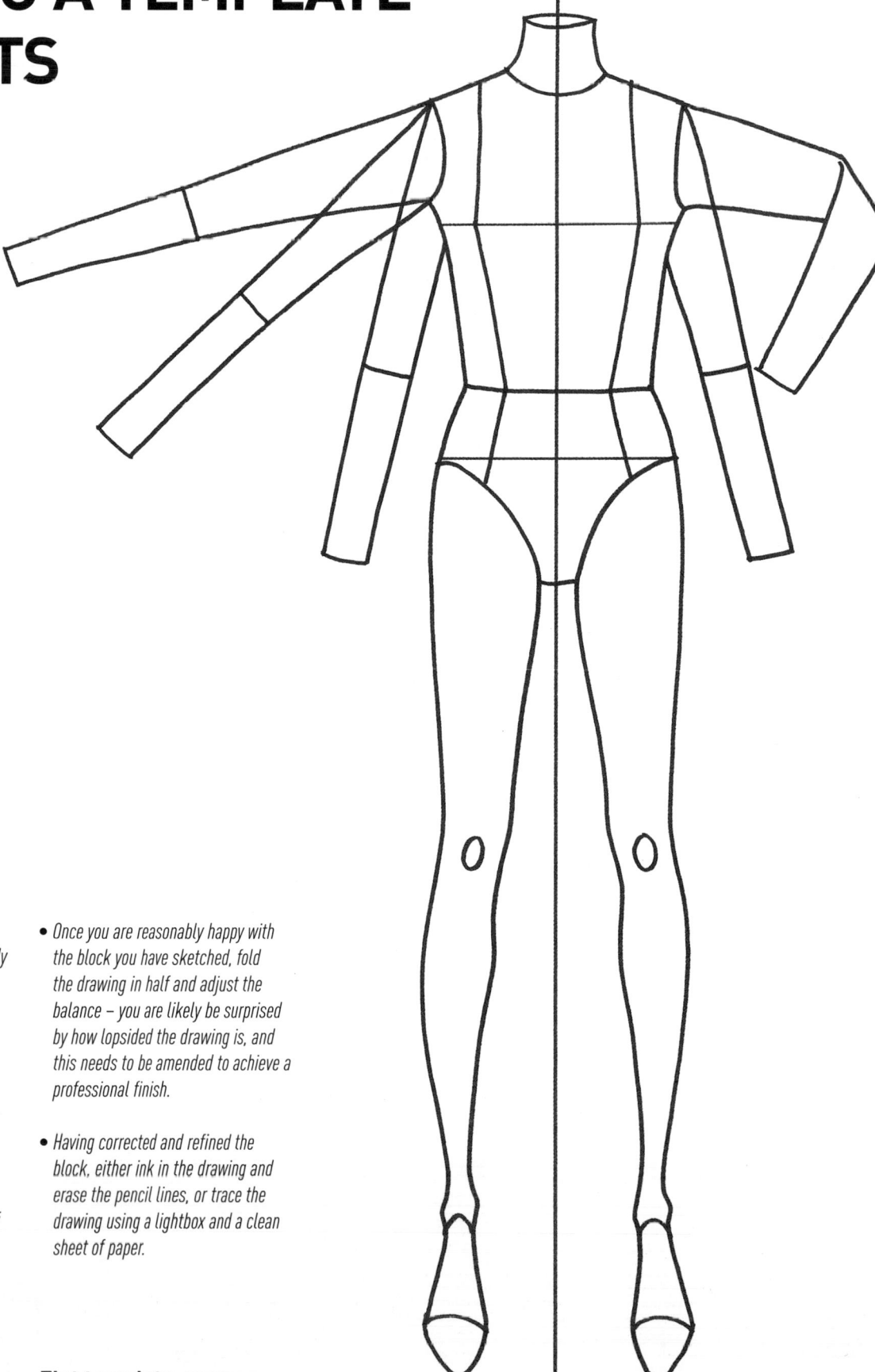

- To create a flat template, first, using pencil, draft an appropriate body 'block'. You should consider the end use of your drawing; the target market for your design is important and designs intended for a younger market will require a different block to that of an older or more classic market. Flat templates do not usually have the exaggerated proportions of a figure template as, especially in the case of technical flats, they are meant to be an accurate representation of a garment.

- Once you are reasonably happy with the block you have sketched, fold the drawing in half and adjust the balance – you are likely be surprised by how lopsided the drawing is, and this needs to be amended to achieve a professional finish.

- Having corrected and refined the block, either ink in the drawing and erase the pencil lines, or trace the drawing using a lightbox and a clean sheet of paper.

Flat template: women

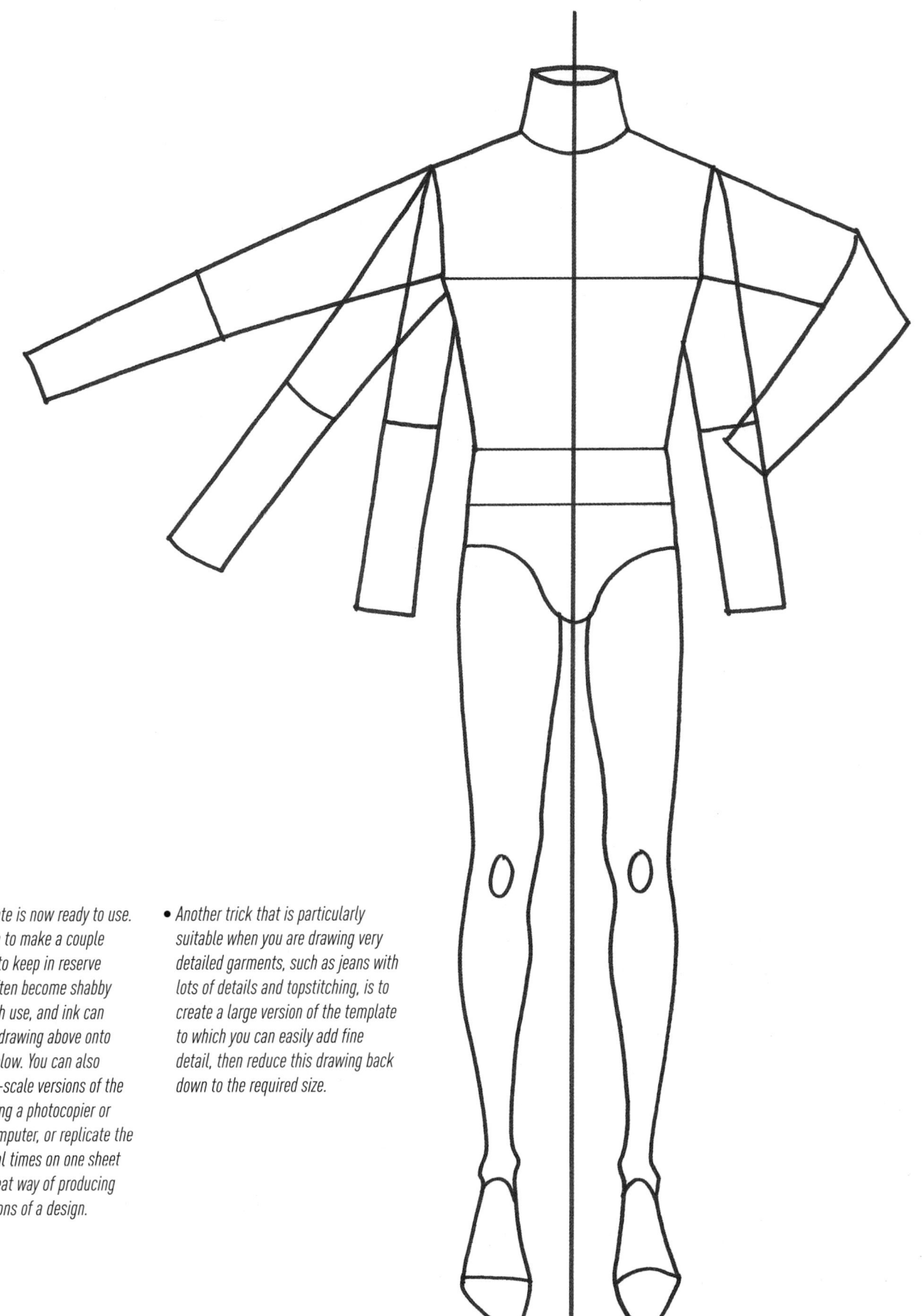

• Your flat template is now ready to use. It is a good idea to make a couple of photocopies to keep in reserve as templates often become shabby and marked with use, and ink can migrate from a drawing above onto the template below. You can also create different-scale versions of the template by using a photocopier or scanner and computer, or replicate the template several times on one sheet of paper as a neat way of producing multiple variations of a design.

• Another trick that is particularly suitable when you are drawing very detailed garments, such as jeans with lots of details and topstitching, is to create a large version of the template to which you can easily add fine detail, then reduce this drawing back down to the required size.

Flat template: men

FLATS: EXAMPLES

You should use a range of pens of different thickness for all types of flats, floats and technical drawings, both for clarity and to avoid monotony. Thicker-line pens will help to define outer edges, flaps and openings, while finer-line pens should be used for top-stitching. Brush pens can help to add a little additional movement and energy to floats and are also helpful when drawing fine and delicate fabrics.

Although primarily a functional drawing, one should not forget that a flat or float still needs to be attractive; it has to look convincing and communicate and sell the design, so keep looking and assessing its appeal and apparent accuracy.

Women's trenchcoat
Outline: *0.8mm fibre-tipped pen*
Seams: *0.3mm fibre-tipped pen*
Pockets and lapels: *0.5mm fibre-tipped pen*
Top-stitching: *0.05mm fibre-tipped pen*

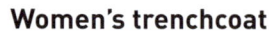

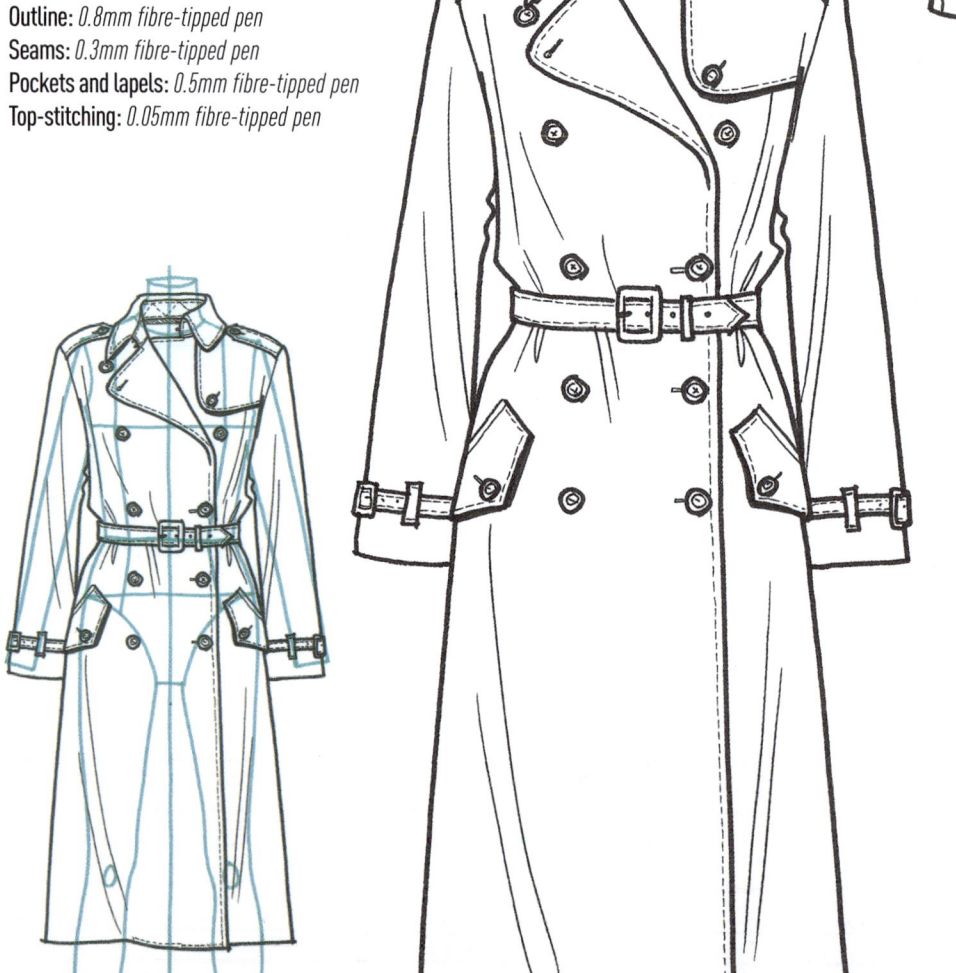

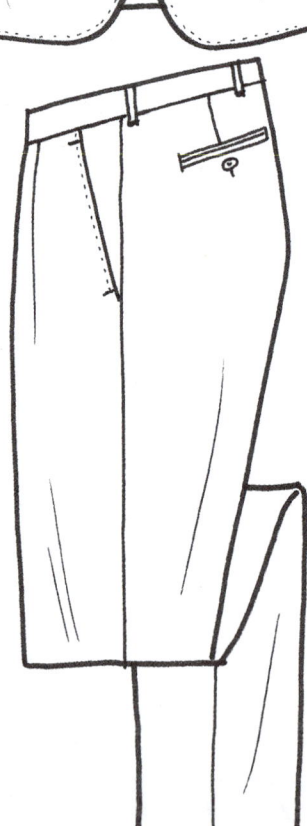

Men's suit
Outline: *0.8mm fibre-tipped pen*
Seams and pockets: *0.5mm and 0.3mm fibre-tipped pen*
Stab-stitching: *0.05mm fibre-tipped pen*

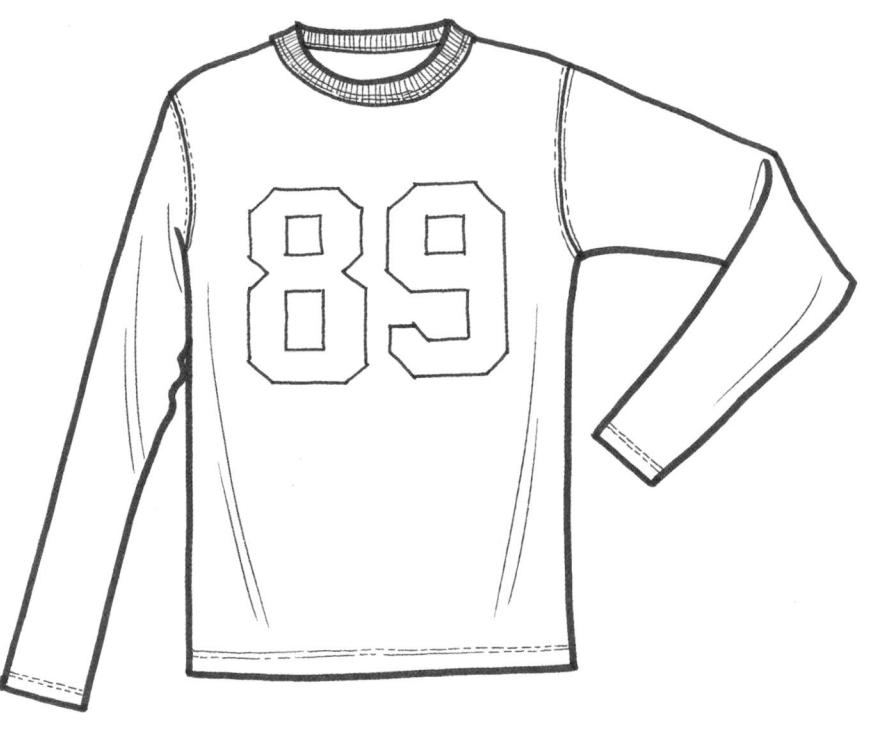

Menswear t-shirt

Outline: *0.8mm fibre-tipped pen*
Seams and neckline: *0.5mm fibre-tipped pen*
Logo/numbers: *0.3mm fibre-tipped pen. An additional tip here is to print out your logo or numbers from a computer, experimenting with scale and font size until you get something that works for the drawing's scale and look.*
Top-stitching: *0.05mm fibre-tipped pen*

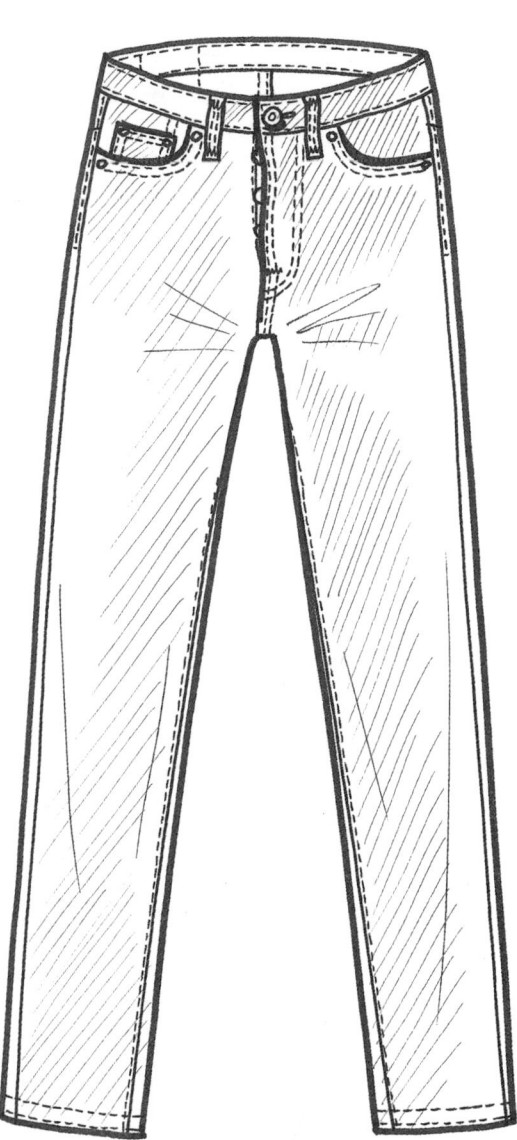

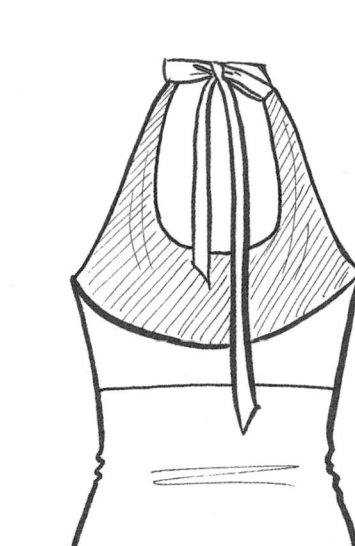

Women's halterneck

Outline: *Brush pen*
Stitching: *0.05mm fibre-tipped pen*
Inside shadow: *0.05mm fibre-tipped pen. For this type of garment, shadow is required to make the drawing easier to read.*

Classic five-pocket jeans

Outline: *0.8mm fibre-tipped pen*
Seams: *0.3mm fibre-tipped pen*
Top-stitching: *0.1mm fibre-tipped pen*
Denim indication (twill): *0.05mm fibre-tipped pen*

TECHNICAL DRAWINGS

The purpose of a technical drawing is to communicate exactly how to make an item of clothing. Whether it is you or a third party who will make the garment, it is down to the designer to analyse and problem-solve at this stage. A technical drawing is a detailed,

disciplined (tight), flat drawing that includes all the essential measurements. It may be necessary to provide additional close-up drawings of particularly complicated details such as pockets and collars that require further explanation.

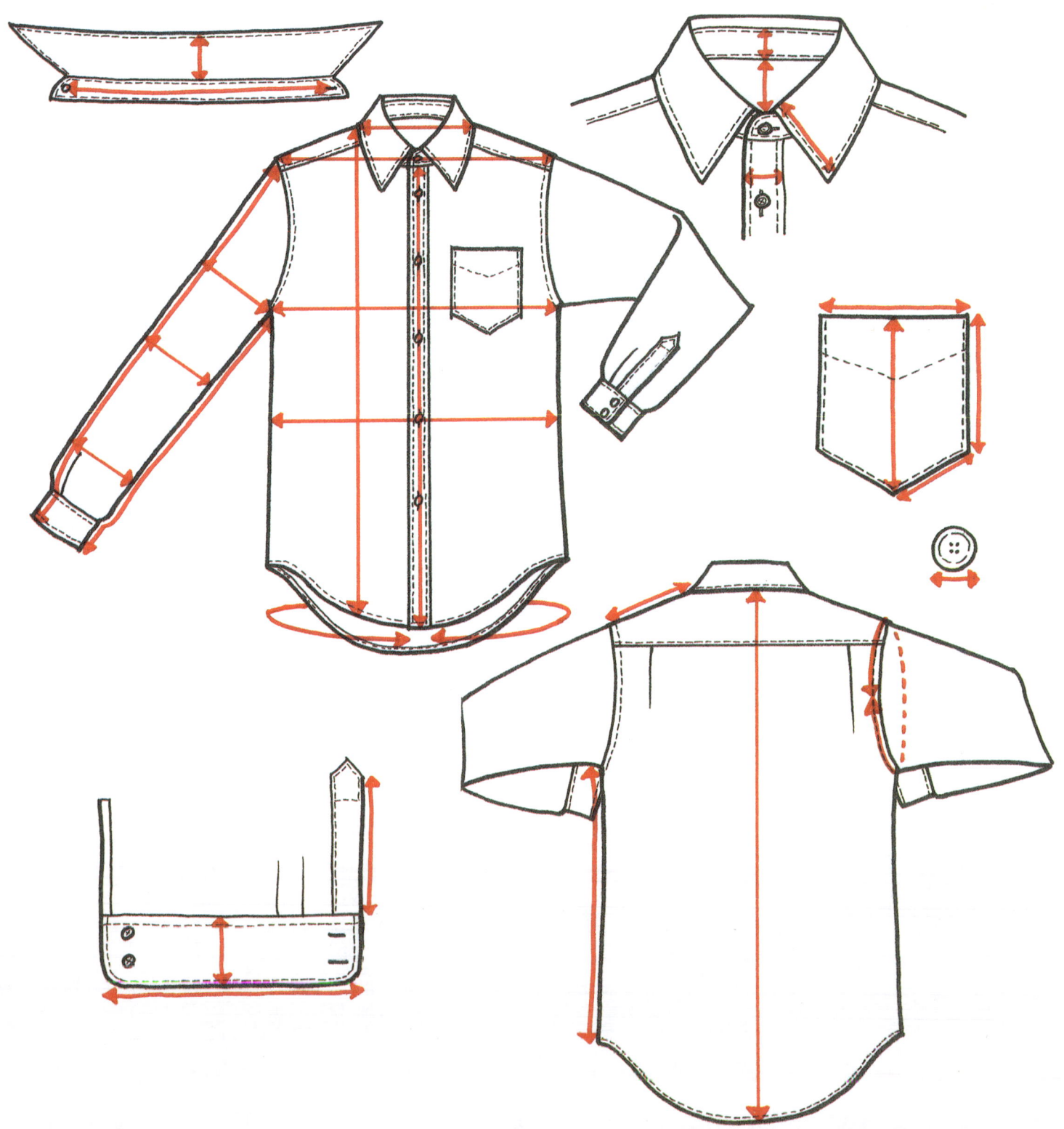

GETTING THE STYLE AND DETAILS RIGHT – MENSWEAR COLLARS AND LAPELS

There are countless styles of shirt collar for both men and women. Influenced by fashion trends, the variations are often simply subtle nuances of line, which over the course of time cause even so-called classics to evolve. However, all originate from half a dozen or so basic designs. These may be subdivided into two main categories: one-piece collars, which are cut from a single piece of fabric and do not have a separate stand; and two-piece collars, which comprise a separate collar and stand.

A collarless top – sometimes called a 'granddad shirt', or a garment with a 'granddad collar' or 'stand collar' – is a shirt that has a collar stand without a collar attached. It originates from the days when formal, starchy collars were made separately and affixed and removed as required, making the shirt easier to launder. It also prolonged the life of the shirt as the collars could be simply replaced when they wore out. The Mao and Nehru collar is a close relative in terms of construction and style.

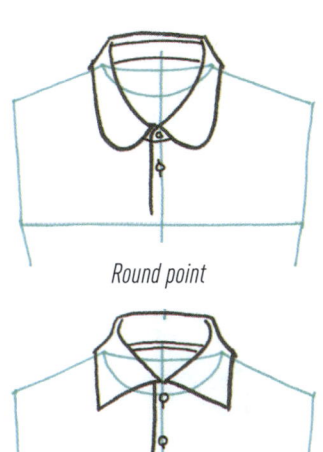

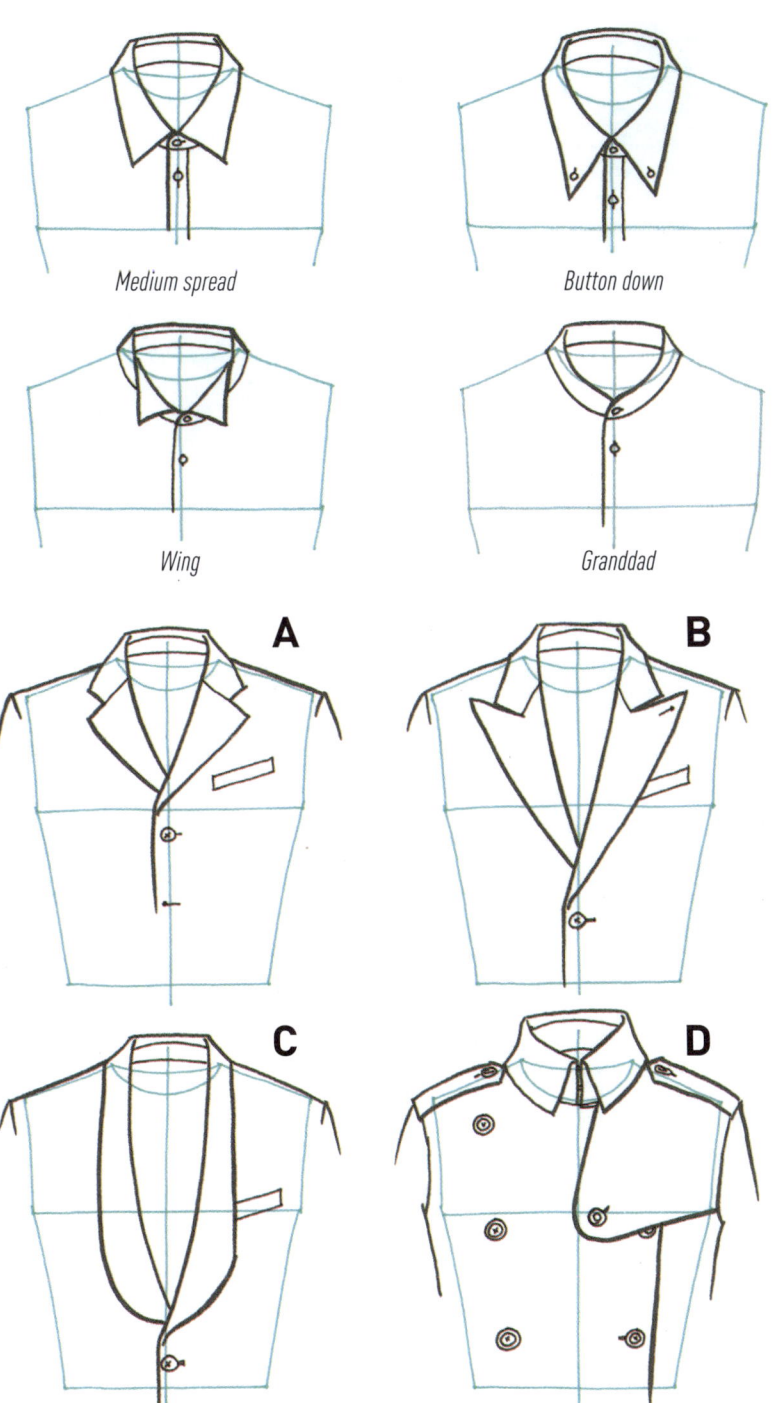

Medium spread

Button down

Round point

Wing

Granddad

Polo

A

B

C

D

There are also endless varieties of jacket collars, lapels or revers, as well as many crossover styles. Cut almost always in at least two parts, collars and lapels can be complex and require close investigation in order that they can be constructed and drawn correctly.

A *Simple notched lapel*
B *Peaked lapel or rever*
C *Shawl collar*
D *Two-part or stand collar, with double-breasted closure and storm flap. (The latter's name refers to a style with military origins that also includes epaulettes.)*

GETTING THE STYLE AND DETAILS RIGHT – WOMENSWEAR NECKLINES, DRAPERY AND SKIRTS

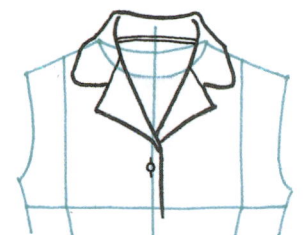

Pyjama collar

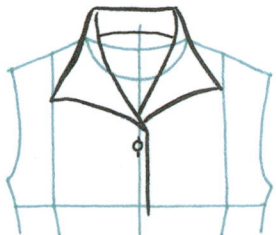

Wing collar (frequently bias cut)

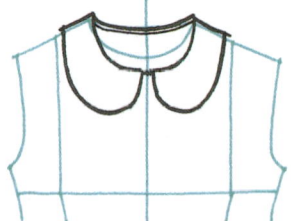

Peter Pan or flat collar

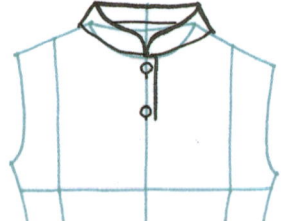

Stand, Mao or Nehru collar

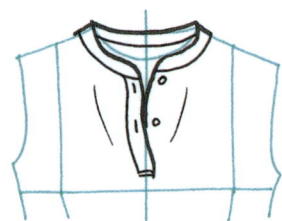

Granddad collar or, when combined with a short placket like this, often known as a Henley style

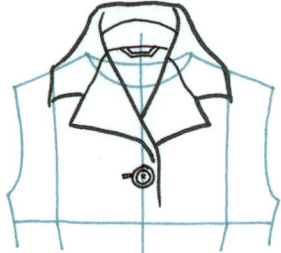

Utility collar – one of the simplest rever collars

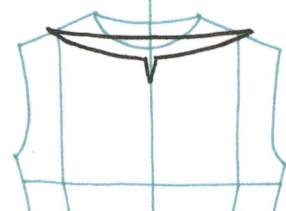

Slash neckline with notch

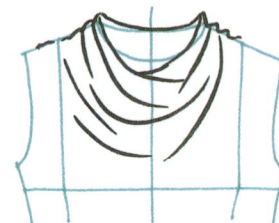

Draped cowl neckline

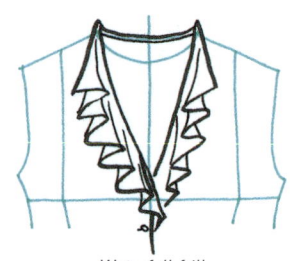

Waterfall frill

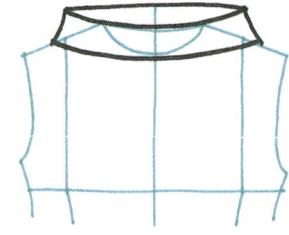

Bateau or boat neckline

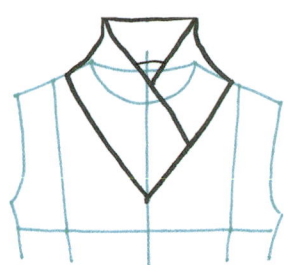

Crossover V inset

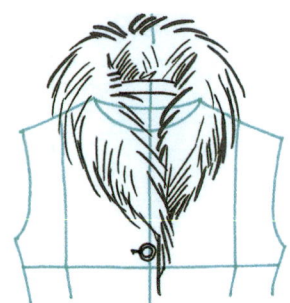

Fur collar

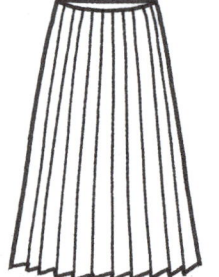

Knife pleats

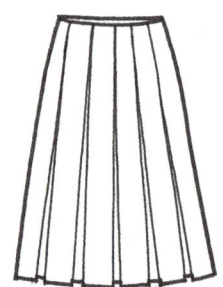

Box pleats

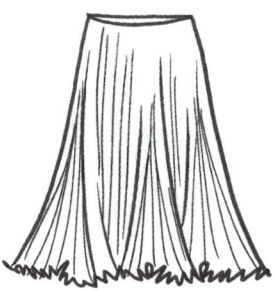

Sunray pleats

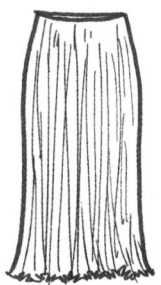

Crystal pleats

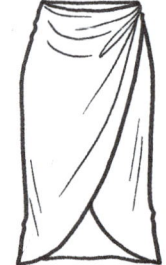

Draped wrap

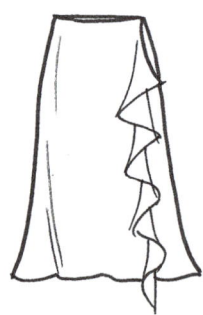

Waterfall frill

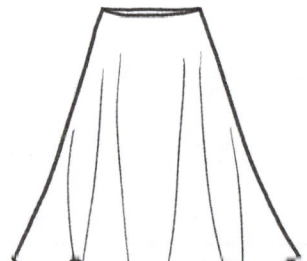

Circular

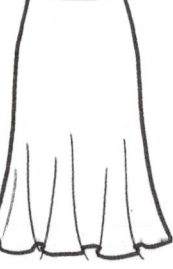

Bias

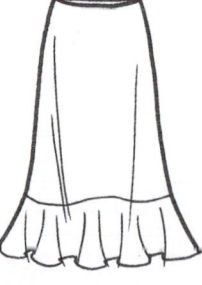

Bias frill

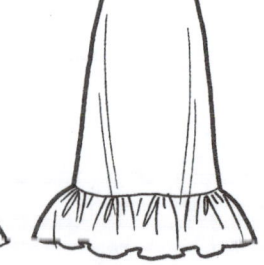

Gathered frill

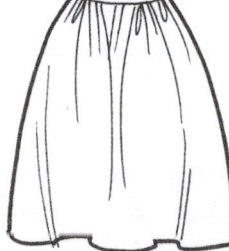

Dirndl

Bias handkerchief

GETTING THE STYLE AND DETAILS RIGHT – POCKETS

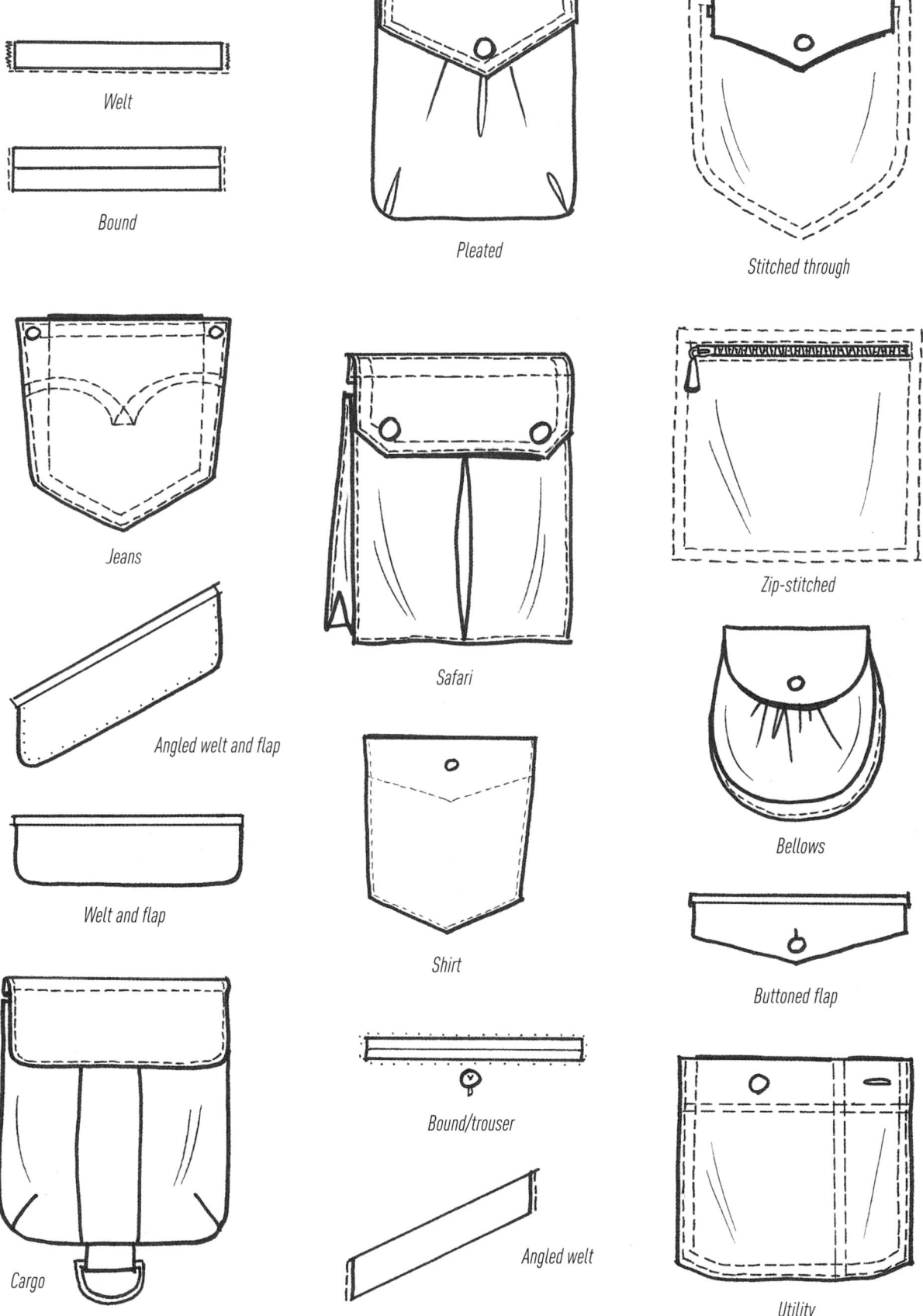

Welt

Bound

Pleated

Stitched through

Jeans

Safari

Zip-stitched

Angled welt and flap

Welt and flap

Shirt

Bellows

Buttoned flap

Cargo

Bound/trouser

Angled welt

Utility

GETTING THE STYLE AND DETAILS RIGHT – STITCHING AND DETAILS

Here we show you some examples of different stitches and finishes, but you are always going to encounter new and different types. The trick is to experiment and to develop your own shorthand versions as you come across different types.

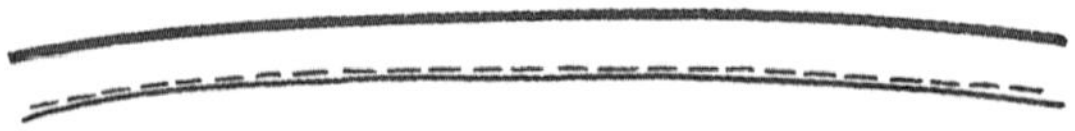

Bound edge

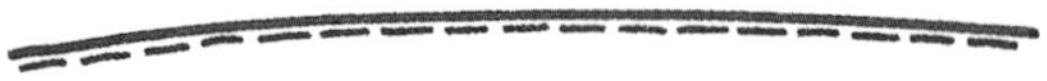

Single

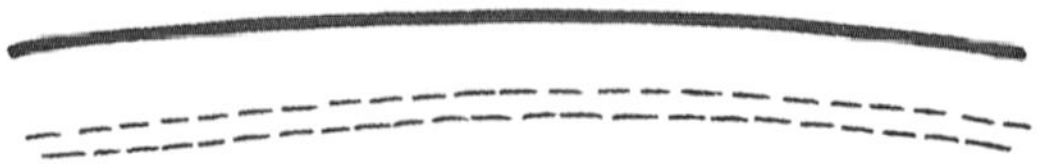

Jersey twin needle

Twin needle

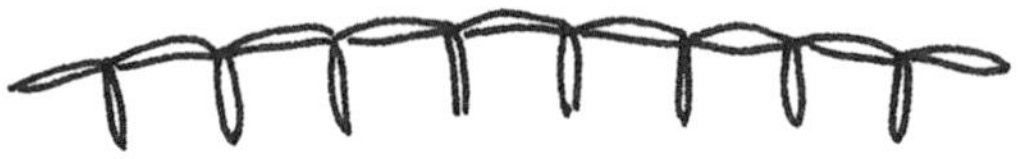

Blanket stitch

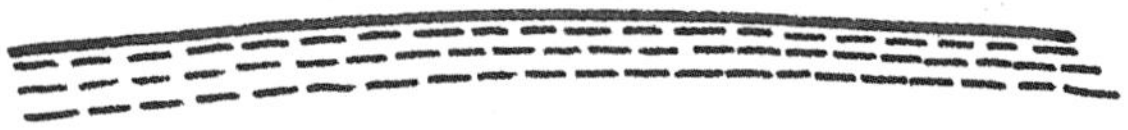

Triple top stitch

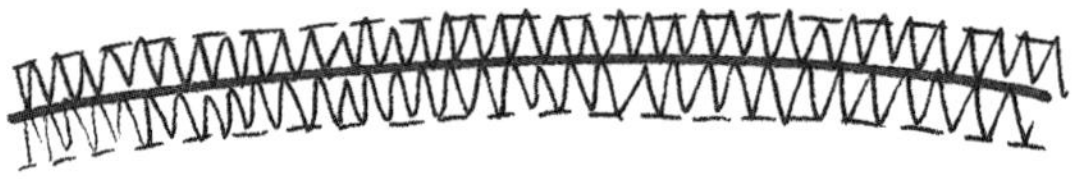

Flat lock/cover seam

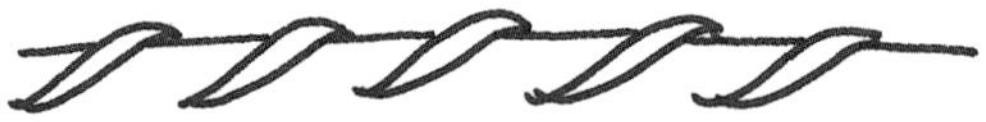

Whip stitch

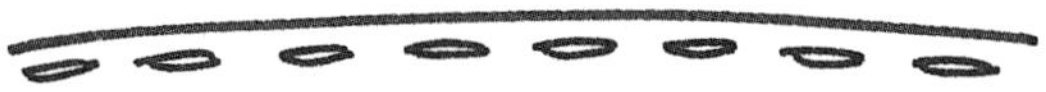

Small saddle

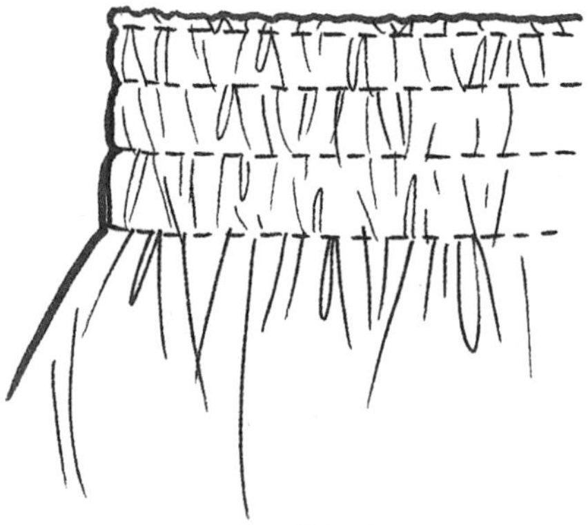

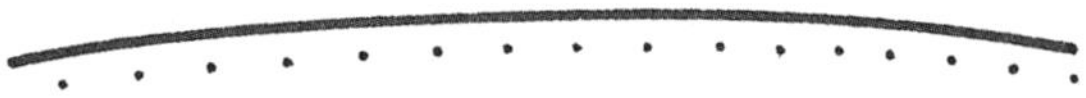

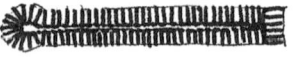

Stabstitch

Shirred

Keyhole buttonhole

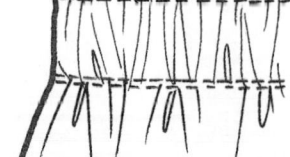

Wide elastic-cased waistband

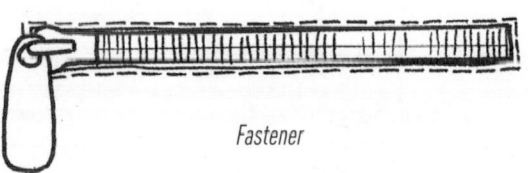

Fastener

KNITWEAR DETAILS

Drawing knitwear has its own particular set of problems and considerations; not only are you drawing the style and detail of the garment, but also the texture, pattern and structure of the knit itself. Again, knowing a little about knitting will inform your ability to draw it. Understanding the characteristics that give the garment its identity, such as a rib, a cable or a jacquard, is key to successfully rendering the idea.

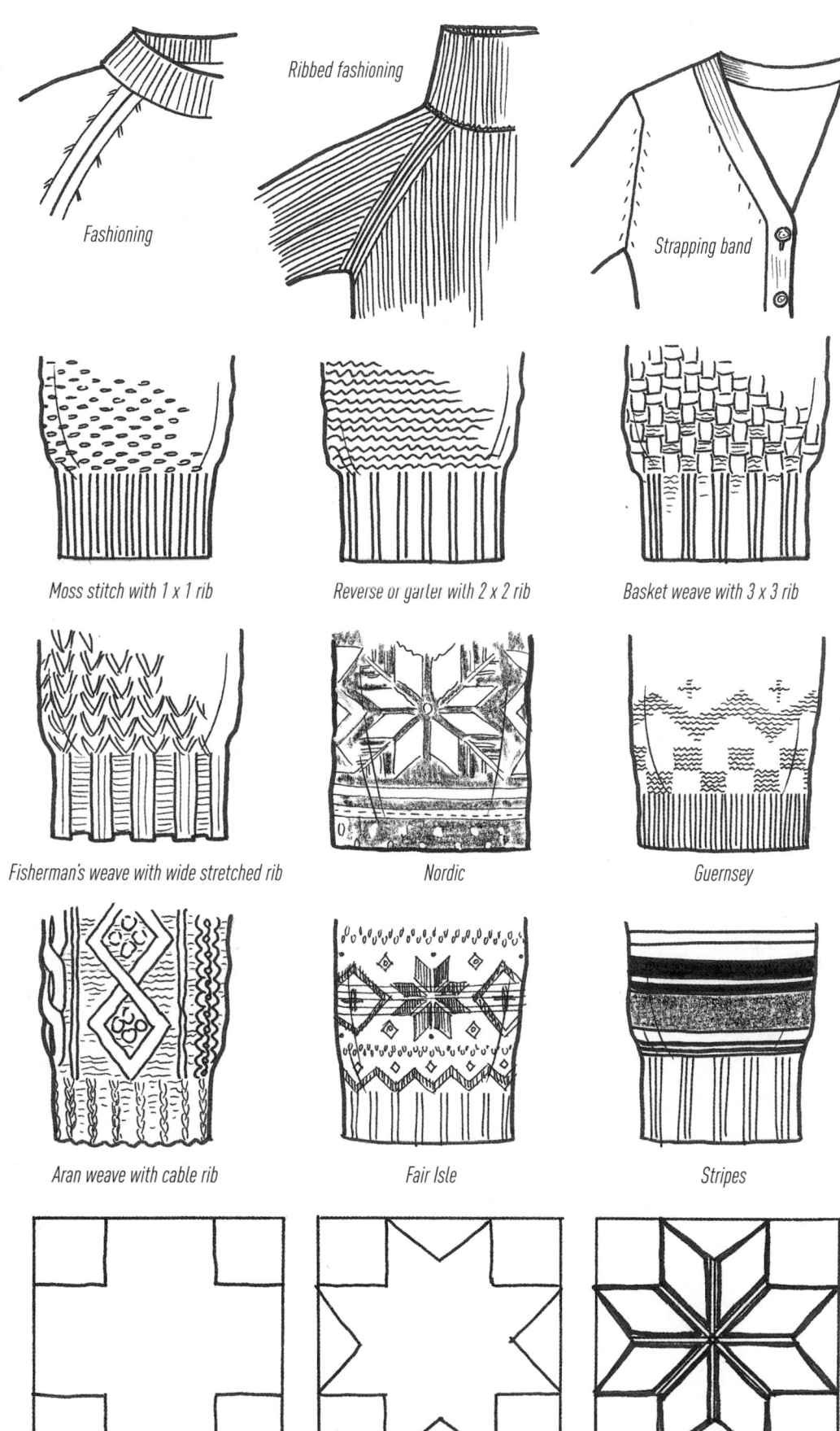

Fashioning

Ribbed fashioning

Strapping band

Moss stitch with 1 x 1 rib

Reverse or garter with 2 x 2 rib

Basket weave with 3 x 3 rib

Fisherman's weave with wide stretched rib

Nordic

Guernsey

Aran weave with cable rib

Fair Isle

Stripes

3 stages cable

3 stages snowflake

DRAWING FABRICS ON FLATS AND FLOATS

A flat drawing, particularly if it is for production purposes and to be accompanied by supporting specifications, will often for clarity consist of a simple outline, without added detail or any indication of the type of fabric used. However, if flats are intended to be more illustrative or are for designing purposes you may choose or need to illustrate fabrics. The manner in which you depict pattern on a flat needs careful evaluation and, as experience will show, it can be too much – too visually confusing and flattening – to fill in all the garment areas with colour. Practice will help you decide the right level of illustration for each job.

There are various ways of showing the fabrics:

- Include a swatch of the actual fabric or a drawn swatch.
- Draw a 'focus circle' showing an enlarged area.
- Draw a suggestion of the fabric in a limited area that fades out to white or a background colour.

Men's raincoat
Outline: *Brush pen*
Seams and pockets: *0.5mm fibre-tipped pen*
Top-stitching: *0.1mm fibre-tipped pen*
Lining: *Chinagraph pencil*
Colour: *Marker pen and chinagraph pencil*

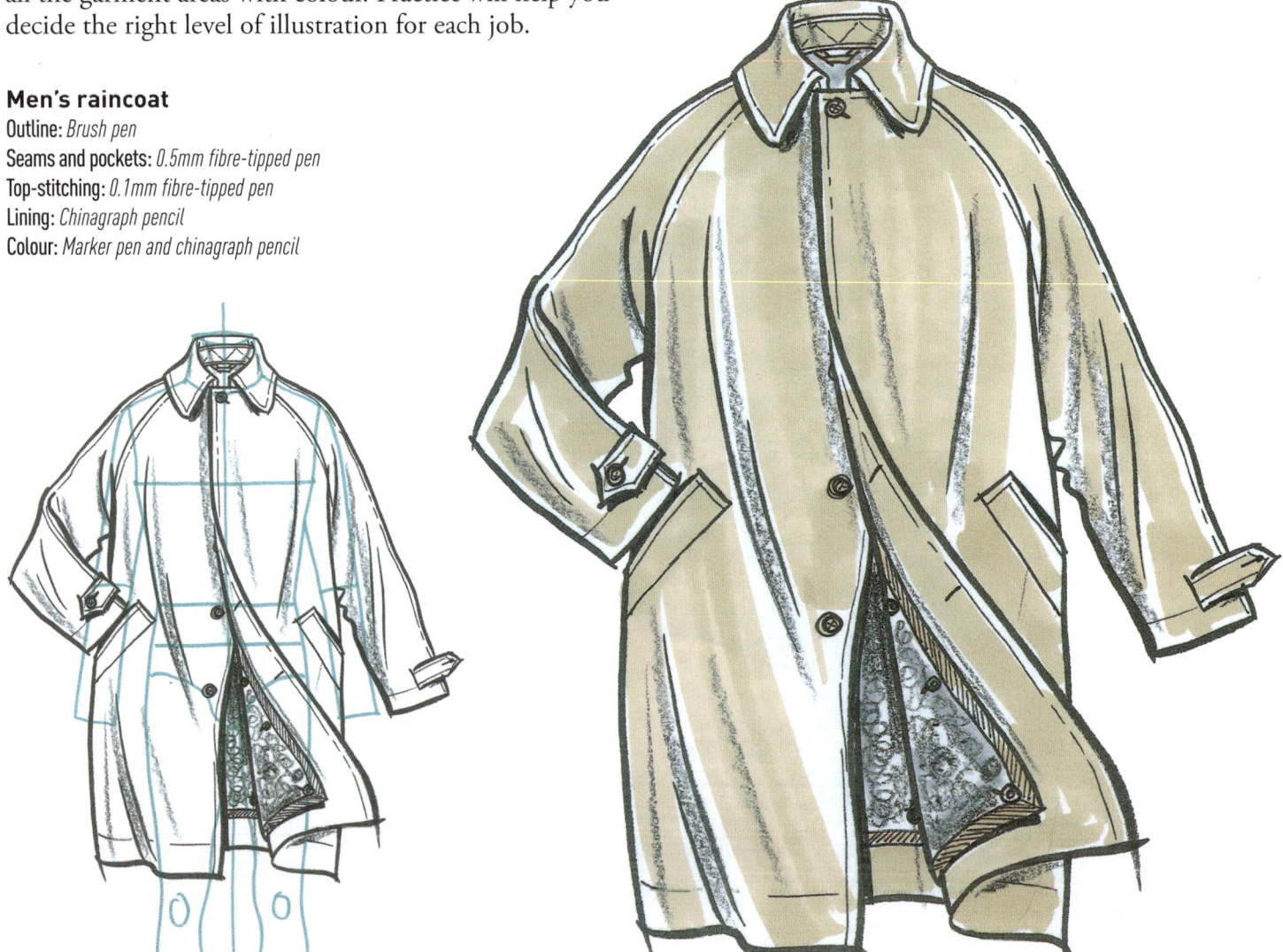

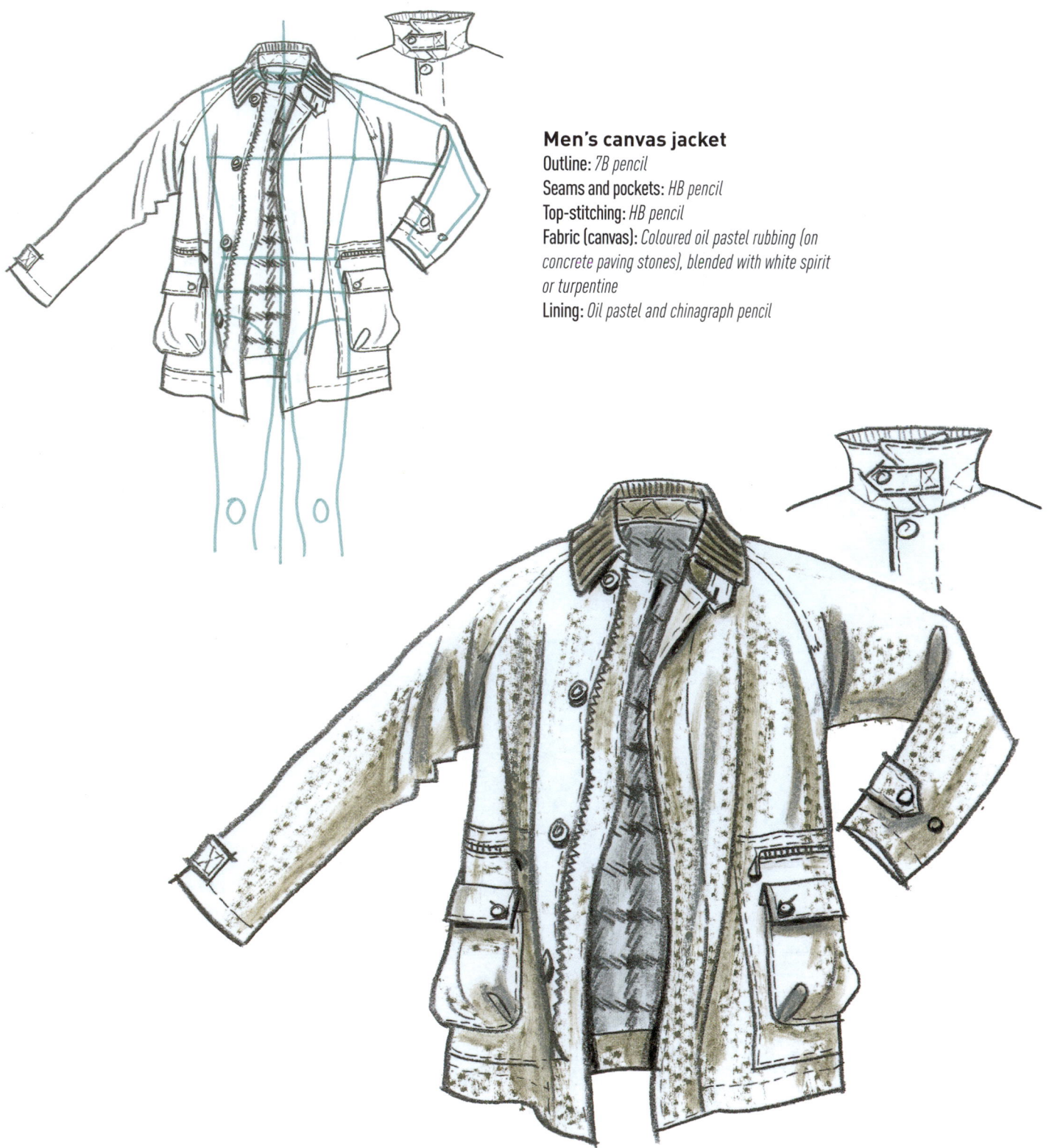

Men's canvas jacket

Outline: *7B pencil*
Seams and pockets: *HB pencil*
Top-stitching: *HB pencil*
Fabric (canvas): *Coloured oil pastel rubbing (on concrete paving stones), blended with white spirit or turpentine*
Lining: *Oil pastel and chinagraph pencil*

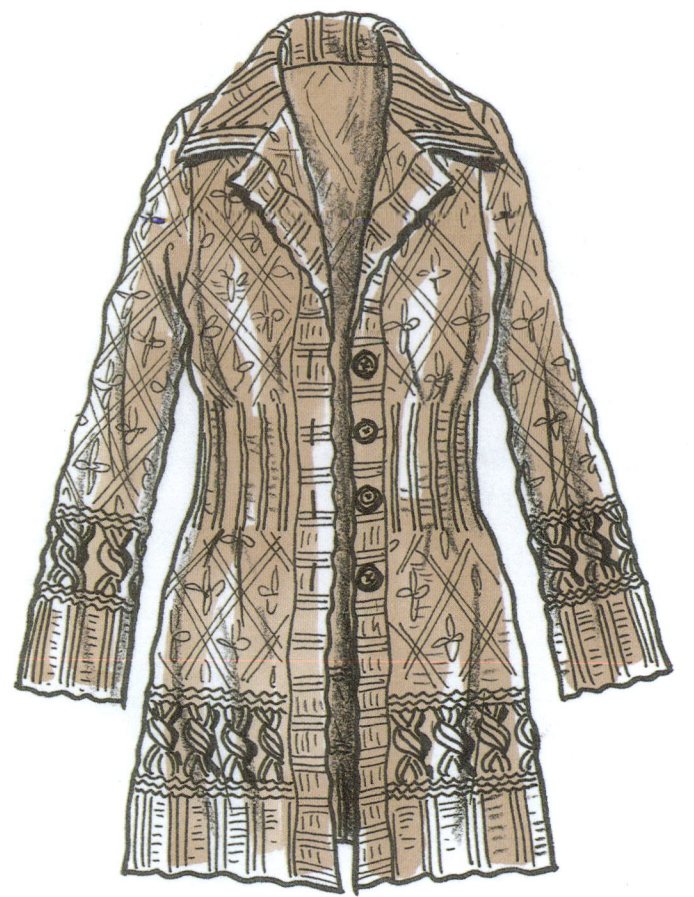

Women's textured-knit cardigan
Outline: *Brush pen*
Stitchwork: *0.3mm fibre-tipped pen*
Stitchwork: *0.1mm fibre-tipped pen and chinagraph pencil for texture and shading*
Colour: *Marker pen*

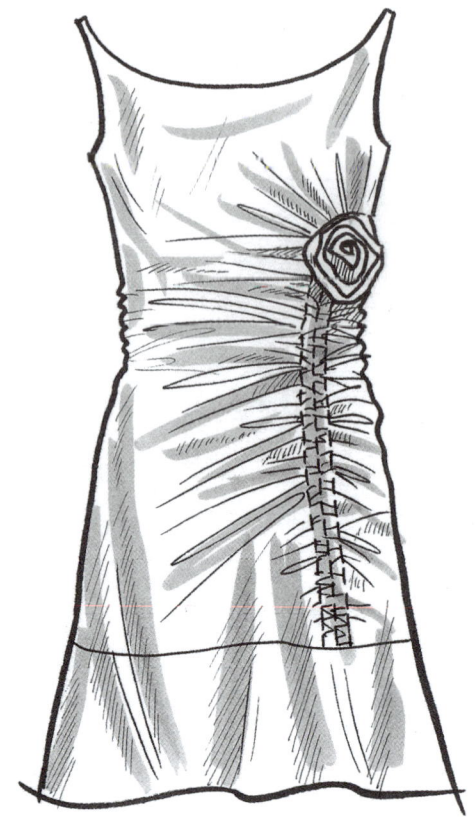

Dress
Outline: *Brush pen*
Gathers: *0.3mm fibre-tipped pen*
Texture and shading: *0.05mm fibre-tipped pen*

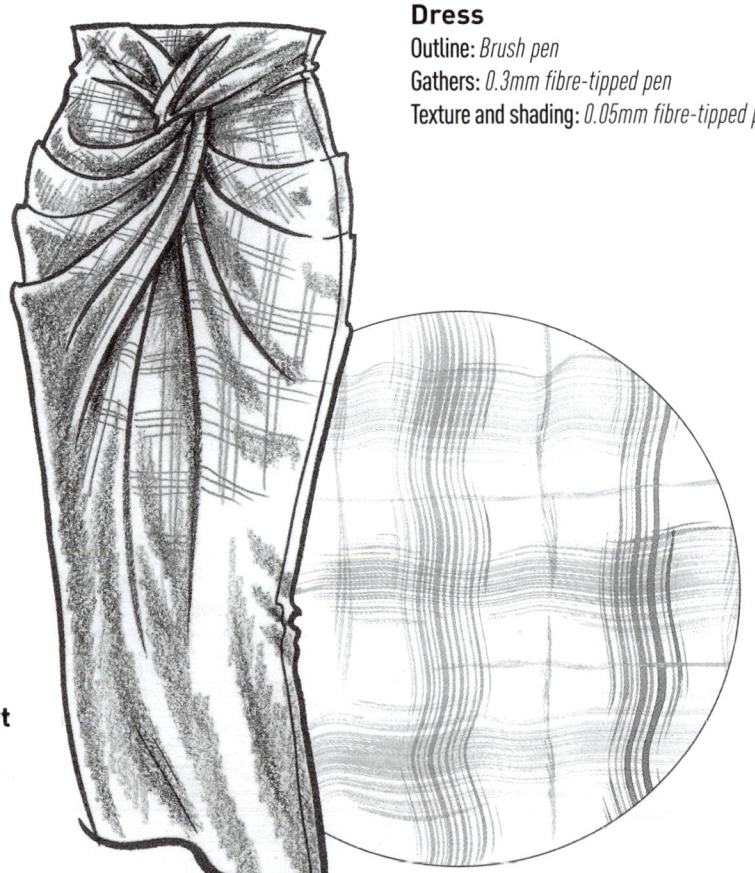

Vintage skirt
Outline: *Brush pen*
Shading: *7B pencil*

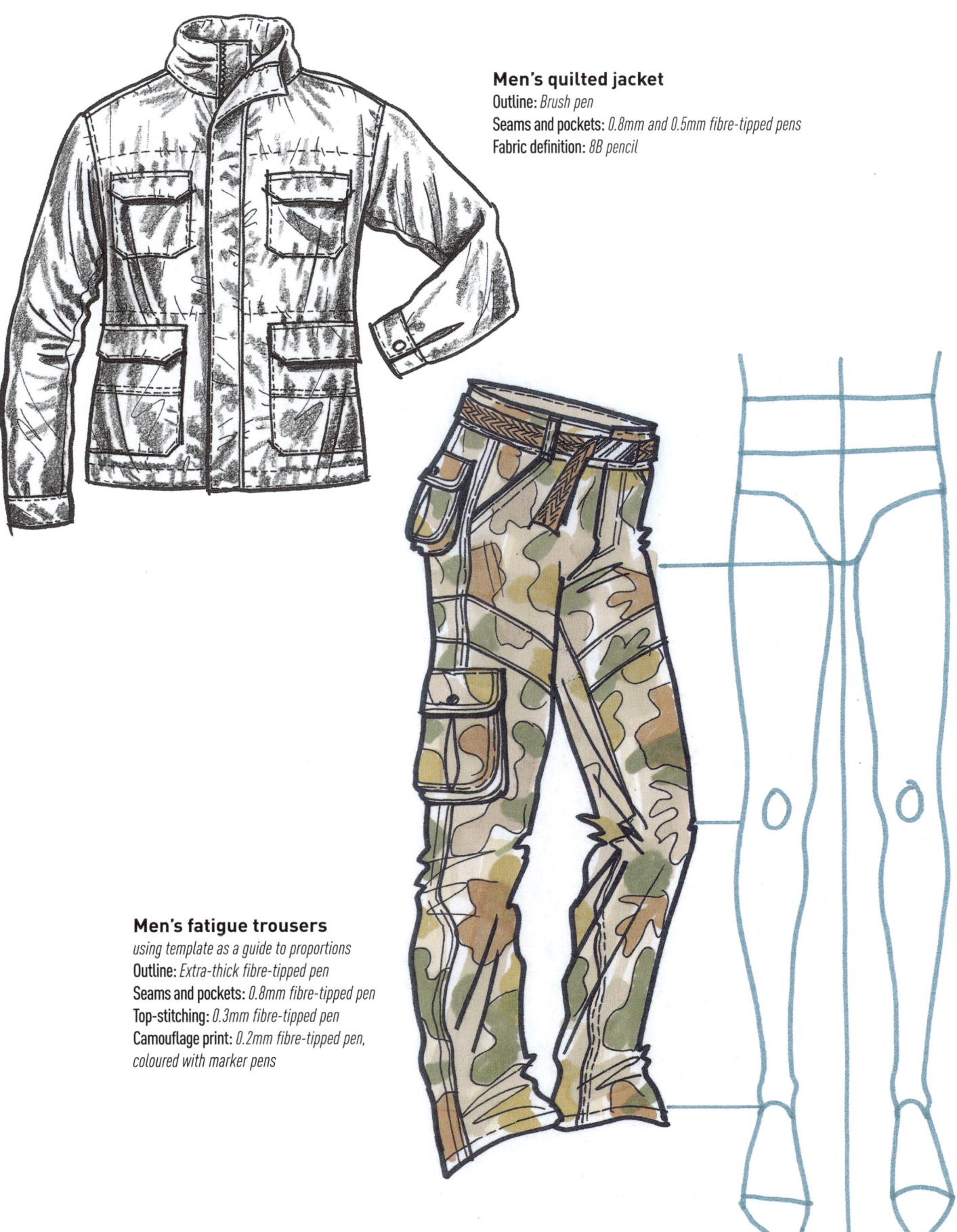

Men's quilted jacket

Outline: *Brush pen*
Seams and pockets: *0.8mm and 0.5mm fibre-tipped pens*
Fabric definition: *8B pencil*

Men's fatigue trousers

using template as a guide to proportions
Outline: *Extra-thick fibre-tipped pen*
Seams and pockets: *0.8mm fibre-tipped pen*
Top-stitching: *0.3mm fibre-tipped pen*
Camouflage print: *0.2mm fibre-tipped pen, coloured with marker pens*

CAD: COMPUTER AIDED DESIGN

In the industry today, flats are increasingly created using a computer. Many designers say it takes longer than hand-drawing, but as long as the illustrator really understands the construction of the garments the results are slicker and generally more accurate and readable. You can certainly make a beautiful job of rendering details such as top-stitching, flat-locking and cover-seaming, so the jeanswear and active sportswear sections of the industry have embraced the facility. However, few designers find designing on a computer spontaneous or flexible enough when coming up with initial concepts, and this is why hand-drawn flats are still so useful.

Illustrator Martina Farrow has had a successful career as a freehand fashion illustrator and has gradually honed her computer illustration skills, from the earlier experiments with cruder programmes to the most sophisticated work using the latest developments. Although most of Martina's work is purely illustrative, her advice on learning to draw and illustrate using computers is equally applicable when drawing flats. Here she talks us through her approach:

To illustrate on an Apple Mac using Adobe Illustrator CS range or a similar programme, it's a good idea first to play with each command in the various toolboxes and settings (as you would when trying out any other materials) to get a feel for their scope, and how you may like to use them.

A logical starting point is establishing the size of the illustration. Open a new document and select its size (e.g. A4) and orientation (landscape or portrait), or select 'Custom' and enter your own artboard's dimensions in the boxes. For commercial work, it is worth bearing in mind the final file size; a bigger artboard just means a bigger file size, which can be more unwieldy to store and email. This does not apply so much for one-off illustrations.

Next, decide if you want to use one of your own digital photographic files as reference and, if so, import that to the new document, and resize it accordingly. I generally then lock the image in place, and begin drawing over it freehand using the pencil tool or use the pen tool to accurately trace the outline. Alternatively you can just begin drawing in the programme as you would if drawing freehand on paper. A Wacom tablet and stylus are often easier to use for drawing than a mouse, so it may be worth considering purchasing these if you intend to do a lot of CAD.

Once the line drawing is complete, delete the reference picture if you have one and have a look at the lines created. These can now be adjusted and edited at their anchor points to give the desired curves and so forth, using the Direct Selection Tool, or similar.

If the finished piece is to be a line-only artwork, there are many different options for line thickness and texture. Experiment using the Stroke menu and Brush libraries. A huge range of gorgeous line thicknesses and effects can be found, including chalk, soft pencil, pastel, ink, watercolour and spatter.

Colour Swatch libraries provide almost every colour range in existence! Stroke and Fill menus generate whatever colour/line combinations you like. Fill outlines with plain colour only, generate your own patterns or delve into the Pattern libraries in the toolbox.

If a specified Pantone colour reference is required, select from the appropriate Swatch library. You can also save your own selections to a personal colour library.

Other useful menus to try are Transparency and Gradient. The Transparency option includes several settings that vary how colour can be applied. For example, Multiply can be used to overlay colours in the same way that they would appear if they were overlapping layers of coloured film.

The Gradient menu is a great device for creating a soft melding of two or more colours. All these effects can be deployed in CMYK or RGB colour or Grayscale.

The decision to add type of any font, in any colour, outline or pattern is easy; simply use the Type tool. There are also many kinds of grids and line shapes contained in the AI toolbox.

Here are some examples of flats drawn using a computer, from a teaching aid by Lynnette Cook.

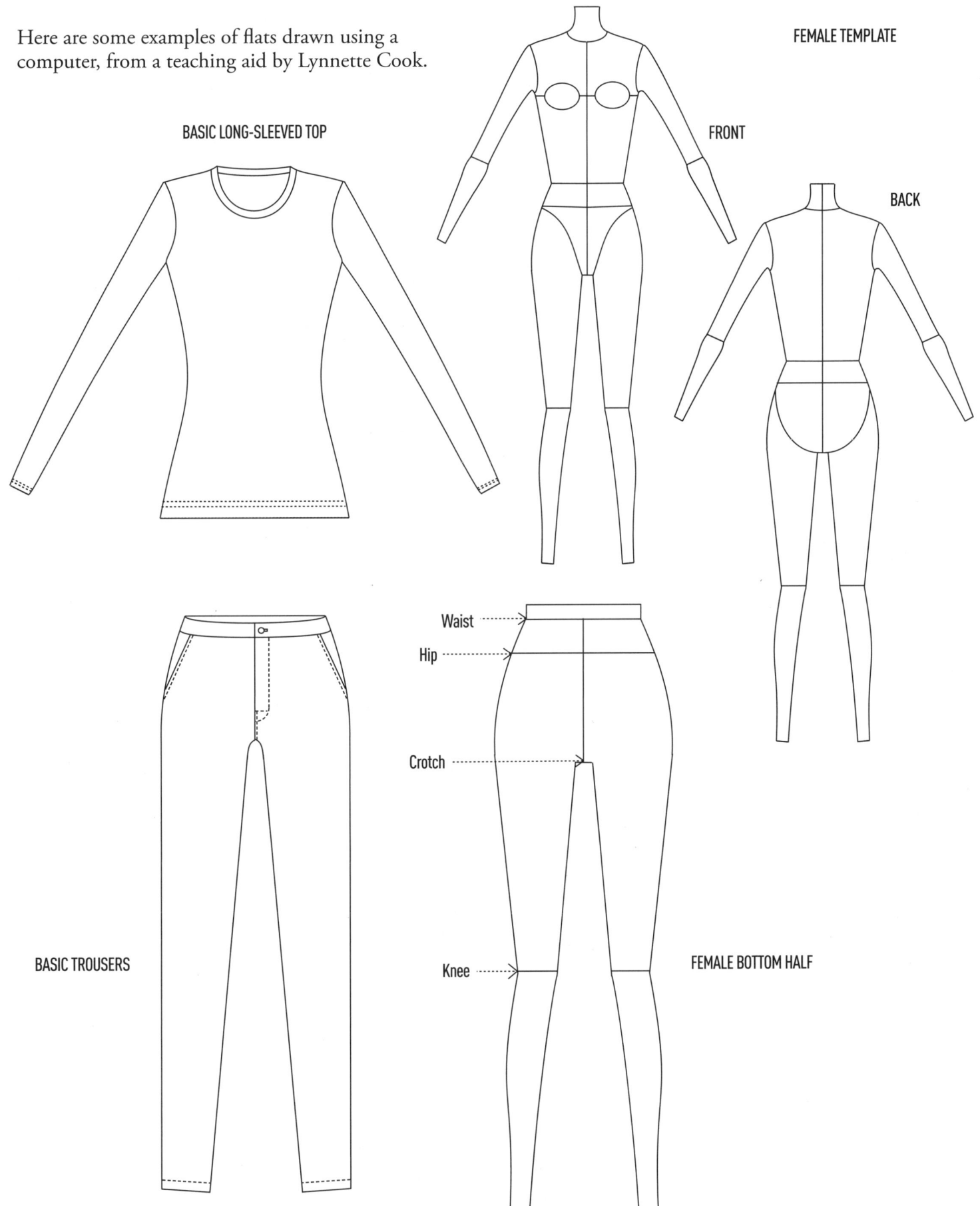

BASIC LONG-SLEEVED TOP

FEMALE TEMPLATE

FRONT

BACK

BASIC TROUSERS

Waist

Hip

Crotch

Knee

FEMALE BOTTOM HALF

TECHNICAL OR SPECIFICATION FLATS USING CAD

These drawings were created in order to communicate the design to a manufacturer. The designs have to stand up on their own, with little more than measurements to further explain them.

It is evident that the designer had to thoroughly understand and anticipate the necessary construction of the design in order to communicate the intentions clearly and accurately.

Mariella Ertl
for ONLY Autumn/Winter 2012/13
Using ILLUSTRATOR

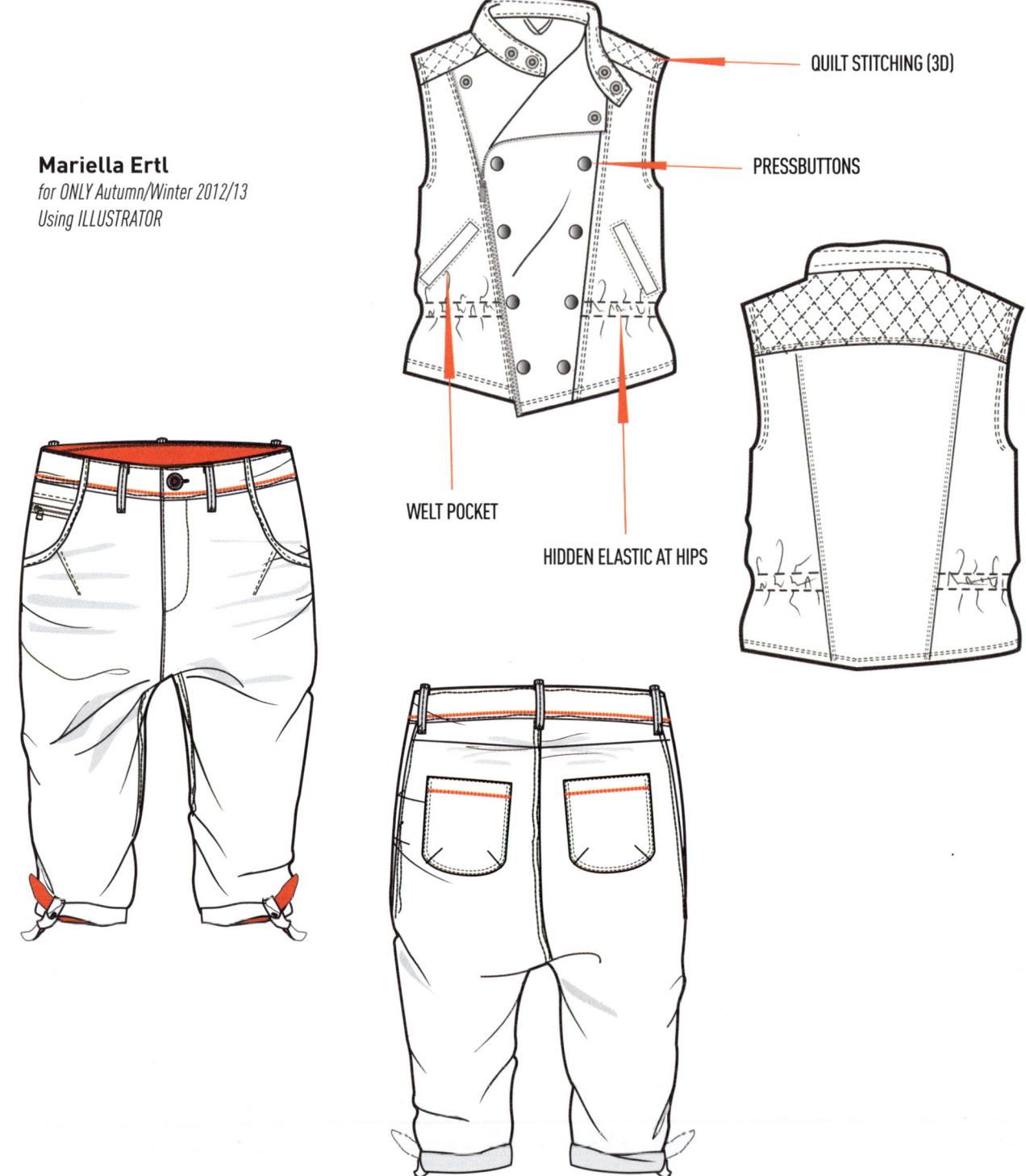

QUILT STITCHING (3D)

PRESSBUTTONS

WELT POCKET

HIDDEN ELASTIC AT HIPS

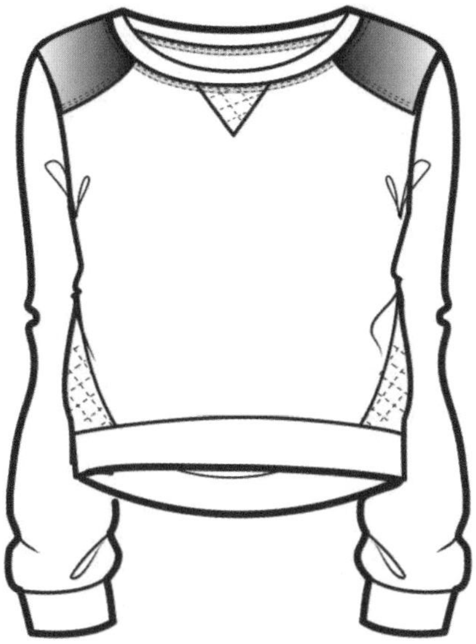

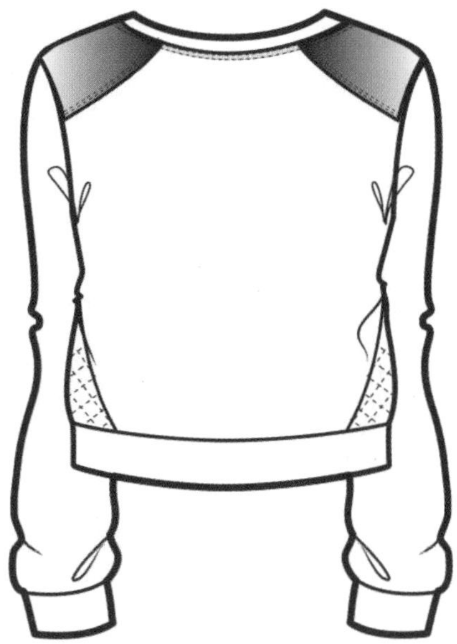

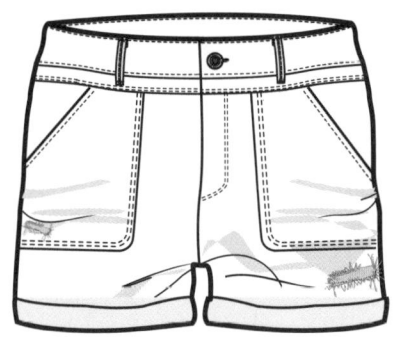

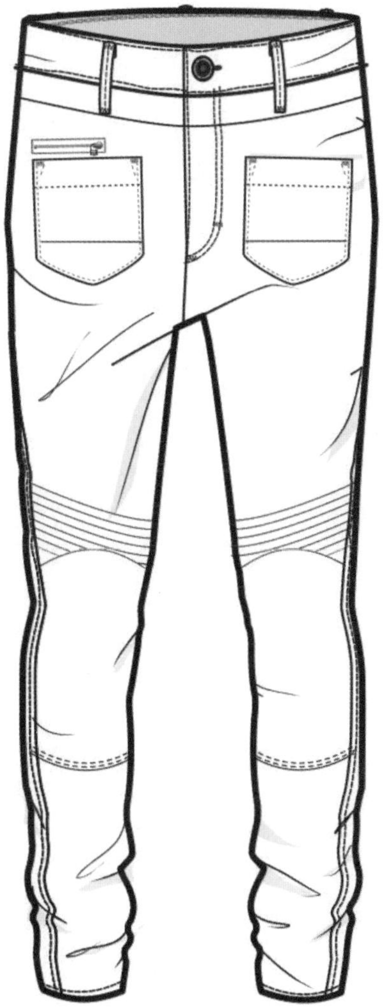

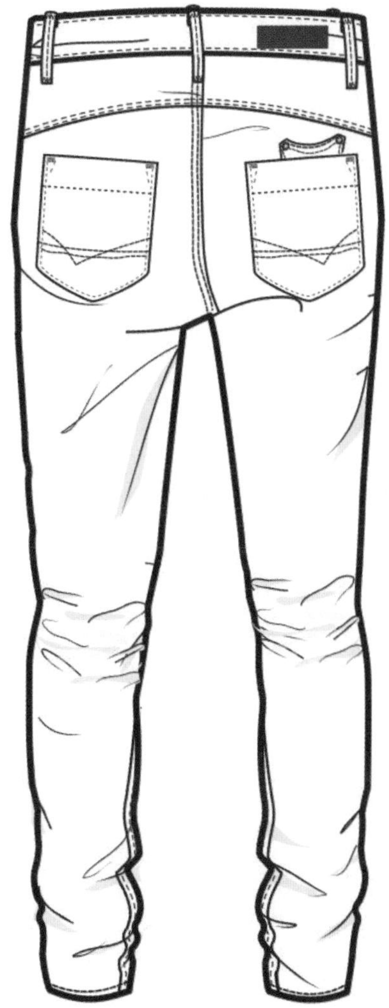

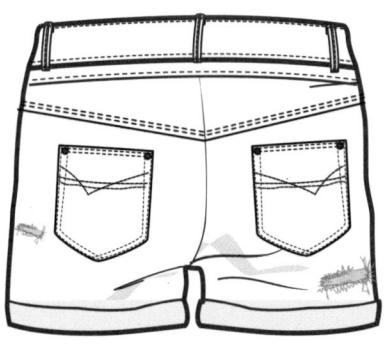

Mariella Ertl
for ONLY Autumn/Winter 2012/13
Using ILLUSTRATOR

COMBINING FIGURES AND FLATS

Using the template from page 43 (J), you can create an outfit by drawing a combination of garments on a figure, perhaps adding colour and rendering the fabric to make them visually appealing. For clarity, these can be accompanied by an individual flat of each garment.

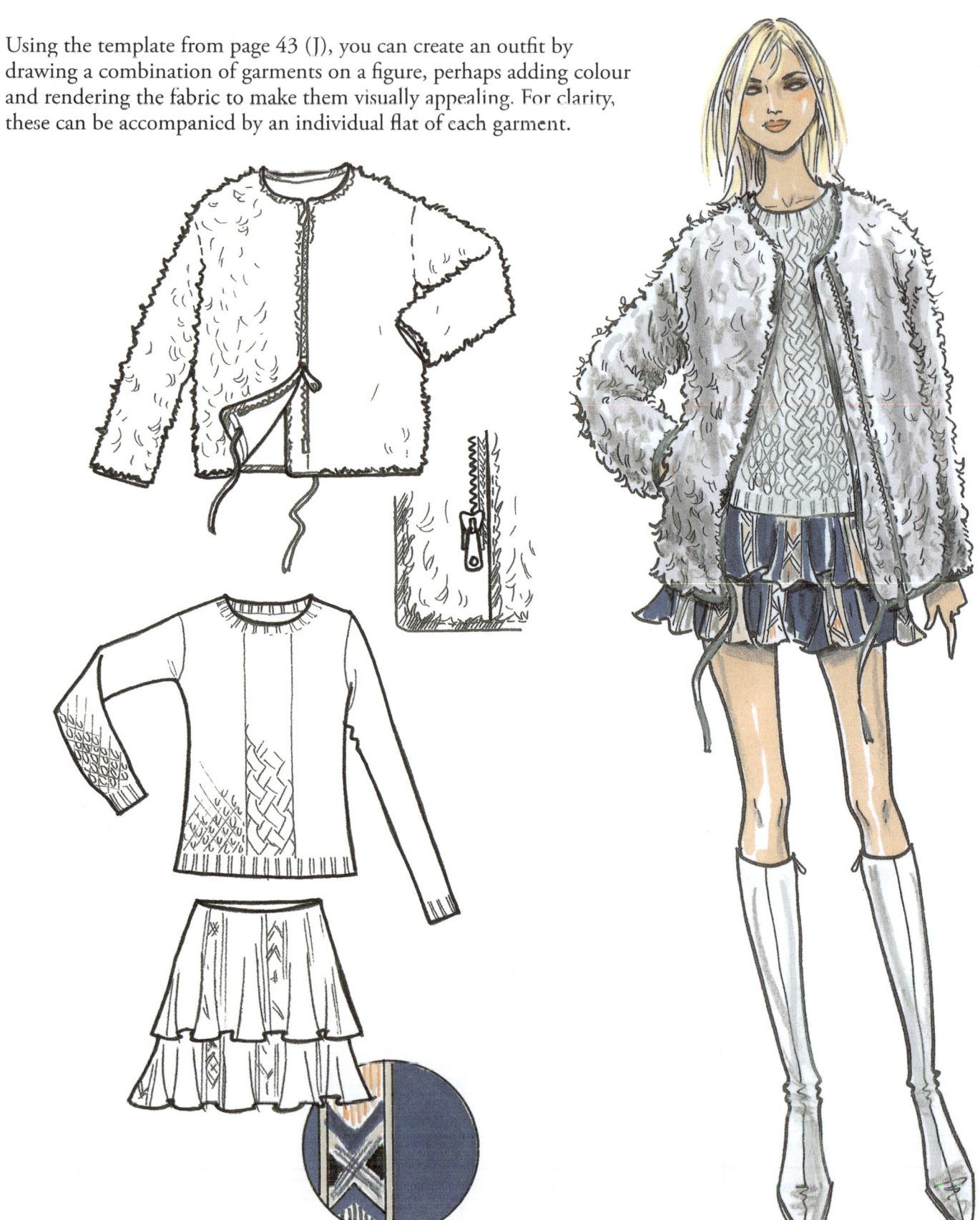

ILLUSTRATIVE FLOATS

This accessorized, finished outfit is based on the template on page 32 and is drawn as a float using soft pencil (8 or 9B). This is the style of illustration that you may expect to see in magazine features about 'must-have looks'.

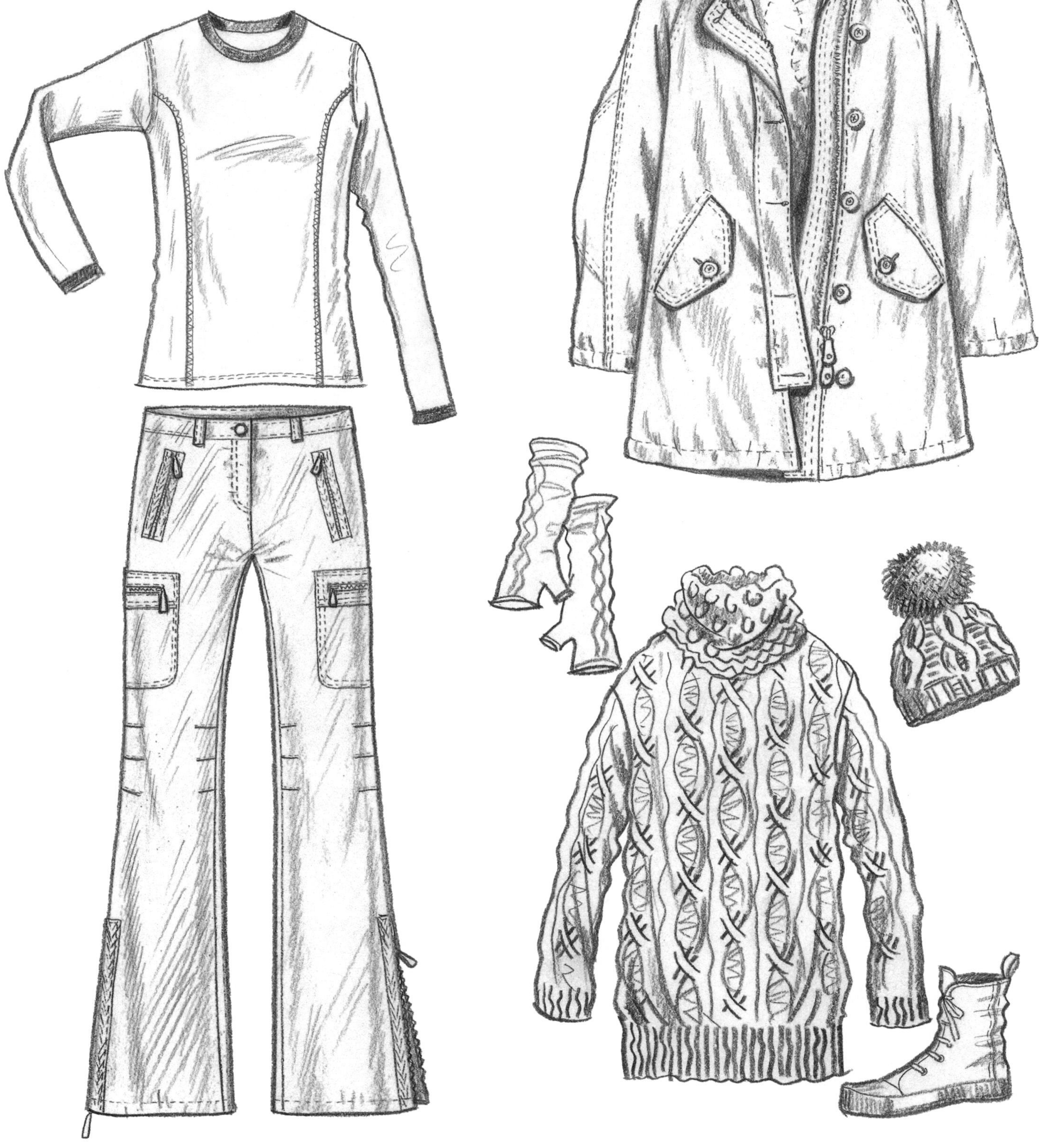

SO, HOW ARE YOU GOING TO DRAW THAT PARKA?

Having grasped the essential skills outlined in this book, and grown in confidence and proficiency, you can now start to push the boundaries and develop your own style. This is likely to include experimenting with different mediums and ways of working, and there are also some tricks of the trade that you can use to help you build a portfolio of work that reflects your own interests, particular skills and abilities, and what is generally known as your own 'handwriting'. Here you can see how the same type of garment can be approached using very different techniques and drawing styles.

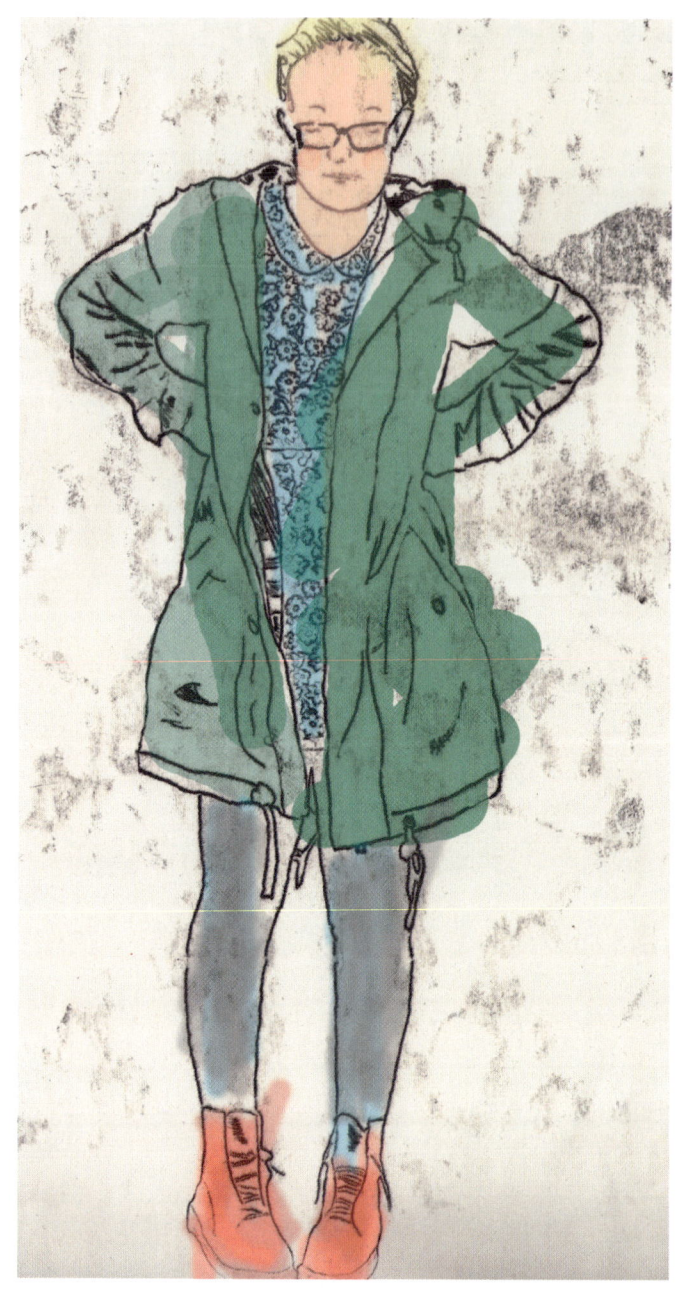

Martina Farrow
Client: *Cambridge University Press*
Agent: *New Division*
Drawn freehand using Adobe Illustrator, this charming artwork for an editorial story on camping features a loosely drawn parka-type garment along with other related paraphernalia.

Alice Fletcher-Quinnell
This lively drawing by Alice Fletcher-Quinnell has a youthful, casual and spontaneous atmosphere. Although the garments are perfectly recognizable, the illustration says less about the finer details of the clothing and far more about a modern fashion attitude. This image was created using monoprinting and Adobe Photoshop.

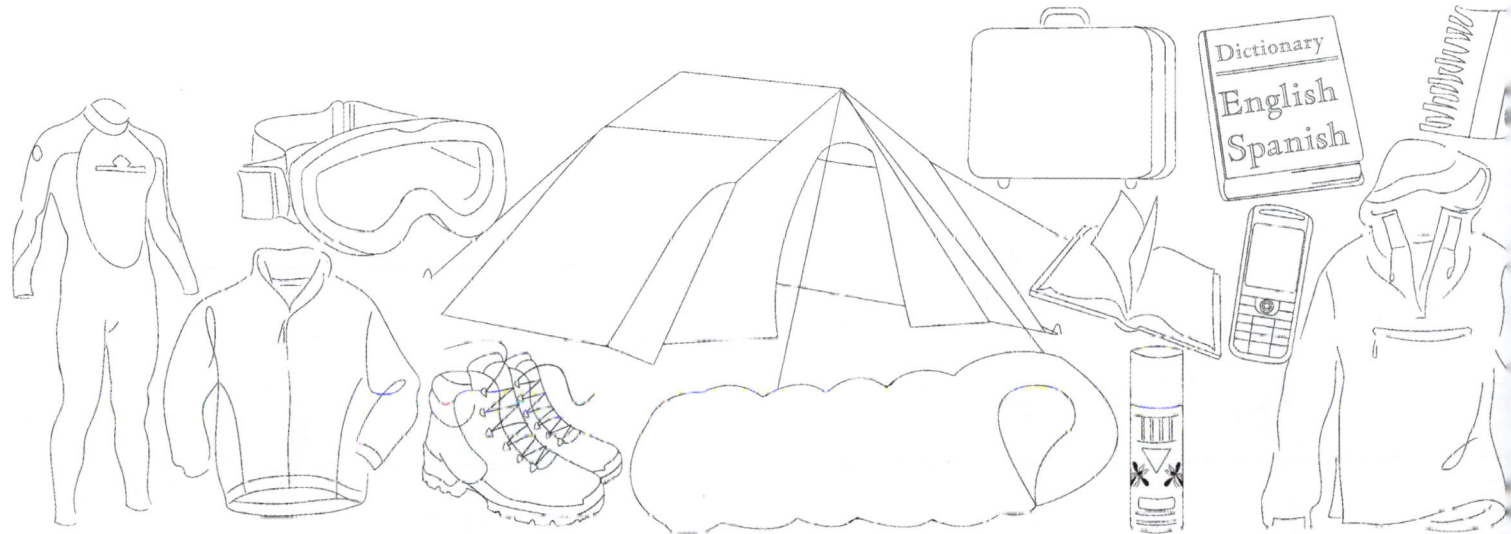

Judith Cheek

This illustration was drawn in a loose, confident style. The outlines of the figure were first sketched in with a soft 6B pencil, then watercolour wash was used to fill in the garments. White highlights were reserved with a wax resist pencil and masking fluid. The simplest watercolour background of a blue sky grounds the figure and provides atmosphere and setting. Detail is accurately portrayed, but not over-complicated.

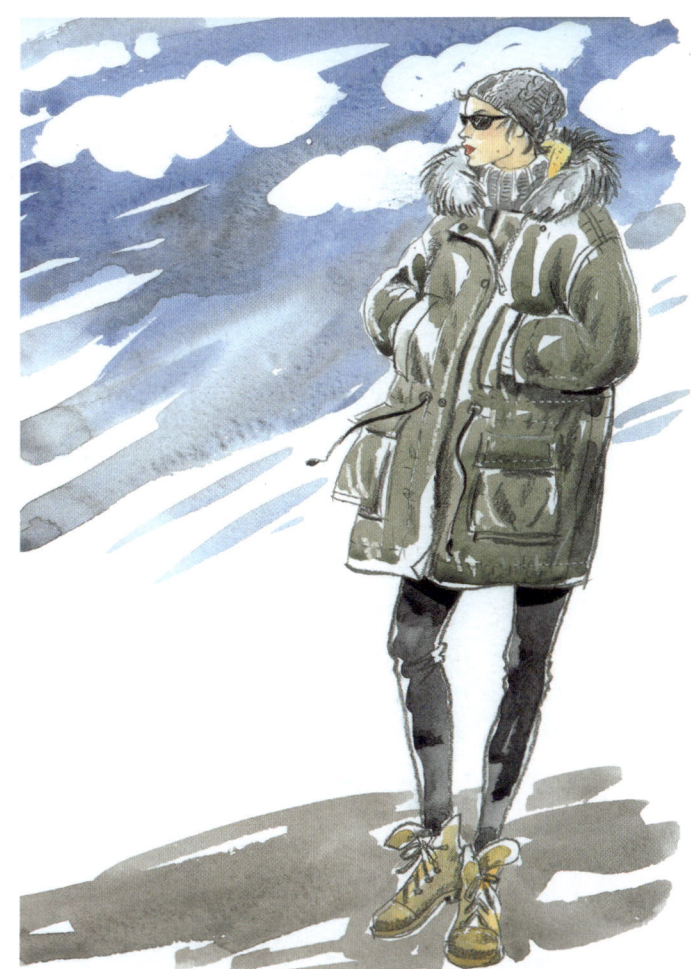

Judith Cheek

This free, quick sketch energetically captures the essence of the stylish juxtaposition of a utilitarian parka with a glamorous party dress.

Judith Cheek

This graphic image was created using collage. First, the simplified figure and garments were cut out from coloured paper and then fixed to a background with adhesive spray. The details of the garment and facial features were then added in pastel, with drawing kept to a minimum so that the lines remain bold and simple.

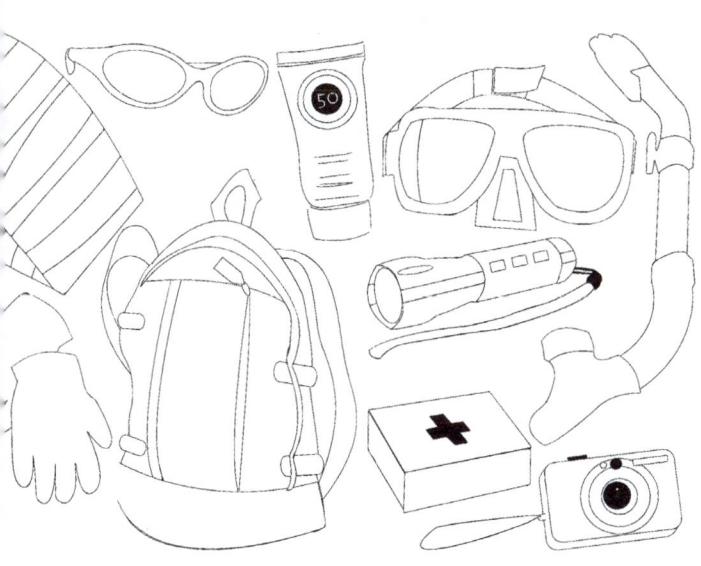

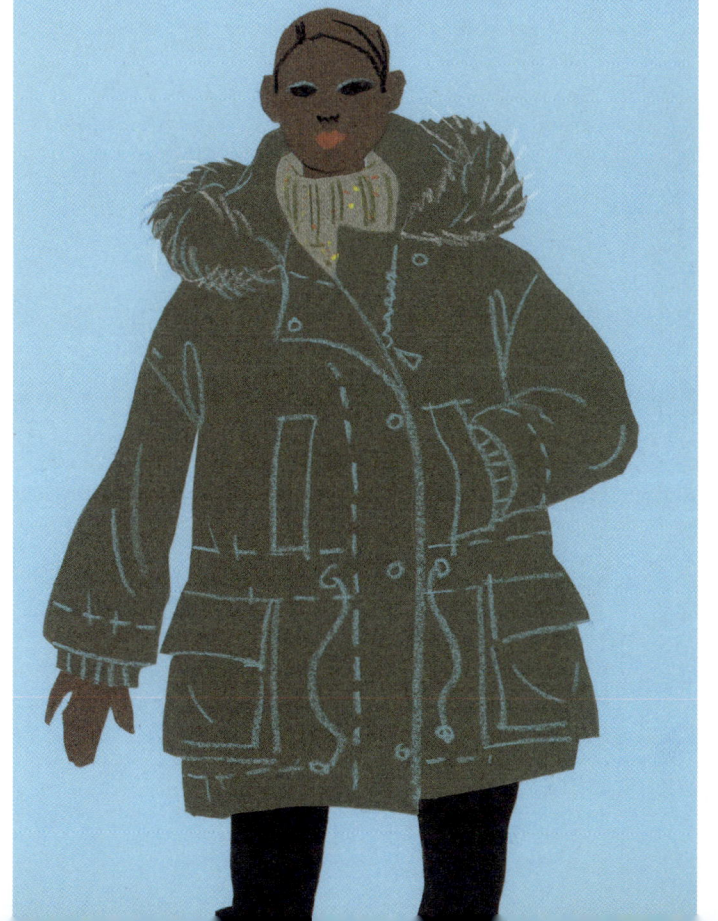

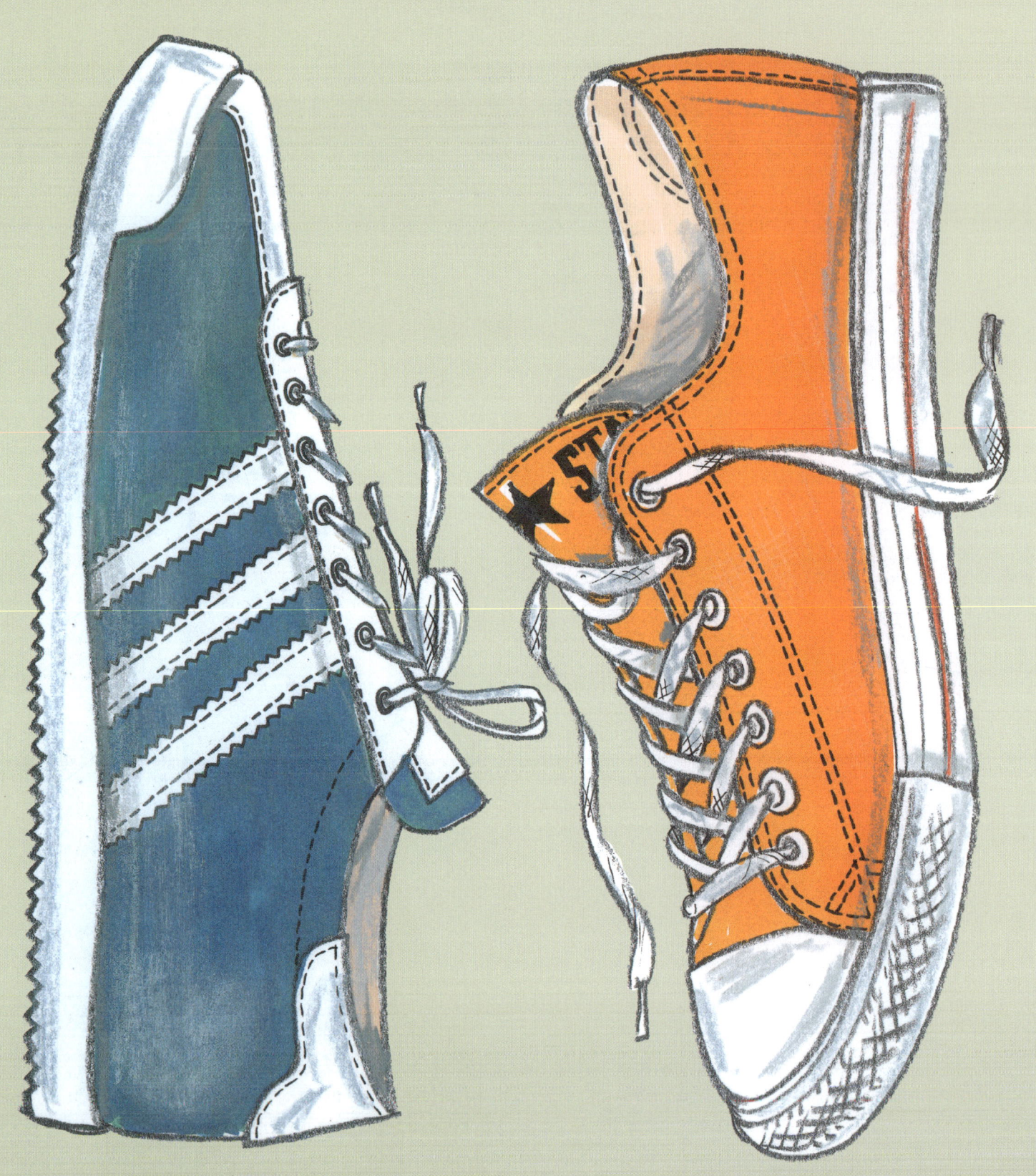

CHAPTER 8

DRAWING ACCESSORIES

Just as fashion expands to encompass ever-developing markets, so the demand for accessories expands too. Every fashion niche now has an accompanying range of accessories and so the scope for designing, drawing and illustrating them has grown.

Drawing accessories can incorporate many of the skills we've learnt already. Since by their very nature accessories are often small and very detailed, a fairly graphic drawing style – midway between that used for drawing designs on a figure and that used for creating flats – is often the most successful means of communication. With a little practice and experimentation you'll soon discover what works best for you and for particular project briefs.

One advantage of drawing garments is that, consciously or not, we acquire visual awareness and knowledge of clothing through wearing and handling it. We understand how the flat shapes that make up the garment have created its form. But with shoes, which hold their shape when we take them off, we

often do not have that extra knowledge of structure and component shapes. A little extra work is usually necessary to carefully observe and visually analyse accessories like shoes.

You may also encounter a slightly different range of materials when drawing accessories. It is important to familiarize yourself with these materials – with leather and suede in various grades and qualities, and with metal clasps and fastenings – not to mention all the other materials that may be used to make or decorate a shoe.

Then there are the practical aspects of the design to consider: for example, a wallet or bag may have a particular mechanism for closing or a way of folding that must be explained in your drawing, so you might decide to draw it open or part-open. If you are drawing a design of your own – of something that has not yet been realized – then you can use the drawing process as a way of problem-solving, drawing and redrawing to refine certain aspects and to come up with the best design.

CREATING TEMPLATES

As with figure drawing, where possible it can be a great help to create a template. Doing this will bring to the fore the first of several questions you need to answer, namely whether you wish to show the item on or off the body. This may be especially relevant when illustrating footwear, for instance, as it may be quite tricky to convey the subtleties of a design if it is not being displayed correctly. This is particularly true of strappy shoes, which may be limp and have very little integral form when viewed off the foot, and so are best shown being worn.

With this in mind, it is a good idea to develop a small range – a library if you like – of useful templates like those shown opposite. These provide a quick and accurate means of depicting a foot in the correct position for each of the different kinds of shoes you wish to draw or design. They are likely to include foot positions for flat and heeled shoes, and perhaps one of each with a leg present for drawing boots. Similarly, it is a good idea to have a bank of templates for well-proportioned heads seen from various angles, torsos, and many hand poses.

In order to create these, simplify the body parts into geometric shapes such as boxes, spheres and triangles and sketch them lightly in pencil. You can then begin to plot out the primary proportions and details. Once you are happy with these, you can complete the details, and finally ink over the finished shape and delete the pencil marks.

When drawing some accessories you may find that conveying scale can be a problem; just how big is that bag or purse? You might notice in magazines that accessories are sometimes photographed with a standard-size object – a lipstick or perfume bottle with a bag, a shoe with a holdall and so on – as this helps to portray the scale of the items. With a little imagination, this is a trick you can employ equally well in your drawings. Dressing a figure with the accessory is also a good way of clarifying its size. A scarf, for instance, can be anything from a small square handkerchief to an enveloping shawl. However, by showing it being worn, the scale and intention becomes obvious.

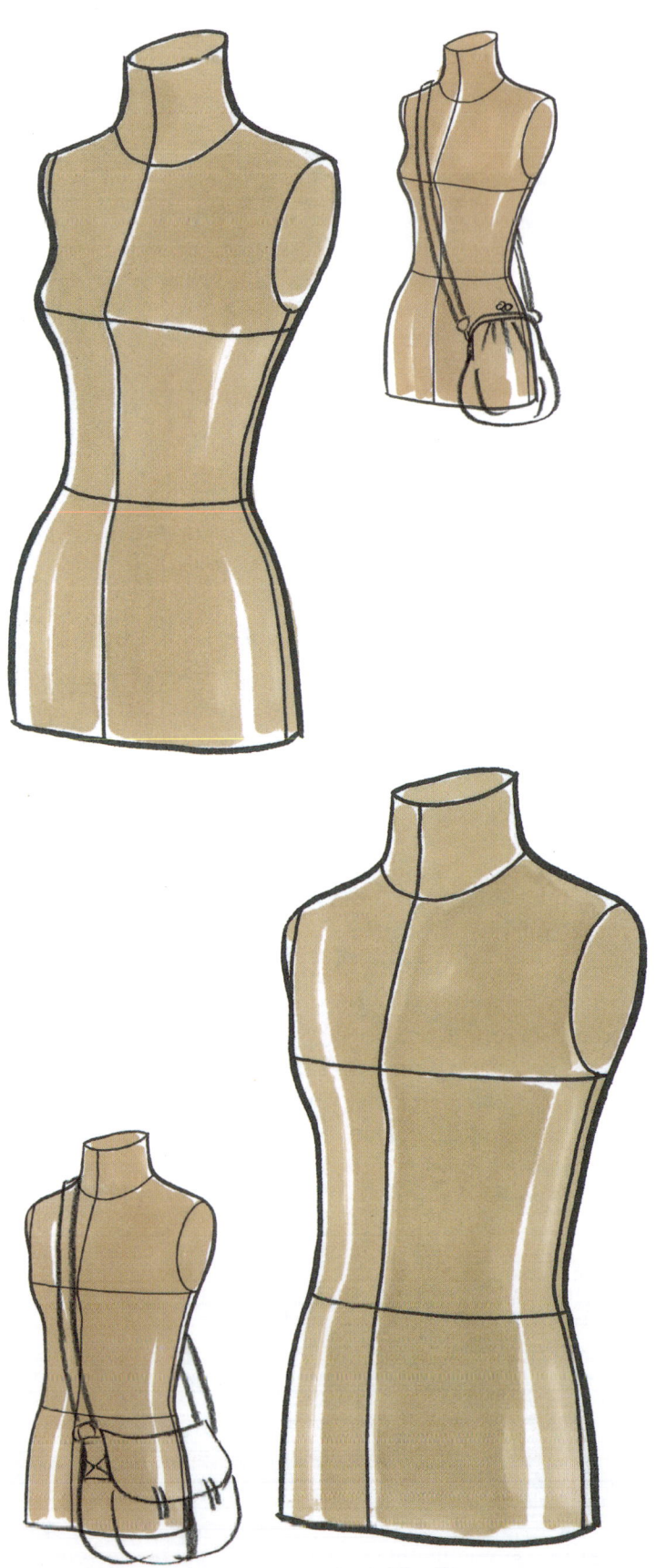

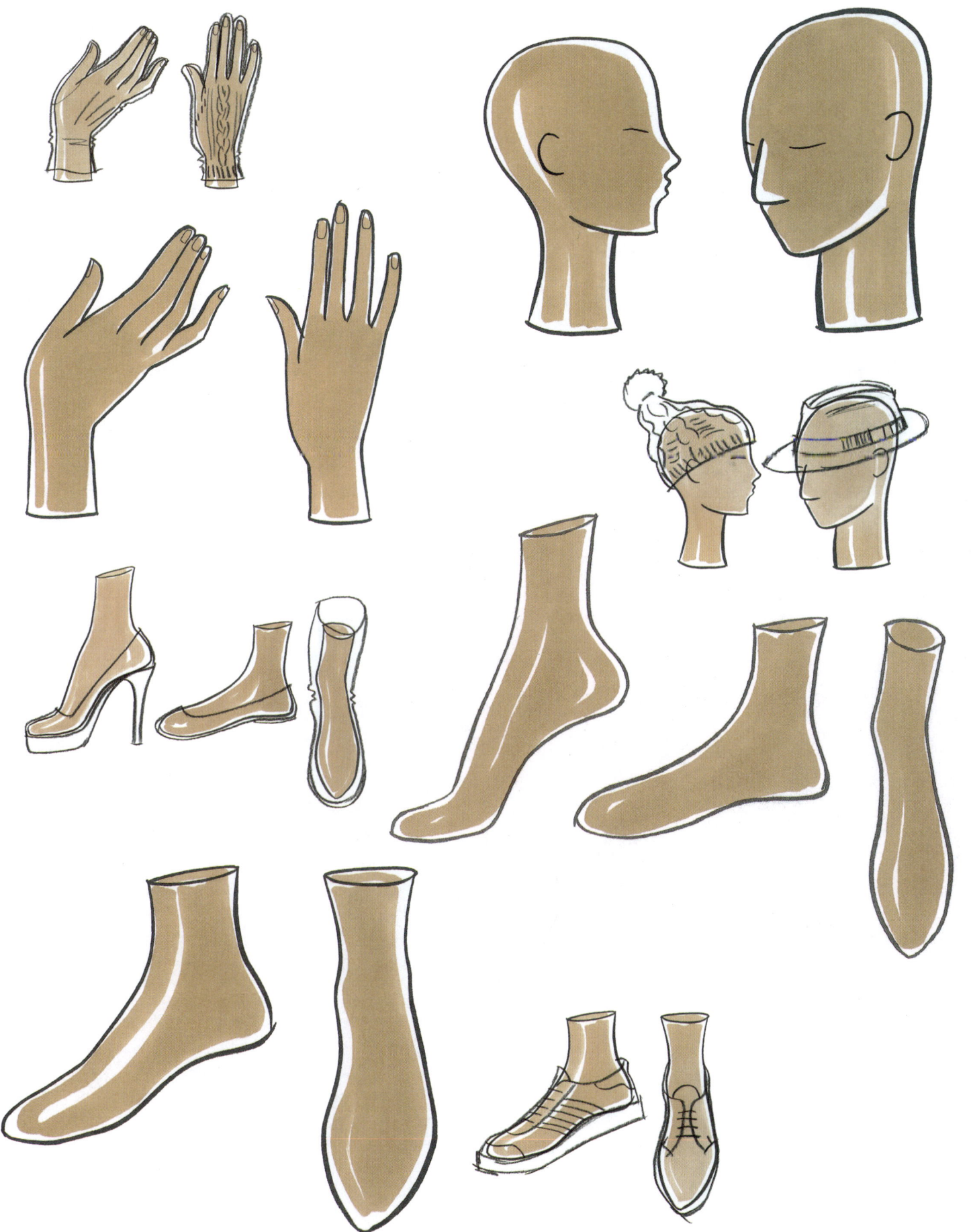

HOW TO DRAW SHOES: WOMEN

These examples show how shoes can be drawn using a range of mediums, including marker pen, pencil, oil pastels, soft crayons and many others. Simple techniques such as rubbings have also been employed. Plan some experimentation time into your schedule so that you can try new techniques and different mediums.

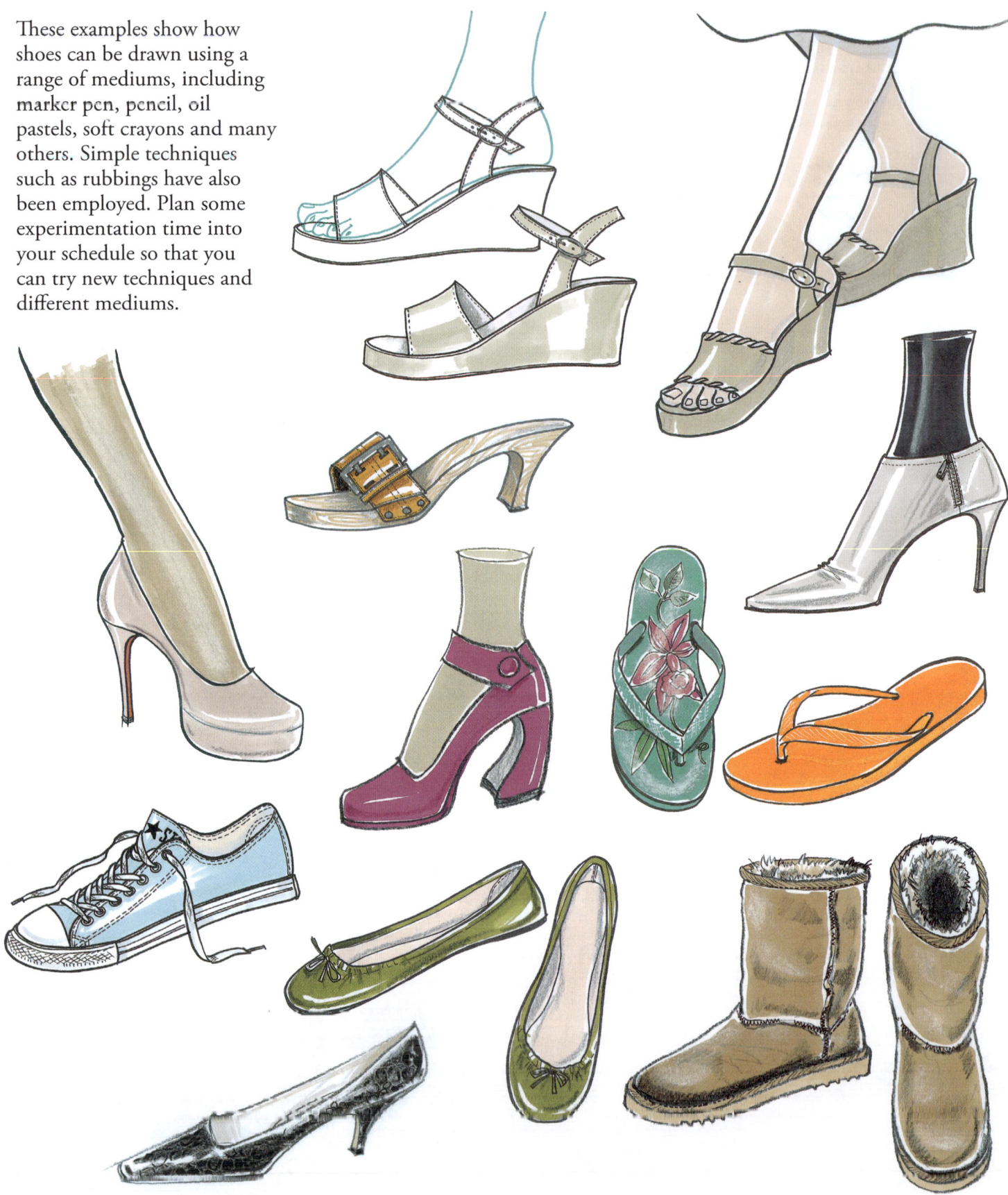

HOW TO DRAW SHOES: MEN

Techniques for drawing men's shoes are the same as for women's. If you are drawing men's and women's shoes on the same page, remember to draw the men's slightly larger, as they probably would appear in reality, so that they read correctly.

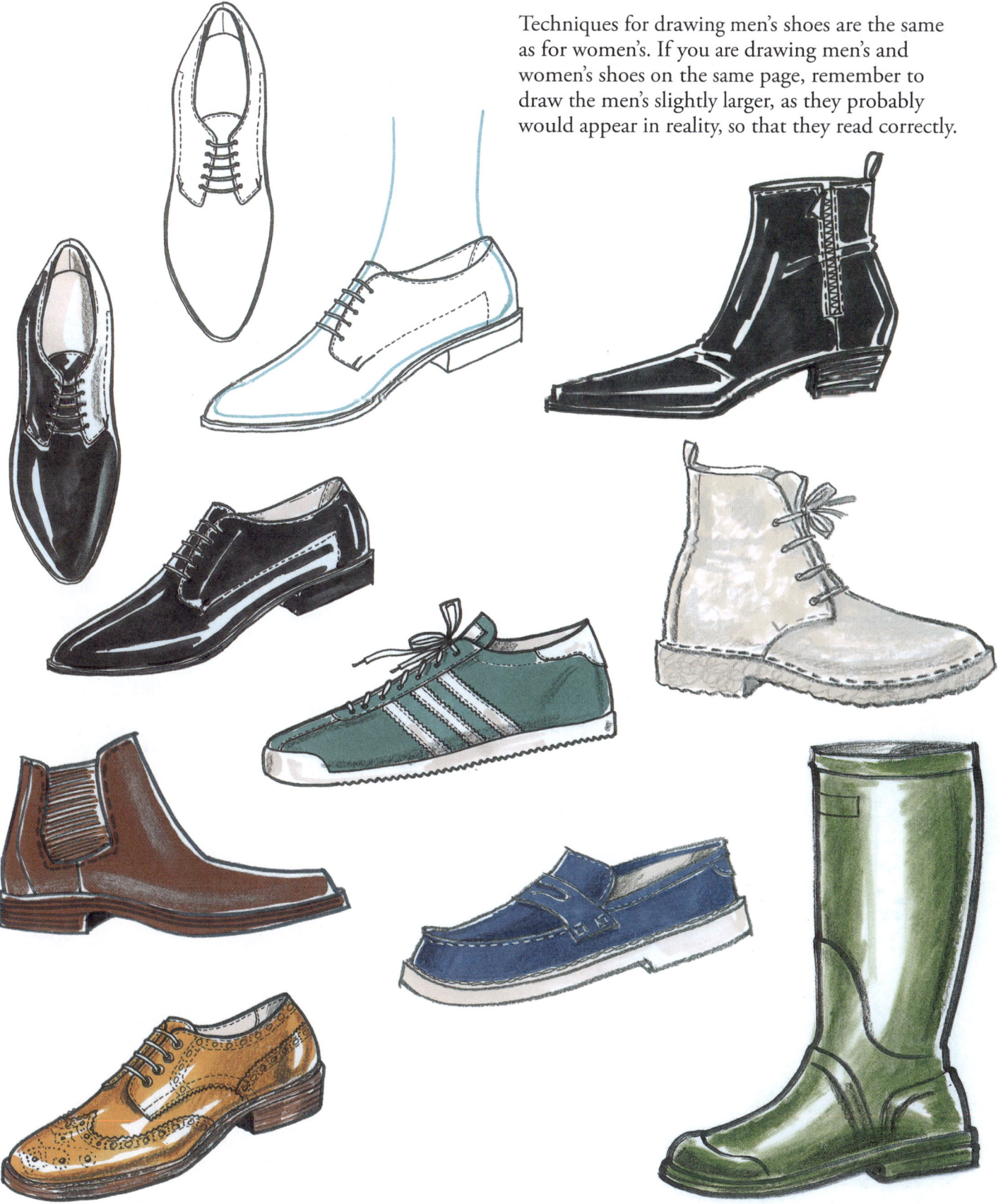

HOW TO DRAW BAGS: WOMEN

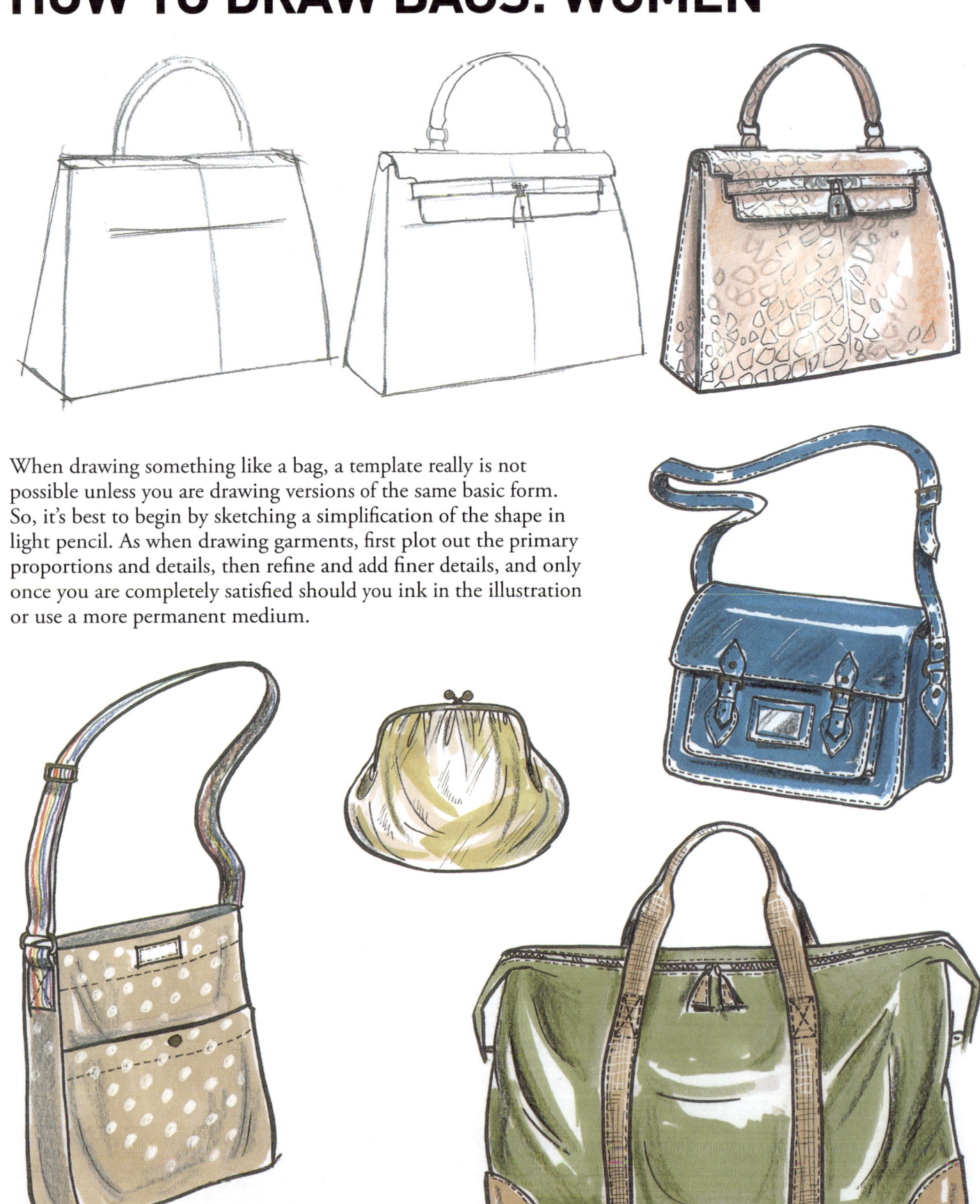

When drawing something like a bag, a template really is not possible unless you are drawing versions of the same basic form. So, it's best to begin by sketching a simplification of the shape in light pencil. As when drawing garments, first plot out the primary proportions and details, then refine and add finer details, and only once you are completely satisfied should you ink in the illustration or use a more permanent medium.

HOW TO DRAW BAGS: MEN

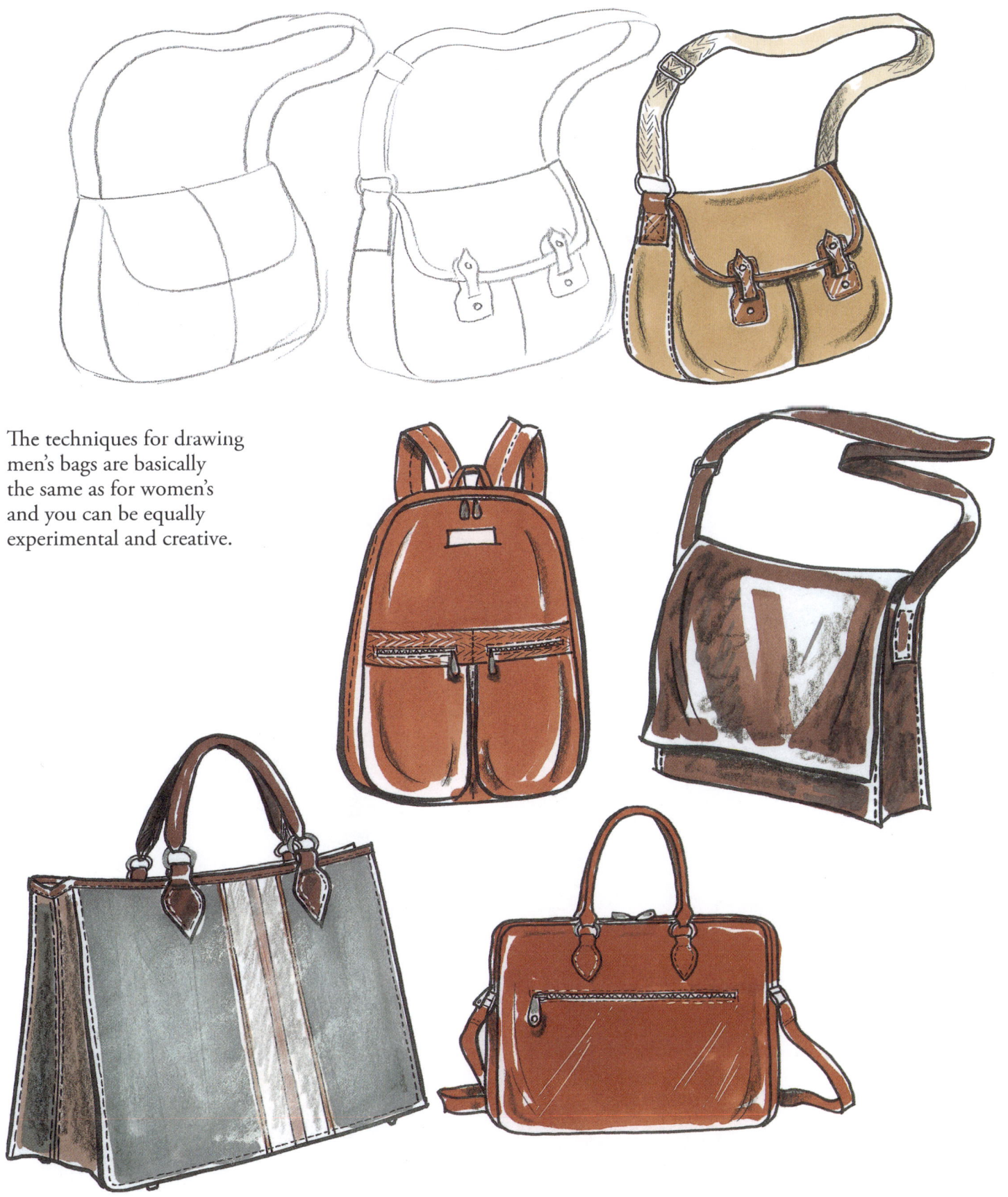

The techniques for drawing men's bags are basically the same as for women's and you can be equally experimental and creative.

GROUPING ACCESSORIES: WOMEN

These layouts or round-ups of accessories are similar to pages you may see in magazines, for instance features on 'How to do the latest look', 'Key must-have pieces' or 'Seasonal gifts'. A range of rendering techniques are employed and the items are arranged in a clever way so that their scales, proportions and intended usage are apparent, and they are shown to their best effect.

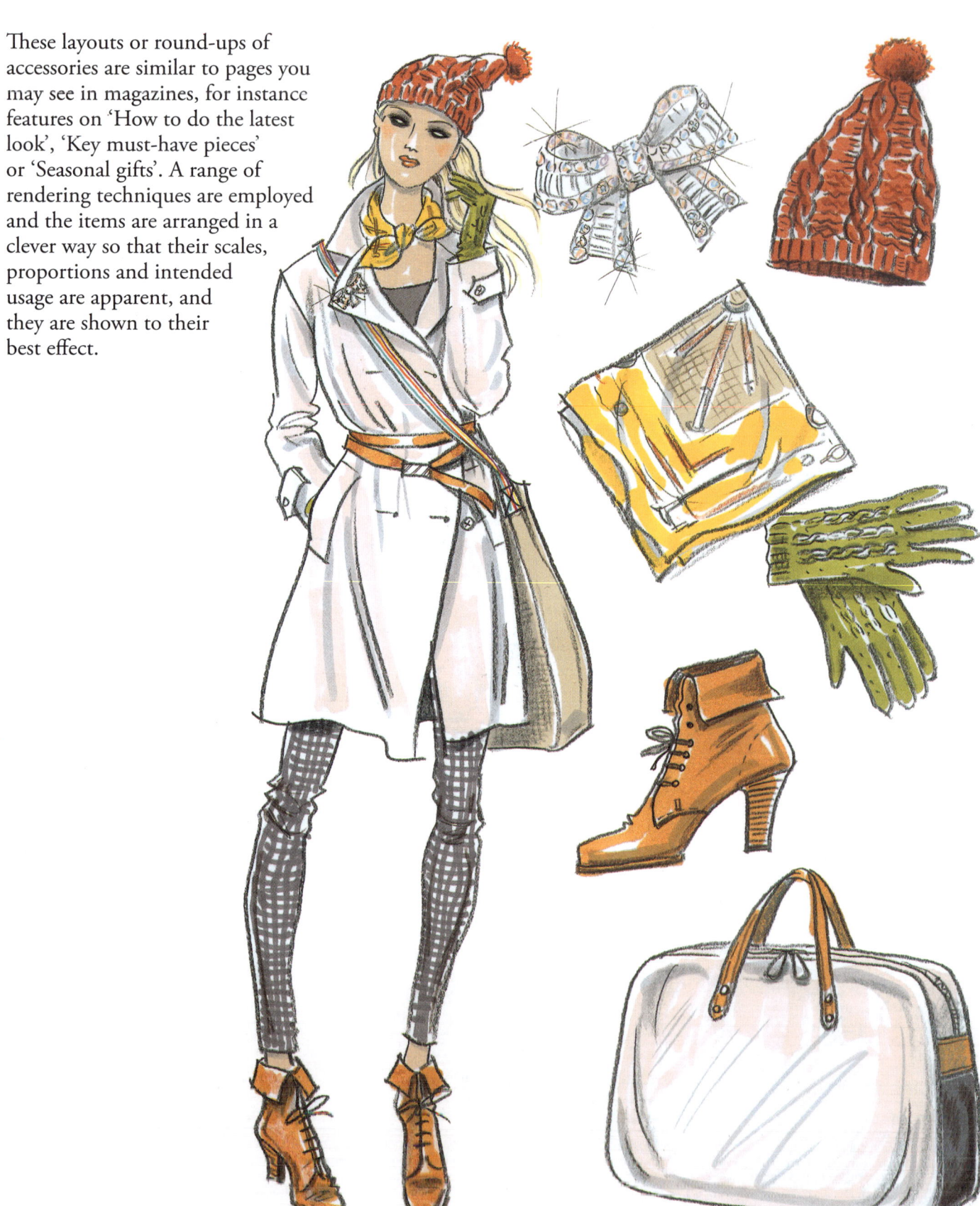

GROUPING ACCESSORIES: MEN

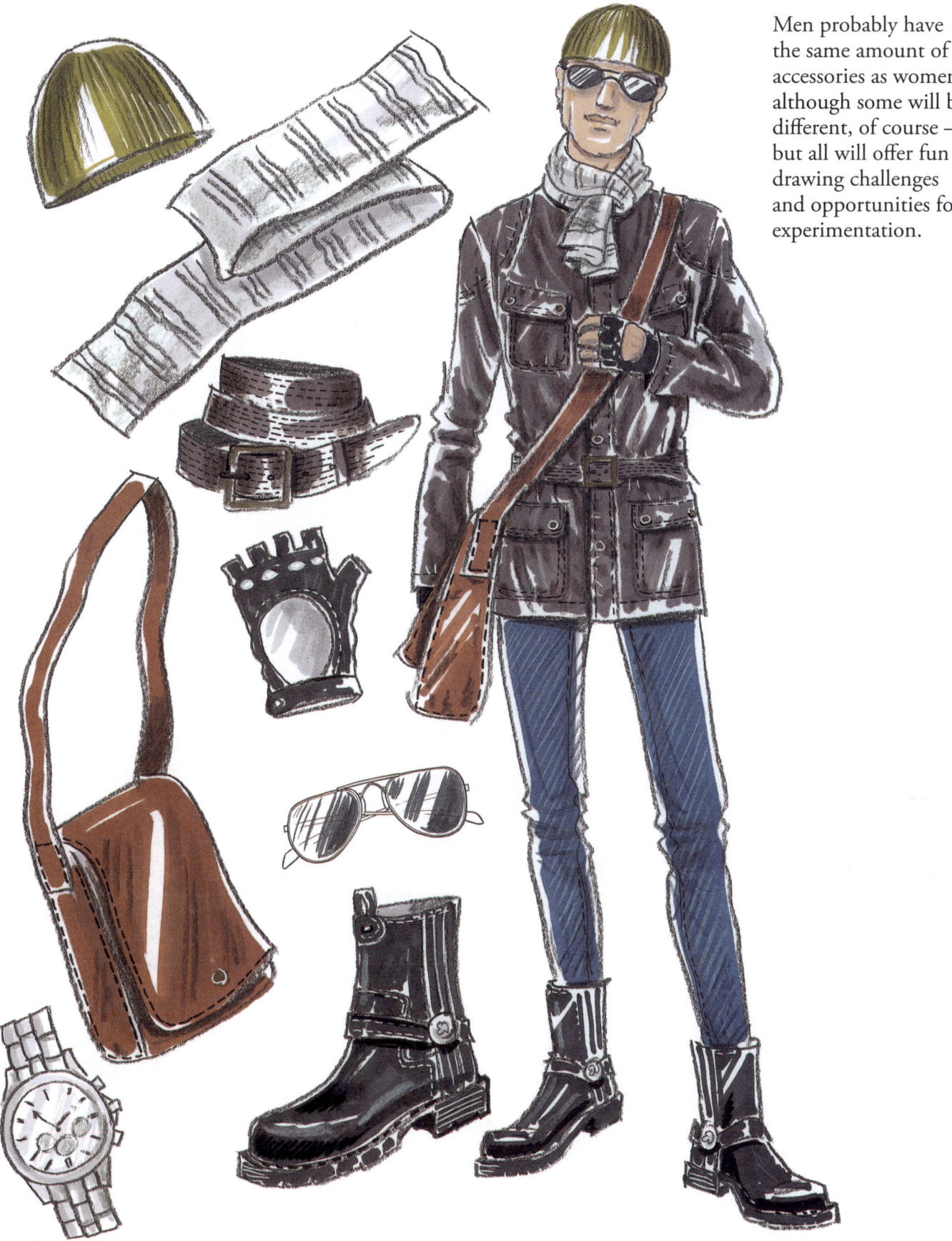

Men probably have the same amount of accessories as women, although some will be different, of course – but all will offer fun drawing challenges and opportunities for experimentation.

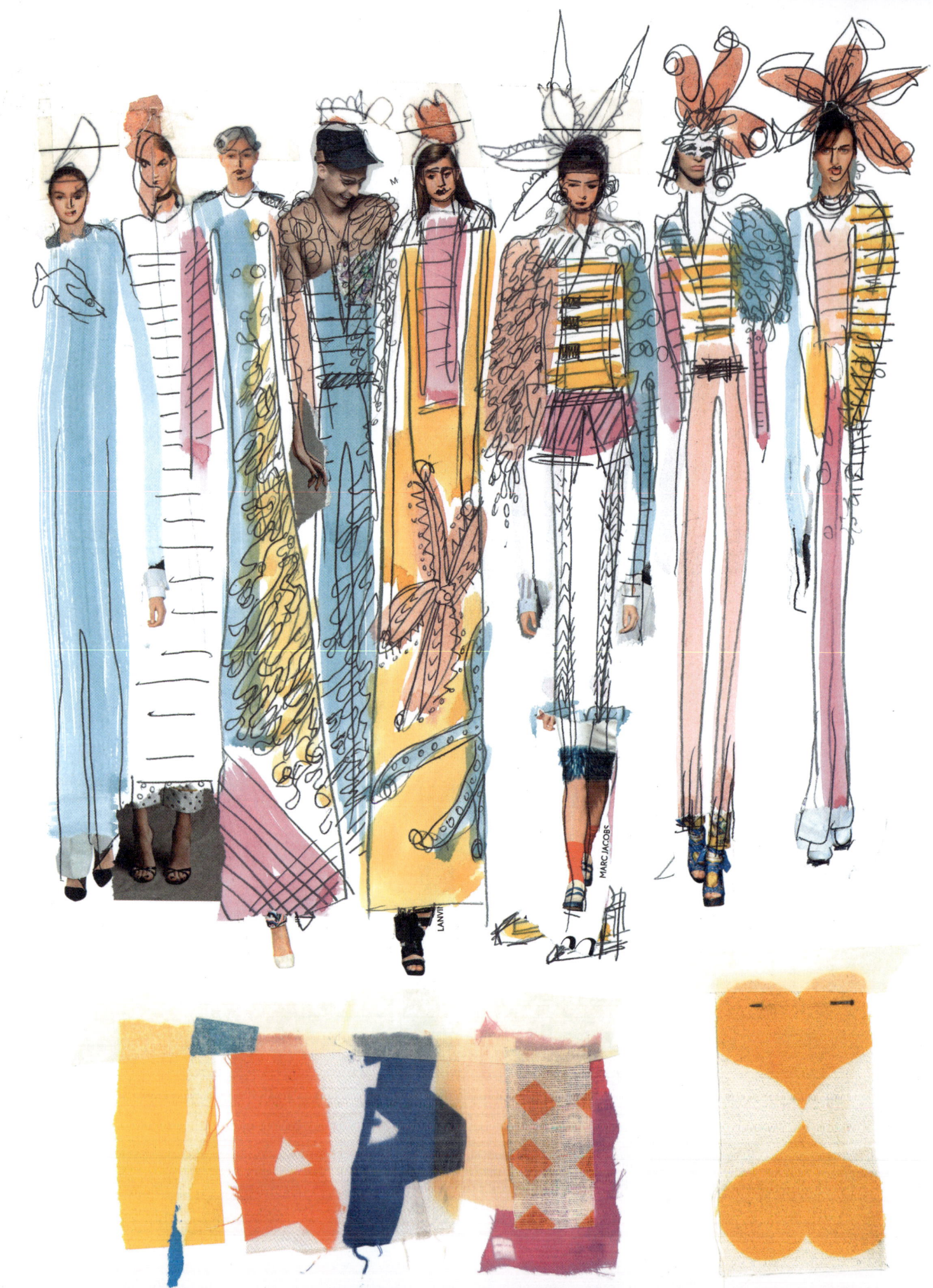

CHAPTER 9

LAYOUT AND PRESENTATION

The presentation of fashion images and ideas is a mixed affair which brings together many influencing and defining factors; it is never static and is itself affected by fashion trends and the zeitgeist. The presentation work can often be considered a fashion image in its own right. What defines a suitable presentation is governed by the nature of the job, the client's expectations, the target market, whether the work is to be delivered digitally or physically, the time span involved, the budget – and that's just the start!

Presentation isn't just something to consider at the end of a project, nor indeed is it something done purely for the approval and benefit of a third party – you are in the process of clarifying and refining for yourself. This method of drawing, illustrating, designing, editing and developing is important and clients may often want to see behind the scenes to get an idea of the work in progress, the way in which ideas are formulated, and how the work has been edited, refined and developed. It is worth remembering that although you may be dealing with someone who is design-literate, they won't necessarily be a designer themselves and may have a limited appreciation of certain design aspects. Seeing an idea explored and developed from conception to finish can often give the client confidence and insight into the validity

of your work. So sketchbooks and design developments are frequently a part of presentation. Sometimes it may be appropriate to produce an edited and polished version of your sketchbook – a kind of fast-forward glimpse into your design process – for the client to view as an introduction to the finished work.

SIMPLICITY AND CLARITY

The brief dictates the elements to be included. While the visual style of the presentation should be sympathetic to and evocative of the theme of the project, it should not confuse or overshadow the content of the work itself. It should not be overcomplicated and should generally be in keeping with current trends for simplicity and clarity. Any text or instructions should be well laid out (it is good practice to get into the habit of noticing and analysing quality fashion magazine layouts and such). Hand written titles and text are not acceptable – computers enable the printing of professional standard graphics cheaply, quickly and easily. Novelty and over-decorative typefaces should generally be avoided; the simple, timeless logos of many high-fashion brands provide a good example of the use of stylish graphics.

It is worth developing a simple style for your name that can be unobtrusively incorporated into the presentation. It is useful and practical to create a label with your name and contact details, which can be readily printed out to stick to the reverse of all physical work submitted. Your work may have a long afterlife in a plans chest or such, and may be rediscovered and appreciated in the light of a follow-up project. We've all left work behind at a meeting or interview; if clearly labelled on the reverse, it can easily be traced and returned to you.

FACING PAGE: *This lively, vibrant illustration by Mary Ratcliffe presents a collection line-up for Alternative Fashion Week at Spitalfields, London. It shows the 'Starfish and Periwinkle Collection' (menswear and womenswear). Ratcliffe says: 'Drawings for digital and screen prints [are] taken from underwater forms. This illustration was worked to show the coordinated colour and overall print mood, to plan styling prior to the catwalk presentation.'*

LAYOUT

Planning and organization are key factors in the successful completion of any project, not least design-driven ones. One of the biggest errors is not to allow enough time at the end to bring a project to conclusion, so it's important to plan for that as you go. Use drawings and sketches to rough out and try different layouts, and allow time for experimentation with different styles, alternative media and techniques so you're not simply ploughing on with your fingers crossed in the final hours.

Components for presentation may typically include: project title; season; client/brand drawings (designs) on a figure and/or as flats or technical drawings; colour palette; fabric swatches; mood/theme or inspiration images; and a brief description of garments or theme-story/legend. Juggling this array of imagery and information while allowing for breathing space and clarity is a skill to be learned and continually honed and refined. The techniques and formats for layout and presentation of design work, mood boards and colour palettes are constantly evolving as trends and technologies themselves progress. Where a number of presentation sheets or boards are necessary, it is important that they all follow the same layout and format as a cohesive whole.

In the tutorial on the following pages Yvonne Deacon simplifies some the possible approaches to a stylish formula, which allows plenty of scope for personality and individuality to shine while conforming to contemporary standards of good design presentation. She shows how traditional methods of layout use negative space, deploy narratives on the page and lead the eye as directed by the artist, using classical compositional rules from fine art. The significance of images is prioritized by their scale and positioning. But how we read images is changing. Through social media, we are becoming more familiar with images presented in new ways. Flickr, Pinterest, Google Images and Instagram all present multiple images in grids or scroll-down formats. Their prioritizing is done in different ways – by impact, by our own interests,

Layout Planning

- Composition

- Juxtaposition

- Meaning

- Narrative

- Cluster and group

- Colour palette

Planning your portfolio for direction content and page layout aiming to show your work to its best advantage, to achieve the best read

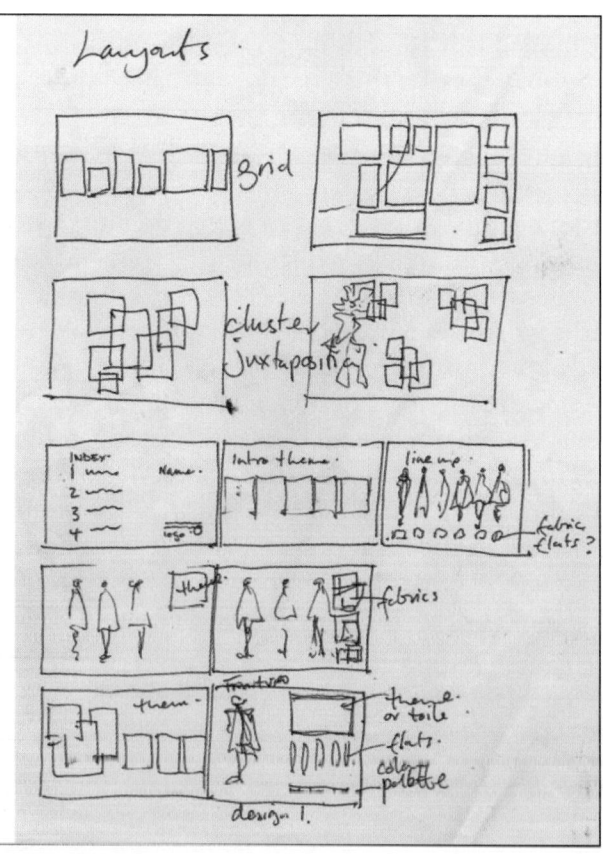

Once you know what material and information you need to include, you can sketch out plans for alternative layouts.

by trails, by 'best people' and 'most popular', by similar associations and related connections – evidence indeed that change and design influences can come from all directions. As designers we need to engage with this technology, remaining open to newness and continually refreshing our views.

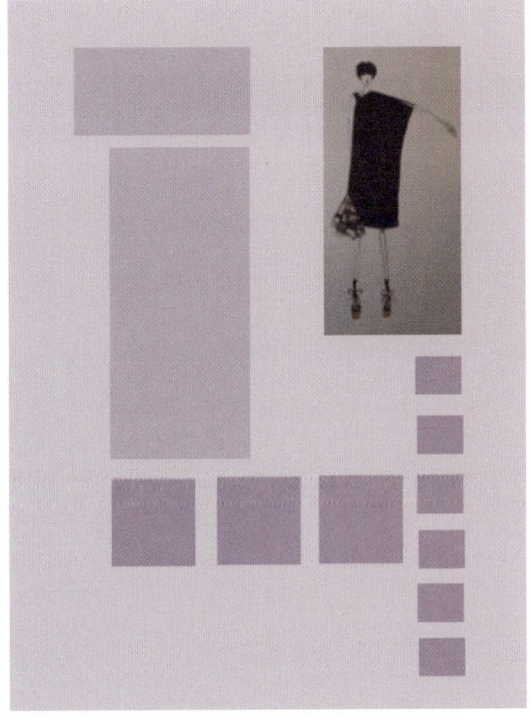

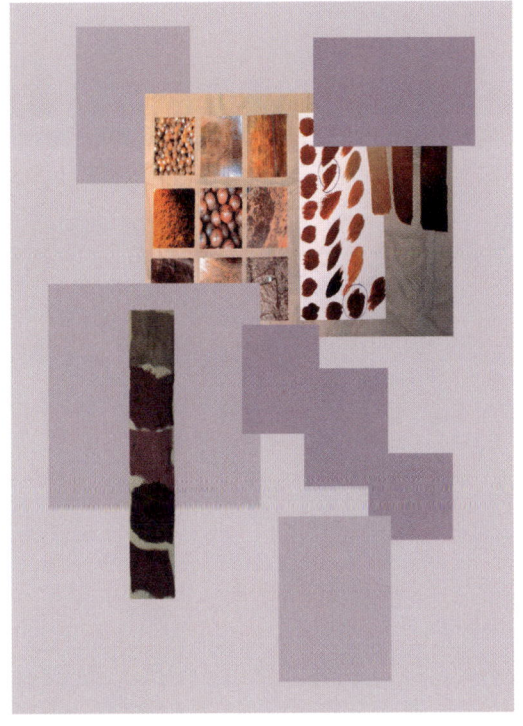

Portrait grid

Portrait tiled grid

These two alternatives for a portrait layout show something of the scope and options open for creative presentation. The positioning of images is crucial to how the board is read; composition itself can help create elements of mood.

The portrait grid (far left) is clear and simple; the eye is led around in a circular direction that is quite calm.

In the portrait tiled grid (near left), energy and rhythm are created by the overlapping images and their strong diagonal direction. The eye criss-crosses around the board, generating a certain visual excitement.

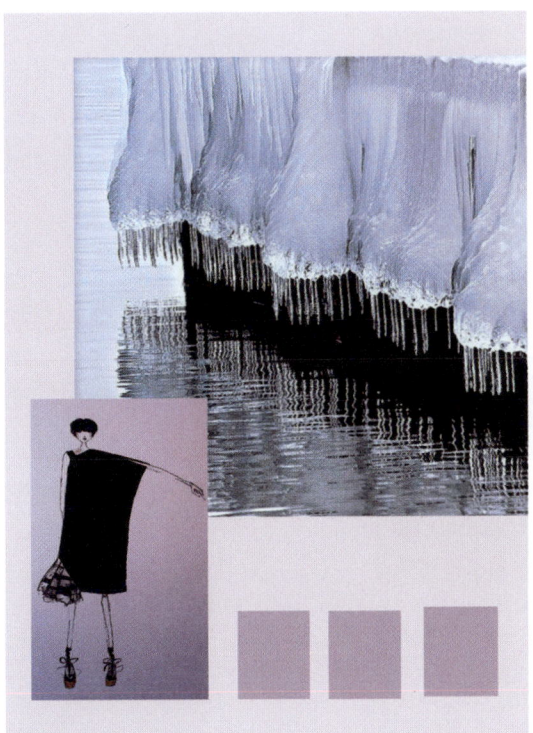

Double page spread, fashion and theme – colour trend

This double page spread opens up yet more scope and opportunities. The partial repeat of the central image provides a dramatic focus and a connecting visual link between the two boards.

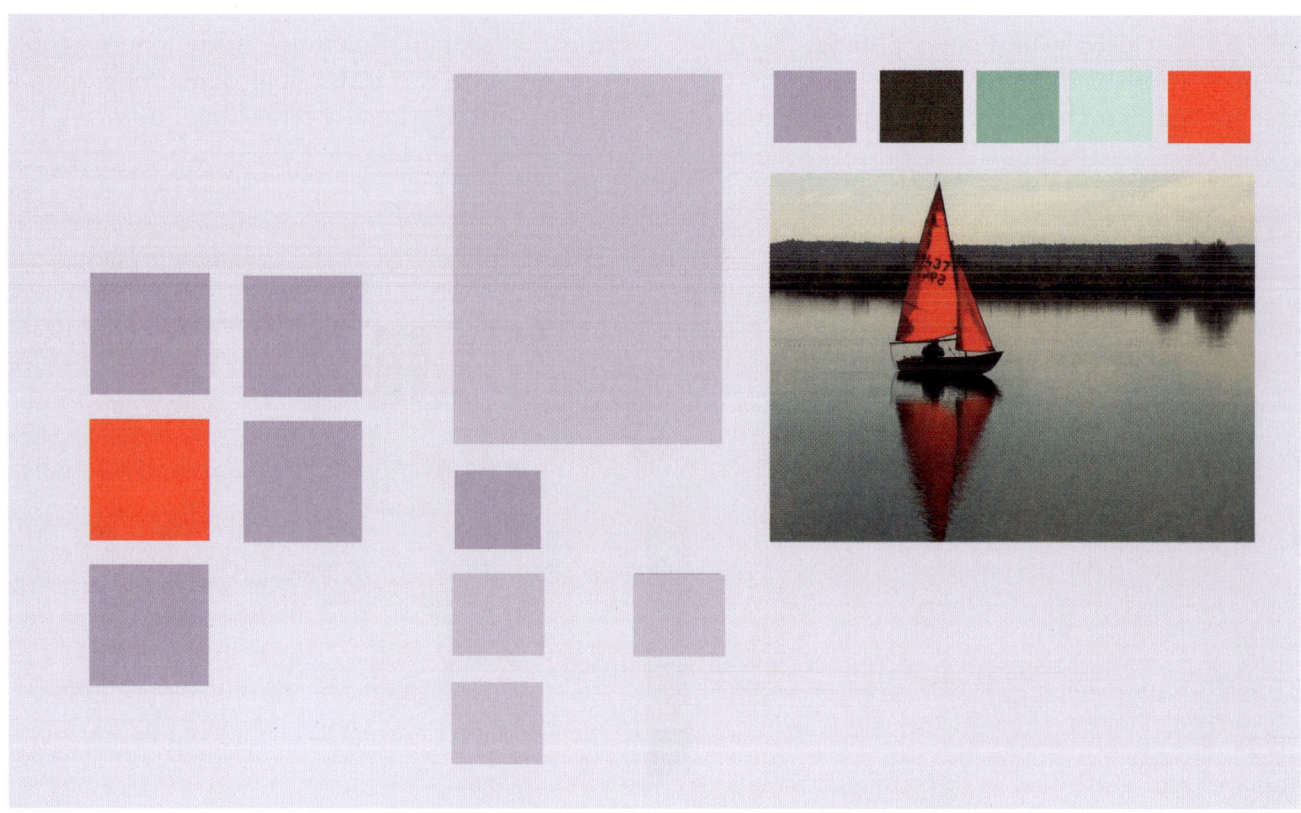

The grid format here is split between uniform and regular groups that balance and contrast in scale and direction. Larger images grab priority, smaller ones take supporting roles and create directional rhythms, leading the eye around the board.

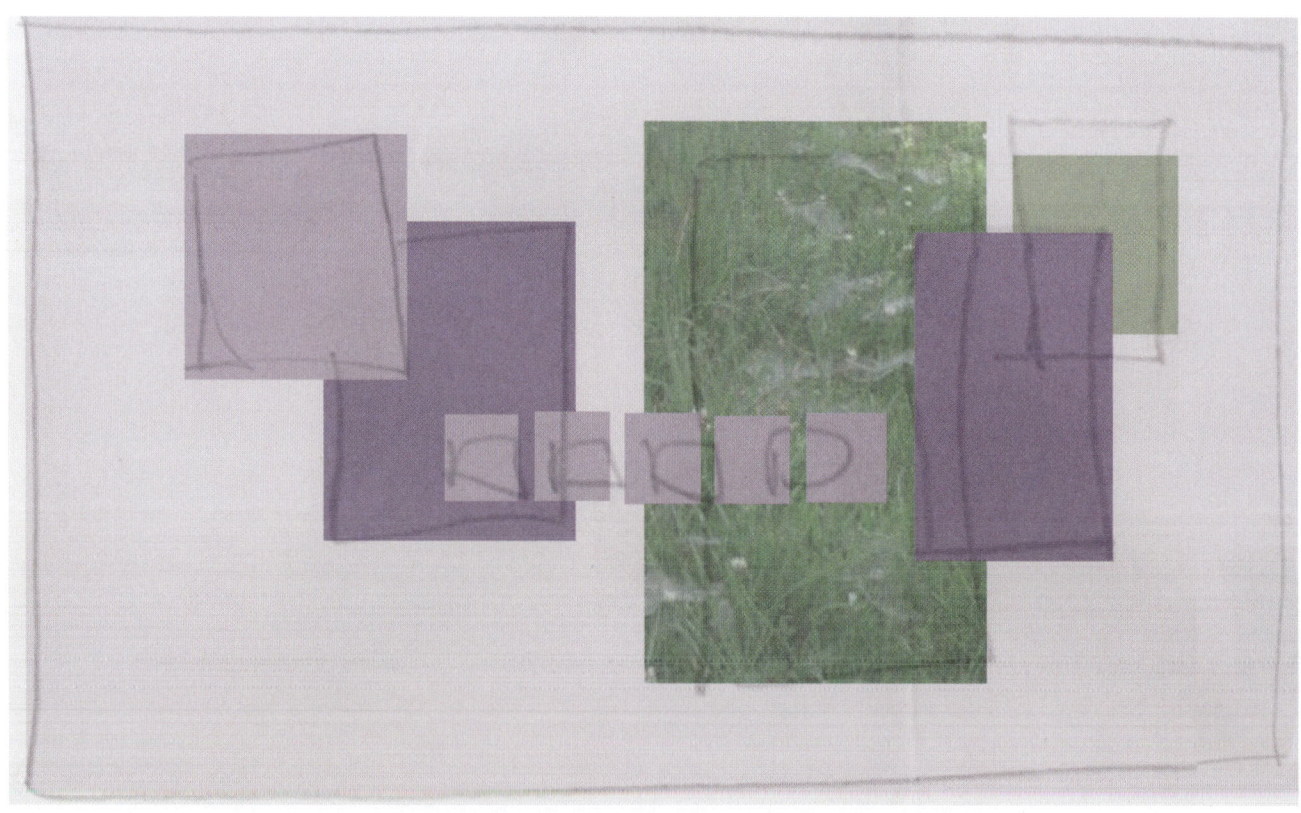

This landscape layout uses tiling to plan where themes, colours and ideas connect. The tiling technique makes strong visual connections that can reinforce narrative and thematic links between images. Variations of scale and proportion add interest.

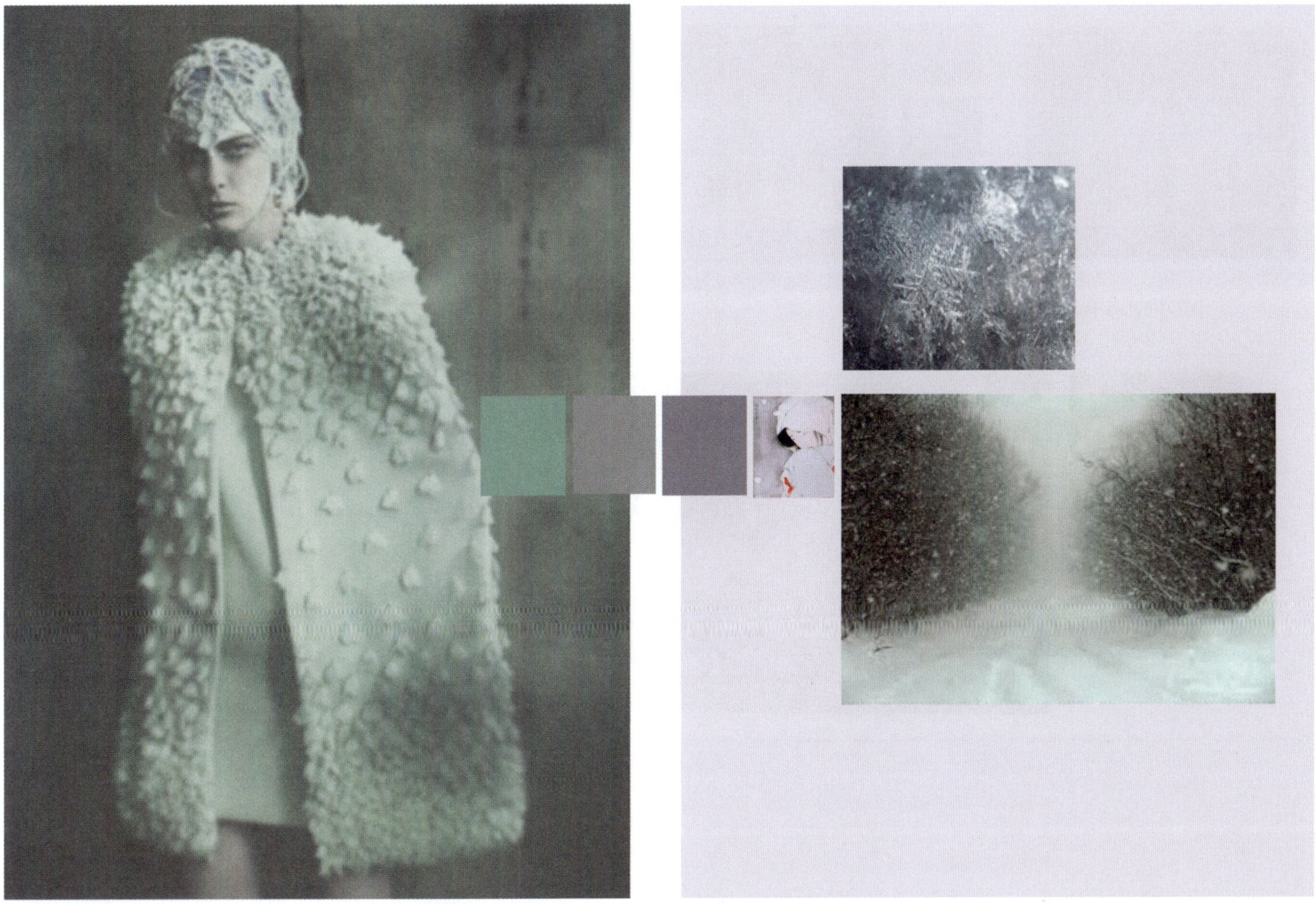

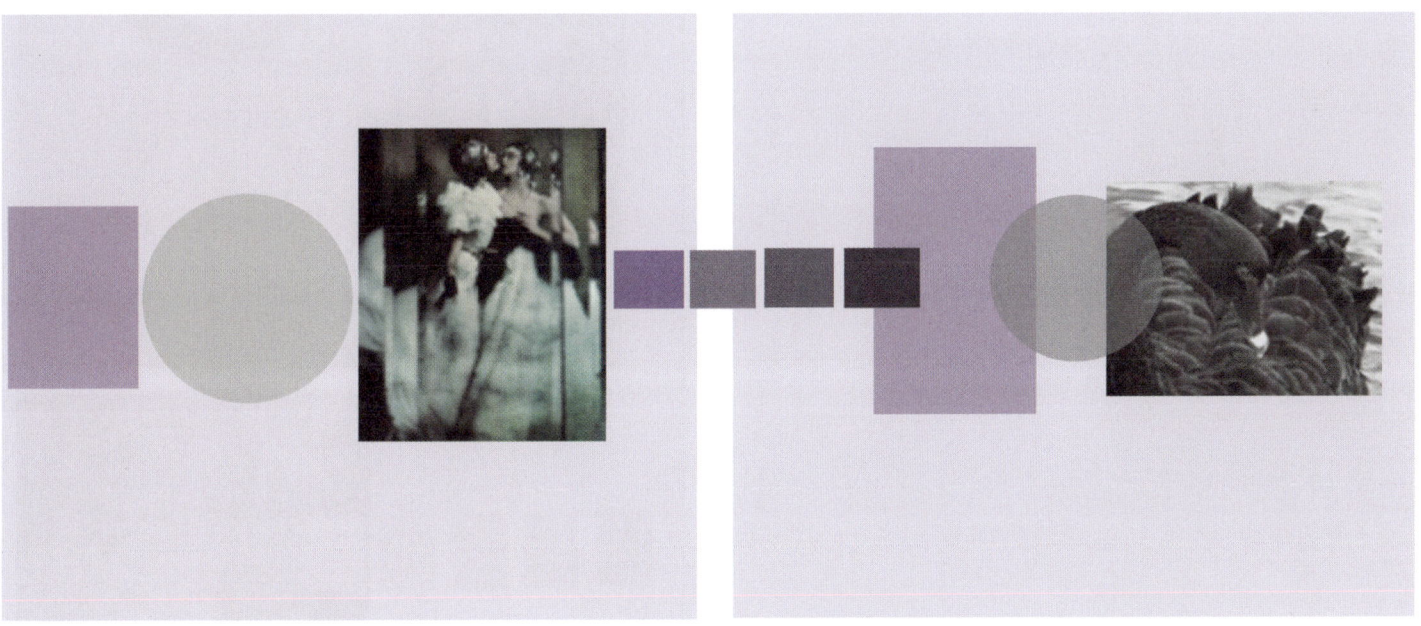

Portrait and landscape combined: the clever use of a large portrait image adds impact and importance to a significant visual. Colours taken from the main photo are used to connect it across the landscape format to its supporting research imagery.

Linear landscape – either grid or tiled: this is a relatively new format we are seeing develop that has a clean, easily read style. It is something like a visual sentence, but can be read left to right and right to left or from any point outwards as though along a horizon.

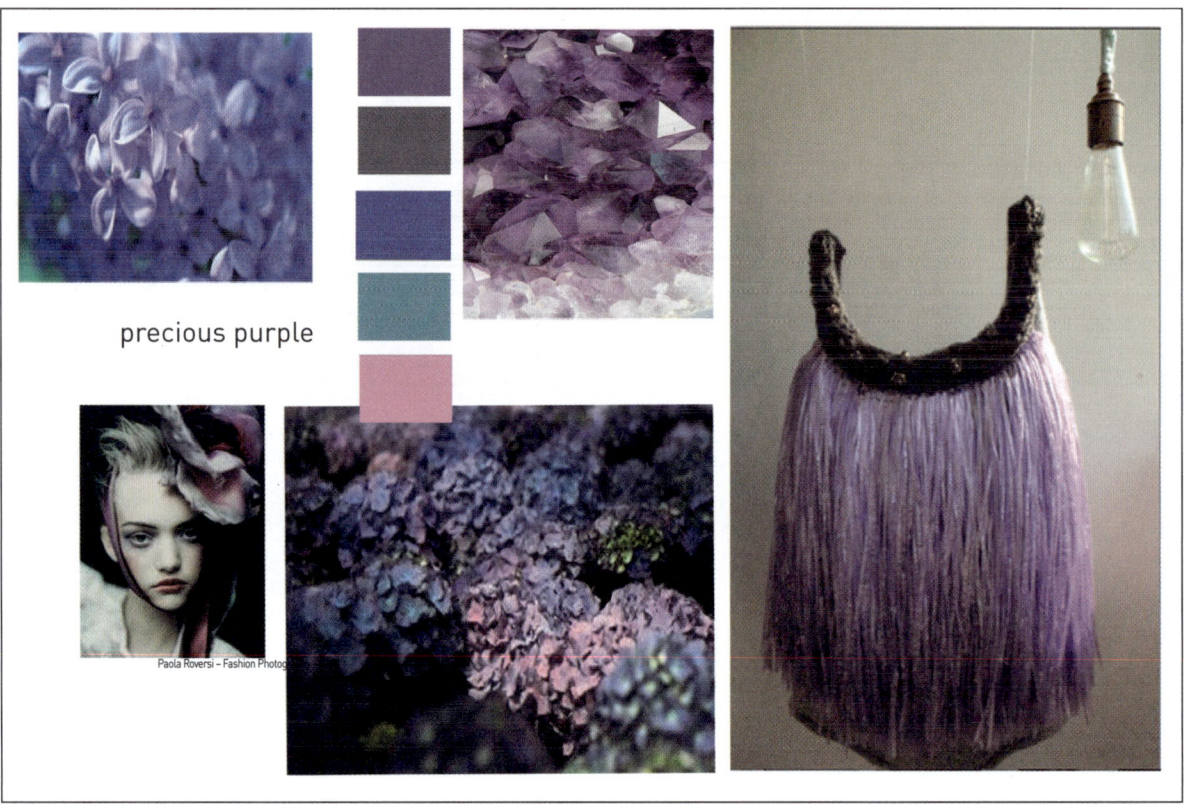

precious purple

Paola Roversi – Fashion Photography

These formats present almost identical information, but each prioritizes different aspects, with quite different visual results. The eye is drawn to different images and prioritizes attention because of variants in scale and positioning.

Grass skirt by Heather Ridley-Moran

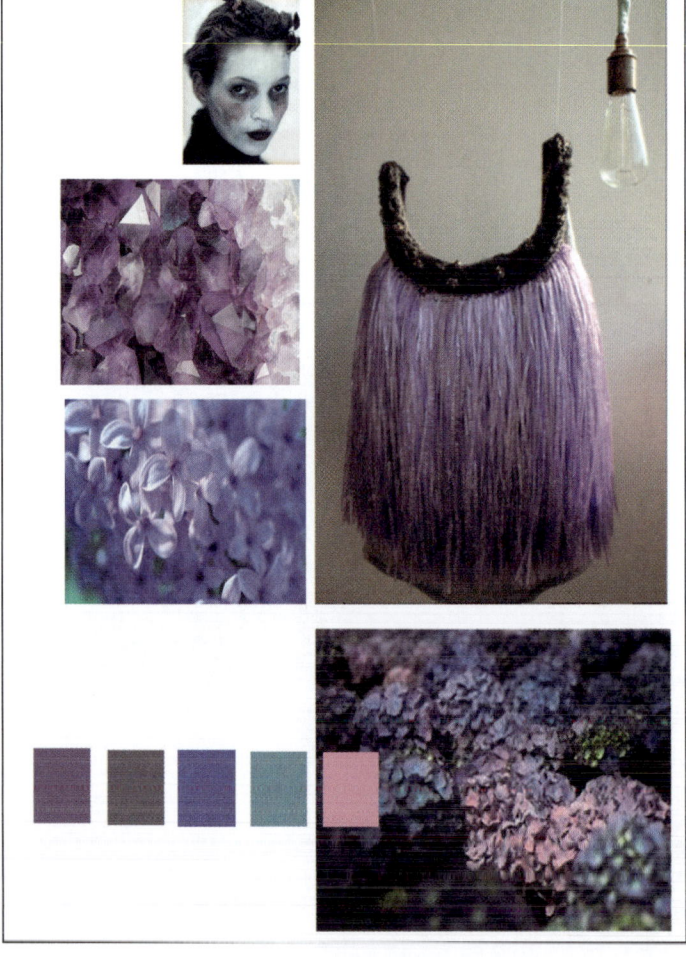

Layout

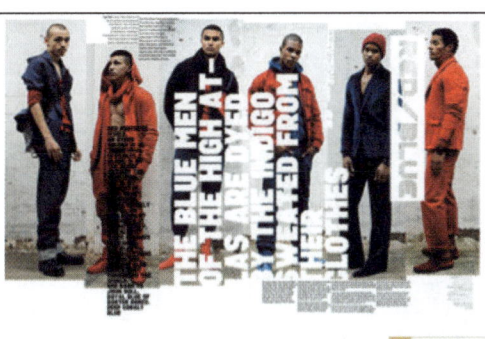

- Use the invisible grid (Neville Brody for The Face, Peter Saville for Factory Records) for original 80s layout technique
- Cluster and group to connect images and juxtapose
- Negative space to lead the eye through
- Rich and confusing
- Isolated and clear
- Ordered
- Not a scrapbook
- What is the page saying? Are you communicating the evocative content and main intent?

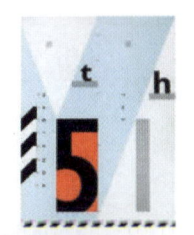

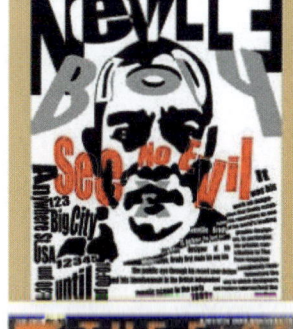

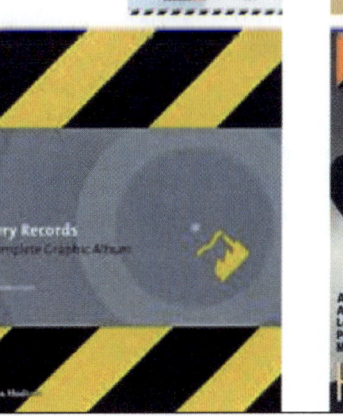

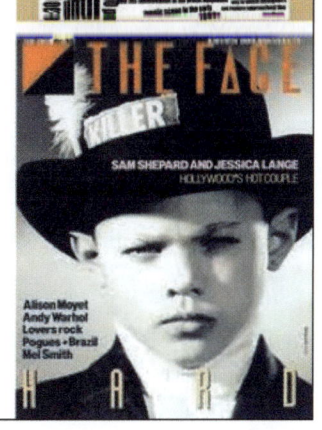

Remembering the key rules of presentation does not prohibit you from experimenting with some unlikely but exciting elements. Here a strong grid and subtle visual links with diagonals contribute to the balance and success of this bold, energetic layout. The text continually leads the eye back to the images.

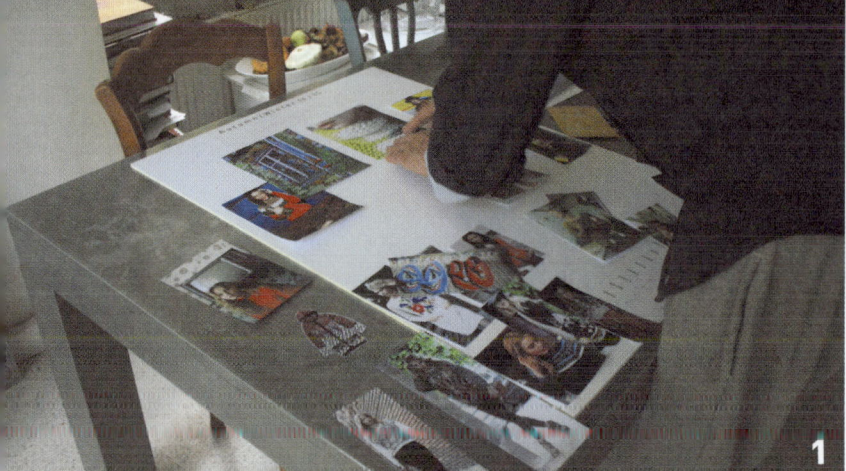

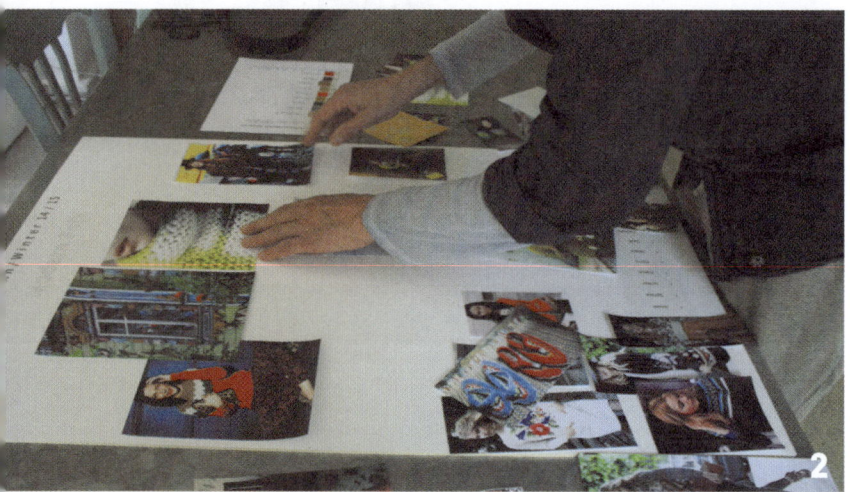

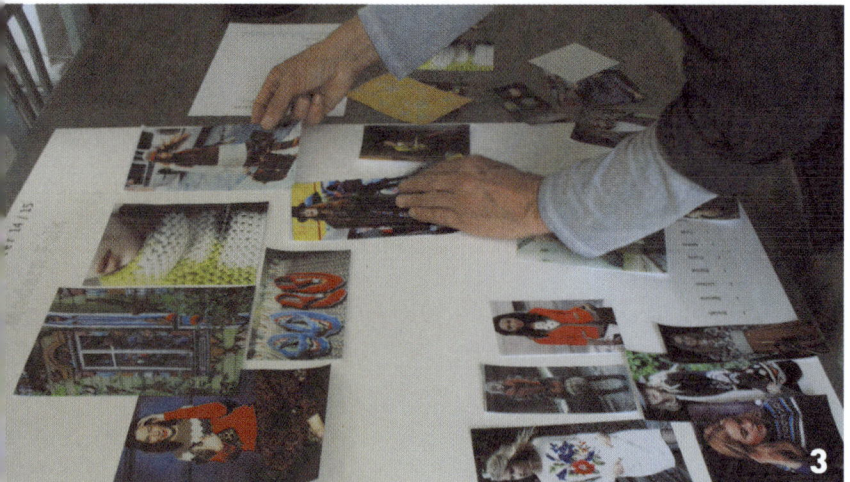

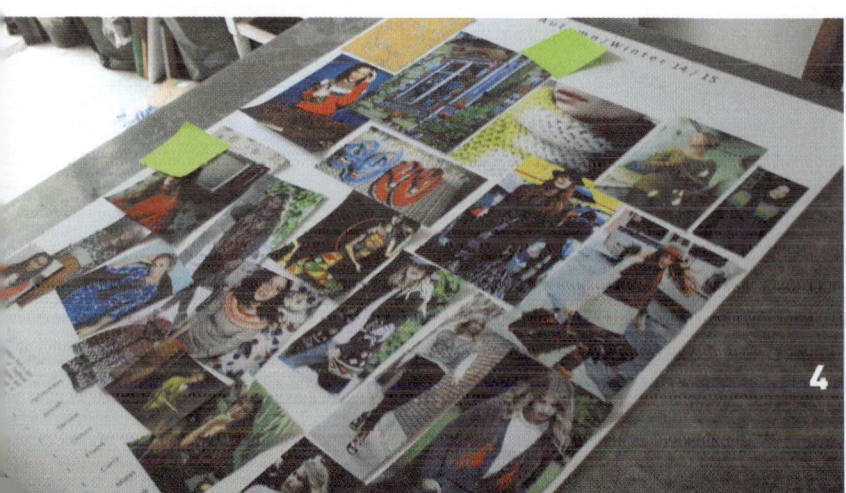

PRESENTATION BOARDS

I am by nature an advocate of simpler, sparer boards – with just perhaps four key images – but the brief for this project for a very commercially driven client required masses of clear, precise information for their buying and design teams.

I assembled one board for each of six themes identifying trends appropriate to their private label brands. Each board included a colour palette, with a short written synopsis of the colour story; comprehensive selections of images identifying a range of key garment types; and all elements and possibilities for each theme. Consequently the boards became image-heavy and needed clever organizing to be clearly defined and as readable and self-explanatory as possible.

The images had to be new, not US originated (to minimize the risk that the customer would already be familiar with them), style-right, and colour-right to reflect the colour palette. So as not to send out confusing messages, they had to be modelled by an appropriate image model (age, demographic, etc). Once all the images were found, I printed them to approximately the right scale, then trimmed and cropped them using a paper trimmer/cutter for speed and accuracy.

I usually have 'working titles' when researching themes until, gradually, final versions of titles are decided. I always use the same typeface every season and each of my clients has a different version of my format – this simplifies the decision-making process and so saves time and ensures continuity. By adhering to my formula, which includes a specific layout, point size for type, title positioning and all measurements kept on record, I stamp the boards with a style recognizable as my own as a kind of subtle branding. Titles, the season and all information required are printed on to Safmat, a printer-friendly transparent adhesive film that can be trimmed and applied to the foam boards I use for such presentations. When working on a set such as this, I will break the tasks down and print and trim all titles and text at once, then stick them to the boards. As all the pictures have already been printed and trimmed, along with a few spares or alternatives, I can arrange them for each theme one board at a time.

1 Start with the strongest or preferred images placed more or less centrally in prime position (although nothing is fixed at this stage).

2 Shift the images around and give some of them an extra trim to get them to fit or read better.

3 Juggle and shift the images as necessary (some will get edited out).

4 Use removable sticky notes to hold some of the images in position or to mark levels and right angles when they are lifted off to apply adhesive spray.

5 Stick down the images, taking care to maintain the exact positions and sequence of any layering.

6 A rubber roller reserved solely for this task (to keep it pristine) is used to flatten all images.

7 Once the images have been stuck in place, it is sometimes necessary to make tiny final trims using a craft knife and a cutting-edge rule.

8 Tiny slivers are trimmed away as some of the images are overlapped to fit or to cover any random text in a photograph. The last stage involves attaching the Pantone chips to the Safmat printed and placed colour palette at the foot of the board.

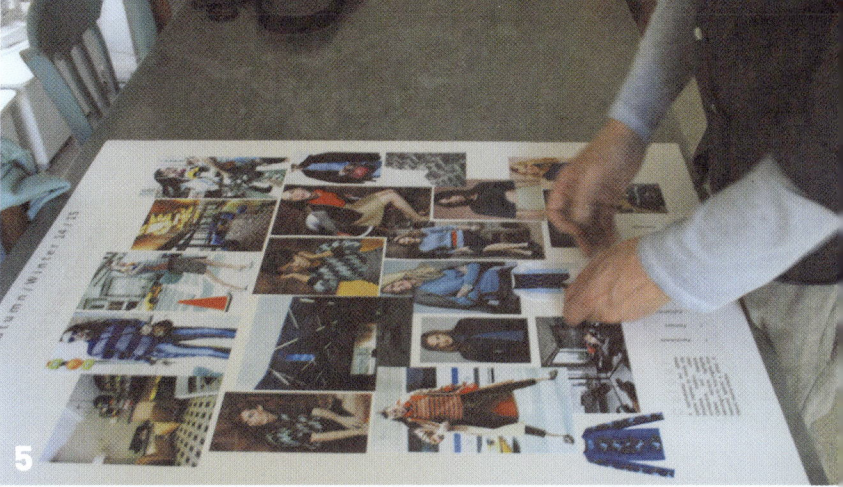

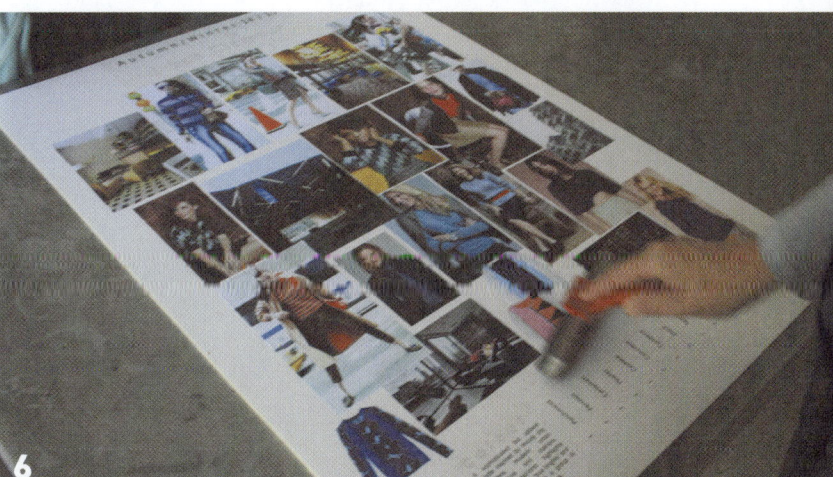

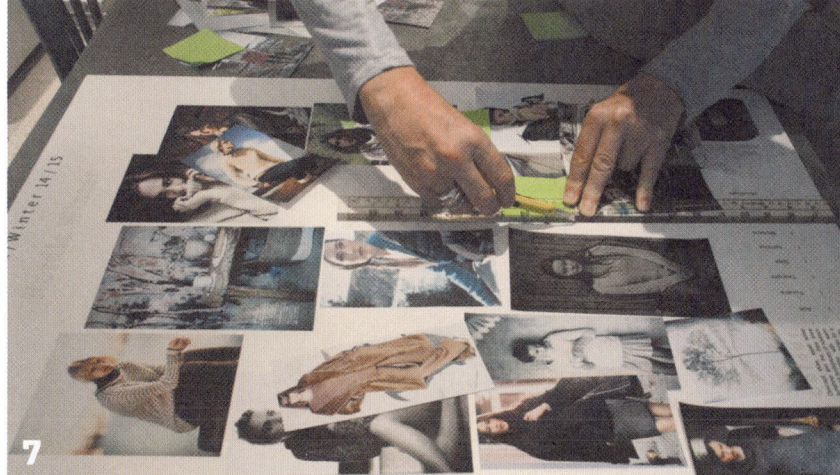

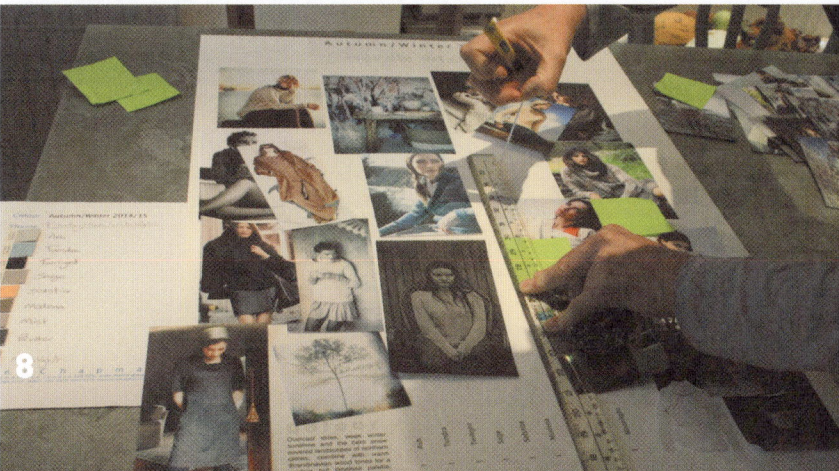

The six A1 boards are finished. While each displays its individual thematic differences, the six present a matching professional set and are ready to pack off to the client. Smaller less image-dense boards are sometimes produced using Photoshop and can be sent electronically or printed out. But for large format presentations such as this, actual boards with accurate colour references are still – for the moment, at least – required by clients for presentations to teams and meetings.

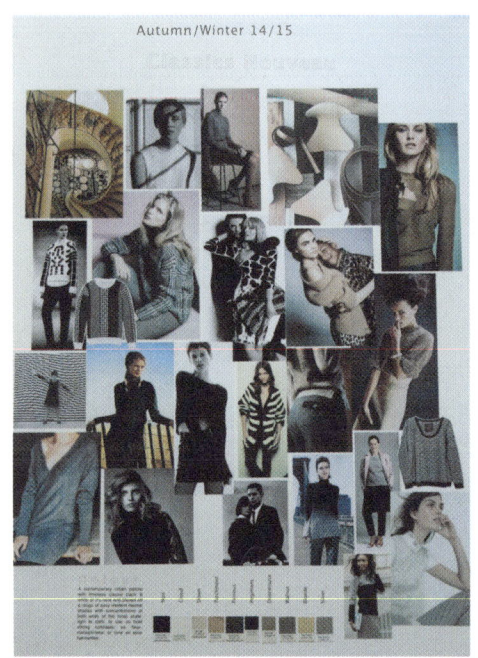

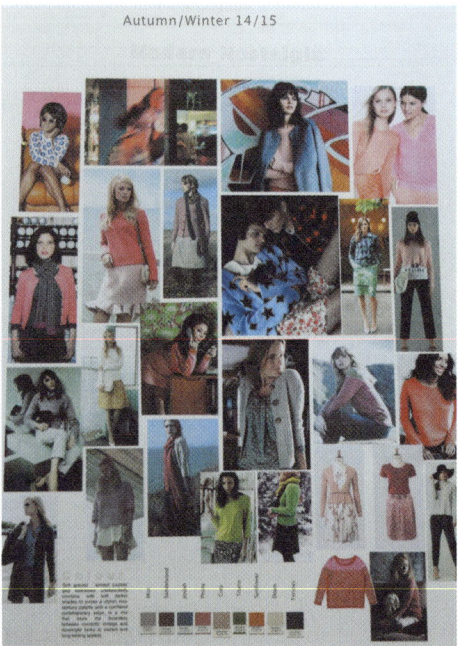

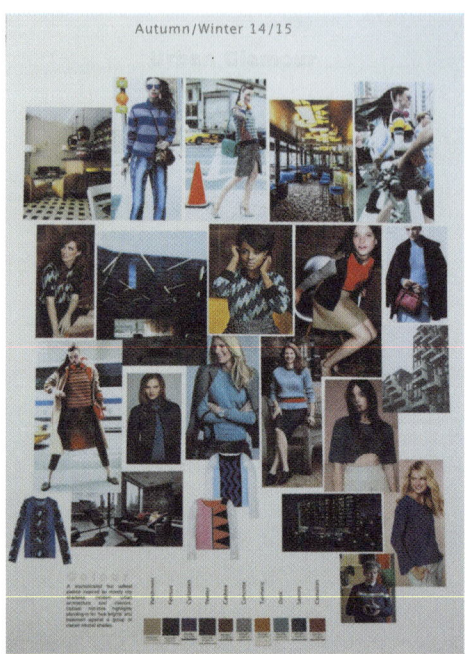

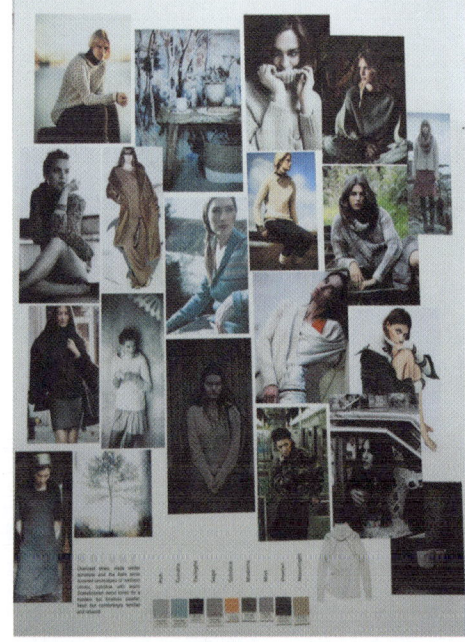

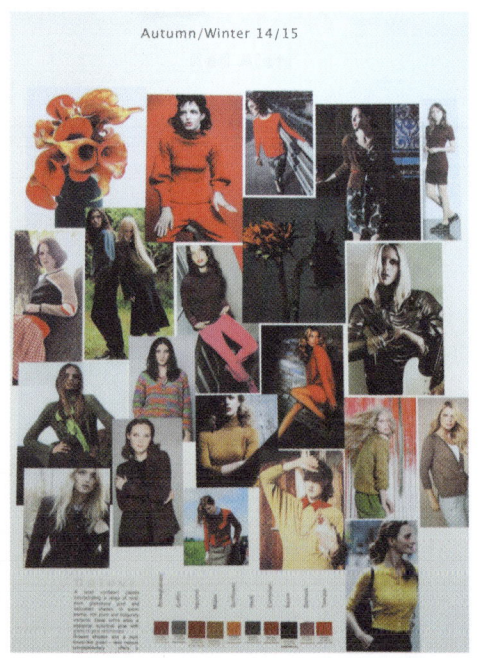

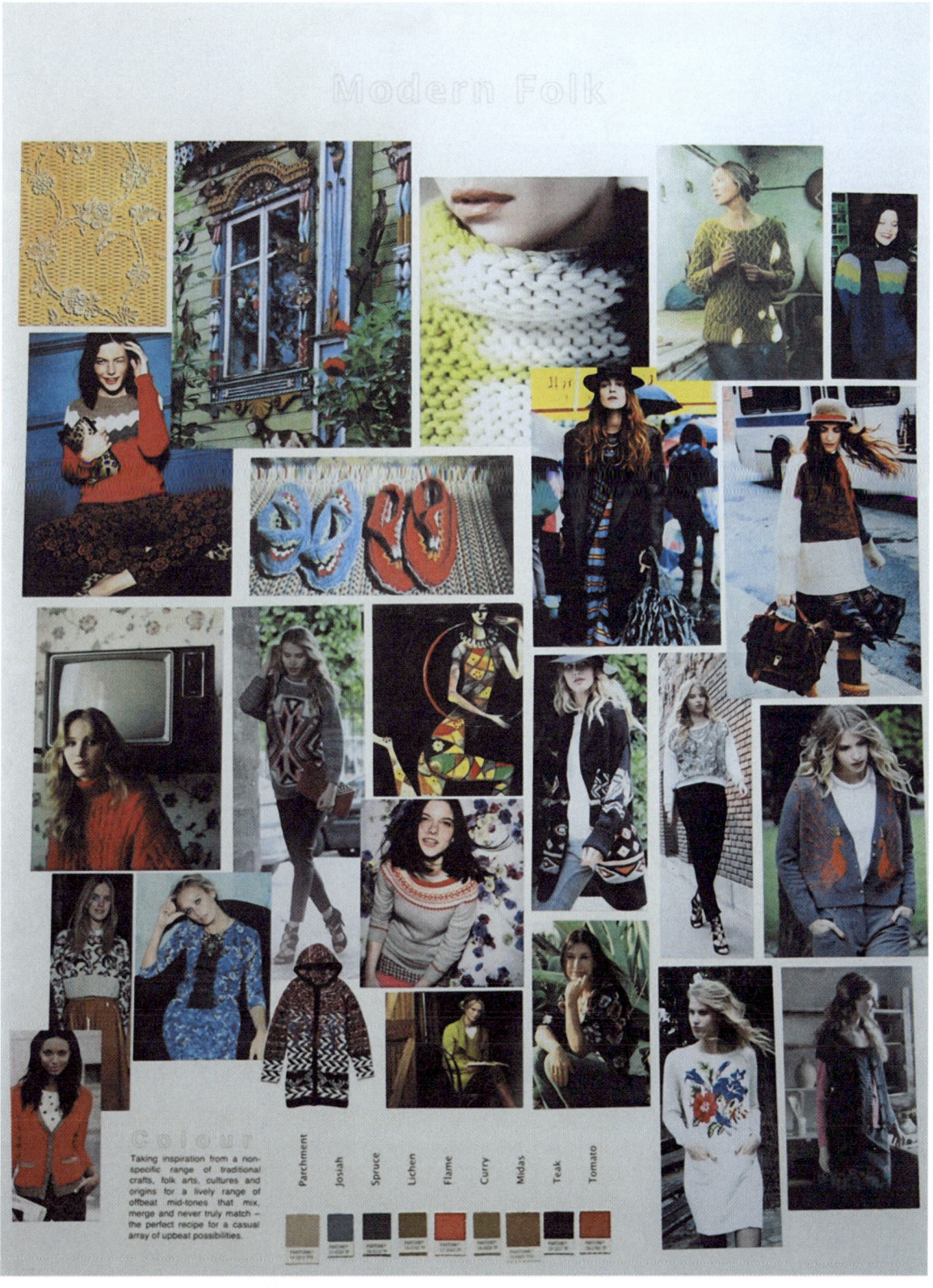

Densely image-laden, the finished presentation boards embrace all the trend influences relevant for each look, while successfully consolidating them under an umbrella theme that covers colour, yarn, pattern, texture, silhouette, detail and styling. The customer is presented with a complete overview of opportunities for trend-driven design ideas for each theme as appropriate for their market levels.

ILLUSTRATION

In these images for a commercial client, the illustrators use different techniques to achieve a loose, free approach to convey moods that are appropriately young and casual.

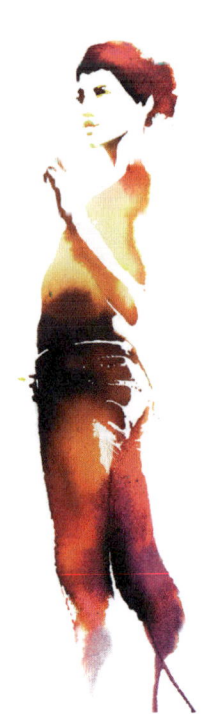
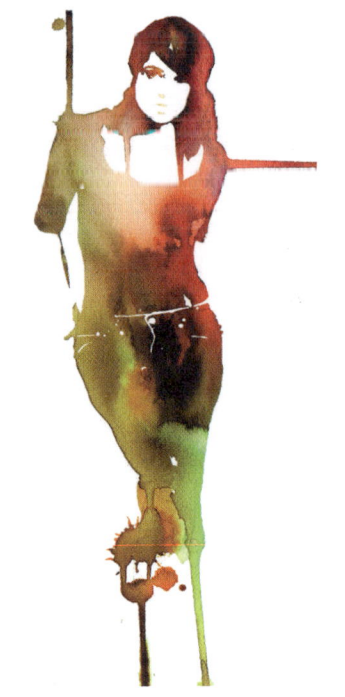
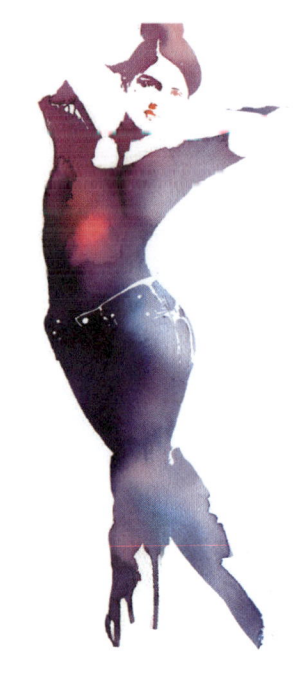

RIGHT: *Three figures, hand-drawn with inks and digitally manipulated, make for strong image and impact. Stina Persson*

BELOW: *In these two lively illustrations hand-drawn figures and loose mark-making are boldly combined through digital enhancement to achieve strong impact. Patrick Morgan*

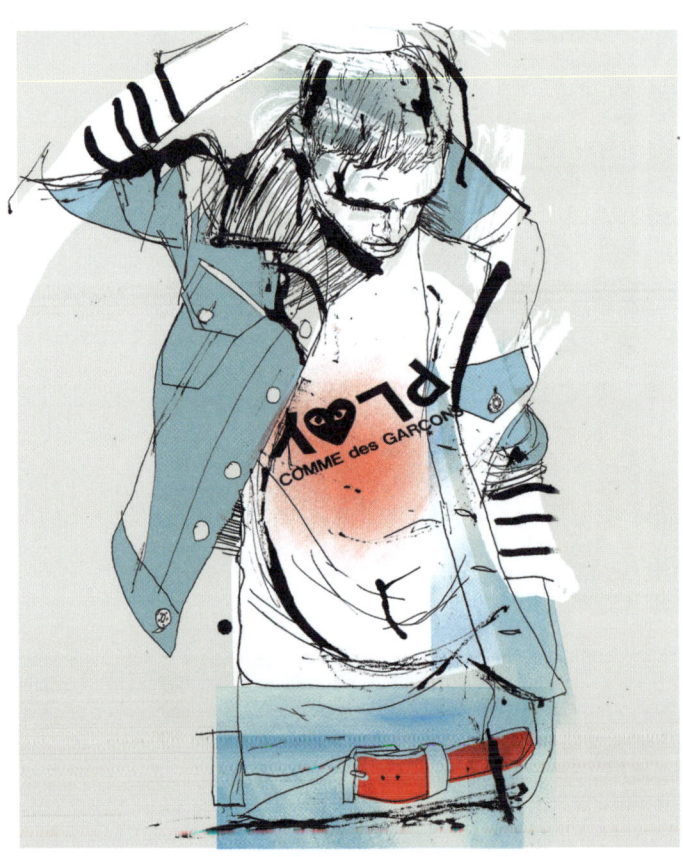

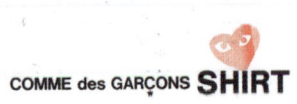

COMME des GARÇONS SHIRT

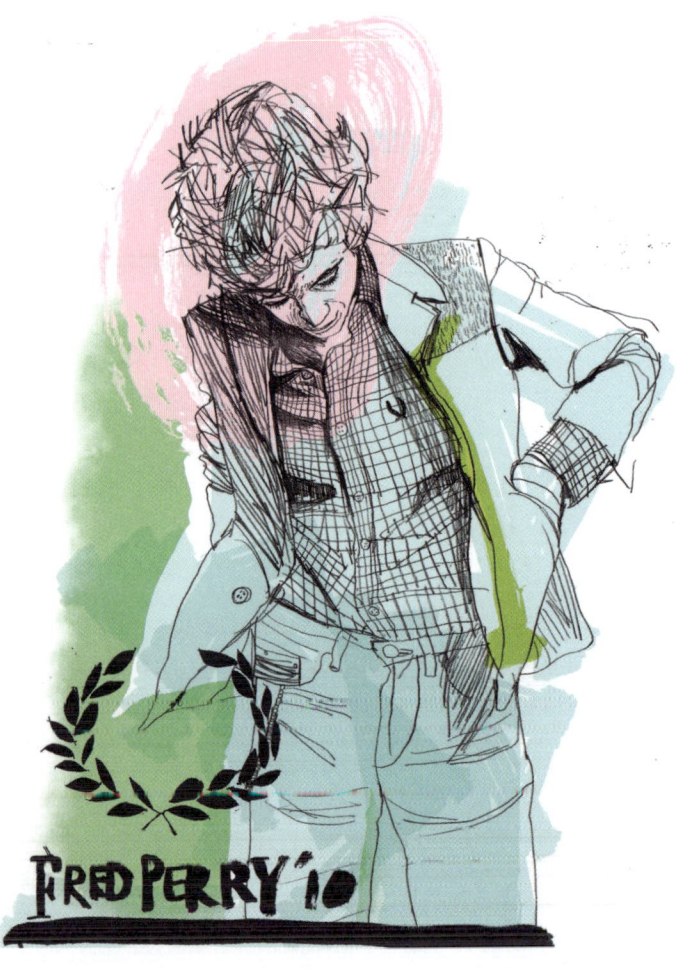

FRED PERRY '10

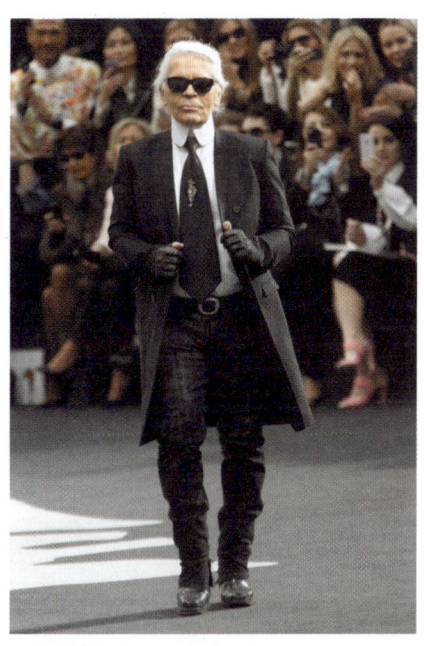

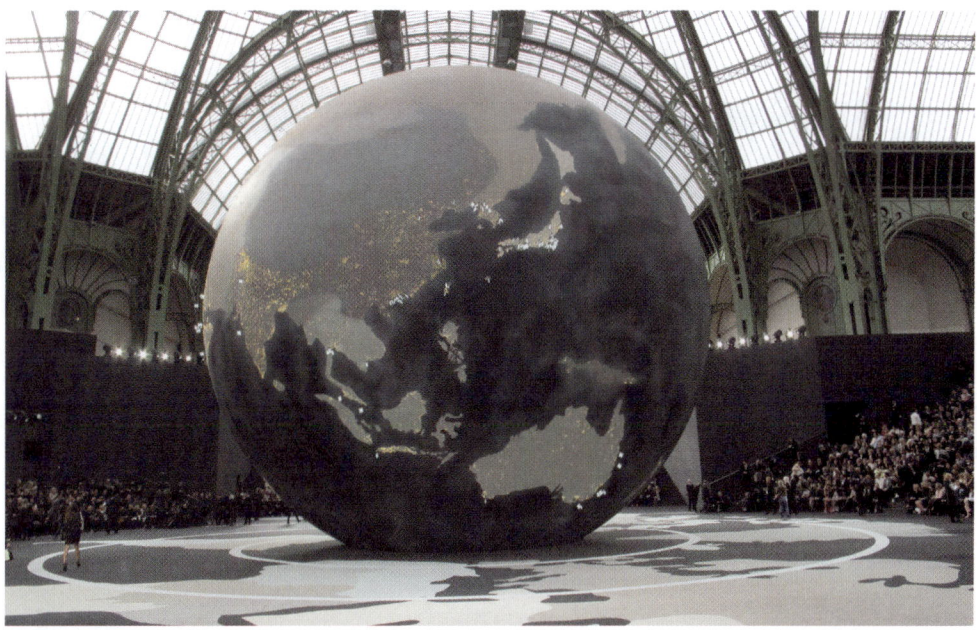

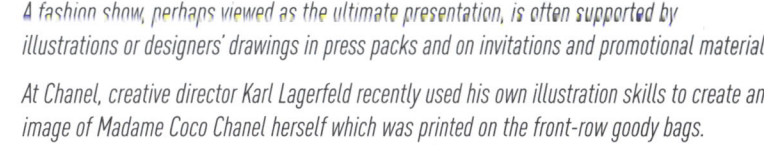

A fashion show, perhaps viewed as the ultimate presentation, is often supported by illustrations or designers' drawings in press packs and on invitations and promotional material.

At Chanel, creative director Karl Lagerfeld recently used his own illustration skills to create an image of Madame Coco Chanel herself which was printed on the front-row goody bags.

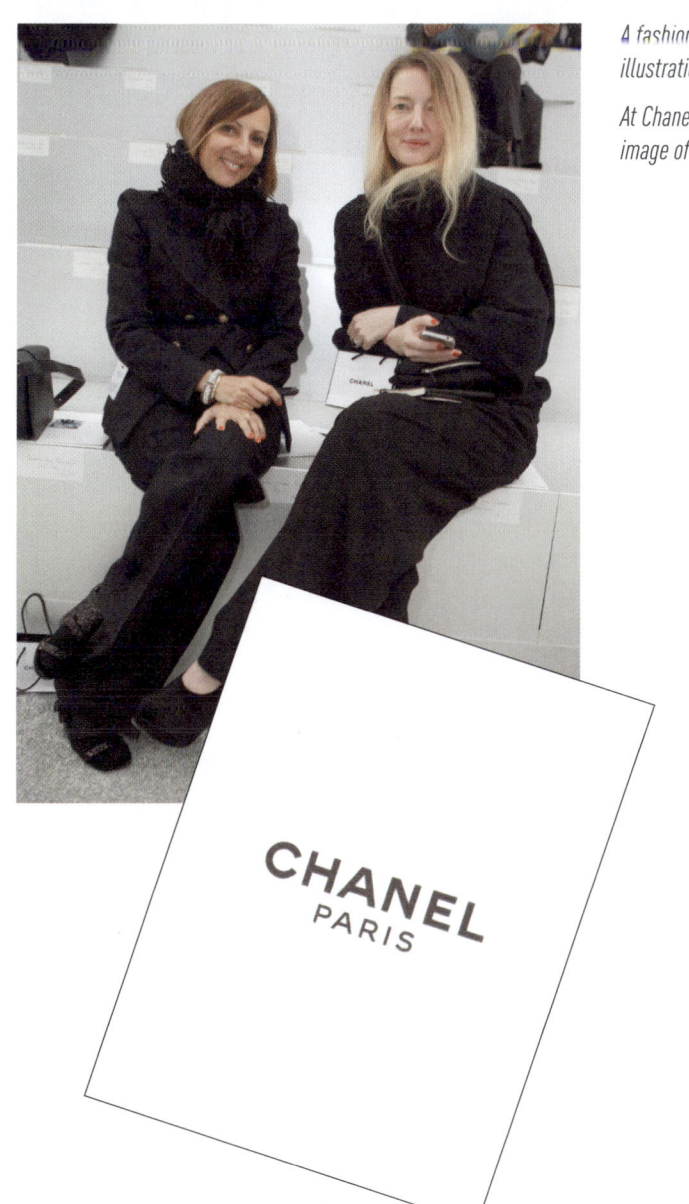

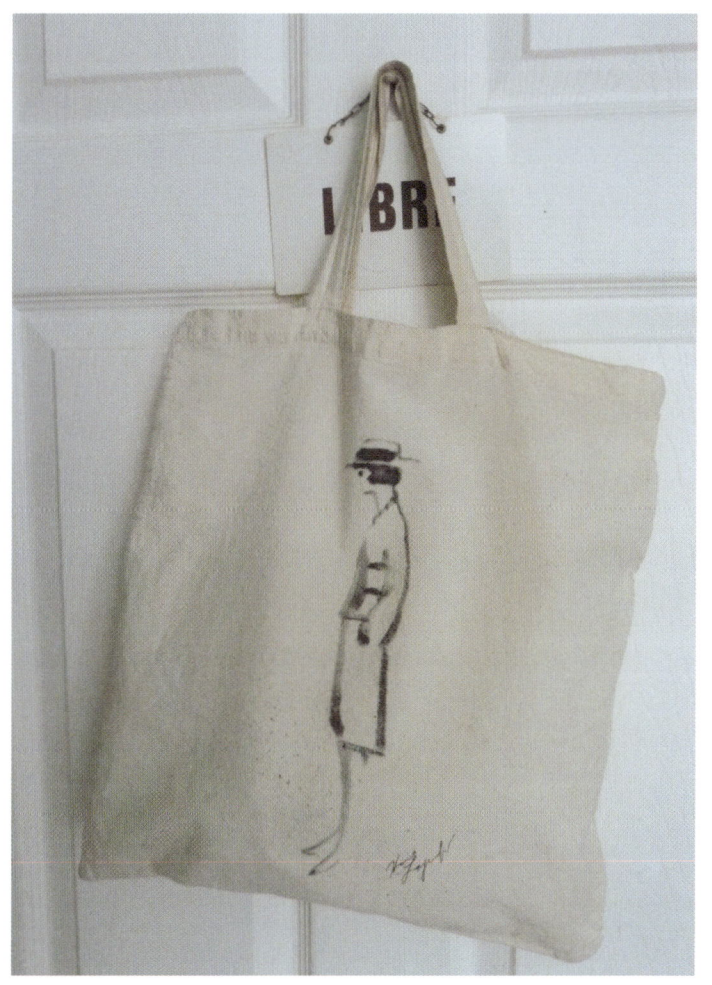

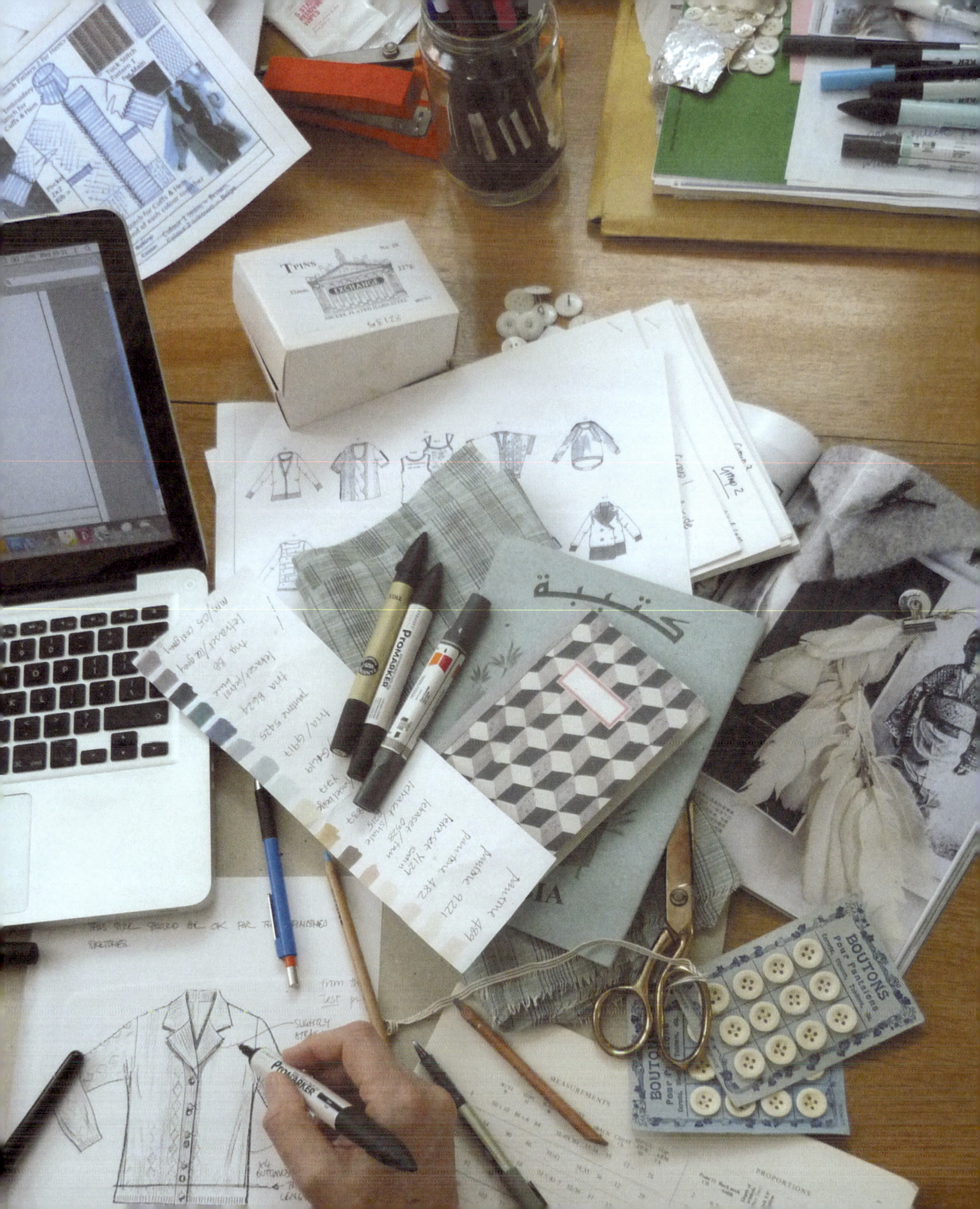

CHAPTER 10

WORKING IN INDUSTRY

Whether employed by a company or self-employed, as most illustrators and many designers are, it is important to be able to follow and adhere to a brief. Industry briefs, like any other, may be well planned and presented, straightforward and clear; but they are not always – your boss or your client may not fully know what they want, be vague about their requests or they may be fickle and change their mind without realizing they have shifted. Perhaps they have asked you to undertake a project without fully grasping its scope or the amount of work involved. The request may be unreasonable or impossible to achieve within the budget or time-span. You may even be briefed 'secondhand' by someone 'down the line' who is passing on requests without fully understanding the task themselves. Always try to get a written brief and don't be afraid to amend it; both parties need to clarify any grey areas and gather together all possible information. If anything is unclear or unspecified, remember it is important to ask questions and get the answers in writing.

AGREEING TERMS

Always get your fee and payment terms agreed and try to secure an advance, particularly if the project is long-running or will involve expenditure on your part. If your client is based overseas, make sure you are paid in your own currency at the agreed rate, not in their currency, as you may lose money in conversion; the client should also cover the cost of any payment transfer fees. Agree in advance how the work will be delivered; if electronically, check the digital resolution needed and ensure that your client is able to receive the right size files, etc. If you have physical (hard copy) to deliver, make sure it is clear who pays for the postage or courier, how long it will take to reach the client, and how much of your time will be involved, as that too should be allowed for in the budget.

When agreeing terms don't forget to take into consideration any other projects you are working on or engagements that may collide. If you think there may be a conflict between projects, alert your client to this and assure them of your discretion and professionalism – and be sure to follow that through! If you are not sure about a new client, check them out online, ask around – has anyone you know done work for them? Before beginning any work always understand your client's business, their market and customers. Check out their product and their stores; ask them how they perceive themselves and their brands they aspire to. It does not make you look silly to ask questions, but you are silly not to.

CAREER PATHWAYS

Career pathways are seldom clear and direct; careers segue along, offers are seized and undertaken. If we are lucky, someone may see talent and potential within us and we might end up in the most undreamt of places – frequently quite happily! The career pathways of the super-successful are familiar to us via the media; but other less prominent people have followed equally creative and rewarding careers and left their significant mark on fashion history.

MALCOLM BIRD

After studying Art Foundation at Rochdale Art College, Malcolm Bird studied fashion design at Manchester and gained an MA in Fashion Design at the Royal College of Art. He went on to be a key figure in the graphic and visual style of some of the most influential magazines and worked for Biba, the iconic fashion brand of the 1960s and 1970s.

Malcolm's illustrations presented here show his characteristic wit and distinctive personal handwriting, while reflecting a strong 1920s and 1930s influence very much in vogue at the time.

'Whilst still studying at Manchester, Honey magazine did an audition from the North and I took my portfolio of fashion drawings, but it was the humorous little drawings I'd added around the edges that they liked. I did illustrations for that issue, and others followed.

'Whilst at the Royal College, I also became a regular contributor to Petticoat, *the weekly 'sister' magazine of* Honey, *and subsequently several other magazines.*

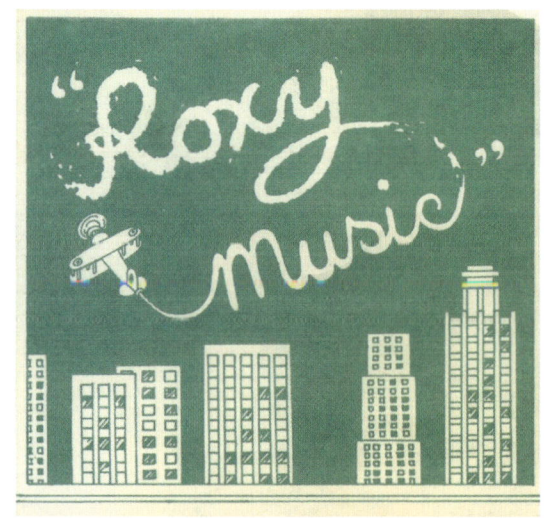

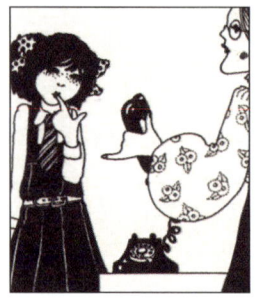

ABOVE: *The first artwork designed for the band Roxy Music in 1971 by Malcolm Bird. It was used, printed on satin, as backstage passes and, in repeat, as a paper poster.*

LEFT: *One of a series of illustrations 'Love through the Letterbox' by Malcolm Bird for* Honey *magazine, circa 1970*

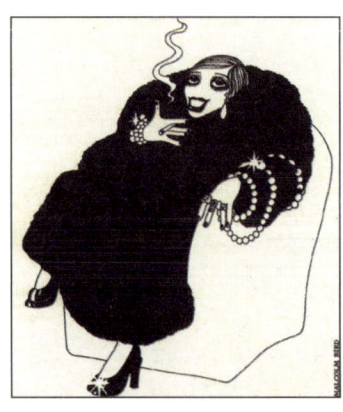

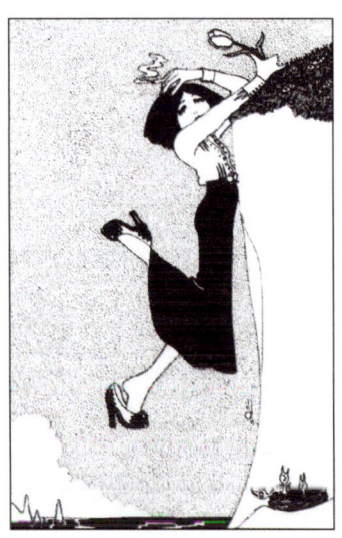

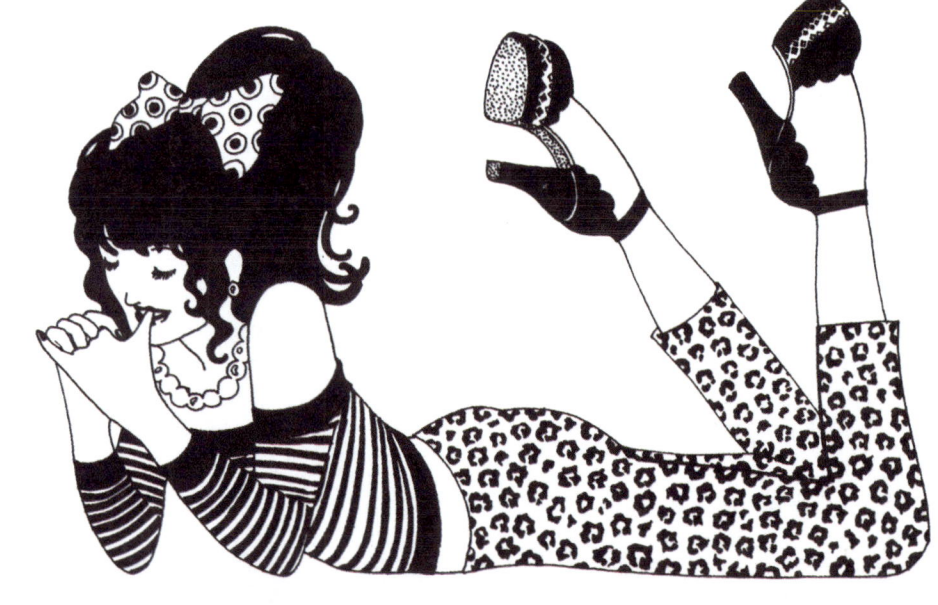

CALENDAR 1972

After leaving college I continued the magazine work, whilst taking a fashion design job three days a week.

'After that – being a huge Barbara Hulanicki fan – I went to work as one of her pattern cutters, and later was a colourist. I also did several interior drawings to promote the store, designed the children's department in the third of her four successive shops, and designed a huge reclining Biba lady cake for a party there. The illustration work continued and I worked regularly for a range of magazines and publications including: Jackie, Fashion Forecast, Vanity Fair, Mother, Woman's Realm, Woman, The Times, Sunday Times, and the Daily Mail, and designed greeting cards for Gallery Five.

'Many of my early magazine drawings were done freehand with a Rapidograph pen. Later, for both magazine and children's book illustration, I used Daler fine surface line and wash card, pencilled in first (tracing off a preliminary rough on a layout pad), using a Rapidograph for the black line and then watercolour for the colour. For black and white work I always use an A4 Bristol Board pad.'

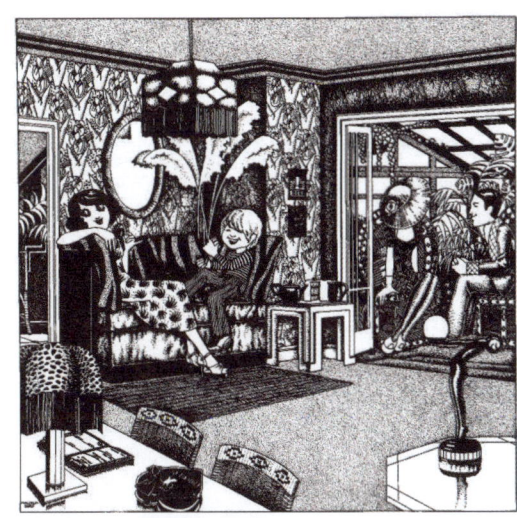

ABOVE: *Malcolm Bird, lounge drawing to promote the Biba brand, 1974*

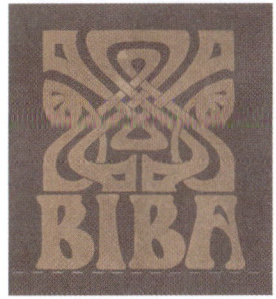

LEFT: *The iconic, Art Nouveau inspired Biba logo*

BELOW: *Bedroom drawing to promote Biba, 1974*

FAR LEFT CENTRE: *Woman smoking in an armchair by Malcolm Bird,* Petticoat *magazine, 1969*

FAR LEFT BOTTOM: *Malcolm Bird, 'How possessed are you?' – a quiz illustration for* Vanity Fair, *1970*

LEFT: *The cover of a calendar to promote Malcolm Bird's work*

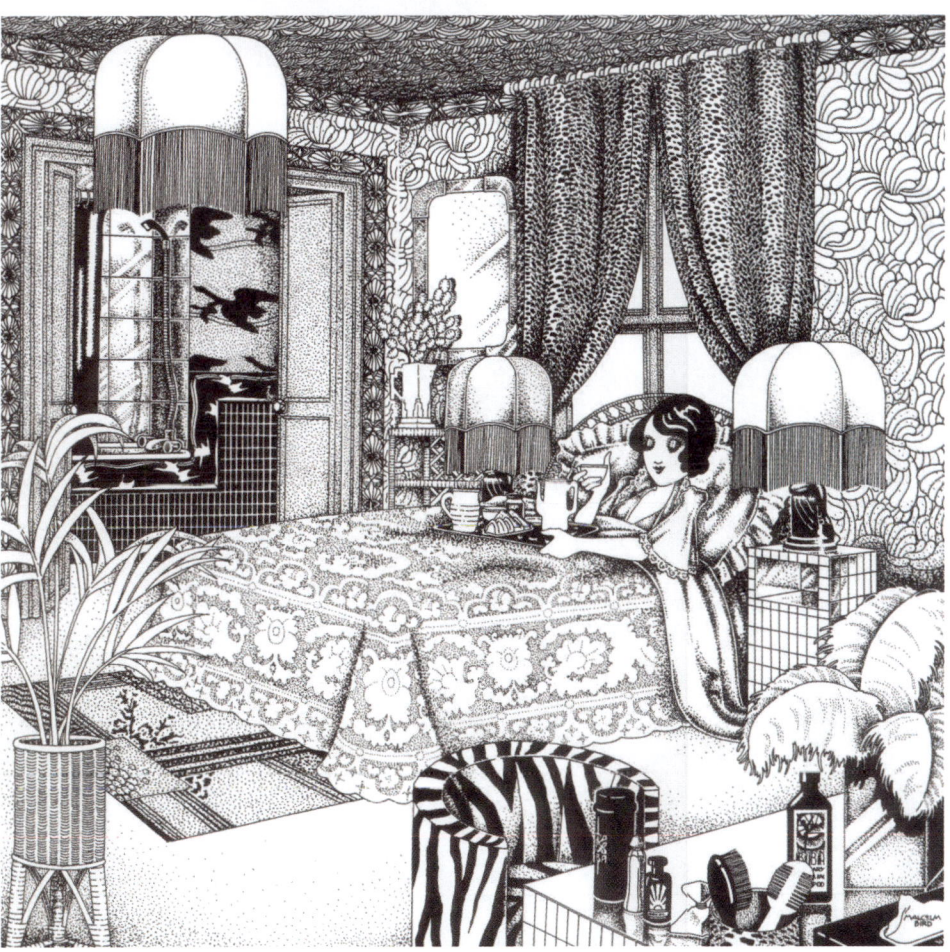

HILARY KIDD

Hilary is a freelance illustrator working for a wide range of clients that include womenswear, menswear and childrenswear. She also does beauty and accessories illustrations, working through agents and with design studios, trend bureaus and directly with brands and magazines.

1 *Insight women's trend forecast artwork, 2005/06. Brush pen, Pantone marker and crayon*

2 *Beauty advertisement, 1980s. Pencil and crayon*

3 *Trade magazine, 1990s. Brush pen, marker and crayon*

4 *Christmas card, 1980s. Brush pen and marker*

5 *Promotional drawing, 2011. Pencil and grey marker*

6 *Insight women's trend forecast, artwork 2008/09. Brush pen, marker and crayon*

7 *Insight women's trend forecast, artwork 2008/09. Brush pen, marker and crayon*

8a and b
International Wool Secretariat, 1996–7, womenswear styling directions. Brush pen, marker and crayon

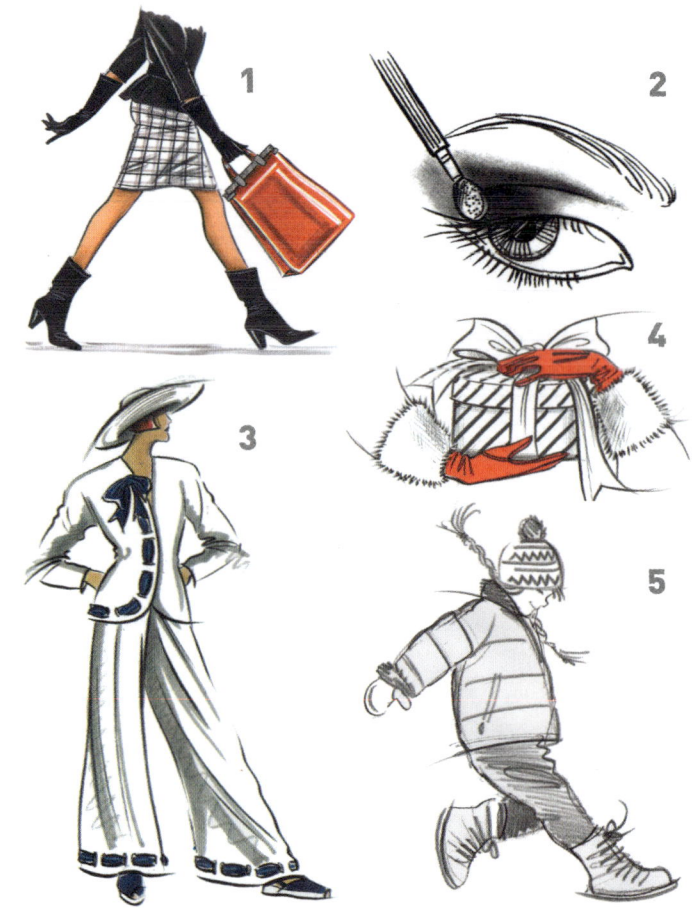

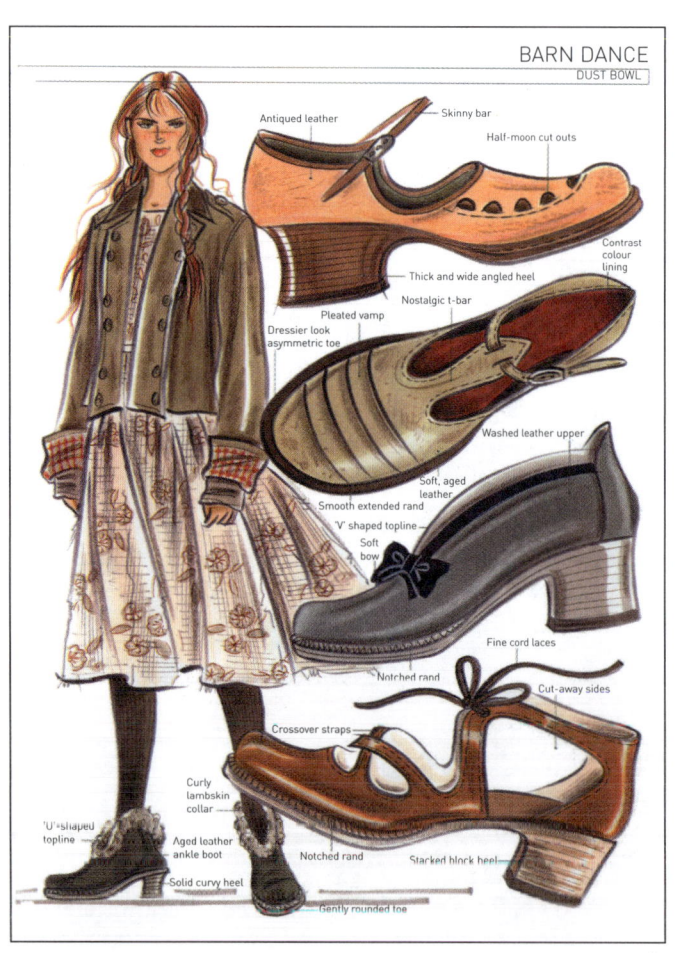

BARN DANCE
DUST BOWL

Antiqued leather
Skinny bar
Half-moon cut outs
Contrast colour lining
Thick and wide angled heel
Nostalgic t-bar
Pleated vamp
Dressier look asymmetric toe
Washed leather upper
Soft, aged leather
Smooth extended rand
'V' shaped topline
Soft bow
Fine cord laces
Notched rand
Cut-away sides
Crossover straps
Curly lambskin collar
'U'-shaped topline
Aged leather ankle boot
Notched rand
Stacked block heel
Solid curvy heel
Gently rounded toe

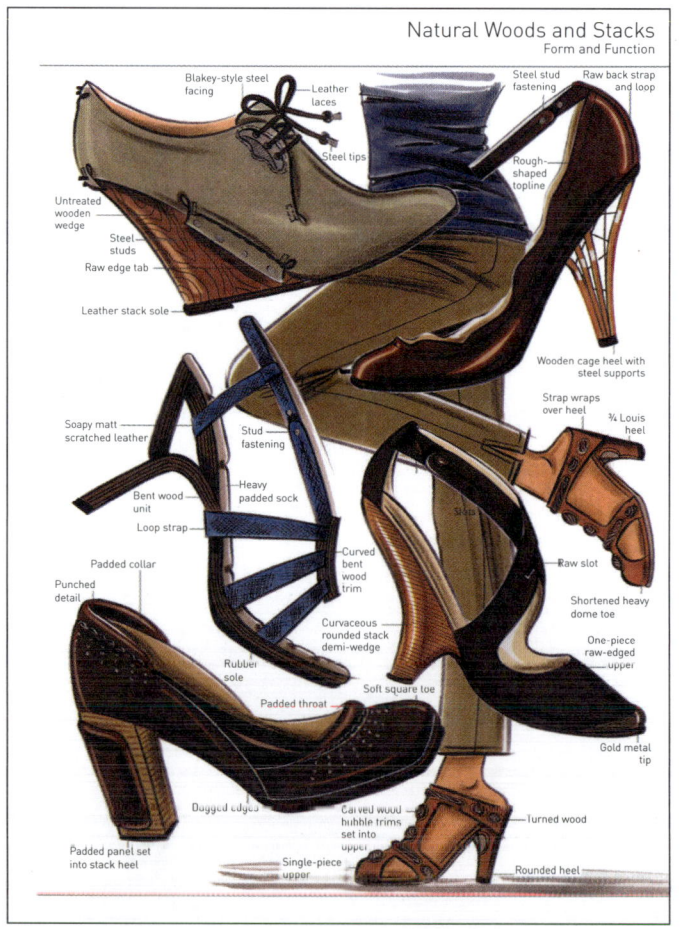

Natural Woods and Stacks
Form and Function

Blakey-style steel facing
Leather laces
Steel stud fastening
Raw back strap and loop
Steel tips
Untreated wooden wedge
Rough-shaped topline
Steel studs
Raw edge tab
Leather stack sole
Wooden cage heel with steel supports
Strap wraps over heel
¾ Louis heel
Soapy matt scratched leather
Stud fastening
Heavy padded sock
Bent wood unit
Loop strap
Curved bent wood trim
Raw slot
Padded collar
Shortened heavy dome toe
Punched detail
Curvaceous rounded stack demi-wedge
One-piece raw-edged upper
Rubber sole
Soft square toe
Padded throat
Gold metal tip
Carved wood bubble trims set into upper
Turned wood
Dagged edges
Single-piece upper
Padded panel set into stack heel
Rounded heel

8a

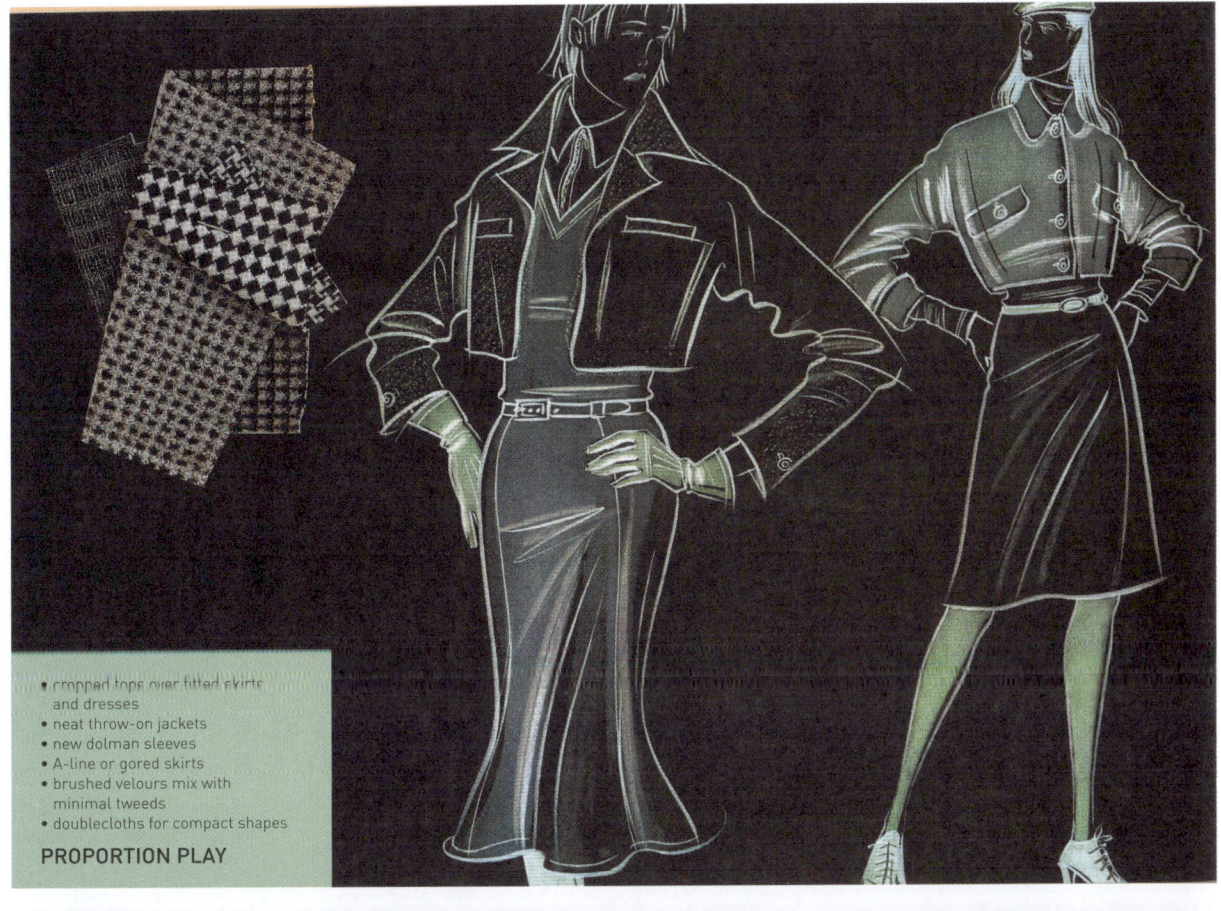

- cropped tops over fitted skirts and dresses
- neat throw-on jackets
- new dolman sleeves
- A-line or gored skirts
- brushed velours mix with minimal tweeds
- doublecloths for compact shapes

PROPORTION PLAY

8b

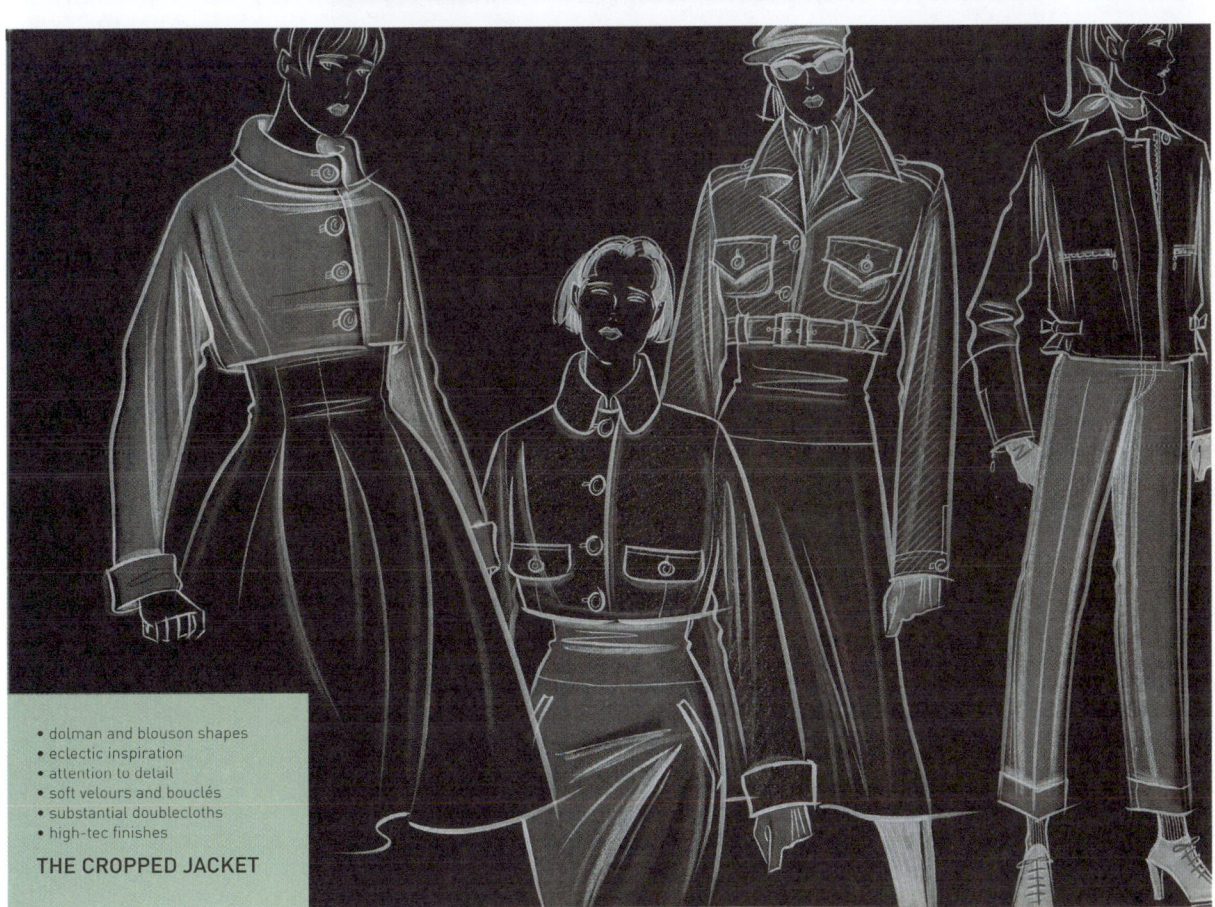

- dolman and blouson shapes
- eclectic inspiration
- attention to detail
- soft velours and bouclés
- substantial doublecloths
- high-tec finishes

THE CROPPED JACKET

CHRISTOPHER BROWN

'I consider myself as an illustrator who records fashion rather than a "fashion illustrator", a slightly different approach which has been popular. I try to create a mood, a feeling or "fantasy" of the collection rather than simply recording the clothes.'

'When visiting the collections, I always sketched, using a camera simply as an aide-mémoire. At first I was rather slow at getting details down but I soon sped up. I feel that unless I draw something I won't remember it.'

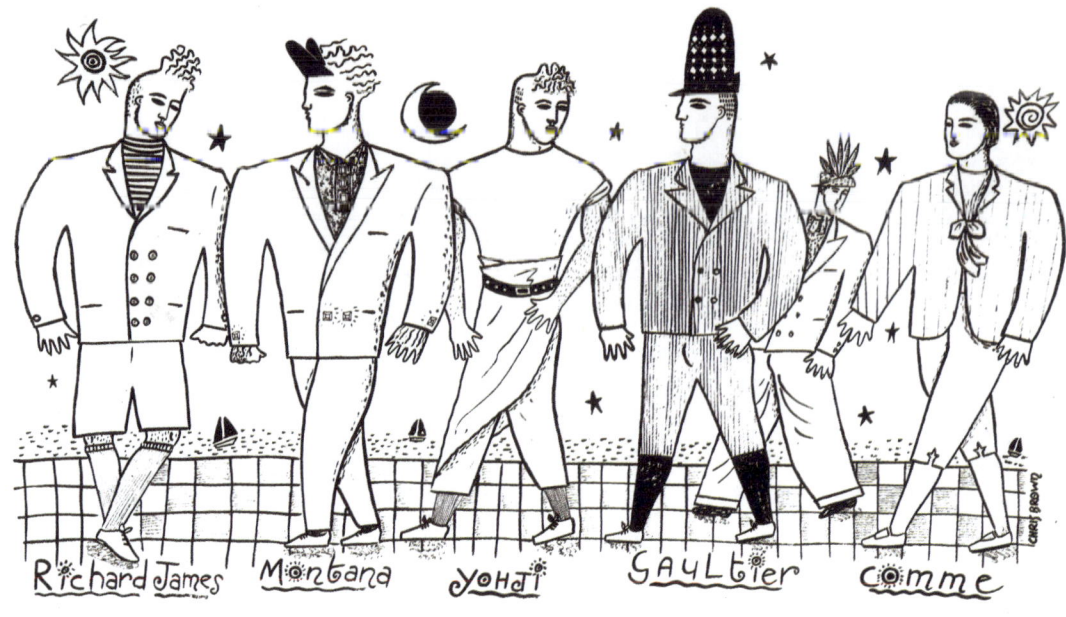

ABOVE: The Times, *double page spread, black and white illustration, ink with brush and dip pen, late 1980s*

BELOW: Sunday Times, *late 1980s, double page spread*

BOTTOM OF FACING PAGE: *'Les Hommes Like It Hot', Sunday Times, 1988–9. Cerruti (left) and Yves St Laurent (right). 'For this article I used my sketches done both in the show and afterwards in the showroom, and I also took photographs to use as additional reference back in my studio for the finished illustrations, which used collage of found and hand-painted papers.'*

'I suggested the article after seeing an YSL show and meeting with Bernard Sanz who became designer in 1987. I was interested in how designers working for famous houses design not for "themselves" but in the spirit of the designer . . . After the article was published Bernard Sanz asked me to design ties for his next collection.'

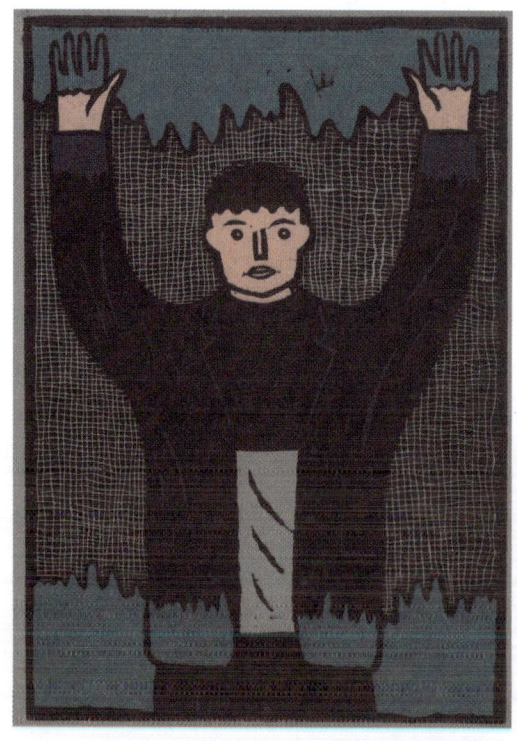

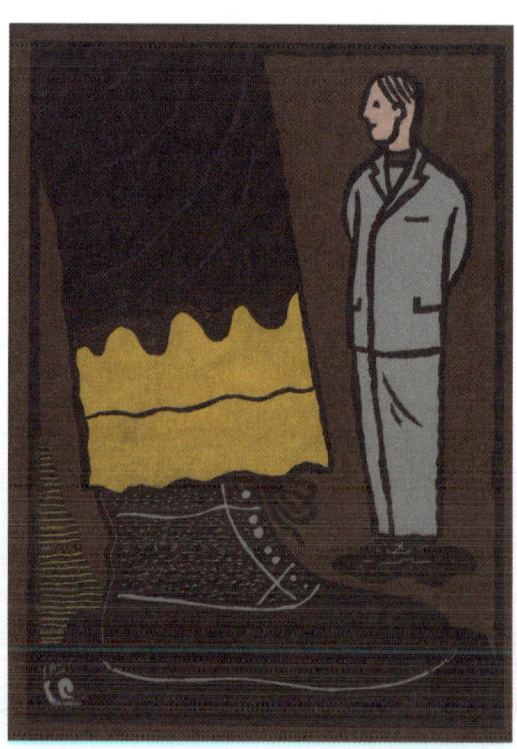

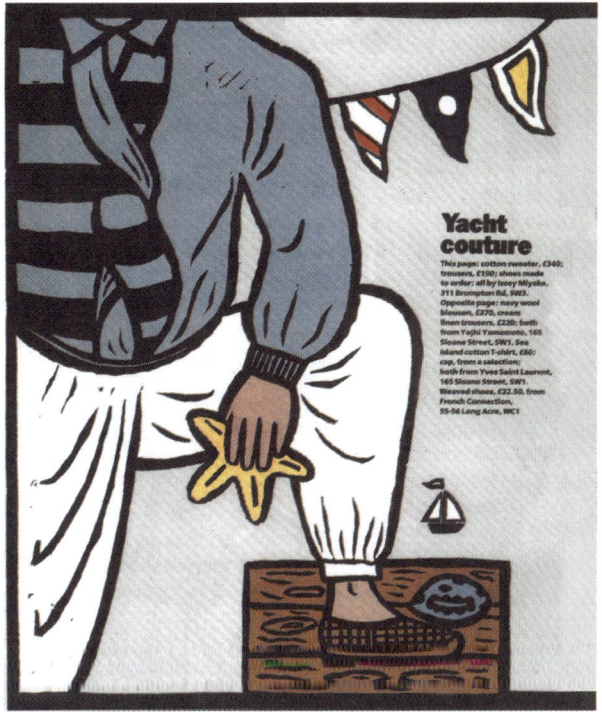

Yacht
couture

This page: cotton sweater, £340;
trousers, £190; shoes made
to order; all by Issey Miyake,
311 Brompton Rd, SW3.
Opposite page: navy wool
blouson, £370; cream
linen trousers, £220; both
from Yohji Yamamoto, 185
Sloane Street, SW1. Sea
Island cotton T-shirt, £80;
cap, from a selection;
both from Yves Saint Laurent,
165 Sloane Street, SW1.
Weaved shoes, £32.50, from
French Connection,
55-56 Long Acre, WC1

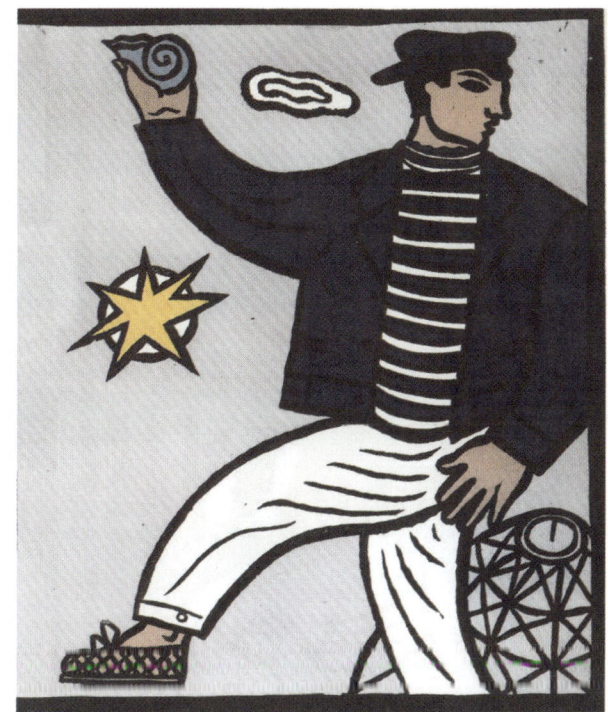

ABOVE: 'This large linocut was one of three spreads for the Sunday Times. It was the first of my "fashion" illustrations for a newspaper although I had previously done work for designers such as Artwork, Jasper Conran, Betty Jackson and Paul Howie.

'It came about because Pedro Silmon, the art director (with whom I had been at the RCA), asked if I was interested in contributing to the men's supplement. I, of course, jumped at the chance and went in and met with him and Caroline Baker the fashion editor.

'I then arranged to get invitations to the shows in Paris sketching. On my return I put together a story based around a summer in my imagination in the south of France. Once I decided which clothes to use, I contacted the designers and borrowed the items to draw using a model to pose for me. Then I transferred the drawings to lino and printed and collaged the final artwork.

'The illustrations won the W.H. Smith Illustration Award.'

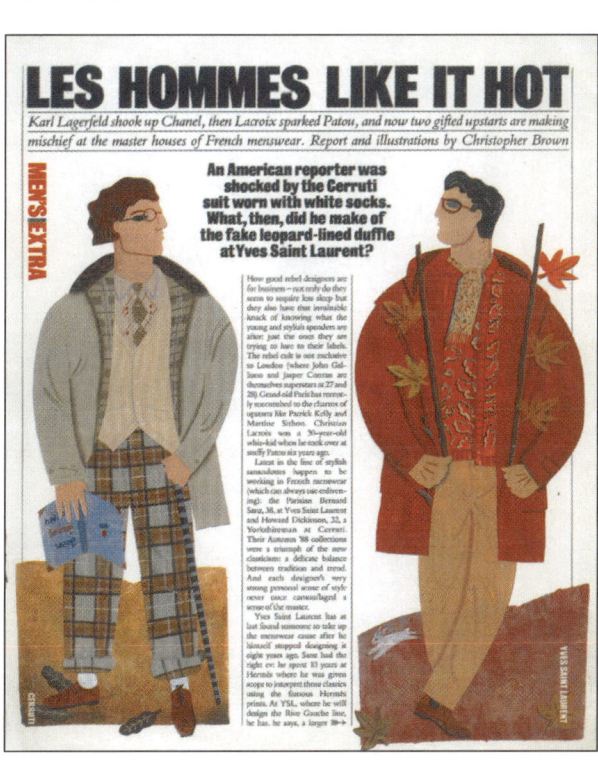

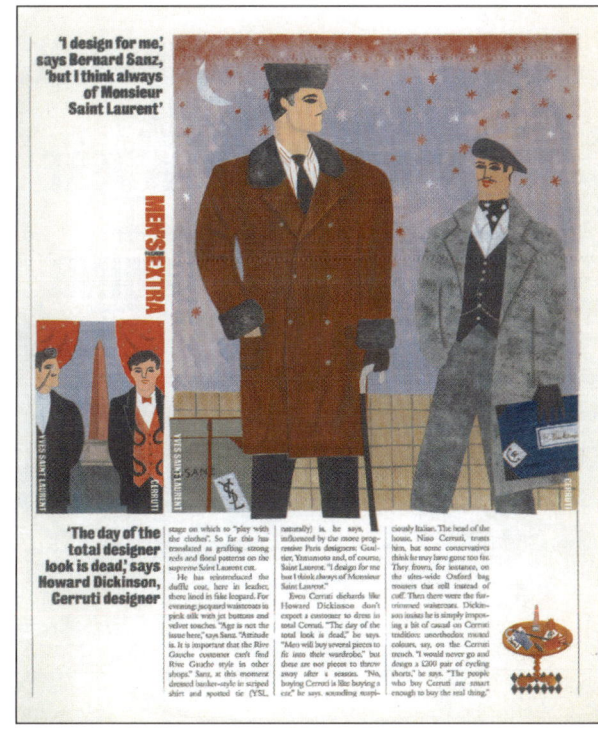

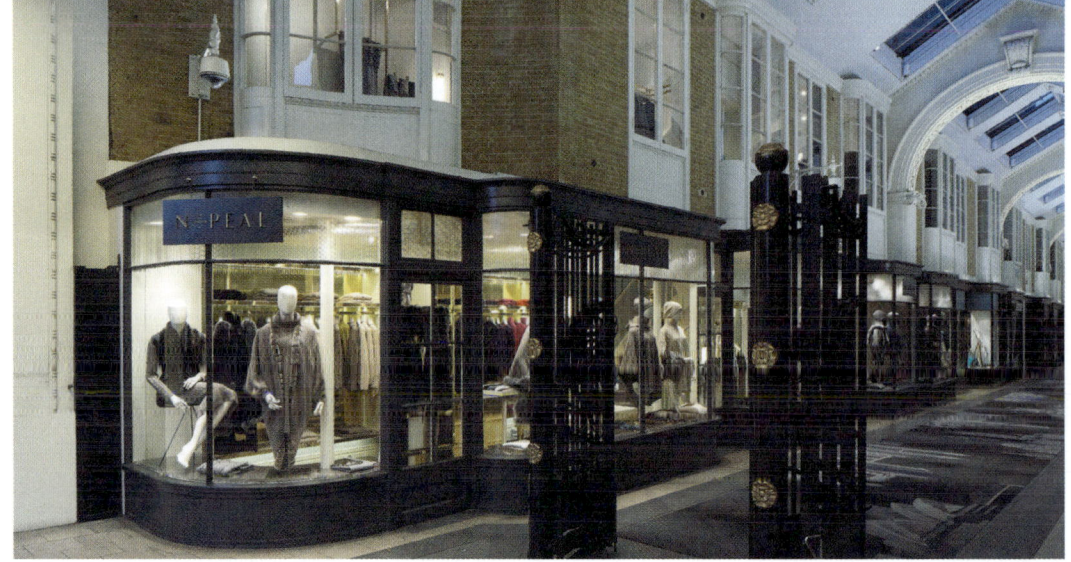

LEFT: *The window of N Peal in Burlington Arcade, London*

BOTTOM LEFT: *Mobile phone camera photographs, quick roughs and notes record the essential details and information while on site with the client's range.*

CATALOGUING AND RECORDING
N PEAL
(19 36)

Founded in 1936 by Nat Peal, this company has traded in luxurious cashmere knitwear from its Burlington Arcade shop for over 75 years. This assignment is an example typical of some of the many 'behind the scenes' roles for a freelance fashion illustrator, which are part of the rich and sprawling support system of the fashion industry.

'For this project, the brief was to sketch the client's knitwear range in a clear and readable style for the purpose of making a complete range plan. This plan was to be used by sales and merchandising teams when organizing, planning and tracking stock.

'I had just a day to work from the samples in the limited space of the company's stockroom to rough out the range. I could then do the final drawings at home in my workroom, a total of 126 pieces. The whole project needed to be completed in just a few days.

'So I arrived armed with layout pads, post-it notes, pens, pencils, a men's and a women's template, bulldog clips and pegs to hold garments in a good shape and my camera-phone to make additional records. A bottle of water and a sandwich completed my kit – it was a busy day!

'I began by making quick roughs, keeping an eye on the time to pace myself. I knew how many pieces I had to record in the available time – so to speed up I took photos of stitches, patterns and details – for accurately checking of proportions when refining my sketches later – all the time keeping a record of the style numbers too.

'The drawings later became an aide mémoire for staff teams to view against the sales figures when designing and range-building the following seasons.'

JUDITH CHEEK

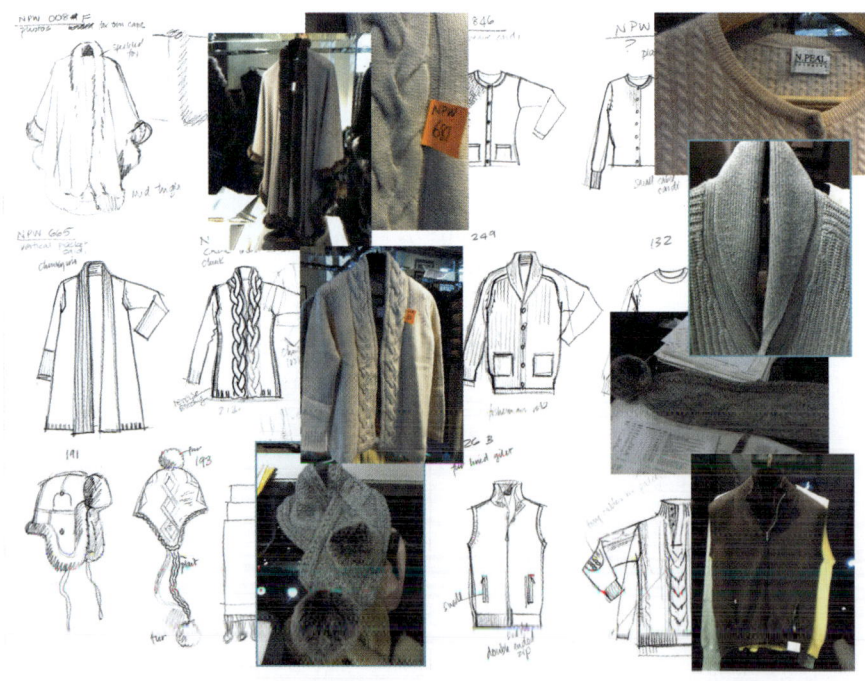

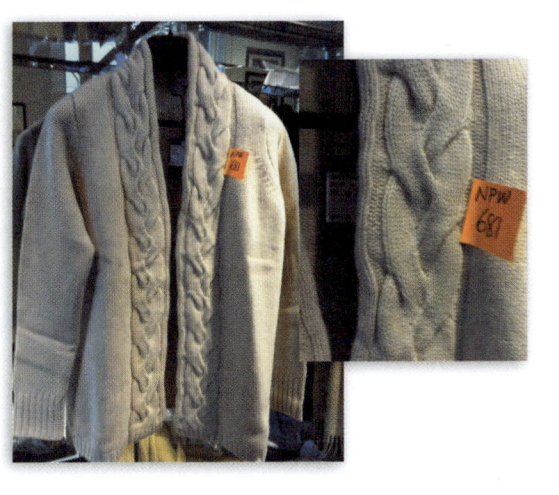

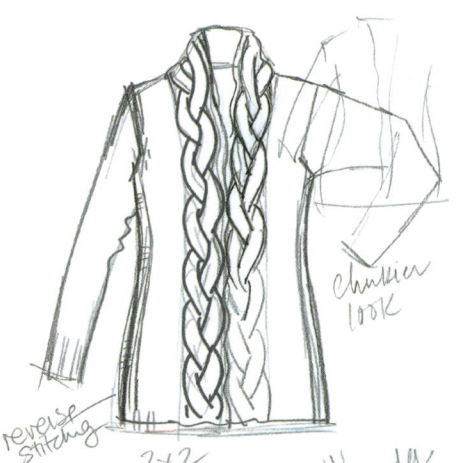

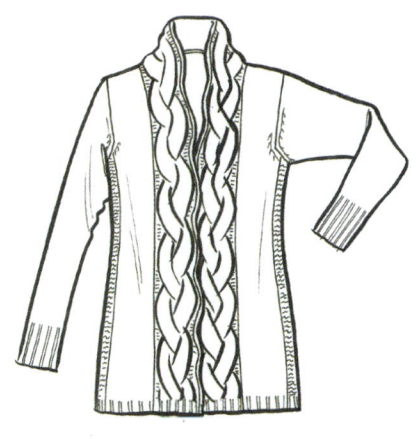

ABOVE: *Photographs, rough sketches and notes made on site help with detail and accuracy when redrawing roughs. The final clear drawings are completed and inked in using a fine fibre-tip and a brush pen.*

BELOW: *The finished drawings provide a clear and readable overview of styles in the range. Simple, precise drawings like this have all manner of end-uses including websites and e-commerce.*

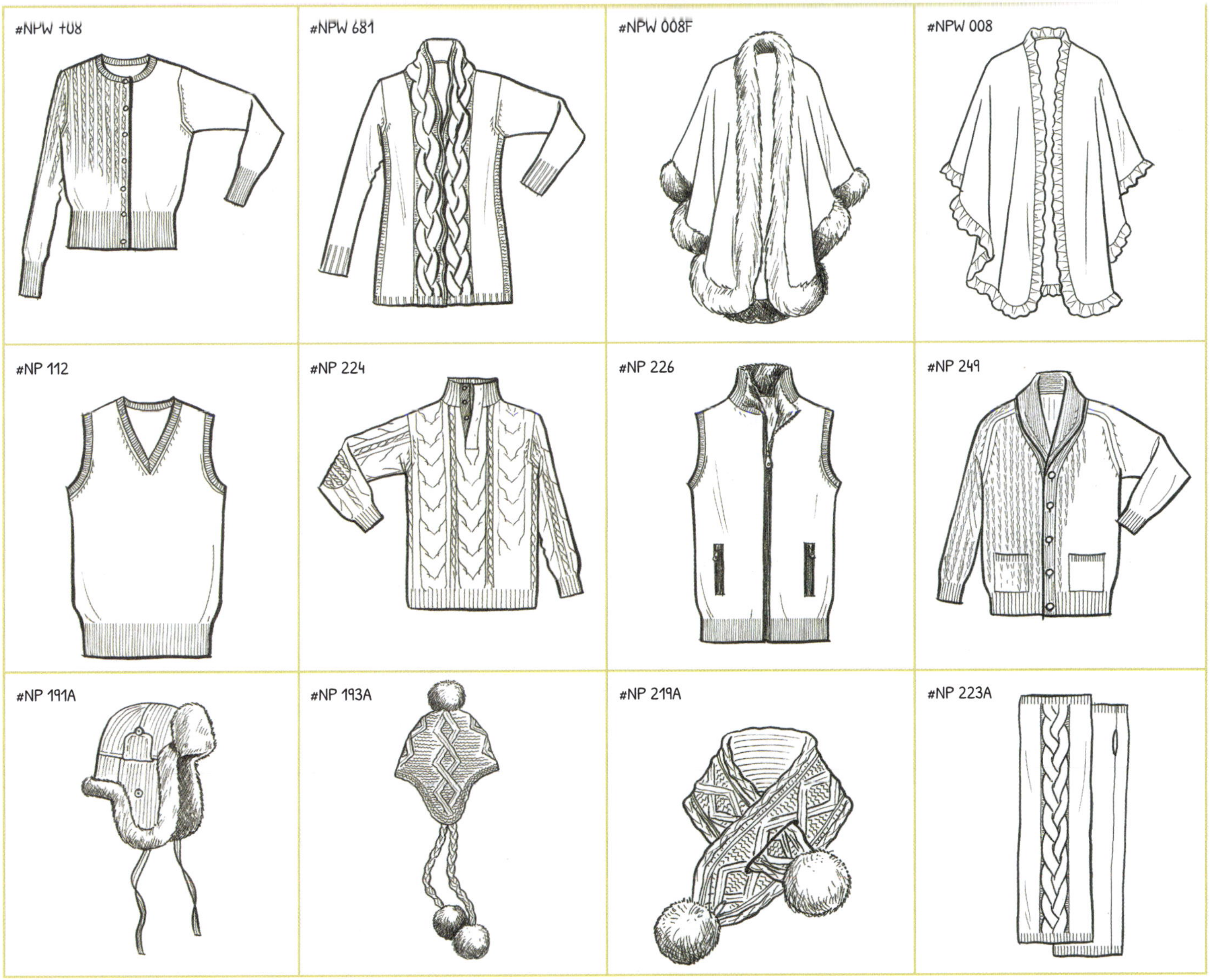

#NPW 408

#NPW 681

#NPW 008F

#NPW 008

#NP 112

#NP 224

#NP 226

#NP 249

#NP 191A

#NP 193A

#NP 219A

#NP 223A

IAN BATTEN

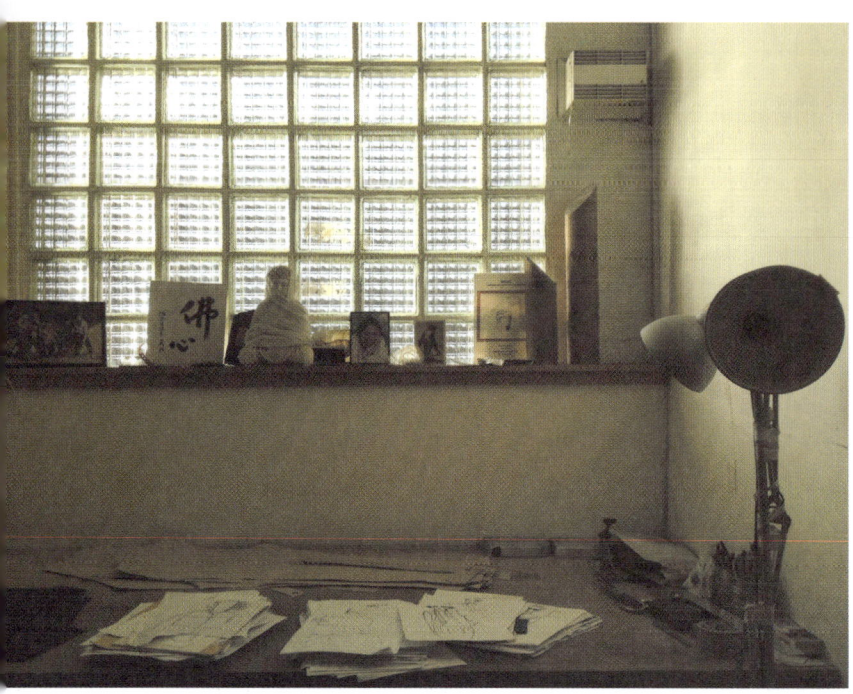

Ian Batten runs his label from a London studio, designing two collections a year for men and women. He works largely with traditional quality British and European cloth mills and he manufactures in the UK. The Ian Batten range sells to selective stores worldwide and directly to an exclusive range of personal clients.

Ian draws initially for himself, to generate and develop ideas. His drawings help him refine and select ideas to go forward into sampling, range planning and, later, production.

IAN BATTEN

LEFT: *Greatly influenced by Japanese design aesthetics, the studio is spare, compact, well-planned and organized.*

BELOW: *Menswear design sketches demonstrate traditional influences and Batten's flair for strong tailoring. The sketches also show fabric allocations and designer's notes for variations.*

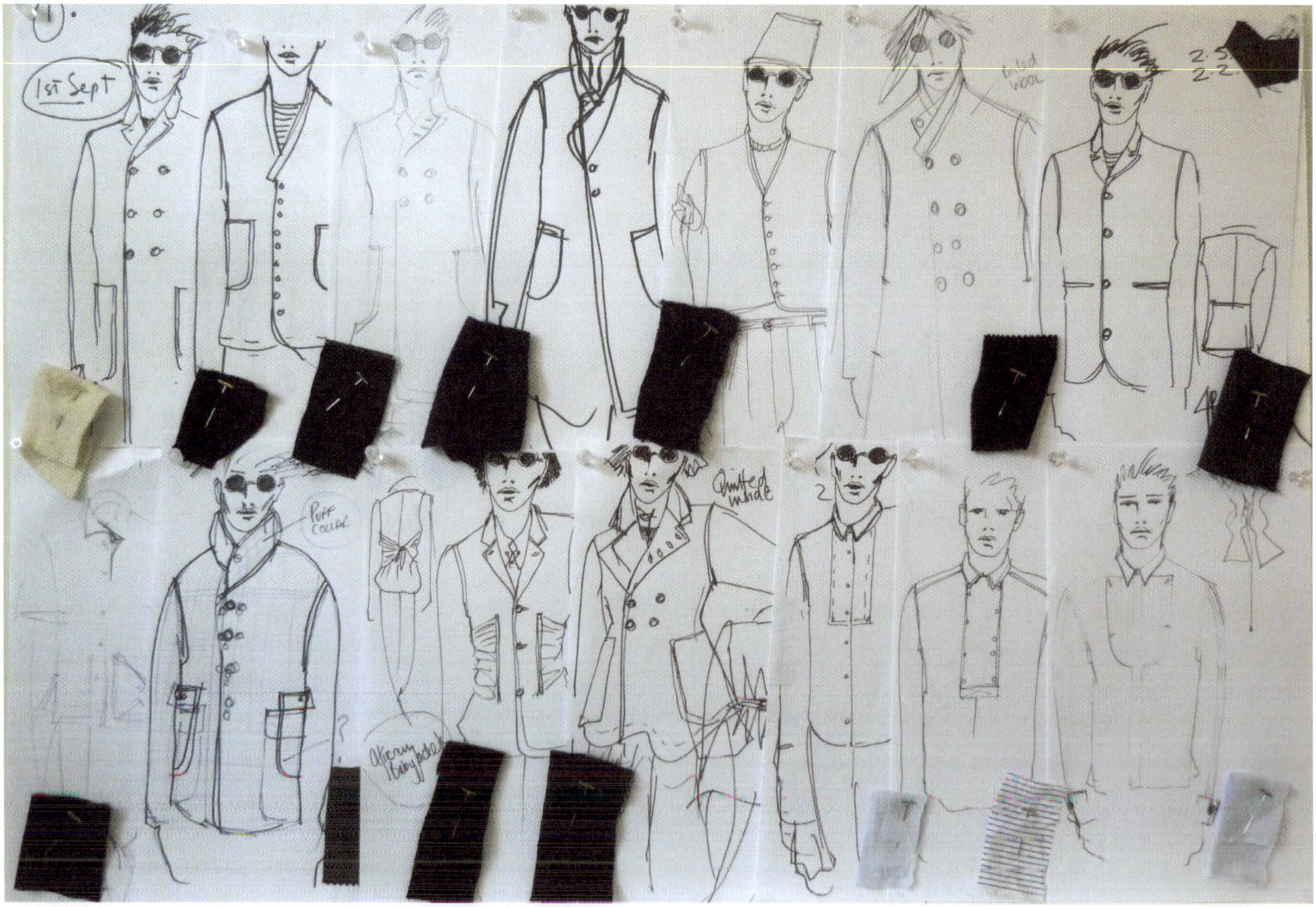

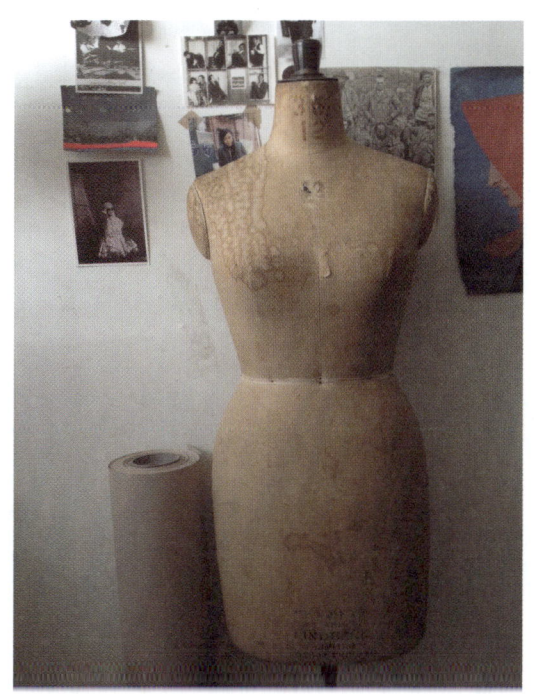

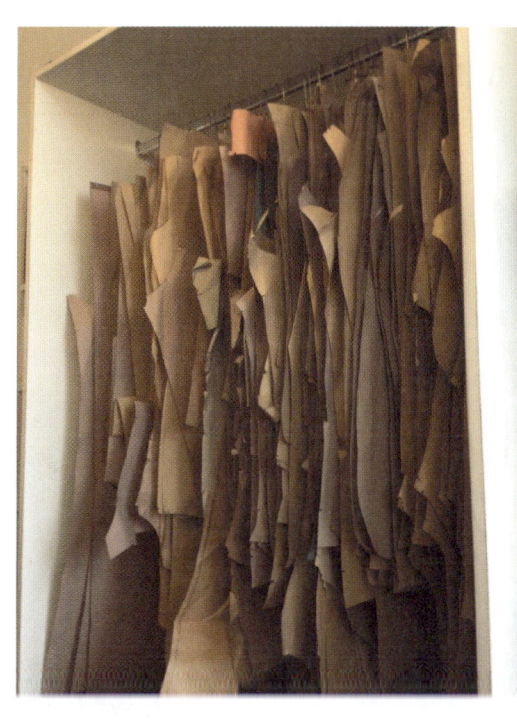

ABOVE: *In a corner of the studio, a tailor's mannequin stands next to selected images and inspirational tearsheets on the wall, creating an unpretentious but stylish still life.*

ABOVE: *Original patterns and blocks are stored away neatly for easy access.*

BELOW: *Womenswear designs reveal a wealth of ideas and share the same strong aesthetic as Batten's menswear sketches.*

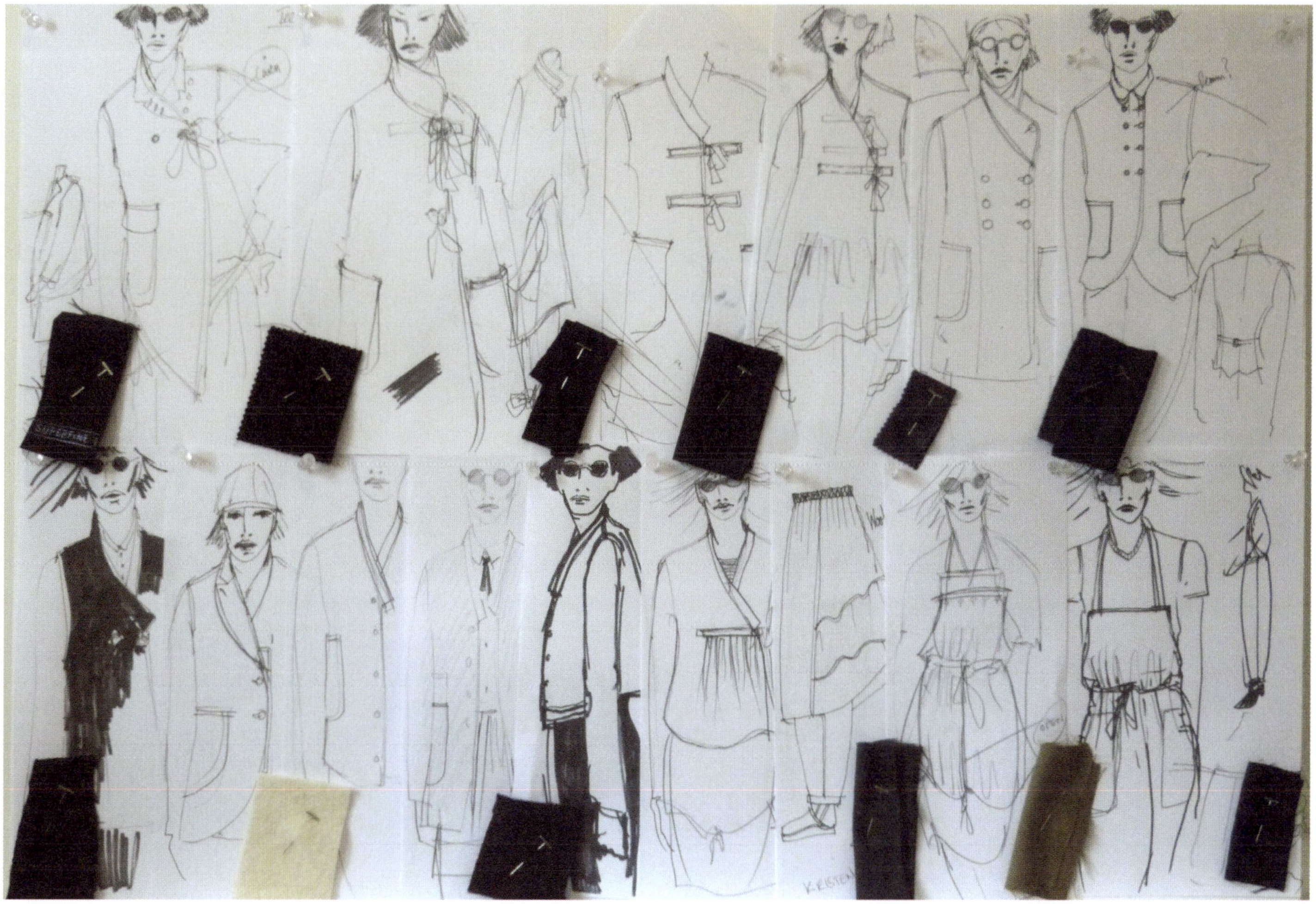

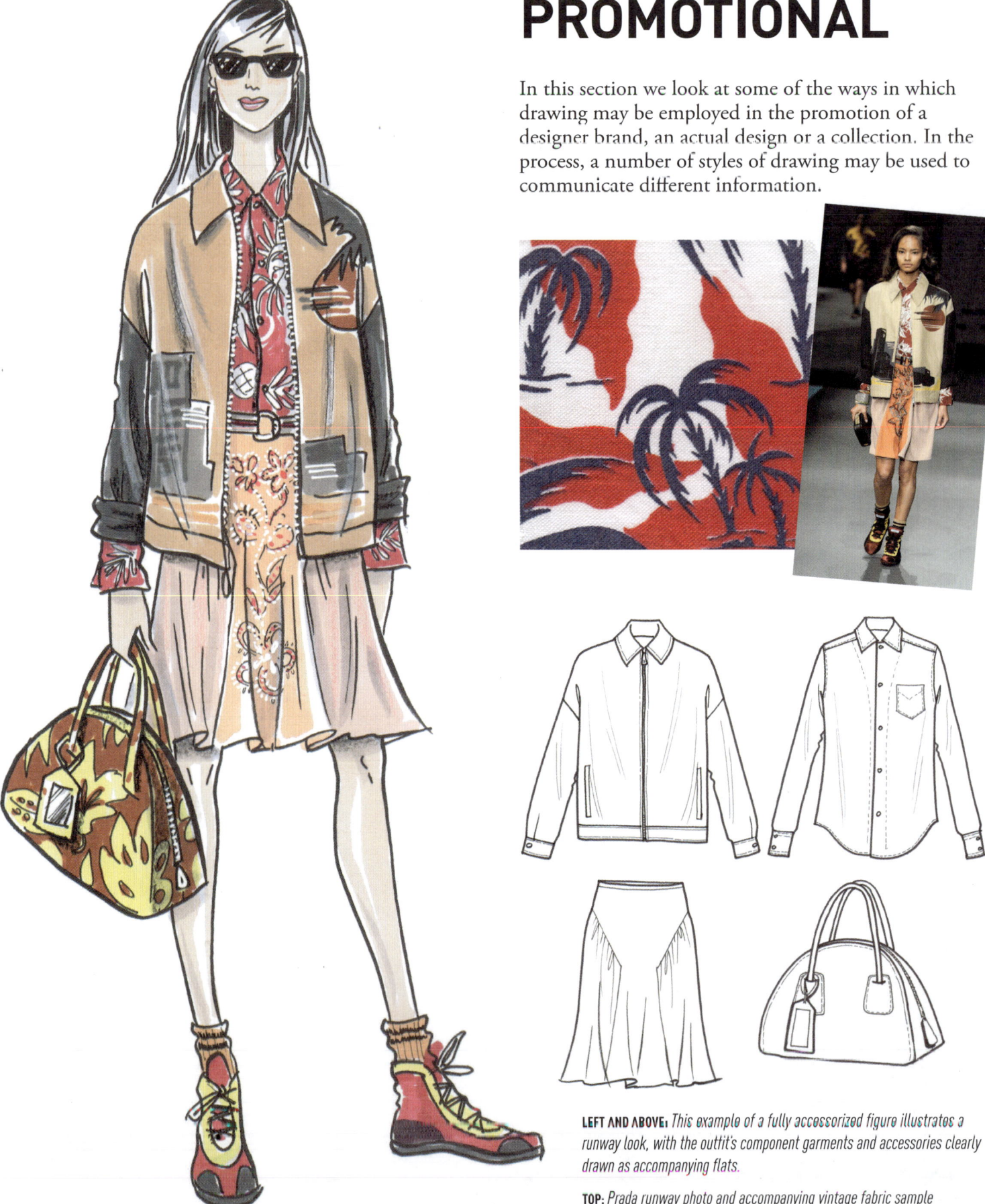

PROMOTIONAL

In this section we look at some of the ways in which drawing may be employed in the promotion of a designer brand, an actual design or a collection. In the process, a number of styles of drawing may be used to communicate different information.

LEFT AND ABOVE: *This example of a fully accessorized figure illustrates a runway look, with the outfit's component garments and accessories clearly drawn as accompanying flats.*

TOP: *Prada runway photo and accompanying vintage fabric sample*

Spring/Summer 2010 Design Ocean Reef

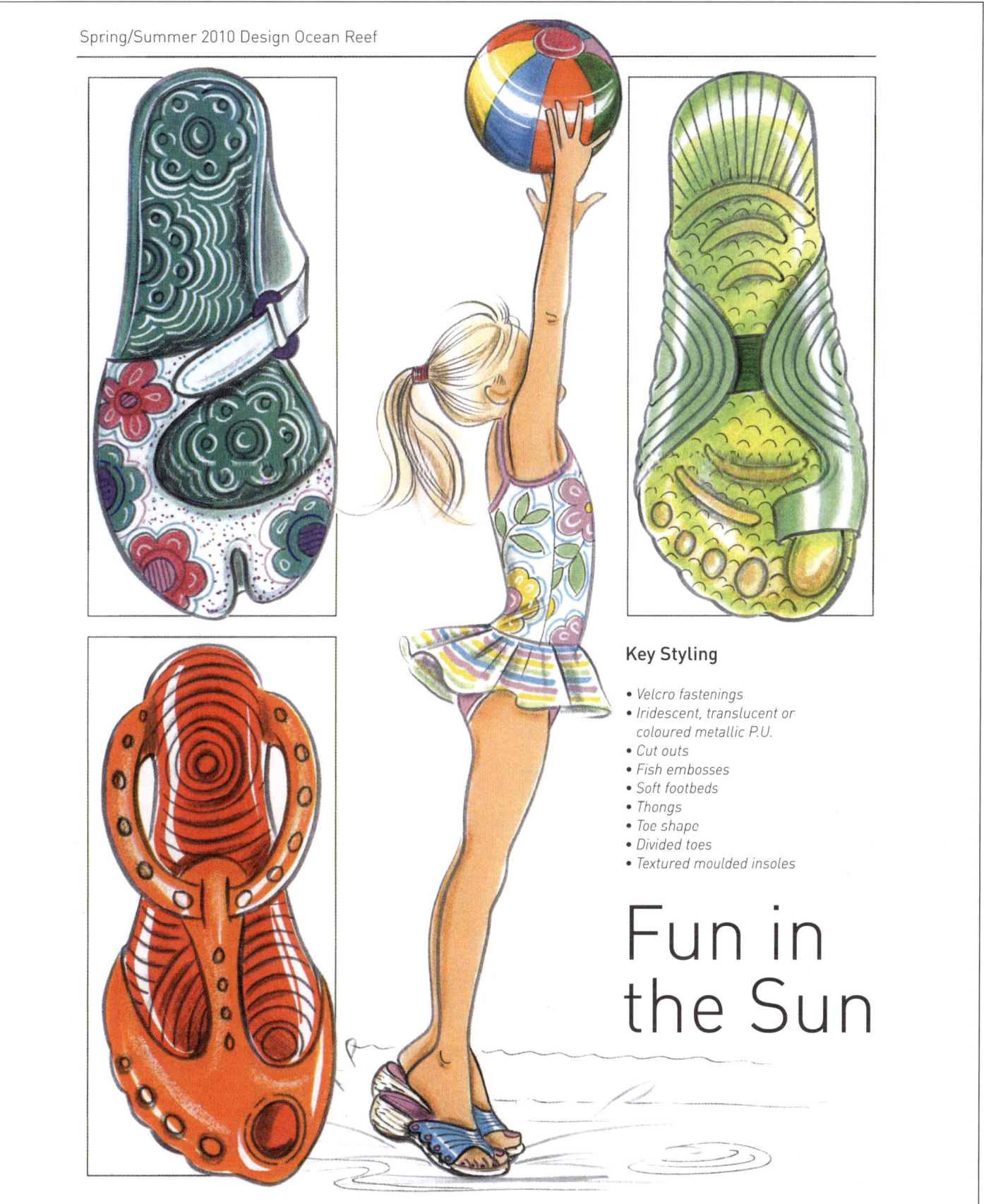

Key Styling

- *Velcro fastenings*
- *Iridescent, translucent or coloured metallic P.U.*
- *Cut outs*
- *Fish embosses*
- *Soft footbeds*
- *Thongs*
- *Toe shape*
- *Divided toes*
- *Textured moulded insoles*

Fun in the Sun

This drawing is less an illustration of actual garments, but is designed to convey the more intangible elements of the mood and atmosphere of the collection. It could be compared to a film poster that tries not to reveal specific details of the movie, but evokes a sense of the story and ambience.

COMMUNICATING DESIGN IDEAS

These pages show two cashmere knitwear projects, womens and mens, for a China-based company. The collections were designed separately, but consecutively, with each following the same work pattern. All communication was done via email. Timing was tight, so drawings and instructions had to be as clear, precise, self-explanatory and foolproof as possible.

'A typical design process would be as follows: to research the customer thoroughly, together with the customer's competitors and the brands to which they aspire; to research colour, yarn, stitches, patterns, styling and silhouette trends. The designer generally works about a year ahead of the season. Ideas are sketched in pencil with appropriate reference information gathered together to inform and inspire. I then select designs to draw in detail with fibre-tip pen, marker pen and crayon. I add a brief description and carefully selected images of related

looks and styles – sometimes vintage, sometimes contemporary – to further explain the look. The designs – approximately 60 – are scanned and sent digitally to the client for selection.'

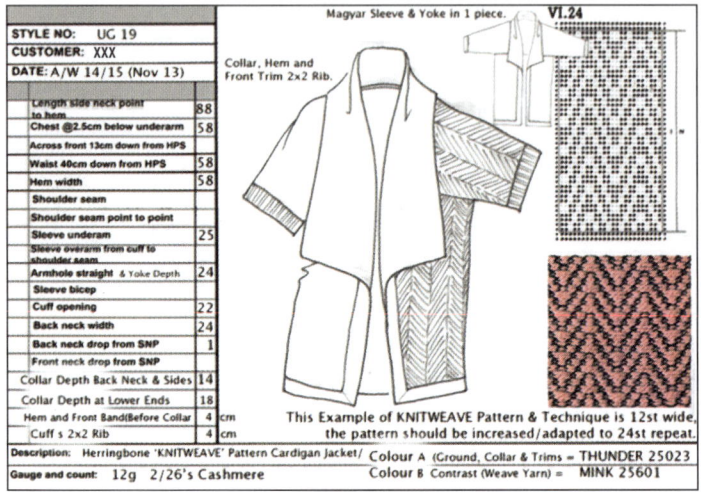

STYLE NO:	UG 19
CUSTOMER:	XXX
DATE: A/W 14/15 (Nov 13)	

Length side neck point to hem	88
Chest @2.5cm below underarm	58
Across front 13cm down from HPS	
Waist 40cm down from HPS	58
Hem width	58
Shoulder seam	
Shoulder seam point to point	
Sleeve underam	25
Sleeve overarm from cuff to shoulder seam	
Armhole straight & Yoke Depth	24
Sleeve bicep	
Cuff opening	22
Back neck width	24
Back neck drop from SNP	1
Front neck drop from SNP	
Collar Depth Back Neck & Sides	14
Collar Depth at Lower Ends	18
Hem and Front Band(Before Collar	4 cm
Cuff s 2x2 Rib	4 cm

Description: Herringbone 'KNITWEAVE' Pattern Cardigan Jacket/ Colour A (Ground, Collar & Trims) = THUNDER 25023

Gauge and count: 12g 2/26's Cashmere   Colour B Contrast (Weave Yarn) = MINK 25601

ABOVE: *Womenswear – a patterned cardigan jacket with magyar sleeves. The hand-drawn design sketch is scanned into an A4 spec sheet using Photoshop, along with details of the stitch and pattern techniques. All necessary measurements are included for manufacturing.*

BELOW: *A composite image of part of the womenswear collection shows how the first design sketches are presented alongside images of related styles to assist in explaining and contextualizing the designs into a fashion look/theme.*

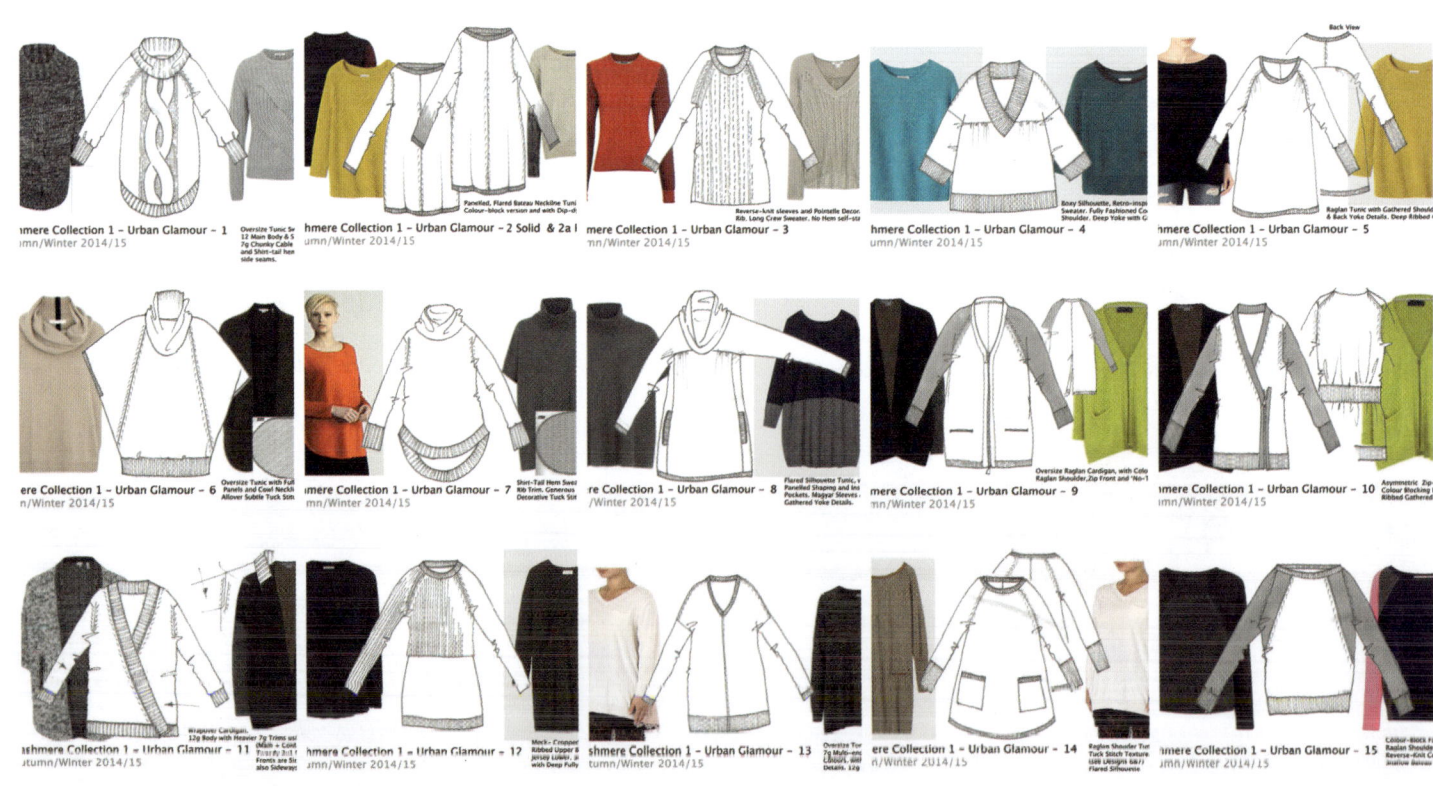

'The selected designs are then scanned into a spec sheet and sent off with key measurements and information, sometimes with additional sheets of information, including close-up or detailed construction sketches and swatches, to ensure accurate interpretation by the sample room.

Additional designs are requested and added at this stage, where the client feels they are needed. The timespan would typically be between six to eight weeks from initial briefing to send-off of final designs and specs.'

NOEL CHAPMAN

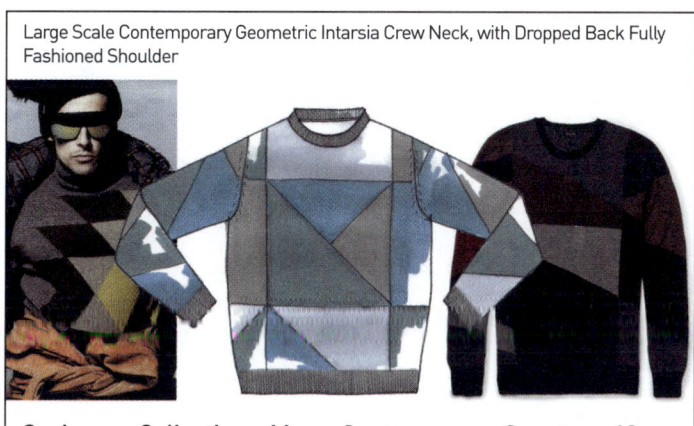

Large Scale Contemporary Geometric Intarsia Crew Neck, with Dropped Back Fully Fashioned Shoulder

Cashmere Collection – Men – Contemporary Country – 69 Autumn/Winter 2014/2015

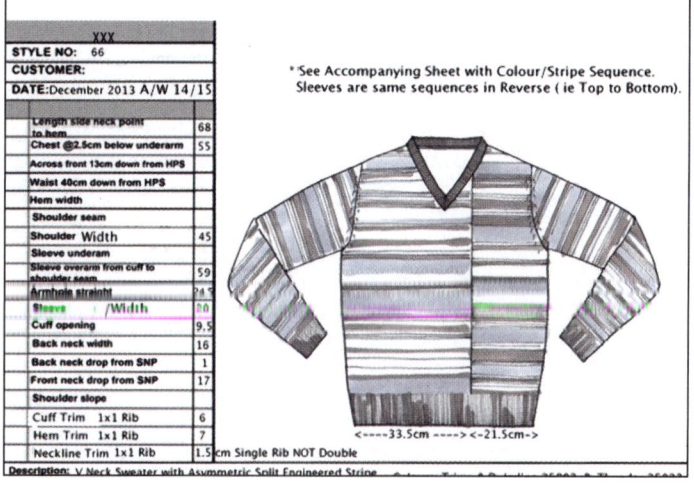

STYLE NO:	66	
CUSTOMER:		
DATE:December 2013 A/W 14/15		
Length side neck point to hem	68	
Chest @2.5cm below underarm	55	
Across front 13cm down from HPS		
Waist 40cm down from HPS		
Hem width		
Shoulder seam		
Shoulder Width	45	
Sleeve underarm		
Sleeve overarm from cuff to shoulder seam	59	
Armhole straight	24	
Sleeve /Width	20	
Cuff opening	9.5	
Back neck width	16	
Back neck drop from SNP	1	
Front neck drop from SNP	17	
Shoulder slope		
Cuff Trim 1x1 Rib	6	
Hem Trim 1x1 Rib	7	
Neckline Trim 1x1 Rib	1.5cm Single Rib NOT Double	

*See Accompanying Sheet with Colour/Stripe Sequence. Sleeves are same sequences in Reverse (ie Top to Bottom).

<----33.5cm ----> <-21.5cm->

Description: V Neck Sweater with Asymmetric Split Engineered Stripe

ABOVE: Menswear for Autumn/Winter 14/15 – first finished design drawing presented for the client with supporting and contextualizing fashion images on A4 sheets.

ABOVE RIGHT: Design sketches are scanned into spec sheets and completed in Photoshop with all key information and instructions added.

BELOW: As with the womenswear image on the facing page, an A4 composite image of part of the menswear collection shows first design sketches alongside images of related styles. The sketches must be clear so that they can be read very small, when they are amalgamated on to range pans and the like.

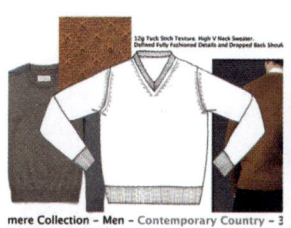

mere Collection – Men – Contemporary Country – 3 mn/Winter 2014/15

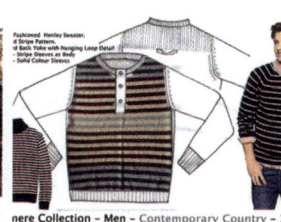

mere Collection – Men – Contemporary Country – mn/Winter 2014/15

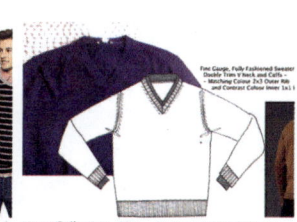

ere Collection – Men – Contemporary Country – 1 nn/Winter 2014/15

mere Collection – Men – Contemporary Country – umn/Winter 2014/15

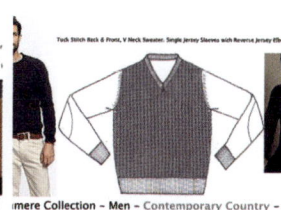

mere Collection – Men – Contemporary Country – 3 mn/Winter 2014/15

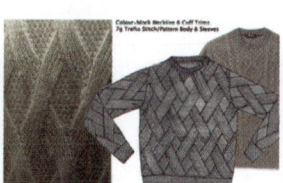

mere Collection – Men – Contemporary Country – 33 n/Winter 2014/15

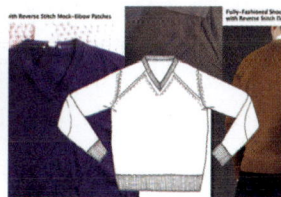

mere Collection – Men – Contemporary Country – 3 umn/Winter 2014/15

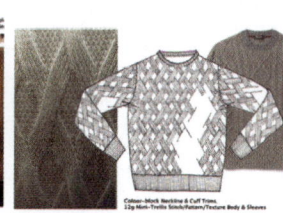

ere Collection – Men – Contemporary Country – 35 /Winter 2014/15

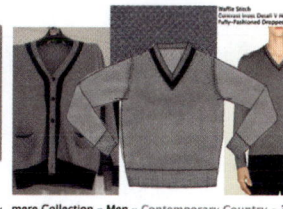

mere Collection – Men – Contemporary Country – 3 umn/Winter 2014/15

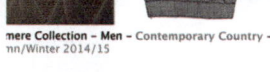

mere Collection – Men – Contemporary Country – 3 mn/Winter 2014/15

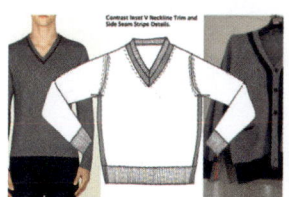

shmere Collection – Men – Contemporary Country – utumn/Winter 2014/15

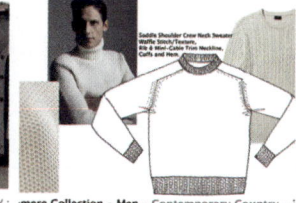

mere Collection – Men – Contemporary Country – mn/Winter 2014/15

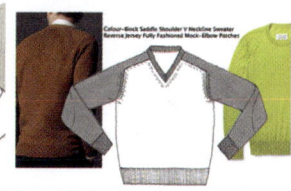

hmere Collection – Men – Contemporary Country – umn/Winter 2014/15

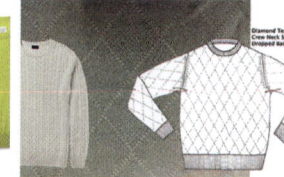

mere Collection – Men – Contemporary Country – 41 /Winter 2014/15

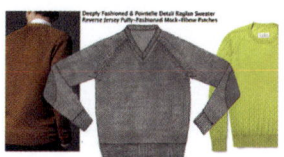

mere Collection – Men – Contemporary Country – mn/Winter 2014/15

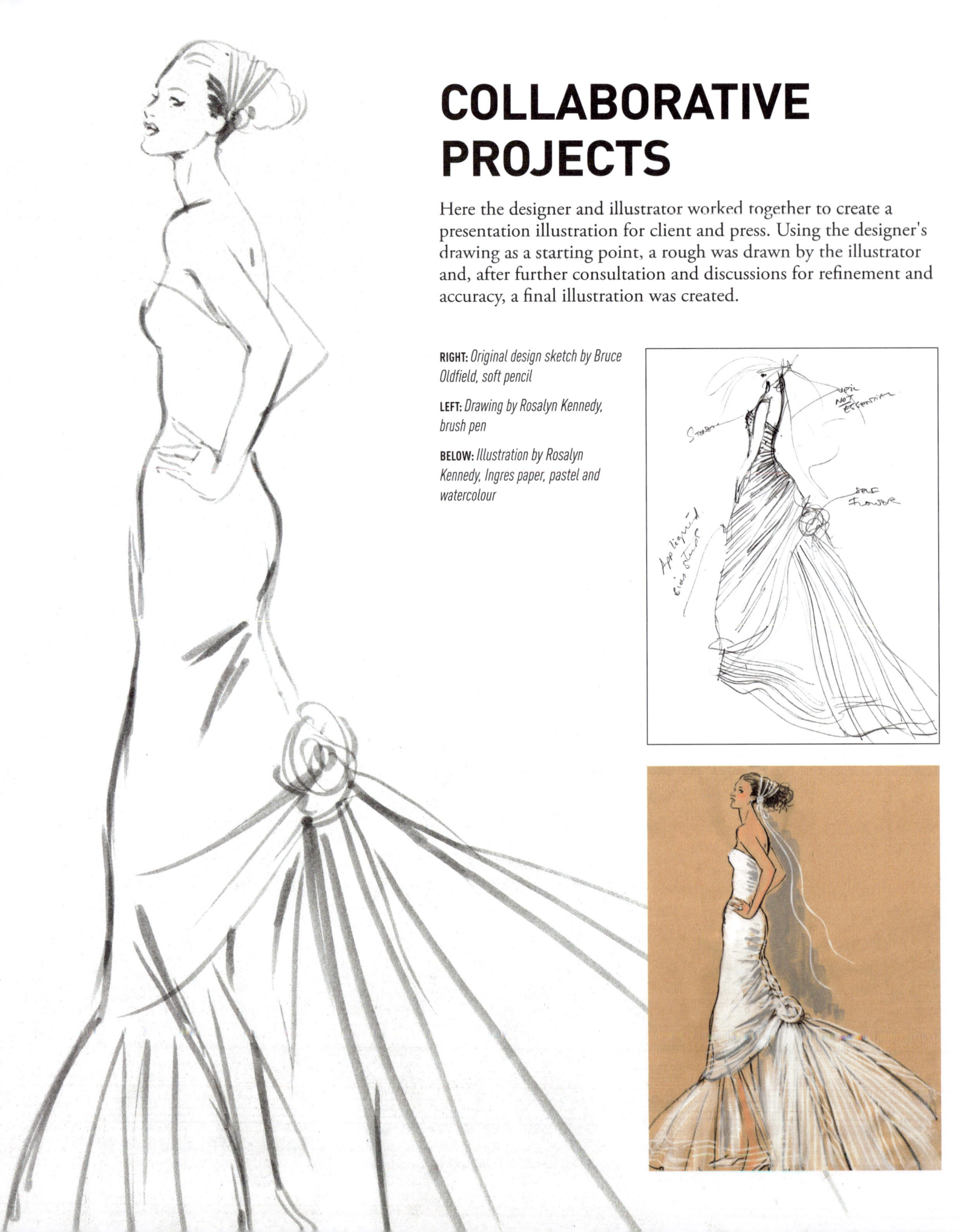

COLLABORATIVE PROJECTS

Here the designer and illustrator worked together to create a presentation illustration for client and press. Using the designer's drawing as a starting point, a rough was drawn by the illustrator and, after further consultation and discussions for refinement and accuracy, a final illustration was created.

RIGHT: *Original design sketch by Bruce Oldfield, soft pencil*

LEFT: *Drawing by Rosalyn Kennedy, brush pen*

BELOW: *Illustration by Rosalyn Kennedy, Ingres paper, pastel and watercolour*

Cherrill Parris-Fox works as an illustrator in the fashion and advertising industries for a variety of high-profile international companies. Most recently she has directed her creativity into fine art projects and become more or less a full-time painter. In a recent collaboration with her fashion and textile designer daughter, Louisa Parris, she produced a witty, delightful series of illustrations to promote Louisa's range of marvellous graphically printed silk scarves and accessories. Louisa sent her mum a 1940s Dick Whittington comic, suggesting the old cartoon sketches typical of *Punch* magazine as an inspiration source.

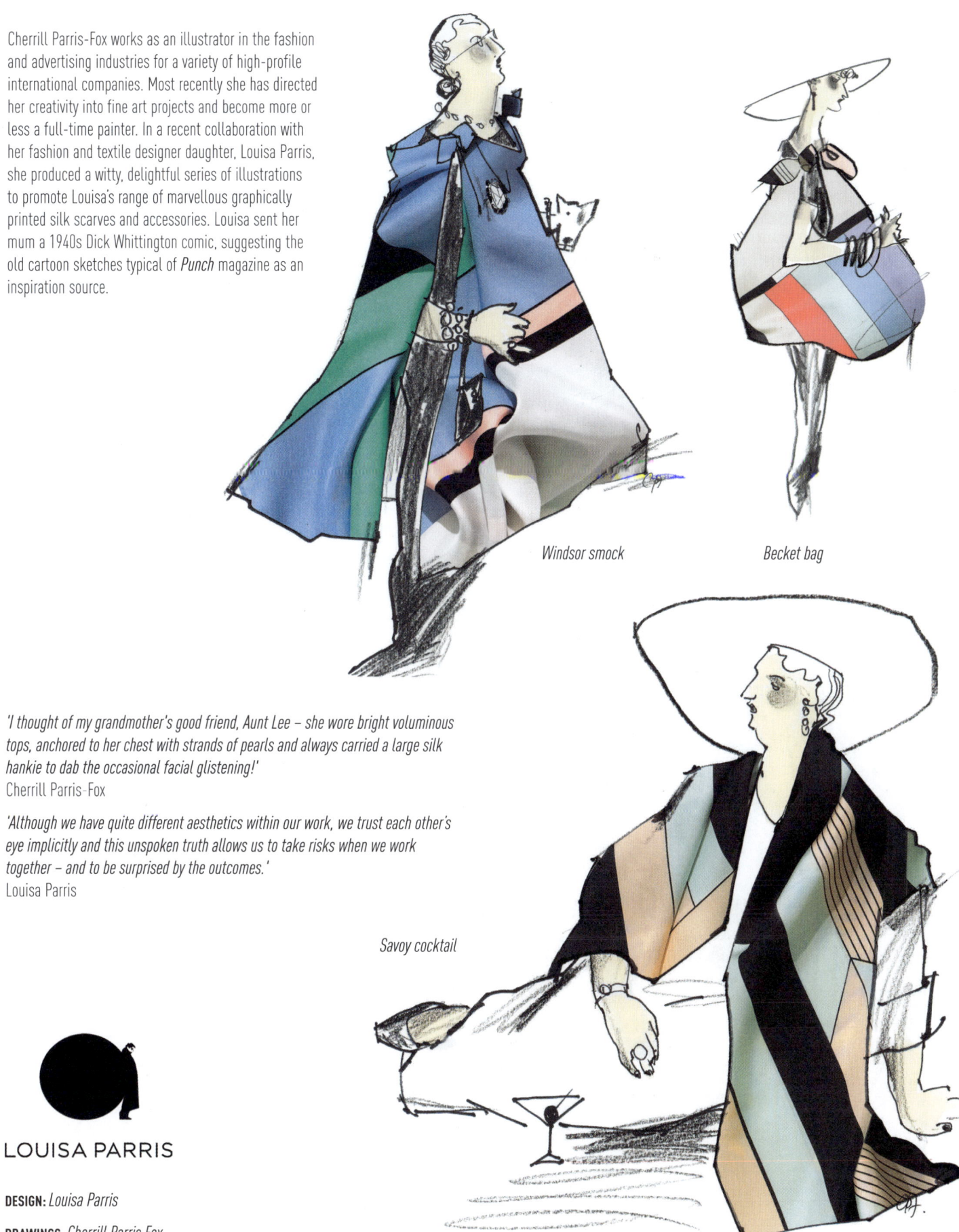

Windsor smock

Becket bag

'I thought of my grandmother's good friend, Aunt Lee – she wore bright voluminous tops, anchored to her chest with strands of pearls and always carried a large silk hankie to dab the occasional facial glistening!'
Cherrill Parris-Fox

'Although we have quite different aesthetics within our work, we trust each other's eye implicitly and this unspoken truth allows us to take risks when we work together – and to be surprised by the outcomes.'
Louisa Parris

Savoy cocktail

LOUISA PARRIS

DESIGN: *Louisa Parris*

DRAWINGS: *Cherrill Parris Fox*

DIVERSITY

The drawings and illustrations on these pages show something of the range and diversity of roles that drawing can play in contemporary fashion – from communicator of strict and precise instruction to image promotion, echo of attitude and creator of ambience and aspiration.

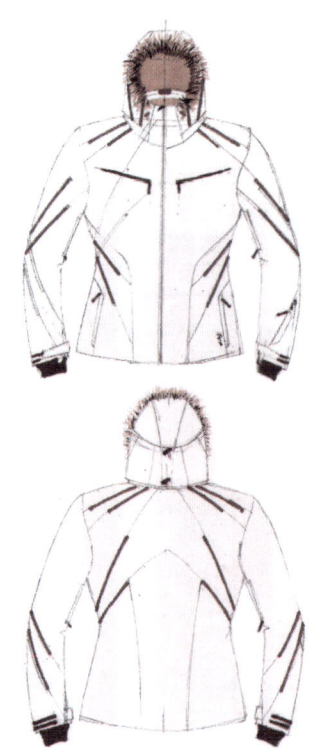

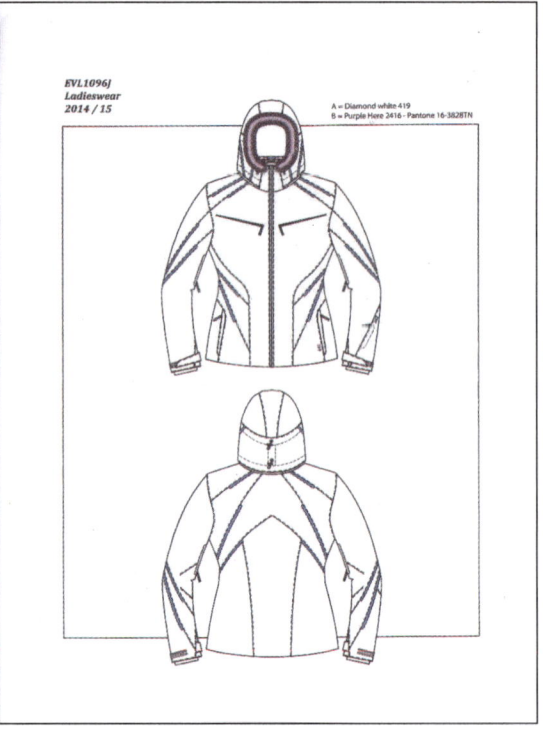

NEAR RIGHT: *Clare Dudley Hart – women's ski jacket, working sketch in pencil, fibre tip pen, marker pen*

FAR RIGHT: *The presentation drawing of the design, digitally generated using Adobe Illustrator*

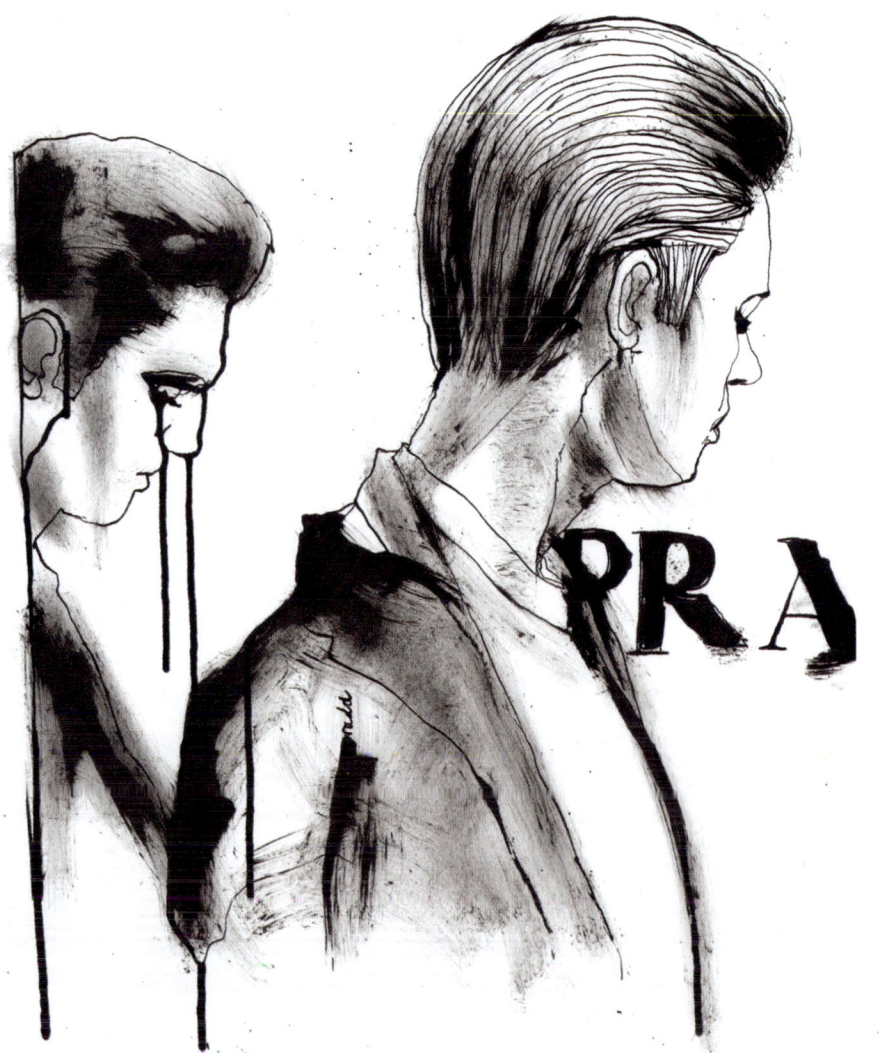

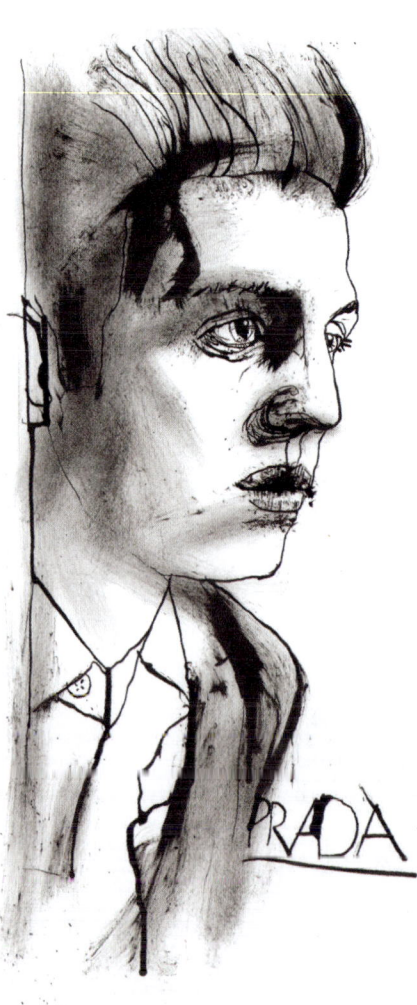

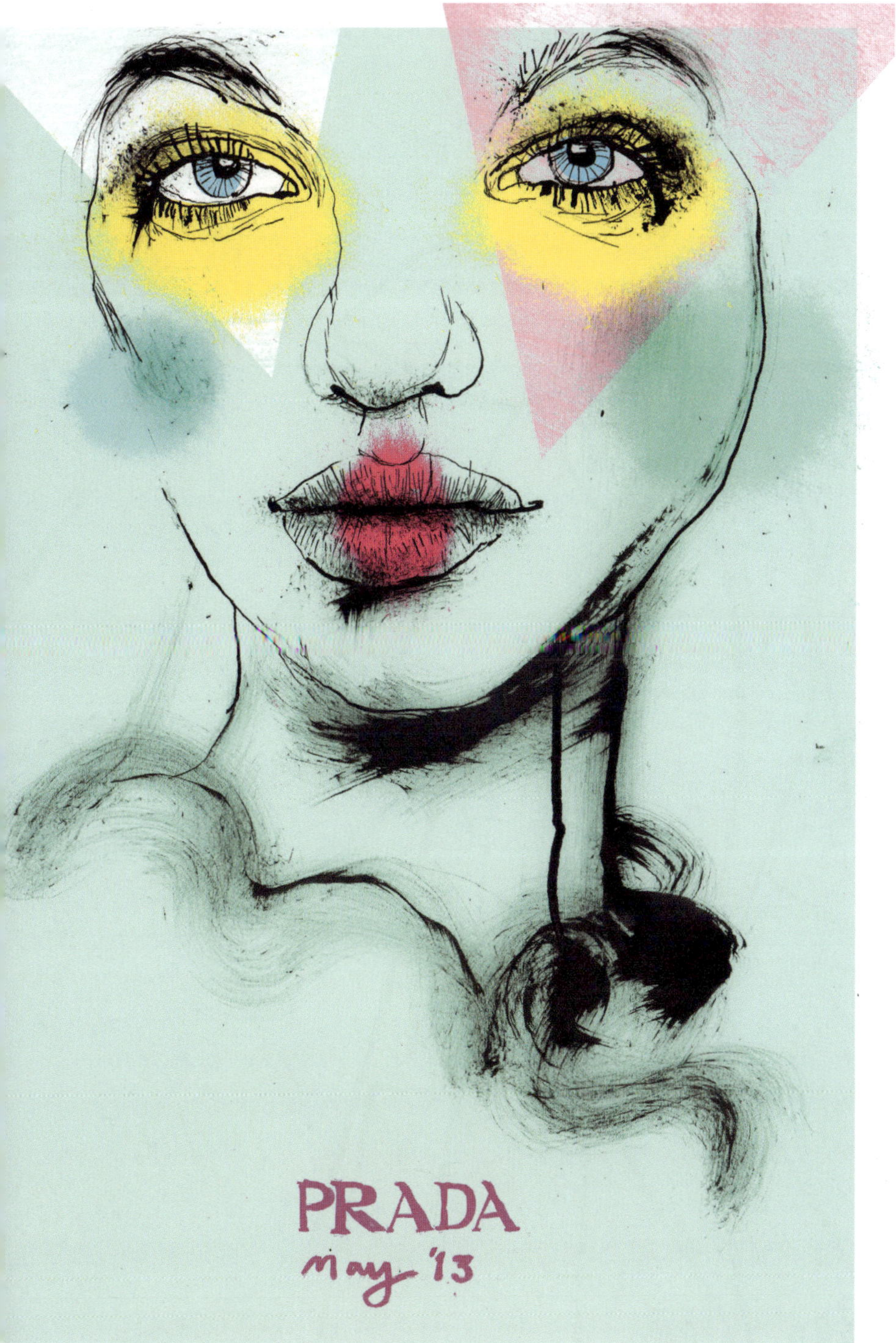

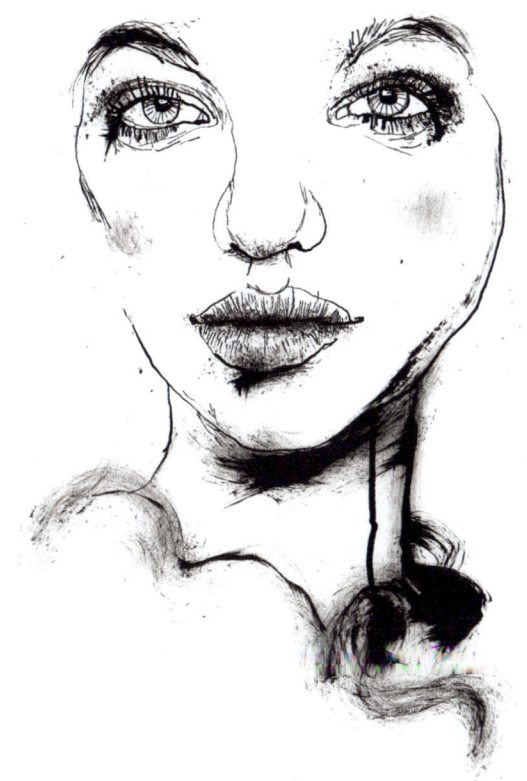

LEFT: *Patrick Morgan – Prada girl, ink and dip-pen, dry brush technique, digitally manipulated*

ABOVE: *The first version of the drawing without added colour*

BELOW: *Patrick Morgan – Chanel. An example in simple mark-making using sponged and masked colour*

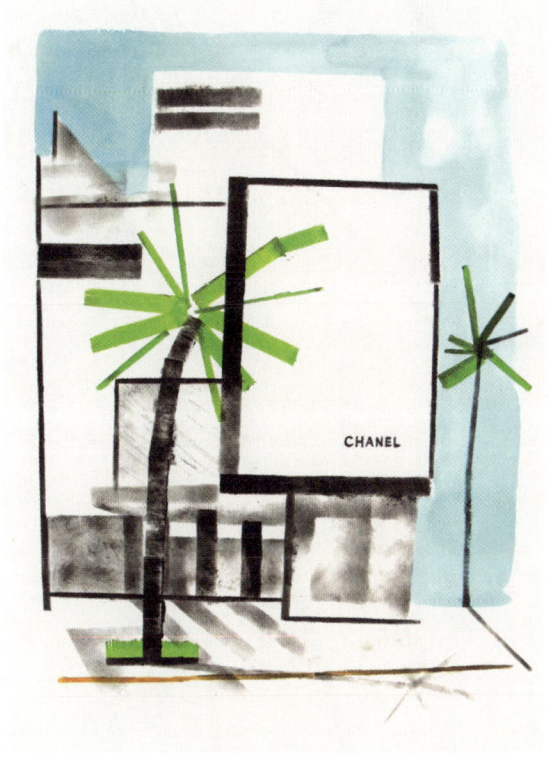

FACING PAGE: *Patrick Morgan – Prada boy, in ink and dip-pen, dry brush technique, digitally manipulated*

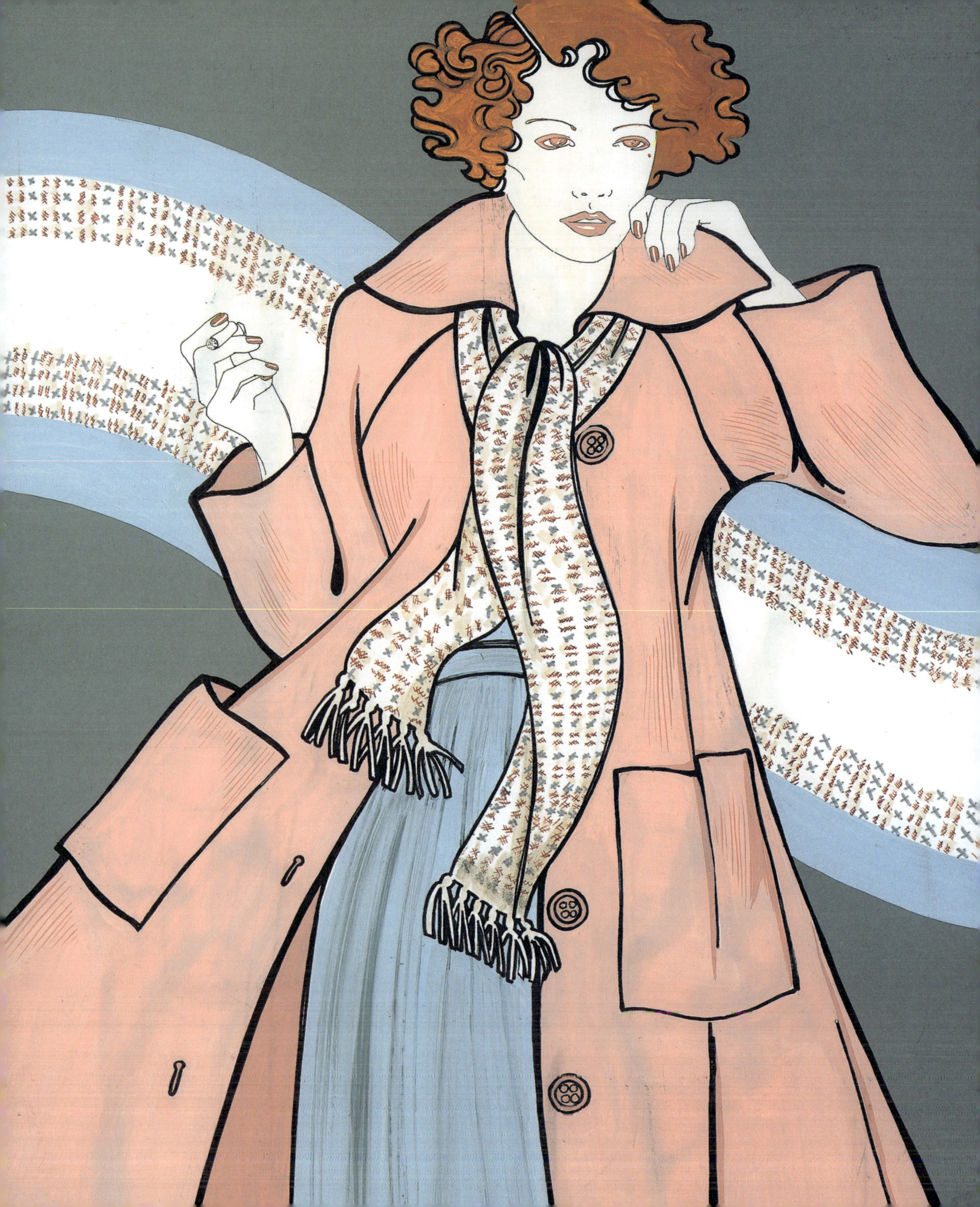

CHAPTER 11

FASHION ILLUSTRATION GALLERY

This chapter showcases a wide range of fashion drawings for prestigious clients by some of the most illustrious international designers, as well as rising talents. Other images have rarely been seen by the public, and reveal the working practices of the artists and designers, including how items are drawn and redrawn to refine proportions and details, the hastily scribbled 'notes to self' that many designers use during the development process, and the more polished, precise and informative drawings used to communicate the design to manufacturers.

In the same way that fashion is cyclical – trends ebb and flow, are revived and refreshed, deconstructed and reassembled – the style of fashion drawings also changes, and this is evident when a vintage artwork is juxtaposed with a more contemporary illustration. While some appear timeless, others provide a stark contrast and offer a glimpse of alternative, individual and inspiring ways of expressing design that could be interpreted and adapted to suit today's technology-assisted methods.

Some drawings fulfil their roles with quiet efficiency, others sing with the energy of their execution, their captured vitality. When viewing some illustrations it is as if we are entering another world and find ourselves mid-story in a fantasy where fashion, clothes and accessories take on starring roles. In others, realism and accurate representation take precedence, and a tighter, less flamboyant but nevertheless graphic style dominates. All are equally valid if the artworks fulfil their briefs.

During the course of this book we have learned some of the rules and requirements of a good drawing – with perhaps the most important being that it is 'fit for purpose'. This end result is achieved through a process of recording and generating ideas in a sketchbook, drawing and refining designs, and constantly accessing and judging a drawing so that the garment or outfit it represents is attractive and technically accurate and conveys the idea behind the project in an appealing manner. However, as we shall see here, some rules can be pushed to their limits (although the design must remain fit for purpose), and it is having the skills to know how and when to do this that is the mark of a great designer or illustrator.

Illustration by Cath Knox

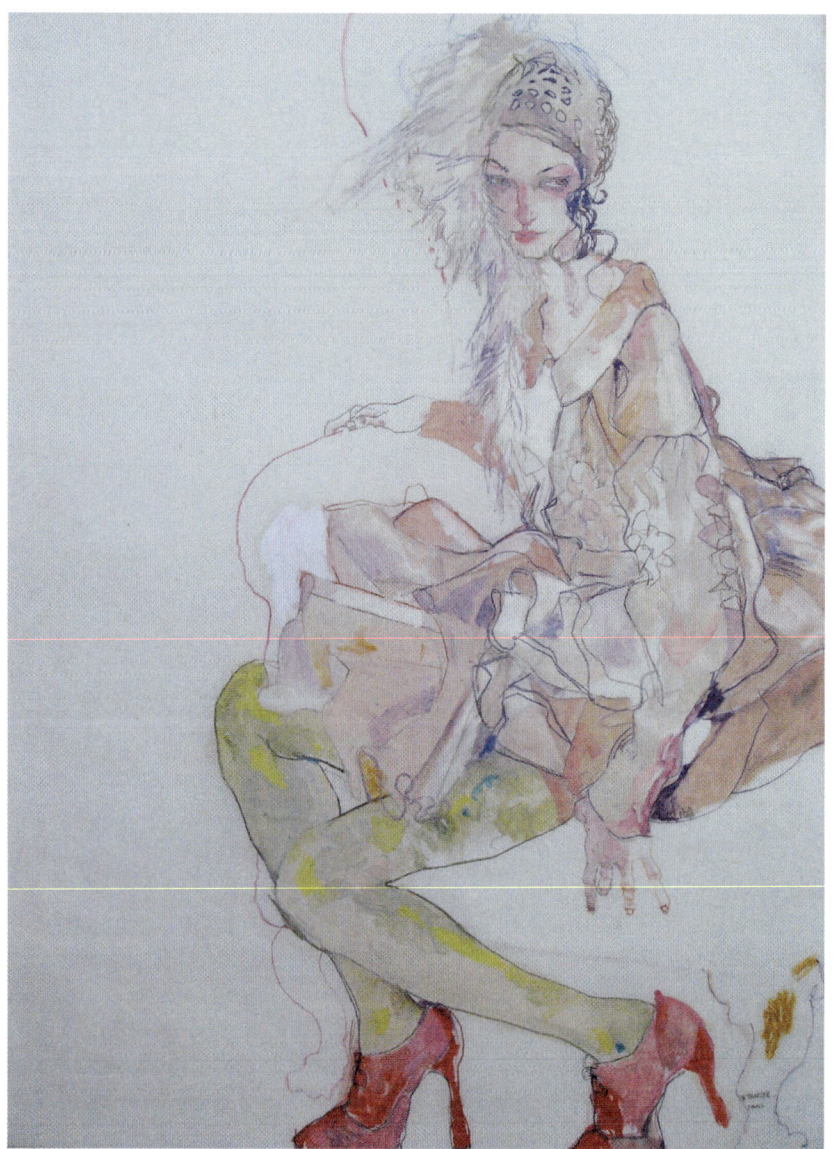

Howard Tangye
'Maya' Galliano girl (Autumn/Winter 2007), drawn in situ in the John Galliano studio in March 2007. Mixed media, including oils, pastel and graphite on paper.

Hilary Kidd
A simple yet effective image drawn with a brush pen

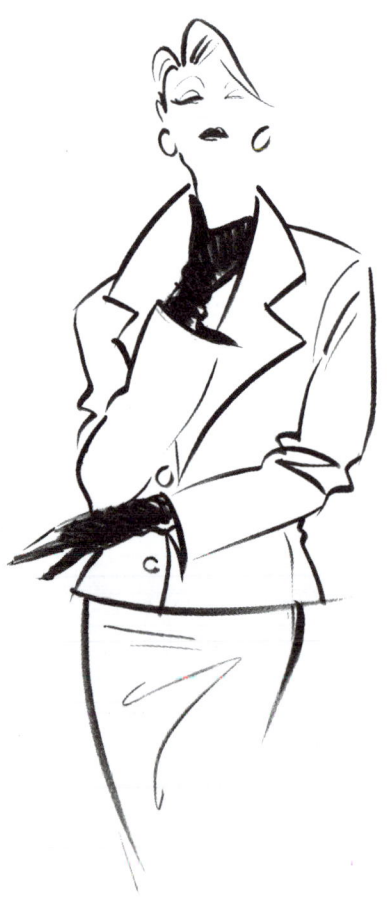

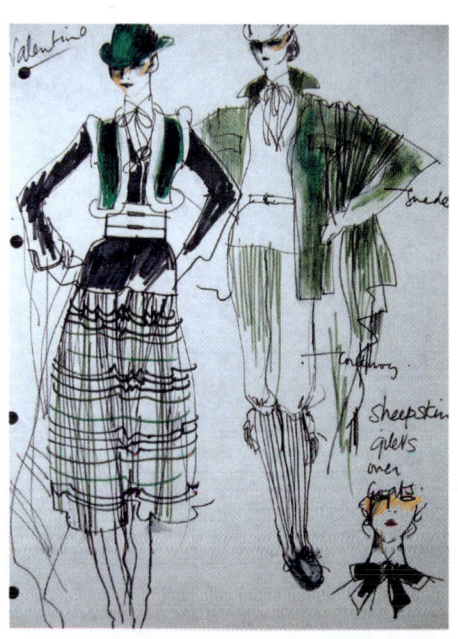

Elizabeth Suter
Drawn at the 'Collections', 1978. Fibre-tipped pen, pencil and marker pens

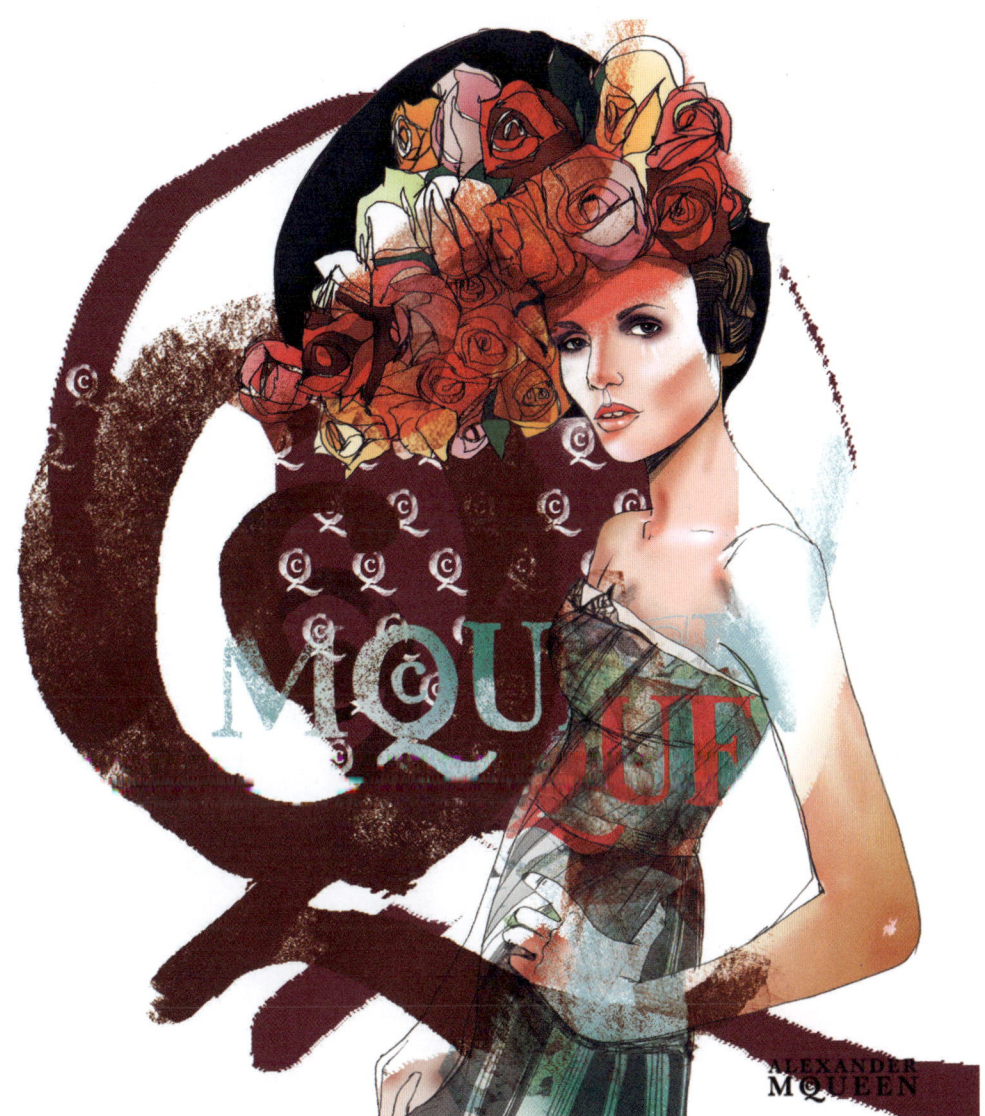

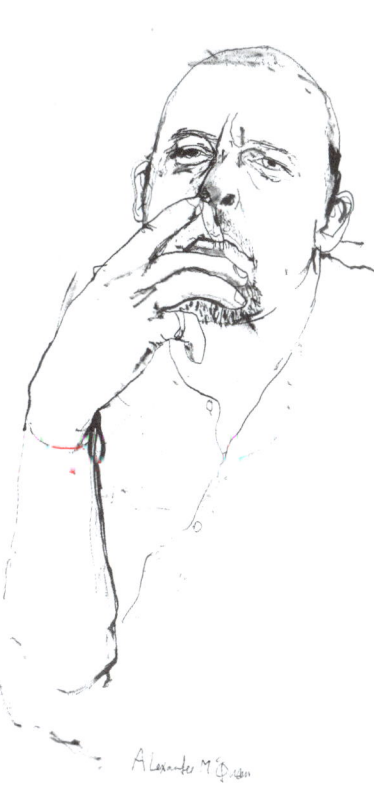

Patrick Morgan
Illustration for Alexander McQueen, created using pen and ink, pencils, crayons, rollers and stencils on 310 Somerset paper. Scanned and colour-managed in Photoshop.

Patrick Morgan
Drawn using pen and ink and pencil on 310 Somerset paper

Claire Fletcher
Illustration using acrylic paint on wood and a collaged doll's dress

Lesley Hurst
Client: Textile View Magazine
*Illustrations created using
Photoshop, collage and
watercolour*

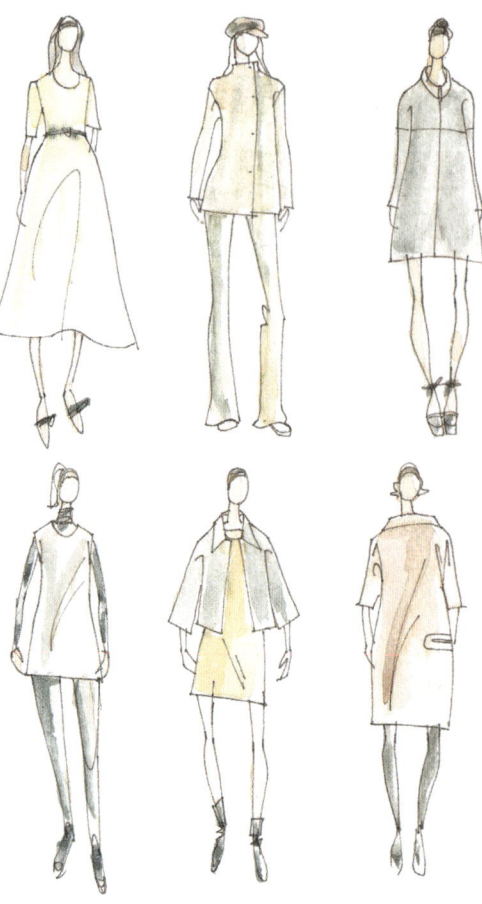

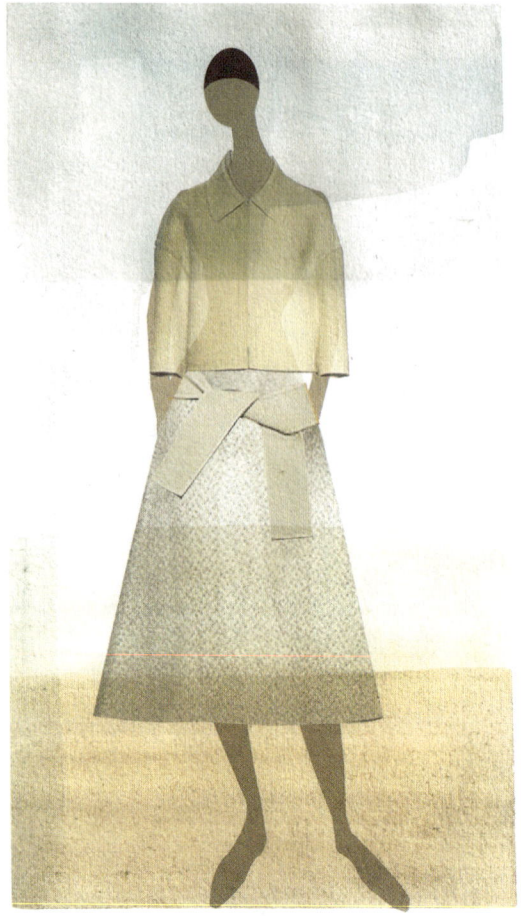

Lesley Hurst
Client: Textile View *Magazine
Illustrations created using
Photoshop, collage and
watercolour*

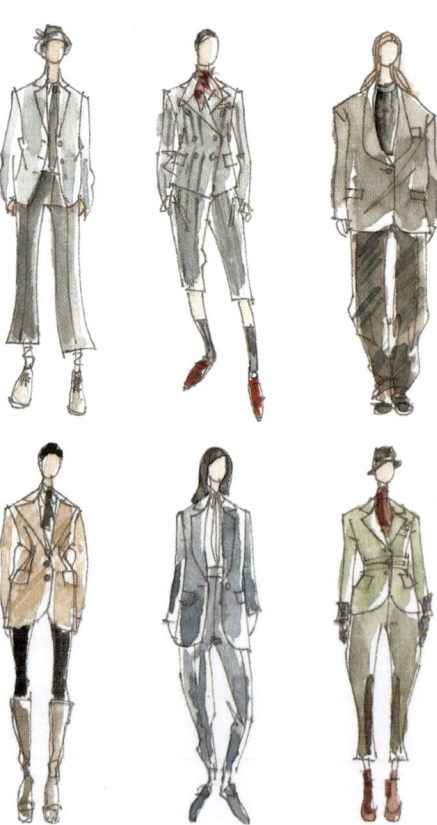

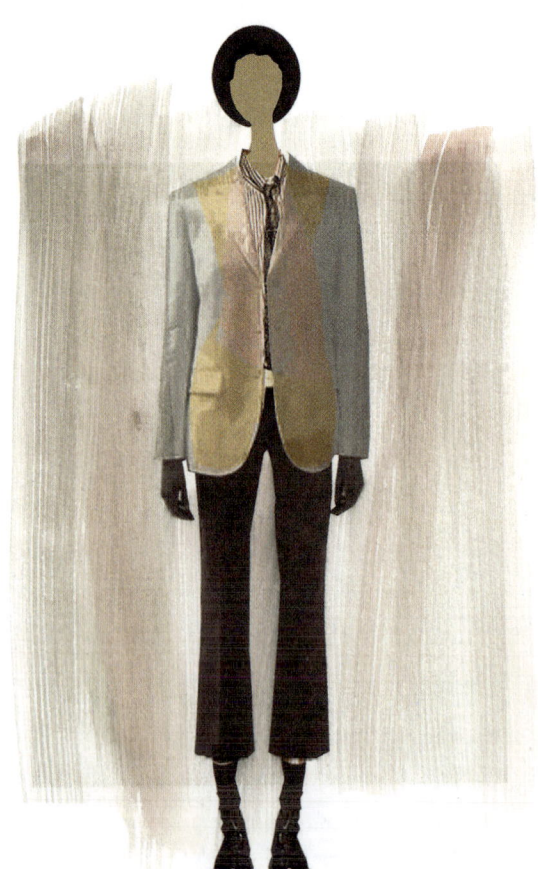

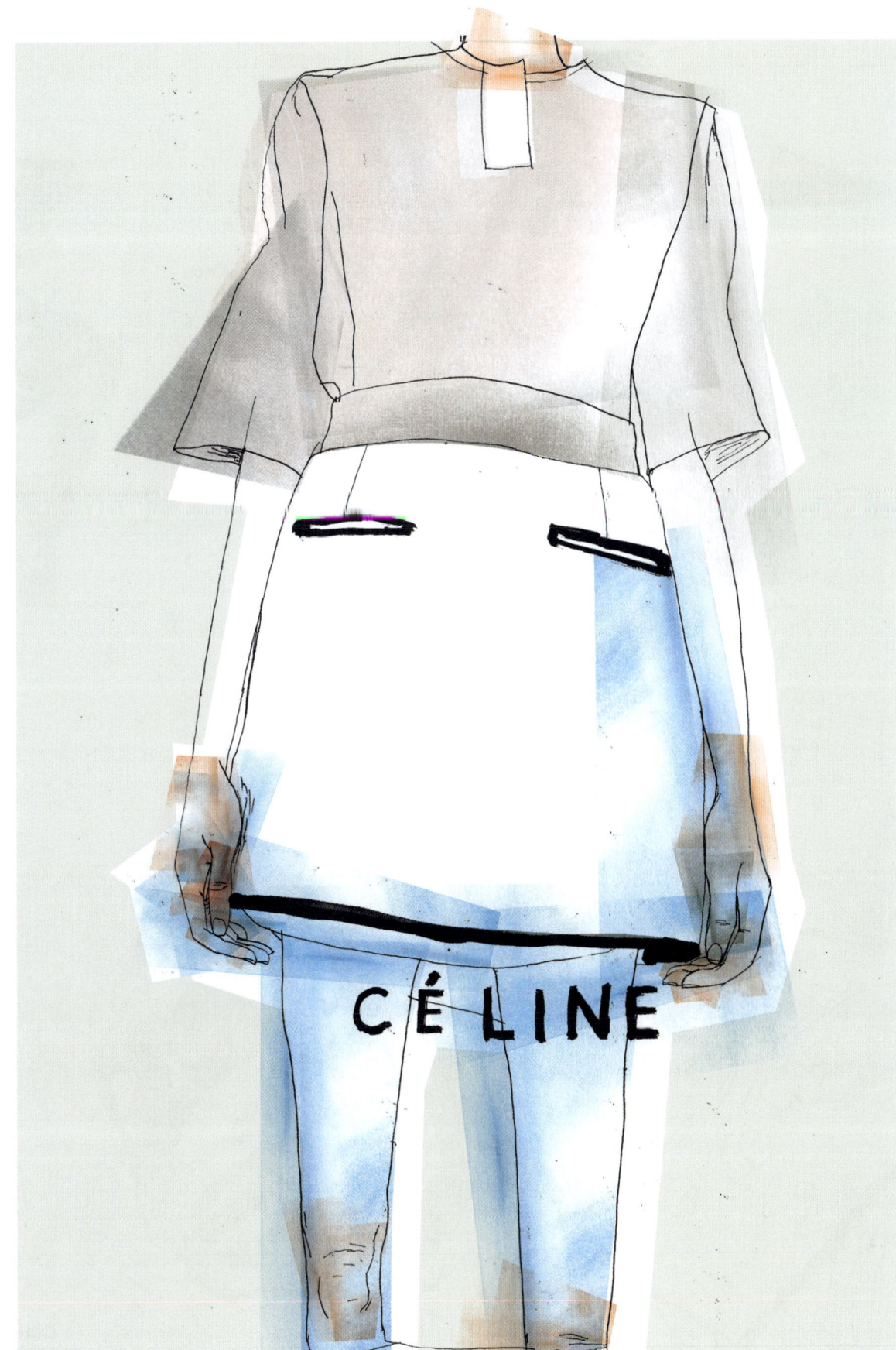

Patrick Morgan

Illustration using pen and ink and pencil along with rollers and stencils on 310 Somerset paper. Scanned and colour-managed in Adobe Photoshop.

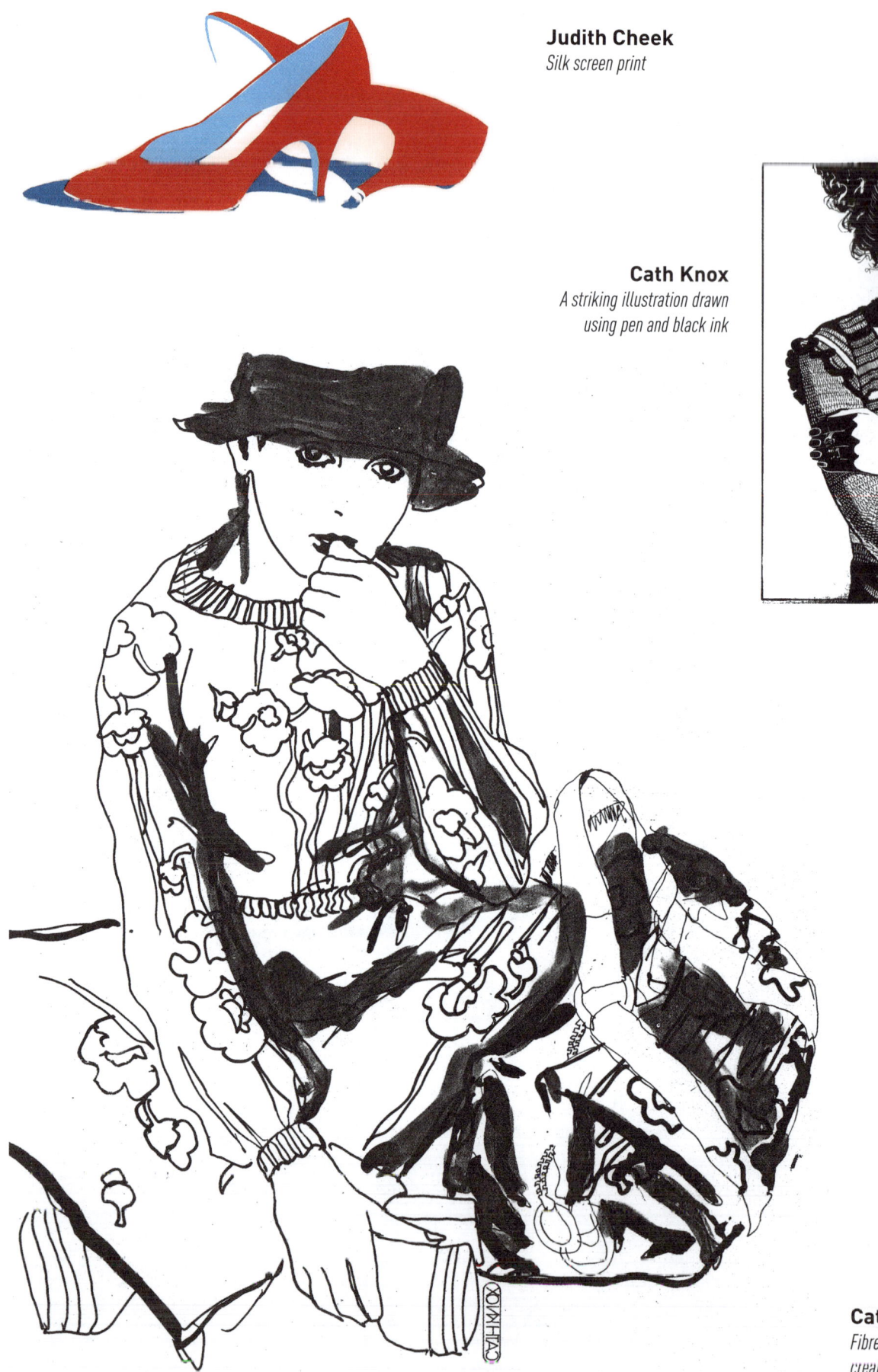

Judith Cheek
Silk screen print

Cath Knox
*A striking illustration drawn
using pen and black ink*

Cath Knox
*Fibre-tipped pen was used to
create this drawing*

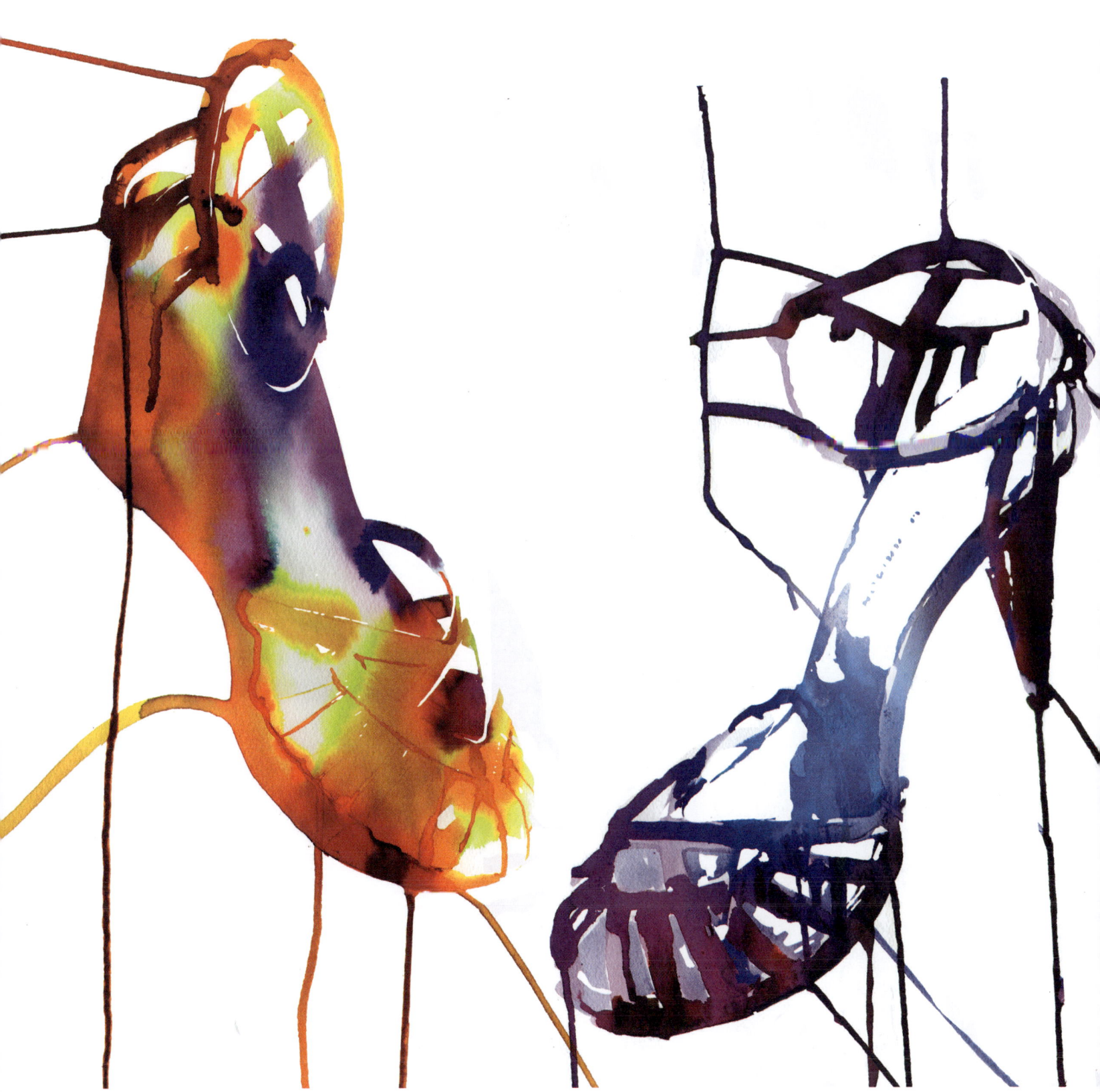

Stina Persson
Client: *Sigerson Morrison, 'Belle'*
Watercolours were used to paint these shoes

Hilary Kidd
*Figures rendered using brush pen,
marker pens and crayon*

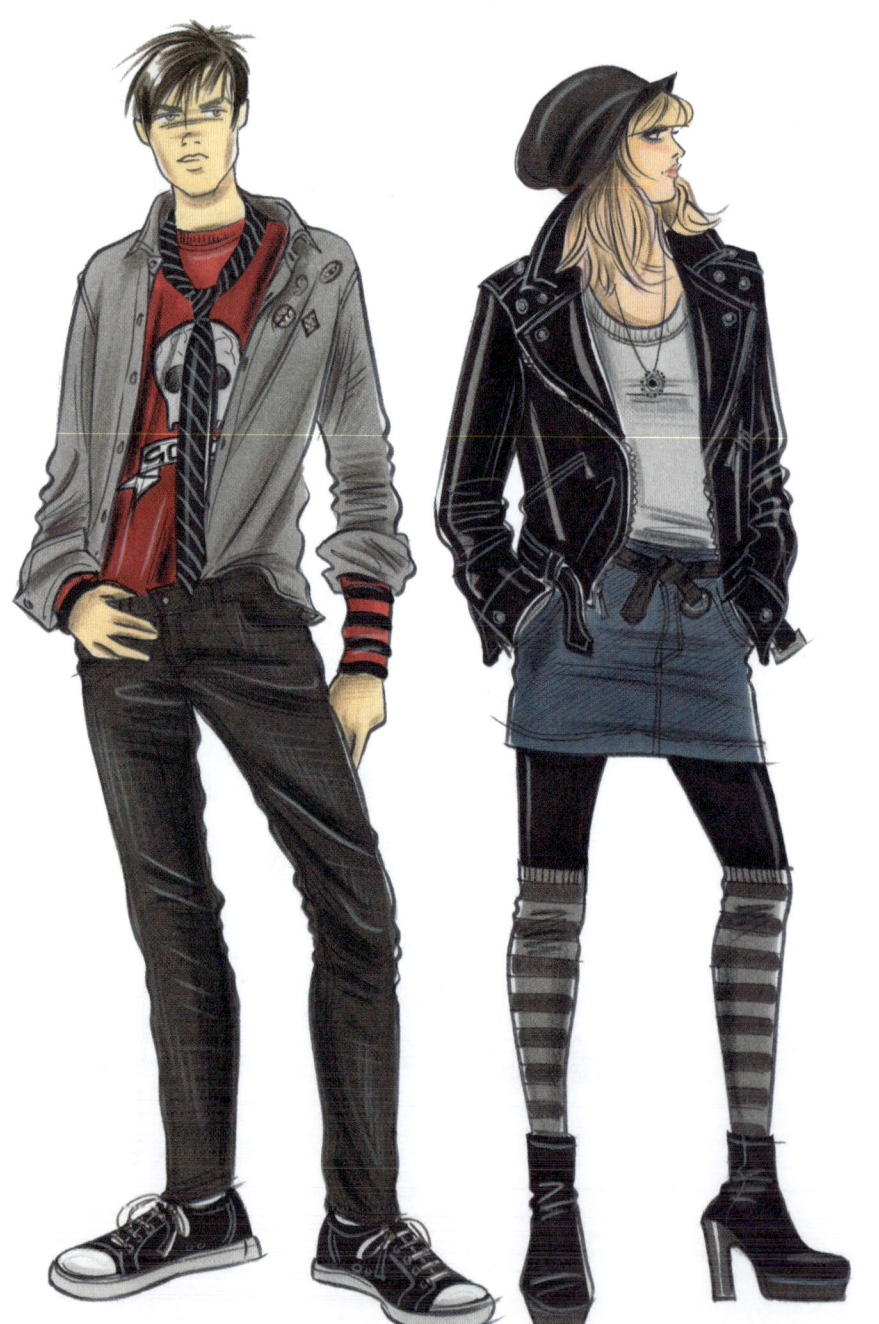

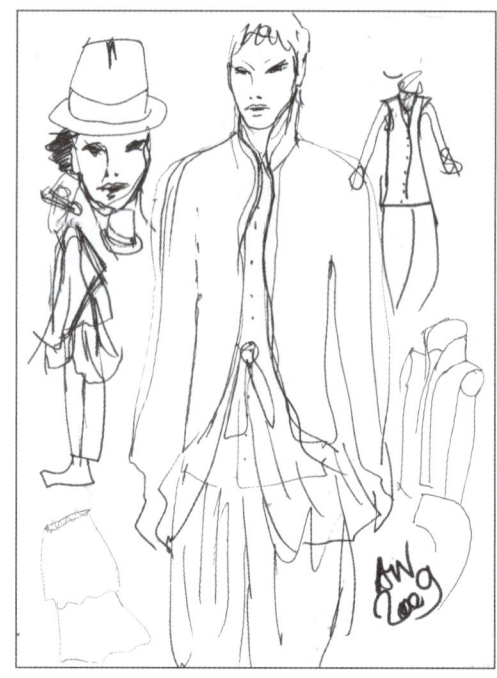

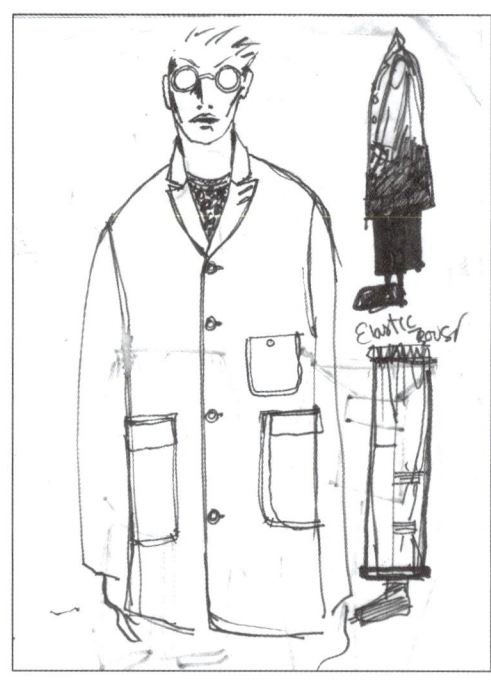

Ian Batten
*Design drawings created using
fibre-tipped pen*

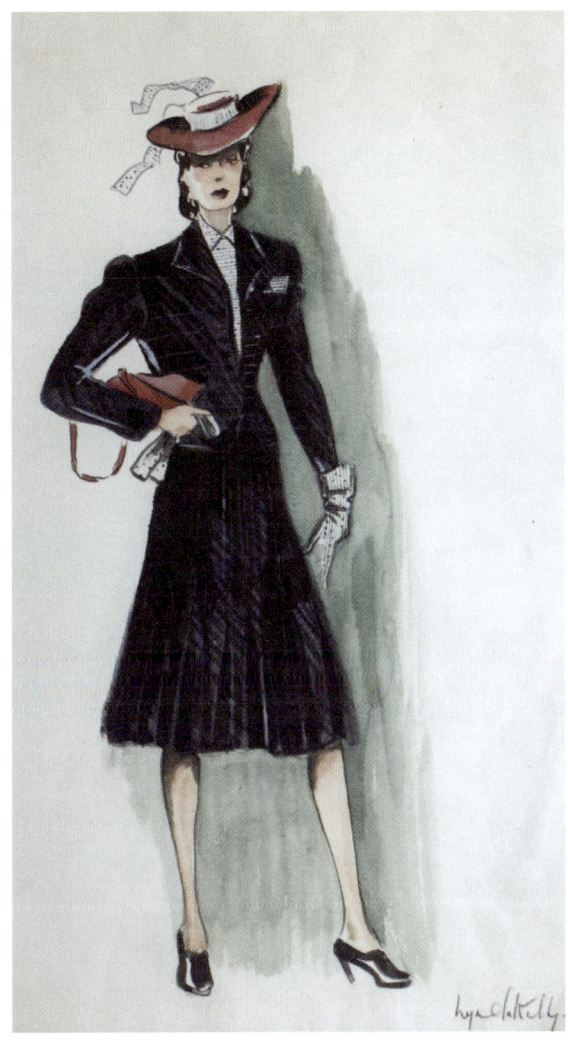

Lynda Kelly
*St Martin's School of Art, 1938–40.
A vintage illustration created
using mixed media, including
watercolours and crayon*

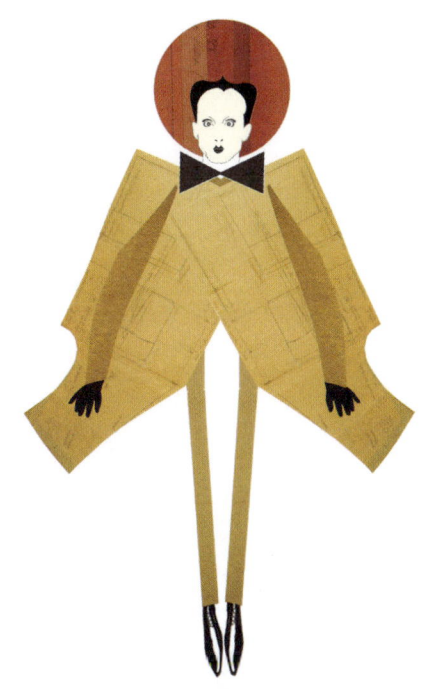

Hormazd Narielwalla
*Exhibited at the 'Markt' exhibition
at SCOPE, New York, this was an
editorial for Coilhouse magazine,
and depicts the late performance
artist Klaus Nomi. It is a digital
collage of vector illustrations and
photographs of tailoring patterns.*

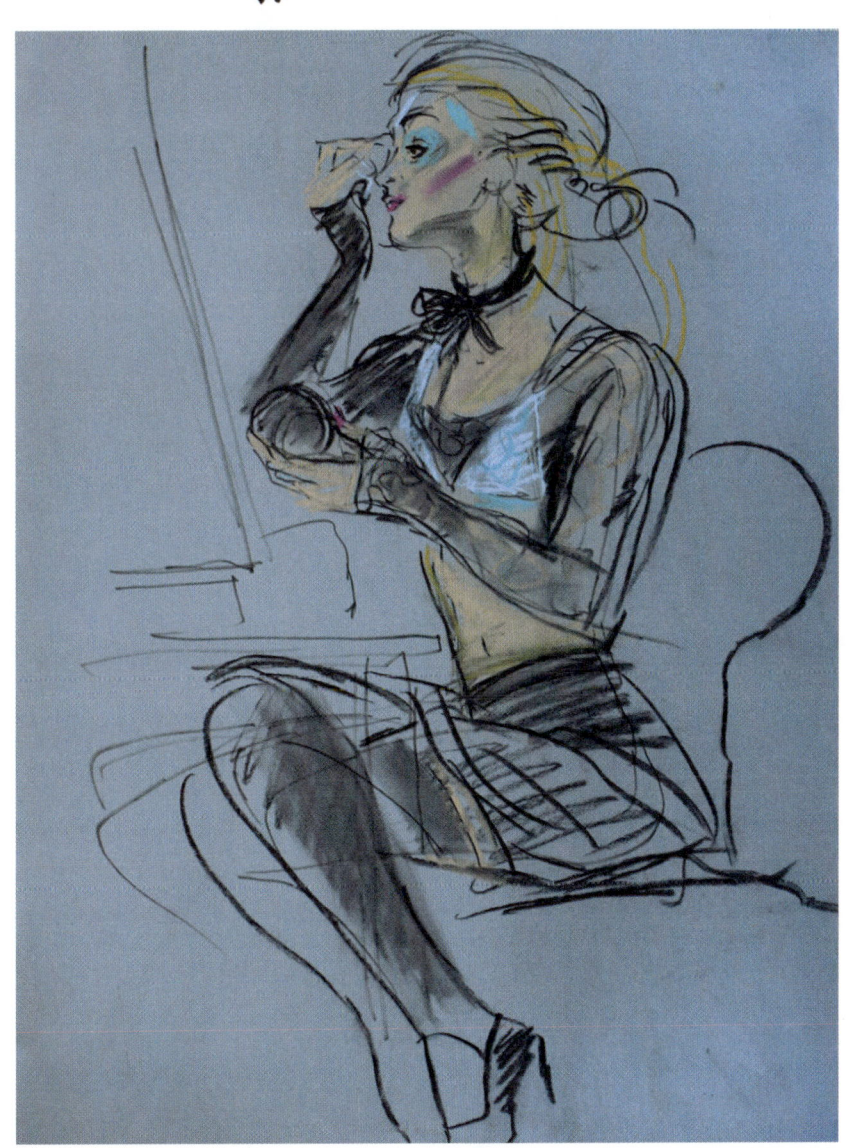

Rosalyn Kennedy
*Illustration using brush pen,
charcoal and soft pastels on
coloured paper*

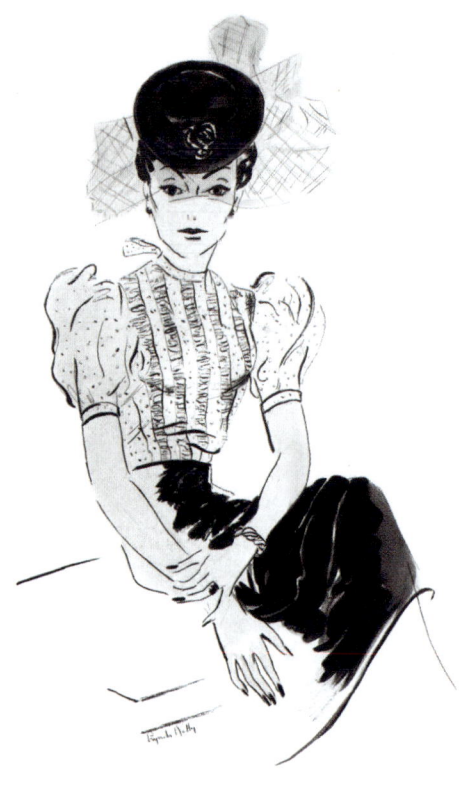

Lynda Kelly
*St Martin's School of Art, 1938–40.
A vintage illustration using mixed
media, including pen and ink and
watercolour wash*

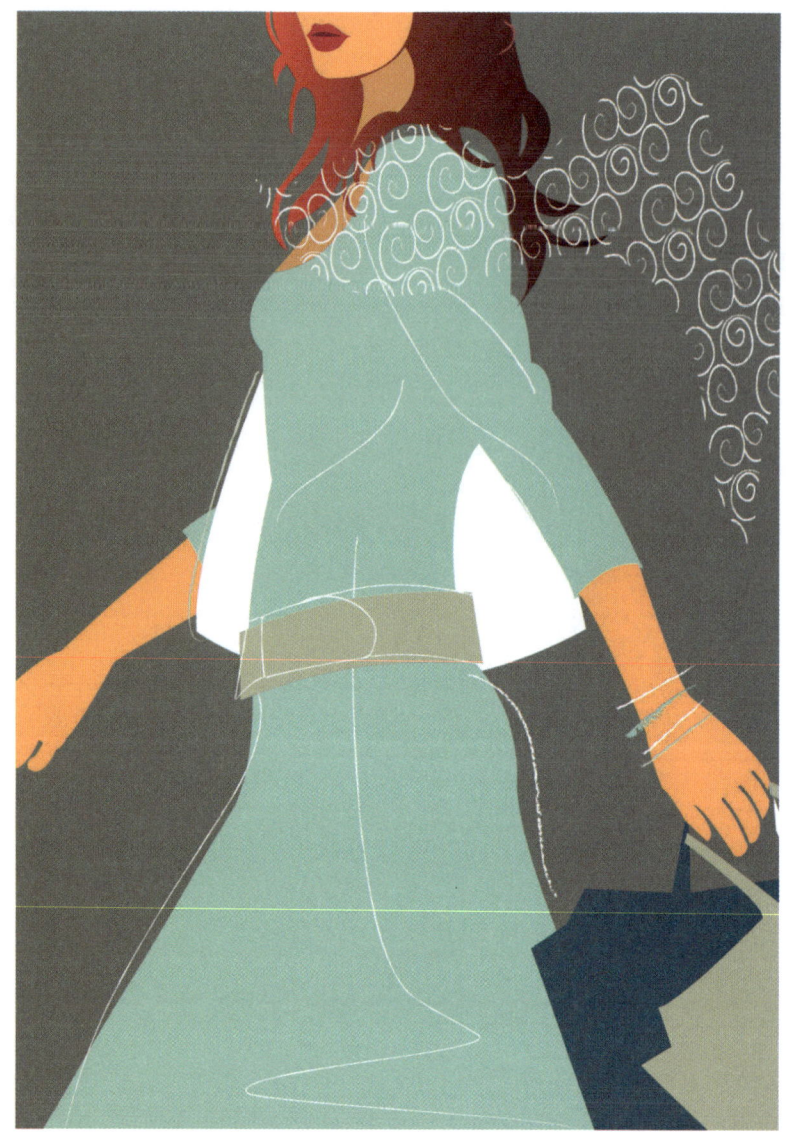

Martina Farrow
Agent: *New Division*
*'Shop', Promotional work 2010/2011
Artwork created using Adobe Illustrator CS3*

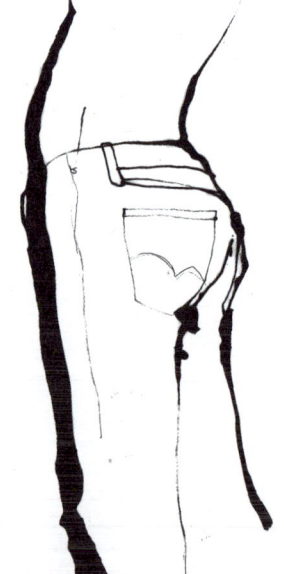

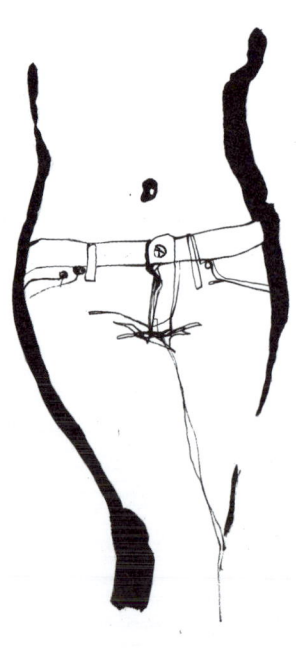

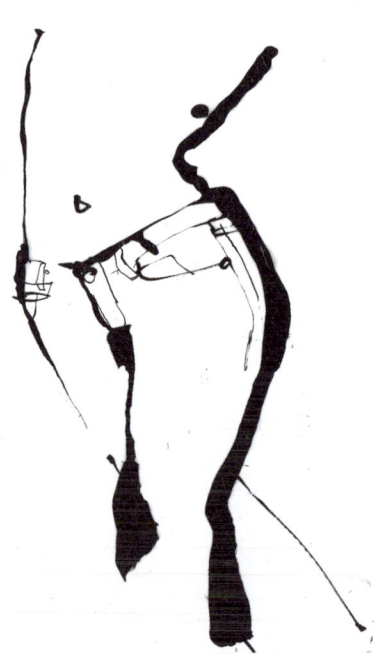

Stina Persson
Client: *Levi's*
*Ink drawings used in-store
and on hangtags for the
2010 'Levi's Curve ID' line*

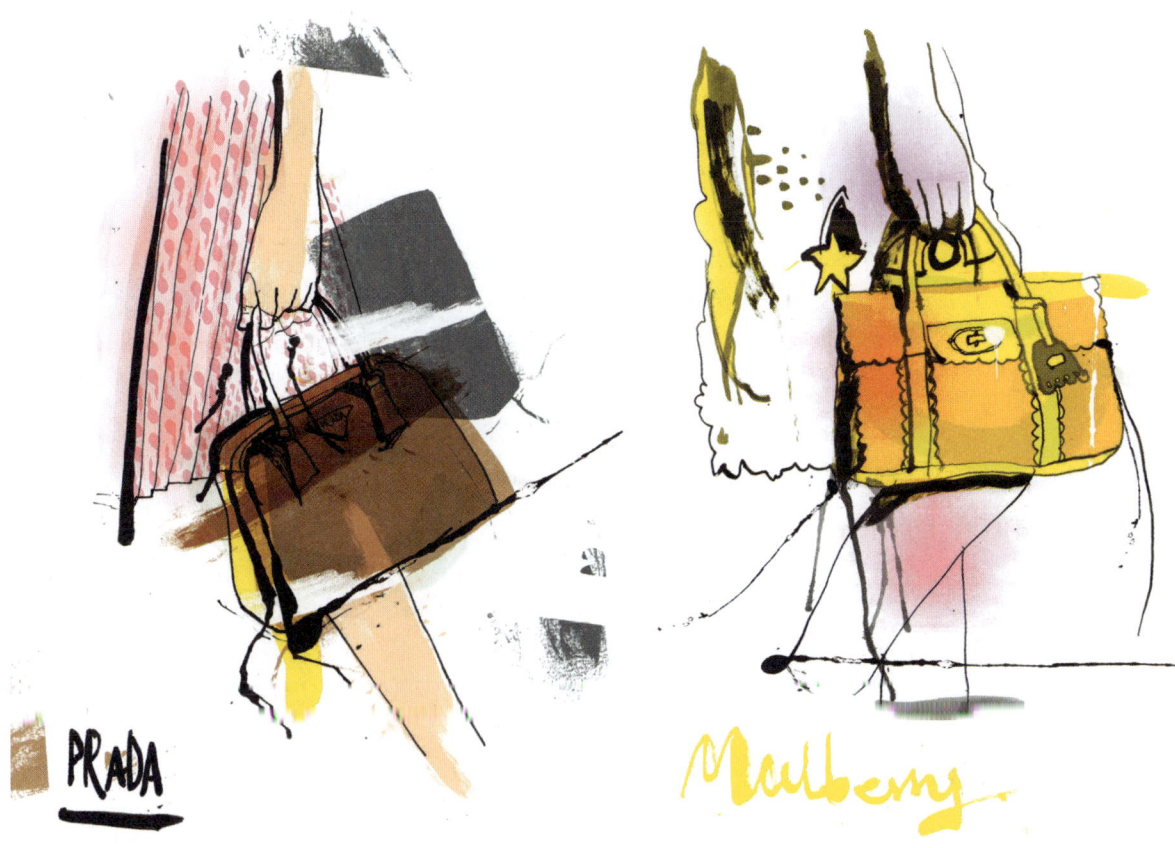

Patrick Morgan

Drawn using pen and ink and pencil on 310 Somerset paper. Brushes, crayons, pens, pencils, rollers and stencils were used for mark-making on block areas. Scanned and colour-managed in Adobe Photoshop.

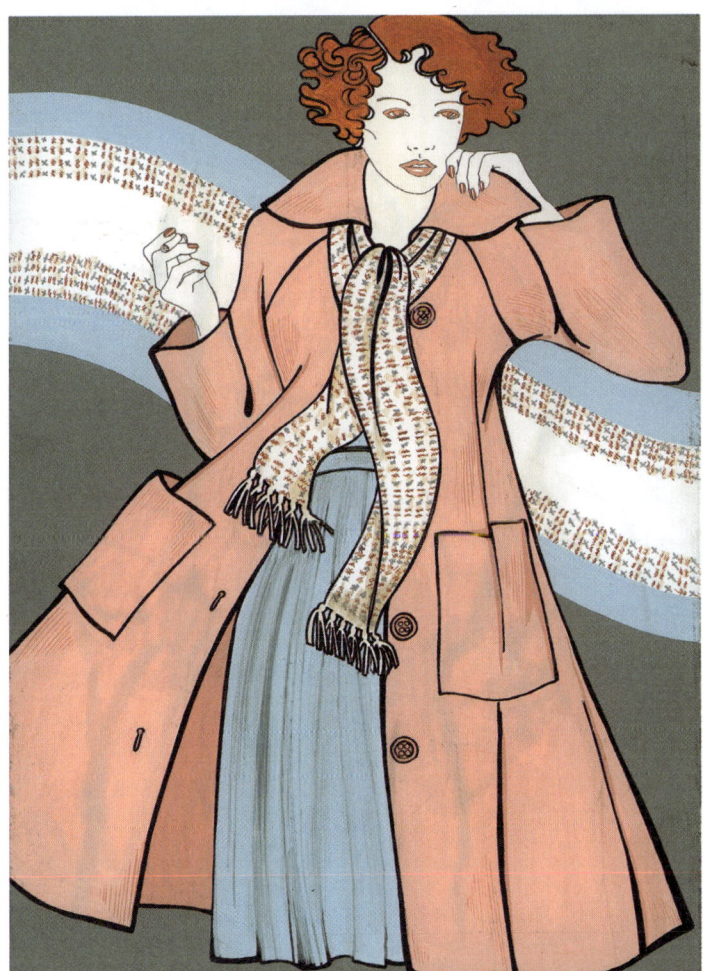

Cath Knox

Ink and gouache were used to create this image

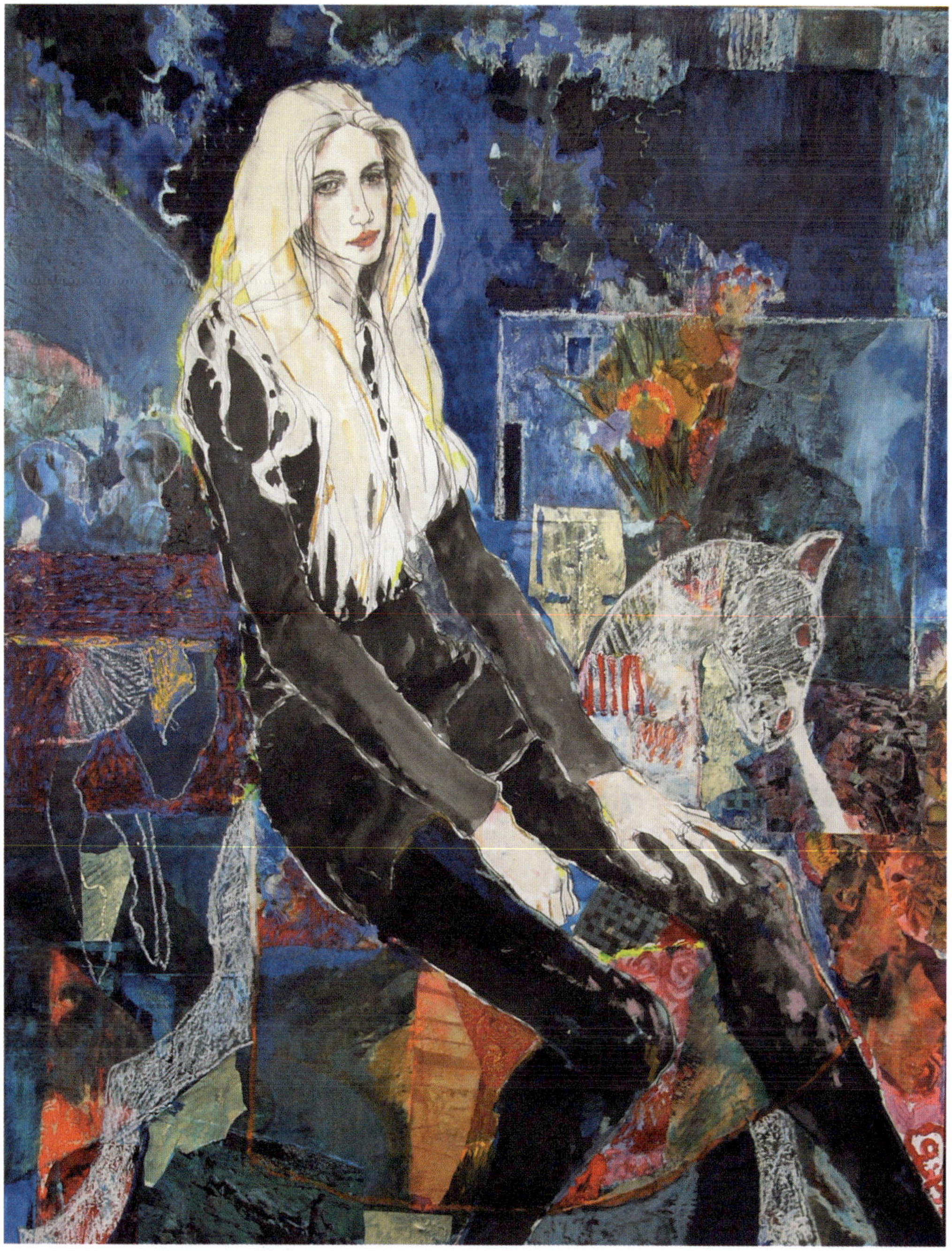

Howard Tangye
'Sue B': a portrait of a friend made using mixed media, including ink and collage of torn paper

Lynda Kelly
St Martin's School of Art, classwork, 1939
A vintage illustration created with mixed media

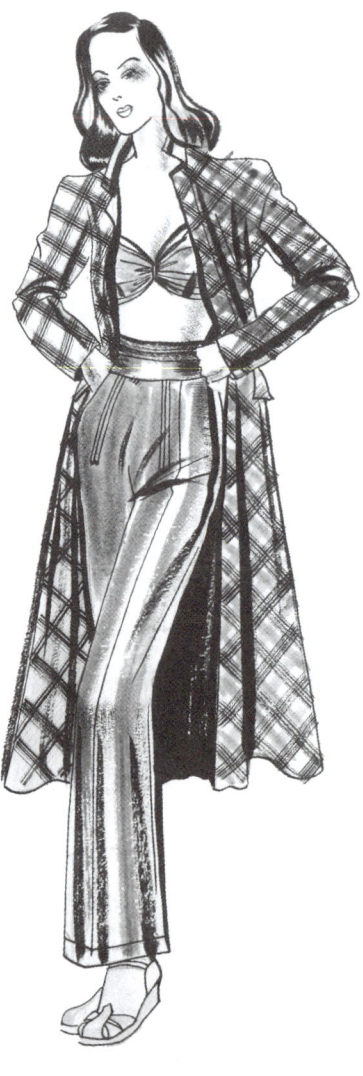

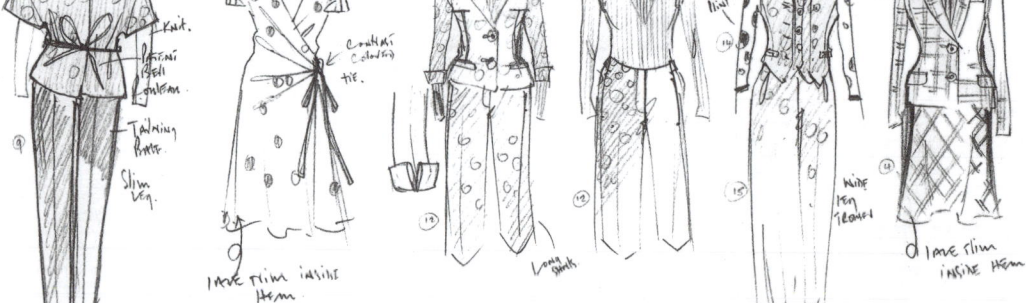

Bruce Robbins
Design drawings in soft pencil

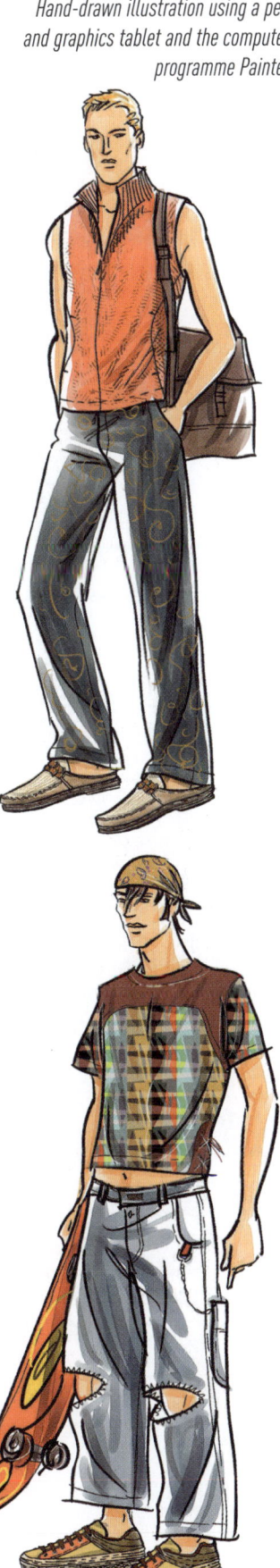

Neil Greer
*Hand-drawn illustration using a pen
and graphics tablet and the computer
programme Painter*

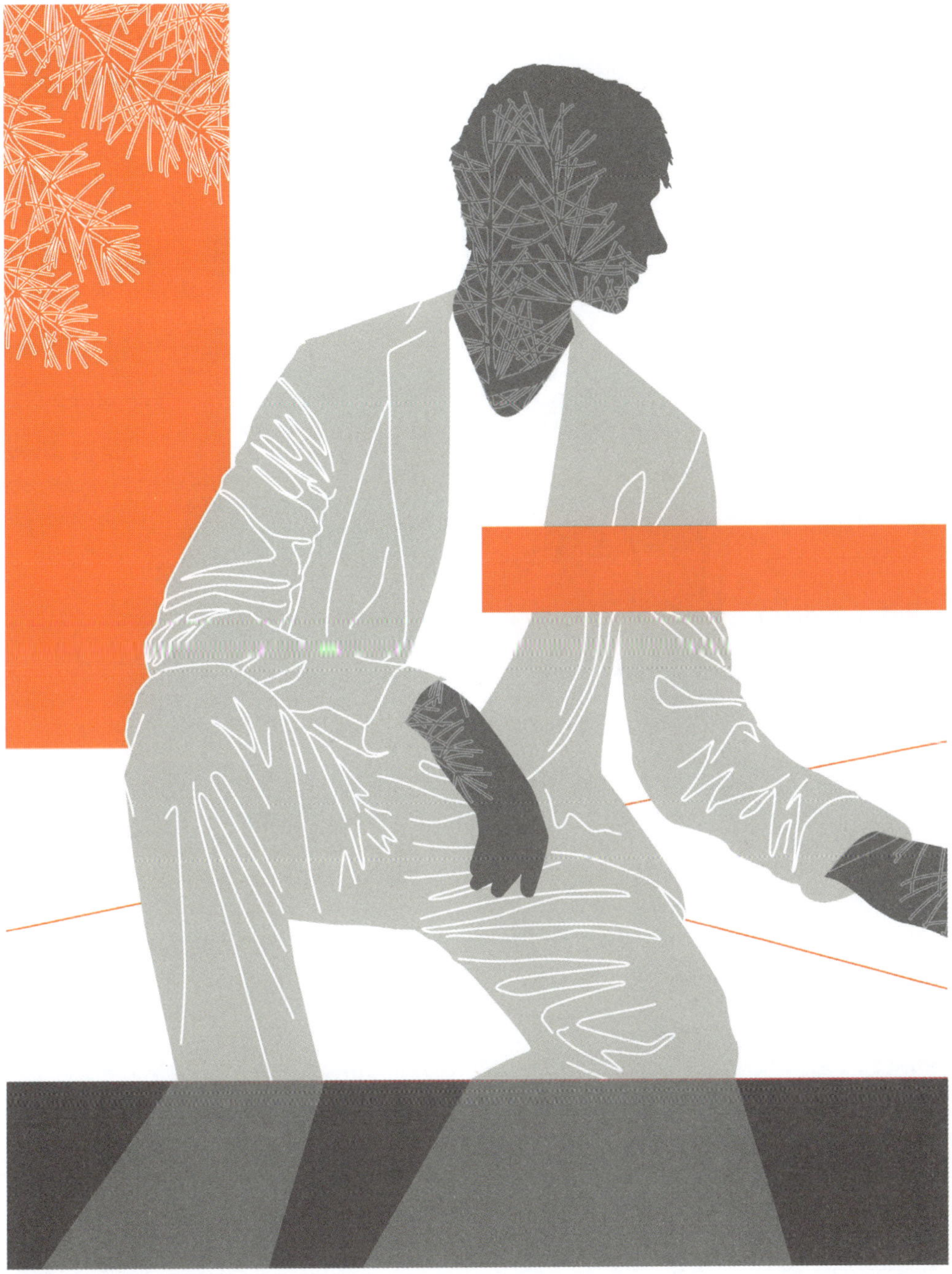

Paul Wearing
Client: Textile View Magazine
Digitally produced illustration

Neil Greer
*Hand-drawn illustration using a pen
and graphics tablet and the computer
programme Painter*

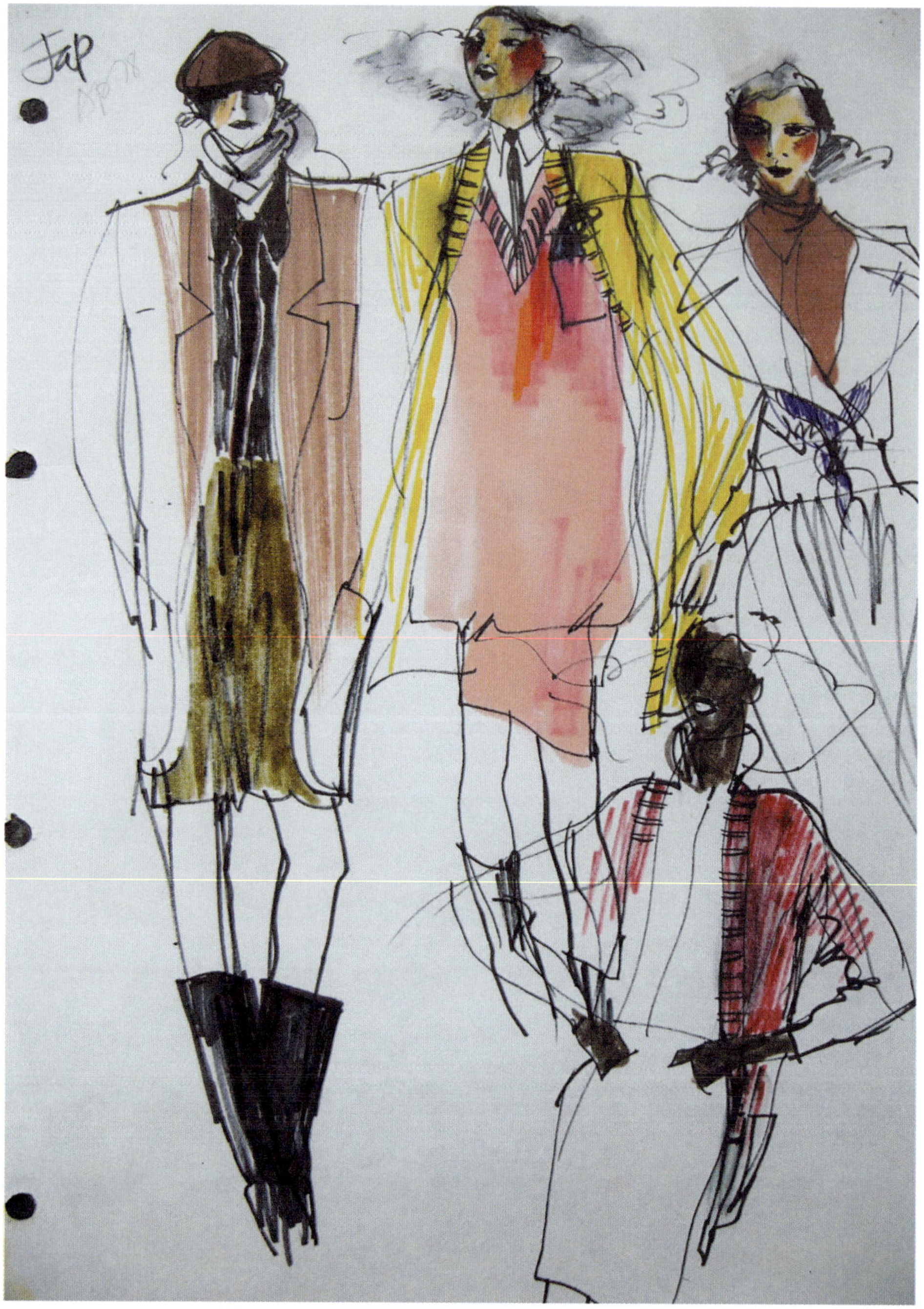

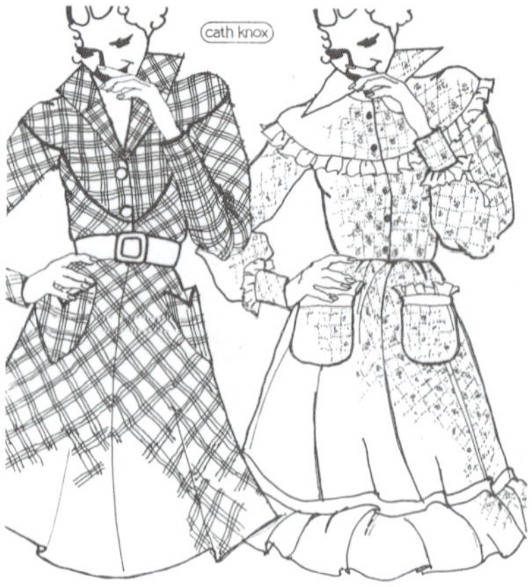

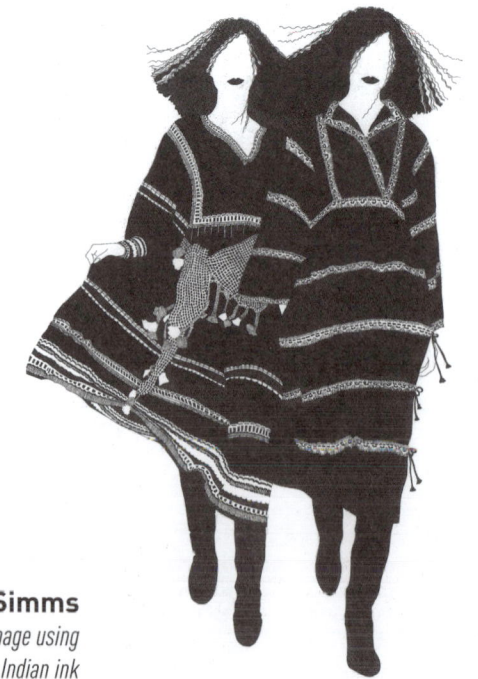

Cath Knox
*Illustration drawn with
fibre-tipped pen*

Elizabeth Suter
*Drawn at the 'Collections' in
1978, using fibre-tipped pens,
pencil and marker pens*

Judith Cheek
Oil pastel illustrations

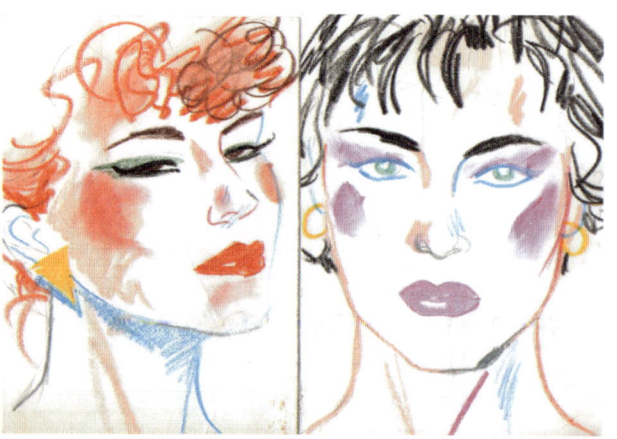

Anthea Simms
*Monochrome image using
Indian ink*

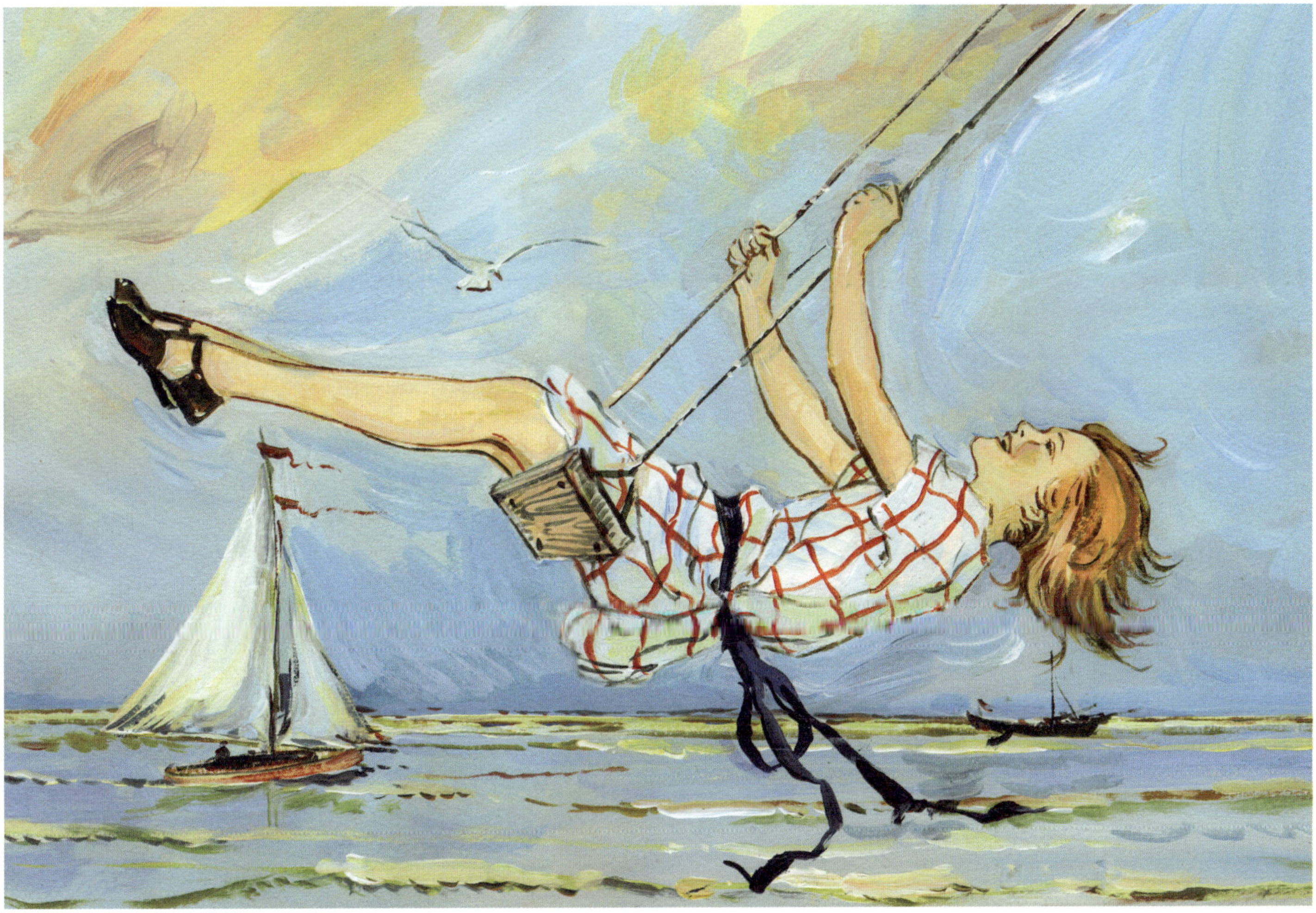

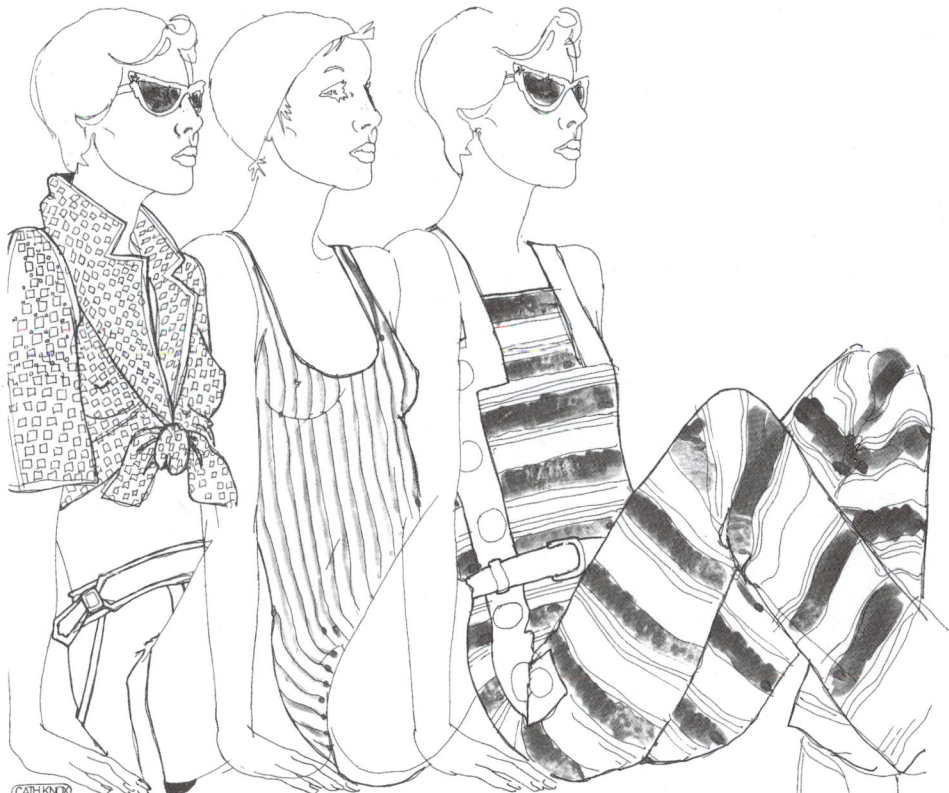

Claire Fletcher
*Illustration using acrylic
paint on paper*

Cath Knox
Client: *Cotton Board, Summer 1975*
Illustration using marker pen and pencil

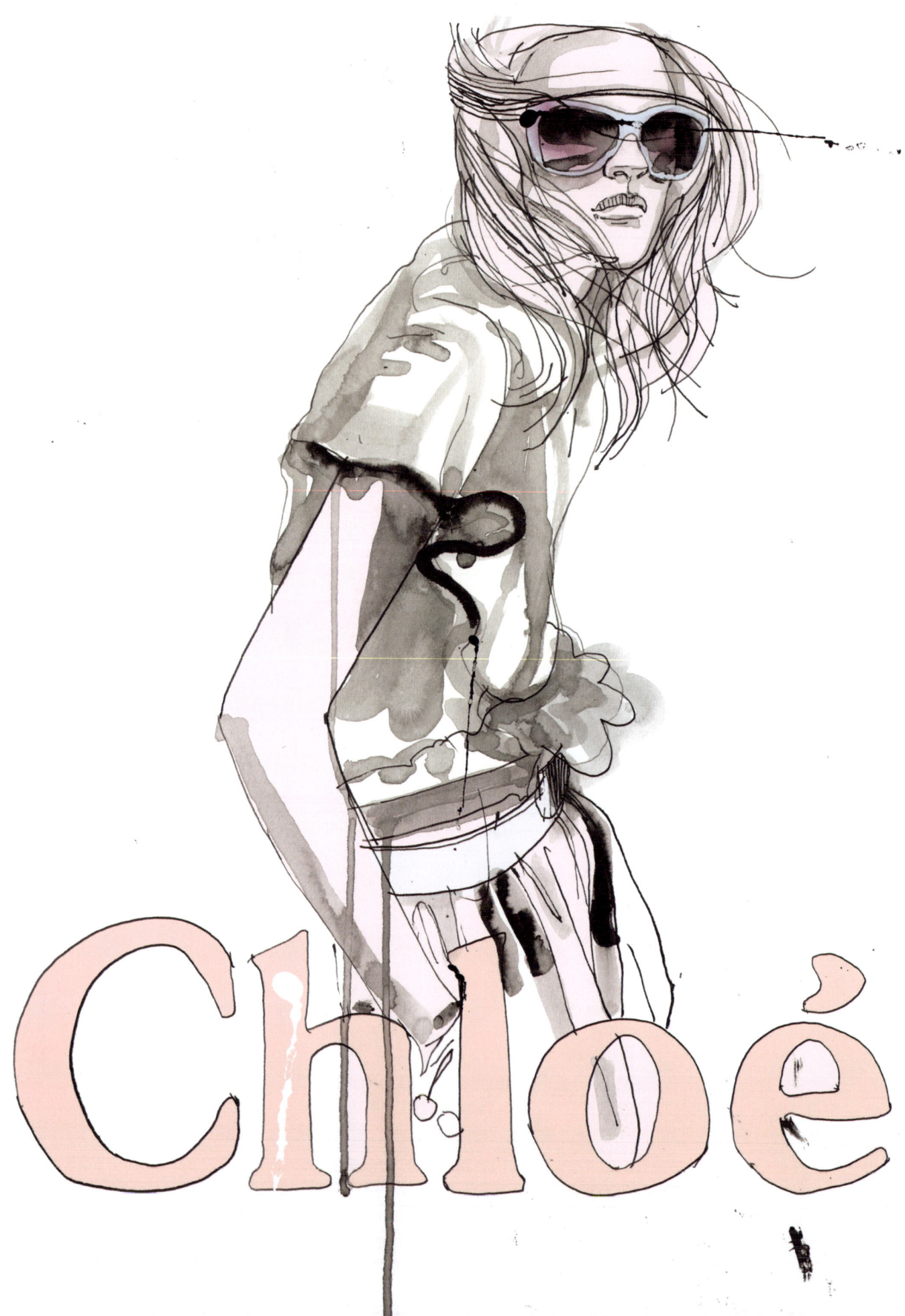

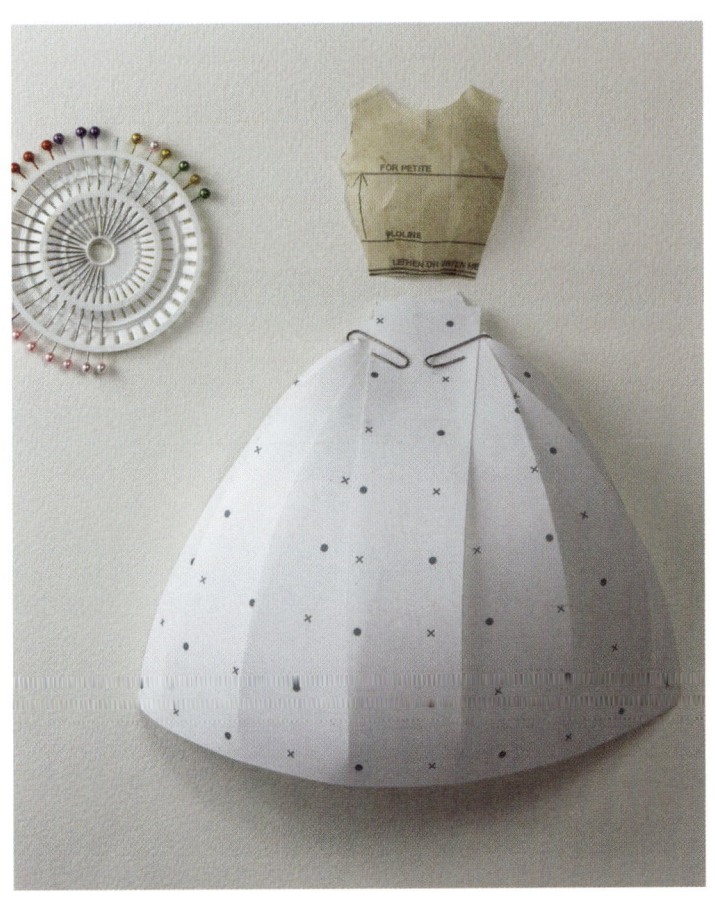

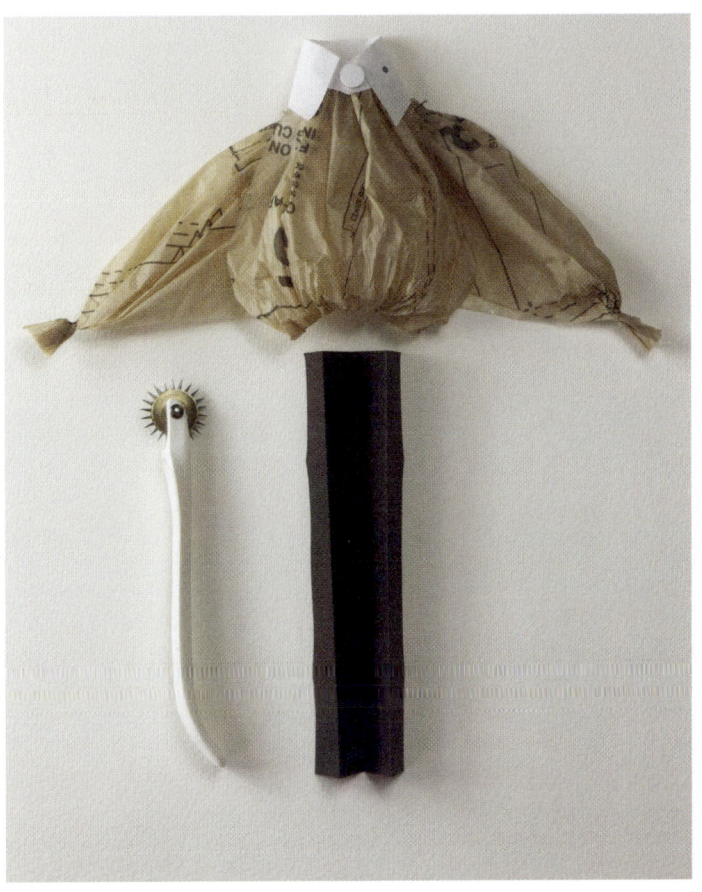

Lesley Hurst
Client: Textile View Magazine
Created with paper collage

Lesley Hurst
Client: Textile View Magazine
Created with paper collage

Patrick Morgan
FACING PAGE: *Illustration drawn with pen and ink and pencil on 310 Somerset paper. Brushes, crayons, pens, pencils, rollers and stencils were used for mark-making on block areas. Scanned and colour-managed in Adobe Photoshop.*

Judith Cheek
Silk screen print.

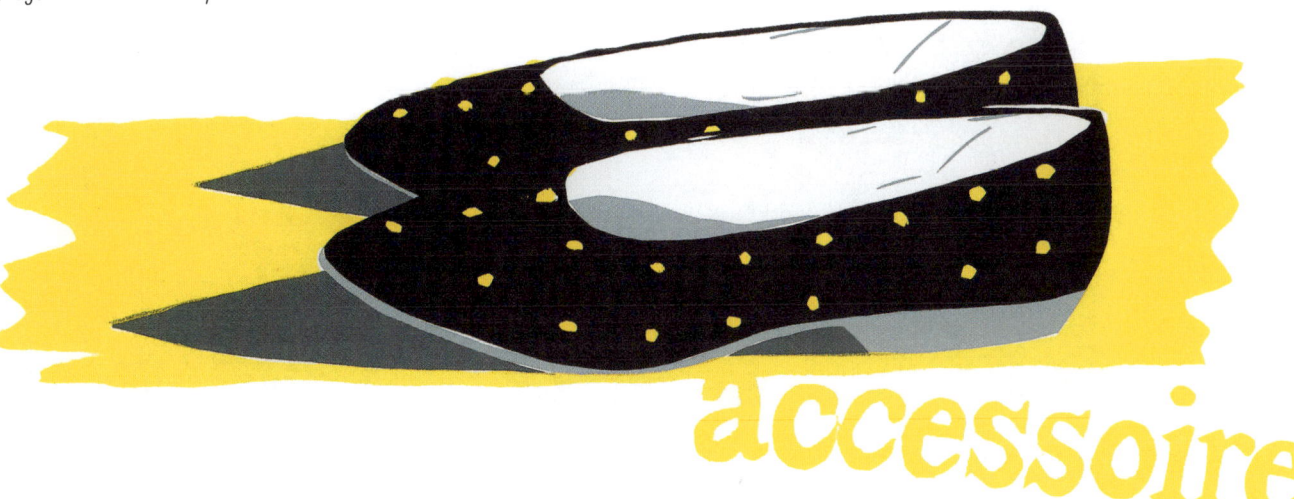

accessoire

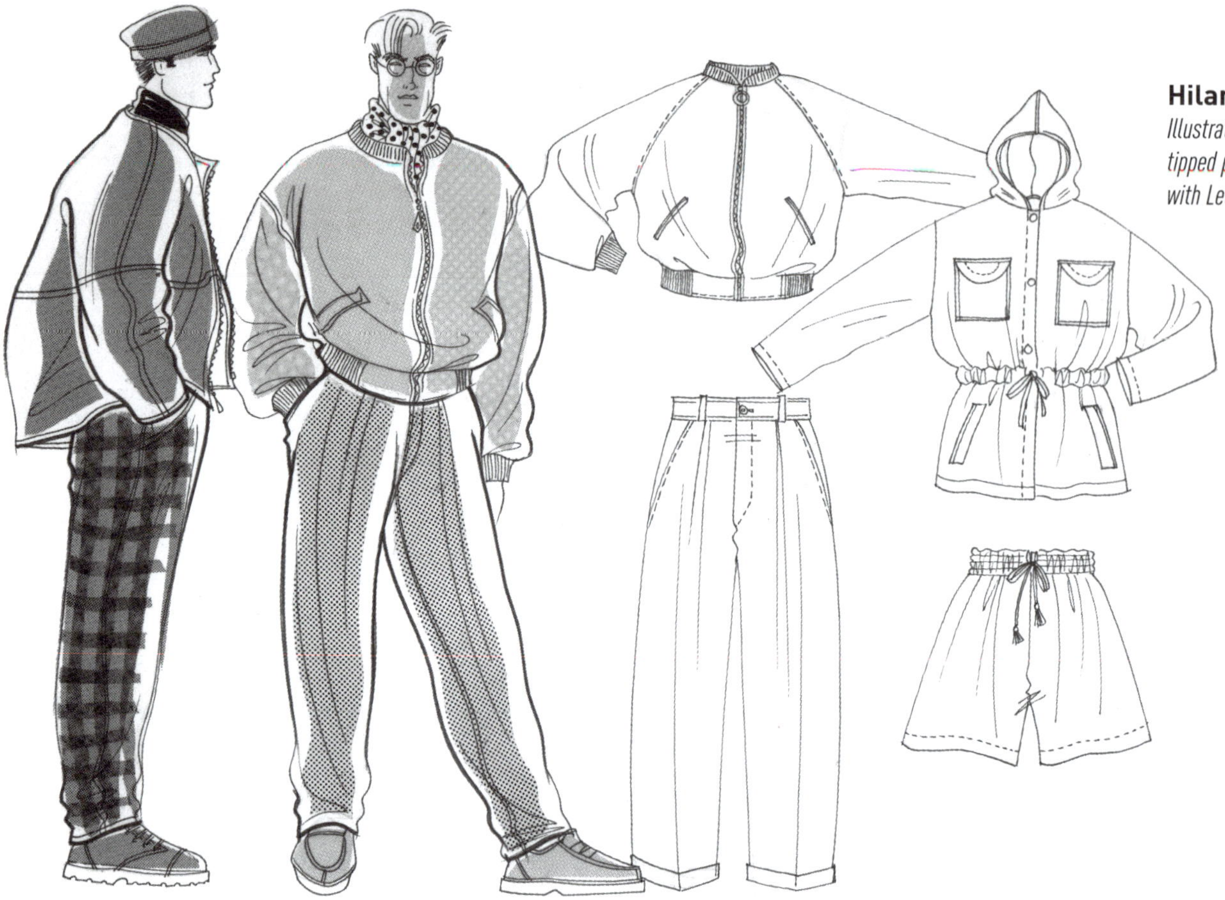

Hilary Kidd
Illustrations using fibre-tipped pens and brush pens with Letratone

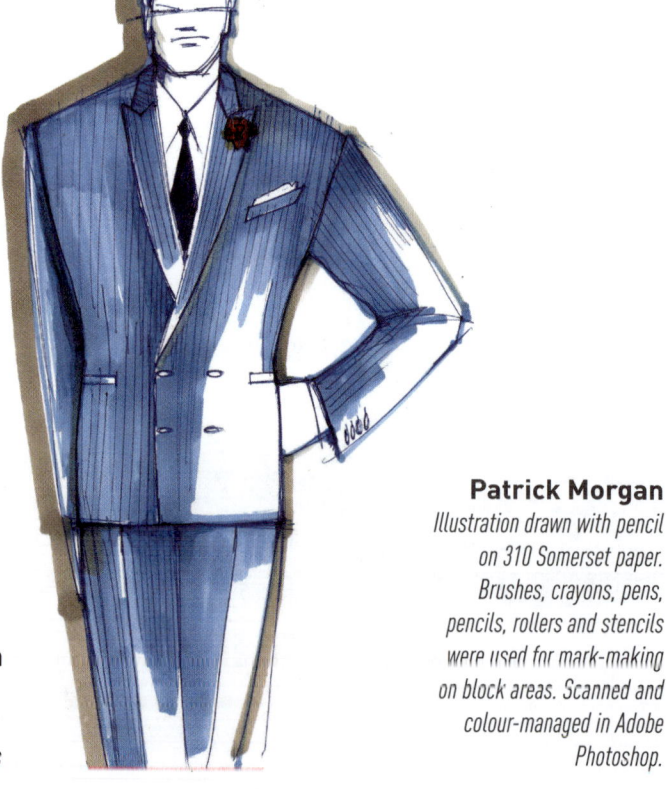

Charlie Allen
'Summer Wedding', drawn with ballpoint pen and marker pens

Patrick Morgan
Illustration drawn with pencil on 310 Somerset paper. Brushes, crayons, pens, pencils, rollers and stencils were used for mark-making on block areas. Scanned and colour-managed in Adobe Photoshop.

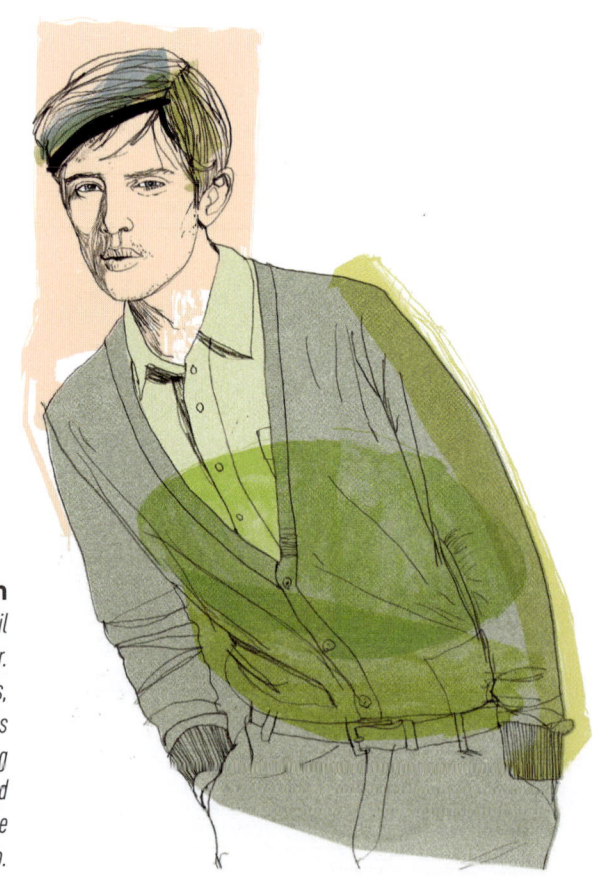

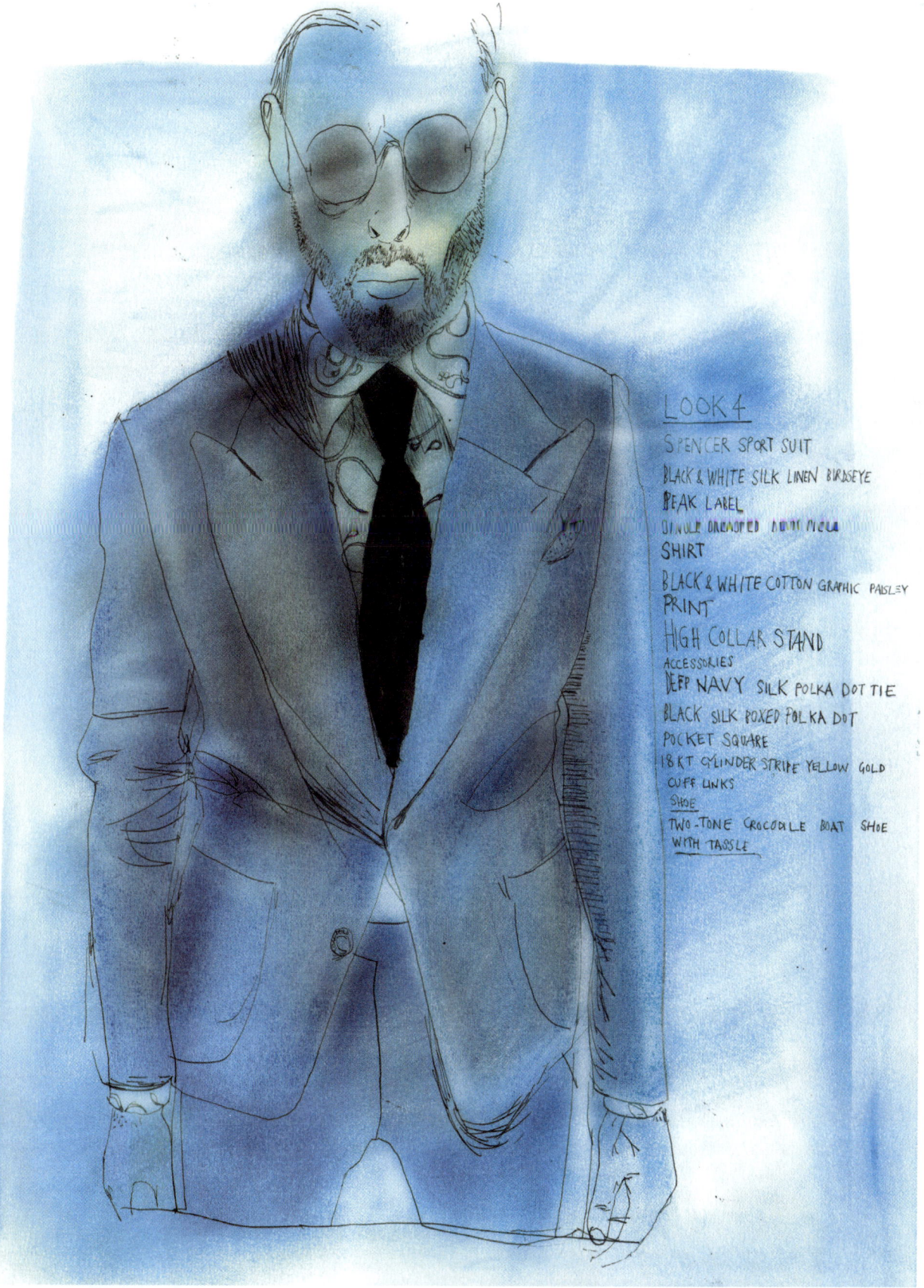

LOOK 4
SPENCER SPORT SUIT
BLACK & WHITE SILK LINEN BIRDSEYE
PEAK LABEL
SINGLE BREASTED
SHIRT
BLACK & WHITE COTTON GRAPHIC PAISLEY
PRINT
HIGH COLLAR STAND
ACCESSORIES
DEEP NAVY SILK POLKA DOT TIE
BLACK SILK BOXED POLKA DOT
POCKET SQUARE
18 KT CYLINDER STRIPE YELLOW GOLD
CUFF LINKS
SHOE
TWO-TONE CROCODILE BOAT SHOE
WITH TASSLE

Patrick Morgan

Image drawn with pen and ink and pencil on 310 Somerset paper. Brushes, crayons, pens, pencils, rollers and stencils were used for mark-making on block areas. Scanned and colour-managed in Adobe Photoshop.

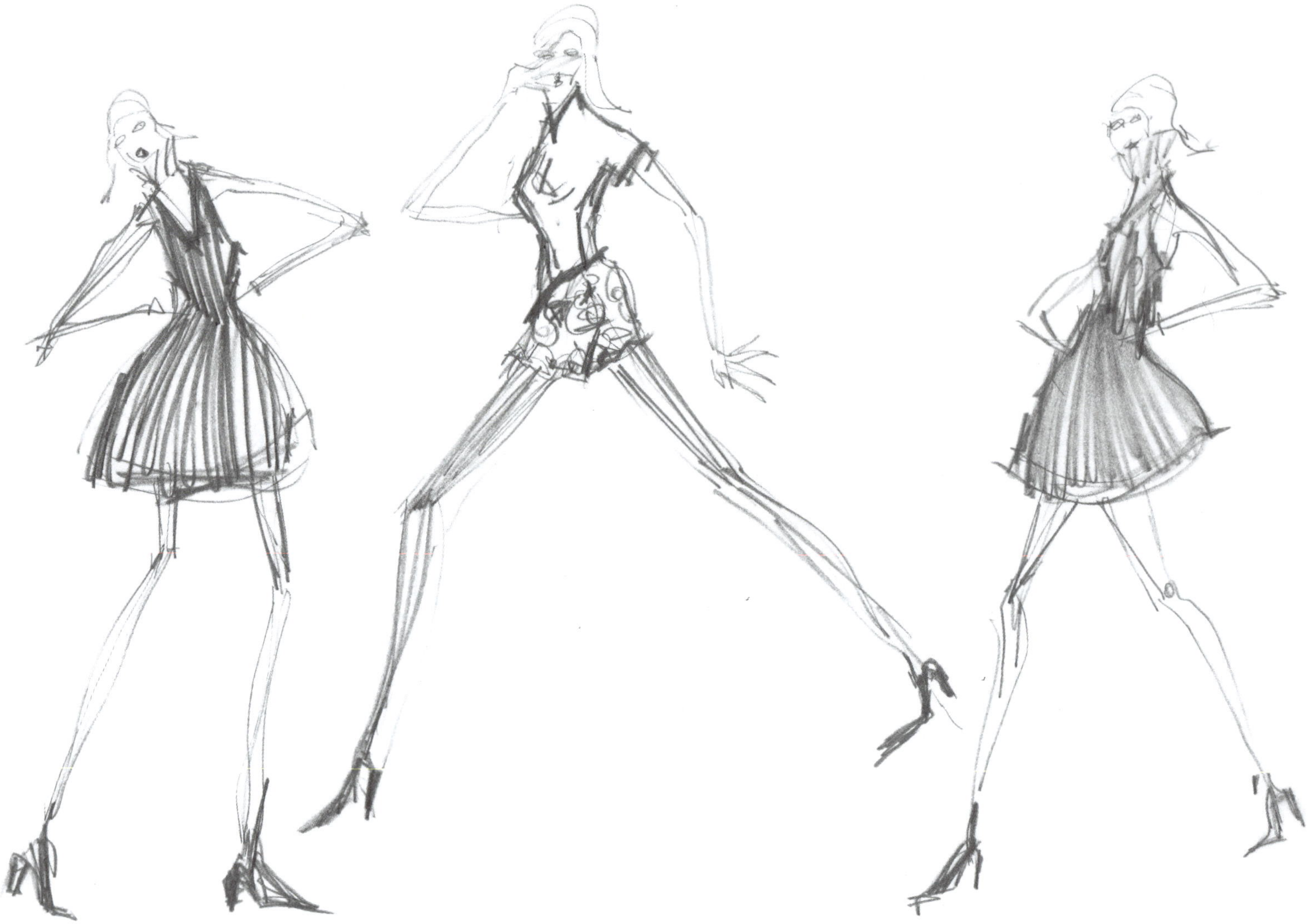

Pik Yee Berwick
Soft pencil sketch

Hormazd Narielwalla
Digital collage

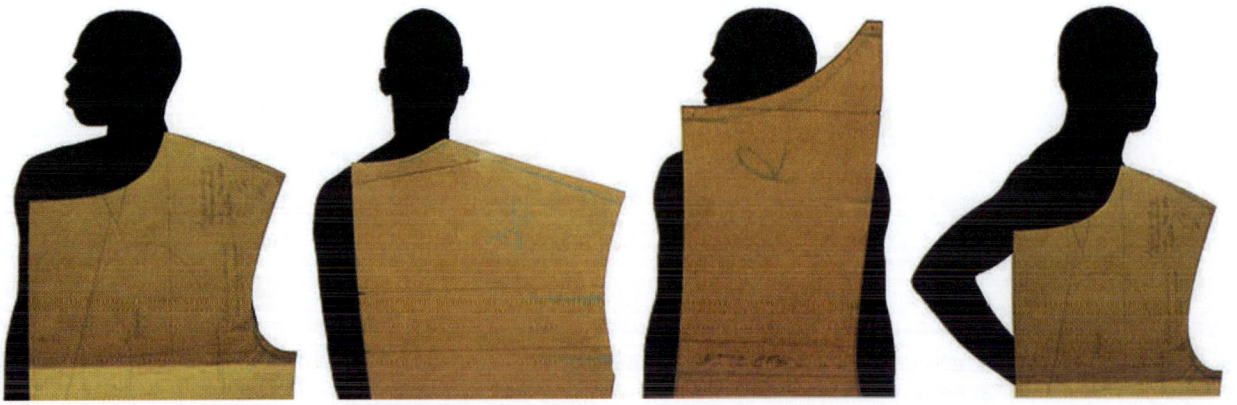

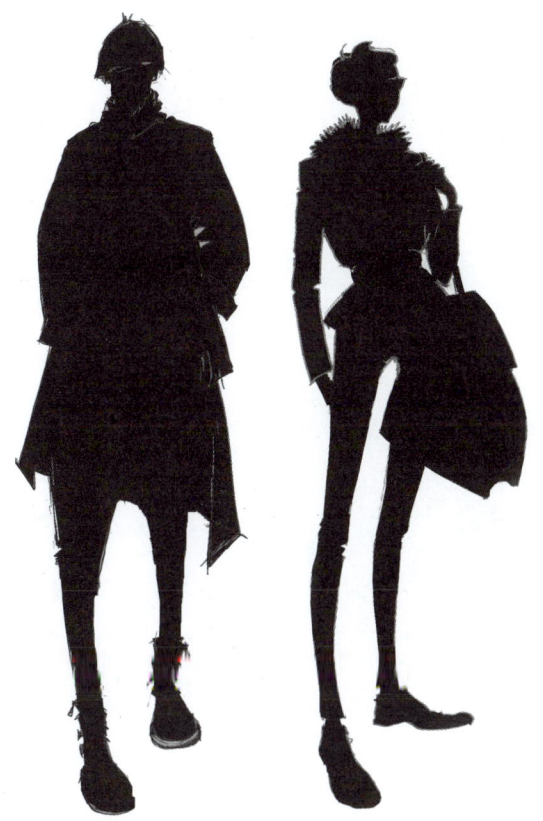

Yvonne Deacon

Here, outlines were sketched in pencil, then the artwork was scanned and outlines were filled in using Adobe Photoshop.

Patrick Morgan

Drawn with black ink and pencil on 310 Somerset paper

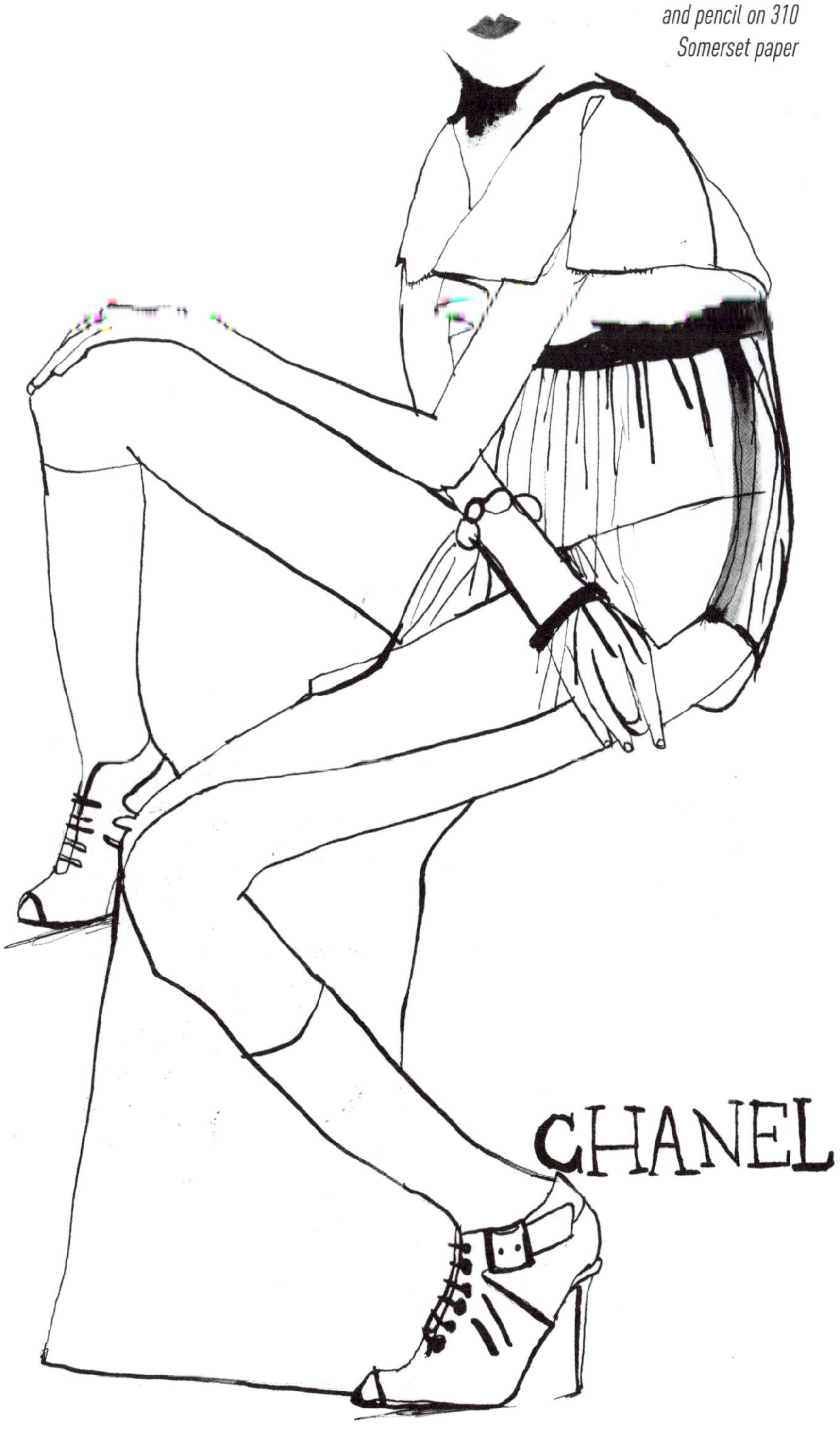

Yvonne Deacon

BELOW: Artwork using pencil, watercolours and an ink splodge collage on paper. Scanned and finished using Adobe Photoshop.

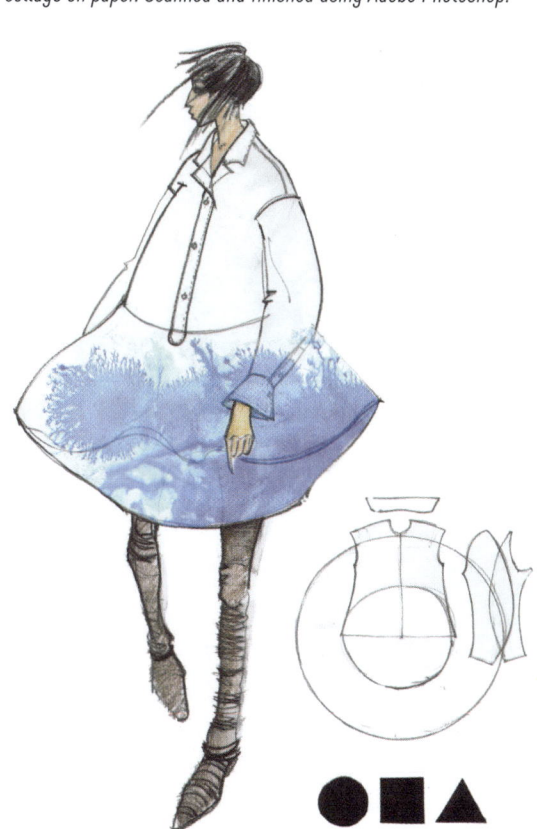

CHANEL

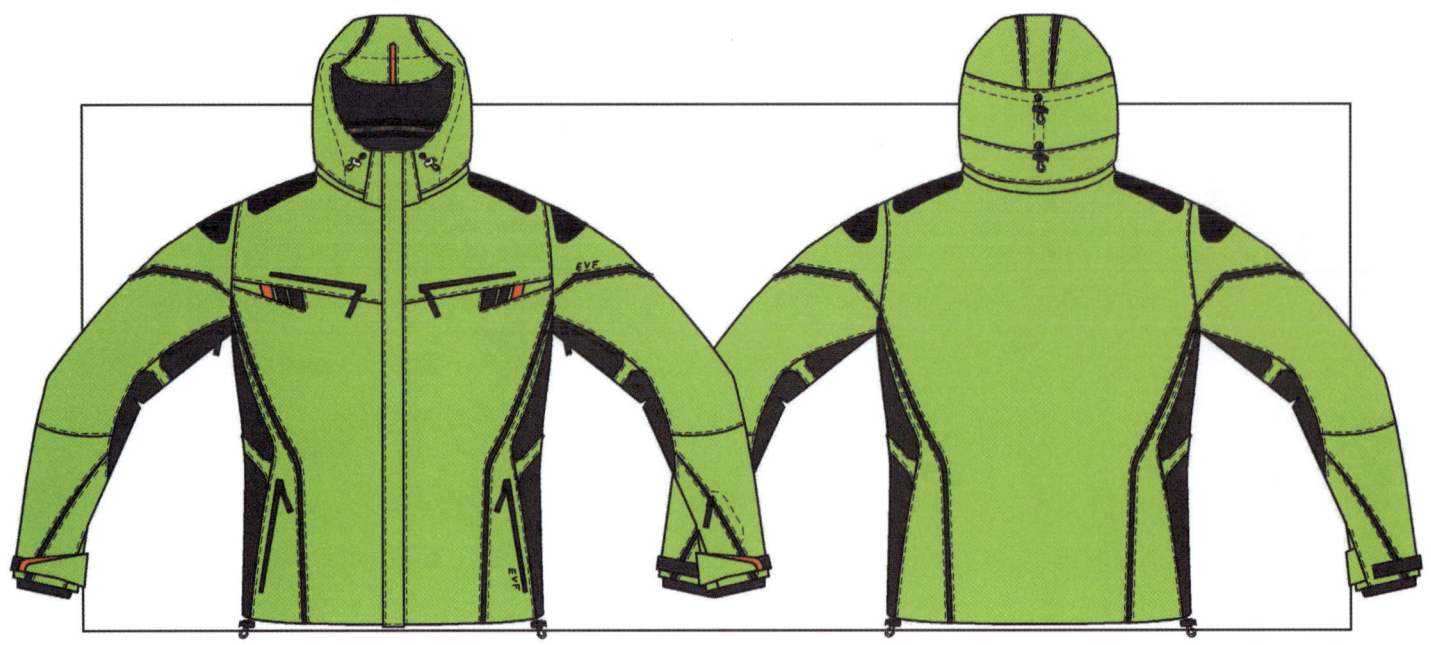

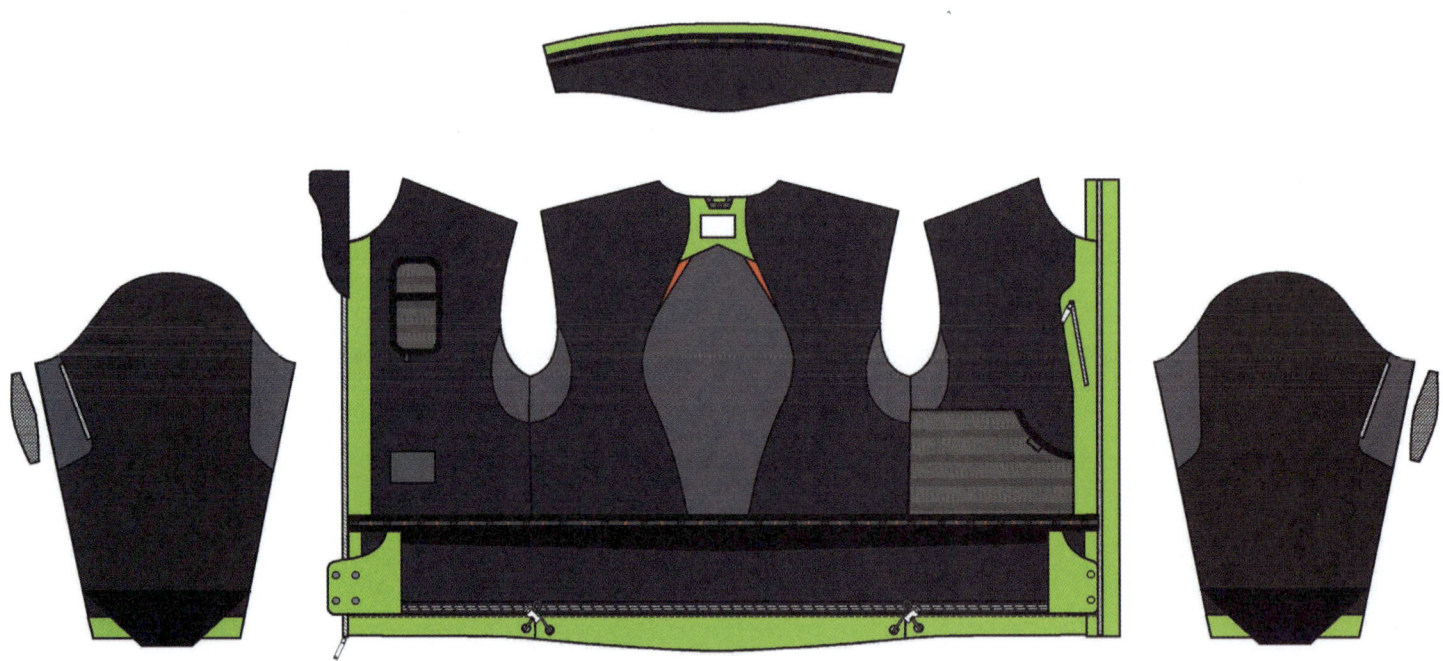

Clare Dudley Hart
Client: *EVF Ltd – Skiwear technical drawings*
Drawings produced digitally

Paul Wearing
FACING PAGE
Client: Textile View Magazine
Digital illustration

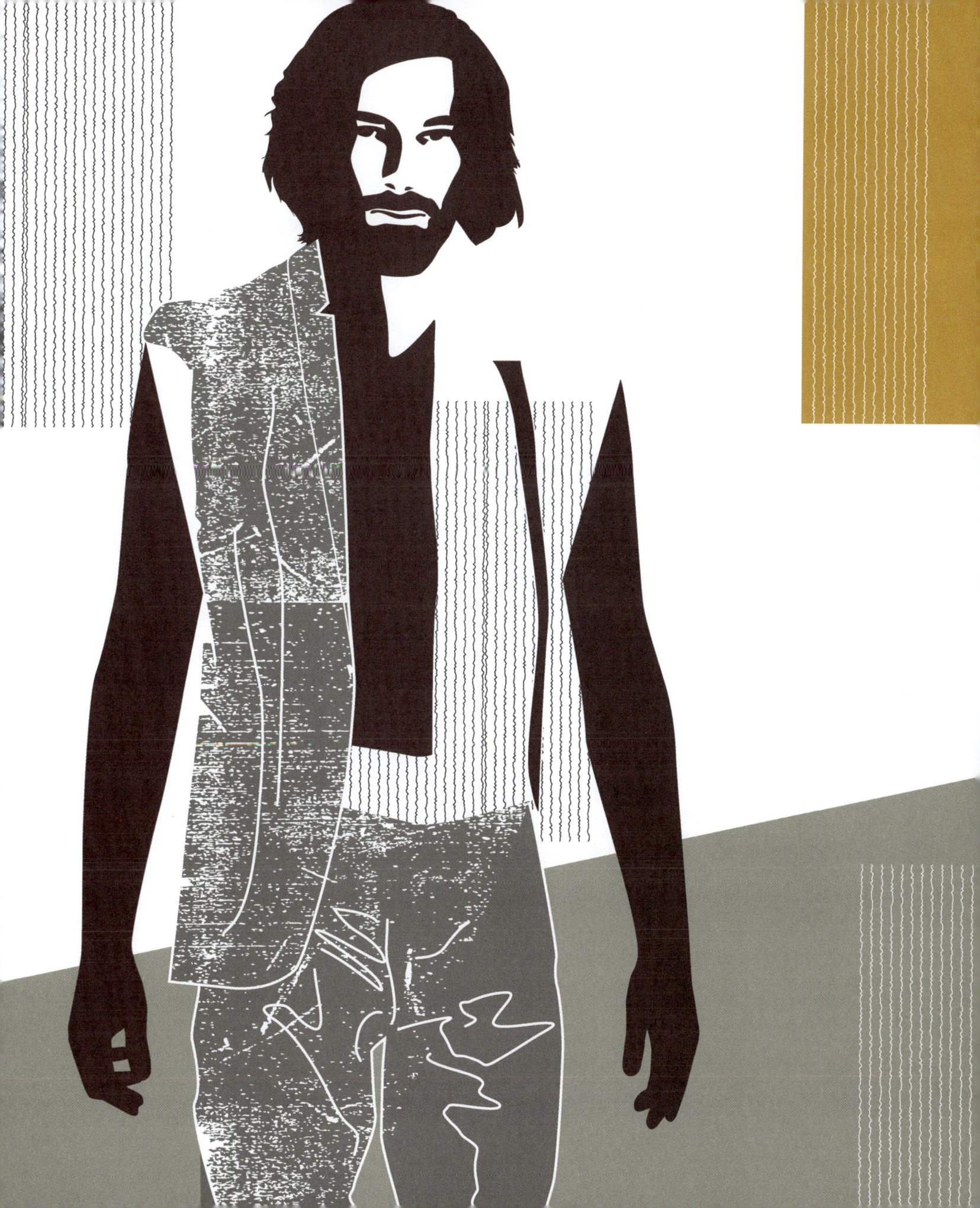

Martina Farrow
Agent: *New Division*
'Floral' - Promotional work 2010/2011
Created using Adobe Illustrator CS3

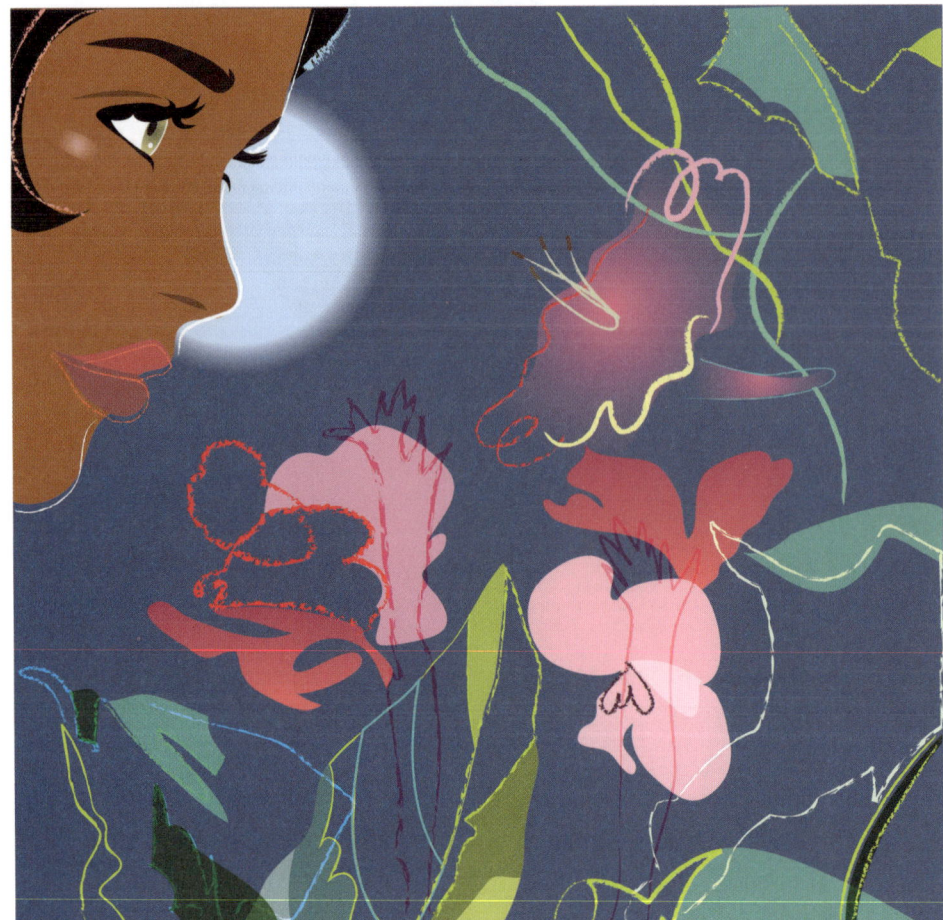

Hilary Kidd
Illustration using brush pen, marker pens and crayon

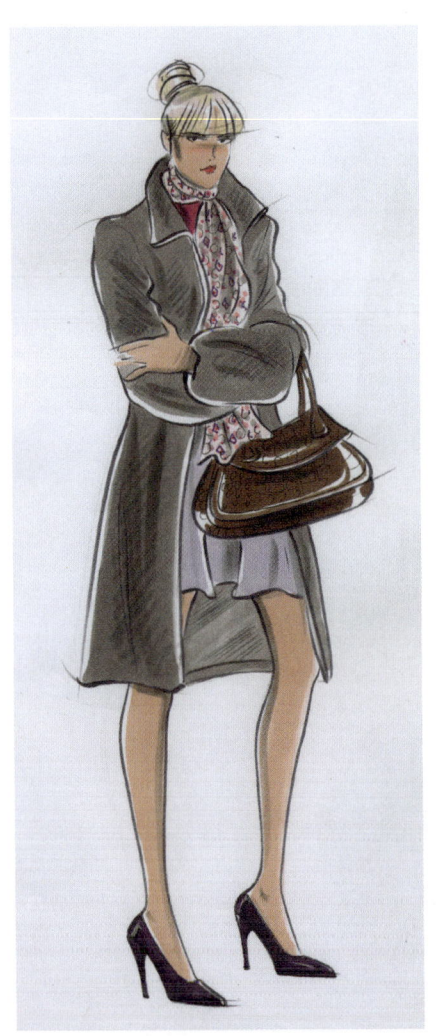

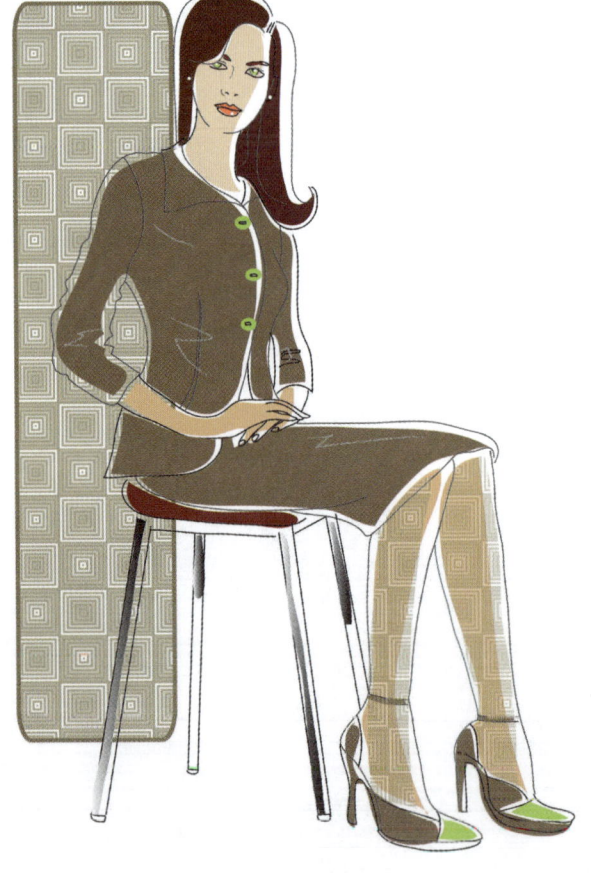

Lynnette Cook
'Lady Lou'
Created using Adobe Illustrator CS3

Rosalyn Kennedy
Illustration using brush pen, pencil,
watercolour and pastel

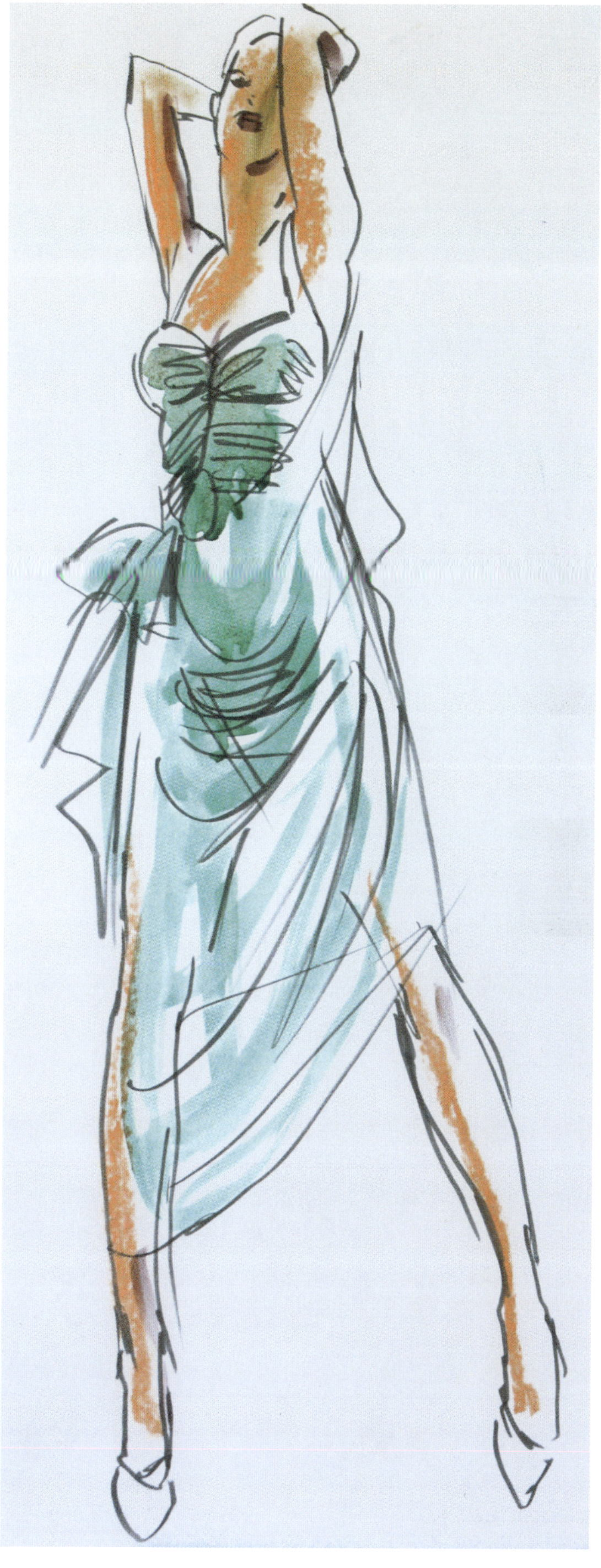

Howard Tangye
'Emilie', a drawing for Elisa Palomino 2009–10
Mixed media on paper

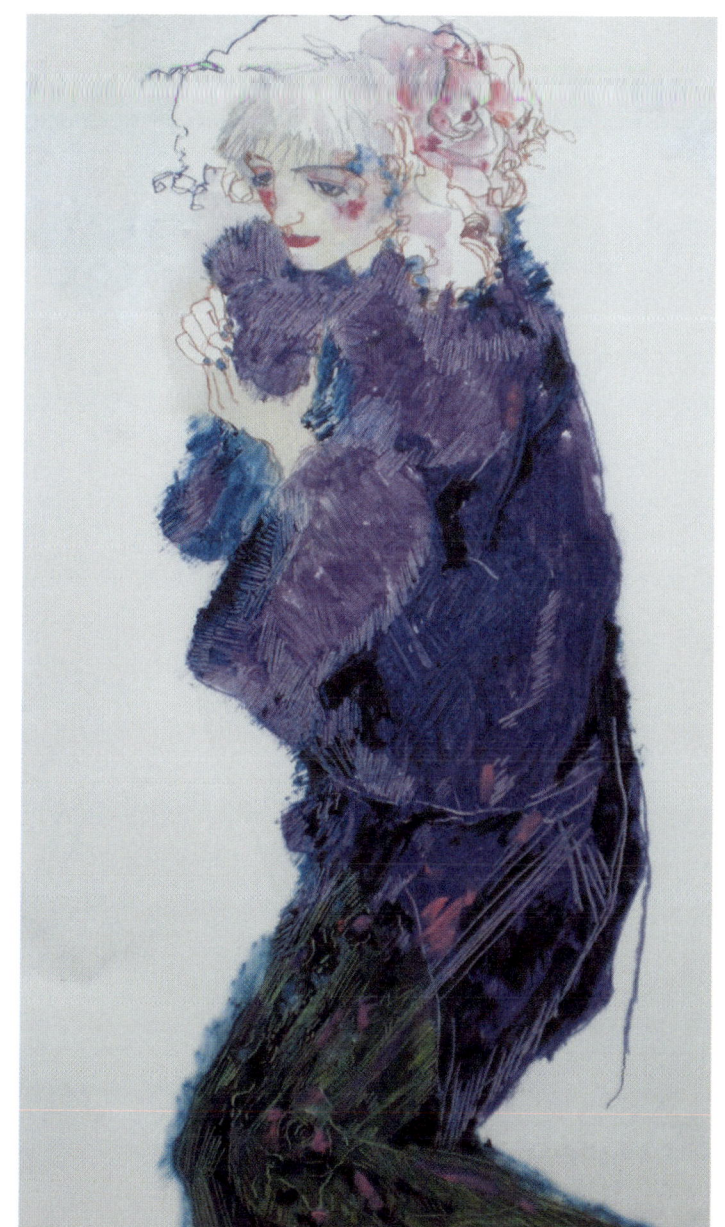

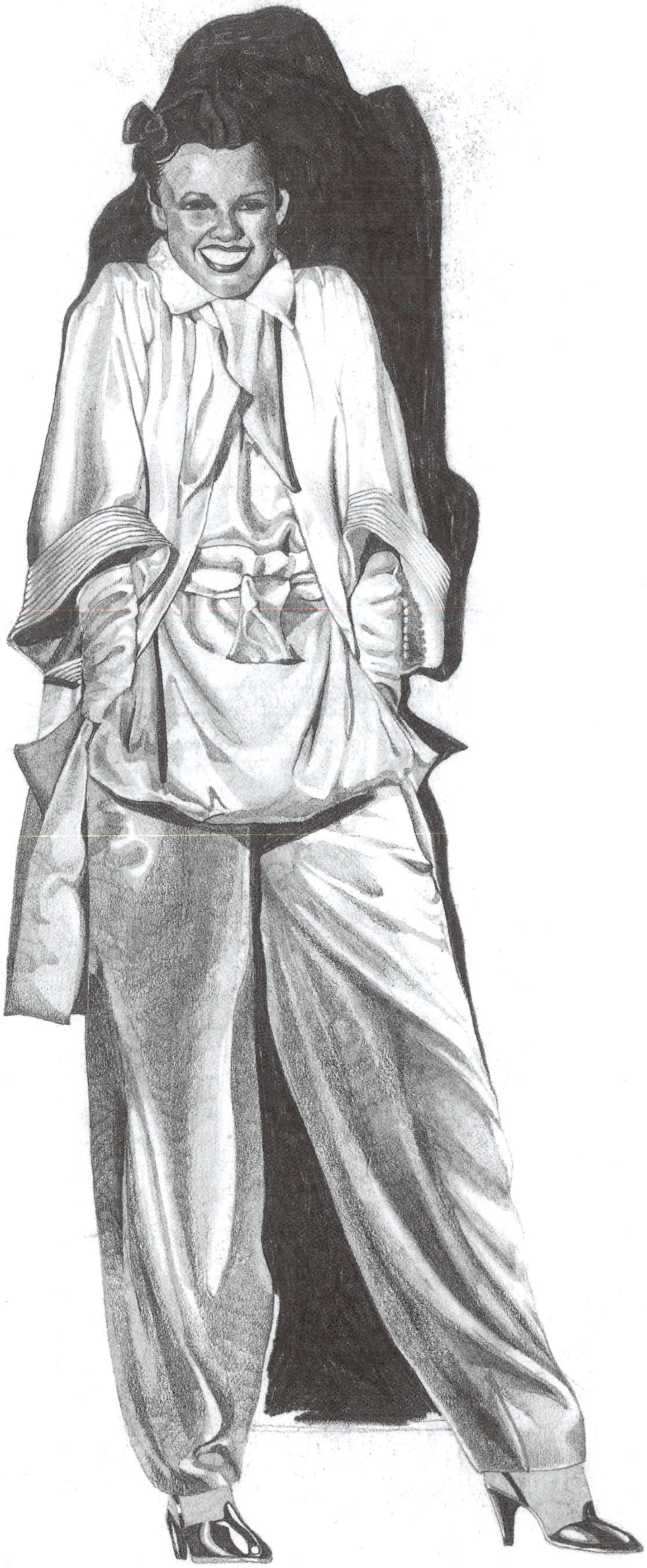

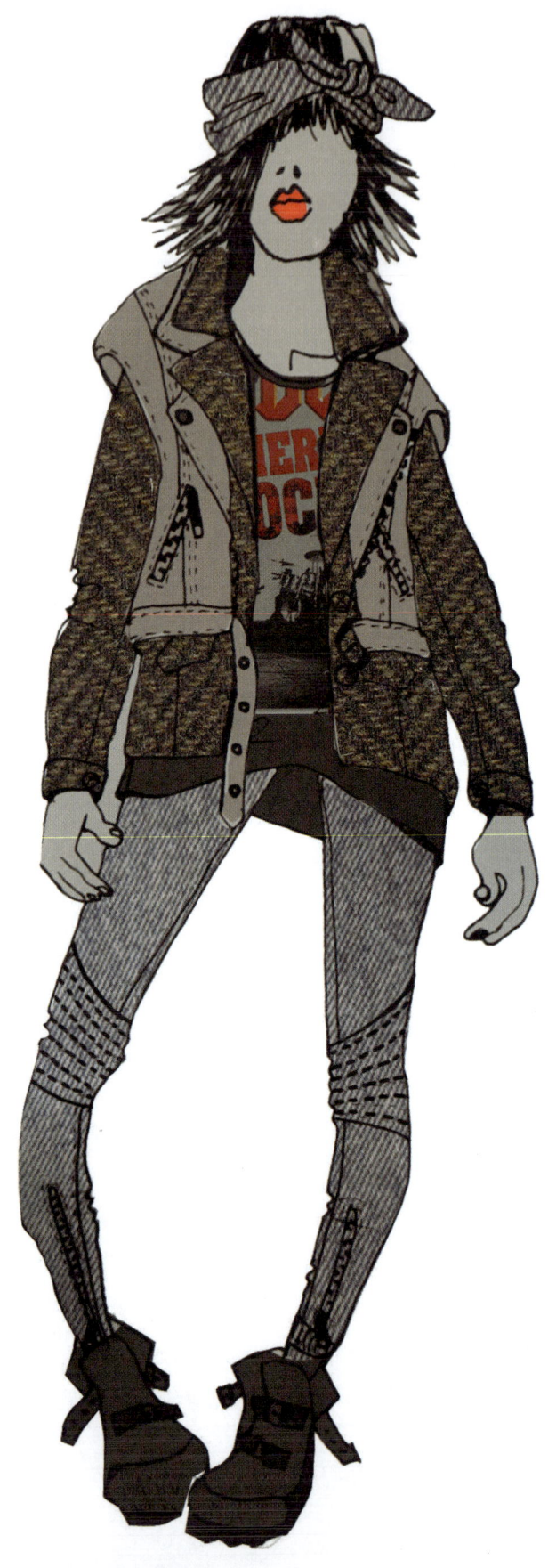

Anthea Simms
Pencil drawing

Katharina Gulde
Client: *ONLY Bestseller*
Hand-drawn and digitally manipulated

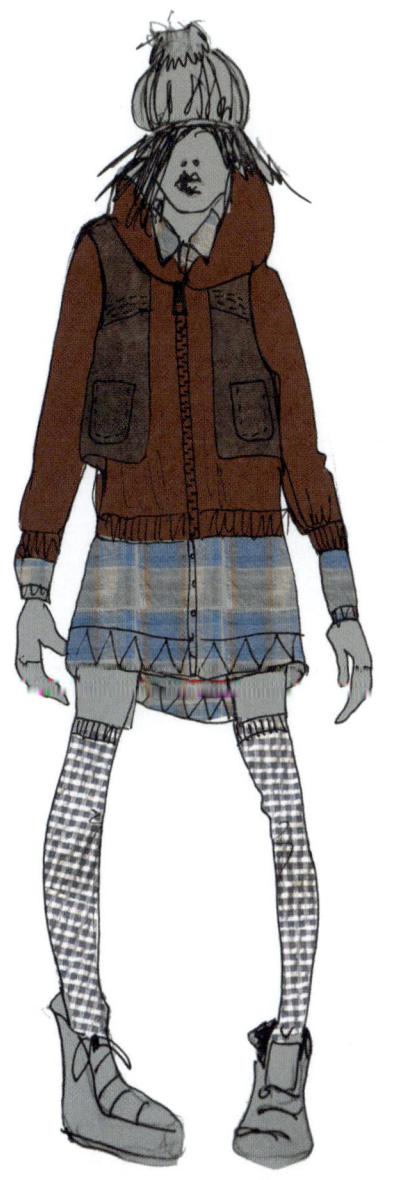

Katharina Gulde
Client: *ONLY Bestseller*
Hand and digital drawing

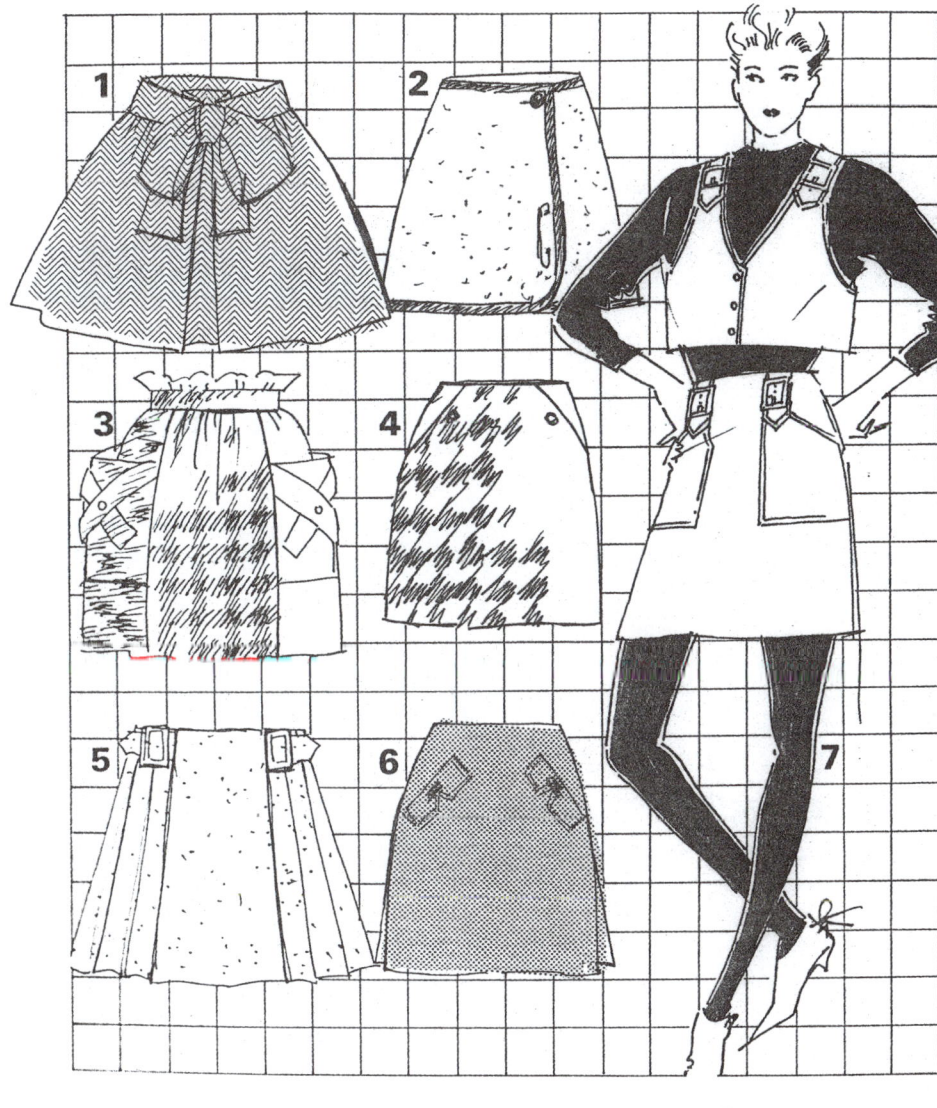

Rosalyn Kennedy
Client: *Nigel French Enterprises*
Fibre-tipped pen with Letratone

Hilary Kidd
Hand-drawn using brush pen, marker pen and chinagraph pencil

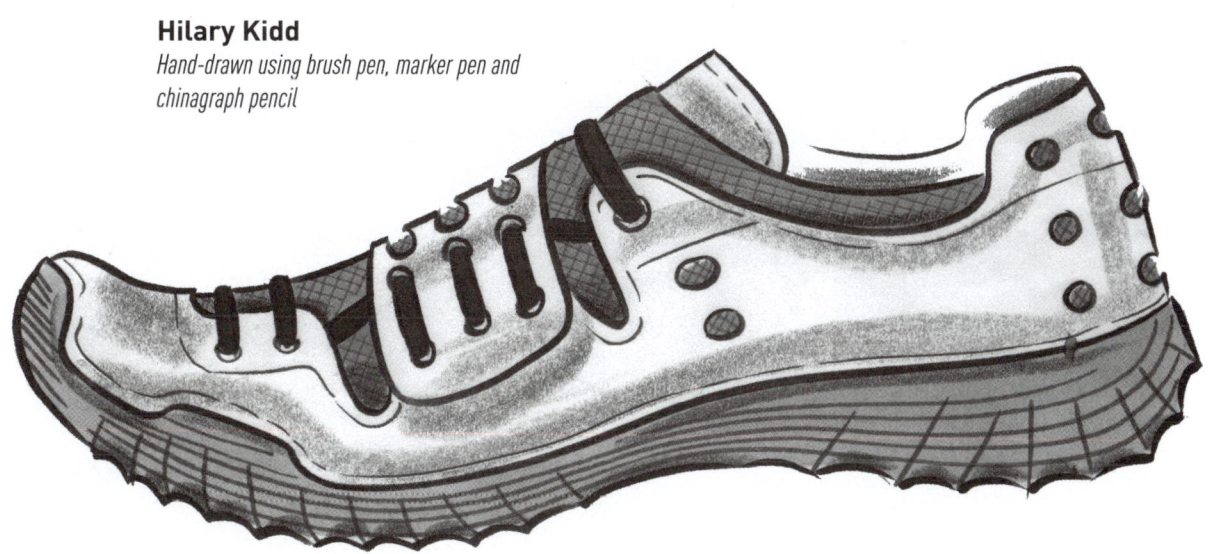

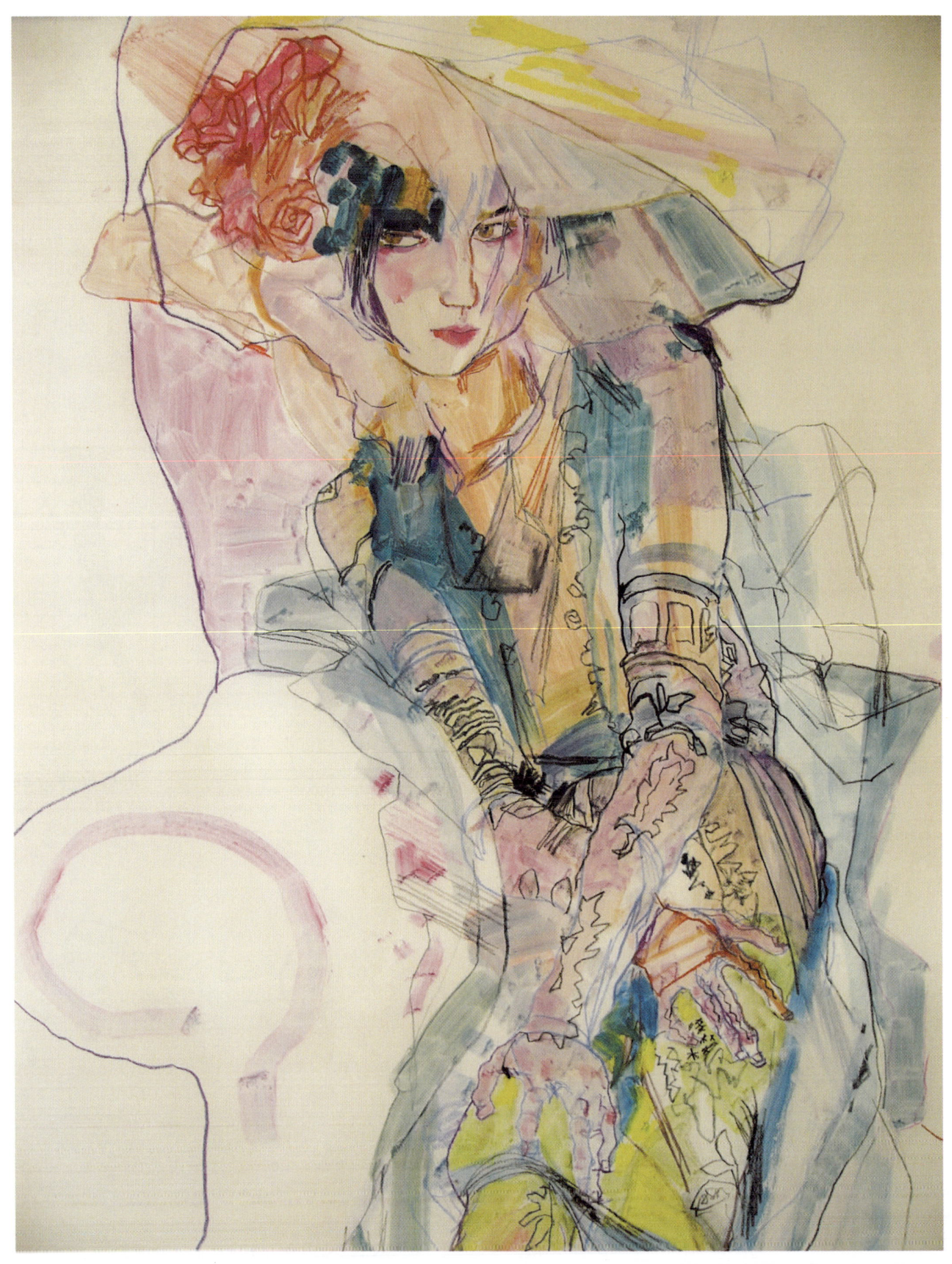

Howard Tangye

FACING PAGE

*'Elodie' Galliano girl (Autumn/Winter 2007), drawn
in situ in the Paris studio of John Galliano. Created
using mixed media on paper.*

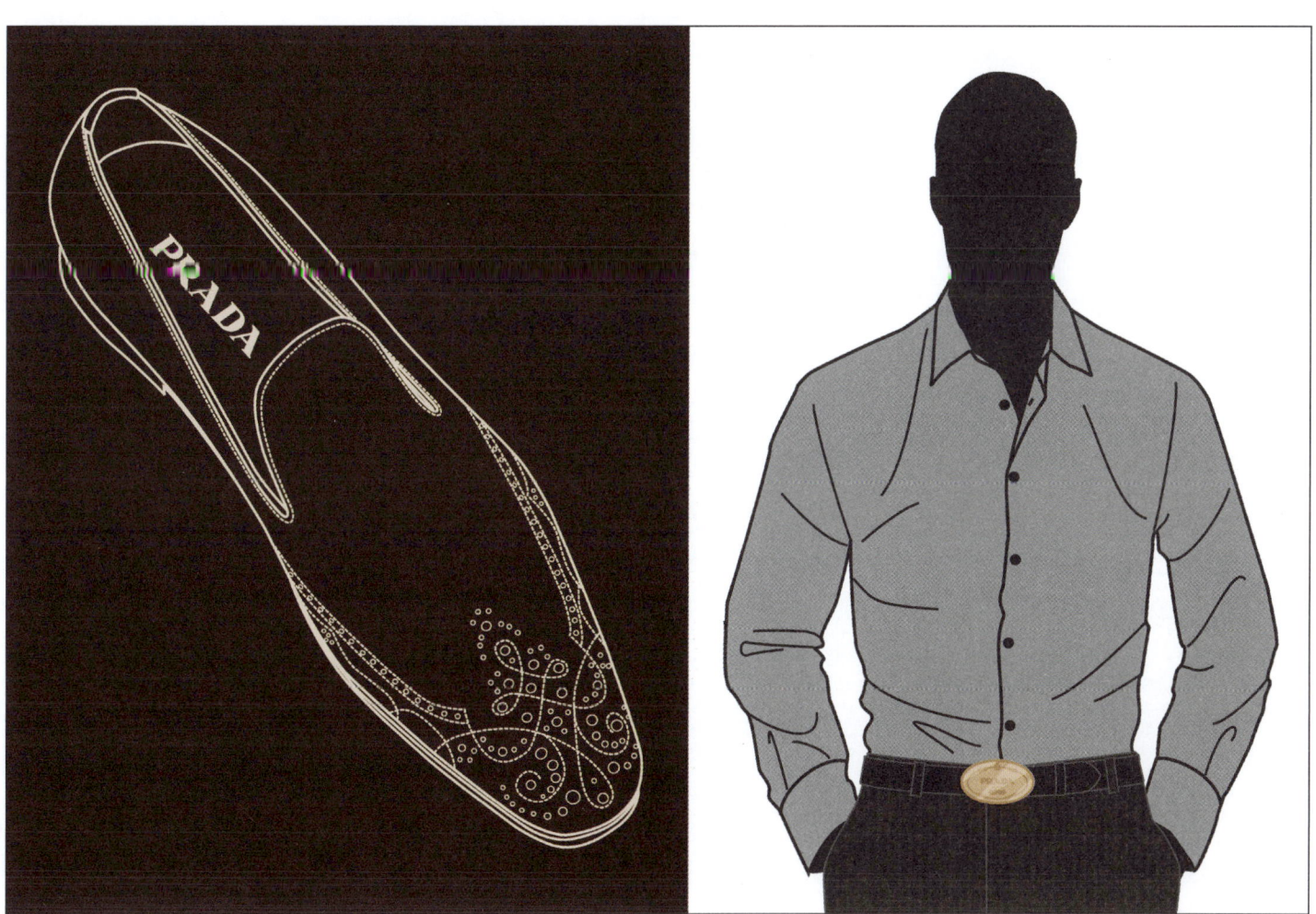

Paul Wearing

Client: *Neiman Marcus – The Book*
Digitally produced illustration

Sophia Kokosalaki
Client: *Christina Gourdain wedding commission*
Hand-drawn and scanned to computer

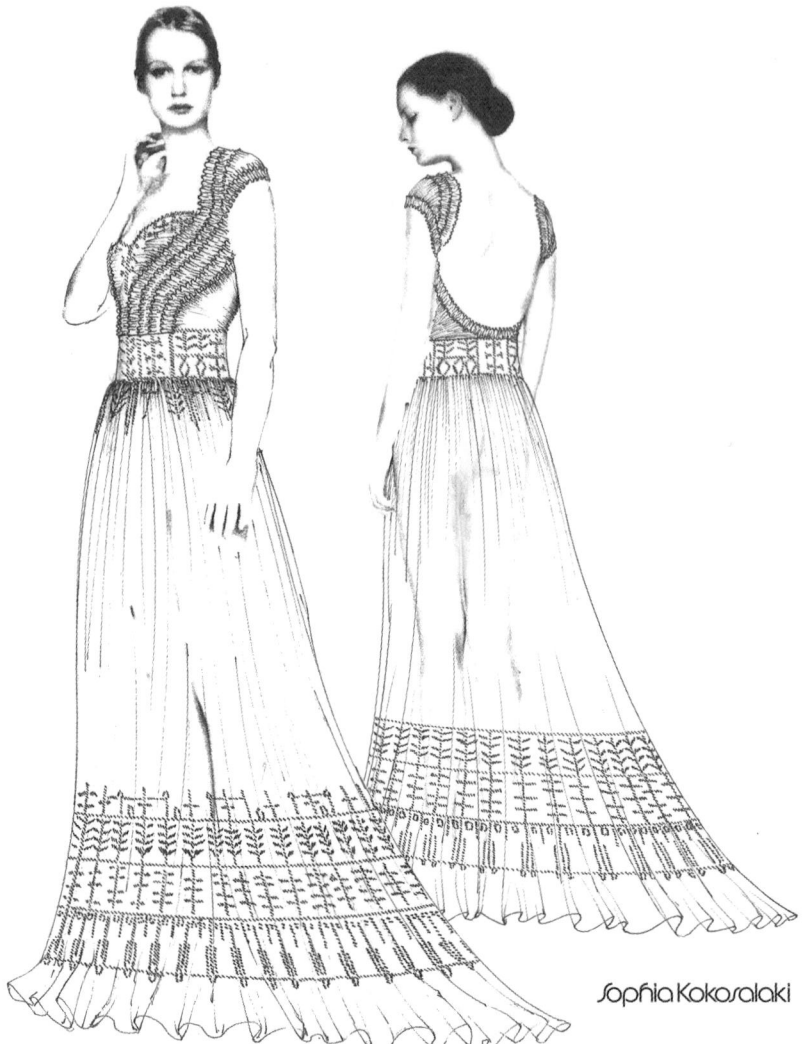

Sophia Kokosalaki

Henrietta Goodden
Client: *Publicity for Italian Lace,*
Autumn/Winter 2006
Roughs/design drawings in pencil
Finished drawing in brush pen, black
crayon and Letratone

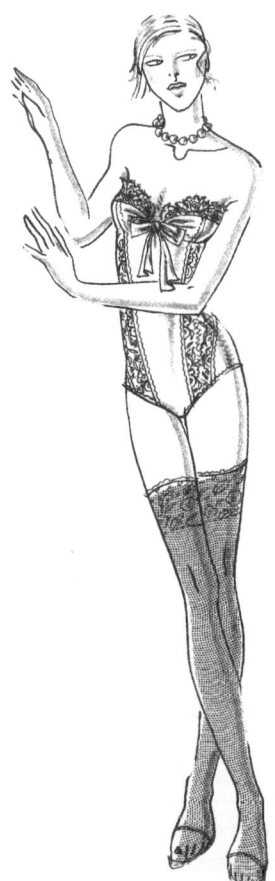

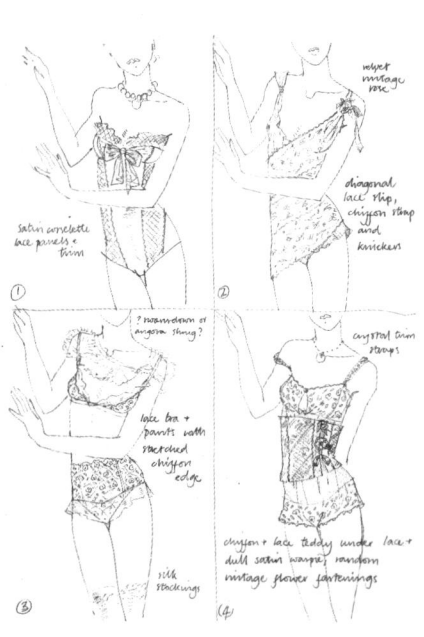

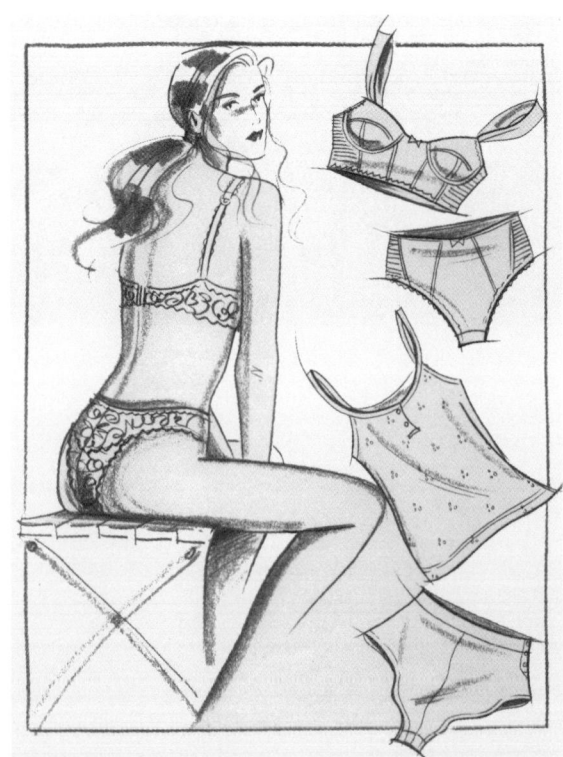

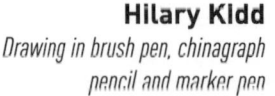

Hilary Kidd
Drawing in brush pen, chinagraph
pencil and marker pen

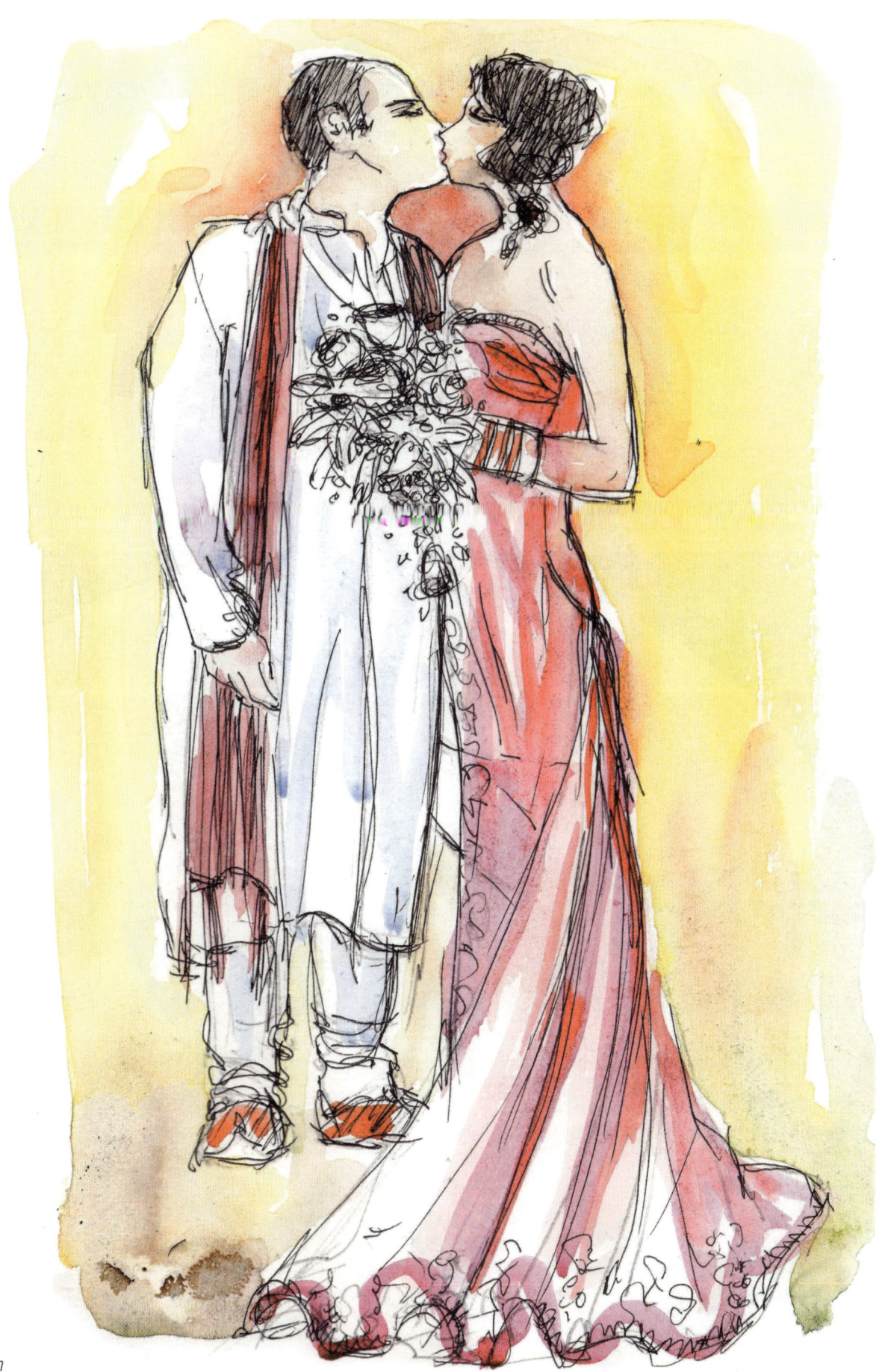

Rosie McClelland
'Wedding', 2011
Pen and watercolour illustration

Paul Wearing
Client: *Neiman Marcus – The Book*
Digitally produced illustration

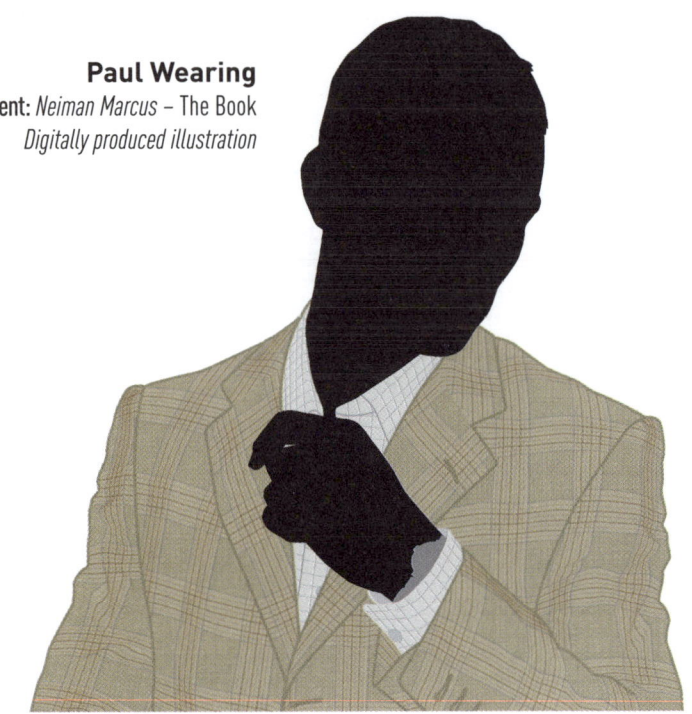

Patrick Morgan
FACING PAGE
Illustration using pen, ink and pencil
on 310 Somerset paper

Hormazd Narielwalla
Client: *Les Garçons de Glasgow*
Illustration of street photographers Daniel
Stern and Jonathan Price – November 2011
Digital collage of tailoring patterns, vector
illustration and photography

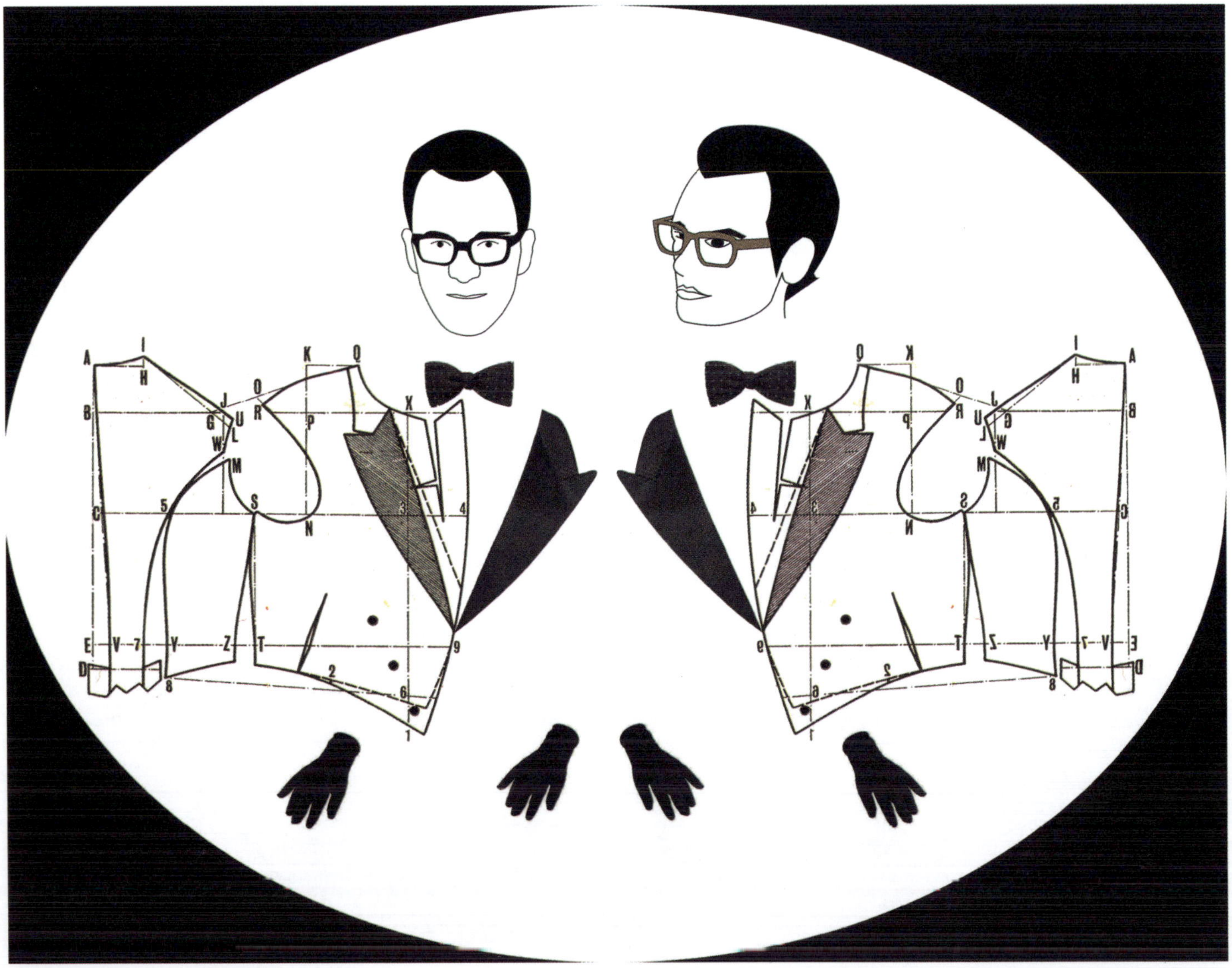

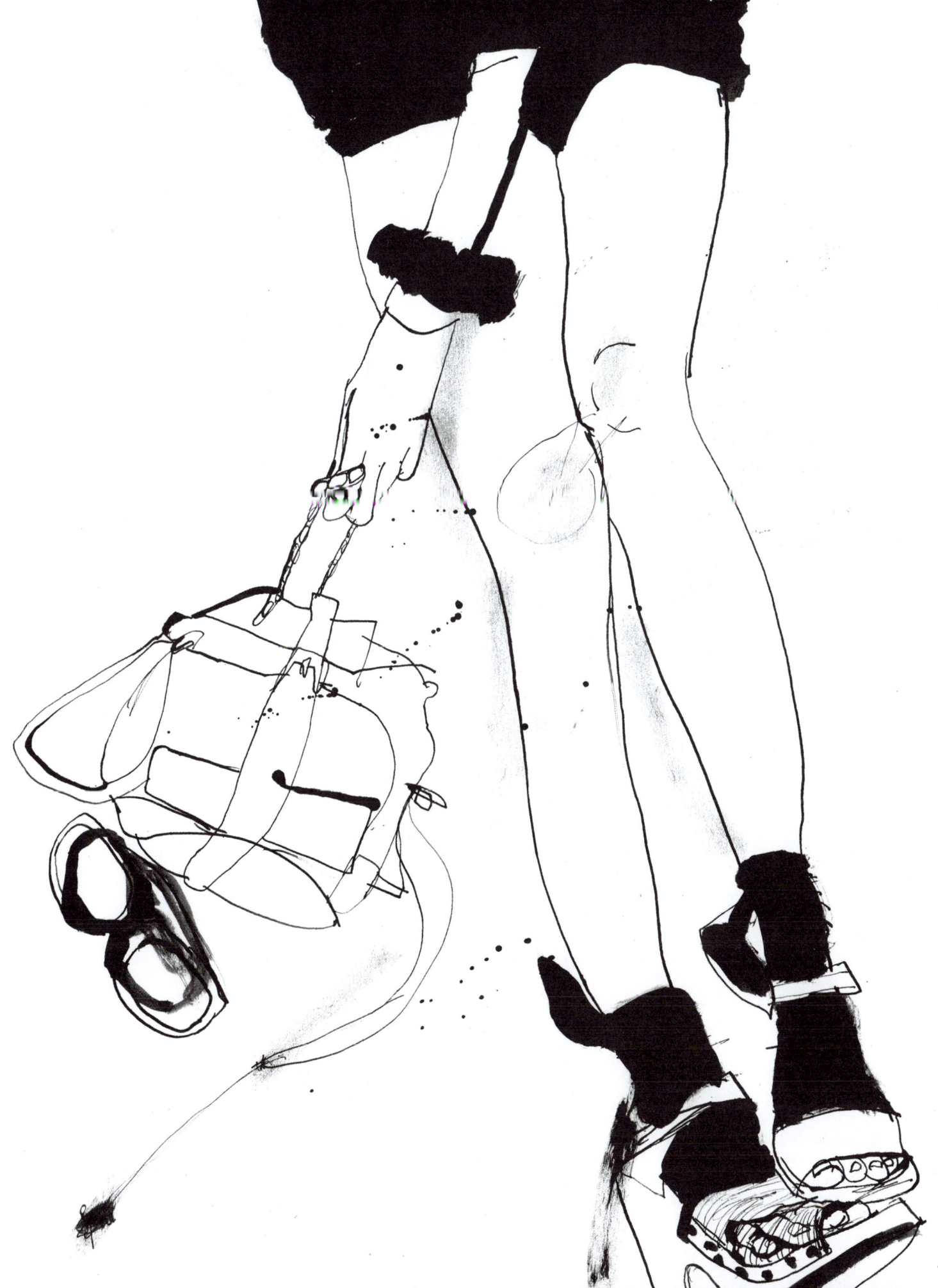

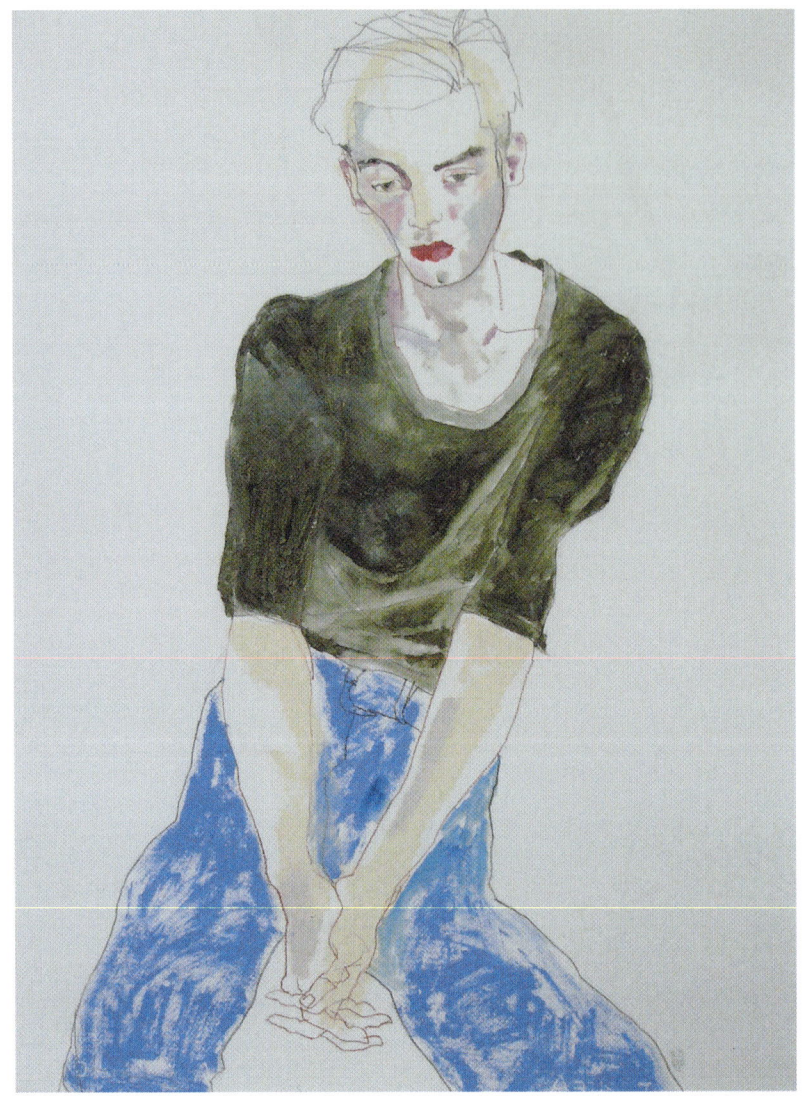

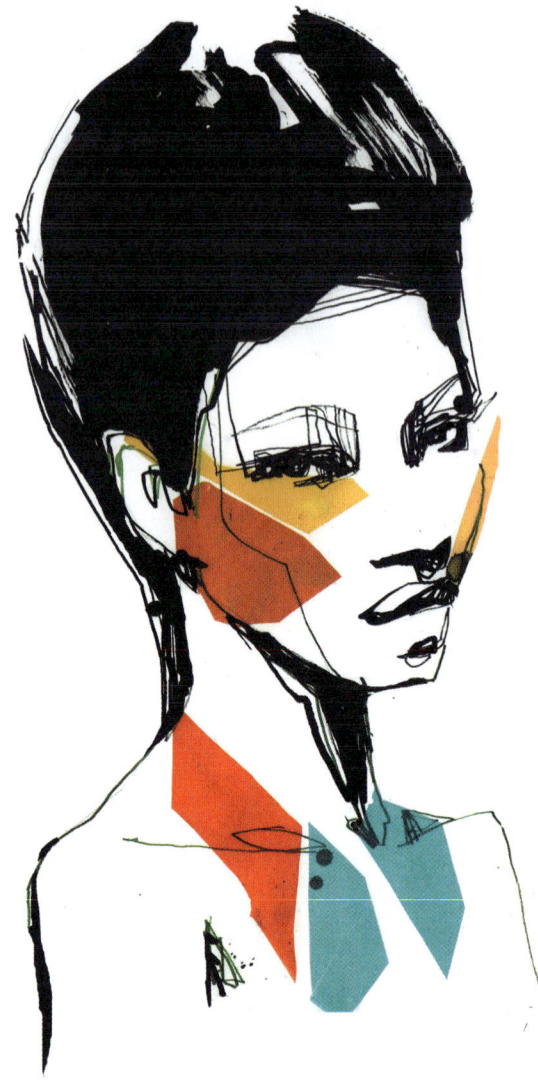

Howard Tangye
'Jake', portrait 2011
Mixed media on paper

Stina Persson
This illustration was created
using ink and cut paper

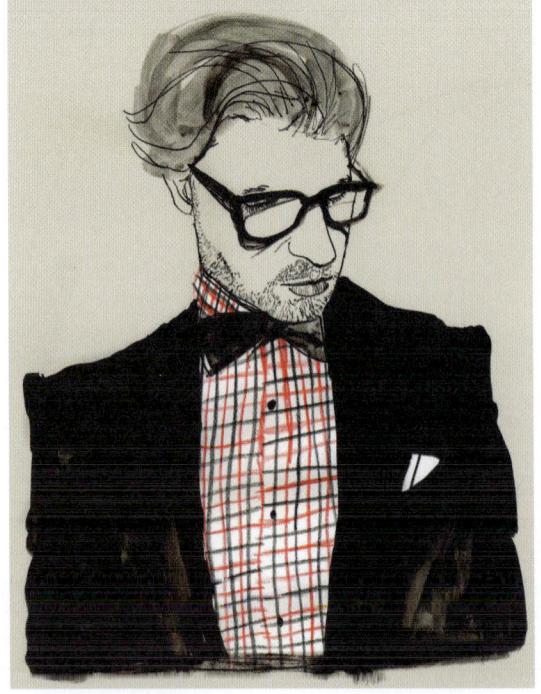

Patrick Morgan
Drawn with pen and ink on 310 Somerset
paper. Brushes, crayons, pens, pencils,
rollers and stencils were used for mark-
making on block areas. Artwork scanned and
colour-managed in Adobe Photoshop.

Patrick Morgan
FACING PAGE: *Drawn with pen*
and ink on 310 Somerset paper.
Brushes, crayons, pens, pencils,
rollers and stencils were used
for mark-making on block areas.
Artwork scanned and colour-
managed in Adobe Photoshop.

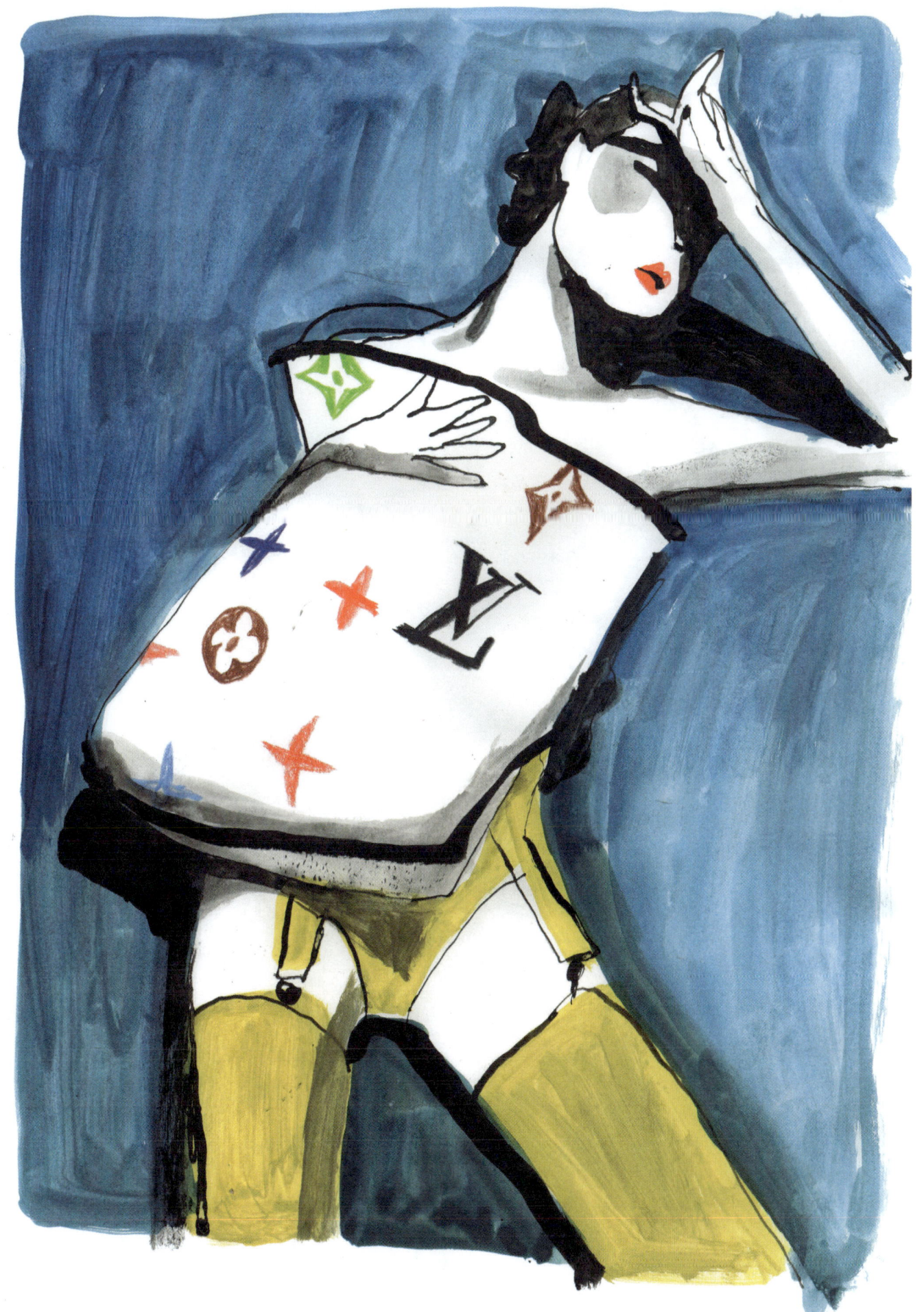

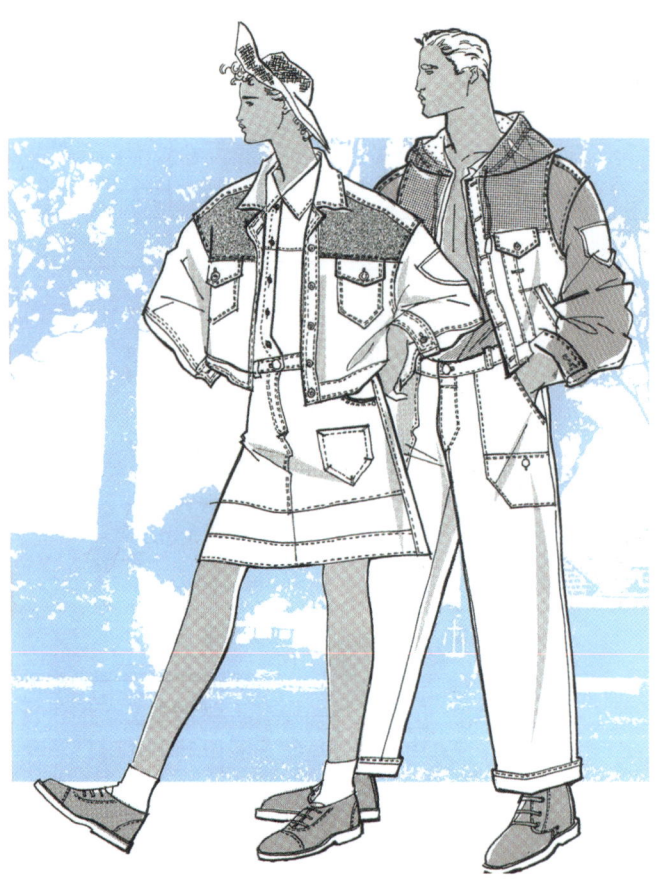

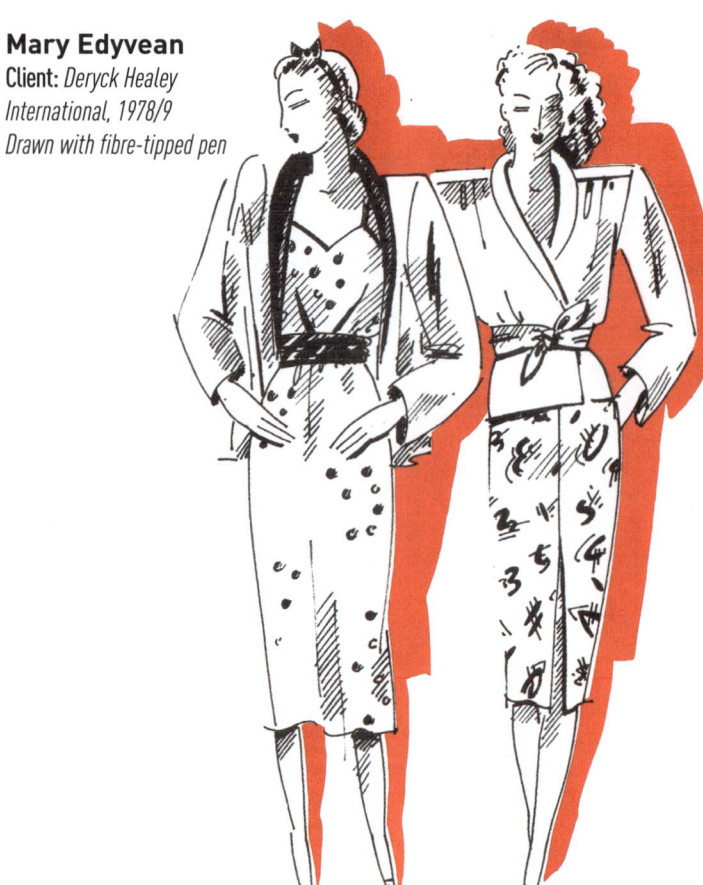

Mary Edyvean
Client: *Deryck Healey International, 1978/9*
Drawn with fibre-tipped pen

Billy Atkin
Client: *Design Intelligence, 1980s*
Drawn with fibre-tipped pen and Letratone

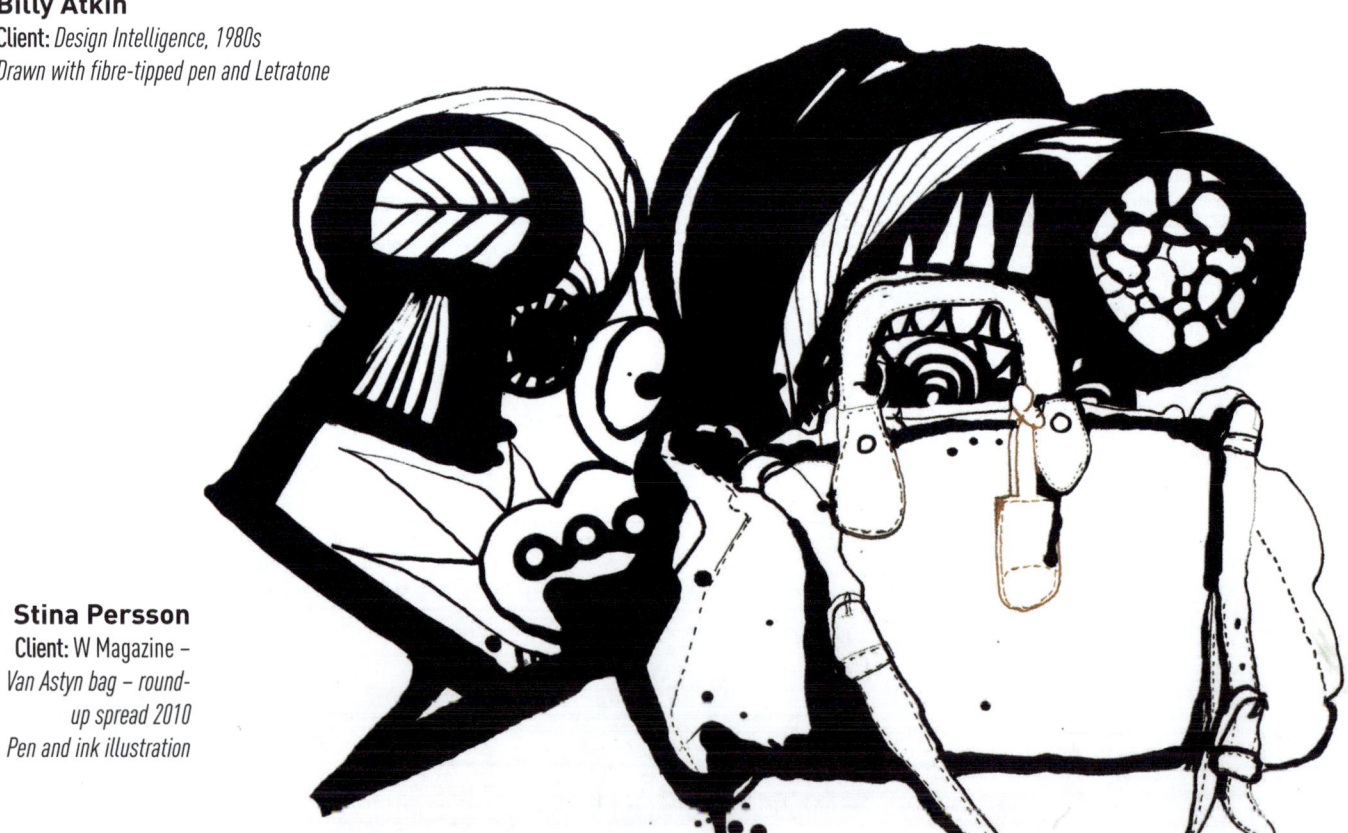

Stina Persson
Client: W Magazine –
Van Astyn bag – round-
up spread 2010
Pen and ink illustration

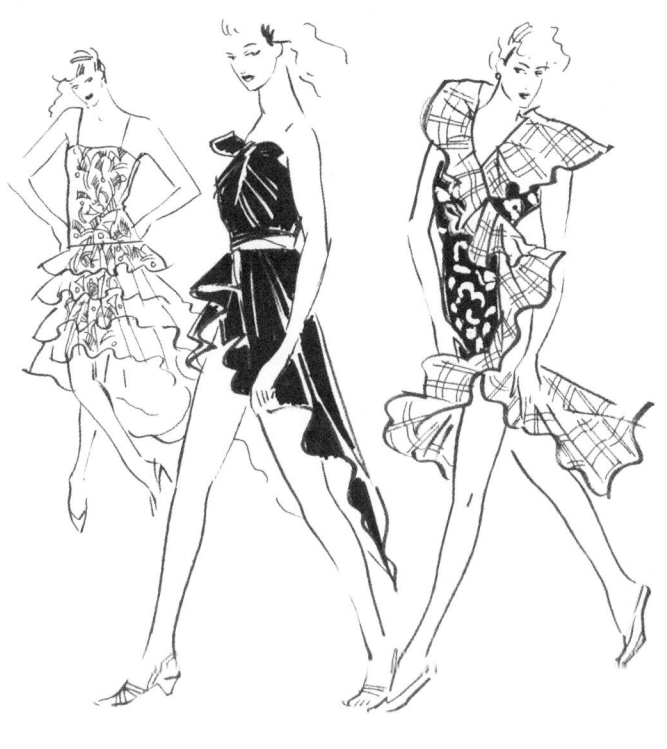

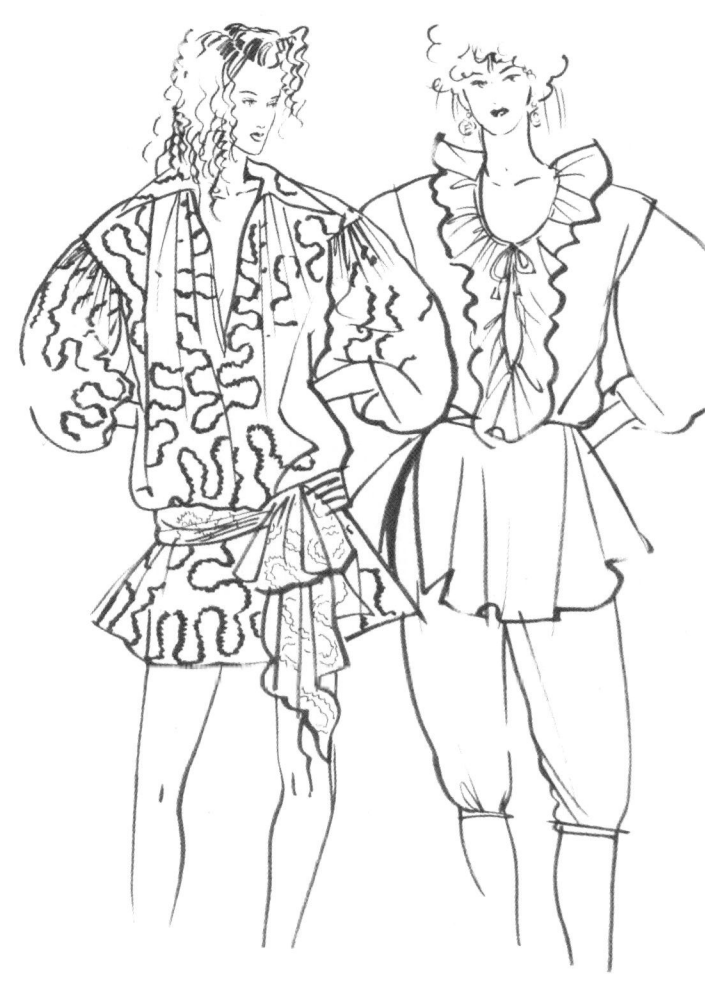

Rosalyn Kennedy
Client: *Prism, 1981*
Illustrations of five figures using fibre-tipped pen

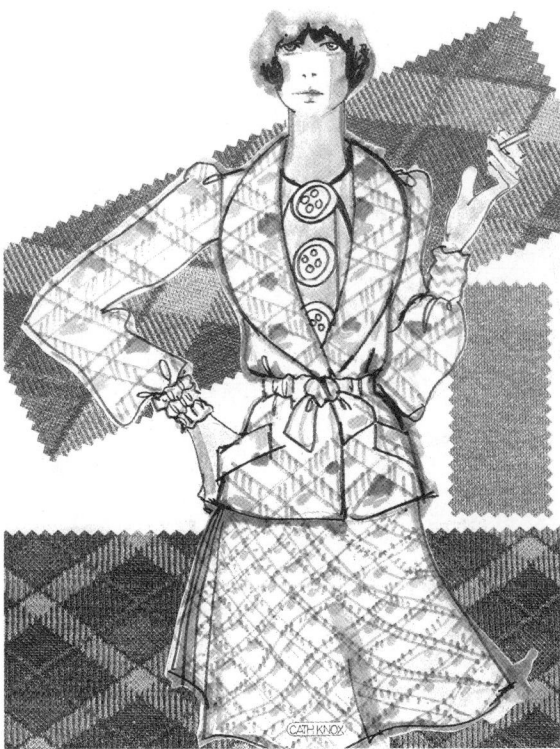

Cath Knox
Two illustrations using collaged fabric swatches with a painted acetate overlay

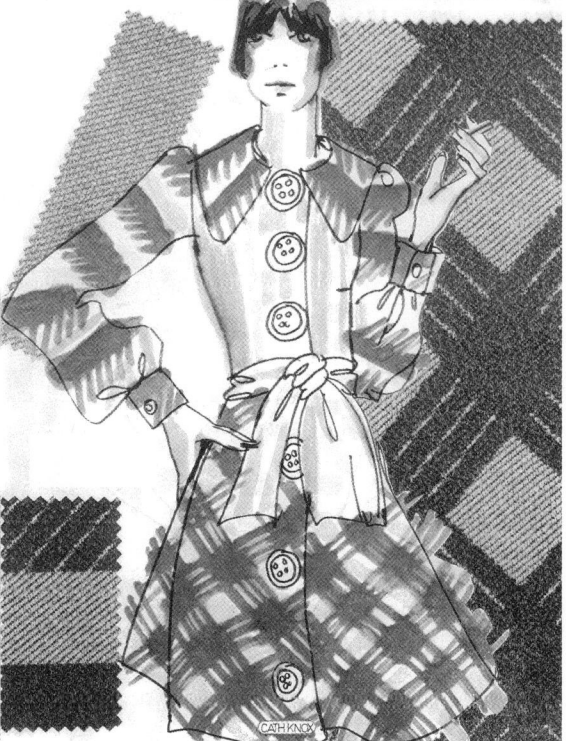

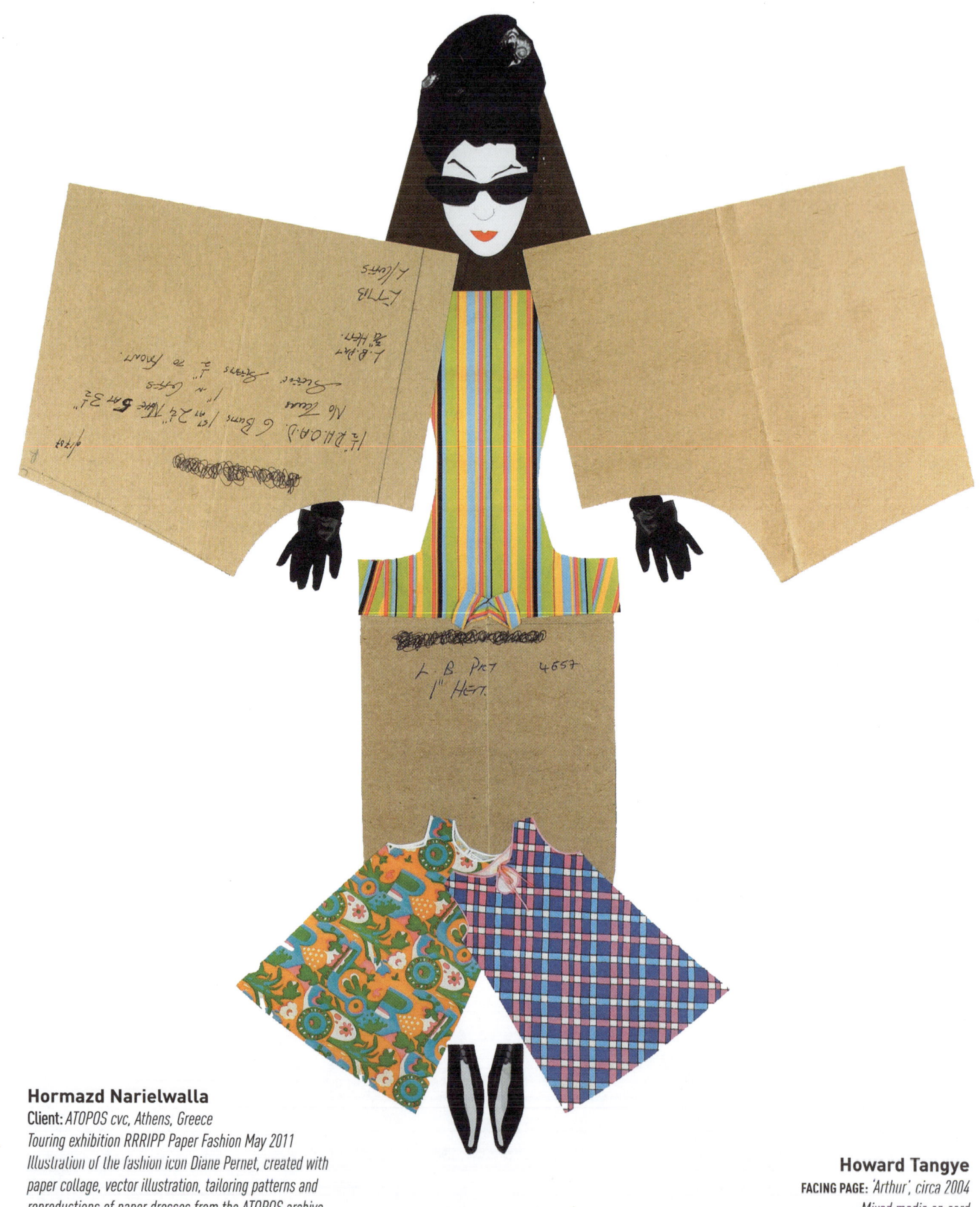

Hormazd Narielwalla
Client: *ATOPOS cvc, Athens, Greece*
Touring exhibition RRRIPP Paper Fashion May 2011
Illustration of the fashion icon Diane Pernet, created with
paper collage, vector illustration, tailoring patterns and
reproductions of paper dresses from the ATOPOS archive.

Howard Tangye
FACING PAGE: *'Arthur', circa 2004*
Mixed media on card

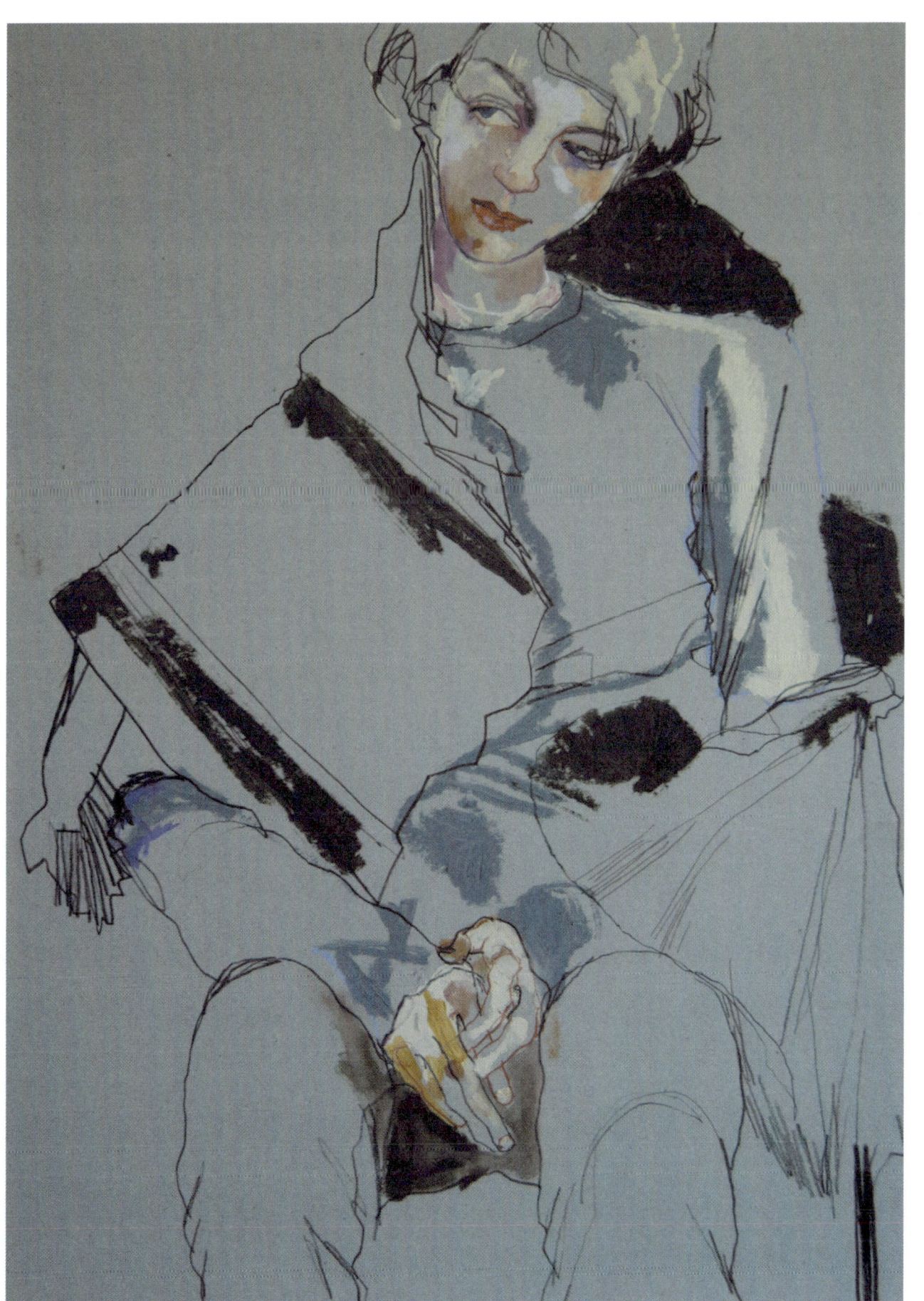

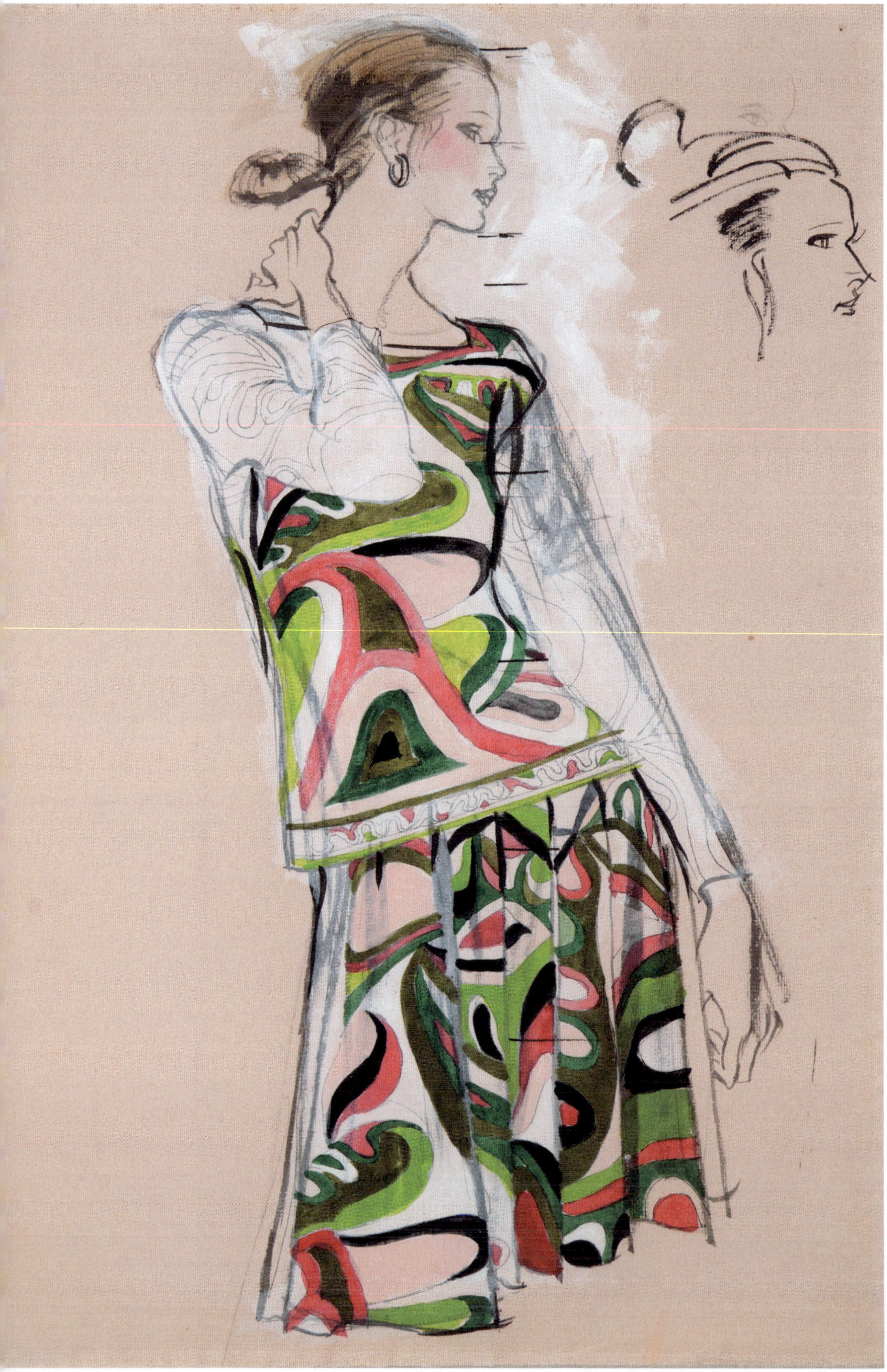

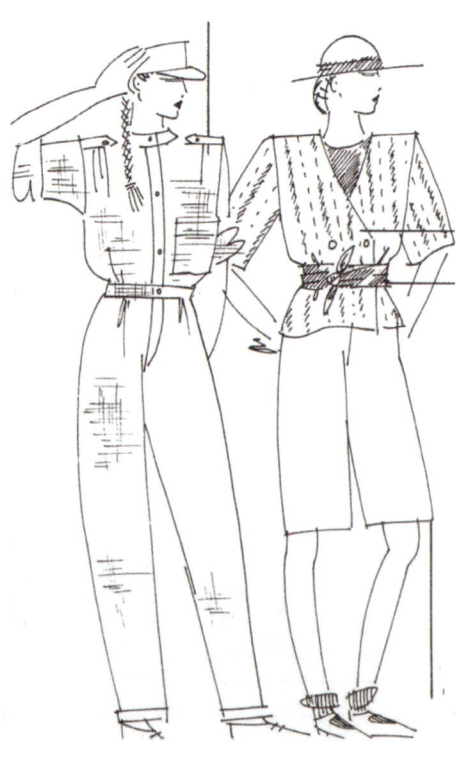

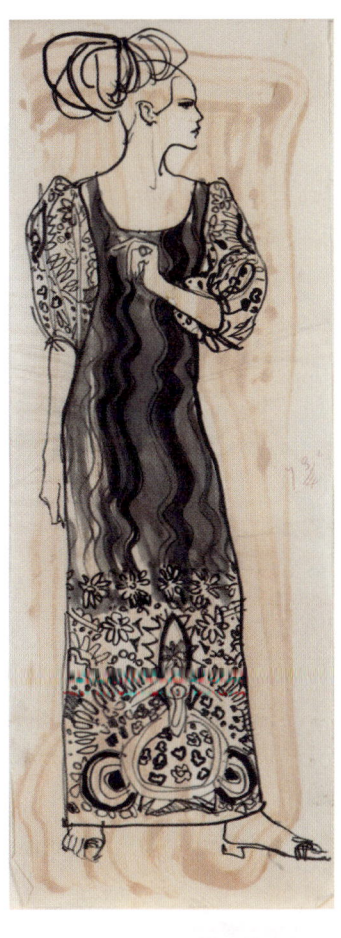

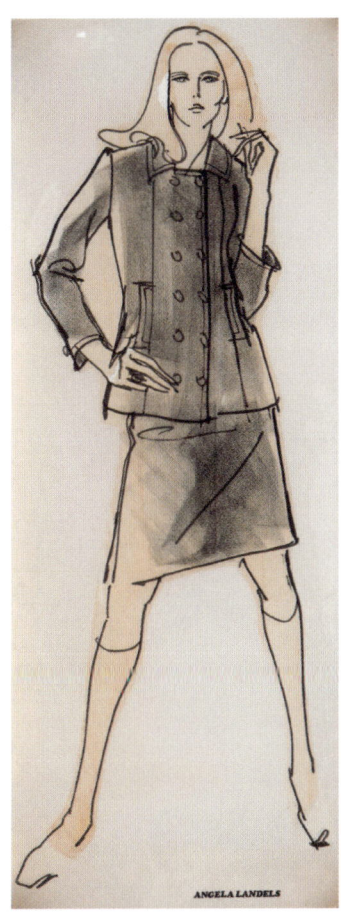

FAR LEFT: *Drawing by Angela Landels (courtesy of Gray Modern & Contemporary Art), Liberty, Princess Lucianna dress circa 1970s, pencil and felt tip, 50 x 18.5cm. Client: Advertisement for Liberty, London*

LEFT: *Drawing by Angela Landels (courtesy of Gray Modern & Contemporary Art), grey suit, 1960s collage, felt tip and charcoal, 68 x 26cm. Client: Liberty, London*

BELOW: *2011 Paul Wearing, digital, adapted from drawing. Created for Neiman Marcus's account holder magazine,* The Book

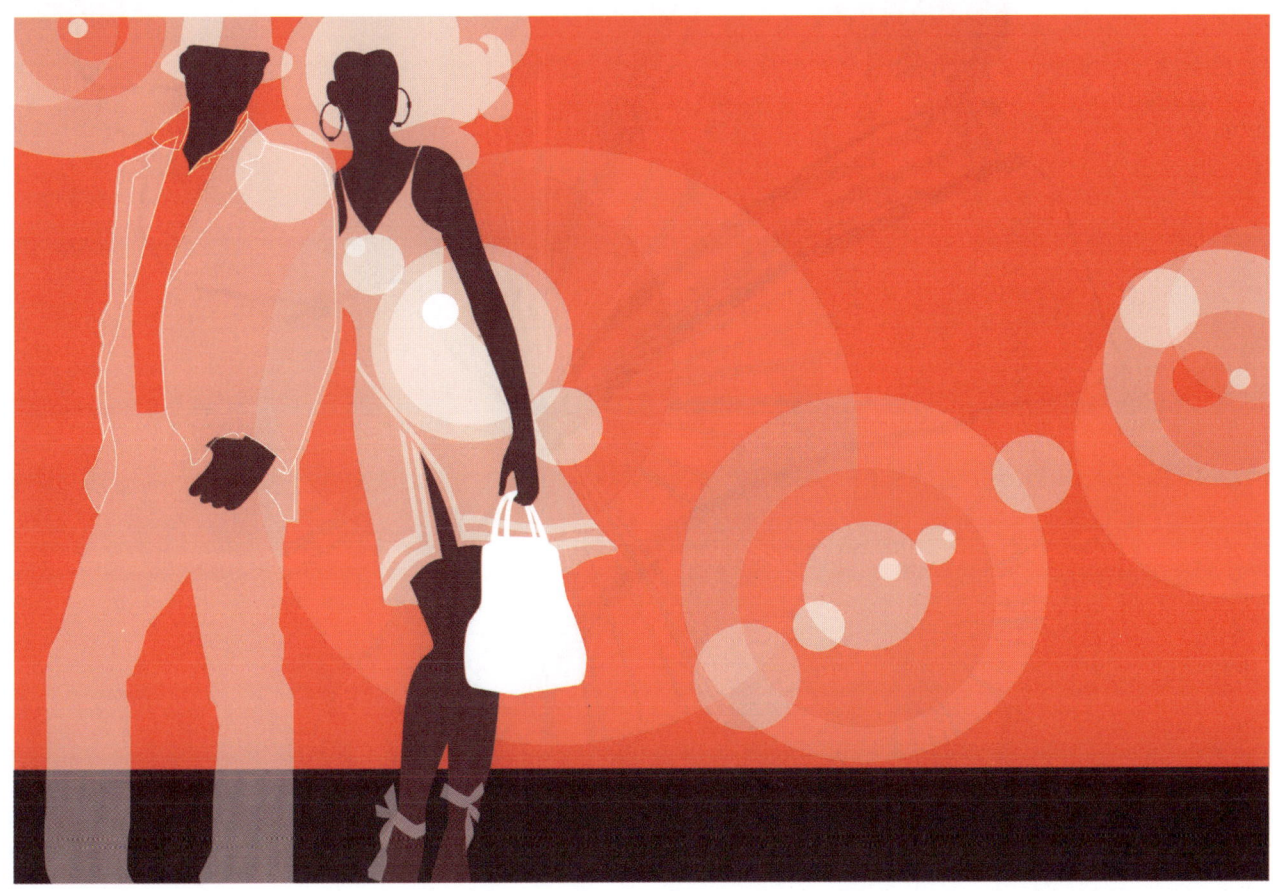

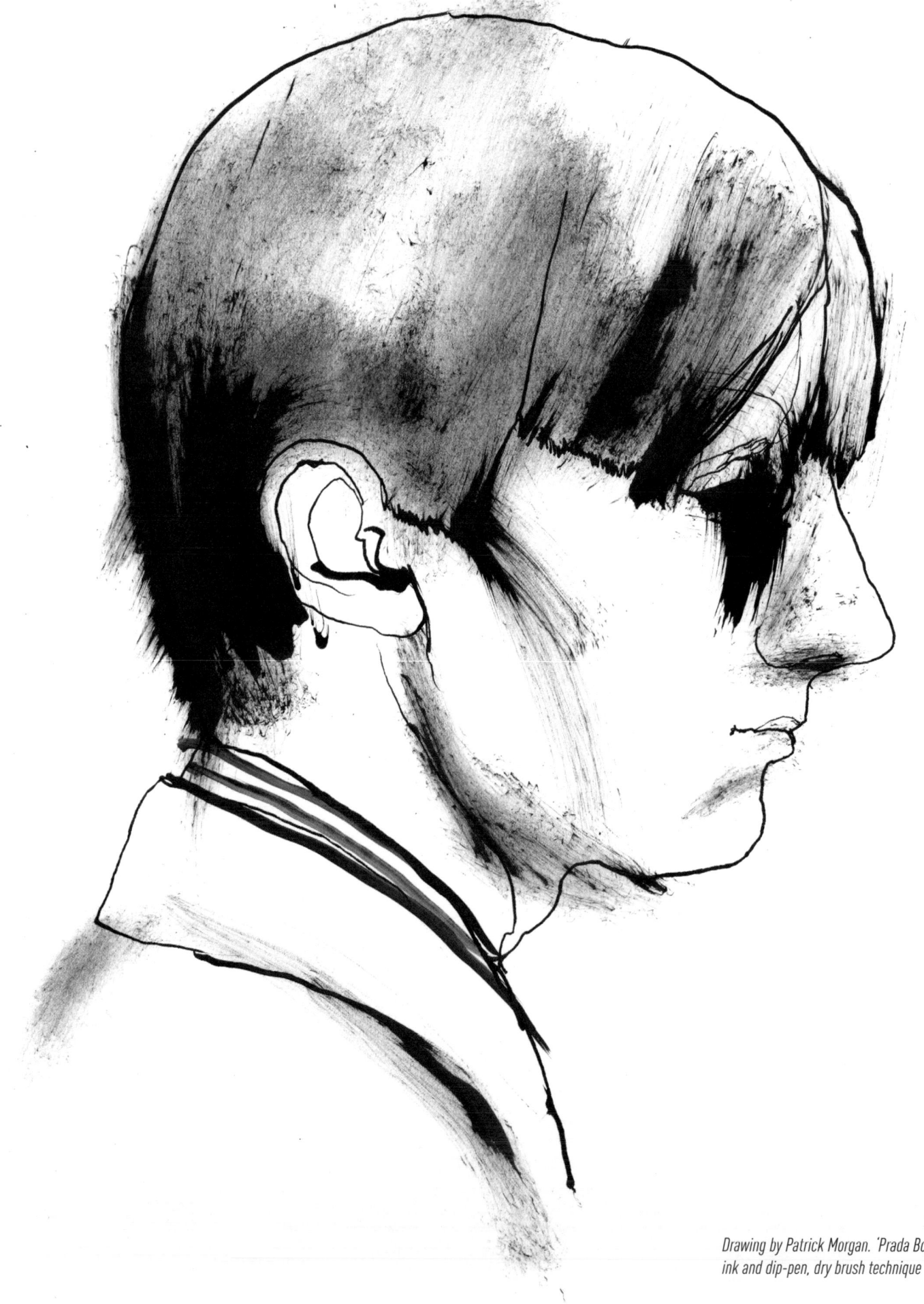

*Drawing by Patrick Morgan. 'Prada Boy',
ink and dip-pen, dry brush technique*

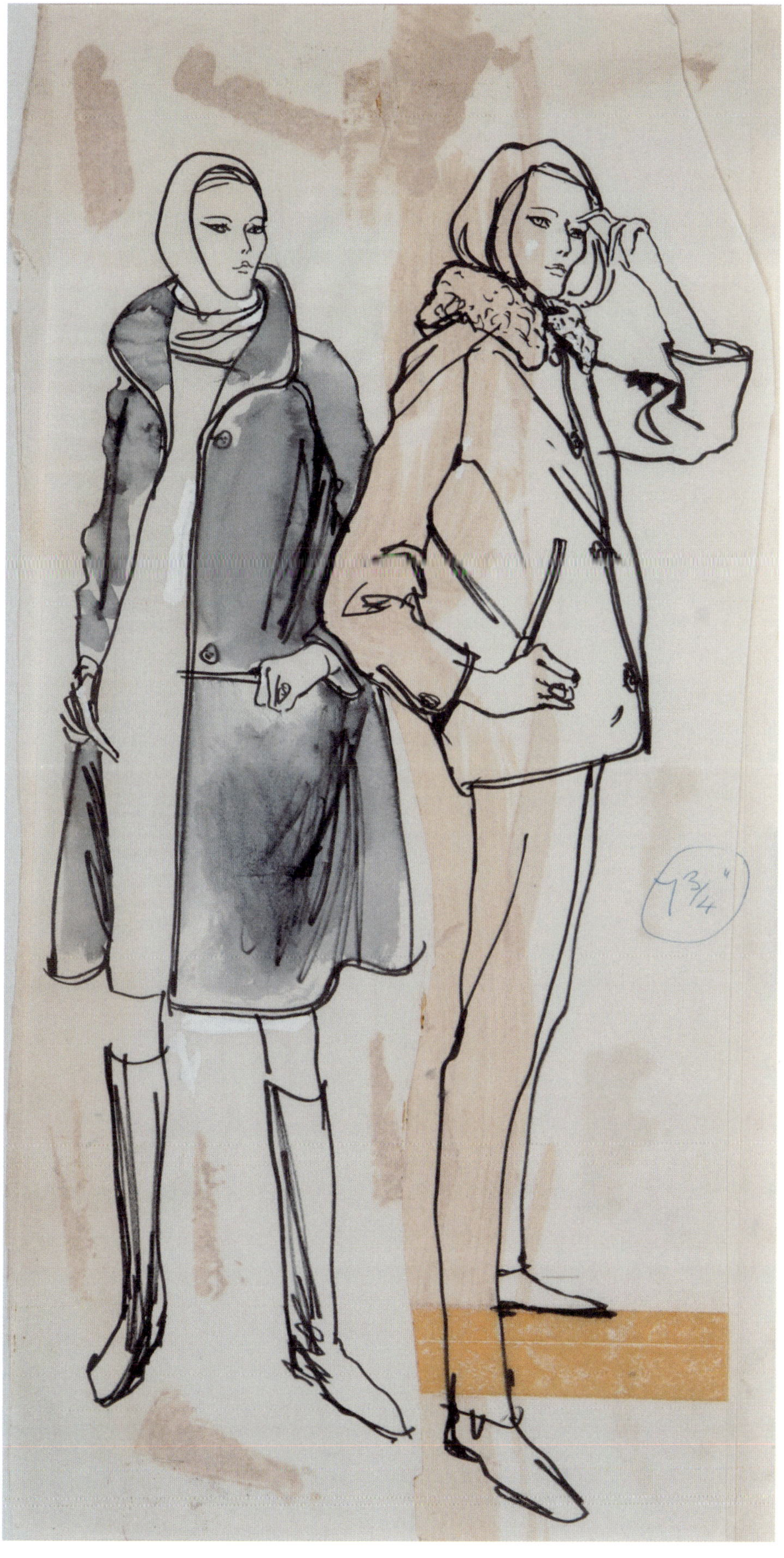

LEFT: *Drawing by Angela Landels (courtesy of Gray Modern & Contemporary Art), winter après-ski wear circa 1960s, featured in the Sunday Times*
BELOW: *Patrick Morgan, 'Prada Girl', ink and dip-pen, dry brush technique*

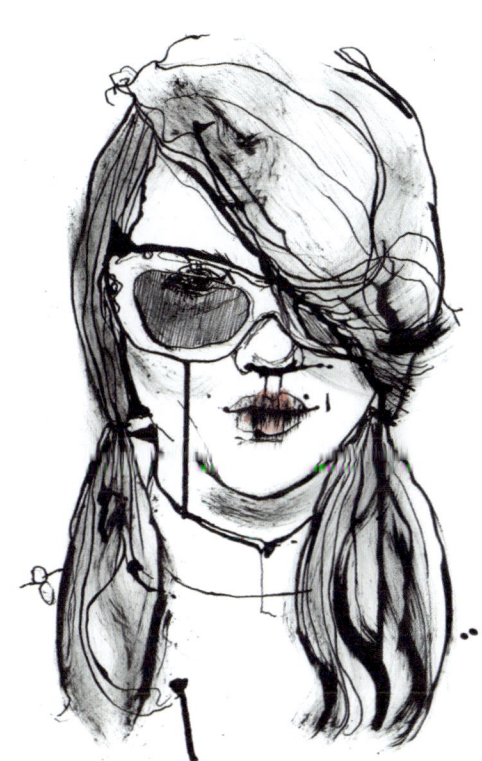

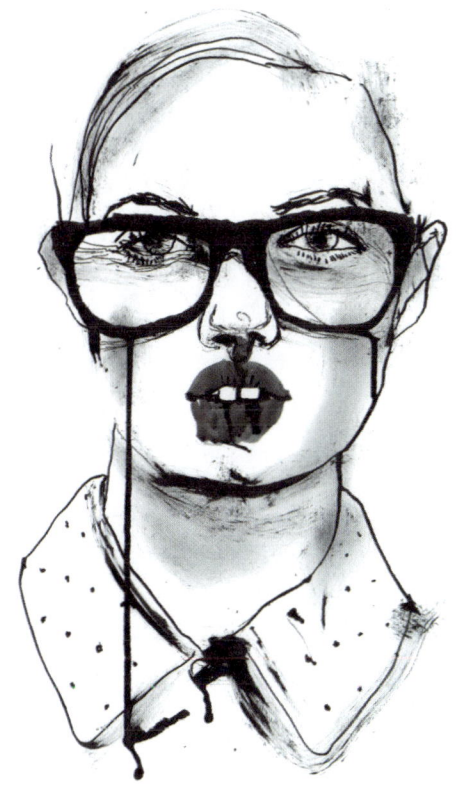

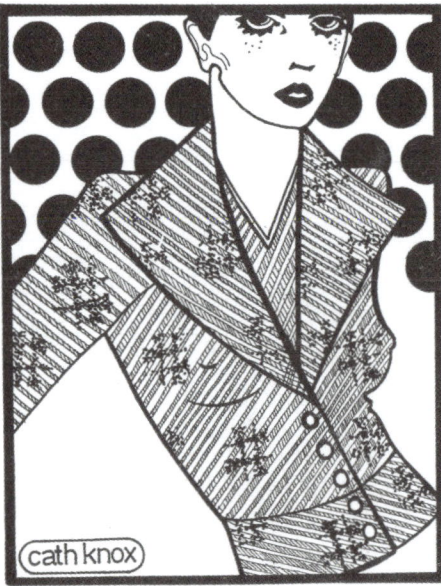

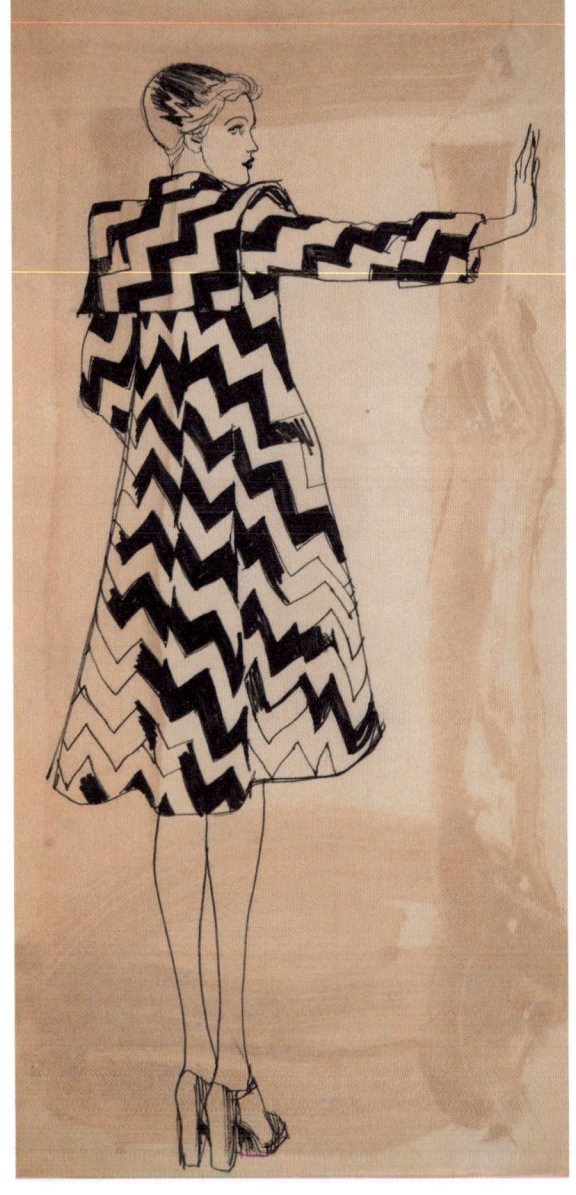

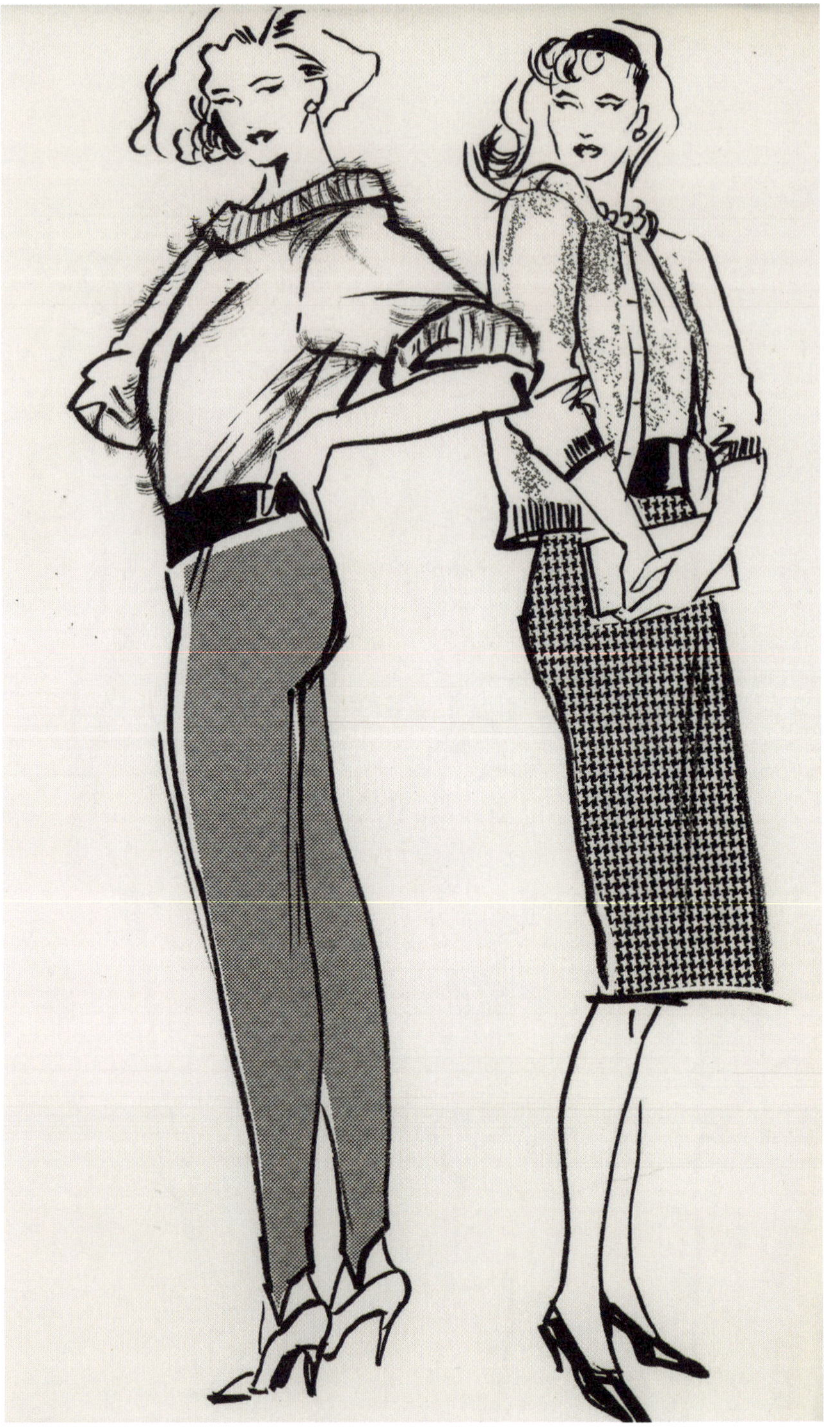

TOP LEFT: *Drawing by Cath Knox, circa 1970s, felt tip (with sticky dots)*

ABOVE: *Drawing by Rosalyn Kennedy, felt tip pen, brush pen and Letratone*

LEFT: *Drawing by Angela Landels (courtesy of Gray Modern & Contemporary Art), circa 1960s, Liberty zig-zag coat, pencil and felt tip pen*

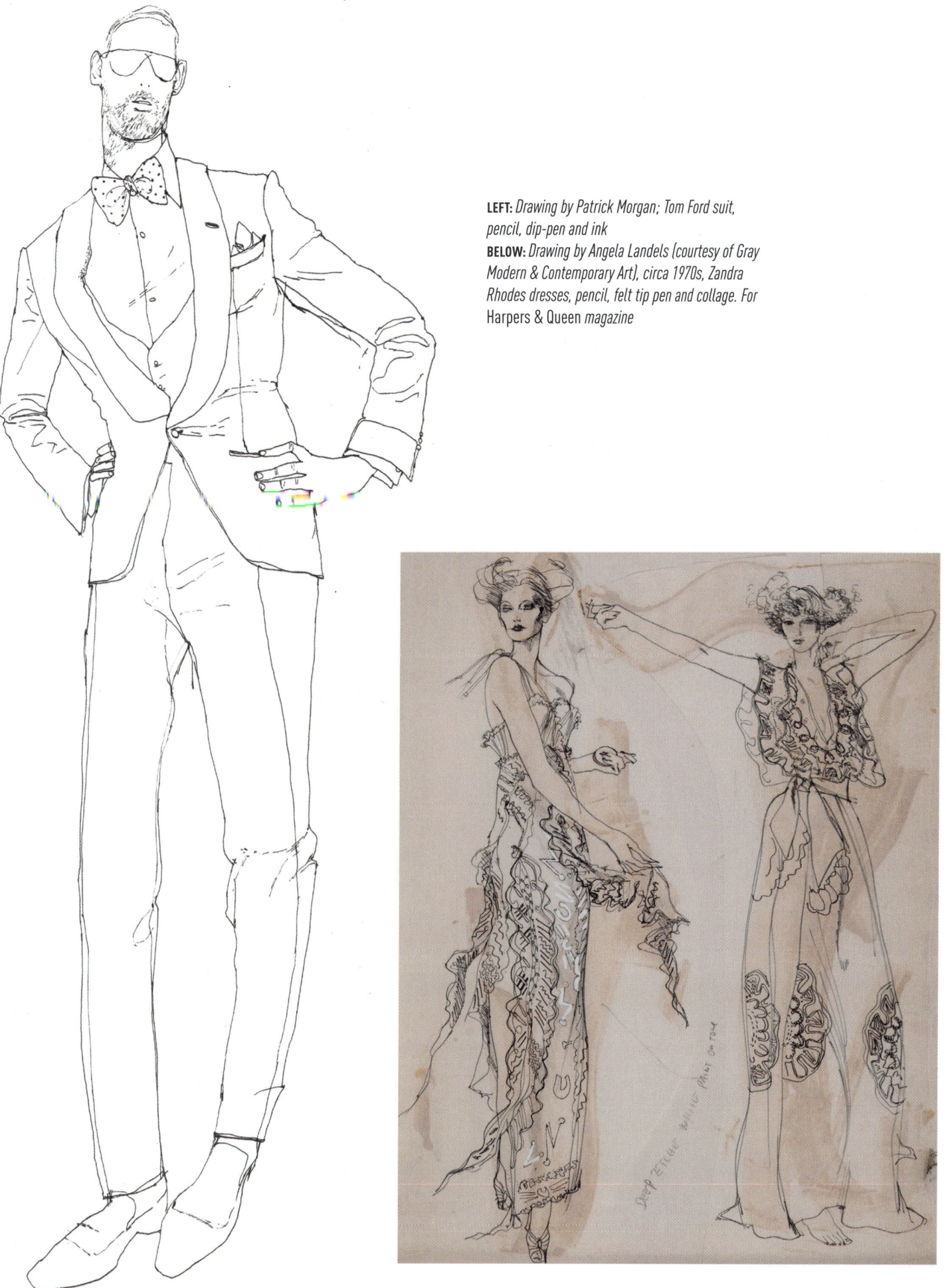

LEFT: *Drawing by Patrick Morgan; Tom Ford suit, pencil, dip-pen and ink*

BELOW: *Drawing by Angela Landels (courtesy of Gray Modern & Contemporary Art), circa 1970s, Zandra Rhodes dresses, pencil, felt tip pen and collage. For Harpers & Queen magazine*

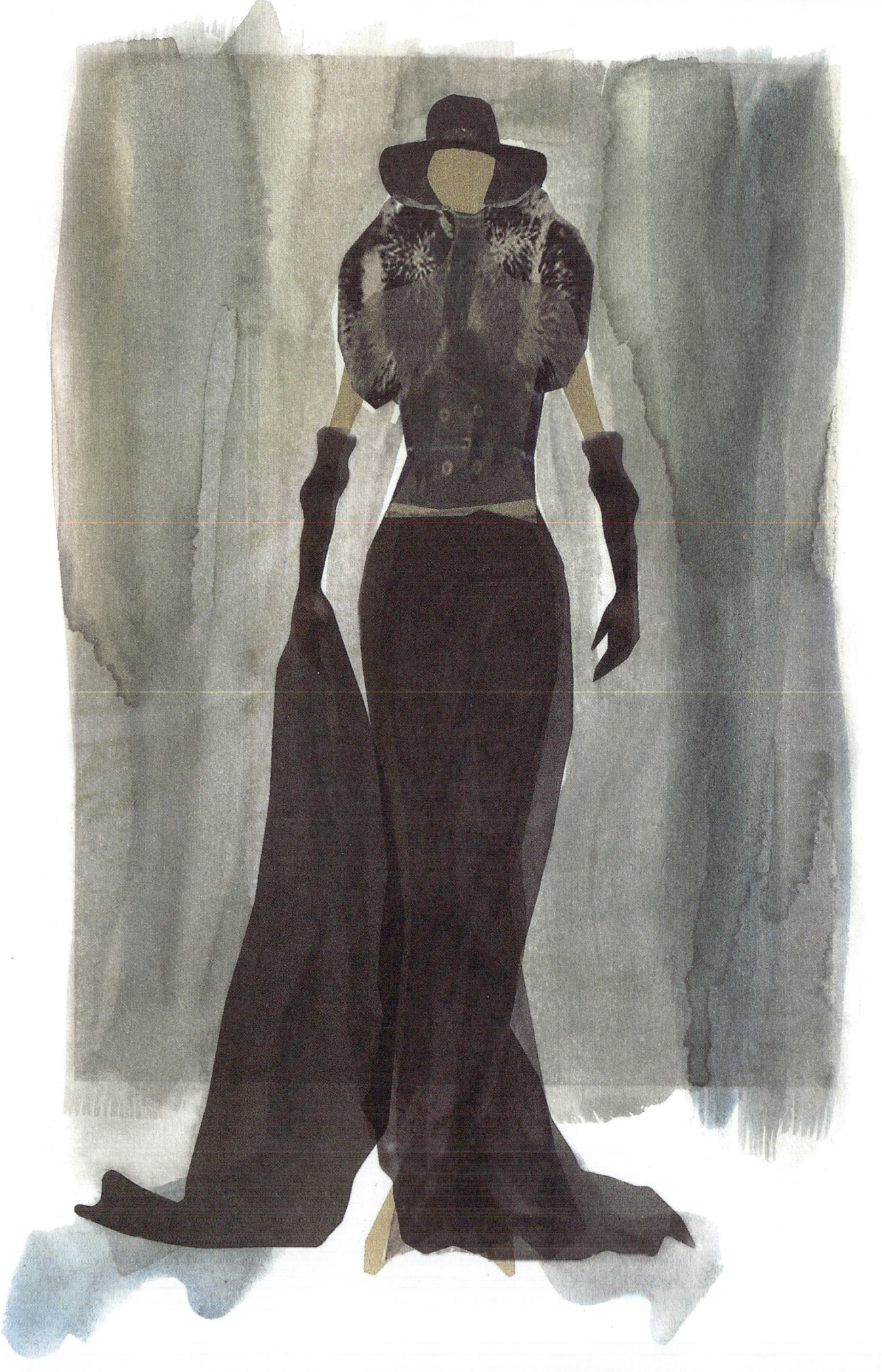

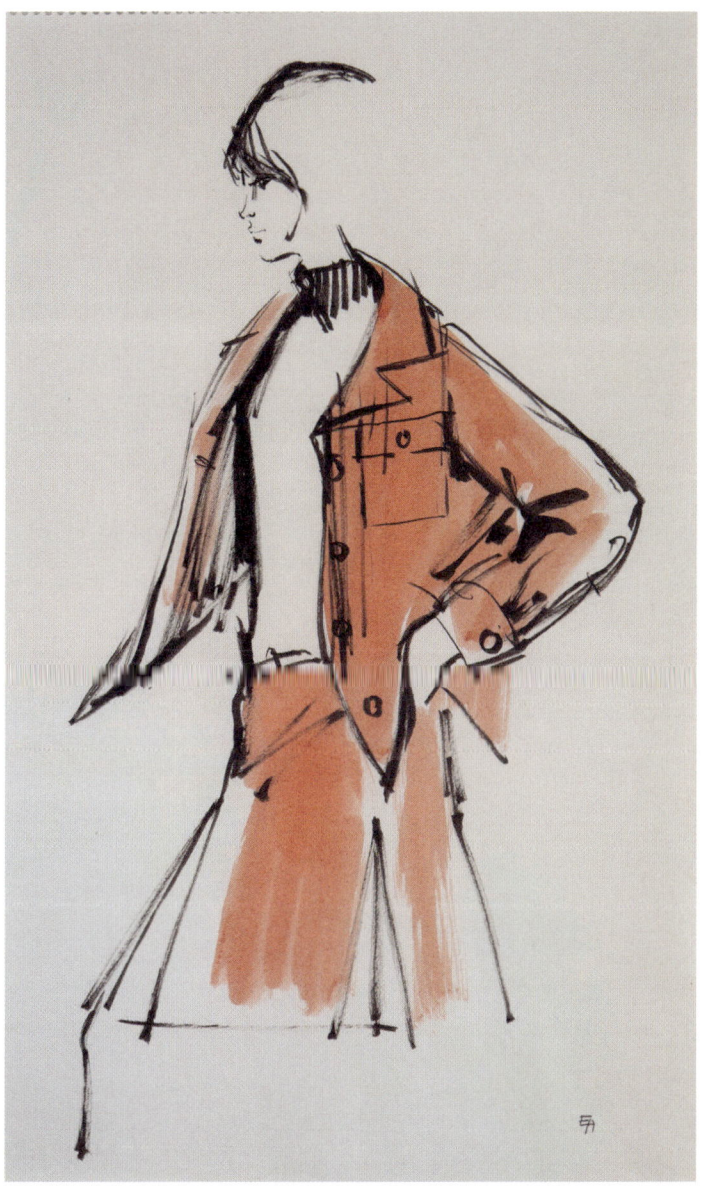

RIGHT: *Drawing by Judith Cheek, fibre tip pen*

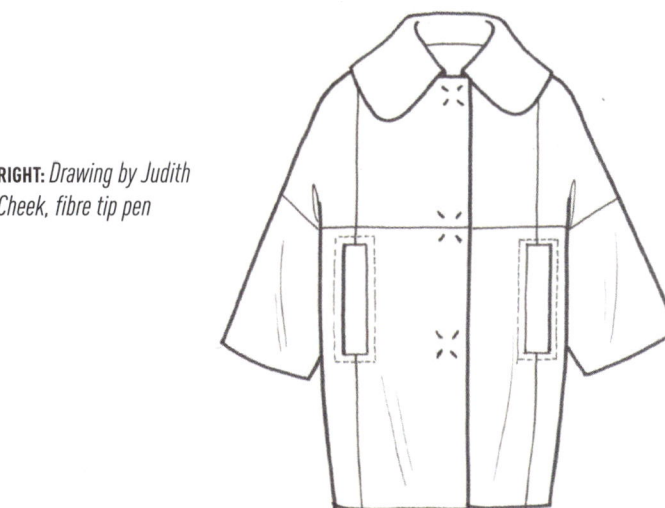

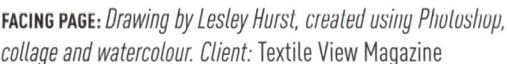

FACING PAGE: *Drawing by Lesley Hurst, created using Photoshop, collage and watercolour. Client:* Textile View Magazine

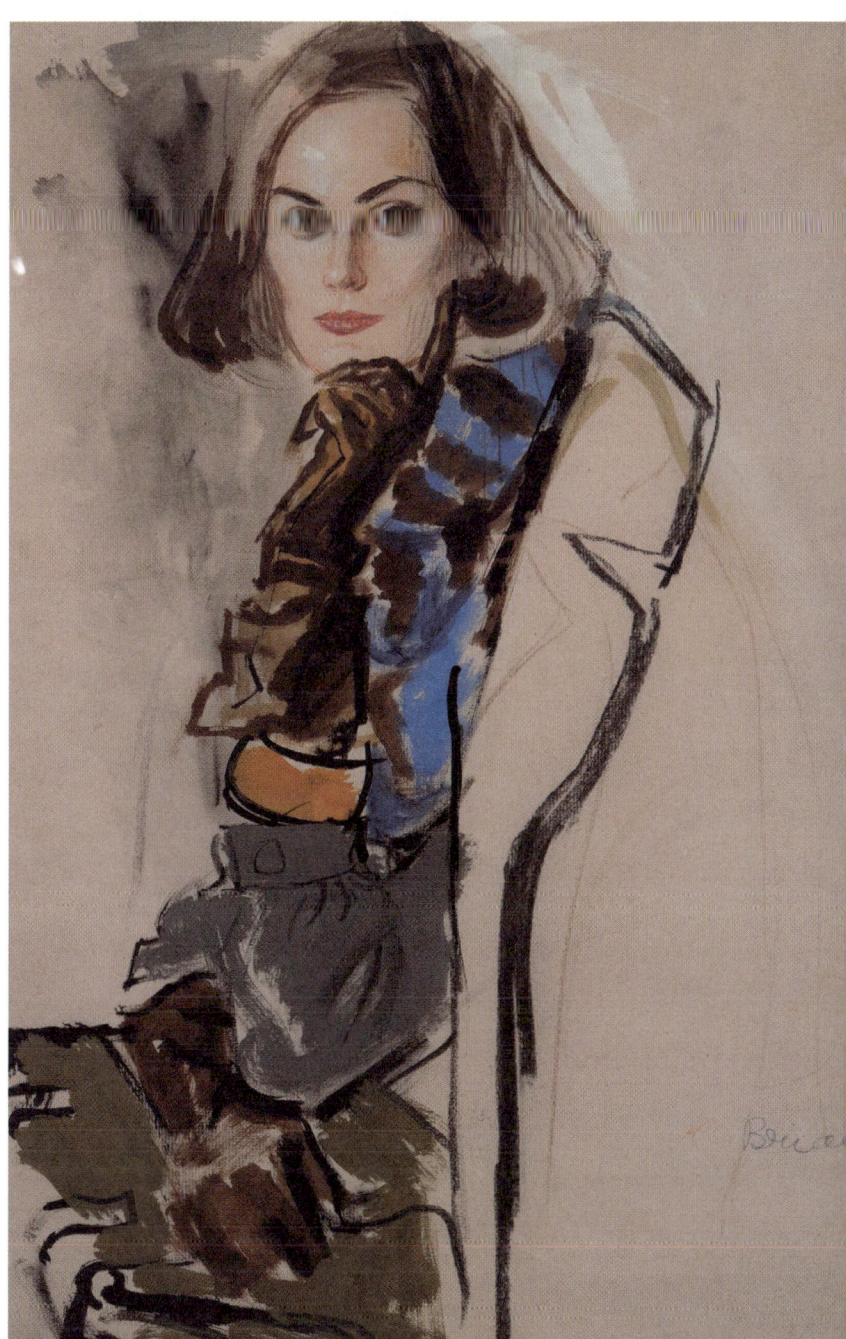

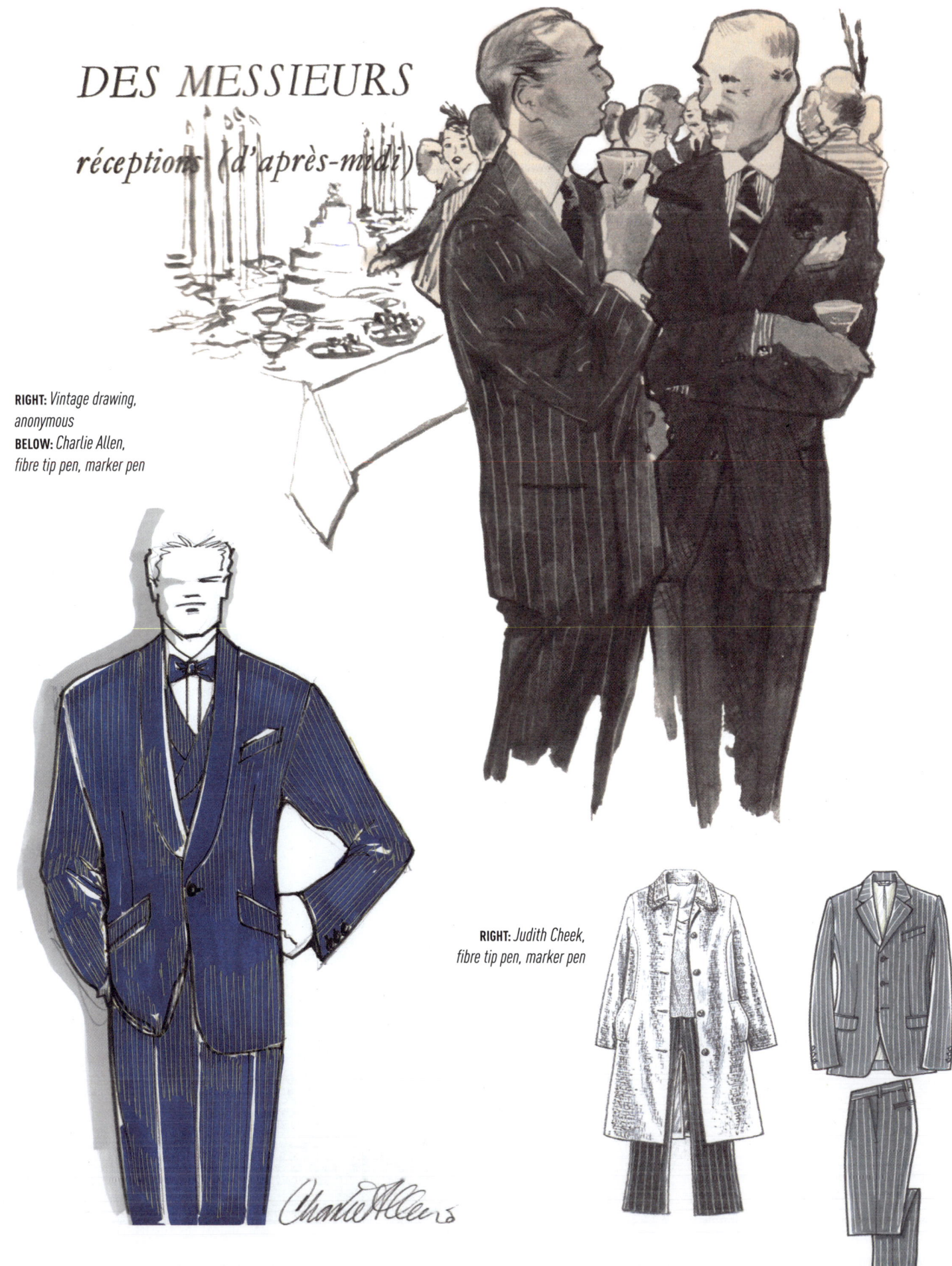

DES MESSIEURS
réceptions (d'après-midi)

RIGHT: *Vintage drawing, anonymous*
BELOW: *Charlie Allen, fibre tip pen, marker pen*

RIGHT: *Judith Cheek, fibre tip pen, marker pen*

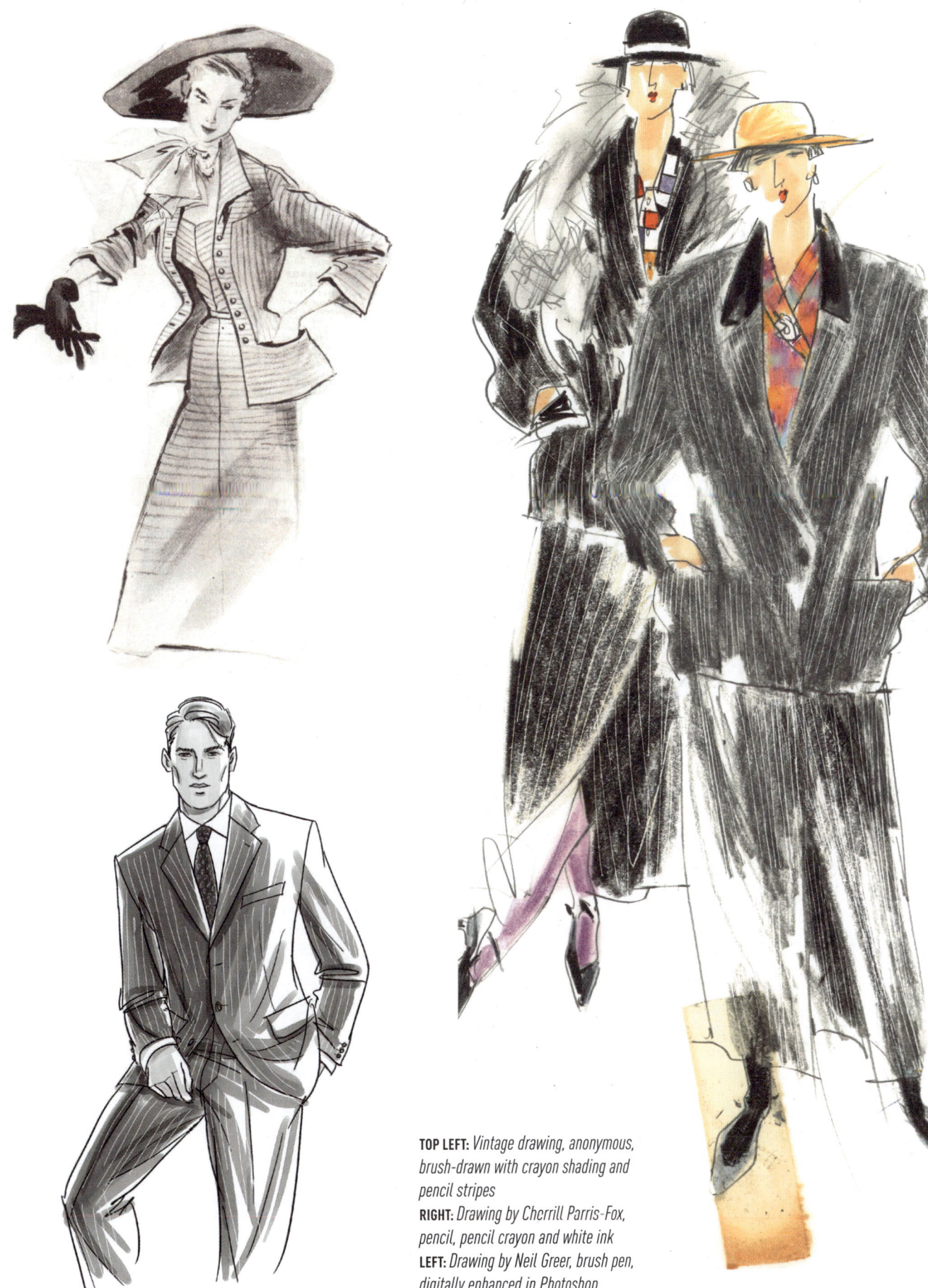

TOP LEFT: *Vintage drawing, anonymous, brush-drawn with crayon shading and pencil stripes*
RIGHT: *Drawing by Cherrill Parris-Fox, pencil, pencil crayon and white ink*
LEFT: *Drawing by Neil Greer, brush pen, digitally enhanced in Photoshop*

DRAWING THE FUTURE

*'Don't worry about what anybody else is going to do.
The best way to predict the future is to reinvent it.'*

ALAN KEY, COMPUTER SCIENTIST

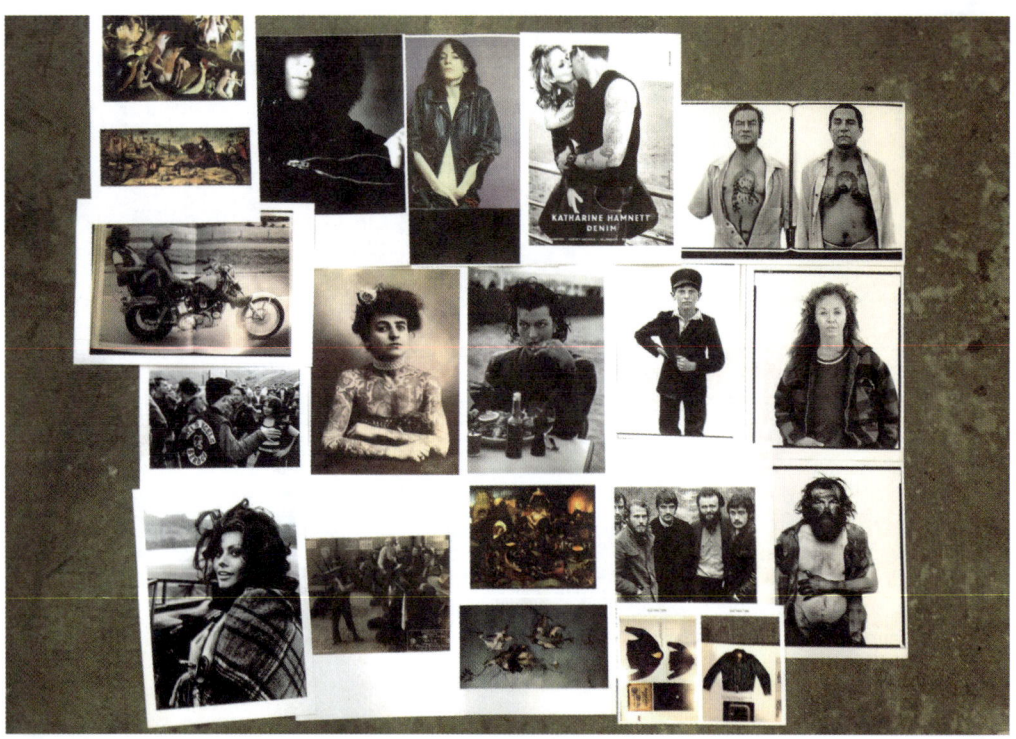

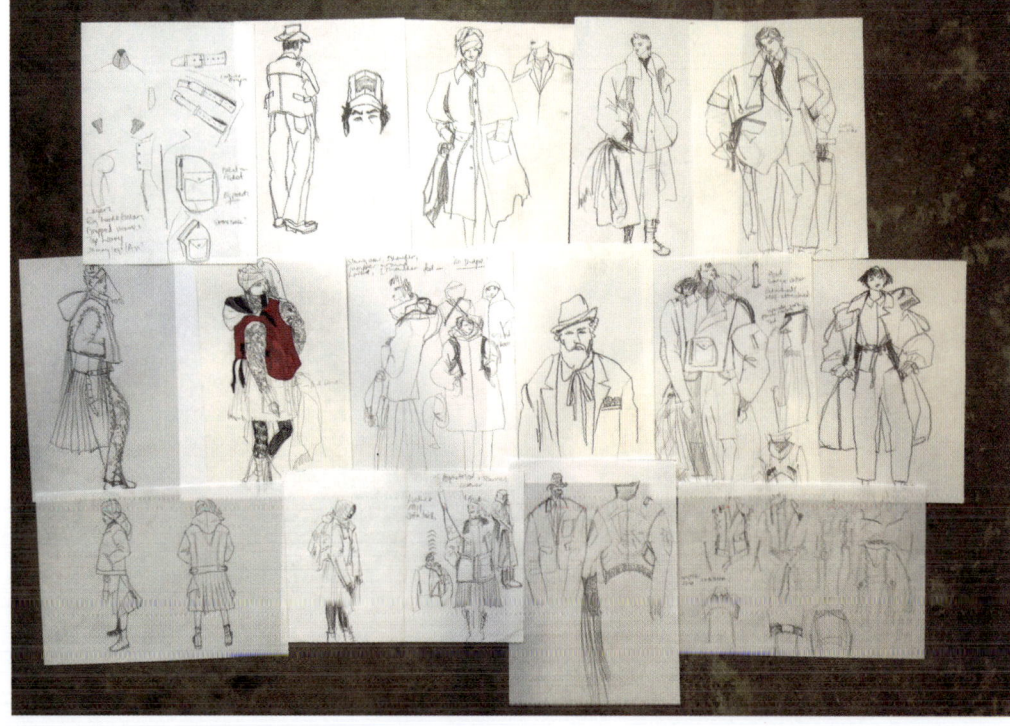

ABOVE LEFT: *'Working Mood Board', collage
of magazine tears, photocopies and print-outs*
LEFT: *Research and investigatory sketches,
design ideas sketches*

In this section, Flora Cadzow presents an edited version of her final degree collection work. Here is her rationale:

'This collection is inspired by a mood, a feeling, an attitude. I took inspiration from various sources that represented this nonchalant, 'give a damn', seriously cool attitude. These included rockers, bikers, cowboys, the American West, the documentary photographs of Richard Avedon, and films such as The Wild One and Django. The most powerful influence came from everyday people, and the way they naturally wore and styled their outfits in a thrown-on manner – mechanics at work with a rag hanging out of their pocket, builders with a hoodie wrapped around their waist, a jumper thrown over the shoulder, a jacket half on, trousers hanging off, zips undone, belts and buckles hanging off, layers of clothing, hands in pockets, sleeves too long.

'My aim is to encapsulate this typically masculine and practical attitude in the clothes themselves, and for the wearer to feel this through them – the point of these clothes is not to be precious, but to be worn.

Fabrics and elements include leather with metal fastenings, satin twill, cotton flannel, organza, fine wool and silk/linen blends.

Prints and embroideries take inspiration from the Italian Renaissance, baroque, religious art, tattoos and other dark but beautiful pieces of art by Thomas Woodruff, Caravaggio, the Chapman brothers, Hieronymus Bosch, and from the darker side of my imagination. Hand-drawing the prints using a tattoo machine has a more raw and rugged look and echoes some of the references.'

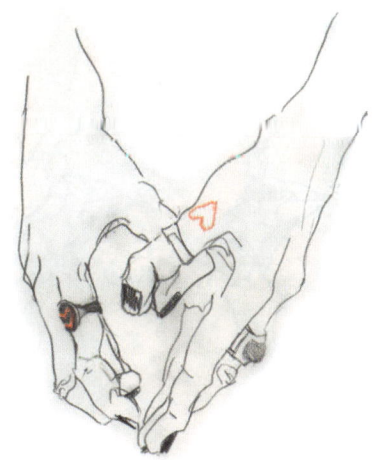

LEFT/BELOW: 'Materials used in all of the drawings and sketches were pencil – I change weights often depending on what it is. Colour was done in oil pastels with white spirit – a tip I learnt from Howard Tangye.'

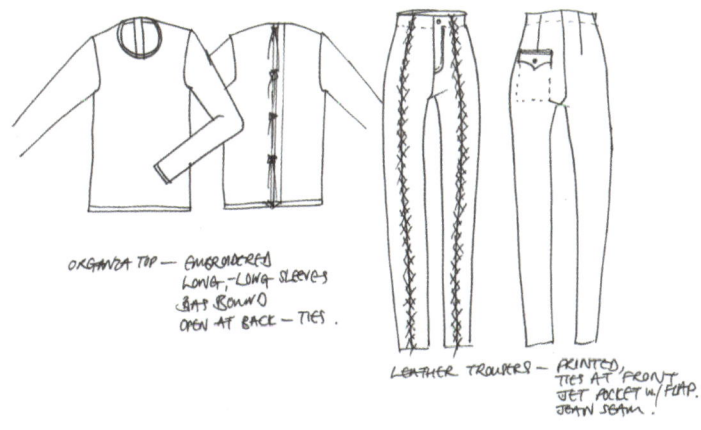

ORGANZA TOP — EMBROIDERED LONG, —LONG SLEEVES BIAS BOUND OPEN AT BACK — TIES .

LEATHER TROUSERS — PRINTED/FRONT TIES AT FRONT JET POCKET w/ FLAP. JEAN SEAM .

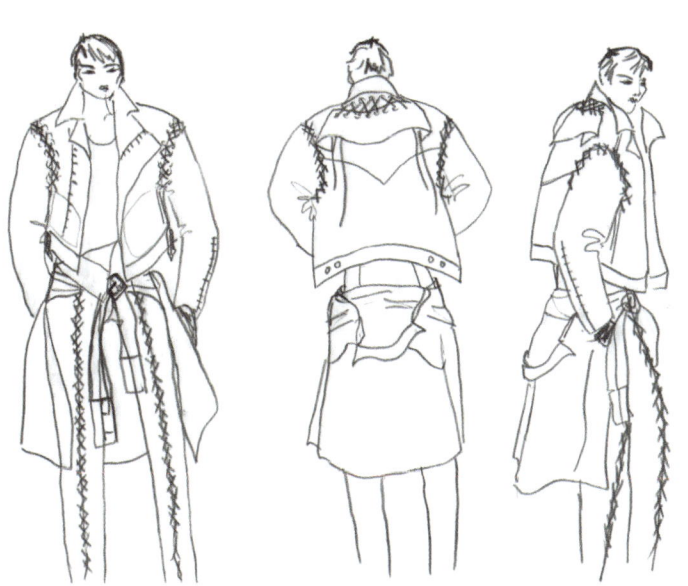

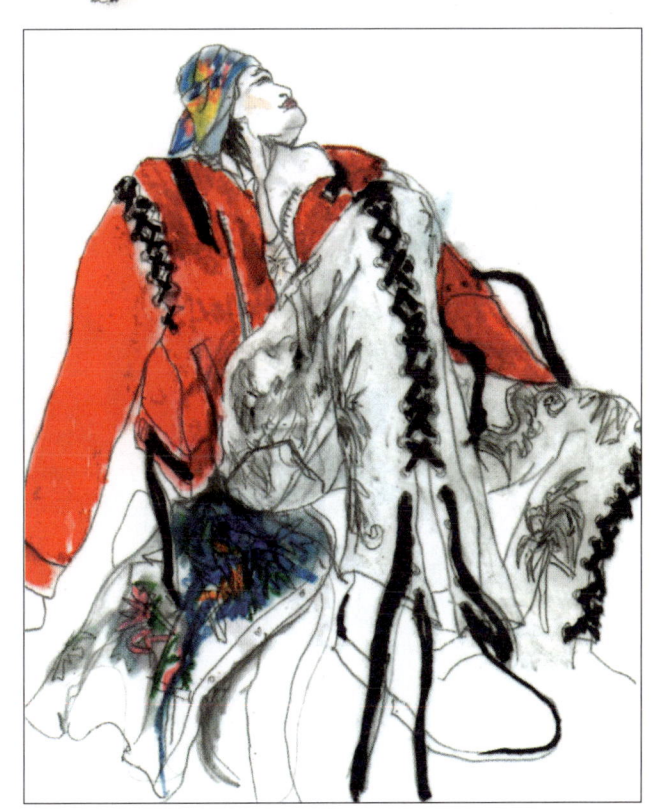

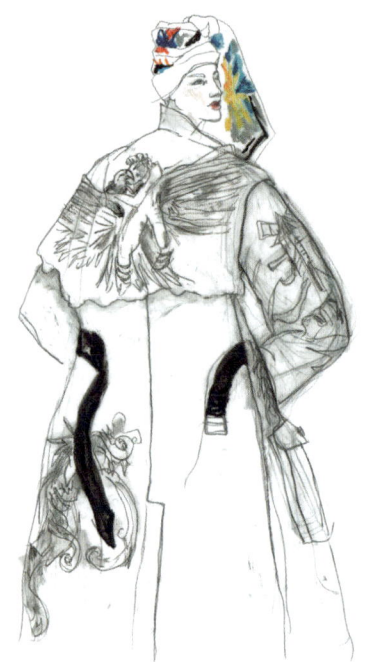

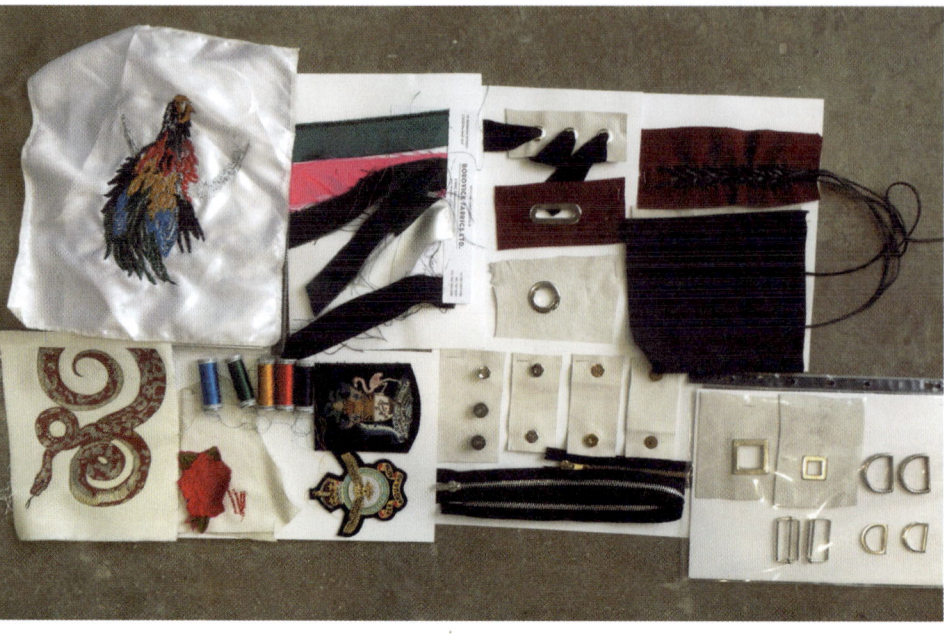

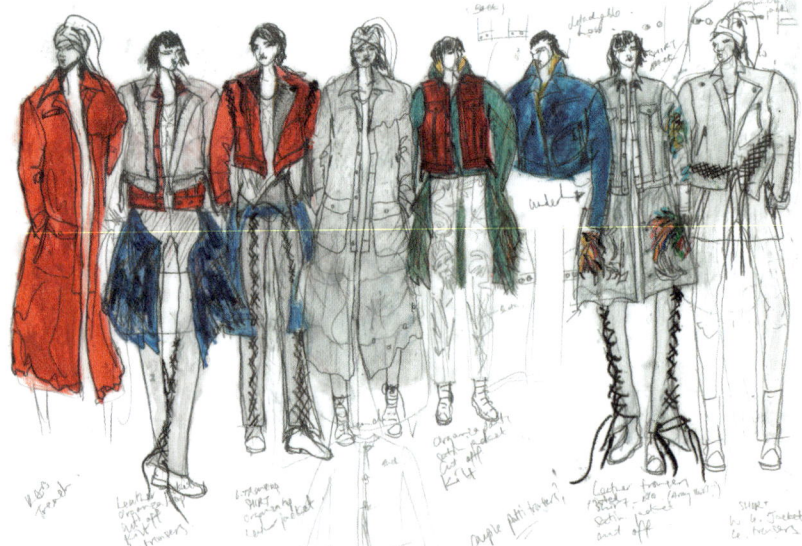

ABOVE: *A selection of fabrics, trims and hardwear used in the designs*
LEFT: *Additional drawing materials include fibre tip pens and marker pens*

'Dream job?! – Erm . . . creative director of the best company! Aim for the top – there is no point in aiming for the middle is there? For me it's not so much about what you do, it's how you do it. What is important to me is that I have a job that allows me to do, see and meet a diverse range of things, places and people. To mix researching, drawing, making, print, textiles, etc. – fuelling my intrigue. I always need to be doing things, I love exploring a diverse range of things, getting excited, learning, I am a curious person, I love adventure.

I love considering how I can use these things and manifest that feeling and make it into clothes. For me, fashion is not just about making pretty dresses – I like design to be relevant, to connect to aspects outside of fashion, to be a reflection of the time and the attitude. Design, it allows me to do all those things – to learn about and explore other cultures, histories and societies. A job that lets me do that is the dream! I am realistic about the corporate reality, but it's nice to hope, and at least try to retain part of that.'

FLORA CADZOW

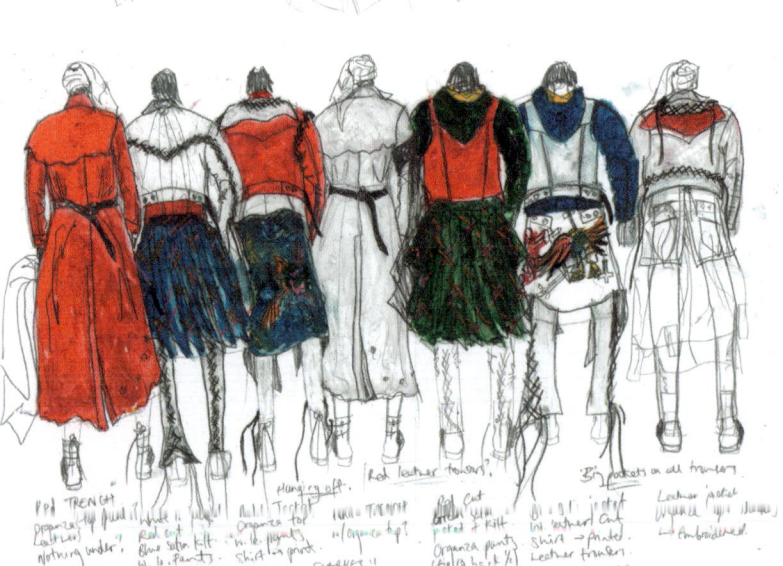

'I no longer listen to the market – creativity sometimes needs a deaf ear.'

JEAN CLAUDE ELENA

A FUTURE IN FASHION

For students applying to university for degree courses in fashion design and fashion related courses, requirements will vary from establishment to establishment and the specific nature or bias of the course. Yvonne Deacon presents some guidelines:

What we look for in a student applying for a place on a fashion course:
• Personality
• Curiosity
• Observation
• Skill

ONLINE SUBMISSION

Before applicants are called for interview there will be a request for an online sample of their work via Flickr webpage or drop box, so that an initial review of the work can be made. Applicants must ensure that this is original personal work containing most of the attributes required for **portfolio**. Page layout, drawing skills, mark-making and colour will be the first things that interviewers see, therefore they need to be effective. Good quality scanning or photography in the correct resolution and size is essential.

PORTFOLIO

If the potential student is called in for interview, the selection panel will first look at the portfolio and sketchbooks for evidence of creative ability, **personality** and the skills necessary to record images to a good standard that recognizes creative lines of thinking in your research. Each student portfolio should demonstrate individual **curiosity** about wider influences and the creative world in relation to the applicant's work and the specialist subject area of fashion. The interview panel will analyze choices made in activating the variety of media and techniques used to render images. They will also assess the skill and quality of drawing, mark-making and **observation** from the essential skills and developments as evidenced in the portfolio.

SKILLS

Drawing is a fundamental and transferable **skill** that applies throughout the art and design disciplines. It is one of the main criteria by which the qualities in the portfolio are judged, and demonstrates an appetite for the subjects of drawing, mark-making and illustration that will reveal the personality of the applicant's work.

Fashion is concerned with the body, therefore confident observational drawings made during clothed life, and in life drawing, are essential components of the portfolio. This demonstrates the development of skill and perception as a personal means of expression.

Compositional skills should reveal the ability, through the 'measuring eye', to judge the position of an image for its impact on the page. Leaving a good space around an image gives it importance and added reverence. Setting out images to connect for theme is a skill where a narrative can be created to lead the eye round a page to induce an understanding of its content and meaning on all levels.

There should be evidence of the careful selection of found or created imagery for size, intensity, depth of colour or tone content, for its juxtapositioning, cluster and spread for rich, intense effects or isolated for clarity and modernity.

The panel is interested in seeing how the work is processed, how research is developed, and to what depth and with what awareness initial ideas are set against a brief, demonstrating how creative problems have been solved and translated into design outcomes and illustrations. It is not always the big, fat sketchbook and portfolio that win the day, but the choices made at all stages for the quality of the work and how it is set out that reveal essential skills for selection.

Careful consideration needs to be given to the order (sequence) of the work in the portfolio. New projects showing best skills should be at the beginning and other skills should be revealed towards the back, usually ending with examples to show off your abilities to good advantage.

INTERVIEW

Once the portfolio and research work have been assessed, group or personal interviews follow. Questions may be asked about the applicant's personal opinion and passions and you will be expected to be able to have an intelligent and informed discussion about your work and the work of others, and to hold opinions about the work of others in the field. You need to be well informed about fashion in general and be able to demonstrate knowledge about contemporary trends and events that are of interest.

WRITTEN WORK

A short essay, rationale or questionnaire concerning the reasons for your application choice may also be requested as you wait for interview.

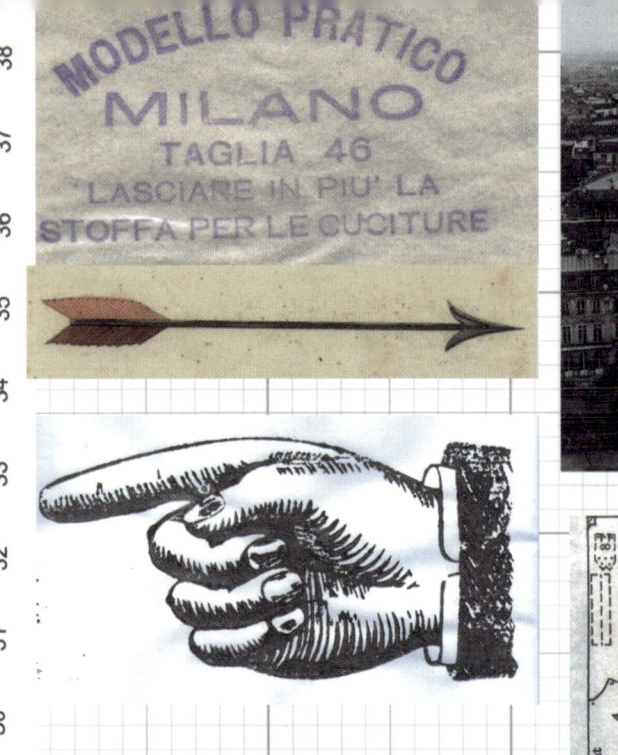

MODELLO PRATICO
MILANO
TAGLIA 46
LASCIARE IN PIU' LA
STOFFA PER LE CUCITURE

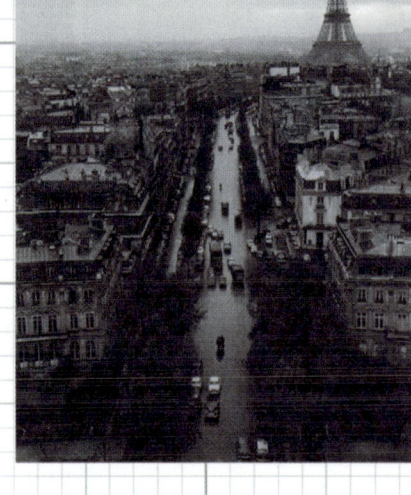

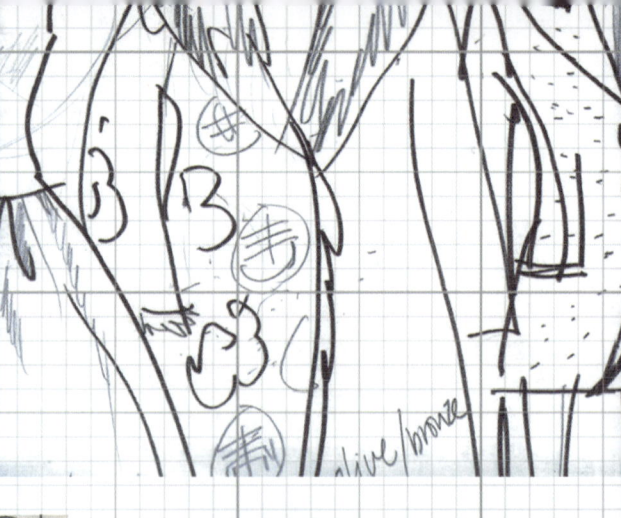

olive/bronze

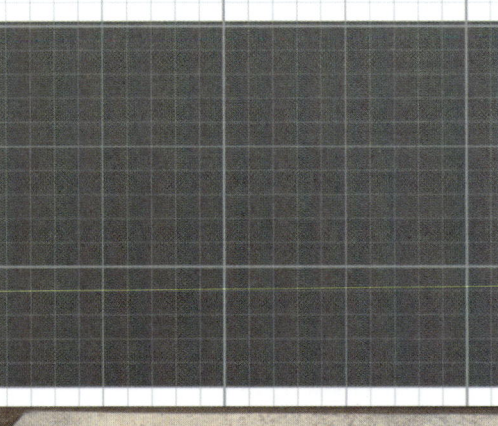

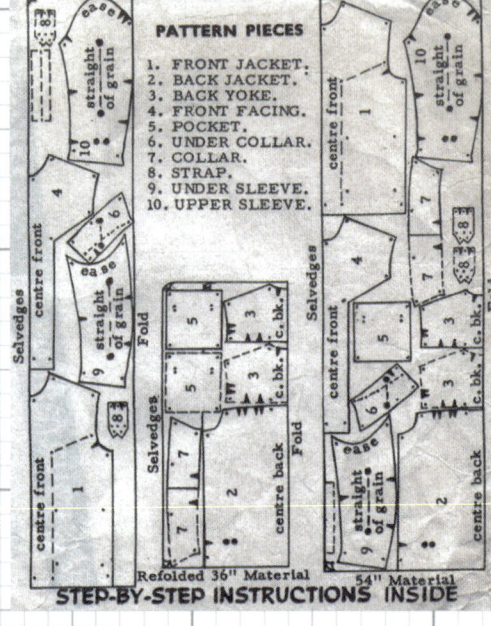

PATTERN PIECES
1. FRONT JACKET.
2. BACK JACKET.
3. BACK YOKE.
4. FRONT FACING.
5. POCKET.
6. UNDER COLLAR.
7. COLLAR.
8. STRAP.
9. UNDER SLEEVE.
10. UPPER SLEEVE.

Refolded 36" Material   54" Material
STEP-BY-STEP INSTRUCTIONS INSIDE

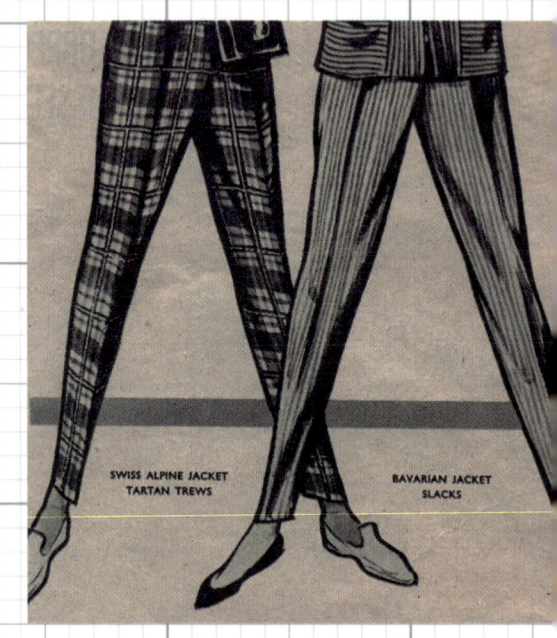

SWISS ALPINE JACKET
TARTAN TREWS

BAVARIAN JACKET
SLACKS

TYO NYC
LON PAR

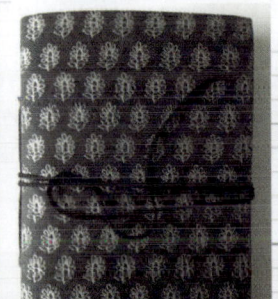

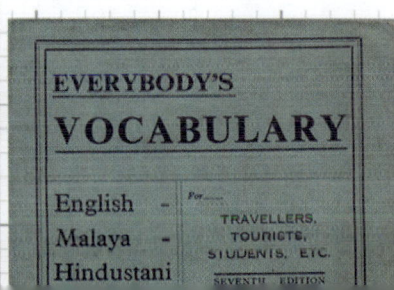

EVERYBODY'S
VOCABULARY

English -
Malaya -
Hindustani

For _____
TRAVELLERS,
TOURISTS,
STUDENTS, ETC.

SEVENTH EDITION

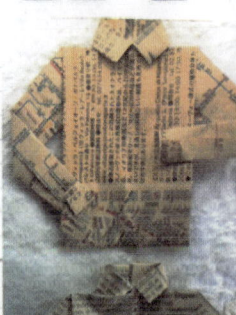

CHAPTER 12

HOW TO SPEAK FASHION

To be successful in any sphere, it is important to be familiar with its terminology and language. This is no less important for fashion designers and illustrators than it is for other professionals, and anyone interested in the fashion trade will benefit from knowing something of its history and traditions and the derivation of specific terms associated with it. Traditional techniques and skills still inform and enhance even the most contemporary and avant garde aspects of the fashion industry, while new phrases and language continue to be imported and taken up as standard.

The importance of learning the correct and universally accepted vocabulary – for your notes, research, understanding of briefs and international communication – is fundamental to any successful career. The aim of this section is, with the inclusion of a little fun, to help inform and inspire you to further study and investigation; to provoke curiosity to discover more; and to encourage you to be diligent and even pedantic about the use of accurate terminology. Your own fashion drawing and design will improve as you gain a sounder knowledge, understanding and appreciation of fashion's crafts and heritage.

We don't attempt to, and cannot be fully comprehensive within the confines of this book, but we hope to explain – along with many established words and regularly used expressions – a few misunderstood ones, to correct a few sloppy ones, and perhaps to revive a few of our favourites which we'd be sad to see disappear. Read on to learn how to speak the language of fashion . . .

INDUSTRY & TECHNICAL TERMS

BESPOKE a custom-made piece of tailoring (particularly menswear); bespoke is also used to refer to custom-made shirts, shoes and boots. Though historically women went to their dressmaker for most of their wardrobe and trousseau, their riding habits and other country attire would often be made *bespoken for*, in the same way as a gentleman's. This service is made to measure and to clients' specific requirements and includes accessories, jewellery and luggage (see also **haute couture**, opposite).

COLLECTION a range of garments which a designer creates for a specific season or label/brand. The term is used increasingly to upgrade and add fashion cachet to all sorts of ranges of products. See also **line-up**, opposite.

COLOURCARD a presentation showing a range of colours for a collection.

COLOUR COMBO an American term for **colour combination**, popularly adopted across the industry.

COLOUR EFFECTS iridescence (also known as **goniochromism**, **pearlescence** or, in France, *changeant*), a phenomenon caused by the angle of light on certain surfaces which gives the appearance of colour changes (typically butterfly wings, soap bubbles and sea shells). It is frequently emulated in fabrics, beads and sequins. Fabrics with these qualities are traditionally known as 'shot', which describes the way a contrasting weft colour, sometimes shiny and light-reflecting, is shot through the warp on the shuttle as it is woven. See also **weave/woven**, page 244.

COLOUR PALETTE a selected range of colours, perhaps focussed on a specific season or range of goods.

COLOUR PIGMENTS see **dyeing & dyes**, page 245.

CROQUIS a template for drawing fashion figures. From the French *croquer*, meaning to draw or sketch quickly, though textile designers also use this phrase for a finished painted or drawn textile design.

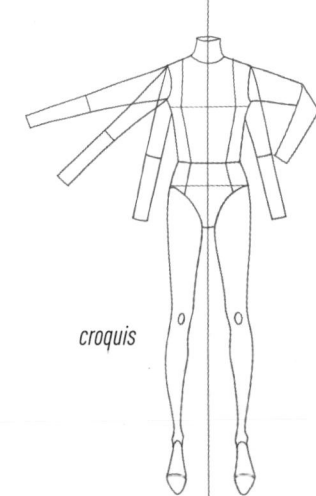

croquis

DANDY generally, a man who dresses flamboyantly with extreme attention to detail. The most famous early dandy was Beau Brummell; others included Lord Byron and Oscar Wilde. Similar terms include **beau**, **gallant** and, perjoratively, **fop**, **coxcomb** and **popinjay**. The end of the 18th century saw the height of dandyism. By the early decades of the 19th century the fashion had acquired some women followers, known as **dandizettes**.

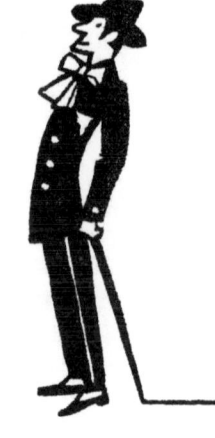

dandy

DATA SHADOW not strictly a fashion term, but used generally and increasingly by fashion companies to describe a person's online shopping and browsing habits that are analysed by marketing companies and used to target their customers for new sales and products.

DELUXE from the French *de luxe* (of luxury) and originally from Latin *luxus* meaning excess.

FASHION the great British designer **Jean Muir**, never too grand to call herself a dressmaker, liked to use the word as a verb – to fashion/to make – to reinforce the notion of the craft of fashion design.

FASHIONISTA a light-heartedly derogatory colloquial term for people in the fashion business or industry.

FLATS drawings of garments as if laid flat, clearly showing all seams, design and construction details, but without the visual complications of fabric pattern, colour or styling.

FLOATS similar to flats, but less rigid, drawn as if animated by an invisible model/wearer.

LAB DIP a swatch of fabric test-dyed to specific colour instructions by the factory for approval by the designer.

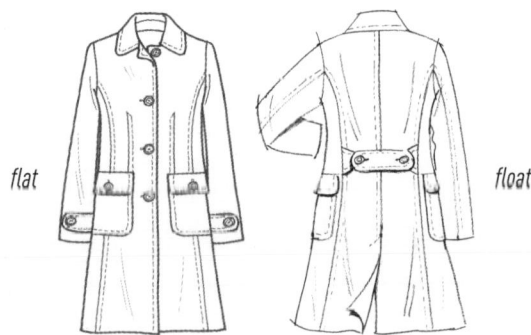

flat   *float*

HAUTE COUTURE literally meaning *high sewing*, this phrase can be traced back to the reign of Louis XVI of France and his 19-year-old queen Marie Antoinette whose love of extravagance and exquisite fashion immortalized the name of her dressmaker, Rose Bertin (1747–1813). Charles Worth, an Englishman working in Paris, is often heralded as the first couturier. Worth opened his atelier in 1858 and, to regulate the craft of haute couture, he founded the Chambre Syndicale de la Couture in 1868. The couturier (only latterly described as the designer, as the emphasis was always placed on craftsmanship rather than simply the design) will make a small selection of garments (models) which are presented to his or her clients. A client chooses a garment which is then specially made, with amendments to suit. An atelier would seldom make more than six costumes of a particular model. Today there are officially 23 designers on the official Chambre Syndicale de la Haute Couture Parisienne calendar. Gowns can take over 800 hours of work and involve the world's most skilled pattern cutters, dressmakers, tailors, embroiderers and beaders. Consequently, daywear starts at around £8,000 ($13,000) – for the rest, the sky is the limit. After the golden age of haute couture in the 1940s and 1950s, the number of customers decreased drastically; but thanks to developing economies it is now estimated that there are 4,000 women worldwide who patronize true couture, an increase of 20–30%, though only a few hundred are regular customers. See also **bespoke**, opposite.

HOMAGE a convenient let-out phrase used when a designer is inspired by or blatantly copies ideas and stylistic characteristics closely identified with another designer.

LINE-UP a row of drawings showing a garment range or collection, or part of one, as if the models were on a runway or catwalk.

LOOK BOOK a book, booklet, pamphlet or such that presents images of a seasonal range or collection, usually given to customers as promotional material. Generally, a look book is also presented online.

MOOD or **THEME BOARD** a small collection of images that evoke the look, mood or theme of a season, trend, product or collection, without showing the actual product itself. Usually assembled early on in the design process as a way to focus.

NEW LOOK in February 1947, as Paris and the rest of Europe struggled to recover from seven years of war,

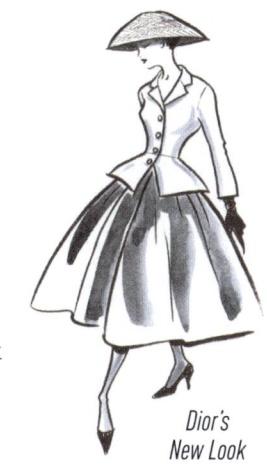

Dior's New Look

Christian Dior opened the House of Dior and launched his first collection, entitled Corolle, for the following winter. Most famous was the Bar Suit, a neo-Victorian silhouette with narrow shoulders and a tiny corseted waistline emphasized by padded hips, with skirts so full that many of them took up to 20 yards of fabric. It was seen simultaneously as a step backwards for women's emancipation, a return to an image of femininity not seen for 30 years or so, a boost to the ailing textile industries and a blatant extravagance in a Europe still blighted by rationing. Carmel Snow, editor-in-chief of *Harper's Bazaar*, echoed a phrase that was popular in the politics of the day, announcing to Dior that: 'Your dresses have such a New Look!' The rest, as they say, is history.

PAPARAZZI the collective term for press photographers who pursue celebrities to get photographs of them. The name is an eponym from the 1960 Federico Fellini film *La Dolce Vita* in which one of the characters is a news photographer named Paparazzo.

PRÊT-À-PORTER literally meaning 'ready to wear', the name was first coined in 1966 when couturier Yves Saint Laurent offered a prêt-à-porter range from his shop in the Rue de Tournon, Paris, which he saw as a step towards the democratization of fashion.

RANGE PLAN a plan of a range or collection, showing all the component styles and pieces. Usually drawn as flats, with colour and fabric options. For selling and promotional use and often included as part of a **look book**, see left.

STRIKE OFF a small swatch of fabric printed by the factory for colour and pattern quality approval before the final seal is placed on the order.

SWATCH colour swatch, design swatch, sample swatch, tension swatch, test swatch . . . A sample of fabric, knit, embellishment or such, used for referencing, colour, fabrication, techniques, compatibility or embellishment, etc.

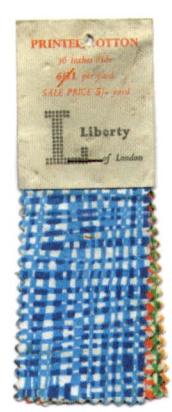

swatch

TEAR SHEET an interesting page or piece of reference cut from a magazine or such, also called a **swipe**.

TECH-PACKS/SPECS a tech-pack is what is sent to a factory to instruct them to make a sample. It includes a spec (specification), which is a flat drawing with measurements, details and swatches of fabric or materials, colour reference, yarn, etc., plus special construction information, including specified threads and stitches, tension and finishing information, such as washing, pressing, etc.

TREND FORECASTING part of the designer's role is to anticipate coming moods and directions, informed by research and awareness, finely tuned antennae and confidence in his/her own instincts. For a few people this is a career in its own right; professionals in this field are called **cool hunters**.

UNISEX a phrase first coined in relation to fashion in the 1960s – fashion's reaction to the sexual identity questioning of the times. A number of designers presented identical clothing on male and female models on the runway, and on the streets hippie couples swapped clothes.

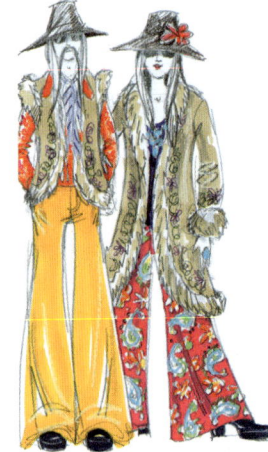

unisex

VINTAGE a catch-all phrase which came into fashion use in the late 1990s and borrowed directly from the wine industry, 'vintage' implies that something is rare and has improved with age – though this is not always strictly true for fashion items! Used to describe and simultaneously upgrade what were previously described unceremoniously as 'old' or 'secondhand' clothes. There is apparently a guideline that recommends pieces should be at least 30 years old to be classified as vintage, but this is frequently only loosely adhered to. The media quickly latched on to this value-laden phrase and it is now applied to anything of non-specific age, from homeware and ephemera to music, food and recipes from a past era, and often without merit.

XXXL a hugely expanding market

ZEITGEIST the mood of the moment, as defined and indicated by the creative, intellectual and fashionable ideas and thoughts of the particular time.

FIBRES, FABRICS, YARNS, DYEING & DYES

Fundamentally, there are three types of fibre – natural, man-made and synthetic.

NATURAL FIBRES (ANIMAL)

ALPACA a long, silky, luxury fibre from the fleece of this South American relative of the llama.

ANGORA from angora rabbits, ethical production involves brushing the hair from the animal rather than plucking or stripping, which injures and eventually kills it.

CAMEL both the coarser outer-hair and the softer under-hair are used.

CASHMERE misleadingly for a luxury wool-like fibre, this comes from angora goats.

LLAMA a similar fibre to alpaca.

MOHAIR we'd like to tell you about a tiny, shy, elusive creature called a Mo, living high up in deepest . . . but no, mohair comes from the angora goat (which may be slightly misleading too, so you had better also read about **angora**, above!)

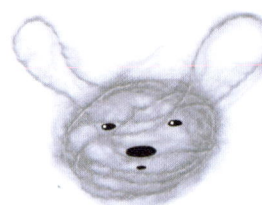

mohair

QIVIUT the soft, downy, waterproof, hypoallergenic wool of the muskox, a rare luxury fibre much prized by the people of Greenland and used to make traditional smokerings (nachaqs) and accessories.

SILK silk fibres are released by dissolving the glue around the cocoon spun by the silk worm, which lives on a particular species of mulberry tree. The whole process is known as **sericulture**.

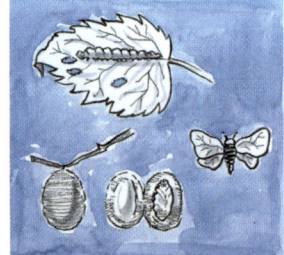

lifecycle of the silk worm

WOOL/LAMBSWOOL/MERINO/WORSTED sheep are sheared to obtain the wool fibre. Young sheep produce a softer fibre known as lambswool. **Merino** is a luxury longer-fibre wool produced mainly in Australia. **Worsted** is a process of spinning wool with longer fibres, keeping them parallel to produce a smoother, tighter yarn and cloth. Woollen spinning produces a looser, fuzzier yarn and cloth.

VICUNA a small animal, similar to the llama and native to the Andes, the vicuna provides the aristocrat of animal fibres, fine and softer than any wool. Forty fleeces are needed to make enough cloth for one coat-length of cloth.

NOBLE FIBRE the collective noun for rare and high-quality fibres such as **alpaca**, **cashmere**, **mohair**, **silk**, **vicuna**, etc.

NATURAL FIBRES (VEGETABLE)

COTTON/ORGANIC COTTON derived from the seed head of the cotton plant, this is the world's most widely grown and used fibre. Vast quantities of chemicals and water are involved in its growth and mass production. As awareness grows of the impact of cotton production on the environment, an increasing number of schemes have evolved for producing organic cotton.

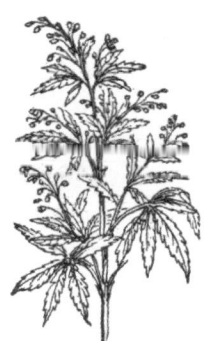

cotton

FLAX/LINEN a **bast** fibre obtained from the fibrous stems of the flax plant.

HEMP a bast fibre similar to coarse **linen**, obtained from *Cannabis sativa*, a relative of the marijuana plant.

JUTE a coarse bast fibre used in a similar way to sisal.

NETTLE a soft, delicate bast fibre that is gaining in popularity. The cultivation of nettles is more ecologically sound than that of most cotton. The hollow fibres give yarns and fabrics a natural insulation, warm in winter and cool in summer.

Cannabis sativa

RAMI a bast fibre from the nettle family, somewhere between coarse cotton and linen, recently gaining popularity as a cheaper alternative.

SISAL a coarse fibre from the *Agave sisalana* plant, frequently confused with hemp, used principally for string, twine, scrim and sacking, etc.

MAN-MADE FIBRES manufactured fibres, as distinct from fibres that occur naturally, made from chemically processed natural vegetable or mineral based materials.

PROTEIN including milk and soya based fibres.

CELLULOSE rayon and viscose, produced largely from wood pulp.

MINERAL including glass fibre, steel, copper and other metals.

SYNTHETIC FIBRES manufactured fibres produced from polymers built up from chemical elements or compounds in contrast to fibres made from naturally occurring fibre-forming polymers. Produced largely via oil and fossil fuels.

ACRYLIC polyester and **polyamide**, and includes **nylon**, often added to blends for its hard-wearing and low-power stretch properties.

ACETATES part cellulose based and part synthetic fibres.

KEVLAR® the registered trademark for a para-aramid synthetic fibre used in personal armour for the military and other protective clothing, such as motorcycle wear.

LYCRA known for its extreme elasticity, this is a trade name for a synthetic form of latex. Known as **Elastane** in most of Europe and in North America as **Spandex** (an anagram of the word 'expands').

FABRICS

BATISTE a fine, sheer cotton or linen cloth, named after the linen weaver who created it, Jean Baptiste.

BOLT a flat, folded way of storing and selling fabrics, usually at the quality end of the market. There is no standard measurement, as loftier fabrics make larger more cumbersome bolts; average lengths may be between 50 and 100 yards. See also **waste** (page 244).

BONDED a composite of two fabrics produced using heat, adhesive or felting.

BOUCLÉ a fabric woven from looped or knotted yarns that create a curly, textured surface. Historically associated with **Coco Chanel** and her famous jackets (see also **yarn**, page 244).

BROCADE taking its name from the French word for 'ornament' – a rich jacquard weave with a raised design, traditionally floral or figurative in origin.

BRODERIE ANGLAISE sometimes called Swiss embroidery, a fine eyelet-embroidered cotton.

CALENDER a mechanized process involving heat and heavy rollers to finish fabrics with a smooth, sometimes lustrous surface.

CALICO a simple plain woven cotton used in various weights for toile making (named after Calicut on India's Malabar coast, from where it originates).

CHAMBRAY a soft cotton fabric where the vertical (warp) threads are coloured and the horizontal (weft) threads are white. Named after Cambrai in northern France.

CHENILLE a tufted pile fabric named after the French word for 'caterpillar'.

CHINO a twill-woven cotton that has been mercerized to increase its strength and lustre. Created for summer uniforms for American armed forces, so lending the name to the casual trousers.

CIRÉ from the French word for 'wax', used to describe fine, showerproof fabrics of a waxy appearance.

CORDUROY a hardworking, ribbed cotton pile fabric originally used to make livery worn by the servants of French kings (*cor du Roi*). Fine versions are **needlecord** or **babycord**. As in knitting, the ribs in the cord are called **wales**, and the cloth is often categorized by the number of wales per inch.

COVERT a twill weave medium or lightweight overcoating fabric with a lightly flecked appearance from the grandrelle yarns made of worsted wool. Its dense surface was thorn-proof and made it suitable for hunting clothes. The name derives from the covert or shelter which the animals sought.

CREPE yarns are twisted to create a dry, wrinkled surface – available in many fabric variations.

CROMBIE a soft overcoating with a raised pile finish. Associated with a classic style of overcoat made of this fabric, 'Crombie' is the registered trade name of J.&J. Crombie Ltd, founded in 1805.

DENIM a robust twill weave (serge) cotton originating from Nîmes in France, *serge de Nîmes*. Traditionally denim is made from blue vertical warp threads woven with white horizontal weft threads. See **weave/woven**, page 244, and **indigo**, page 245.

DOBBY a fabric featuring all over woven repeats, which can take the form of a texture or a coloured pattern. They are woven using a special heddle (header) on a jacquard-type loom.

DOUBLE FACE **face** or **face-side** – the right side of the fabric. **Double face** means fabric that is double sided, sometimes with contrasting colours or pattern with plain. Plated knitwear or knitted fabrics can be similarly created using a technique that feeds a particular yarn only to the back of the stitch.

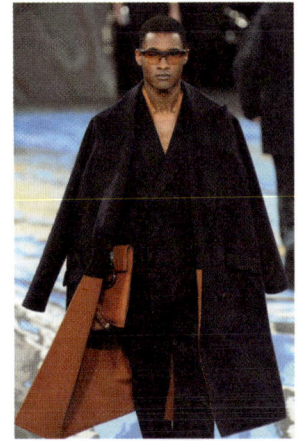

double face

EMBELLISHED/EMBELLISHMENT somewhat all-encompassing words for fabrics enhanced with one or more techniques or processes, including **beads** and **sequins** (also called spangles or by the French *paillettes*), studs or eyelets. **Appliqué:** a method whereby additional motifs, fabrics and materials are applied with stitches, heat or other techniques. **Embossed:** a technique of producing pattern in relief by applying heat and pressure with an engraved roller or plate on to fabric in a process similar to **calendering**.

EMBROIDERY an array of decorative stitch-based techniques applied to pre-existing ground fabrics by hand or machine.

EMBROIDERY LACE a lace construction created by stitching on to a pre-existing ground of tulle, net or dissolvable net to produce a decorative effect (see **lace**, facing page).

FELT non-woven felt is created by applying heat, moisture, friction and pressure to layers of primarily woollen fibres until they matt together. **Woven felt** is created similarly by applying moisture, friction and pressure to loosely woven primarily woollen fabric until the surface becomes dense and matted.

FERRANDINE a luxury silk and wool fine blend cloth.

FINE the correct description for quality, delicate or micro-gauge fabrics (rather than 'thin'). See also **noble fibre**, page 240.

FLANNEL a light twill weave woollen or worsted fabric, slightly napped on one side. The name originates from the Welsh word *gwlamen* meaning 'allied to wool'.

FLOAT a term used in both knitting and weaving where secondary colours are traversed across the back of the fabric surface.

FUR many volatile arguments exist in favour of and against fur. Undoubtedly, many animals bred for fur have a miserable existence even before meeting their end. In Scandinavia, a method is being developed which avoids killing animals; the moult of mink and foxes is collected and processed to produce single and 2-ply yarns which is then woven into fabrics.

GABARDINE originating in Spain in the Middle Ages (the Spanish word *gabardina* means 'protection from the elements'). A fine twill woven cotton or wool cloth; a later version in waterproof Egyptian cotton was adopted by a certain London tailor, Thomas Burberry.

GINGHAM from the Malayan word *gingan*, a simple cotton fabric with even checks of colour, usually plus white. Frequently associated with school and nurses' uniforms.

GRAIN the direction of threads (the warp and weft) of a fabric; when garment patterns are cut down along the grain, they are cut parallel to the **warp**; when cut across the grain, they are cut parallel to the **weft**.

GUIPURE strictly speaking, an embroidery with no visible background, with bars and threads joining the motifs. The name derives from the French word *guipe*, a cord around which silk is rolled.

HABOTAI one of the very many types of silk fabrics; soft and downy, it takes colour excellently.

HANDFEEL how the fabric feels to the hand, an inaccurate but widely used way of assessing the success or appeal of a fabric.

IKAT a pattern made by binding areas of the warp before dyeing; a certain amount of bleeding, capillary action and discrepancy means that, when woven, the pattern has an attractive blurred and smudged definition.

INKLE a linen thread or tape for making laces (not many people know this, but we think they should – it's such a good name!).

JACQUARD an elaborate loom invented in 1802 by Joseph Marie Jacquard to mechanize the production of brocade and damask patterned fabrics. Since its invention, any pattern-woven fabric or ribbon is generally referred to as a 'jacquard'. See also **knitwear** (page 247).

JERSEY see **jerseywear & knitwear** (page 247).

LACE a fine, open-work fabric with a background of net or mesh with patterns worked simultaneously or applied later by looping or twisting. Made by hand with bobbins, needles or by machinery. Lace-type fabrics can be created by knitting, crochet, tatting, darning, embroidering, macramé and weaving.

LAMÉ a fabric in which either the warp or weft threads are metallic in appearance. From the French verb *laminer*, 'to flatten', from the days when real metals were used to create such fabrics.

LOFTY the trade term for bulky, but light and springy fabrics.

LUREX the registered brand name of a type of metallic-look yarn. Fabrics made of this yarn are frequently similarly called **lurex fabric**.

MADRAS from the Indian city, more or less a jolly multicolour version of **gingham**.

MERCERIZED of cotton thread that has been treated with sodium hydroxide to increase its lustre and affinity for dye – also known as 'pearl cotton'. The process was invented by John Mercer in 1844 and improved by H.A. Lowe in 1980.

MOIRÉ from the French verb *moirer*, 'to water'; wavy watermark type patterns characterize this lightly ribbed, taffeta-like fabric.

MOUSSELINE or **MOUSSELINE DE SOIE** a sheer or semi-sheer fabric, like chiffon, but crisper and paper-like.

MULL similar to **calico** (see page 241), these days mull is almost solely used for **toile** making; its Indian name means 'soft and pliable'.

NAP any pile to the surface of a fabric.

NEP when a garment has nep, it means that the fabric has been woven in such a way that some of the fibres protrude from the main surface.

OTTOMAN a heavy, corded silk-type fabric with crosswise ribs. **Grosgrain** and **petersham** are similar in ribbon form, used for waistbands, trims and finishes.

OXFORD a heavy cotton used largely for shirts or summer suiting.

PAISLEY a curved, pine-cone shaped motif named a *boteh*, originating in India. When the British East India Company imported patterned shawls from Kashmir, the craze drove manufacturers to produce their own versions printed on to fine wool challis. The Scottish town of

Paisley became a specialist, producing printed versions of these shawls and the name was forever linked.

PINSTRIPE a finely striped fabric that can be interpreted in almost any fibre combination. Wider striped versions are sometimes called **chalk stripe**, particularly in woollen versions where the stripe becomes broken-up somewhat.

POPLIN a plain, medium-weight woven cotton.

QUILTING a way of increasing the loft of fabrics by sandwiching a filling between and stitching them together. Used for warm linings or as design feature in its own right.

RASCHEL a warp knitted lacy fabric made on a machine of the same name. Very popular in the 1920s and 1930s; subsequently revived by the Italian company Missoni in the 1970s.

SATIN a **silk, rayon/viscose** or such fabric characterized by a smooth, shiny face and a dull back. Excellent draping qualities are part of its appeal, though it is tricky to handle because of its slipperiness.

SEERSUCKER a rippled, striped, textured fabric taking its name from an old Persian word meaning 'milk and sugar'.

SELVEDGE a selvedge on either side of a woven material is general, but not invariable. *Solve* is the Scandinavian name for a heddle (part of a loom). The name means the end or the edge of the material. The threads at the edges are threaded double to make the edge stronger. The selvedge is always threaded plain, the real pattern beginning after the selvedge. Some cloths will have the name of the mill woven through the selvedge as a guarantee of authenticity and endorsement of quality.

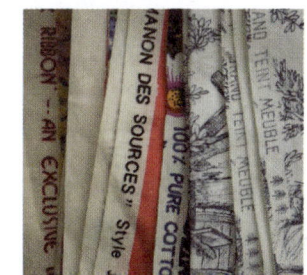

printed selvedge

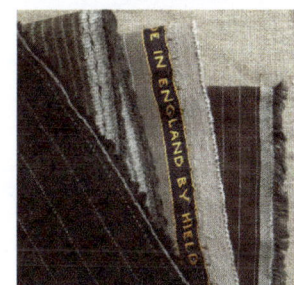

woven selvedge

SHODDY along with linen paper, perhaps one of the earliest examples of recycling – a generally inferior yarn or cloth made from the shredded fibres of waste woollen cloth and clippings (also sometimes known as **mungo**).

SUITING usually taken to refer to fine **worsted** cloths, traditionally used for tailored suits.

TARTAN AND PLAID the traditional woven woollen clan fabrics of Scotland. **Hunting plaids** are more subtly coloured than dress plaids. The square repeats of the plaid are known as **setts**.

TOILE DE JOUY famous printed cotton fabrics from Jouy in France, which first appeared in the 18th century. Usually one colour – Madder red, French or China blue, Olive green or, occasionally, black – all on white or ecru ground. The designs feature flowers or pictoral landscapes with figures.

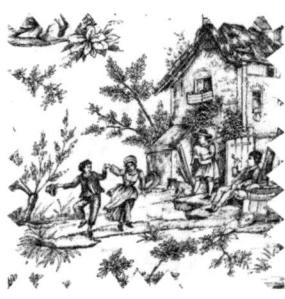

toile de jouy

TWEED an all-encompassing name for a vast array of traditional woven cloths, including **estate tweeds**, a family of traditional tweed cloths originally woven for countrywear on the great estates of England and Scotland and including all the great classics; **gunclub**, **hound's tooth**, **shepherds**, **Glenurquhart**, **Rothiemurchus**, **Wyvis** etc. **Prince of Wales check**: a varient of Glenurquhart check much favoured and popularized by HRH Prince Edward Prince of Wales (later the Duke of Windsor) in the 1920s and 1930s. **Harris tweed**: spun, dyed and woven in the Scottish islands of Harris and Lewis for over 300 years, Harris tweed has been much favoured by Vivienne Westwood and other designers and is now a registered trademark. **Donegal**: a tweed fabric originally hand-woven in County Donegal, Ireland, and characterized by a speckled, neppy surface. See also **nep**, page 243. **Hound's tooth**: a two-colour, broken-check cloth; also called **dog's tooth**. Smaller versions frequently informally called **puppy tooth**.

TWILL a diagonal rib or grain achieved as part of the weaving sequence.

VELVET a short, thick pile fabric, usually woven double. The fabric is cut apart to create the pile. With **cut velvet**, the pattern is a raised brocaded surface on a plain ground. With **façonne velvet/devoré**, the pile is eaten away (devoured) via a printing process to create a pile/non-pile design, sometimes with a sheer chiffon-like ground.

VENETIAN a luxury worsted wool satin-like fabric with a soft, polished surface.

WARP AND WEFT the warp is the length threaded on the weaving loom; the weft is the thread woven across the warp (across the width of the loom). When warp and weft stripes are combined, a check or plaid is produced.

WASTE Cabbage: the fabric a garment manufacturer has left over after production is complete. The manufacturer may illegally make additional identical garments or simply use the fabric to make alternative garments for sale covertly. **Fents**: a length of fabric sold by the mill, usually at a mill shop, sometimes in a trial colourway that never went into production or with unusual colour changes throughout the length which occurred during trialling. Usually sold by weight. **Remnant**: a length of fabric sold by a fabric merchant from what is left at the end of a roll or bolt. It is sold by the piece, take it or leave it.

WEAVE/WOVEN fabrics are woven on a weaving **loom**. A few traditional fabrics are still hand-woven. Weave designers generally still hand-weave their first samples. Hand-woven fabrics can be described as **hand-loomed**.

WOOLLEN SPUN generally loose, fuzzier finished yarn and fabrics made with shorter fibre wool.

WEIGHT cloth quality is calculated by the weight in grams per square metre and written as GSM or gm/^{2}. Some traditional fabrics are still sold in imperial measurements – oz/yd^2 = ounces per yard squared.

ZEBRA an eternally popular monochrome pattern, successfully interpreted by a huge range of designers, including Coco Chanel, Bridget Riley, Mary Quant and Roberto Cavalli.

YARN
YARN & FABRIC COUNT
yarn count is calculated by thickness of the yarn end and the number of twists. Fabric is the number of ends to the inch.

BALL/ BOBBIN/ CHEESE /CONE/ HANK/ REEL/SHUTTLE/ SKEIN/ SPOOL different ways of buying and using yarn and thread.

BOUCLÉ a looped or knotted decorative yarn. See also **bouclé fabric**, page 241.

CHINE a French word meaning 'speckled'; two threads (ends) of contrasting colours or tones are twisted together.

GIMP a helically wrapped and spun yarn which has a crimped, irregular texture.

GRANDRELLE a 2-ply twisted yarn of two colours, or two tone, sometimes one yarn having a lustre to create a matt and shine contrast.

JASPE similar to chine, usually jaspe yarns have one end black and the other end colour.

MAL-FLAMME literally 'badly spun', an uneven, slubbed or rustic-looking yarn.

MÉLANGE the French word for 'mixture', yarns are comprised of mixed tones.

PLY the number of ends twisted together to make a yarn – 2-ply, 3-ply, etc.

ROVING YARN unspun or loosely spun yarns.

TWIST the way ends of yarns are spun together.

DYEING & DYES

BLUE WOOL SCALE this measures and calibrates the permanence and light-fastness of dyes.

GARMENT DYE a process where garments are made in un-dyed cloth and dyed as whole garments, begun so that garments could be dyed closer to the season in fashionable colours, but now frequently used purely for its soft, washed/aged look.

PIECE DYE a similar process for knitwear, in which the garment parts (pieces) are dyed and then assembled by linking.

OVER DYE (*ton sur ton*) a process whereby base colours or patterns are dyed over to produce tone-on-tone effects in garments or fabrics.

TIE DYE a process where the garment or fabric is tied tightly in areas so that when dyed, areas and patterns are not exposed to the dye and remain undyed.

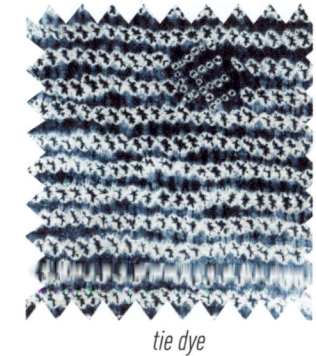

tie dye

YARN DYE a knitwear phrase which describes using yarn that is already dyed (see **piece dye**, above).

OMBRE derived from the French for shade or shadow – a colour effect achieved in dyed or woven fabrics so that they change gradually from dark to light or from one colour to another (also known as **dégradé**).

MADDER an evergreen plant native to Asia and the Old World, the roots of which produce beautiful pink/red colours and dyes, known as madder and sometimes as Turkey Red.

INDIGO a blue pigment extracted from the leaves of the *Indigofera tinctoria* plant. One of the oldest and most treasured dyes it used to be known as 'blue gold'. Still valued above its synthetic rivals, indigo is responsible for our ongoing love affair with denim and its connotations of authenticity and democracy.

KHAKI legend has it that during a safari, a hunter dressed in customary white leant upon a cashew tree and the gum permanently stained his jacket. It was realized that this was a most suitable camouflage colour. The cashew has been a natural source of khaki dye ever since.

CUT & CONSTRUCTION

ASYMMETRIC/SYMMETRIC most garments, like most people, are more or less symmetrical, or even, on both sides. Double-breasted features make a nod towards asymmetry, but true asymmetry has a deliberate absence of balance. Garments may typically have one shoulder, one sleeve, or be a combination of fitted and flare. Japanese designers Rei Kawakuba for Commes des Garçons and Junya Watanabe, in particular, have recently pushed the limits of asymmetry to extremes with some extraordinary, challenging, but exciting collections exploring this oeuvre.

BIAS to cut fabric crosswise to the grain of the cloth (at 45 degrees). A technique pioneered by Mme Madeleine Vionnet in the 1920s which utilizes the natural stretch of the cloth to create a gentle cling and drape rather than a straight/free-hanging silhouette. The technique, all but forgotten and neglected, was revived and further explored by John Galliano in the early 1980s and has since gained popularity thanks to much improved production techniques.

BIAS BINDING a narrow tape cut from cloth at a 45 degree angle. Used for binding seams and sometimes appropriate for finishing hems, necklines and tricky curved edges, etc.

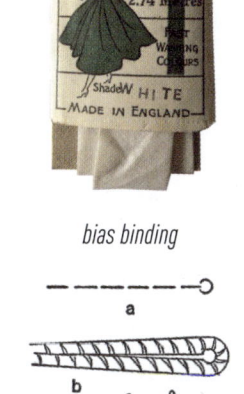

bias binding

BLIND HEM/BLIND STITCH a method of hemming that is almost invisible. When sewing, only a single thread of the outer fabric is caught.

BLOCK or **BODY BLOCK** the basis of a pattern, cut according to a standard size or to the fit of an individual for following garments pattern or design (see also **toiles**, page 247).

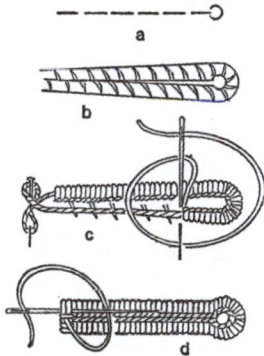

hand-stitched keyhole buttonhole

BUTTONHOLES these are traditionally hand-finished, but now more usually machine-stitched. Tailored and heavier fabric garments traditionally have **keyhole** buttonholes to facilitate functioning. Fabric or bound buttonholes, sometimes called **jet** or **jetted** buttonholes, can be made using self or contrasting fabric, sometimes used on the bias.

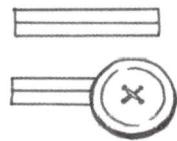

jet or jetted buttonhole

CONSTRUCTION the way in which a garment is made, referring to methods, techniques, etc.

CUT the way in which a garment is cut, the fabric grain, silhouette and line. See **silhouette & line** (page 247) and **grain** (page 242).

DECONSTRUCTED the ideas first appeared in fashion in the late 1980s, the term 'deconstructed' applied a few years later and borrowed from theories on architecture that had been evolving throughout the 1960s and 1970s. Ideas were apparently simultaneously explored by a handful of designers across the globe, including avant garde Japanese designers Rei Kawakuba for Commes des Garçons and Yohji Yamamoto, the Belgian designer Anne Demuelemeester (one of the Antwerp Six), and Parisian Anne Valerie Hash. This disparate group of rebellious spirits were united in trying to challenge the traditions of construction and the accepted standards of making and finishing of garments. Seams exposed, and edges left raw, unfinished and un-hemmed, were just some of the characteristics. Aspects of tailoring normally hidden internally, but involving great skill and craftsmanship, were proudly exposed and transferred to the outside of garments to be enthusiastically admired by the sympathetic cognoscenti.

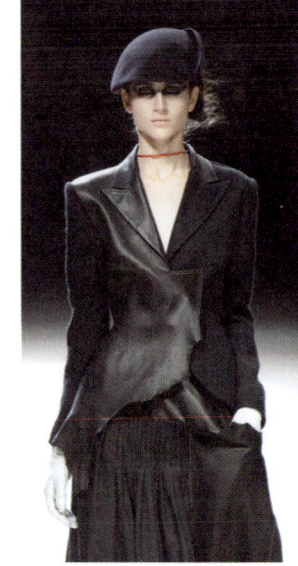

deconstructed

FIT/FITTING/FIT MODEL the toile or first sample garment is usually examined for fit as well as aesthetic interpretation compared to the design drawing. The garment is usually tried on a model whose measurements are perfectly standard size (a **fit model**). During the fitting process, alterations may be drawn and written on the toile, or pinned on the garment and meticulously noted for amendment. More recently, digital photographs have also become part of this procedure.

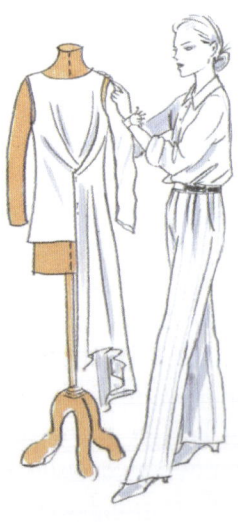

fit / fitting / fit model

GRADING & SIZING once perfected and sold, garment patterns are graded up and down according to standard international size grades. Quality garments are refitted again in each of the sizes to make sure the fit is correct.

HEMLINES shaped, handkerchief, asymmetric, shirt-tail, hi-lo. See also **blind hem**, page 245. The circumference of the hemline is known as the **sweep**.

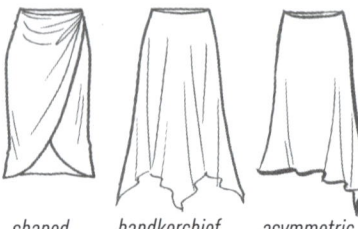

shaped   *handkerchief*   *asymmetric*

INTERFACING a layer of woven or non-woven fabric layered on a garment to support and facilitate shaping. Sometimes stitched, otherwise fused with heat (fusable interlining).

LINE often used to describe the simplified cut, defining outline or silhouette of a single garment or the common denominator which unifies a collection. A number of silhouettes have evolved along various lines that have since become standard references. We can probably thank the Empress Josephine (1763–1814) for popularizing the high-waisted empire line, also known as Directoire after the French Directoire period 1795–9. See also **line-up**, page 239.

PATTERN MAKING
PATTERN BLOCK/SEWING PATTERN/LAY the **pattern block** is usually the first version of the pattern, perfecting the basic silhouette. The pieces and panels that make up the garment design are known as the **garment pattern** or, domestically, as the **sewing pattern**. The arrangement of pattern pieces on the fabric, correct to grain, match and nap and for best, most economic use of the fabric, is called the **lay**.

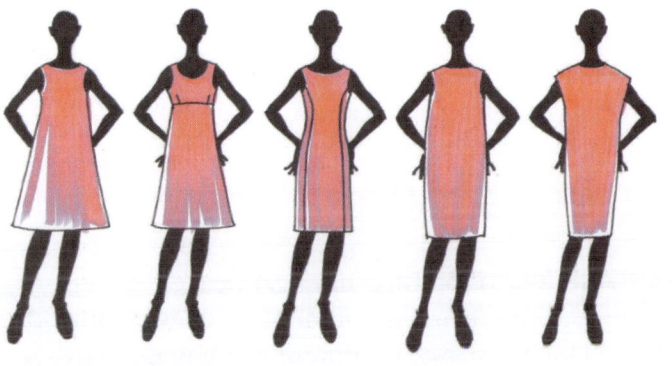

A-line   *empire line*   *princess*   *sack /shift*   *Y-line*

SCISSORS different types include dressmaking, embroidery, paper, pinking, tailor's shears, snips.

SILHOUETTE & LINE in 1760, Etienne de Silhouette (1709–67) was the unsuccessful French minister of finance to King Louis XV. So brief was his tenure that it led to public ridicule and he became associated with anything penny-pinching and cheap (*à la Silhouette*). At the same time there was a fashion for simple portraits cut in outline, like a shadow, from black paper. It was not long before the name Silhouette was linked with this inexpensive alternative to portrait painting.

silhouette

STAND/DRESS STAND/ MANNEQUIN/ DRESS FORM a stuffed, modelled facsimile of the human torso, accurately made to standard sizes or custom-made. Sometimes also unfortunately called a 'dummy'.

TOILES the series of mock-up garments made in calico (sometimes called muslin) to develop, refine and perfect a design before using the final fabric. Every detail should be fully trialled and resolved at this stage, being aware that the choices of weights of calico should be appropriately matched as closely as possible to the end fabric's characteristics. Jersey garments are similarly toiled in substitute jersey fabric. A designer may work on several toiles to develop the perfect version of his or her design, beginning by working solely on the silhouette. This may then be used as a block for future design variations and garments, creating continuity and a strong identity within a collection.

dress stand

GARMENTS & ACCESSORIES, JERSEYWEAR & KNITWEAR

GARMENTS

BODICE a garment for the upper body, neck to waist, or the top or upper section of a complete dress or coat. Derived from earlier times when the bodice of a dress was separate from the skirt.

BUSTIER originally a form-fitting garment worn as part of underwear, more recently worn as outerwear.

CORSET a body-shaping, smooth-fitting garment, usually extending from under the bust to the waist or hips. Originally boned, with metal, wood or whalebone, later substituted with plastics and Lycra to enforce a silhouette. Modern versions are more fetish than foundation.

CROWN not just for royalty, but also the top part of a hat or sleeve.

CULOTTES short knee breeches worn throughout Europe from the late Middle Ages to the early 19th century. During the French Revolution (1789–99), working-class rebels were known as the *sans-culottes* (without culottes) – those who rejected aristocratic dress. Today the term is applied to almost any short or cropped trousers, sometimes a close relative of the split skirt.

FROCK originally a loose, long garment with wide sleeves worn by monks and priests – hence the word 'de-frock' for when they left the clergy. By the 16th century a frock had evolved to become a woman's dress or gown, unfitted and comfortable for wear in the house. By the 17th century it was a loose working garment for men and women, sometimes called a smock frock and sometimes buttoning all the way down the front.

GAUCHO traditional wear of the South American cowboy; wide-hemmed, mid-calf-length trousers, similar to a split skirt.

KAFTAN sometimes **caftan** or **qaftan** – traceable back to biblical times and the Middle East. A long, loose, open-sleeved tunic, displaying the under-garment sleeves and split at the sides.

SHIRT/BLOUSE traditionally we consider shirt to be masculine and blouse to be feminine, but originally a blouse was a peasant garment worn by both sexes.

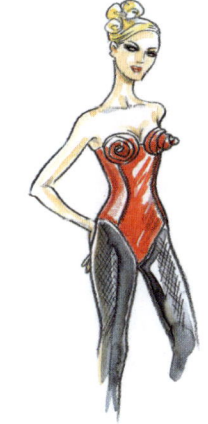

Gaultier bustier

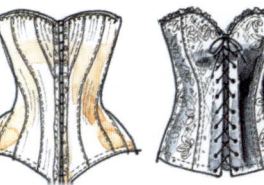

corsets

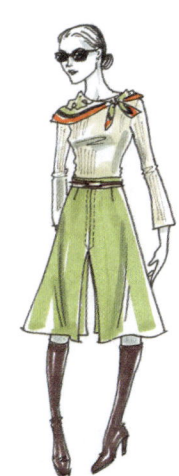

culottes

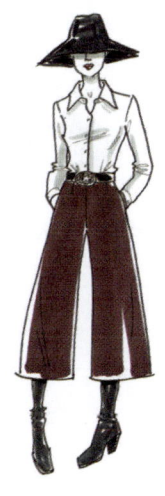

gaucho

The shirt was underwear for men only, not intended to be seen. As men's clothes became more sober throughout the 19th century, the shirt with collar and cuffs that we recognize today became accepted formal attire. The blouse became accepted office wear towards the end of the 19th century for the growing number of working women, a look popularized by the Gibson Girls drawn by Charles Dana Gibson.

SHIRTWAISTER the style probably first appeared in the 1940s. Later versions became little more than extended or oversized shirts, frequently worn belted or cinched.

SINGLET/VEST originally an undergarment only, now worn as outerwear and active sportswear. In North America a vest is a waistcoat and a singlet, curiously, is a **wife beater**.

SMOCK traditionally worn by rural workers and closely related to the shirt and peasant blouse. Associated with artists and craftspeople, particularly in the 19th century. A strict pull-on version became the traditional workwear of Cornish fishermen and was immortalized in the paintings of the Newlyn School of artists in the 19th and 20th centuries.

TANK a simple, sleeveless garment with wide, built-up shoulders and no opening or fastening. Usually made in jersey or knit fabrics. Originating in the USA, from the one-piece bathing suits of the 1920s worn in tanks (swimming pools). **Tank dress** – an extended form.

TOP a word to be avoided at almost any cost (please!) – there are far better and more accurately descriptive names you can use.

TROUSERS to put it grandly, a bifurcated garment worn by both sexes. Styles, silhouettes, cuts and variants are many and include **bootleg**, **drainpipe**, **harem**, **jodphur**, **loons**, **Oxford bags**, **sailor**, **slacks**, **track**, **trews**, **palazzo** and **zouaves**.

WRAP in 1974, a little-known New York designer, Diane von Furstenberg, encouraged by the famous editor of US *Vogue*, Diana Vreeland, launched her jersey wrap dress. It was an immediate success. By 1976, she had sold over 1,000,000 of them. Relaunched in 1997, the famous wrap dress is now considered a perennial and classic design.

ZOOT SUIT a big trend look associated with black musicians of the 1930s and 1940s, most famously the Cotton Club's top-billing Cab Calloway. Typified by an oversized, long, wide-shouldered jacket, baggy and exaggeratedly tapered trousers, often light or flamboyantly coloured, and accessorized. In the 1980s, the look was successfully revived, along with elements of the musical genre, by Kid Creole.

COATS & JACKETS

ANORAK a waterproof hooded jacket fastening with a zipper, with a drawstring at the bottom. It became popular during World War 2, when warm, quilted or fur-lined versions were worn by pilots. The name is thought to derive from similar Eskimo garments from which the anorak may be traced. See also **cagoule**, below.

BIKER JACKET a motorbike jacket of black leather, with zip fasteners and stud closures; a perennial fashion favourite since the youthquake days of the 1950s. Famously worn by Marlon Brando for his iconic role in *The Wild One* (1953).

BLOUSON a loose blouse-type jacket, gathered or reduced at the waist to create the characteristic silhouette.

CABAN a short warm coat, similar to a **reefer jacket** (see facing page), worn by Breton fishermen for centuries. Originally white – *kap gwenn* means 'white cloth' in Breton – it changed to navy blue during the early 19th century.

CAGOULE/CAGOUL/KAGOULE/KAGOOL a short, waterproof, hooded jacket; many versions pull on over the head rather than opening completely. Otherwise

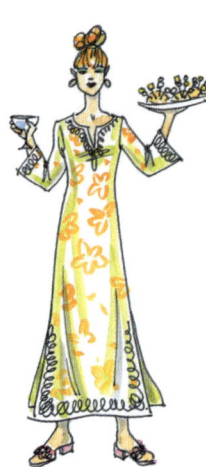

kaftan

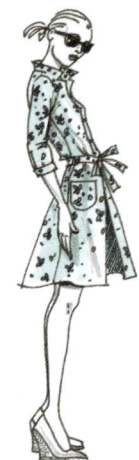

shirtwaister

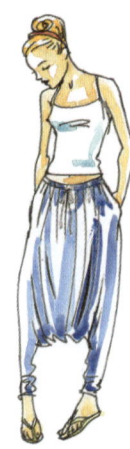

zouaves

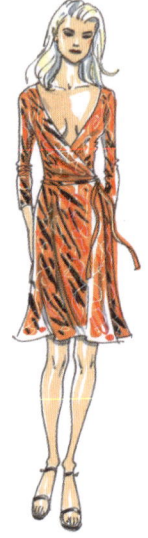

wrap dress

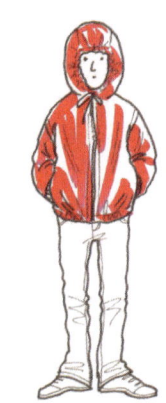

anorak

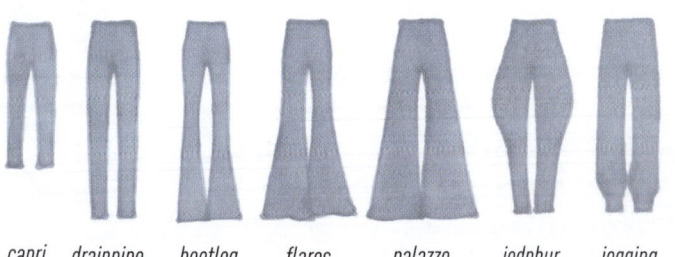

capri   drainpipe   bootleg   flares   palazzo   jodphur   jogging

blouson

almost indistinguishable from an anorak, taking its name from the French *cagoule*, meaning 'hood'. Some well-designed versions fold away into their own chest pocket or small sack.

CAPE from *Batman* to *Dracula* and *Miss Marple* by way of Courrèges, there are endless variations from grand and tailored country classics to sci-fi fantasy. A sleeveless garment worn around the shoulders, open or fastened at the front; sometimes with openings for hands or arms.

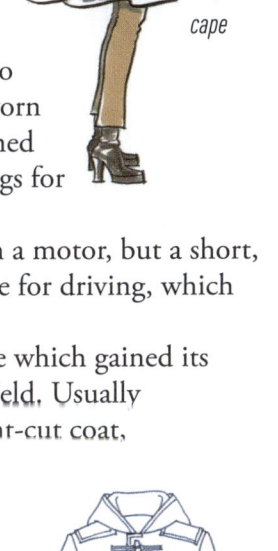
cape

CAR COAT no, not a hybrid coat with a motor, but a short, hip-length tailored coat, comfortable for driving, which first appeared in the early 1960s.

CHESTERFIELD a classic overcoat style which gained its name from the 4th Earl of Chesterfield. Usually a fly fronted, single-breasted, straight-cut coat, characteristically with a velvet top collar. Variations include double-breasted and more fitted versions.

CROMBIE see **fabrics**, page 242.

DUFFEL/DUFFLE COAT the Belgian town of Duffel gave its name to a heavy, woollen woven cloth and subsequently to the warm protective coats for the military and navy. Traditionally vent-less, with a double layered yoke, large collar or a hood and fastening with wooden or horn toggles.

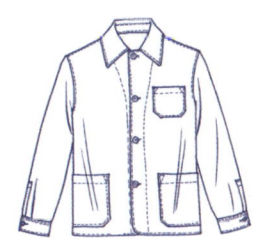
duffle coat

ENGINEER'S JACKET a boxy cotton drill or denim utility jacket, with breast and hip pockets and close-fastening cuffs as a safeguard for engineers using machinery.

FLYING or **AVIATOR JACKET** a short usually leather jacket with utility pockets, maybe a double closure of zip and buttoned flap, tight knitted rib cuffs and waist and, often, a mouton collar, typically worn by pioneer aviators and World War 2 pilots.

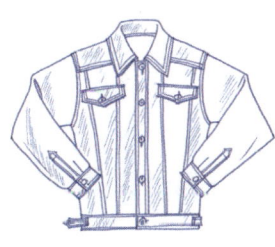
engineer's jacket

JEANS JACKET a short, shirt-style, usually close-fitting denim utility jacket.

INVERNESS a tweed overcoat with a deep cape attached, as typically worn by Sherlock Holmes.

jeans jacket

JERKIN/GILET/BODY WARMER a sleeveless jacket, waist- or hip-length; padded and down versions have revived the look.

GREATCOAT originally a voluminous, extra-heavy fur-lined coat, belted and reaching mid-calf or longer, worn by British soldiers. Officers wore a shorter version, known affectionately as a **British Warm**.

HARRINGTON a short, zip-up casual jacket with a band collar, first made in the 1930s by British companies Grenfell of Burnley and Baracuta of Stockport. Frank Sinatra and Steve McQueen apparently both wore the Baracuta G9 jacket, as did Elvis Presley in his 1958 film *King Creole*. But when Ryan O'Neal wore one in the cult 1960s soap opera *Peyton Place*, his character Rodney Harrington gave the jacket its popular name.

MACKINTOSH a waterproof coat named after the Scottish chemist Sir Charles Mackintosh who invented a rubberized cotton fabric in 1823.

REEFER JACKET (also known as a **PEA COAT**) a warm coat with wide revers, double-breasted, short hip length, similar to a **caban**, see opposite, worn by the American Navy in the early 18th century and later by Navvies. The name can be traced back to 1846, when the pilot schooner USS *Reefer* famously led task forces in the Mexican–American War.

TRENCHCOAT a long, belted rain or showerproof coat worn by officers in the trenches in World War I. Typified by a short, caped-yoke back and storm flaps at the front. Versions with a deep inverted pleat from back waist to hem were for riding, similar to those still worn by British mounted police today.

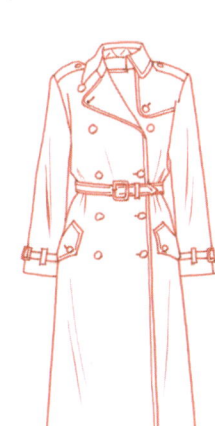
trenchcoat

ACCESSORIES

COWL a tall funnel-like collar, sometimes a completely separate entity, worn like a scarf. Versions with an inbuilt twist follow the principle of a Mobius band. Often mistakenly called a snood, which is a net for the hair. There is an Eskimo (Inuit-Yupik) version of the cowl, known as a smokering (nachaqs).

FASCINATOR little more than an alice band with pretensions – a poor excuse for a proper hat.

MUFF a tube of fur or warm cloth into which the hands are inserted for warmth.

MUFFLER a long scarf.

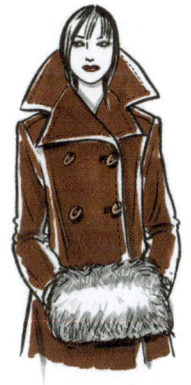
muff

SCARF a square or rectangle of cloth usually worn at the neck or on the head.

TIPPET a scarf worn draped round the neck by ecclesiastics or a separate fur collar worn as a warm accessory around the neck.

SHOES/HEELS see illustration of some different types below.

SNOOD traditionally, a close-fitting cloth hood, more often made of net or a mesh-like fabric, last popular in the 1940s. See also **cowl**, page 249.

JERSEYWEAR & KNITWEAR

JERSEY the name of the island that gave us the particular style of sweater now more commonly known by the name of its neighbouring island, Guernsey. Jersey has subsequently given its name to all knitted structures and to fabric sold by the metre, as other fabric, and cut, sewn and constructed in more-or-less similar ways to woven fabric. Jersey garments made in this way are often referred to as **cut & sew** garments.

ARAN a style of fisherman's sweater traditionally knitted in ecru wool. Typified by a rich mix of cable patterns and textured stitches.

CABLE a crossover knitted stitch resembling ropes, typically found in traditional folk knitwear such as Aran sweaters.

FAIR ISLE a traditional style of knitwear pattern from the Fair Isles off the coast of Scotland, typified by multiple small-scale geometric patterns combined in many subtle colours.

GUERNSEY a style of fisherman's sweater, more or

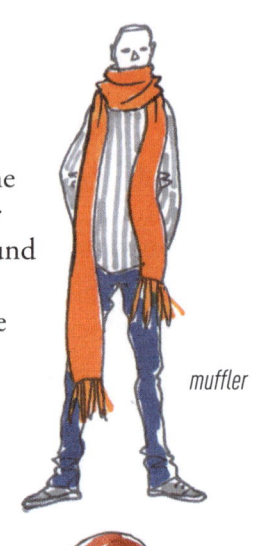

muffler

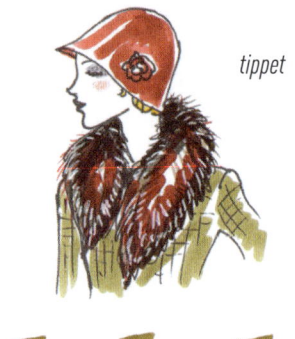

tippet

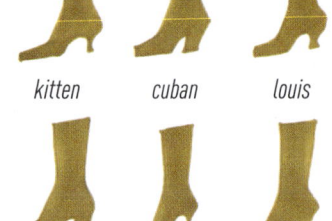

kitten   *cuban*   *louis*

platform   *stiletto*   *wedge*

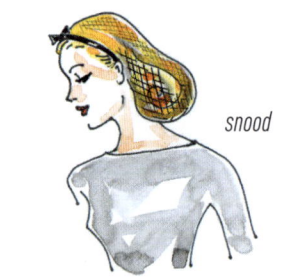

snood

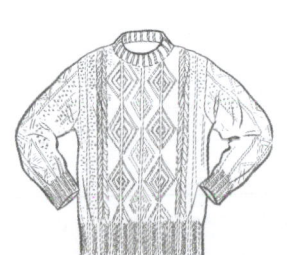

Aran sweater

less square and loosely based on a smock, originating centuries ago on the island of Guernsey in the English Channel. Yorkshire fishermen have long called their navy blue sweaters **guernseys** or **ganseys**.

GAUGE in much the same way that in hand-knitting different yarns are knitted on thicker or thinner needles depending on the thickness of the yarn, in machine knitwear it is the number of needles across the needle bed that dictates the gauge. The higher the gauge number, the finer the knit.

KNITWEAR a knitted garment, a **sweater**, but no longer called a **pullover** or a **jumper**.

MATELOT the French word for sailor, used to describe the perennially popular navy-and-white striped sweaters and T-shirts originally worn by sailors and first brought into the fashion arena by Coco Chanel.

INTARSIA a technique for knitting large-scale patterns without using floats.

JACQUARD patterns created in knitwear with floats; the name borrowed from a woven pattern system.

SINGLE JERSEY a plain knit structure producing a right (jersey) and wrong (reverse) side.

DOUBLE JERSEY a generic term for a range of weft knitted fabrics made on a rib or interlock basis.

WEFT KNITTING machine-knitted fabric or garments made on a flat bed or circular bed machine.

CROCHET related to knit in that it is a system of interconnecting loops, but using a single needle to create fabrics and trims. There is no machine version, crochet can only be handmade.

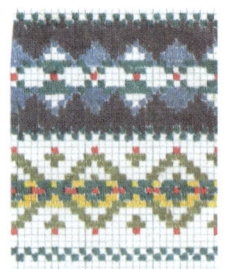

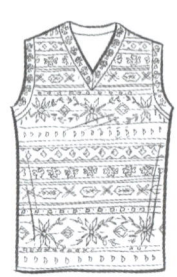

fair isle

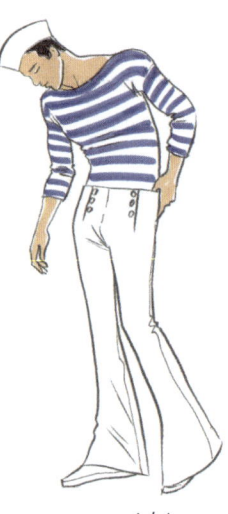

matelot

GARMENT DETAILS & PARTICULARS

COLLARS

COLLAR generally consisting of three parts, the stand, where it is joined to the neckline, the top and the under collar.

SPREAD the distance between the points of a collar.

CUTAWAY as the name suggests, a widely spread collar with the front edges cut away.

FUNNEL a tall, upstanding collar.

COWL a soft draped neckline, created by cutting the bodice with fullness and on the bias.

HIGHWAYMAN an historic feature, with a tall or extended stand.

MOUTON a sheepskin or shearling top collar.

PETER PAN a flat turned-down collar, named after the J.M. Barrie character.

SAILOR as typified by the traditional sailors' uniform, a flat collar, large and square at the back, forming a V at the centre front. Sometimes called a **middy** collar, from midshipman.

TURTLE a shallow, standaway collar reminiscent of its namesake.

WING a formal collar with turned-down corners resembling wings. An earlier form, with curved or rounded corners, is known as a **butterfly collar**.

LAPELS, REVERS, ETC.

Lapel: the front, turned part of a jacket collar. **Rever**: a large lapel. **Notch**: the V-shape cut out where the lapel meets the collar. **Gorge seam**: the visible turned-back part of the join. A **peaked rever** is a stylistic variation.

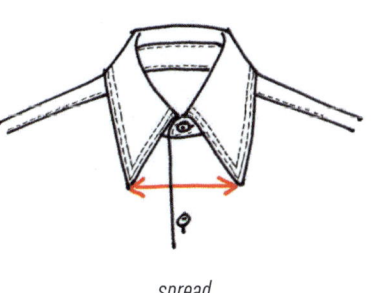
spread

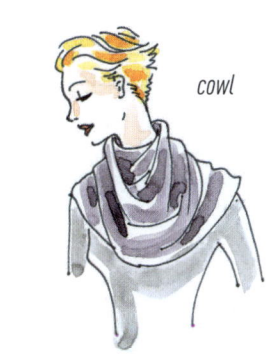
cowl

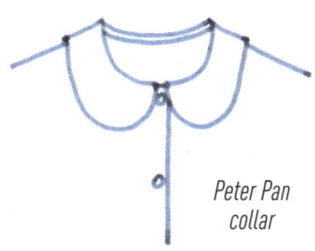
Peter Pan collar

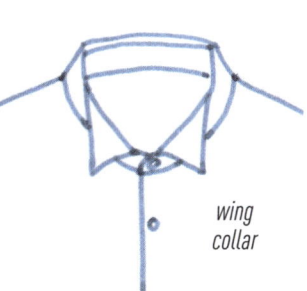
wing collar

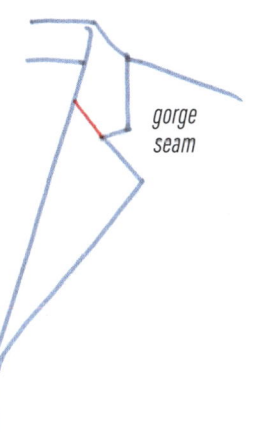
gorge seam

NECKLINES

BATEAU French for 'boat' – a more glamorous way of describing this attractive, shallow, wide neckline.

CREW NECK a high, close-fitting round neckline usually finished with a trim, as in T-shirts.

DÉCOLLETÉ/DÉCOLLETAGE a very low neckline, popular in Directoire times and various periods in history, particularly for evening-wear, often displaying the cleavage.

HALTER a strap from the garment front or built-up bodice which passes round the back of the neck to support the garment.

JEWEL a wider, lower version of a crew neckline that can display neck jewellery.

POLO NECK / POLO COLLAR confusion, always, here! In Europe, a **polo neck** is a high, close-fitting turned-down collar; in the US this is called a **roll neck**. A **polo collar** is a simple, square-cut collar typically found on **polo shirts**.

SWEETHEART a low-ish neckline, cut in two more-or-less semicircular curves, so that the bodice resembles a heart shape.

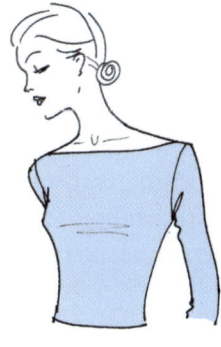
bateau

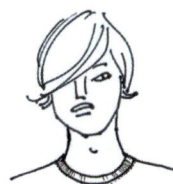
crew neck

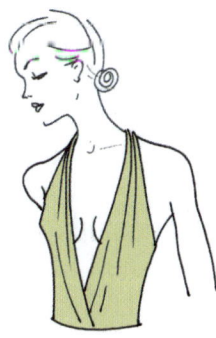
décolleté/décolletage

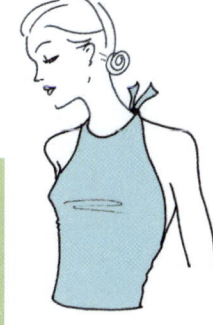
halter

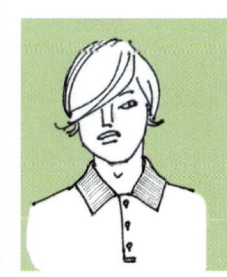
polo neck

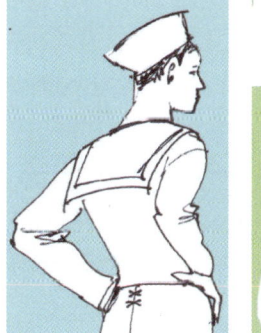

sailor

polo collar

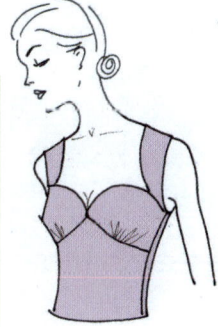
sweetheart

DART a shaped tuck, pointed at one or both ends, created to control excess material and develop fit. Similarly, pintuck, smocking and ruching are all ways of controlling and creating volume and shape. See **pleat**, below.

DRAPE the way in which fabric falls and hangs. Used also to describe a way of developing a style directly on the dress stand, known as **modelling**.

EPAULETTE from the French word *epaule*, meaning 'shoulder'. A largely decorative ornament or strap at the shoulder, originally on the naval or military uniforms of officers, later used to display rank at all levels and widely adopted as a fashion detail.

FROG FASTENING a decorative fastening consisting of a looped braid and knotted button, versions of which are loosely based on Chinese and oriental costume.

GALLOON metallic braid, lace or other trimming as used on dress military uniforms.

GODET a usually triangular-shaped fabric inset, often stitched into a hemline to create fullness.

dart

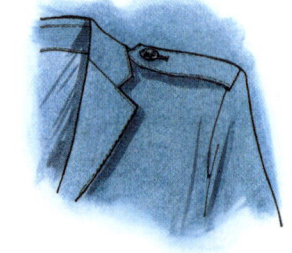

drape

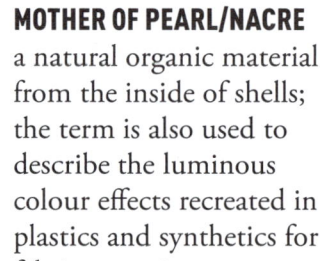

epaulette

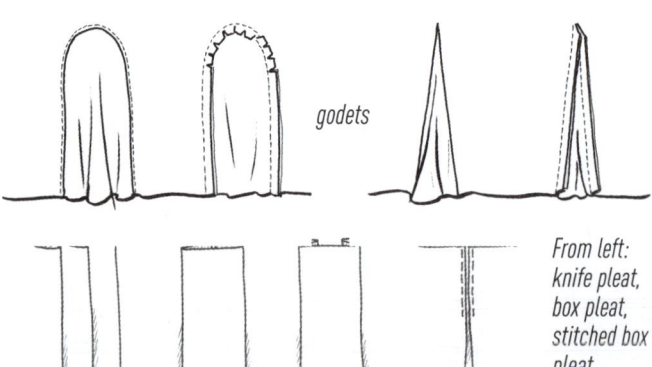

godets

From left: knife pleat, box pleat, stitched box pleat

GUSSET an insert of fabric into a garment seam for added strength, movement or expansion.

HABERDASHERY sometimes called **notions**, in North America **findings**, a range of delightful phrases that encompass all the bits and pieces of the sewing and fashion workroom, from pins and needles, threads and buttons to linings, interfacings and a myriad of things besides.

MITRE the name of a bishop's or archbishop's hat; in fashion it is more commonly encountered as square-cut collar profile or as a way of finishing right-angled corners.

MONOGRAM the stylized initials or crest of the owner/wearer of the garment. These days more likely to be substituted by a company logo.

MOTHER OF PEARL/NACRE a natural organic material from the inside of shells; the term is also used to describe the luminous colour effects recreated in plastics and synthetics for fabrics, sequins, etc.

PLEAT a fold of fabric, to control fullness; popular variations include **knife**, **box**, **sunray** and **crystal**. *Plisse*, the French word for pleat, is used specifically to describe a narrow, sometimes uneven or puckered pleat.

gusset

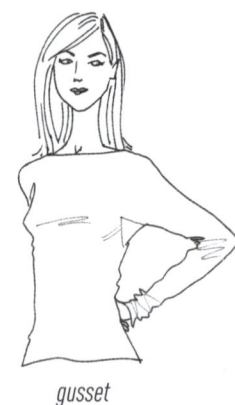

haberdashery

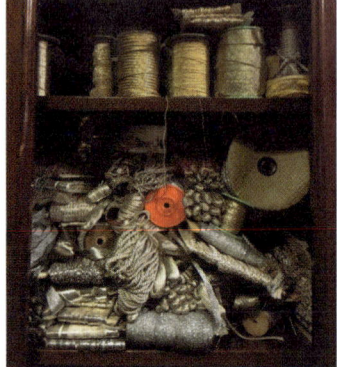

monogram

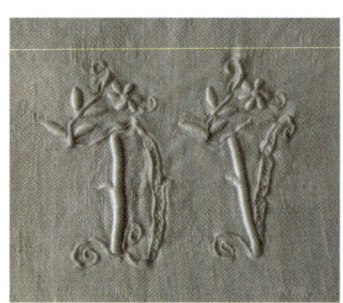

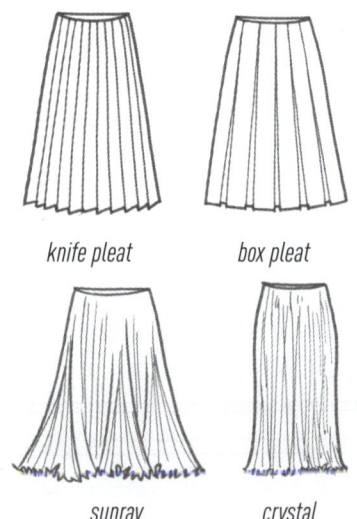

knife pleat   *box pleat*

sunray   *crystal*

POCKETS there are numerous variations, including bellows, flap, bound, jetted, smile, frontier, accordion, patch and welt.

RISE the depth of the crotch seam from the top of the leg to the waist or top of the garment.

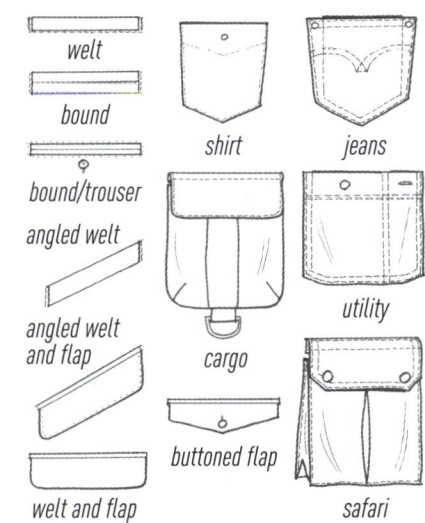

welt

bound

bound/trouser

angled welt

angled welt and flap

welt and flap

shirt

jeans

cargo

buttoned flap

utility

safari

SHOULDERS, SLEEVES & ARMHOLES

SADDLE the sleeve has an extension along the top of the shoulder into the neckline.

SET IN a standard or regular sleeve, set in to the body of the garment.

MAGYAR taking its name from the traditional costumes of the Magyar people of the Urals, the term is used to describe a deep sleeve cut all in one piece with the body. Very deep versions, where the sleeve comes from near the waist, are often called **batwing** sleeves – for obvious reasons.

DOLMAN traditionally a long loose Turkish robe dating back to the 16th century, open at the front with wide sleeves, now generally used to describe a deep-set, wide, loose sleeve.

saddle shoulder

set in sleeve

magyar (batwing)

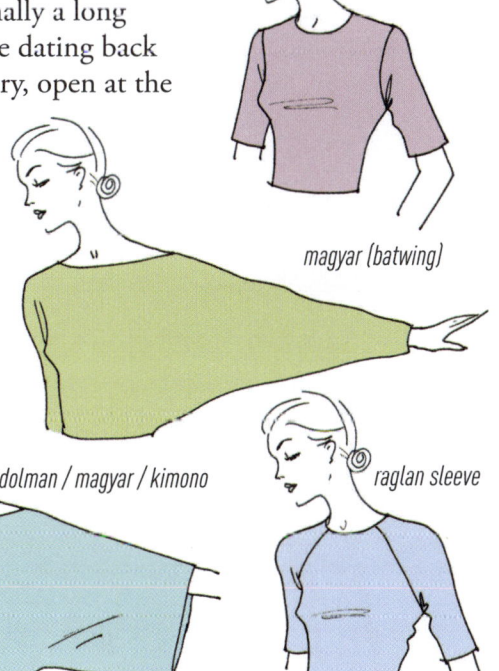

dolman / magyar / kimono

raglan sleeve

RAGLAN sometimes also called raglan shoulder, named after Lord Raglan (1788–1855), a British commander in the Crimean War. The sleeve is extended more or less diagonally across the body from underarm to collarbone. Sometimes the name is also used to describe a type of overcoat.

STORM FLAP typically the shaped flap at the shoulder or neckline that covers the neck opening on a trenchcoat as a double closure.

TAB the fabric strap at a cuff, neckline or sleeve that facilitates closure or holds rolled up sleeves in place, etc. Also the opening placket on shirt cuffs.

VENT from the old French word for 'to let out air' and from the Latin for 'wind', a vent is a split at the sides or centre back of a coat or jacket.

WELT the finishing band at a hemline or pocket top. In knitwear this may be the ribbed hemline or pocket trims.

YOKE a panel or section, sometimes shaped and usually of double fabric, at the shoulder usually of a shirt or jacket that supports the rest of the garment. The classic **cowboy shirt** presents a fine example.

ZIP the history of the zip fastener or zipper is long and convoluted. First versions date back to the mid-19th century, but in its crude early forms its potential uses were undervalued. Later developments, patent issues, production problems and rights were not resolved until the early 1920s. But the zipper was largely overlooked by the fashion industry for another decade or so. It was only after a financial deal between the Canadian division of the Lightning Fastener Company and the Italian couturier Elsa Schiaparelli that she used zips in her winter 1935–6 collection, characteristically shocking buyers by using them exposed as unexpected design features, that they made their slow but eventual acceptance into high fashion.

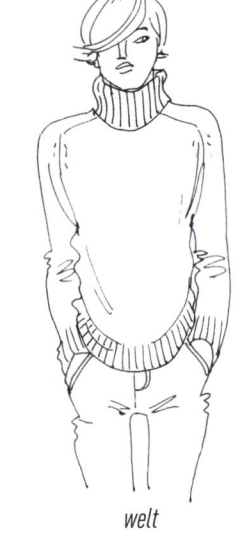

welt

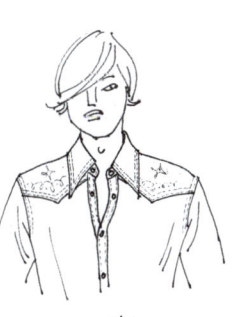

yoke

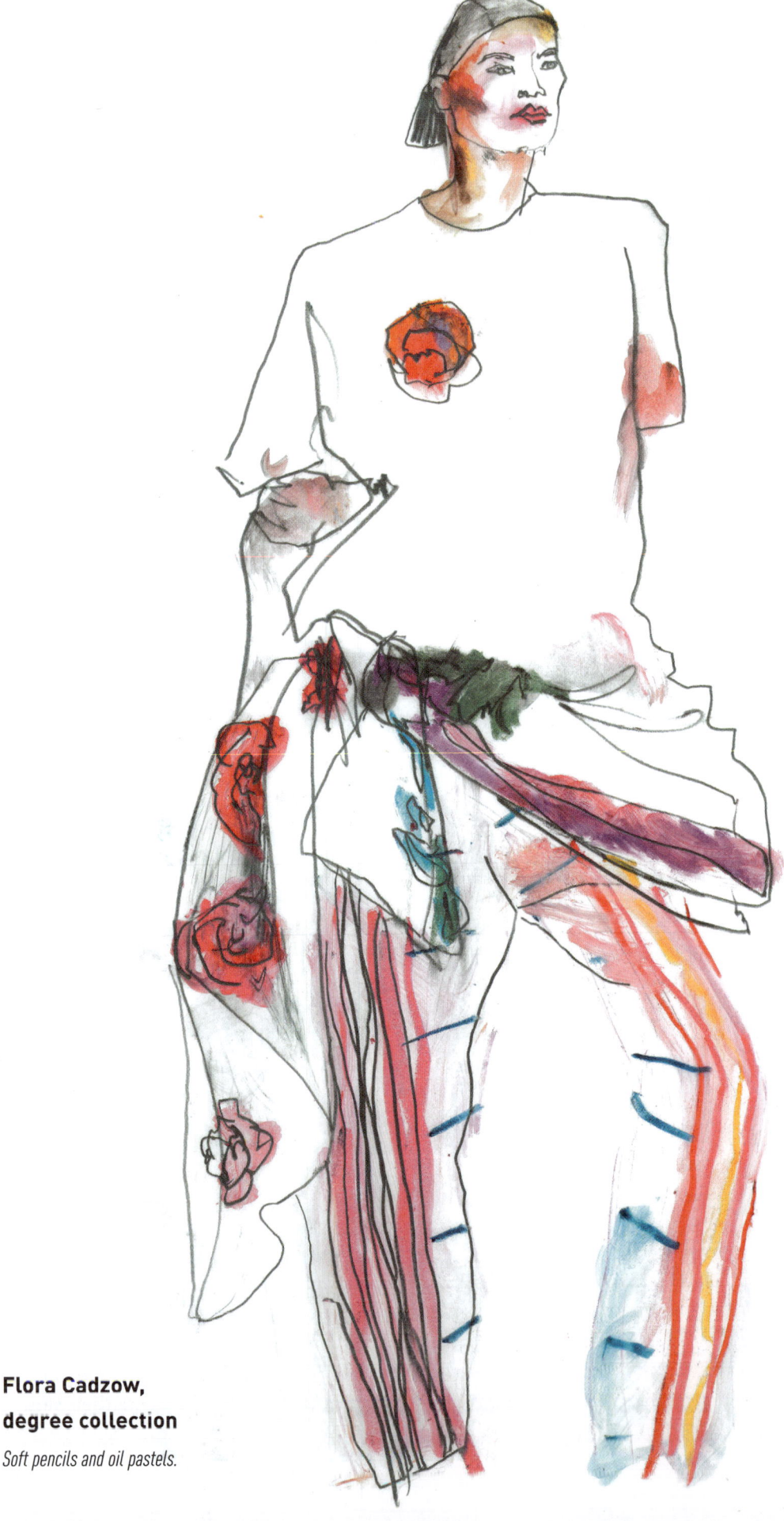

**Flora Cadzow,
degree collection**

Soft pencils and oil pastels.

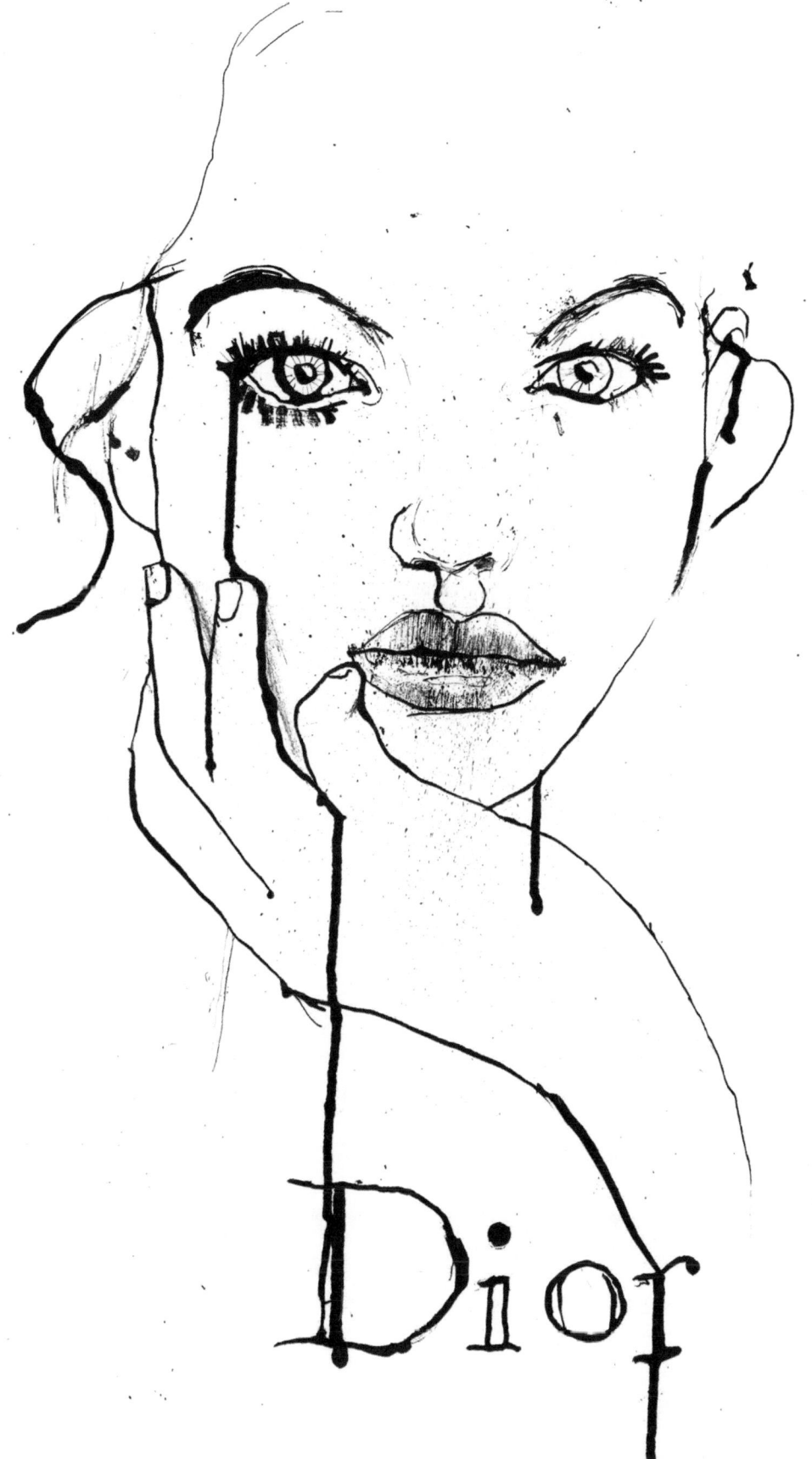

**Patrick Morgan,
commercial artist**

Ink and dip-pen, dry brush technique.

CONTRIBUTORS

Charlie Allen
www.charlieallen.co.uk

Ian Batten
www.ianbatten.com

Pik Yee Berwick
berwick1@nyc.rr.com

Malcolm Bird
www.malcolm-bird.co.uk

Christopher Brown
chrissbrown@btinternet.com

Flora Cadzow
fcadzow@gmail.com

Massimo Casagrande
www.massimo-casagrande.com

Noel Chapman
noelchapman.co.uk

Judith Cheek
judith.cheek@btinternet.com

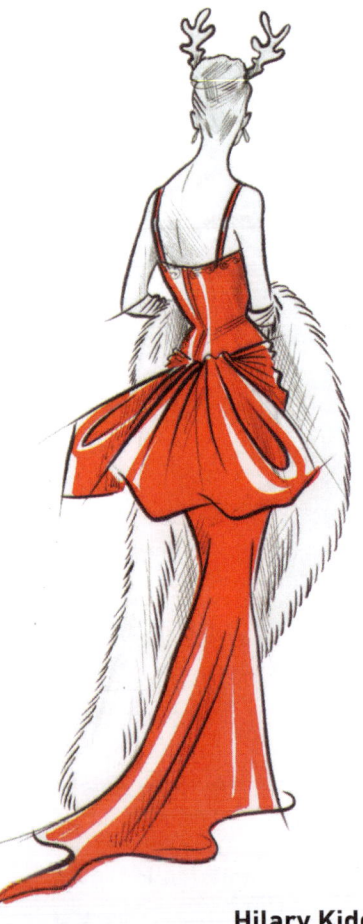

Hilary Kidd

Brush and marker pen.

Lynnette Cook
coookbook@yahoo.co.uk

Yvonne Deacon
yvonnedeacon@googlemail.com

Mary Edyvean
mary.wilson2010@hotmail.co.uk

Mariella Ertl
mariellaertl@gmx.de

Martina Farrow
www.martinafarrow.com

Claire Fletcher
www.clairefletcherart.com

Henrietta Goodden
henri@post.com

Gray Modern & Contemporary Art
www.graymca.co.uk

Neil Greer
neiltendenz@aol.com

Katharina Gulde
www.katharinagulde.com

Clare Dudley Hart
clarehart@btinternet.com

Christopher Heeney
www.christopherheeney.com

Lesley Hurst
lesley.hurst@virgin.net

Rosalyn Kennedy
rosalynkennedey@hotmail.com

Hilary Kidd
www.hilarykidd.co.uk

Sophia Kokosalaki
www.sophiakokosalaki.com

Rosie McClelland
www.rosiemcclelland.co.uk

Patrick Morgan
www.patrickmorgan.co.uk

Hormazd Narielwalla
www.narielwalla.com

Bruce Oldfield
www.bruceoldfield.com

Louisa Parris
www.louisaparris.com

Cherrill Parris-Fox
www.parrisfox.com

N. Peal
www.npeal.com

Stina Persson
www.stinapersson.com

Alice Fletcher Quinnell
fletcherquinnellalice@googlemail.com

Mary Ratcliffe
maryratcliffe8@gmail.com

Heather Ridley-Moran
www.hridleymoran.co.uk

Bruce Robbins
bdrobbins@btinternet.com

Mitchell Sams
m@mitchellsams.com

Anthea Simms
www.antheasimms.com

Howard Tangye
www.howardtangye.com

Textile View Magazine
www.view-publications.com

Paul Wearing
www.paulwearing.co.uk

Niki Zachiardis
for her vintage magazine collection

We would also like to extend our gratitude and send a very special thank you to Dick Knox for permission to use Cath Knox's lovely illustrations.

PICTURE CREDITS

Christopher Brown: page 238, Oscar Wilde linoprint; Noel Chapman: pages 158–9, 172–3, 252; Judith Cheek: pages 102, 170, 171; Lynn Goldsmith: page 232, Patti Smith portrait as part of collage © Lynn Goldsmith 1976; Christopher Heeney: pages 72, 156–7; Mitchell Sams: pages 174, 242; Anthea Simms: pages 161, 246; Ann-Marie Ward: pages 64, 107 and 161 (bottom right)

FABRIC AND STILL LIFE CONTRIBUTORS

Butlers Emporium
70 George Street
Hastings
TN34 3EE
UK

The Cloth Shop
www.theclothshop.net